"Hans Boersma's *Seeing God* is the most significant and theologically comprehensive treatment of this topic in English since Kenneth Kirk's classic *The Vision of God*. And, far more than Kirk, Boersma provides the invaluable service of breaking down the barriers (mostly barriers of misconception) separating differing Christian traditions, East and West, Orthodox and Catholic and Protestant. This is theological reflection of the most illuminating kind."

— DAVID BENTLEY HART
author of *Atheist Delusions* and
The Beauty of the Infinite

"Christian theology has traditionally identified the beatific vision as the ultimate end of humanity. But what does it mean to 'see God'? How can we pursue such an end if it is beyond our understanding? Building on his exemplary 'sacramental ontology,' Hans Boersma here offers us a 'sacramental teleology' in which the end of humanity—the *visio Dei*—is revealed sacramentally *within* the created order. A profound and important work."

— SIMON OLIVER
Durham University

"Only Hans Boersma could write this book. With a superb command of the Scriptures and of the Reformed, Protestant, and Catholic traditions, he revisits the neglected topic of beatific vision and reminds us what it is to see God in Christ. An energizing book from one of today's best theologians."

— JANET SOSKICE
University of Cambridge

"*Seeing God* is a subtle yet sustained polemic against the notion that the Christian eschaton is simply an improved version of the universe as we know it, and that Christian Platonists—Nyssen, Augustine, Dante, Jonathan Edwards, C. S. Lewis—were all wrongheadedly otherworldly. Boersma's breviary for sacramental ontology, advocating a more 'vertical' kind of theology and spirituality, deserves consideration among so-called Christian materialists and contemporary proponents of the 'renewed cosmos' approach to eschatology."

— MICHAEL MCCLYMOND
Saint Louis University

SEEING GOD

*The Beatific Vision
in Christian Tradition*

Hans Boersma

WILLIAM B. EERDMANS PUBLISHING COMPANY
GRAND RAPIDS, MICHIGAN

Wm. B. Eerdmans Publishing Co.
2140 Oak Industrial Drive N.E., Grand Rapids, Michigan 49505
www.eerdmans.com

27 26 25 24 23 22 21 20 19 18   1 2 3 4 5 6 7 8 9 10

ISBN 978-0-8028-7604-1

Library of Congress Cataloging-in-Publication Data

Names: Boersma, Hans, 1961– author.
Title: Seeing God : the beatific vision in Christian tradition / Hans Boersma.
Description: Grand Rapids : Eerdmans Publishing Co., 2018. |
    Includes bibliographical references and index.
Identifiers: LCCN 2017059820 | ISBN 9780802876041 (hardcover : alk. paper)
Subjects: LCSH: Heaven—Christianity. | Beatific vision—History of doctrines.
Classification: LCC BT848 .B64 2018 | DDC 236/.24—dc23
    LC record available at https://lccn.loc.gov/2017059820

To Jim Houston,
friend and mentor

The Glance

When first thy sweet and gracious eye
Vouchsaf'd ev'n in the midst of youth and night
To look upon me, who before did lie
        Weltring in sinne;
    I felt a sugred strange delight,
Passing all cordials made by any art,
Bedew, embalme, and overrunne my heart,
        And take it in.

Since that time many a bitter storm
My soul hath felt, ev'n able to destroy,
Had the malicious and ill-meaning harm
        His swing and sway:
    But still thy sweet originall joy,
Sprung from thine eye, did work within my soul,
And surging griefs, when they grew bold, control;
        And got the day.

If thy first glance so powerfull be,
A mirth but open'd and seal'd up again;
What wonders shall we feel, when we shall see
        Thy full-ey'd love!
    When thou shalt look us out of pain,
And one aspect of thine spend in delight
More then a thousand sunnes disburse in light,
        In heav'n above.

—George Herbert

CONTENTS

CONTENTS

Contents

CONTENTS

Contents

FOREWORD

"Blessed are the pure in heart, for they shall see God": in this beatitude the Lord speaks of the vision of God as a reward for purity of heart, and for all traditional forms of Christianity the "beatific vision," gazing on God in utmost joy, is the ultimate goal of Christian living, the fulfillment of our Christian discipleship. Perhaps because so much is invested in it, conceptions of the beatific vision have differed among the Christian traditions, sometimes very sharply; some Christian traditions speak of it in terms of deification and transfiguration, while other traditions shun these terms, fearful of eliding in some way the fundamental distinction between Creator and creature; the place of the body in what is often perceived as a fundamentally spiritual experience adds complications. The notion of some final transforming vision is not confined to Christianity, or even to the Judeo-Christian tradition; most religious and indeed philosophical traditions envisage some final condition of union with the ultimate, expressed, though it must be, in tentative and often contradictory terms. The Christian traditions of the beatific vision owe something to pagan antecedents, not least the Platonic tradition, as Hans Boersma makes clear in an early chapter.

In this remarkable book, Hans Boersma explores what a range of Christian thinkers have made of the notion of a final beatific vision. It is not a history of the beatific vision in Christian thought as such (which seems never to have been attempted), but an exploration of powerfully significant ways, sometimes linked, sometimes divergent, that are to be found in Christian history. The range of thinkers and traditions explored is remarkable: from Platonic and patristic notions; to a striking variety of approaches found in the medieval period, both in the East and in the West; to Protestant approaches, again manifesting enormous variety, from the Reformation on-

xiii

ward. Two poets are explored in depth: Dante and John Donne. Boersma achieves this almost incredible task by bringing to his sources a remarkable intellectual and imaginative sympathy; he is not uncritical, but his criticisms are based on patient and learned understanding. (The footnotes, which often creep up the page, make clear the breadth of his research.) Several times Boersma engages in comparison between apparently sharply contrasting figures—Aquinas and Palamas, Symeon the New Theologian and John of the Cross, Bonaventure and Nicholas of Cusa—not to mention the tensions found between early modern Puritans and Dutch Reformed: these explorations are invariably careful, fair, and immensely illuminating.

Underlying explicit concern with the beatific vision itself, there is another recurring leitmotif, what Boersma calls "sacramental ontology," that is, the notion, characteristic of the ancient and medieval world, that reality is symbolic, both in the sense that the material world discloses spiritual reality, which is expressed through the material lending it meaning, and in the way in which, throughout the material, animal, human world, there is an interlocking symbolism that draws on the fundamental spiritual-material symbolism and reveals a kind of cosmic sympathy, reaching throughout the whole created order. The notion that everything has a purpose, a telos, links the sacramental ontology with the beatific vision as the goal of humankind, if not of creation.

One talks nowadays about an "ecumenical theology," which sometimes runs the risk of being so respectful of disagreement as to tend to blandness. Hans Boersma seems to me a one-man ecumenical movement, as he explores with a rare skill the different ways of thinking that have expressed Christian faith and hope. There is nothing bland about his exploration, which rather delights in tension and difference. Reading this book, I was reminded of the observation of Antoine de Saint-Exupéry: "Linked to our brothers [and sisters] by a common goal which is situated outside ourselves, only then do we breathe and experience shows us that to love is not to gaze at one another, but rather to look together in the same direction." If ecumenism is indeed the fruit of mutual love among Christians, then it might find fulfillment by looking, as Hans Boersma encourages us, "together in the same direction," that is, toward the beatific vision promised to the pure in heart.

ANDREW LOUTH
Professor Emeritus, University of Durham, UK
Honorary Fellow, Vrije Universiteit, Amsterdam

ACKNOWLEDGMENTS

This book has its origin in a course on the beatific vision, which I taught in various versions at Regent College in Vancouver, at Saint Louis University (SLU), and at Nashotah House (Wisconsin). The interactions with my students greatly helped mature my thinking on the topic of the beatific vision. I owe a special word of thanks to the board of governors and the administration of Regent College. They graciously allowed me to devote two full years to research and writing, the first one as the Danforth Visiting Chair in Theological Studies at Saint Louis University (2015–2016) and the second as a sabbatical leave at the Theologische Universiteit Kampen (TUK; Netherlands) (2016–2017). This extended hiatus from my teaching duties has allowed me to focus intensely on the topic of this book, for which I am most grateful. I also thank my colleagues at SLU for inviting me to take up the Danforth Chair and for the wonderful opportunity this offered me to do some in-depth study. The hospitality that the TUK offered me was marvelous, and it was a true blessing to spend time reading and writing in the beautiful medieval city of Kampen.

Numerous family members, students, colleagues, and friends have read parts of this book and offered corrections and suggestions. Their help has simply been invaluable. They have pulled me out of culs-de-sac, encouraged me to stay on the main road, cautioned me against problematic shortcuts, and pushed me to explore different avenues. Of course, I am ultimately responsible for the book as it is, but I am keenly aware of how much I have benefited from the input of others. It is a blessing to have children who read my work and think along with me—Gerald, John, Corine, Jonathan, and Pete. I owe much to the comments and suggestions offered by Michael Allen, Khaled Anatolios, Silvianne Aspray, Fr. John Behr, Todd Billings, Sarah

Coakley, Richard Cross, Edwin Chr. van Driel, Fr. Simon Gaine, OP, Jay Hammond, George Harinck, Russell Hillard, Matthew Levering, Dominic Manganiello, Michael McClymond, Gerald McDermott, Mark McInroy, David Meconi, SJ, Nomi Pritz-Bennett, Tracy Russell, Lydia Schumacher, Tom Schwanda, Jeanne Shami, Austin Stevenson, Kyle Strobel, Matthew Thomas, and Derek Witten. My research assistants, Austin Stevenson and Brian Dant, are simply among the best; their assistance went well beyond the call of duty. Thanks, Brian, for your fabulous work on the index! Finally, a special word of gratitude to Alec Arnold: Thank you so very much, not only for your hard work as my research assistant, for faithfully reading and offering commentary on every chapter, and for the drawing of Plato's cave (in chapter 2), but especially also for your (and Crystal's) gracious hospitality during my stay in Saint Louis!

It has been a privilege to try out some of my ideas through several speaking engagements. It was a particular honor and joy to deliver the annual Herman Bavinck Lecture at the TUK, which gave me an opportunity to study Abraham Kuyper's theology of the beatific vision. I also offer a warm thank-you to Chad Raith for inviting me to do a presentation for the Paradosis Center at John Brown University; Paul Gavrilyuk for organizing a superb colloquium, "Rethinking the Tradition," at the University of St. Thomas; Kees van der Kooi for the opportunity to speak at the Bavinck Center for Reformed and Evangelical Theology at the Vrije Universiteit of Amsterdam; and Warren Smith and Paul Griffiths for asking me to deliver the Duke Lecture at the Boston Colloquy in Historical Theology. I also thank James Ernest and Michael Thomson and their colleagues at Eerdmans Publishing for their backing of this project and for the careful professional support throughout the process. I also appreciate the permission to republish two articles: "Becoming Human in the Face of God: Gregory of Nyssa's Unending Search for the Beatific Vision," *IJST* 17 (2015): 131–51, and "Blessing and Glory: Abraham Kuyper on the Beatific Vision," *CTJ* 52 (2017): 205–41.

Finally, my wife Linda has supported me throughout this process, in part by putting up with a lengthy absence while I was in Saint Louis. She also read the entire manuscript, offering numerous suggestions. Most importantly, I see in her face the light of God shining in my life, for which I am eternally grateful.

ABBREVIATIONS

ACQR	*American Catholic Quarterly Review*
ACW	Ancient Christian Writers
Adv. Prax.	Tertullian, *Adversus Praxean*
AncPhil	*Ancient Philosophy*
ANF	*The Ante-Nicene Fathers*
AnM	*Annuale Mediaevale*
Ascent	John of the Cross, *The Ascent of Mount Carmel*
AugStud	*Augustinian Studies*
BBGG	*Bollettino della Badia Greca di Grottaferrata*
Beat.	Gregory of Nyssa, *Homilies on the Beatitudes*
BLE	*Bulletin de littérature ecclésiastique*
CA	Thomas Aquinas, *Catena aurea*
Cant.	Gregory of Nyssa, *In Canticum canticorum* (*Homilies on the Song of Songs*)
CH	*Church History*
Civ. Dei	Augustine, *De civitate Dei* (*On the City of God*)
ClQ	*Classical Quarterly*
Comm.	*Calvin's Commentaries*
Conf.	Augustine, *Confessiones* (*Confessions*)
Cons.	Augustine, *De consensu Evangelistarum* (*Agreement among the Evangelists*)
CTJ	*Calvin Theological Journal*
Dark Night	John of the Cross, *The Dark Night*
De divinis nominibus	Thomas Aquinas, *In librum beati Dionysii De divinis nominibus exposition*
Dem.	Irenaeus, *Demonstratio apostolicae praedicationis* (*Proof of the Apostolic Preaching*)

Div. quaest.	Augustine, *De diversis quaestionibus octoginta tribus* (*Eighty-Three Different Questions*)
DN	Pseudo-Dionysius, *The Divine Names*
Doctr. chr.	Augustine, *De doctrina Christiana* (*On Christian Teaching*)
DOP	*Dumbarton Oaks Papers*
DVD	Nicholas of Cusa, *De visione Dei* (*On the Vision of God*)
Eccl.	Gregory of Nyssa, *In Ecclesiasten homiliae* (*Homilies on Ecclesiastes*)
Enarrat. Ps.	Augustine, *Enarrationes in Psalmos* (*Expositions of the Psalms*)
Enn.	Plotinus, *Enneads*
Ep.	Augustine, *Epistulae* (*Letters*)
ET	English translation
Eun. 2	Gregory of Nyssa, *Contra Eunomium liber II* (*The Second Book against Eunomius*)
FC	Fathers of the Church
FcS	*Franciscan Studies*
FirAn	John Donne, *The First Anniuersarie*
FP	*Faith and Philosophy*
FZPhTh	*Freiburger Zeitschrift für Philosophie und Theologie*
Gen. litt.	Augustine, *De Genesi ad litteram* (*The Literal Meaning of Genesis*)
GNO	*Gregorii Nysseni Opera*
GOTR	*Greek Orthodox Theological Review*
Haer.	Irenaeus, *Adversus haereses* (*Against Heresies*)
HLQ	*Huntington Library Quarterly*
Hom.	Gregory Palamas, *Homilies*
HTR	*Harvard Theological Review*
IJST	*International Journal of Systematic Theology*
Inst.	Calvin, *Institutes of the Christian Religion*
Itin.	Bonaventure, *Itinerarium mentis in Deum* (*The Soul's Journey into God*)
ITQ	*Irish Theological Quarterly*
JES	*Journal of Ecumenical Studies*
JHP	*Journal of the History of Philosophy*
JHRP	*Journal for the History of Reformed Pietism*
JMRCul	*Journal of Medieval Religious Cultures*
JPT	*Journal of Psychology and Theology*
JR	*Journal of Religion*
JTS	*Journal of Theological Studies*

J Value Inq	*Journal of Value Inquiry*
L&T	*Literature and Theology*
LCL	Loeb Classical Library
Macr.	Gregory of Nyssa, *Vita s. Macrinae* (*Life of Saint Macrina*)
Metaph.	Aristotle, *Metaphysics*
ModTh	*Modern Theology*
MT	Pseudo-Dionysius, *Mystical Theology*
NB	*New Blackfriars*
NedTT	*Nederlands Theologisch Tijdschrift*
NPNF II	*A Select Library of Nicene and Post-Nicene Fathers of the Christian Church*, Second Series
NTL	The New Testament Library
NV Eng	*Nova et Vetera*, English edition
Op. hom.	Gregory of Nyssa, *De hominis opificio* (*On the Making of Man*)
OSAP	*Oxford Studies in Ancient Philosophy*
PACPhA	*Proceedings of the American Catholic Philosophical Association*
Par.	Dante, *Paradiso*
Perf.	Gregory of Nyssa, *De perfectione* (*On Perfection*)
PG	Patrologiae Cursus Completus: Series Graeca
Phaedr.	Plato, *Phaedrus*
Phys.	Aristotle, *Physics*
Pol.	Plato, *Politicus* (*Statesman*)
ProEccl	*Pro Ecclesia*
Proslogium	Anselm, *Proslogium* (*Proslogion*)
PTMS	Princeton Theological Monograph Series
Purg.	Dante, *Purgatorio*
Quant. an.	Augustine, *De quantitate animae* (*The Greatness of the Soul*)
Red. art.	Bonaventure, *De reductione artium ad theologiam* (*On the Reduction of the Arts to Theology*)
RelS	*Religious Studies*
Rep.	Plato, *Republic*
RSR	*Recherches de science religieuse*
RTAM	*Recherches de théologie ancienne et médiévale*
SA	Studia Anselmiana
ScEs	*Science et esprit*
SCG	Thomas Aquinas, *Summa contra Gentiles*
SecAn	John Donne, *The Second Anniuersarie*

Sent.	Thomas Aquinas, *Scriptum super Sententiis*
Sermons	John Donne, *The Sermons of John Donne*
SJT	*Scottish Journal of Theology*
SMC	*Studies in Medieval Culture*
SP	*Studia Patristica*
ST	Thomas Aquinas, *Summa theologiae*
STC	Alfred W. Pollard and G. R. Redgrave, eds., *A Short-Title Catalogue of Books Printed in England, Scotland, and Ireland and of English Books Printed Abroad, 1475–1640*
Super Matth.	Thomas Aquinas, *Super Evangelium S. Matthaei Lectura*
SVTQ	*St. Vladimir's Theological Quarterly*
Symp.	Plato, *Symposium*
TC	*Textual Cultures*
TDNT	*Theological Dictionary of the New Testament*
Theaet.	Plato, *Theaetetus*
Thomist	*The Thomist: A Speculative Quarterly Review*
Tim.	Plato, *Timaeus*
TMA	*The Merton Annual*
Triads	Gregory Palamas, *Triads in Defense of the Holy Hesychasts*
Trin.	Augustine, *De Trinitate* (*The Trinity*)
TS	*Theological Studies*
TSLL	*Texas Studies in Literature and Language*
UTQ	*University of Toronto Quarterly*
VC	*Vigiliae Christianae*
VCSup	Supplements to Vigiliae Christianae
Vit. Moys.	Gregory of Nyssa, *De vita Moysis* (*The Life of Moses*)
VT	*Vetus Testamentum*
Wing	Donald Goddard Wing et al., eds., *A Short-Title Catalogue of Books Printed in England, Scotland, Ireland, Wales, and British America, and of English Books Printed in Other Countries, 1641–1700*
WJE	*The Works of Jonathan Edwards*
WSA	The Works of Saint Augustine: A Translation for the 21st Century
WTJ	*Westminster Theological Journal*

INTRODUCTION

Why Beatific Vision?

Why beatific vision? Why make the claim that seeing God is the purpose of our life? One way to respond to this question is by evoking the tradition. To use Michael Polanyi's term, it is by lovingly "indwelling" the tradition that we come to see its inner strength.[1] At the same time, however, I do not simply want to make an appeal to the Christian tradition—even though it is true that this indirectly also involves an appeal to the Scriptures that inform this tradition. Appealing to a formal authority (such as tradition) is unlikely to convince all on its own. We must also ask what it is within the material contents of the doctrine of the beatific vision that has rendered it compelling to many in the history of the church as the telos of human existence.

First, however, we should explore what is and what is not implied in the claim that the beatific vision is our final aim. Throughout this book, when I speak of the beatific vision as the human telos, I am keenly aware that I am using a metaphor that, though present in Scripture itself, originates from human experience. That is to say, vision is a metaphor taken from everyday life, which we use to speak of the happiness for which we hope in the hereafter. Metaphors, as I understand them, derive their power from the way they function in relation to other words or descriptions and to the realities that they describe.[2] Metaphoric language that involves our relation to God

---

1. Cf. Michael Polanyi's discussions of "indwelling" a language, a cultural heritage, and moral teachings in *Knowing and Being: Essays by Michael Polanyi*, ed. Marjorie Grene (Chicago: University of Chicago Press, 1969), 148; and *The Tacit Dimension* (Garden City, NY: Doubleday, 1966), 16–18.

2. See further my discussion of metaphors in Hans Boersma, *Violence, Hospitality, and*

is particularly complex. These kinds of metaphors speak of a supernatural reality that we cannot directly access through the senses or through the abstraction of intellectual thought. The reliability of our metaphors depends, therefore, upon divine revelation. Whenever we use a metaphor to talk about our relationship to God, we implicitly make the claim that, in some manner, God stands behind our use of the metaphor in question.

This book does not argue that the language of vision fully or adequately describes our eschatological relationship with God. After all, as I just indicated, the language of vision gives us *only* a metaphor. That is not a negative thing; I am convinced that metaphors are the stuff of which all human language is made, and they allow us to make sense of the world around us. On my understanding even God makes use of our human web of metaphors when he stoops down to reveal himself to us. But we do need to remember the limits of metaphors—and indeed of all human language—particularly in describing our relationship to God. Just as our naming of God is always only analogous (because God infinitely transcends the human realities on which our verbal signs are based), words such as "vision" fail to describe our relationship with God in a straightforwardly univocal manner. Our access to God is always indirect: we do reach God, God himself, but we reach him obliquely—sacramentally—in and through human signs. By making the claim that the language of *visio Dei* is uniquely suitable to describe our ultimate relationship to God, therefore, I am not at all suggesting that I fully or adequately comprehend what our telos is like.

It is also true that Scripture (and the Christian tradition) uses a great variety of metaphors to refer to the reality of our relationship with God. Jesus himself, in his parables, often speaks of the coming kingdom—which comes about in his own telling of the stories—through all kinds of different metaphors. Just in the one chapter of Matthew 13, Jesus speaks of the kingdom's coming in a wide variety of ways. It is like the sowing of seed (Matt. 13:1–9, 18–23), which an enemy counters by sowing weeds (13:24–30, 36–43). The kingdom is like a mustard seed that a man sows in his field (13:31–32). It is like leaven that a woman hides in her flour (13:33). Again, Jesus compares the kingdom to a treasure hidden in a field (13:33) and to a pearl of great value (13:45–46). Both the treasure and the pearl are worth everything one owns (13:44, 46). The kingdom is also like a net that a fisherman throws into the sea to gather in fish (13:47–50). These are just the so-called kingdom parables

---

the Cross: Reappropriating the Atonement Tradition (Grand Rapids: Baker Academic, 2004), 99–114.

in Matthew's Gospel. In other parables, Jesus employs yet different metaphors to give expression to the eschaton and the events leading up to it: the parables of the wicked tenants (Matt. 21:33–44; Mark 12:1–11; Luke 20:9–16), the wedding feast (Matt. 22:1–14; Luke 14:16–24), the budding fig tree (Matt. 24:32–35; Mark 13:28–31; Luke 21:29–33), the faithful servant (Matt. 24:43–51; Mark 13:34–37; Luke 12:35–48), the ten virgins (Matt. 25:1–13), the rich fool (Luke 12:16–21), and the barren fig tree (Luke 13:6–9). No one parable, picture, or metaphor adequately or fully describes the reality of the eschaton.

Likewise, the final two chapters of the Bible speak of the eschaton by means of a dizzying array of images. The eschatological reality is spoken of as "a new heaven and a new earth" (Rev. 21:1). Here we find a "holy city," the "new Jerusalem," which comes down from heaven, and which with a mixing of metaphors is also called "a bride adorned for her husband" (21:2, 9–10). The adorned city is described in great detail (21:11–27). The same reality is also depicted with paradisal images: the water of life flows through the city, and the tree of life yields its fruit on both sides of the river (22:1–2). This garden city (again, a mixed metaphor) houses God himself, along with his people: "Behold, the dwelling place of God is with man" (21:3). Both of these broad-stroke metaphors and many of the numerous metaphors that John uses to fill in the smaller details (far too many to try to outline here) are rooted in the Old Testament. John knows that the only way to "make sense" of the glory of the eschaton is through recourse to numerous earlier, already known realities. He uses these depictions to arrive at something of an analogous approximation of the eschaton.

Nonetheless, not all these metaphors are equally suitable to describe our ultimate end. As far as I can see, for at least three reasons, theologians throughout the tradition have privileged the metaphor of vision.

The first reason is that it is simply a key metaphor in much of the Scriptures. Despite the plurality of images that we just noted in the two last chapters of Revelation, the metaphors of light and vision do play a particularly central role here. Saint John emphatically states that "the city has no need of sun or moon to shine on it, for the glory of God gives it light, and its lamp is the Lamb. By its light will the nations walk" (Rev. 21:23–24). John mentions the beatific vision explicitly when he comments: "They will see his face, and his name will be on their foreheads. And night will be no more. They will need no light of lamp or sun, for the Lord God will be their light, and they will reign forever and ever" (22:4–5). Furthermore, throughout these final chapters of the Bible we are struck by the brightness of the new Jerusalem: the "radiance" (21:11) of the many shining jewels, the pure gold that is like "clear glass" (21:18), the numerous jewels on the foundations of the city walls (21:19–21), the pure gold of the city street, which is like "transparent glass" (21:21), and the water of life that is "bright as crystal"—all these images convey the impression of a city marked by unalloyed luminosity. I cannot give an overview here of the metaphor of seeing God in the Scriptures as a whole, but I trust that the theologians discussed throughout the book (as well as the biblical passages dealt with in the concluding chapter) will further demonstrate the biblical centrality of the metaphor of seeing God.[3]

Second, though it is true that each of our five senses gives some kind of apprehension of God, they do not all function in the same way. It seems to me that, at least in some sense, vision has priority over the others. To illustrate this, consider a meditation the Dutch neo-Calvinist theologian (as well as journalist and statesman) Abraham Kuyper published in his 1891 book *Voor een distel een mirt (A Myrtle for a Brier)*, in which he reflects on the relationship between vision and sacrament. Kuyper observes that God has made the eye infinitely more beautiful than the ear and has created it in a more exalted position than the ear.[4] The eye took priority in paradise, while the ear has become prominent merely as a result of the Fall. Kuyper does not mean to suggest that the sense of hearing is unimportant; it is by listening that we are saved. Nonetheless, he claims that, in the hereafter, the eye will again take the place of pride, since saved sinners are promised that they will see God face-to-face.[5] It is, therefore, a matter of great importance that God does not *speak* to us in the sacraments, but that we *see* him there.

3. The long tradition of reflection on the beatific vision is based primarily on the biblical promise that after death believers will see God face-to-face (cf. Job 19:26–27; Matt. 5:8; John 17:24; 1 Cor. 13:12; 2 Cor. 5:7; and 1 John 3:2). Also important are descriptions of theophanic appearances to Old as well as New Testament saints (e.g., the Lord's appearing to Abraham [Gen. 18]; Jacob [Gen. 28 and 32]; Moses [Exod. 33–34; Num. 12:7–8; Heb. 11:27]; Micaiah [1 Kings 22:19]; Isaiah [Isa. 6:1–5]; Ezekiel [Ezek. 1:4–28; 8:1–4]; Peter, James, and John [Matt. 17:1–8 and pars.]; Paul [Acts 9:3–9; 2 Cor. 12:1–4]; and John [Rev. 1:12–16; 4–5]), which occur despite repeated biblical claims that no one can see God (cf. Exod. 33:20; John 1:18; 1 Tim. 6:16; 1 John 4:12). Passages that speak more broadly about life before God in terms of vision or light also receive a lot of attention (e.g., Pss. 27; 36:9; 80:19; Isa. 26:10; 53:2; 64:4; 66:14; Matt. 18:10; John 14:8–9; 1 Cor. 2:9; 2 Cor. 3:18; 4:6; and Rev. 21:23–24). Where the influence of Gregory of Nyssa and of Dionysius has been prominent, reflection on these passages is often linked with attention to texts that speak of God's self-revelation in terms of darkness (cf. Exod. 20:21; 24:18; Ps. 18:11; Song 2:3; 5:2, 5–6).

4. Abraham Kuyper, "Hetgeen onze oogen gezien hebben," in *Voor een distel een mirt: Geestelijke overdenkingen bij den Heiligen Doop, het doen van belijdenis en het toegaan tot het Heilig Avondmaal* (Amsterdam: Wormser, 1891), 12–13.

5. Kuyper, "Hetgeen onze oogen gezien hebben," 13–14.

Kuyper situates this vision of God in the sacrament in between the *symbolic* vision of God in the tabernacle and the temple and the *real* vision of God in the hereafter.[6] Since neither of these is available to us today, God gives us a vision of himself in the sacraments. In the marvel of the sacraments, claims Kuyper, "the ear moves into the background, and the spoken word merely provides assistance. Meanwhile, the eye—and through the eye also the soul itself—is active, and you discern something of a holier touch of the divine life than you can ever experience through the Word."[7] The eye allows for a kind of communion with God that the ear cannot experience. In short, although in our fallen state hearing serves a remedial role, it is vision that has priority and perdures into eternity.

The final reason the beatific vision is a particularly apt metaphor to describe our eschatological happiness is that there is a kind of congruity between the human eye (and its power) and the being of God. I will discuss this point in detail in chapter 8, in connection with Dante. Dante's journey is a journey from language to vision. That is to say, as he moves up the spheres of paradise, words increasingly fail to describe what he sees. Words, for Dante, are tethered to the plurality of this-worldly, created objects. That does not make them useless by any means; they are like sacraments (*sacramenta*) that lead us to the reality (*res*) of God. Unlike words, however, vision captures its object all at once. What is more, vision—certainly on the ancient understanding—reaches out to unite viewer and object.[8] And transformation ("transhumanizing," Dante calls it) cannot but be the result of such union with God. Vision, therefore, is "theocentric" in a way that the other senses are not. The beatific vision, in its perpetual gaze on God in Christ, centers like nothing else on enjoying him. None of the biblical metaphors that I mentioned above—mustard seed, banquet, city, and even the image of the bride-groom relationship—quite match that of vision. This does not at all render them superfluous. It is simply that they are less ultimate than vision. No other metaphor implies the same thorough change in human beings, transfiguring them to be like God. And no other metaphor implies the same continuity of attachment to God (even if on this point the metaphor of the bride-groom relationship comes close).

6. Kuyper, "Hetgeen onze oogen gezien hebben," 15–16.
7. Kuyper, "Hetgeen onze oogen gezien hebben," 17.
8. For more detailed discussion, see chap. 8, section entitled "Sending forth Its rays / It is the source of every good."

History and Analogy

Our longing for this vision of God ensures that eschatology can never turn into an afterthought, which we deal with once everything else has been said. To be sure, the Christian faith is a historical religion, marked by a history of salvation that leads to a climactic denouement at the end of time. In his book *Eschatology*, Hans Schwarz points out the uniqueness of the Christian faith in that it has a linear rather than a cyclical concept of time, a "time arrow that has a definite starting point and a definite goal."[9] By combining the belief that there is only one true God (monotheism) with the notion that this God is the one who has created and redeemed everything (universalistic), the Judeo-Christian understanding regards God as the God not of the past but of the future.[10] "Yahweh," comments Schwarz, "provided the origin of the world; he is active in it and will provide its redemption. This latter part came to its fulfillment in the Christian faith when the history of Jesus of Nazareth was understood as the decisive redemptive act of God."[11] The Christian faith, Schwarz helpfully reminds us, is a historical faith, predicated on the conviction that God leads the world through time to its climactic redemption of a "new world" (παλιγγενεσία) (Matt. 19:28). In this sense, the *eschata* are literally the last things—the events surrounding the end of history.

All of this is true as far as it goes: inasmuch as the beatific vision is our telos or end, eschatology deals with "last things." In the course of the previous century, however, a number of theologians have reminded us that salvation history is not simply a gradual moving forward from one event to the next. Karl Barth rightly saw that we should treat the eschaton not just horizontally (as something that will happen at the end-time) but also vertically (calling us into judgment today).[12] Oscar Cullmann took Christ to be the "midpoint" of history,[13] and he compared Christ's victory on the cross to the Allied forces' securing of a beachhead on D-day at Normandy in 1944, while V-day would have to wait one more long, harsh winter.[14] For Cullmann, the Christ event

---

9. Hans Schwarz, *Eschatology* (Grand Rapids: Eerdmans, 2000), 7.

10. Schwarz, *Eschatology*, 10.

11. Schwarz, *Eschatology*, 12.

12. Barth's revolutionary statement in this regard came in the second edition of his *Römerbrief*: Karl Barth, *The Epistle to the Romans*, trans. Edwyn C. Hoskyns (Oxford: Oxford University Press, 1968).

13. Oscar Cullmann, *Christ and Time: The Primitive Christian Conception of Time*, trans. Floyd V. Filson, rev. ed. (Philadelphia: Westminster, 1964), 18.

14. Cullmann, *Christ and Time*, 84, 87, 145–46.

(D-day) inaugurated the eschaton in the midst of history. Jürgen Moltmann took his starting point in Revelation 1:4 ("Grace to you and peace from him who is and who was and who is to come"), arguing that the verb "to come" (ἔρχομαι) implies that "God's Being is in his coming" because the "linear concept of time is broken through" by the use of the verb "to come" rather than "to be."[15] The eschaton was not a straightforward chronological *futurum* but was instead the eschatological arrival of the *adventus* of God.[16]

These approaches all have their strengths and weaknesses, but each in its own way reminds us that a linear understanding of history—while, as far as I can tell, broadly consonant with the Scriptures—does not provide us with a complete picture. One way to point up the inadequacy of a linear understanding is by complementing it with the image of a spiral: a spiral keeps coming back to the same place. Or, at least, in some sense it does; in reality, on each turn, the circle always comes around at a point just a little higher than before. A spiral view of history, therefore, is an analogous view of history, in that it recognizes both similarities and differences between the past and the present. To say that history functions like a spiral, then, does not reduce it to a cycle. In a cyclical understanding, nothing really new happens; all we have is repetition. An analogous or spiral view of history recognizes both similarity and difference between various moments in time.

The well-known twentieth-century patristics scholar Jean Daniélou often drew attention to this analogical or spiral functioning of history in the early church's understanding. He claims that the search for similarity within dissimilarity lies behind the patristic understanding of biblical typology:

> In the gradual unfolding of God's design, there appears a system of analogies between his successive works, for all their distinct self-sufficiency as separate creative acts. The Flood, the Passion, Baptism and the last Judgement, are closely linked together in one pattern. In each instance, though at different levels, there is a divine judgement on the sinful world, and a divine clemency whereby a man is spared to be the beginning of a new creation. Hence arises a new kind of symbolism, which is characteristic of the Bible. Its specific difference is historicity, for it denotes a relationship between various events belonging to sacred history. It is called *typology*,

---

15. Jürgen Moltmann, *The Coming of God: Christian Eschatology*, trans. Margaret Kohl (Minneapolis: Fortress, 1996), 23. See also *God in Creation: A New Theology of Creation and the Spirit of God*, trans. Margaret Kohl (San Francisco: Harper and Row, 1985), 133.

16. Moltmann, *The Coming of God*, 25.

from the wording of two passages in the New Testament: one where it is said of Adam that "he was the type (τύπος) of him who was to come" [Rom. 5:14]; and another where baptism is called the "type (ἀντίτυπος)" of the Flood [1 Pet. 3:21].[17]

According to Daniélou, the fathers detected a "system of analogies" (or spirals) within God's successive works in history, which means that they discerned typological resemblances throughout history.[18]

This understanding of analogy or typology is grounded in a high view of divine providence. The "similarity axis" of analogy is the result of the faithfulness of God in history; seeing that the same God is at work throughout time, we would expect to discover similarities within the linear unfolding of history, which result from the faithfulness of God's character. Typology reaches beyond this-worldly cause and effect because it sees historical events as grounded within the eternal character of divine providence. Matthew Levering, in his superb book entitled *Participatory Biblical Exegesis*, makes the point that we can go beyond an atomistic, linear understanding of history if we take seriously that history is an "ongoing participation in God's active providence."[19] Earlier moments in history can be types or analogues of subsequent events inasmuch as they are all grounded within the faithful character of God's overarching providence. Thus, an analogical or typological understanding of history upstages a modern, purely linear understanding of history, and it does so in the conviction that we can trace the faithful character of God through history.

Edward Pusey, the nineteenth-century Hebrew scholar from Christ Church, Oxford, was deeply intrigued by the "similarity axis" of the various historical moments in time. He usually characterized the link between (Old Testament) prophecy and (New Testament) fulfillment not as a relationship between type and *antitype* but as a relationship between type and *archetype*. The reason is that, for Pusey, all of history centers on Christ. He is the model, as it were, on which all other similarities within history are patterned. Christ is the very character of God's faithfulness, and the similarities found in his-

17. Jean Daniélou, *The Lord of History: Reflections on the Inner Meaning of History*, trans. Nigel Abercrombie (1958; reprint, Cleveland: Meridian/World, 1968), 140.

18. For further discussion of the relevance of Daniélou's views for biblical interpretation, see Hans Boersma, *Scripture as Real Presence: Sacramental Exegesis in the Early Church* (Grand Rapids: Baker Academic, 2017), 83–92.

19. Matthew Levering, *Participatory Biblical Exegesis* (Notre Dame: University of Notre Dame Press, 2008), 1.

tory (or the Scriptures) as leading up to Christ are all patterned after Christ as the archetype. Thus, although chronologically many historical types may precede the Christ event, ontologically Christ precedes them and is their origin (ἀρχή). He is, as it were, the providential master plan on which all of history is patterned. As George Westhaver puts it: "That which most fulfils the meaning of the types of the Old Testament, and which is also the fundamental reality of which they are copies or images, can be described as the Archetype or the substance of the type."[20] The similarities within history, therefore, are grounded in Christ as the archetype of God's faithfulness—or, to put it more theologically, as the substance or essence of the character of God.

We may speak, therefore, of Christ (the archetype) as the sacramental reality (*res*) in which the various historical events (the types) inhere or participate as sacraments (*sacramenta*). Pusey articulates the relationship as follows: "It has been well said, that God has appointed, as it were, a sort of sacramental union between the type and the archetype, so that as the type were nothing, except in as far as it represents, and is the medium of conveying the archetype to the mind, so neither can the archetype be conveyed except through the type. Though the consecrated element be not the sacrament, yet neither can the soul of the sacrament be obtained without it. God has joined them together, and man may not and can not put them asunder."[21] For Pusey, Christ—who in his person is the embodiment of the eternal Word or Son of God—is the sacramental reality (*res*) in which sacramental types (*sacramenta*) find their truth or identity.

In the incarnation, therefore, the reality of the eschaton truly has arrived. As the true human being, Christ is the telos of history. In his archetypal reality human beings find their true identity—the way they are meant to be. We could say, therefore, that we are human inasmuch as we are conformed to Christ. As we become more and more like Christ, we become more truly ourselves. It is not our past, therefore, but our future that properly tells us who we are. As imperfect types, our identity is grounded sacramentally—or, we could also say, teleologically—in Christ. Once we recognize Christ as the archetype of history, we also discover the teleological drive and the sac-

20. George Westhaver, "The Living Body of the Lord: E. B. Pusey's Types and Prophecies of the Old Testament" (PhD diss., Durham University, 2012), 168.

21. Edward Pusey, "Lectures on Types and Prophecies in the Old Testament" (unpublished lectures, 1836), 23. I am indebted to George Westhaver for providing me with an electronic copy of Pusey's lectures.

ramental character of history: the future reality of the archetype is already present within the shadowy types of history.

Sacramental Ontology and the Beatific Vision

A sacramental understanding of the beatific vision takes seriously the teleological character of history. A sacramental ontology closely links nature and the supernatural, earthly and heavenly realities, reason and faith, Old Testament Scriptures and gospel truth. In each of these doublets, the former participates in the latter, and the latter is really (or sacramentally) present within the former. A sacramental ontology treats the first item in each of the pairs as the sacrament (*sacramentum*), and the latter as the reality (*res*). I have elsewhere explained in greater detail what I understand by a sacramental ontology[22] and what its implications are for our interpretation of Scripture.[23] In this book, I take the next step and ask the question: What are the implications of a sacramental ontology for our understanding of the beatific vision?

We usually deal with the topic of sacramental ontology by using vertical or spatial metaphors. When we think of this-worldly, natural realities participating in the supernatural, divine life, we conjure up in our minds a picture of earthly realities ascending or going up: the journey is anagogical (literally, upward-leading). Similarly, when we say that God in Christ is sacramentally present in this world, we tend to think of a supernatural descent into this world. God makes himself really present in the created order. Whether in our imagination we move from the bottom up (through language of participation) or from the top down (speaking of real presence), the metaphor is spatial or vertical.

In connection with the beatific vision, however, we have to think in horizontal or temporal categories. We anticipate seeing God at the end of our lives and, particularly, at the end of history. The telos or purpose of our lives is the vision of God (*visio Dei*) in Christ. Hence, we could interpret life as a pilgrimage to a sacred place and—as I do in the final chapter of this book— treat history as an apprenticeship that aims at acquiring a skill. The sacred place is the face of God, and the skill the beatific vision. As we will see in this

22. Hans Boersma, *Heavenly Participation: The Weaving of a Sacramental Tapestry* (Grand Rapids: Eerdmans, 2011).
23. Boersma, *Scripture as Real Presence*.

book, theologians through the history of the church have been convinced that the beatific vision is the ultimate reality (*res*) at which we aim. It is the only proper telos of our life. (To be precise, it is not *our vision* but *God in Christ* that is the sacramental reality at which we aim. Speaking somewhat improperly, we can say that we aim for the beatific vision. This vision beatifies us—literally, makes us happy—inasmuch as it unites us to God.) The doctrine of the beatific vision broadens our understanding of sacramental ontology by drawing attention to horizontal or temporal metaphors: we anticipate the face of God at the end of time. The only reality worthy of being called the sacramental truth (*res*) of our lives is the end-point of our lives: God in Christ.

The underlying assumption in this study is that the telos of the beatific vision lies embedded in our human nature. That is to say, we are true to the way God has made us when we make the vision of God our ultimate desire. Once we have arrived at the final cause or telos of our lives (God in Christ), we will be truly ourselves. We will have arrived at our true being, Christ—the sacramental reality of the *totus Christus*, as Saint Augustine typically calls it.[24] I will unpack this teleological relationship between our nature as humans and Christ as our eschatological goal in greater detail in chapter 1. In doing so, I am inspired by Henri de Lubac's rearticulation of the sacramental relationship between nature and the supernatural, which he famously articulated in his 1946 book *Surnaturel*.[25] I have benefited tremendously from reading de Lubac, and I think he was right to draw attention to the fact that the beatific vision as human beings' final cause lies embedded in some manner in our nature. (At the same time, I think it is important to acknowledge that our desires are not always in sync with our nature. Sometimes we surreptitiously make other things our ends, and by doing so we act against our nature.) In this book, I will not rehearse in any detail the Catholic debate surrounding the supernatural. Instead, I will go beyond the broader metaphysical issue of the sacramental relationship between nature and the supernatural to the question of what it means to conceive of the beatific vision sacramentally. If the beatific vision is our ultimate telos, then how does God's economy—or,

24. Cf. Michael Cameron, "The Emergence of *Totus Christus* as Hermeneutical Center in Augustine's *Enarrationes in Psalmos*," in *The Harp of Prophecy: Early Christian Interpretation of the Psalms*, ed. Brian Daley and Paul R. Kolbet (Notre Dame: University of Notre Dame Press, 2015), 205–26.

25. See my discussion of the broader *nouvelle théologie* movement in Hans Boersma, *Nouvelle Théologie and Sacramental Ontology: A Return to Mystery* (Oxford: Oxford University Press, 2009).

as I call it in the last chapter of this book, God's pedagogy—work in line with this ultimate end? I am particularly interested, therefore, in how the future end of the beatific vision links up with the vision that God gives us already today. Saint Paul insists that "we walk by faith, not by sight" (2 Cor. 5:7). At the same time, faith too is a kind of vision, even if we only "see in a mirror dimly" (1 Cor. 13:12). We need to ask, therefore, how God's pedagogy (God's gift of a partial vision of him today) prepares us for the future face-to-face vision of him.

Theologies of the beatific vision have struggled with the question of how to speak of the object of the vision. What do we mean when we say we hope to see God? The church fathers typically shied away from saying that in the beatific vision we will see the essence of God. The reason, I think, is their quite appropriate fear that we might end up claiming it is possible to comprehend God exhaustively. The divine attribute of invisibility—illustrated by the biblical notion that one cannot see God and live (cf. Exod. 33:20; John 1:18)—prevented the fathers from claiming that we can ever see the divine essence. The same salutary caution lies behind the Eastern distinction between God's essence and his energies, along with the claim that we participate only in the latter. In this book, I am with the church fathers and the Orthodox in emphatically maintaining that we will never comprehend or exhaust the nature of God; there is always more of the infinite God to apprehend, and this is why I endorse Gregory of Nyssa's concept of an "eternal progress" (*epektasis*) in the being of God.

This *epektasis*, however, means progress within the *being* of God. That is to say, whether or not we use the language of divine energies, we do need to confess that the beatific vision is a vision of God's very own character as revealed in Christ. As we will see in chapter 3, few theologians had as thoroughly a christological understanding of what it means to see God as did Gregory of Nyssa. If it is within the eternal tabernacle, or with our eyes fixed on the heavenly groom—both images of Christ, on Nyssen's understanding—that we see God himself, then this must entail that we see the true or faithful character of God in Christ. Seeing God in Christ, therefore, is at the same time a vision of God's nature or God's essence. (After all, Scripture itself already intimates that we will become partakers of the divine "nature" [φύσεως; 2 Pet. 1:4].) Indeed, it is precisely *inasmuch as we see Christ that we see the very character of God and so participate also in who he is, that is to say, in his being or essence.* No matter how deeply we enter into the being of God—or, as the cover of this book depicts it, no matter how many icons we impose on top of each other—in the end we are still faced with the face of

12

Christ, for in him alone do we see the essence of God.[26] The debate between East and West has been bedeviled by the fear (on the part of the East) that to see the essence of God means to leave Christ behind. This apprehension seems understandable to me, considering what I think is a christological deficiency in Thomas Aquinas's understanding of the *visio Dei*. Nonetheless, whether we see only shadowy sacraments here on earth (in creation, theophanies, or Scripture) or in the future attain to the heavenly reality itself, either way we see God's true character or essence in Christ. Whenever we see God—both today and in the eschaton—we see him in Christ. And (astounding mercy!) there is always infinitely more to see.

This book mostly approaches the key issue obliquely. Throughout, I am interested in what theologians in the past have said about the beatific vision and in what it meant for them to treat it not just as our goal but also *as the sacramental end that, in some ways, is already present in our lives*. To the degree that we live in sync with the final end for which God has created us, we are already being habituated to seeing God in the here and now of our everyday lives. While we may reserve the language of "beatific vision" for the ultimate, eschatological goal, this sacramental reality must, in some ways, already become present in our lives today. Our day-to-day lives must be shaped not by the "purely natural" world of immanent cause and effect. Rather, it is the ultimate telos of the beatific vision that determines our priorities and molds our desires.

In my understanding, therefore, it would be very odd if the human telos of the *visio Dei* had no link with a spirituality of contemplation here on earth. Just as the pilgrims would sing the Songs of Ascent (Pss. 120–134) on their pilgrimage to Jerusalem, so we contemplate Christ in anticipation of the face-to-face vision of God in Christ. *A truly sacramental understanding of the beatific vision, therefore, points us to the recognition of the real presence*

26. On the book cover, the four circles are comprised of the following icons (starting from the center): (1) the face of Christ in a twelfth-century *acheiropoietos* ("not made by hands") icon from the Assumption Cathedral in the Kremlin, Moscow, currently held in the Tretyakov Gallery in Moscow; (2) the halo of the thirteenth-century Christ Pantocrator in the Deesis mosaic of the Hagia Sophia in Istanbul; (3) the gown—along with the Greek and Latin Gospel text—from the Christus Pantocrator mosaic in the apse of the Catholic cathedral of Cefalù, Sicily (ca. 1130); (4) part of a Christ Pantocrator icon—with the Gospel text in Church Slavonic—that the Vysotsky Monastery in Serpukhov (south of Moscow) received from Constantinople between ca. 1387 and 1395 and that is currently housed in the Tretyakov Gallery in Moscow. The Gospel text in the last two icons is that of John 8:12: "I am the light of the world. Whoever follows me will not walk in darkness, but will have the light of life." I am indebted to Daniel Galadza for his expertise in Church Slavonic.

of Christ already in this life, in anticipation of the beatific vision of God in the hereafter. Few have put it better than the Puritan theologian Isaac Ambrose: "Consider that *looking unto Jesus* is the work of heaven. . . . If then we like not this work, how will we live in heaven?"[27] Ambrose's sentiment is the one I will trace throughout this book. Whenever a theologian enjoins us to like the very work that we will do eternally in heaven, we may be confident we're dealing with a theologian who has a sacramental understanding of the beatific vision. The work on earth may be only a preliminary and shadowy sacramental anticipation, but it is sacramental nonetheless—preparatory practice that already participates in the reality itself.

Chapter Outline

Should you need a shortcut to reading this book, I would recommend going through chapters 1 and 13. Those who wish to know how I connect the beatific vision to the broader question of a sacramental ontology, and perhaps wonder what happened historically to cause the decline of the doctrine of the beatific vision, may want to read chapter 1 ("Plausibility and Vision"). Here I discuss how a sacramental ontology provides the plausibility structure for the beatific vision, and I turn to Saint Anselm's *Proslogion* as an example of a sacramental approach to the beatific vision. I then discuss Hans Urs von Balthasar (Swiss Catholic) and Herman Bavinck (Dutch Reformed) as theologians who sideline the doctrine of the beatific vision. In chapter 13 ("Pedagogy and Vision") I most fully explain my own understanding of the beatific vision. There I treat the doctrine of the beatific vision by characterizing our journey toward it as a pedagogical process of apprenticeship. I discuss four characteristics of the beatific vision that I think are of paramount importance within this apprenticeship: divine providence, teleology, Christ-centeredness, and transformation. Each of these four characteristics contributes to the divine purpose of enabling us to see God as he is in Christ. I will argue that God trains us to see his character (that is to say, his essence) by transforming our eyes and mind.

Those with more patience or time may wish to read the intervening chapters as well, in each of which I deal with one (or more) theologian's treatment

---

27. Isaac Ambrose, *Looking unto Jesus a view of the everlasting Gospel, or, the souls eying of Jesus as carrying on the great work of mans salvation from first to last* (London, 1658; Wing A2956), 1.3.7 (p. 46).

of a topic that relates directly to the beatific vision. The overall presentation is straightforwardly diachronic. The three central sections of the book deal with early Christian thought (part 1), medieval thought (part 2), and Protestant thought (part 3), respectively. This division does not imply the pretension of a fulsome history of the doctrine of the beatific vision. To my knowledge, such a book does not exist—neither Kenneth Kirk's 1928 Bampton Lectures nor Vladimir Lossky's *The Vision of God* really provides such a history.[28] Since numerous theologians in the tradition have regarded the beatific vision as our final end, the theological reflection on it is expansive, and it would require something like Bernard McGinn's six volumes on the history of spiritual theology (*The Presence of God*)—only with a narrower focus on the beatific vision—to do this task properly. I am keenly aware of the historical limitations and gaps of this book. My excuse is that I simply don't pretend to write an entire history of the doctrine.

What I have done instead is to match key issues pertaining to the beatific vision with individual theologians. The one exception to this is the opening chapter of part 1 (on early Christian thought). In this chapter (chap. 2, "Philosophy and Vision") I discuss Plato and Plotinus, because I thought it important to trace their thought, both so as to analyze how they positively impacted the later Christian theology of the beatific vision and to discuss their limits and shortcomings vis-à-vis a Christian approach to the doctrine. Each of the subsequent chapter deals with one or more theologians in relation to a topic that is of importance for the doctrine of the beatific vision. For example, I deal with the question of eternal progress (*epektasis*) in chapter 3 ("Progress and Vision"), focusing on Gregory of Nyssa. In chapter 4 ("Anticipation and Vision"), I raise the much-disputed question of whether or not Augustine thought it possible to share in some way in the beatific vision today.

Part 2, on medieval theology, begins with a discussion of the transfiguration—a major topic in the history of Christian thought—in chapter 5 ("Transfiguration and Vision"), in connection with Gregory Palamas and Thomas Aquinas. While the vision of light is obviously central to the beatific vision, we experience both light and darkness in our lives, and in chapter 6 ("Mystical Union and Vision") I discuss their relationship by looking at

28. Kenneth E. Kirk, *The Vision of God: The Christian Doctrine of the Summum Bonum; The Bampton Lectures for 1928* (London: Longmans, Green, 1932); Vladimir Lossky, *The Vision of God*, trans. Asheleigh Moorhouse, 2nd ed., Library of Orthodox Theology 2 (1963; reprint, Leighton Buzzard, UK: Faith Press, 1973).

Symeon the New Theologian (theologian of light) and John of the Cross (theologian of darkness). The question of whether the beatific vision is primarily a matter of understanding or of enjoyment—an issue on which medieval scholastic theologians disagreed—is the focus of chapter 7 ("Faculties and Vision"), and I deal with it by juxtaposing Bonaventure and Nicholas of Cusa. Next, in chapter 8 ("Speech and Vision"), I turn to the role of vision in relation to speech, and here I look at Dante Alighieri, since in his *Paradiso* he reflected deeply on the respective roles of both.

The section on Protestant thought (part 3) begins in chapter 9 with a discussion of John Calvin ("Accommodation and Vision"), who is not usually read with an eye to his understanding of the beatific vision, but who did consider the topic carefully, and whose pedagogical approach made a substantive contribution.[29] The "new philosophy" of the following century played an important role in rupturing the sacramental unity between heaven and earth, and in chapter 10 ("Modernity and Vision") I trace John Donne's mournful awareness of this and discuss how in his poetry and sermons he put forward the beatific vision as a biblical antidote. The Reformation tradition was by no means homogeneous, and I compare in chapter 11 ("Christ and Vision") several English Puritans with the Dutch neo-Calvinist Abraham Kuyper, asking especially the question of how Christology functioned in their respective approaches. Chapter 12 ("Mediation and Vision") provides an exposition of the beatific vision in Jonathan Edwards's theology (in comparison with Thomas Aquinas). My discovery of Edwards's theology of the beatific vision has been a highlight for me, and I hope that my appreciation of his sacramental and christological treatment of the beatific vision will prove contagious.

---

29. I am much indebted to James Ernest for encouraging me to explore Calvin's views on the beatific vision.

CHAPTER 1

PLAUSIBILITY AND VISION

The Beatific Vision in Modernity

Sacramental Teleology

The final end of human beings is the vision of God. To some, this truth may seem self-evident: What greater good could we possibly look forward to? It would be foolhardy, however, for me simply to assume that every reader of this book will immediately be sympathetic to this claim. Some readers may well wish to challenge the plausibility of using the metaphor of the vision of God (*visio Dei*) for eternal life. The prospect of seeing God may have been central to patristic and medieval readers of Scripture, but perhaps there is good reason we have left behind many of the elements of a premodern worldview. Our values are not the same as those of our forebears. Otherworldliness, aversion to materiality, and ascetic self-denial characterized an outlook that our society no longer recognizes as its own. Instead, the earth and its future viability, the material well-being of all its inhabitants, and justice in human relationships have become today's primary concerns. With this shift from heavenly to earthly concerns, the notion of "seeing God" may come across as an implausible metaphor to describe the eschaton.

It is incumbent on me, therefore, to make a case for the plausibility of the beatific vision. I want to begin by asking what has happened to the traditional teaching of the beatific vision. Why is it so unfamiliar to many of us? Why does the Pauline promise of a face-to-face vision of God hardly seem like a promise at all? The answer, I think, is that the beatific vision no longer fits within the broader framework of our lives. It is the way in which we look at things (and people) and the way we treat them that make us shrug our shoulders about the beatific vision. In short, the doctrine of the beatific vision is an ill fit within the changed plausibility structures of our society.[1] Moreover, it is my conviction that we have every reason to challenge the modern plausibility structure as an illusory construct, which has concealed the real world with its final end from our view.[2]

So, what is it about our changed plausibility structures that makes us turn away from the beatific vision? Most basically, I suggest, it is that *we have done away with the belief that the purpose (telos) of things lies sacramentally embedded within them*.[3] To be sure, it is possible to think of ends or purposes in different ways. Just because someone rejects the idea that purposes are sacramentally embedded within things (or people) doesn't mean he can no longer talk about purposes at all. It is possible, at least theoretically, to conceive of purposes as lying outside of things or objects. Still, this is not a very promising way of looking at ends. In this book I go on the assumption that once we say that the telos of a thing is extrinsic to it—rather than being sacramentally embedded in it—the logical next step is to give up on teleology altogether. The basic reason for this is that if the purpose of a thing is not inherent in its nature, we are forced to decide, in an arbitrary way, what purpose to assign to it or give it. If the end of a thing is not objectively present to it, the best we can do is to assign it subjectively. The interminable conflicts to which this inevitably gives rise have led to the postmodern resignation that we may as well give up on a shared vision of ends altogether. A world that is solely defined by its material DNA, therefore, is a world without purpose.

1. The notion of "plausibility structure," which I use in much of this chapter, derives from Peter L. Berger, *The Sacred Canopy: Elements of a Sociological Theory of Religion* (Garden City, NY: Doubleday, 1967), 45: "Each world requires a social 'base' for its continuing existence as a world that is real to actual human beings. This 'base' may be called its plausibility structure."

2. It will be clear that, despite using the language of "plausibility structure," I don't come at this topic from a sociological perspective. While our culture's plausibility structure may render it more difficult (or at least less likely) to sustain the doctrine of the beatific vision, I am convinced that a sacramental ontology is not one of a number of social constructs but is in line with the way things actually are, so that we must retrieve the doctrine of the beatific vision.

3. While doctrinal attention to the beatific vision has drastically diminished, the topic has continued to garner attention among historians of doctrine, no doubt as a result of the ubiquity of the doctrine in the history of Christian thought. See, most notably, Kenneth E. Kirk, *The Vision of God: The Christian Doctrine of the Summum Bonum; The Bampton Lectures for 1928*, 2nd ed. (London: Longmans, Green, 1932); Vladimir Lossky, *The Vision of God*, trans. Asheleigh Moorhouse, 2nd ed., Library of Orthodox Theology 2 (1963; reprint, Leighton Buzzard, UK: Faith Press, 1973); Christian Trottmann, *La Vision béatifique des disputes scolastiques à sa définition par Benoît XII*, Bibliothèque des écoles françaises d'Athènes et de Rome 289 (Rome: École française de Rome, 1995); Severin Valentinov Kitanov, *Beatific Enjoyment in Medieval Scholastic Debates* (Lanham, MD: Lexington, 2014).

Both Greek philosophy and most of the history of Christian thought maintained that final causality—the notion of purpose or telos—is embedded in the nature of things. That is to say, things exist for a purpose, and this end is sacramentally embedded within the nature of things. Aristotle famously puts it this way in book 2.8 of his *Physics*: "If it is natural for a spider to make its web and it also serves some purpose, if their fruit is the reason that plants grow leaves, and nourishment is the reason they grow their roots downwards rather than upwards, then it is clear that this type of causation is present in naturally occurring events and objects."[4] For Aristotle, then, all natural realities have their purpose or telos built in, as it were.[5] Christian theology operates no differently—at least, traditionally it has not. Thomas Aquinas describes the "final cause" as the "first of all causes," and he adds that an agent, whether rational or otherwise, is naturally inclined toward a particular end (*finis*).[6] Aquinas was by no means an exception in Christian thought. He speaks for a widespread Christian tradition whose ontology or metaphysic I would describe as sacramental.[7] It is a metaphysic in which final causes are inherent in created objects; the identity or reality (*res*) of any given object lies, most fundamentally, in its telos.[8] The appearance that we see with our physical eyes does not determine what something ultimately

---

4. *Phys.* 199a26–32; quotation comes from Aristotle, *Physics*, trans. Robin Waterfield, ed. David Bostock (Oxford: Oxford University Press, 1996). Of course, I do not claim that Aristotle is "sacramental" in the Christian sense of the term. The Christian (ecclesial) sacraments are on my understanding unique, since it is in and through them that God gives saving grace. Here I use the word "sacramental" in a broader, analogical sense. We could say, therefore, that Aristotle was "sacramental" in an analogical fashion.

5. Aristotle seems to identify formal and final causes (*Phys.* 198a25–26). John A. Vella explains this as follows: "Consider a human infant. The form of a human being is present in the infant. The form of a human being also contains within it the ultimate goal of the human infant, i.e. to mature and achieve human flourishing. This end is common to all things that possess the form of a human being. So in a crucial sense, the ends of a thing are part of the form of a thing" (*Aristotle: A Guide for the Perplexed* [New York: Continuum, 2008], 79).

6. *ST* I-II, q. 1, a. 2.

7. I describe in greater detail what I understand by a sacramental ontology in Hans Boersma, *Heavenly Participation: The Weaving of a Sacramental Tapestry* (Grand Rapids: Eerdmans, 2011).

8. This does not mean that discernment of the telos is always easy from a Christian understanding. Because we only "see in a mirror dimly" (1 Cor. 13:12) and so do not have full participation in the truth, distinguishing true ends from false ends is often difficult. See my reflections on this topic in Hans Boersma, "Analogy of Truth: The Sacramental Epistemology of *Nouvelle Théologie*," in *Ressourcement: A Movement for Renewal in Twentieth-Century Catholic Theology*, ed. Gabriel Flynn and Paul D. Murray (Oxford: Oxford University Press, 2012), 157–71.

is. Rather, it is the hidden reality that we can access only with spiritual eyes that gives an object its true identity. Our own identity too lies in the future; we are what we become.

Now, we live in a constructivist world. To the extent that we still think of ends or purposes, we tend to conceive of them either as freely chosen (in the case of human beings) or as extraneously imposed upon objects (in the case of animals, plants, and other objects). That is to say, to the extent that we still think of purposes or aims, we treat them as extrinsic to the nature of things. The very term "final *cause*" strikes us as odd. We regard purposes as outcomes, not causes. We look at purposes as contingent end-points that we have chosen and that could easily have been different. But for the premodern mind-set, a final cause was actually a cause. That is to say, the finality of an object or a human being lay in some manner "embedded" within it, and as such, you could say that the telos "pulled" or "drew" the thing or the person. Aquinas, therefore, used the language of "rational appetite" (for human beings) or "natural appetite" (for other objects).[9] For Aquinas, and for the Christian tradition that he inherited, objects and humans have an "appetite" (*appetitus*) for their final end that is inherent in their nature.

Modernity has been loath to accept the idea that the telos of a thing is inherent in its nature. Francis Bacon, in his *Novum Organum* (1620), was particularly disdainful of final causality. In defense of experimental science, he insisted that we ought to begin with the objects as we have them in front of us and as we access them with the senses. He rejected out of hand, therefore, the notion that ends belong to the nature of things. The notion of a final cause, he writes, "is a long way from being useful; in fact it actually distorts the sciences except in the case of human actions."[10] René Descartes was similarly skeptical of the usefulness of final causality. Within a mechanistic universe, he could not see how final causes could have a place. Descartes's epistemic "humility" comes to the fore in his *Meditations on First Philosophy* (1641): "Since I now know that my own nature is very weak and limited, whereas the nature of God is immense, incomprehensible and infinite, I also know without more ado that he is capable of countless things whose causes are beyond my knowledge. And for this reason alone I consider the customary search for final causes to be totally useless in physics; there is considerable rashness in thinking myself capable

9. *ST* I-II, q. 1, a. 2.

10. Francis Bacon, *The New Organon*, Aphorisms 2.2, ed. Lisa Jardine and Michael Silverthorne (Cambridge: Cambridge University Press, 2000), 102.

of investigating the purposes of God."[11] Therefore, even if things did have a final end embedded within them, Descartes was skeptical of our ability to figure out what it might be. We would need a God's-eye view of reality to determine the end of things. Baconian and Cartesian skepticism about final causality has undoubtedly served the interests of experimental science and technology. But it also meant a rejection of the Greek philosophical and the Christian theological traditions.[12]

The rejection of a sacramental teleology—the belief that there is an inherent link between this-worldly things (including humans) and their final end—meant a break between the appearances of things and their purpose. Put differently, the seventeenth-century experimental sciences discarded the Christian assumption of an inherent (sacramental) link between the sensible thing and its final goal. With the philosophical assumptions of Bacon and Descartes, it became impossible to accept that human beings were *meant* for the beatific vision—or, to put it differently, that it was natural for their rational appetite to long for the vision of God. It is not surprising that these seventeenth-century developments went hand in hand with the rise of "pure nature" (*pura natura*) in theology. It is a development that has been much discussed, particularly as a result of the twentieth-century debates surrounding Henri de Lubac's *Surnaturel* (1946).[13] I will not rehearse here the debates between neo-Thomists and the *nouvelle* theologians, primarily because both

11. *The Philosophical Writings of Descartes*, trans. John Cottingham, Robert Stoothoff, and Dugald Murdoch, vol. 2 (Cambridge: Cambridge University Press, 1984), 239. Cf. René Descartes, *Principles of Philosophy* 1.28, trans. and ed. Valentine Rodger Miller and Reese P. Miller, Synthese Language Library 15 (Dordrecht, Neth.: Kluwer Academic, 1983), 14: "Finally, concerning natural things, we shall not undertake any reasonings from the end which God or nature set Himself in creating these things (and we shall entirely reject from our philosophy the search for final causes): because we ought not to presume so much of ourselves as to think that we are the confidants of His intentions."

12. For a well-known article that presents a much more positive perspective than mine, see M. B. Foster's famous essay, "The Christian Doctrine of Creation and the Rise of Modern Natural Science," *Mind* 43 (1934): 446–68.

13. For this debate, see, for instance, John Milbank, *The Suspended Middle: Henri de Lubac and the Renewed Split in Modern Catholic Theology*, 2nd ed. (Grand Rapids: Eerdmans, 2014); David Grumett, "De Lubac, Grace, and the Pure Nature Debate," *ModTh* 31 (2015): 123–46; Steven A. Long, *Natura Pura: On the Recovery of Nature in the Doctrine of Grace* (New York: Fordham University Press, 2010); Bernard Mulcahy, *Aquinas's Notion of Pure Nature and the Christian Integralism of Henri de Lubac: Not Everything Is Grace*, American University Studies 7: Theology and Religion 314 (New York: Peter Lang, 2011). On de Lubac more generally, see Jordan Hillebert, ed., *T&T Clark Companion to Henri de Lubac* (London: Bloomsbury T. & T. Clark, 2017).

sides were firmly convinced of the importance of final causality and, there-fore, of the link between a thing and its purpose. By contrast, modernity has ended up denying the very notion that the purpose of a thing is given with its nature. This rendered the loss of the notion of the beatific vision all but inevitable. Since all purposes or ends are now humanly "constructed" rather than inherent in nature itself, many consider it outlandish to look for such ends beyond the pleasures that the material, sensible world affords.

Seeking the Face of God: Anselm's *Proslogion*

Let's delve a little more deeply into the question of how in premodern so-ciety the beatific vision fit within the plausibility structure of a sacramen-tal teleology. We see this illustrated with particular clarity in Saint Anselm (1033–1109). Indeed, few theologians have rendered the doctrine of the be-atific vision as plausibly and persuasively as he. His *Proslogion* (1078), mostly known for its ontological argument for the existence of God, makes clear that the plausibility structure of Anselm's world was fundamentally that of a sacramental teleology. Anselm may have been tempted by the foolishness of unbelief, but he refused to give up on the search for the telos for which he was made, and so already in the first chapter he calls out: "I was created to see thee, and not yet have I done that for which I was made."[14] Anselm thought the telos of the beatific vision constituted his identity. It was, we could also say, the plausibility structure of his sacramental ontology that made it possible for him to keep searching for the vision of God as his final end. Anselm's treatment of the beatific vision, therefore, presents us with an example of a sacramental, premodern treatment of the beatific vision.

Throughout his *Proslogion*, the Benedictine abbot of Bec is engaged in a search for God—whom he famously describes as "that than which noth-ing greater can be conceived" (*aliquid quo nihil maius cogitari possit*) (2).[15] Anselm begins the first chapter of his treatise with an attempt to arouse his reader to the contemplation of God: "Enter the inner chamber of thy mind;

14. Anselm, *Proslogium* 1. Hereafter, I refer to the paragraph numbers from this work in parentheses in the text; quotations come from Anselm, *Proslogium*, in *Basic Writings*, trans. S. N. Deane, 2nd ed. (Chicago: Open Court, 1962).

15. Captured in syllogistic form, Anselm's ontological argument that God exists runs as follows: "That than which nothing greater can be conceived" exists in our mind. But it is greater to exist in reality than to exist only in the mind. Therefore, "that than which nothing greater can be conceived" must also exist in reality (*Proslogium* 2–4).

shut out all thoughts save that of God, and such as can aid thee in seeking him; close thy door and seek him. Speak now, my whole heart! speak now to God, saying, I seek thy face; thy face, Lord, will I seek (Psalms xxvii. 8). And come thou now, O Lord my God, teach my heart where and how it may seek thee, where and how it may find thee" (1). By turning to Psalm 27, Anselm takes his reader on a pilgrimage to the summit of human existence, a face-to-face encounter with God.

Anselm's search is one in which he prayerfully pleads with God in faith to reveal himself.[16] Anselm immediately identifies God as the one who lives in "unapproachable light" (1 Tim. 6:16), so that the pressing question becomes: "Who shall lead me to that light and into it, that I may see thee in it?" (1). Anselm struggles with the question of how to move from the sensible world to the transcendent realm of God. At times, he seems to despair of ever entering this divine light, since he has never even seen God and so does not even know what to look for: "I have never seen thee, O Lord, my God; I do not know thy form. What, O most high Lord, shall this man do, an exile far from thee?" (1). Still, Anselm confesses that his desire is for nothing less than God himself. Seeing God is the purpose for which he has been created, and as a result Anselm embarks on his quest in the trust that the final end for which he is made is the beatific vision itself.

It is possible to see the light only if the light first shines on us. Put in the terminology of this study: the sacramental reality (*res*) of the ultimate telos must make itself known in created form (*sacramentum*) if we are to share in it. Anselm recognizes this dependence on divine revelation: "Teach me to seek thee, and reveal thyself to me" (1). And he follows this up with a request for proper understanding: "Give me, so far as thou knowest it to be profitable, to understand that thou art as we believe" (2). At this point, Anselm offers his famous "definition" of God: "And, indeed, we believe (*credimus*) that thou art that than which nothing greater can be conceived" (2, translation slightly changed). Anselm does not rationally try to argue what God is like. He confesses that God utterly transcends anything that the human

16. Cf. Anselm's famous comment: "For I do not seek to understand that I may believe, but I believe in order to understand. For this also I believe,—that unless I believed, I should not understand" (*Proslogium* 1). Gregory Schufreider rightly comments, "We cannot assume that the fact that Anselm's argument is preceded and followed by prayers is irrelevant to it as a proof, nor can we assume that reason is simply defending Christian faith, as if it does not itself have a vested interest in its own theological grounding through the narrative that the prayers provide" (*Confessions of a Rational Mystic: Anselm's Early Writings* [West Lafayette, IN: Purdue University Press, 1994], 100).

mind might be able to imagine—a confession that he recognizes is grounded in faith. Both Anselm's argument that this God exists and his own, personal search for him are, therefore, utterly dependent on divine revelation and on God illuminating his understanding.[17]

Anselm's treatise, then, is a mystical handbook that, like so many other theological works of medieval Christianity, aims to lead the reader to the contemplation of God. The rational argument that Anselm gives for the existence of God makes sense only within a relationship in which God enlightens the understanding and in which the believer deeply desires to see God himself.[18] In fact, the growth in understanding itself *constitutes*, for Anselm, the answer to his plea that he might see God. Far from being an autonomous, rationalist endeavor to secure the existence of God by means of an "ontological argument," therefore, Anselm's treatise is an exercise in mystagogy, taking the reader by the hand "to the contemplation of God" (*ad contemplandum Deum*) (preface). From the beginning, Saint Anselm acknowledges that he depends on the sacramental reality of the divine light entering his creaturely existence.

Contemplation—the alignment of the human mind with the being of God—is thus the purpose of Anselm's rational argument for the existence of God. The spiritual aim of the treatise is to draw his readers toward the final cause, who has come to them and now pulls them from within. This goal of contemplation is entirely in line with the ultimate hope of the beatific vision itself. According to Anselm, human beings will be perfectly aligned with the being of God when the saints enter his light and see him in glory. Earthly contemplation of God (*contemplatio Dei*) is, therefore, a provisional or initial way of seeing God (*visio Dei*). It is a sacramental sharing in the ultimate reality of the vision of God. Anselm's aim with the *Proslogion* is not simply to present an argument for the existence of God; he would have been unlikely to rely on a strictly rational argument, since such an argument would presuppose the neutral ground of pure nature (*pura natura*). Anselm is deeply aware that if the Christian faith holds true, and God creates and sustains everything, then a rational argument for God's existence makes sense only within the context of the confession that the transcendent God is sacramentally present in all things: "For yesterday and to-day and to-morrow

17. Cf. Schufreider, *Confessions*, 109–10.

18. Jacob Holsinger Sherman rightly suggests that Anselm's "adorative intellect" is "the key to our holding together central but seemingly disparate features over which critics otherwise stumble" (*Partakers of the Divine: Contemplation and the Practice of Philosophy* [Minneapolis: Fortress, 2014], 76).

have no existence, except in time; but thou, although nothing exists without thee, nevertheless dost not exist in space or time, but all things exist in thee. For nothing contains thee, but thou containest all" (19). For Anselm, God contains all and is present in all. This belief of the participation of all created things in God's being precludes, therefore, a purely rational argument for the existence of God.[19] All genuine understanding of God belongs to contemplation of God, which in turn is an anticipation of the final vision of God.

Anselm knows that his understanding of God is quite inadequate. Even after he has presented his argument for the existence of God, Anselm's journey for more light continues. Or rather, Anselm gives the impression that he has hardly even made any progress at all. Confessing again his blindness—"I tried to rise to the light of God, and I have fallen back into my darkness" (18)—Saint Anselm again turns to Psalm 27, as he pleads with God: "Do thou help me for thy goodness' sake! Lord, I sought thy face; thy face, Lord, will I seek; hide not thy face far from me (Psalms xxvii. 8). Free me from myself toward thee. Cleanse, heal, sharpen, enlighten the eye of my mind, that it may behold thee. Let my soul recover its strength, and with all its understanding let it strive toward thee, O Lord. What art thou, Lord, what art thou? What shall my heart conceive thee to be?" (18). Anselm may have conjoined his understanding to the truth that God exists, but he is still only able to confess *that* God is rather than *what* God is. The desire of the psalmist to see the sacramental reality of God's face still animates every fiber of Anselm's being, and it continues to do so through to the very end of the treatise.

The reason God's light is unapproachable is that he is beyond our imagination or comprehension. Anselm is frustrated because the very "definition" of God that he has used to prove God's existence is inadequate. Anselm is forced to acknowledge that God is not only "that than which nothing greater can be thought" but beyond human thought itself: "Therefore, O Lord, thou art not only that than which a greater cannot be conceived, but thou art something greater than can be conceived (*maius quam cogitari possit*)" (15; capitalization and translation slightly changed). Anselm—like Gregory of Nyssa and Dionysius before him—recognizes that God is not simply the greatest being our minds can conjure up. To speak truthfully about God means to recognize that our positive, kataphatic language of God falls short,

---

19. Even as Anselm ostensibly expresses frustration at his inability to see God, he acknowledges that he exists by being enveloped in the light of God's vision: "How far removed art thou from my vision, though I am so near to thine! Everywhere thou art wholly present, and I see thee not. In thee I move, and in thee I have my being [cf. Acts 17:28]; and I cannot come to thee. Thou art within me, and about me, and I feel thee not" (*Proslogium* 16).

so that in line with the negative, apophatic tradition we admit the failure of human discourse and confess God's light to be unapproachable. God remains shrouded in darkness. For Anselm, it is only once we come to heaven to enjoy the triune God as the *unum necessarium* (cf. Luke 10:42) that we will experience fullness of joy (23).[20] "The reason we cannot comprehend the extent of the joy of heaven," explains Gavin Ortlund, "is that, in this life, we cannot yet comprehend how much we will know and love God there."[21] Only in heaven will our lack of comprehension and satisfaction give way to the fullness of knowledge, love, and joy. It is, therefore, only in the last few chapters of the *Proslogion* (24–26), when Anselm praises the prospect of heavenly understanding, love, and joy, that he truly envisages the successful completion of his ascent toward the sacramental reality of the vision of God.

This book can do no better than Anselm. It is not possible to offer a rational argument explaining why the beatific vision constitutes our final end. Anselm's sacramental ontology does, however, provide the plausibility structure—the only true and ultimately sustainable one, as I see it—within which the *unum necessarium* is the telos of the beatific vision. He takes us on a mystagogical pilgrimage, which has its own power of persuasion. I do not want to be misunderstood as suggesting that rhetoric by itself is supposed to convince us of the finality of beatific vision. No matter how aesthetically pleasing Anselm's treatise may be, and no matter how important the role of beauty and harmony may be for him,[22] he recognized that it is the supernatural end of the beatific vision itself—rather than this-worldly rhetoric—that ultimately persuades. In the final analysis, Anselm's rhetoric persuades only inasmuch as it is true. Only when the illuminating revelation of God grants

20. Cf. the discussion in Gavin Ortlund, "Ascending toward the Beatific Vision: Heaven as the Climax of Anselm's *Proslogion*" (PhD diss., Fuller Theological Seminary, School of Theology, 2016), 218–29.

21. Ortlund, "Ascending toward the Beatific Vision," 250. Ortlund treats the final three chapters of the *Proslogion* as the climax of Anselm's search for the vision of God. Robert McMahon similarly comments: "Anselm the narrator achieves new understandings in the course of his quest; he longs to experience God, and in the end he is led to a foretaste of the beatific vision and its overflowing joy" (*Understanding the Medieval Meditative Ascent: Augustine, Anselm, Boethius, and Dante* [Washington, DC: Catholic University of America Press, 2006], 161).

22. Anselm speaks of harmony in God in *Proslogium* 17; and in *Cur deus homo*, he is very concerned that, in a fitting manner, God restore cosmic harmony and beauty through Christ's redemption (e.g., 1.15 [in *Basic Writings*, pp. 208–10]; 1.19 [pp. 222–25]). Cf. Stephen M. Garrett, *God's Beauty-in-Act: Participating in God's Suffering Glory*, PTMS 196 (Eugene, OR: Pickwick, 2013), 136–37.

us a glimpse of the vision of God can we recognize the truth itself.[23] Anselm trades neither in the rationalism of *pura natura* nor in the emotivism and fideism of *pura narratio*. It is because Anselm's eyes of faith have met with the light of the face of God that he has become convinced that the beatific vision constitutes his sacramental end and, as such, will supply him with his true humanity.

Dynamic Communion: Hans Urs von Balthasar

We witness the modern decline of the plausibility structure of a sacramental ontology—and of the corresponding sense that the future telos of created objects is inscribed in their nature—within both Catholic and Protestant theology.[24] In the absence of this plausibility structure, the notion of the beatific vision has increasingly come to be regarded as curious and unconvincing. I plan to illustrate this by drawing attention to criticisms of the beatific vision in the theologies of the Swiss Catholic Hans Urs von Balthasar and of the Dutch neo-Calvinist Herman Bavinck. Before explaining and critiquing their treatments of the beatific vision, I should clarify that I have a great deal of respect for both theologians. Both have made significant contributions within their respective theological traditions. And although I will question their treatments of the beatific vision—inasmuch as their overly this-worldly depictions of the hereafter detract from the sacramental reality of the beatific vision—neither Balthasar nor Bavinck was ignorant of the problems of modernity. In fact, it is possible to detect significant elements of a participatory or sacramental ontology in their theology.[25] To my mind, therefore, both

23. After presenting his argument for the existence of God, Anselm comments: "I thank thee, gracious Lord, I thank thee; because what I formerly believed by thy bounty, I now so understand by thine illumination, that if I were unwilling to believe that thou dost exist, I should not be able not to understand this to be true" (*Proslogium* 4).

24. To be sure, the Reformation's focus on the Word implied, to some extent, a devaluation of vision. The Lutheran theologian Allen G. Jorgenson goes so far as to suggest that "if medieval thinkers were enamored with a beatific vision, Luther proposed a beatific hearing in its stead" ("Martin Luther on Preaching Christ Present," *IJST* 16 [2014]: 46). But this generalization needs significant nuancing, both because many Calvinists (including John Donne, Jonathan Edwards, and Abraham Kuyper) followed Augustine in treating vision as the noblest of the senses and because the loss of teleology (and the corresponding decline of the doctrine of the beatific vision) has also affected Catholic theology.

25. I have made the case for this in connection with Balthasar in Boersma, *Nouvelle Théologie*, 117–35. Regarding Bavinck, Wolter Huttinga has drawn attention to participation

Balthasar and Bavinck would have had very good reason to speak more positively about the beatific vision than they did. The fact that both nonetheless opted mostly to criticize the tradition on this topic is an indication that, at key points, their theology was out of sync with the sacramental metaphysic underlying the Christian tradition.[26]

For Hans Urs von Balthasar (1905–1988), the eschatological future is primarily one in which, through Christ, we will participate in the personal life of the triune God.[27] In the last volume of his *Theo-Drama*, Balthasar explains that the Scriptures hold out to us the promise of participation in the divine life. This participation is not just a future anticipation; already today we are born of God as his children and are endowed with the Holy Spirit. Balthasar explains that the Farewell Discourse of John's Gospel speaks of the indwelling of the Father and of the Son in the believers (John 14:23) as well as of the indwelling of the Spirit, who will lead them into all the truth (16:13).[28] The First Epistle of John picks up on this indwelling of the divine persons in the believers (1 John 2:29; 3:9; 4:7; 5:1–4, 18). At the same time, explains Balthasar, this is merely "the preliminary, earthly stage of an ineffable union that is to come," of which John speaks in the famous passage of 1 John 3:1–2. Comments Balthasar: "What is to come will in no way replace the grace of being begotten of God and of being his children; it can only be illuminated by the truth of this relationship: 'But we know that when he appears we shall be like [*homoios*] him' (3:2)—which must refer, not to

in Bavinck in *Participation and Communicability: Herman Bavinck and John Milbank on the Relation between God and the World* (Amsterdam: Buijten & Schipperheijn Motief, 2014).

26. This is perhaps most evident in the critical attitude that both display toward Christian Platonism. For Balthasar, see, e.g., Edward T. Oakes, "Balthasar and Ressourcement: An Ambiguous Relationship," in *Ressourcement: A Movement for Renewal in Twentieth-Century Catholic Theology*, ed. Gabriel Flynn and Paul D. Murray (Oxford: Oxford University Press, 2012), 278–88. Bavinck sharply criticizes Neoplatonism throughout his *Reformed Dogmatics*, often pairing it with Gnosticism: *Reformed Dogmatics*, vol. 1, *Prolegomena*, trans. John Vriend, ed. John Bolt (Grand Rapids: Baker Academic, 2003), 122, 148; vol. 2, *God and Creation*, trans. John Vriend, ed. John Bolt (Grand Rapids: Baker Academic, 2004), 103, 105, 327, 431; vol. 3, *Sin and Salvation in Christ*, trans. John Vriend, ed. John Bolt (Grand Rapids: Baker Academic, 2006), 52; vol. 4, *Holy Spirit, Church, and New Creation*, trans. John Vriend, ed. John Bolt (Grand Rapids: Baker Academic, 2008), 72, 706.

27. Hans Urs von Balthasar, *Theo-Drama: Theological Dramatic Theory*, vol. 5, *The Last Act*, trans. Graham Harrison (San Francisco: Ignatius, 1998), 425–70. For the following discussion of Balthasar, I gratefully make use of Alec Andreas Arnold, "Christ and Our Perception of Beauty: The Theological Aesthetics of Dionysius the Areopagite and Hans Urs von Balthasar" (ThM thesis, Regent College, 2015).

28. Balthasar, *Theo-Drama*, 5:427.

God's essence, but to his personal exchange of love."[29] Rather than insist on a Thomist understanding of a vision of the divine essence (or, for that matter, an Eastern understanding of participating in the divine energies), Balthasar opts for a more personal approach in which human beings will freely come to participate within the communion of the free exchange of love in the interpersonal, triune life of God.[30]

Balthasar's first objection to the notion of the beatific vision is that it implies distance vis-à-vis God: we, as the viewers, would be removed from God as the object of our vision. As such, Balthasar believes that the notion cannot do justice to the promise of eschatological participation in the dynamic, interpersonal love of the triune persons. In his essay "Eschatology in Outline," Balthasar observes that the notion of the beatific vision does have biblical grounding (Matt. 5:8; 1 Cor. 13:12; 1 John 3:2; Rev. 22:4) and that it has often functioned prominently within Christian theology. He acknowledges, therefore, that we should not simply "want to bypass this thought of the 'vision of God.'"[31] Nonetheless, Balthasar goes on to explain that both in the Old Testament and in ancient Greece, the notion of seeing God kept the believer at a remove from God as the object of the vision: "In both cases there remained a certain 'contrast,' a stance of one over against the other, which the Christian view of the 'vision' of God must move beyond and at whose stage it must not be allowed to terminate."[32] Balthasar therefore wants to take his starting point in a different metaphor, namely, that of the living

---

29. Balthasar, *Theo-Drama*, 5:427 (brackets in original).

30. Balthasar's doctrine of the Trinity is beyond the purview of this chapter. But it may be apropos to observe that he holds to a social doctrine of the Trinity, with the three divine persons forming something closely akin to a divine family of persons. See Karen Kilby, "Hans Urs von Balthasar on the Trinity," in *The Cambridge Companion to the Trinity*, ed. Peter C. Phan (Cambridge: Cambridge University Press, 2011), 213.

31. Hans Urs von Balthasar, "Eschatology in Outline," in *Explorations in Theology*, vol. 4, *Spirit and Institution*, trans. Edward T. Oakes (San Francisco: Ignatius, 1995), 441. Balthasar makes similar brief comments acknowledging the beatific vision in "Some Points of Eschatology," in *Explorations in Theology*, vol. 1, *The Word Made Flesh*, trans. A. V. Littledale with Alexander Dru (San Francisco: Ignatius, 1989), 258; and in *The Glory of the Lord: A Theological Aesthetics*, vol. 1, *Seeing the Form*, trans. Erasmo Leiva-Merikakis, ed. Joseph Fessio and John Riches (San Francisco: Ignatius, 1983), 186. I am grateful to Mark McInroy for pointing me to these references.

32. Balthasar, "Eschatology in Outline," 441. At the end of his discussion on eschatological participation in the divine life, Balthasar comments: "In this chapter we have been exploring the depths of what theology, all too abruptly, calls 'visio beatifica.' It is a participation in the life of God himself, but as such it is a completion and perfection of something that began in the Incarnation of the Logos" (*Theo-Drama*, 5:470).

water that Jesus offers the Samaritan woman (and us) to drink: "Whoever drinks of the water that I will give him will never be thirsty again. The water that I will give him will become in him a spring of water welling up to eternal life" (John 4:14).[33] Since Jesus claims that this living water is a gift that we in turn pass on to others (cf. John 7:37), the metaphor seems to Balthasar more useful than that of vision. With the notion of living water, "we can feel the most overwhelming experience of God, an awakening to the presence of God that is much more than vision: it is a *participation* in the very surging life of God himself."[34] Thus, whereas vision suggests distance between viewer and object, living water implies the very presence of God in us and through us in others.[35] According to Balthasar, therefore, the Christian notions of participation and deification are better served by the metaphor of living water than by that of vision.[36]

Balthasar's second objection is that the notion of seeing God seems static. It entails the end of human creative activity. Balthasar comments: "The Book of Revelation speaks of a new heaven and a new earth (Rev 21:1). To depict the latter would be idle; but it is certain that the absolute creativity of the divine life-process—which has now become the open medium of the creature—does not strangle the creatures' own creativity, as if they were meant to be banished into a deedless vision. Rather, in a way that is hard to detect, God's creativity challenges the creativity of creatures to move beyond itself."[37] Similarly, Balthasar suggests that "eternal blessedness can by no means consist of a mere *visio*, but must involve genuine, creative activity."[38] Presumably,

33. Balthasar, "Eschatology in Outline," 441.

34. Balthasar, "Eschatology in Outline," 442.

35. Similarly, Balthasar writes, "Eternal life in God cannot consist merely in 'beholding' God. In the first place, God is not an object but a Life that is going on eternally and yet ever new. Secondly, the creature is meant ultimately to live, not over against God, but in him. Finally, Scripture promises us even in this life a participation—albeit hidden under the veil of faith—in the internal life of God: we are to be born in and of God, and we are to possess his Holy Spirit" (*Theo-Drama*, 5:425).

36. We should keep in mind that Balthasar maintains the eternal particularity of finite beings by suggesting that their distinctiveness is guaranteed by the distinctiveness of the eternal Logos, within which they exist. See Thomas G. Dalzell, *The Dramatic Encounter of Divine and Human Freedom in the Theology of Hans Urs von Balthasar*, Studies in the Intercultural History of Christianity 105 (Bern: Peter Lang, 2000), 198.

37. Balthasar, "Eschatology in Outline," 443.

38. Balthasar, *Theo-Drama*, 5:486. Similarly, Balthasar speaks of "all the vitality of spontaneous, free, inventive living" in heavenly bliss (5:410). Cf. Nicholas J. Healy's explanation: "According to Balthasar, our understanding of the meaning of the beatific vision must be guided by interpersonal communion as the definitive form or structure of the relationship between

the reason for this is that Balthasar thinks that in the eschaton human be-ings, in their finite freedom and particularity, are taken up into the eternal otherness of the Son.[39] According to Balthasar, within the Son's life, human beings retain their own, active life, in dialogue with the infinite freedom of God. Since God is not "pure-act perfection" but a "dynamic event of love," "that event must be thought of as providing space for the creature in such a way that he or she is not merely a passive spectator but an active participant in it."[40] Although Balthasar does not specify what the continuing "creativity" of human beings in the eschaton will consist of,[41] their continuing dynamic activity in the hereafter is of obvious importance to him, particularly since he contrasts it with "a deedless vision."

The remainder of this book will make clear how theologians through-out the Christian tradition have understood the beatific vision. But Balthasar presents an unfortunate caricature of this tradition. Alyssa Pit-stick seems correct to me when she suggests that Balthasar "misunder-stands the beatific vision developed in Catholic theological tradition as something like a movie, and not at all as the union of God with the soul in the most intimate and living communion."[42] Historically, the doctrine of the beatific vision went hand in hand with theologies of deification and participation in God, both of which are aspects of the tradition that Balthasar was rightly eager to maintain. It seems strange that Balthasar failed to note that, for much of the tradition, vision (as well as knowledge) implies union with the object of one's vision. In any case, the notion that the vision of God would keep him at a distance seems odd in light of the

---

God and creature. Correspondingly, all of the elements that contribute to the perfection of true communion—elements such as self-surrender, creativity, receptivity, mystery, and even surprise—must be constitutive aspects of the 'beatific vision'" (*The Eschatology of Hans Urs von Balthasar: Being as Communion* [Oxford: Oxford University Press, 2005], 180).

39. Dalzell, *Dramatic Encounter*, 198.

40. Dalzell, *Dramatic Encounter*, 201.

41. Balthasar does dwell at length on the metaphors of meal and marriage, but he makes clear that they are in no way to be taken literally: "They are elevated 'apophatically' in order to portray heaven fulfilling (and overfulfilling) the dimension of human intimacy through an entirely different intimacy with God" (*Theo-Drama*, 5:470).

42. Alyssa Pitstick, *Light in Darkness: Hans Urs von Balthasar and the Catholic Doctrine of Christ's Descent into Hell* (Grand Rapids: Eerdmans, 2007), 172. Cf. also Dalzell, *Dramatic Encounter*, 201: Balthasar "thinks that 'beatific vision' suggests a static gazing at the divine es-sence whereas he believes his conception of the trinitarian dynamism excludes the possibility of eternal life being reduced to the endless contemplation of the divinity."

tradition's fairly unified witness that the beatific vision implies sharing in the divine life.[43]

Balthasar's second objection does lay bare a real disagreement with the earlier, particularly the Thomist, tradition. For Thomas Aquinas, the beatific vision had meant that one arrives at eternal rest; since the saints see the essence of God, further "movement" into the divine life is excluded.[44] To be sure, several Eastern and Protestant theologians—for example, Gregory of Nyssa, Gregory Palamas, Thomas Watson, and Jonathan Edwards—took a different approach from that of Aquinas. They all regarded deification as an eternal progress (*epektasis*) into the infinite divine life. But neither the Thomist understanding of seeing the divine essence nor the alternative view of an eternal progress into the divine life assumed a further deployment of human creativity. The reason is that for both of the traditional views, the beatific vision terminates in God himself, not in other objects or relationships.

Balthasar creates room for the continuation of this-worldly, temporal elements in the eschaton. He does so particularly by means of his fascinating but speculative doctrine of analogy.[45] Balthasar maintains that Christ is the analogy of being, and he concludes from this that the humanity of Christ—and hence created existence more broadly—must be included in our understanding of God.[46] For Balthasar, therefore, the eternal, dramatic life of the Trinity includes the presence of the temporal world of becoming, which, in an analogous sense, obtains a place within the life of God.[47] In terms of eschatology, the implication is that the world of becoming and of time has a place—albeit in an analogical sense—in the life of God. Therefore, despite

43. Cf. Andrew Louth's comment that already for Plato, the "act of *theoria* is not simply consideration or understanding; it is union with, participation in, the true objects of true knowledge. It bespeaks, as Festugière says again and again, 'un sentiment de présence'—a feeling of presence, of immediacy" (*The Origins of the Christian Mystical Tradition: From Plato to Denys* [Oxford: Oxford University Press, 1981], 3).

44. *SCG* 3.48.3. Michael Allen provides a helpful introduction to Aquinas's views on the beatific vision and on contemplation in "The Active and Contemplative Life: The Practice of Theology," in *Aquinas among the Protestants*, ed. Manfred Svensson and David VanDrunen (Oxford: Wiley Blackwell, 2018), 189–206.

45. Balthasar develops this notion especially in *A Theology of History* (1963; reprint, San Francisco: Ignatius, 1994).

46. Cf. the discussion in Healy, *Eschatology*, 93–104.

47. See Angela Franz Franks, "Trinitarian *Analogia Entis* in Hans Urs von Balthasar," *Thomist* 62 (1998): 533–59; Matthew Levering, "Balthasar on Christ's Consciousness on the Cross," *Thomist* 65 (2001): 567–81; Bernhard Blankenhorn, "Balthasar's Method of Divine Naming," *NV* Eng 1 (2003): 245–68.

Balthasar's strong advocacy of participation and deification, his emphasis on continuing creativity, activity, and surprise in the hereafter takes away from his otherwise markedly theocentric approach. Or, at least, it seems that for Balthasar the world of becoming obtains a place within the being of God.[48] Not to put too fine a point on it, perhaps for Balthasar it is less the case that this-worldly objects are (sacramentally) marked by their final cause than that God is marked by this-worldly realities. As such, Balthasar's view of continuing human creativity and activity within the triune life of God seems a fairly marked departure from earlier understandings of the beatific vision.

No "Melting Union": Herman Bavinck

Dutch neo-Calvinism has generally been less than enamored with traditional teachings on the beatific vision. According to neo-Calvinists, rather than gaze eternally into the face of God, we will carry our cultural accomplishments over into the hereafter, and also in the eschaton we will be actively engaged in social and cultural endeavors of various kinds. Neo-Calvinists sometimes inveigh sharply against traditional views of the hereafter, supposedly characterized by an otherworldly, heavenly outlook, a body-soul dualism, and a benighted captivity to a Christian Platonist mind-set.[49] One of the more common tropes in this connection is the apparently insufferable idea of eternally singing psalms or playing harps on the clouds.[50] Neo-Calvinism has typically disregarded, and at times explicitly rejected, the traditional doctrine of the beatific vision.[51]

Herman Bavinck (1854–1921), who along with Abraham Kuyper provided the original theological animus for Dutch neo-Calvinism, was sharply crit-

---

48. Blankenhorn comments that it seems as though for Balthasar "potency as such is act as such, and becoming as such is being as such" ("Balthasar's Method of Divine Naming," 245).

49. See, for example, J. Richard Middleton, *A New Heaven and a New Earth: Reclaiming Biblical Eschatology* (Grand Rapids: Baker Academic, 2014), 21–34.

50. Anthony A. Hoekema, *The Bible and the Future* (Grand Rapids: Eerdmans, 1979), 274; Middleton, *New Heaven and a New Earth*, 174; N. T. Wright, *Surprised by Hope: Rethinking Heaven, the Resurrection, and the Mission of the Church* (New York: HarperOne, 2008), 105–6. Wright is not a neo-Calvinist, but especially in his eschatology he is influenced by neo-Calvinism. The notion of playing harps in the hereafter goes back to the book of Revelation (Rev. 5:8; 14:2; 15:2).

51. James K. A. Smith has rightly cautioned in this regard against an "eclipse of heaven" in his book *How (Not) to Be Secular: Reading Charles Taylor* (Grand Rapids: Eerdmans, 2014), 49–50. See also Michael Allen, *Grounded in Heaven: Recentering Christian Hope and Life on God* (Grand Rapids: Eerdmans, 2018).

ical of the theology of the beatific vision in the Christian tradition.[52] Before I explain the how and why of his criticism, however, I should note that Bavinck did not oppose the notion of the beatific vision per se. He explicitly affirms, for example, the eschatological future as "the state of the children of God, as participation in the divine nature, as the vision of God, as eternal life, as heavenly bliss, and so forth," and he adds that "on this issue there is no disagreement between Rome and us."[53] Bavinck, therefore, appears to take for granted that, in the hereafter, we will see God face-to-face. Virtually all of his positive references to the beatific vision, however, are just passing remarks. Although he nowhere denies the future of our face-to-face vision of God, he was clearly not of a mind to dwell on it at any length.

In his chapter "The Blessings of the Redeemed" in the final volume of his *Reformed Dogmatics*, Bavinck does present a slightly longer discussion of the beatific vision. Here he speaks of "contemplation (*visio*), understanding (*comprehensio*), and enjoyment of God (*fruitio Dei*)" as making up the "essence of our future blessedness," and he acknowledges that the redeemed will see God "directly, immediately, unambiguously, and purely."[54] Bavinck concludes this (still quite brief) discussion by commenting, "Thus contemplating and possessing God, they enjoy him and are blessed in his fellowship: blessed in soul and body, in intellect and will."[55] Here Bavinck appears quite traditional in his articulation of the beatific vision—even insisting on a direct, immediate vision of God. Still, it remains true that by far the majority of Bavinck's affirmations of the beatific vision are perfunctory.

For the most part, Bavinck was sharply critical of the tradition of the theology of the beatific vision. He placed the large majority of his comments on the topic in a polemical context over against Roman Catholicism, and he elaborated at length on his disapproval. His concerns were fourfold.[56]

52. In contrast to Bavinck, Kuyper warmly embraced the doctrine of the beatific vision. See chap. 12 below. For a solid introduction to Bavinck's overall thought, see James Perman Eglinton, *Trinity and Organism: Towards a New Reading of Herman Bavinck's Organic Motif*, T&T Clark Studies in Systematic Theology 17 (New York: T. & T. Clark, 2012).

53. Bavinck, *Reformed Dogmatics*, 2:542. For similar affirmations of the beatific vision, see 1:229; 2:183, 191, 395; 3:225, 347; 4:130, 257, 633, 642, 722.

54. Bavinck, *Reformed Dogmatics*, 4:722.

55. Bavinck, *Reformed Dogmatics*, 4:722. Bavinck mentions the dispute on whether the future blessedness will formally consist of knowledge (Thomas Aquinas) or of love (Duns Scotus), and he appears taken with Bonaventure's view, which he claims combines the two (4:722).

56. For a similar listing of Bavinck's concerns, see Dmytro Bintsarovskyi, "God Hidden and Revealed: A Reformed and an Eastern Orthodox Perspective" (PhD diss., Theologische Universiteit Kampen, 2018).

First, Bavinck was particularly troubled with the notion that in the hereafter believers would come to know the very essence of God. None of the church fathers held out the prospect of seeing the essence of God, maintains Bavinck.[57] Repeatedly, he discounts the idea of deification, implied in the teaching that we will see God *per essentiam*, as the outcome of the deplorable influence of Neoplatonism and of Dionysius on the Catholic tradition.[58] Rejecting a future vision of God's essence, Bavinck comments:

> Every vision of God, then, always requires an act of divine condescension (συγκατάβασις), a revelation by which God on his part comes down to us and makes himself knowable. Matthew 11:27 ["All things have been handed over to me by my Father; and no one knows the Son except the Father, and no one knows the Father except the Son and anyone to whom the Son chooses to reveal him"] remains in force in heaven. A corollary of vision of God in his essence would be the deification of humanity and the erasure of the boundary between the Creator and the creature. That would be in keeping with the Neoplatonic mysticism adopted by Rome but not with the mysticism of the Reformation, at least not with that of the Reformed church and theology.[59]

Bavinck's misgivings are obvious: vision of the divine essence implies deification, which in turn implies a denial of the creator-creature distinction.[60]

Quoting Gregory the Great, Prosper of Aquitaine, and Bernard of Clairvaux,[61] Bavinck illustrates how this teaching took hold within Catholic thought and ultimately became officially accepted at the Council of Florence (1438–1445), according to which, explains Bavinck, the saints, "immediately upon their entrance into heaven, would obtain a clear vision of the one and triune God as he really is—nevertheless in proportion to the diversity of their merits, the one more perfectly than the other."[62] Bavinck claims that this teaching implies a corporeal "melting union,"[63] a "mystical

---

57. Bavinck, *Reformed Dogmatics*, 2:188.

58. Bavinck, *Reformed Dogmatics*, 2:188, 191, 539; 4:73. The later Dutch Reformed theologian Klaas Schilder proffers similar objections (*Wat is de hemel?*, ed. Koert van Bekkum and Herman Selderhuis, introduction by Barend Kampuis [1935; Barneveld, Neth.: Nederlands Dagblad, 2009], 186–96).

59. Bavinck, *Reformed Dogmatics*, 2:190–91 (brackets in original).

60. Cf. R. H. Bremmer, *Herman Bavinck als dogmaticus* (Kampen: Kok, 1961), 191–92.

61. Bavinck, *Reformed Dogmatics*, 2:188–89.

62. Bavinck, *Reformed Dogmatics*, 2:189.

63. Bavinck, *Reformed Dogmatics*, 2:539.

fusion,"[64] or a "substantial union"[65] between God and the soul, and he expresses concern about the lack of distinction between creator and creature in Catholic teaching.[66] Bavinck repeatedly, vehemently, and elaborately expresses his disagreement with the notion of seeing the divine essence.[67] Thus, Bavinck was particularly intent to uphold the creator-creature distinction, and he was convinced that Catholic teaching was incapable of properly maintaining it.

Second, Bavinck objected to the way in which the beatific vision has served to buttress a separation between nature and the supernatural.[68] He remonstrates against "contemplation of God (*visio Dei*) in a Catholic sense, a contemplation to which human nature can only be elevated by a superadded gift (*donum superadditum*)."[69] Bavinck explains that, in Catholic thought, the light of glory (*lumen gloriae*) functions as a created gift that elevates the intellect so that it can see the essence of God.[70] Bavinck maintains that, on this understanding, the light of glory will, by implication, turn humans into "different beings."[71] While Catholics maintain that supernatural grace is required to arrive at the beatific vision, Bavinck objects to the way this functions in Catholic thought: the notion of a "superadded gift" fails to recognize that in the eschaton we will not leave behind God's created gifts of nature. The future life, according to Bavinck, "is a genuinely natural life but unfolded by grace to its highest splendor and its most bountiful beauty."[72] Bavinck's depiction of Catholicism as teaching a strict separation between nature and the supernatural is perhaps understandable in the light of neo-Thomist scholasticism, but in light of the broader tradition— including Thomas Aquinas—he could certainly have presented a more nuanced portrayal of Catholic teaching.

64. Bavinck, *Reformed Dogmatics*, 2:542.
65. Bavinck, *Reformed Dogmatics*, 4:73.
66. Bavinck, *Reformed Dogmatics*, 2:539.
67. Bavinck does acknowledge that in the Catholic tradition the vision of God "does not amount to comprehension" (and that it differs in proportion to merit), but he immediately adds that "this doctrine nevertheless resulted in the deification of humans" (*Reformed Dogmatics*, 2:189). Bavinck also admits that some Reformed theologians "considered such an essential vision of God not impossible," mentioning in particular Heinrich Bullinger, Amandus Polanus, and John Forbes (2:190).
68. See in particular Bavinck's lengthy critique of the separation between nature and the supernatural in *Reformed Dogmatics*, 2:542–48.
69. Bavinck, *Reformed Dogmatics*, 4:722. Cf. 2:543; 3:577.
70. Bavinck, *Reformed Dogmatics*, 2:189.
71. Bavinck, *Reformed Dogmatics*, 2:191.
72. Bavinck, *Reformed Dogmatics*, 4:722.

Third, Bavinck was troubled that Catholicism treats the beatific vision as the result of merit—often understood as condign merit—so that believers can properly "earn" their eternal reward of the beatific vision. For the Catholic tradition, maintains Bavinck, infused grace enables a person "to do such good works as could *ex condigno* (by a full merit) earn eternal blessedness, the vision of God *per essentiam*."[73] Whatever we may think of Bavinck's objection here, it does not concern the Catholic dogmatic construction of the beatific vision per se. At this point, he is concerned not so much with the beatific vision itself as with the way believers *arrive* at this vision. Considering the frequency with which he mentions the beatific vision being the result of condign merit, it was clearly an important issue for him.

Finally, Bavinck expresses concern about the Catholic teaching regarding the immediate character of the beatific vision. To be sure, we have already seen that Bavinck himself also affirms a vision in which believers will see God "directly, immediately, unambiguously, and purely."[74] Mediation is out of the question, Bavinck remarks in the same context, in the sense that our fellowship with God will not be "interrupted by any distance, or mediated by either Scripture or nature."[75] Bavinck's worry, however, is that the Catholic understanding of the beatific vision leaves Christ behind: "Eternal life is our portion here already and consists in knowing God in the face of Christ (John 3:16, 36; 17:3). Christ is and remains the way to the Father, to the knowledge and vision of God (Matt. 11:27; John 1:18; 14:6; 1 John 3:2b)."[76] Bavinck insists that eschatology is "rooted in Christology and is itself Christology."[77] Accordingly, he suggests that the Son will continue to mediate our access to God in the eschaton: "The Son is not only the mediator of reconciliation (*mediator reconciliationis*) on account of sin, but even apart from sin he is the mediator of union (*mediator unionis*) between God and his creation."[78] Unfortunately, Bavinck does not elaborate how this continuing mediation relates to the vision of God or in what sense we may rightly claim that this vision is direct or immediate if it is also mediated by Christ.

73. Bavinck, *Reformed Dogmatics*, 2:539. Cf. 1:512; 2:544; 3:577; 4:241, 635.
74. Bavinck, *Reformed Dogmatics*, 4:722.
75. Bavinck, *Reformed Dogmatics*, 4:722.
76. Bavinck, *Reformed Dogmatics*, 2:543. Cf. also Bavinck's reference to Matt. 11:27 in 2:190 as quoted above (n. 59).
77. Bavinck, *Reformed Dogmatics*, 4:685.
78. Bavinck, *Reformed Dogmatics*, 4:685. Cf. J. Todd Billings, *Union with Christ: Reframing Theology and Ministry for the Church* (Grand Rapids: Baker Academic, 2011), 85.

Perhaps most remarkable about Bavinck's treatment of the beatific vision is that, although he frequently and in great detail presents his objections to a Catholic understanding, he nowhere explains in any detail how he himself positively understands the doctrine. This is particularly odd, seeing that both the Reformed scholastics and Puritan theologians would have given him the tools with which to arrive at an understanding that would have avoided some or all of his objections. It is also interesting—but historically somewhat less surprising—that Bavinck never reflects on Eastern Orthodox discussions of the beatific vision. After all, here the Dionysian influence precluded the idea of a vision of the divine essence. The Greek (Palamite) distinction between essence and energies—traceable in its origins to the fourth-century Greek fathers and perhaps even to Saint Irenaeus in the second century—circumvented the problems that Bavinck detected in the medieval tradition of the West. For the East, the vision of God is not the result of a created light of glory, and the feared separation of nature and the supernatural is thereby avoided. Nor does, for the Orthodox, this vision of God imply that the saints will see the divine essence. It would have been interesting to hear from Bavinck how he thought one should positively articulate the doctrine of the beatific vision.

But I suspect there is a reason Bavinck did not have a great deal of interest in developing a theology of the beatific vision: the overall drift of his eschatology is simply too this-worldly to do so. He begins his chapter "The Renewal of Creation" by explaining that Scripture does not teach the destruction of the present world.[79] Rather than expecting a "brand-new creation," we should look forward to a "re-creation of the existing world," and Bavinck claims that this "renewal of the visible world highlights the one-sidedness of the spiritualism that limits future blessedness to heaven."[80] Although the New Testament contains "some spiritualization" of the Old Testament, our future blessedness is in no way confined to heaven.[81] The kingdom of heaven will be a visible kingdom.[82] Bavinck acknowledges that we should not take the images of Revelation 21 and 22 literally, but he quickly adds that "they are not illusions or fabrications, but this-worldly depictions of otherworldly realities. All that is true, honorable, just, pure, pleasing, and commendable in the whole of creation, in heaven and on earth, is gathered up in the future city of God—renewed, re-created, boosted to its highest

79. Bavinck, *Reformed Dogmatics*, 4:716–17.
80. Bavinck, *Reformed Dogmatics*, 4:717.
81. Bavinck, *Reformed Dogmatics*, 4:718.
82. Bavinck, *Reformed Dogmatics*, 4:718: "Whereas Jesus came the first time to establish that kingdom in a spiritual sense, he returns at the end of history to give visible shape to it."

glory."[83] Bavinck goes out of his way to underscore continuity rather than discontinuity between this world and the next.[84]

Similarly, while he acknowledges that the notion of Sabbath is a biblical metaphor to describe the eschaton, Bavinck immediately makes sure that we do not draw erroneous conclusions from this. The theme of rest does not preclude people being assigned various tasks, in line with their individual characters and personalities.[85] The future rest will be an active rest. Certainly, we should not think of the future kingdom as one of "blessed inaction."[86] Although "knowing and enjoying God" are the "core and center" of eternal life, Bavinck cautions that the Christian tradition has often overlooked that this communion with God "no more excludes all action and activity in the age to come than it does in the present dispensation."[87] Bavinck seems more at ease with an eschaton that continues the regular workweek than with an eschaton that celebrates Sabbath rest.

As he nears the completion of the final volume of his *Reformed Dogmatics*, Bavinck waxes eloquent about the combination of action and contemplation in the eschaton: "The service of God, mutual communion, and inhabiting the new heaven and the new earth undoubtedly offer abundant opportunity for the exercise of these offices [of prophet, priest, and king], even though the form and manner of this exercise are unknown to us. That activity, however, coincides with resting and enjoying. The difference between day and night, between the Sabbath and the workdays, has been suspended. Time is charged with the eternity of God. Space is full of his presence. Eternal becoming is wedded to immutable being."[88] Bavinck does not explain here how exactly rest and work will be united (or, perhaps, coincide) in the hereafter. What becomes clear from this analysis, however, is that Bavinck was at pains to highlight the earthly, visible,

---

83. Bavinck, *Reformed Dogmatics*, 4:719–20.

84. To be sure, the underlying structure of Bavinck's reflections appears soundly Pauline: "Just as the caterpillar becomes a butterfly, as carbon is converted into diamond, as the grain of wheat upon dying in the ground produces other grains of wheat, as all of nature revives in the spring and dresses up in celebrative clothing, as the believing community is formed out of Adam's fallen race, as the resurrection body is raised from the body that is dead and buried in the earth, so too, by the re-creating power of Christ, the new heaven and the new earth will one day emerge from the fire-purged elements of this world" (*Reformed Dogmatics*, 4:720).

85. Bavinck, *Reformed Dogmatics*, 4:727, 729.

86. Bavinck, *Reformed Dogmatics*, 4:727.

87. Bavinck, *Reformed Dogmatics*, 4:727. Throughout this last chapter of his *Reformed Dogmatics*, the polemical target is what Bavinck calls "the abstract supernaturalism of the Greek Orthodox and Roman Catholic Churches"; the Reformation, he claims, "in principle overcame this supernaturalistic and ascetic view of life" (4:721).

88. Bavinck, *Reformed Dogmatics*, 4:729.

this-worldly character of the new heaven and the new earth.[89] Whereas formally he acknowledged that the beatific vision is the "core and center" of eternal life, in actuality it never really took on this role within his eschatology. Bavinck was simply too much interested in the hustle and bustle of human activity in the hereafter to give any real thought to a positive articulation of the beatific vision.

Conclusion

Neither Hans Urs von Balthasar nor Herman Bavinck directly challenged the doctrine of the beatific vision. Perhaps Balthasar came closer to doing so than did Bavinck; he seems to have been troubled by the distance between God and the believer that he thought is implied in the metaphor of vision, while Bavinck acknowledged, at least formally, the central place of the beatific vision in the hereafter. Clearly, however, although neither theologian directly challenged the doctrine of the beatific vision, both ended up sidelining it as the ultimate human telos.

In some respects, the two theologians differed significantly from each other in the reservations they brought to the fore. Balthasar objected that a beatific vision would eternally keep the creator at bay, while Bavinck worried instead that it would melt creator and creature together. Balthasar, though by no means enamored of the doctrine of the beatific vision, did celebrate the theology of deification that it implies, while for Bavinck deification was the most serious problem with the way theologians had treated the beatific vision in the past. In several respects, therefore, Balthasar and Bavinck were significantly at odds with one another. Balthasar, while expressing his reservations regarding the beatific vision, remained Catholic in his anticipation of sharing in the interpersonal love of the triune God; Bavinck, while formally acknowledging the centrality of the beatific vision, wanted to be Reformed in his opposition to a vision of the essence of God.

The two theologians nonetheless did share a sensibility that I suspect grounded their common demotion of the *visio Dei*. Both wished to shift the weight to other biblical metaphors describing the hereafter. Both prioritized the elements of communion, activity, and perhaps creativity as central to life

89. In his chapter summary, Bavinck puts it as follows: "While the kingdom of God is first planted spiritually in human hearts, the future blessedness is not to be spiritualized. Biblical hope, rooted in incarnation and resurrection, is creational, this-worldly, visible, physical, bodily hope" (*Reformed Dogmatics*, 4:715 [emphasis omitted]).

in the eschaton. Both insisted that diversity and particularity have a legitimate place in the new heavens and the new earth. The reason for this, I suspect, is that both Balthasar and Bavinck wanted to create room in their theologies for the continuation of this-worldly, temporal elements in the eschaton. Balthasar did so by means of his fascinating but speculative doctrine of analogy, which allowed him—in and through Christ—to give the world of becoming and of time a role within the eternal life of God. Bavinck does not seem to have thought through the eschatological future in a similar christological and Trinitarian fashion. Still, perhaps even more than Balthasar, Bavinck was interested in doing justice to the integrity of created realities in the eschaton.[90]

Balthasar and Bavinck did not provide identical dogmatic articulations of the eschaton. Nonetheless, by highlighting the social, dynamic, and active character of the eschaton, both ended up with a remarkably this-worldly eschatology. Both rendered the eschaton and the life of God comprehensible to human thought in ways that the Christian tradition had previously eschewed.[91] In both cases, one of the casualties of these modern conceptions of the eschaton was the doctrine of the beatific vision. Again, I do not want to overplay the criticism. It certainly isn't the case that either Balthasar or Bavinck rejected the teleological plausibility structure of the Christian tradition. Moreover, Balthasar's focus on eternal fellowship in the divine life of the triune God means that his eschatology remained theocentric in a way that other views—including that of Bavinck—did not. Nonetheless, when we make activity, surprise, and creativity central to our understanding of the hereafter, it becomes more difficult to retain the singular focus that the earlier tradition had on seeing God in Christ. Balthasar and Bavinck both introduced this-worldly realities into their theologies of the consummation in ways that the tradition had not. As a result, in both approaches the doctrine of the beatific vision became much more difficult to sustain. The shortcomings in both approaches give ample reason to turn once again to the Christian tradition for a retrieval and rearticulation of an unambiguously theological (God-focused) and christological doctrine of the beatific vision.

---

90. For Balthasar, the ultimate focus is on interpersonal, dynamic fellowship with the persons of the Trinity; Bavinck, by contrast, tends toward a much more variegated continuity of every aspect of the created order. Put differently, eschatological bliss, for Balthasar, is theocentric; Bavinck turns much more directly to the renewal of creation. Or, again, for Balthasar, creation has a place in the eschaton only *within* the personal communion of the Trinity; Bavinck treats created realities in the eschaton as separate from the being of God.

91. Cf. Karen Kilby's criticism that Balthasar simply knows too much about the inner workings of the Trinitarian life ("Hans Urs von Balthasar," 217–18).

PART 1

BEATIFIC VISION IN
EARLY CHRISTIAN THOUGHT

CHAPTER 2

PHILOSOPHY AND VISION

Plato, Plotinus, and the Christian Faith

Theology, Philosophy, and the Beatific Vision

The Christian hope of seeing God face-to-face in the hereafter is grounded in the Scriptures. At the same time, when Christians articulated the biblical teaching of the beatific vision, they typically did so in dialogue with non-Christian sources. In particular, the Platonic tradition has been influential on the development of the doctrine of the beatific vision. Christian Platonism—that is to say, by far the majority of the history of Christian thought—has typically worked on the assumption that the Platonic tradition, for all its flaws, anticipated Christian revelation in important ways and, therefore, is helpful to give expression to the truths of the Christian faith, including the teaching of the beatific vision. In line with this tradition of Christian Platonism, I am convinced that it is unhelpful to operate with binaries: Christianity *or* Platonism, theology *or* metaphysics. Theologians in the premodern tradition typically did not treat their faith commitments in such a binary fashion.

This is not to say that Christians uncritically or naively adopted extrabiblical categories in their articulation of theological truth claims. Not every philosophical system was equally suitable for such articulation, and some were considered downright antithetical to the Christian faith. Recognizing that philosophies invariably involve overarching, metanarratival claims regarding one's view of the world, one's understanding of reality, one's conception of the divine, as well as one's grasp of what it means to be human, Christians often asked rather directly how compatible particular philosophical systems were with the Christian faith. Christian thinkers, therefore, were keenly aware of the potential dangers that philosophies might pose to their

45

deepest-held Christian convictions. And by no means was the Platonist tradition excluded from such critical evaluation.[1]

Indeed, Christians in the early church had good reason for their wary attitude. The famous philosopher Porphyry (ca. 234–ca. 305) represents one example of the opposition between Platonism and Christianity in late antiquity. Porphyry defended Neoplatonism, along with traditional pagan religiosity, over against Christianity in books such as *Against the Christians* and *Philosophy from Oracles*. Porphyry knew the Christian Scriptures, about which Origen had taught him a great deal in Caesarea.[2] Porphyry objected to what he called the "unreasoning faith" of the Christians, which he maintained one could observe in the biblical confession that all things are possible with God. For God to be able to do all things would imply that he can act contrary to nature, which surely is not a reasonable thing to believe.[3] The Christian faith—and, in particular, Christianity's basic reliance on authority rather than reason—was at a foundational level irreconcilable with the Hellenistic approach to reality. Indeed, Robert Wilken, in his book *The Christians as the Romans Saw Them*, comments that in the second century at least, Christians were typically wary of the negative impact that pagan philosophy might have on the Christian faith: "Only a few enterprising intellectuals, and only after more than one hundred years of Christian history, had begun to take the risk of expressing Christian beliefs within the philosophical ideas current in the Greco-Roman world. Most Christians were opposed to such attempts." In fact, Wilken goes on to say, "In the few places in early Christian sources where philosophy is mentioned up to the mid-second century, the term was always used pejoratively."[4] Even though this attitude shifted to some extent in the third and fourth centuries, the differences between Christianity and Hellenism were too great for Christians simply to lapse into a naive acceptance of Hellenistic philosophy.[5]

1. I have outlined some of the great tradition's reservations regarding the Platonic tradition in Hans Boersma, *Heavenly Participation: The Weaving of a Sacramental Tapestry* (Grand Rapids: Eerdmans, 2011), 33–35.

2. For the interaction between Porphyry and Origen, see Anthony Grafton and Megan Williams, *Christianity and the Transformation of the Book: Origen, Eusebius, and the Library of Caesarea* (Cambridge, MA: Belknap Press of Harvard University Press, 2006), 64–66.

3. Robert L. Wilken, *The Christians as the Romans Saw Them* (New Haven: Yale University Press, 1984), 161.

4. Wilken, *Christians*, 79.

5. Jaroslav Pelikan prefers to speak of a "'dehellenization' of the theology that had preceded it," rather than of a Hellenization of the gospel (*The Emergence of the Catholic Tradition (100–600)*, vol. 1 of *The Christian Tradition: A History of the Development of Doctrine* [Chicago:

Therefore, when Christians in the early church did come to accept Platonic or Plotinian categories, they did so only inasmuch as these notions could be incorporated fruitfully within an overarching Christian philosophy—a Christian way of life. Jaroslav Pelikan, in his 1992–1993 Gifford Lectures on the Cappadocians—Basil of Caesarea, Gregory of Nyssa, and Gregory Nazianzen—argues that the Cappadocians "stood squarely in the tradition of Classical Greek culture, and each was at the same time intensely critical of that tradition."[6] Pelikan's in-depth reading of the Cappadocian fathers makes clear that both aspects are true: they were obviously shaped by the Hellenic world around them (and in particular by the Platonist tradition), but they could also be sharply critical of it. What Pelikan argues with regard to the Cappadocians largely holds true for the later Christian tradition more broadly. This complex attitude of Christians vis-à-vis the Platonic tradition shaped the development of the doctrine of the beatific vision.[7]

It should not cause surprise that theologians were not always in complete agreement on which elements of the Platonic tradition to appropriate, and in which manner, in connection with the doctrine of the beatific vision. We don't need to move very far into the history of the development of the doctrine to see differences emerge on various fronts. And in this book I hope to explore some of them. Nonetheless, throughout most of the history of Christian thought—until the rise of modernity—the beatific vision was regarded as the central telos of human existence. Largely, therefore, the tradition has been in agreement that the *visio Dei* is humanity's ultimate aim. One reason for this consensus has been the fruitful dialogue between Christianity and the Platonic tradition. Time and again theologians would turn to Plato and Plotinus for inspiration on how to articulate the biblical truth that we long to see God face-to-face. In fact, it is probably fair to suggest that it is Christian Platonism that sustained the biblical teaching of the beatific vision in Christian doctrine and spirituality throughout the centuries.

University of Chicago Press, 1971], 55). Cf. Robert L. Wilken's comment that a more apt expression than "hellenization of Christianity" would be "Christianization of Hellenism" (*The Spirit of Early Christian Thought: Seeking the Face of God* [New Haven: Yale University Press, 2003], xvi).

6. Jaroslav Pelikan, *Christianity and Classical Culture: The Metamorphosis of Natural Theology in the Christian Encounter with Hellenism* (New Haven: Yale University Press, 1993), 9.

7. For a helpful account of the relationship between theology and philosophy throughout the Christian tradition, see Andrew Davison, *The Love of Wisdom: An Introduction to Philosophy for Theologians* (London: SCM, 2013).

Plato's *Symposium*: Diotima and the Sight of Beauty

In what follows, I will present a fairly straightforward account of how Plato and Plotinus understood some of the central metaphysical teachings that Christians typically link to the doctrine of the beatific vision. The following account is certainly not intended to demonstrate a seamless continuity between Platonism and Christianity. I will purposely avoid the expression "beatific vision" in connection with Plato and Plotinus, despite the centrality of vision and contemplation in their philosophies, and despite Plotinus's use of the term "blessed sight" (ὄψις μακαρία). In what follows, therefore, I will point to continuities as well as discontinuities between Platonism and the Christian tradition. Both are important for understanding the doctrine of the beatific vision in Christian thought.

The Athenian philosopher Plato (ca. 428–ca. 348 BC) deals with themes related to the Christian belief in the beatific vision in three of his works in particular: the *Symposium* (most notably Diotima's famous speech on love); the *Republic* (the three allegories of the sun, the divided line, and the cave); and the *Phaedrus* (the myth of the winged soul). In the *Symposium* we join a spectacular dinner party, which becomes the context for six discourses in praise of love. In the fifth one, the handsome young poet Agathon insists that because Love (ὁ Ἔρως) is the most beautiful and the best of all the gods, it is also the most blissful.[8] Agathon's speech makes a deep impression, for it is the only one thus far that has genuinely praised the excellence of Love itself—rather than just the benefits that it brings us—and this seems to place Agathon in the lead position for winning the prize for the finest encomium on Love.

When Socrates himself takes the floor next, however, he presents a quick and devastating deconstruction of Agathon's speech. Socrates makes clear that he used to be of the same opinion as Agathon, namely, "that Love is an important god and must be accounted attractive" (201e). However, Diotima, the priestess from Mantinea, corrected Socrates's opinion, clarifying that Love, as the child of Poverty and Plenty, is always in need. Love is neither immortal nor mortal, neither rich nor destitute, neither to be identified with knowledge nor with ignorance (203e).[9] In short, Love cannot be the object of

---

8. *Symp.* 195a. Hereafter, references from this work will be given in parentheses in the text; quotations come from Plato, *Symposium*, trans. and ed. Robin Waterfield (Oxford: Oxford University Press, 1994).

9. I take it that Diotima genuinely represents Plato's own views. It also seems to me that Andrea Nye is mistaken when she comments: "Beauty, for Diotima is not a universal, it is a

our loves (since Love remains a needy vagrant) but is, instead, itself a lover of knowledge (204b–c).[10] Love is neither a human being nor a god but is, instead, a daemon (δαίμων), an important spirit, who serves as a mediator between gods and men (202d–e).

Diotima's demotion of the status of Love raises the question of who or what the object of Love's love might be. If Love does not stand at the top of the ladder as the ultimate object of our pursuit, then what constitutes the final object of Love's own pursuit? Through a back-and-forth discussion, Socrates eventually ends up agreeing with Diotima's summary statement that "the object of love is the permanent possession of goodness for oneself" (206a). This permanent possession of the Good (τὸ ἀγαθόν) will render a person "happy" (εὐδαίμων) (204e–205a). Thus, it seems that Goodness takes the place of Love as the final object of our love.

Socrates's discourse on goodness soon gives way, however, to talk about immortality and beauty (τὸ καλόν). Initially, he maintains that also beauty is not the final object of one's love, and that what we pursue instead is "birth and procreation in a beautiful medium," so that beauty is instrumental, and thus secondary (206e). We look for beautiful objects in order to give birth—physically or mentally—through an attractive medium. The reason for this desire to procreate is that procreation renders us virtually immortal and so gives us permanent possession of the Good and hence offers us immortality as the ultimate aim of love (206b–207a). At the very end of the speech, Socrates again makes clear that immortality is the aim of Love: "So there you are, Phaedrus—not forgetting the rest of you. That's what Diotima told me,

---

fact about a particular embodied person, the fact that he or she inspires creative intercourse that will result in good things for the community" ("The Subject of Love: Diotima and Her Critics," *J Value Inq* 24 [1990]: 140). Though it is true that Diotima (and, I believe, Plato himself) is interested in communal affairs, the first part of Nye's comment is pretty much the direct opposite of what Diotima explicitly states.

10. In an astounding move, Socrates places himself into the position of the daemon of Love, commenting on Love that "he's a vagrant, with tough, dry skin and no shoes on his feet. He never has a bed to sleep on, but stretches out on the ground and sleeps in the open in doorways and by the roadside" (*Symp.* 203d). The comment is highly paradoxical, considering that the aim of the speech is to move the listeners away from individual bodies to universal Forms. Alcibiades, who tries to seduce Socrates, limits himself to the pursuit of the beauty of one body, that of Socrates, whom he regards as unique. As Richard Foley observes, quoting Alcibiades: "Socrates' commitment to the pursuit of moral excellence is so extraordinary, that, in the end, it makes him unique, 'he is like no one else in the past and no one in the present—this is by far the most amazing thing about him'" ("The Order Question: Climbing the Ladder of Love in Plato's *Symposium*," *AncPhil* 30 [2010]: 71–72).

and I believe her. As a believer, I try to win others as well round to the view that, in the business of acquiring immortality, it would be hard for human nature to find a better partner than Love. That's the basis of *my* claim that everyone should treat Love with reverence, and that's why I for one consider the ways of love to be very important" (212b). Love, for Socrates, is an "important spirit," a mediator, who leads us to the object of our love, namely, immortality.[11]

The *Symposium*'s relegation of Love to a mere means points up an important difference between Platonism and Christianity. Christians, unlike Plato, identify God as love, and Saint John's first epistle describes this love not as the needy love of Plato's ἔρως, but as the self-giving love (ἀγάπη) that we witness in the incarnation: "Anyone who does not love does not know God, because God is love (ἀγάπη). In this the love of God was made manifest among us, that God sent his only Son into the world, so that we might live through him" (1 John 4:8–9). To be sure, a Christian vision does not simply oppose self-giving ἀγάπη to the needy character of the Platonic ἔρως.[12] The erotic love of desire serves a key function in the economy of redemption, seeing as it is the catalyst for the Christian search for the vision of God. Nonetheless, the explicit identification of God as love (ἀγάπη) in the Christian tradition significantly affects our understanding of who God is and of what love is. If it is true that the eternal Word of God takes on human flesh and so becomes love incarnate, then this implies that the enjoyment of this love in the beatific vision is the ultimate aim of human love.

Thus, whereas Plato's Love—personified in Socrates's self-description of a needy vagrant—reaches beyond itself for the greater good of immortality, Christians know nothing greater than God's love in Christ. It is this love that is on display, therefore, in the beatific vision. The beatific vision—on my understanding of it, at least—is first and foremost a christological doctrine.

11. Luce Irigaray charges Diotima with inconsistency and hence failure in her speech. Irigaray argues that in the first part of the speech, Love functions as a "mid-point or intermediary" between lovers, while later on love gets reduced to a mere "means to the end" ("Sorcerer Love: A Reading of Plato's *Symposium*, Diotima's Speech," trans. Eleanor H. Kuykendall, *Hypatia* 3, no. 3 [1989]: 32). In this second part, says Irigaray, Diotima "used Love itself as a *means*. She cancelled out its intermediary function and subjected it to a *telos*" (44). I am not convinced that Diotima (or Socrates) is inconsistent. From the outset, Diotima deconstructs the lofty position of Love and makes clear that Love must be superseded.

12. This is widely recognized to be the basic problem in Anders Nygren's *Agape and Eros: The Christian Idea of Love*, trans. Philip S. Watson (Chicago: University of Chicago Press, 1982). Nygren's dichotomous treatment has perhaps been most profoundly critiqued in Pope Benedict XVI's encyclical *Deus caritas est* (2005).

"Whoever has seen me has seen the Father," Jesus says to Philip (John 14:9). In no way does the beatific vision take us beyond Jesus Christ. To be sure, some in the Christian tradition may not have accented appropriately the christological character of the beatific vision (although we will see that the great tradition has generally been remarkably christological in its articulation of the beatific vision). In this book I will be critical of elements of the tradition that seem to me insufficiently christological. Particularly, it seems to me problematic to substitute the essence of God for the incarnate Christ as the "object" of our eternal vision. Here I have in mind particularly Saint Thomas Aquinas (1224/25–1274) and the tradition that follows from him, which links the beatific vision to the essence of God. The result, I think, is that Christology has become insufficiently central to the doctrine of the beatific vision.[13] On my understanding, to see Christ is to see the essence of God.

Although Socrates says that immortality is the ultimate object of love, it is nonetheless beauty—and our vision of it—that features most prominently in the last section of Diotima's speech. Possessing Goodness turns out to be identical to seeing beauty.[14] Diotima may earlier have depicted beauty (τὸ καλόν) as simply the medium that gives birth to immortality, but here she clearly suggests that beauty is the ultimate aim of human desire and that the vision of this beauty is the final satisfaction of human desire or love. We could almost say that immortality, rather than being the end in itself, is simply the eternal *mode* in which we come to possess Goodness or see beauty. To be sure, for Plato it is probably not an either/or issue (either immortality or beauty as ultimate aim). After all, Diotima has already made clear that Love is an intermediate between "mortal" humans and "immortal" gods. Immortality, therefore, is not *just* a reference to the permanence of the possession of Goodness (or of the vision of beauty). Achievement of immortality is also an indication that human beings have become divine—and in the process have left even the daemon of Love in the dust. Thus, Socrates appears to link the soul's vision of beauty with divinization as the ultimate aim of the soul's ascent. This aspect of Platonic thought proved particularly fruitful in the Christian tradition. Also there, as we will see, the beatific vision (and the theology of beauty) has been closely linked with *theōsis* or divinization.

13. See my discussion in chap. 5, section entitled "Christian Spirituality and Beatific Vision."
14. Andrew Louth goes so far as to suggest that Plato's "ultimate aim is the vision of the Forms and, beyond and above them, of the Supreme Form of the Good or the Beautiful" (*The Origins of the Christian Mystical Tradition: From Plato to Denys* [Oxford: Oxford University Press, 1981], 15).

Diotima begins her discourse on the vision of beauty by making clear that one arrives at this vision through a number of steps.[15] We start out by loving just one person's beauty. Next, upon the realization that the beauty of all bodies is one and the same, we become capable of loving any and all beautiful bodies in the world. Third, we move from valuing physical beauty to the recognition that mental beauty is greater. This in turn makes us see the attraction of people's activities and institutions rather than their physical beauty. In the fifth stage, we are actually able to see the beauty in the things that people know. Love of knowledge now becomes the medium in which we are able to reason and think in beautiful, expansive ways. Finally, this leads to the sixth stage of contemplation, of which Diotima warns Socrates (and Plato's readers) to take particular note:

"Try as hard as you can to pay attention now," she said, "because anyone who has been guided and trained in the ways of love up to this point, who has viewed things of beauty in the proper order and manner, will now approach the culmination of love's ways and will suddenly (ἐξαίφνης) catch sight of something of unbelievable beauty—something, Socrates, which in fact gives meaning to all his previous efforts. What he'll see is, in the first place, eternal; it doesn't come to be or cease to be, and it doesn't increase or diminish. In the second place, it isn't attractive in one respect and repulsive in another, or attractive at one time but not at another, or attractive in one setting but repulsive in another, or attractive here and repulsive elsewhere, depending on how people find it. Then again, he won't perceive beauty as a face or hands or any other physical feature, or as a piece of reasoning (λόγος) or knowledge (ἐπιστήμη), and he won't perceive it as being anywhere else either—in something like a creature or the earth or the heavens. No, he'll perceive it in itself and by itself (καθ' αὐτὸ μεθ' αὐτοῦ), constant and eternal, and he'll see that every other beautiful object somehow partakes (μετέχοντα) of it, but in such a way that their coming to be and ceasing to be don't increase or diminish it at all, and it remains entirely unaffected." (*Symp.* 210e–211b)

---

15. Cf. A.-J. Festugière's comment: "It is clear that one cannot move directly from the infinity of tangible things to the uniqueness of the Form. This ascent, therefore, takes place by way of stages or degrees. Each of these stages is characterized by an effort to extract oneself more and more completely from matter, in order to reach an ever more spiritual level, closer to the invisible" (*Contemplation et vie contemplative selon Platon*, 2nd ed., Le Saulchoir: Bibliothèque de philosophie 2 [Paris: Vrin, 1950], 165 [translation mine]).

Diotima nears the climax of her speech. She makes clear that one attains to the vision of beauty through six steps, in which one moves from particular, material objects to the immaterial Form of beauty itself. The distinction between particular, material objects and eternal Forms will become crucial in the Christian tradition—although there it is the eternal Logos who functions, as it were, as the repository of the Forms.[16] As a result, in the Christian tradition, the telos of all human desire is the vision of the incarnate Christ—the Form of beauty in Christ's glorified human flesh.

Three elements stand out in Diotima's description of the vision of beauty. First, it is a sudden experience. To be sure, as we have seen, the soul has prepared for this moment in orderly fashion by means of distinct stages. But when the vision of beauty comes, it nonetheless arrives "suddenly" (ἐξαίφνης). The vision may not be entirely unexpected, but it is still something that cannot be controlled or manipulated. In a significant sense it comes, we could say, from the outside, almost as a gift[17]—though for Plato there is no personal "giver" of this vision, seeing that at the level of beauty or Goodness (the world of the Forms) we have come beyond the realm of the gods. Still, the sudden character of the vision points to its gratuitous nature.

Second, this same term ("suddenly") also alludes to the rapturous or ecstatic character of the vision—something also witnessed to in the biblical narrative (2 Cor. 12:1–4) and the Christian tradition. The ecstatic nature of the experience is evident from the mode of apprehension. Each of the previous stages concerned objects of sense experience or of rational knowledge. In this final stage, however, Socrates carefully and explicitly cancels out both of these modes of perception. What we have here is not a perception of beauty as a "face or hands or any other physical feature." Nor is it "a piece of reasoning or knowledge." The vision of beauty leaves behind both the senses and discursive knowledge. Neither the physical senses nor the intellect enables us to perceive beauty itself. Diotima thus turns out to be a mystagogue who leads her initiates beyond ordinary modes of knowing.

Third, the person who sees beauty in this final stage perceives it "in itself and by itself" (καθ' αὐτὸ μεθ' αὑτοῦ). To be sure, Diotima does not suggest that the vision of beauty "in itself and by itself" devalues either bodily or

16. We should also keep in mind that, although the matter-spirit distinction is important for the Judeo-Christian tradition, matter and spirit are not the most important metaphysical categories. Instead, the distinction between uncreated and created is most important here.

17. Cf. Louth, *Origins*, 13: "The final vision of the Beautiful is not attained, or discovered: it *comes upon* the soul, it is revealed to the soul. It is outside the soul's capacity; it is something given and received. One might speak here of rapture or ecstasy."

intellectual objects. To the contrary, this ultimate vision is precisely that which "gives meaning to all his previous efforts." Bodily or intellectual objects may not be of ultimate significance—for Diotima, that place of priority is reserved for beauty itself—but the existence of the eternal Form of beauty does not render particular beautiful objects meaningless. Instead, all the previous steps—and thus their engagement with the material world—aimed at this vision of beauty "in itself and by itself" as the final goal. Indeed, every beautiful object in some way "partakes" (μετέχοντα) of this beauty, insists Diotima. It is the doctrine of participation that gives significance to material objects and to our sensible and intellectual apprehension of them.[18]

When Diotima goes through the various stages one more time—Socrates turns out to be a slow learner—she highlights the anagogical (ascending) character of the process. Socrates should use the things of this world as "rungs in a ladder," insists Diotima (*Symp.* 211c). The sight of true beauty at the top of the ladder is such an astonishing experience that one must prize it above all else:

> "What else could make life worth living, my dear Socrates," the woman from Mantinea said, "than seeing true beauty (αὐτὸ τὸ καλόν)? If you ever do catch sight of it, gold and clothing and good-looking boys and youths will pale into insignificance beside it. At the moment, however, you get so excited by seeing an attractive boy that you want to keep him in your sight and by your side for ever, and you'd be ready—you're far from being the only one, of course—to go without food and drink, if that were possible, and to try to survive only on the sight and presence of your beloved. How do you think someone would react, then, to the sight of beauty itself, in its perfect, immaculate purity—not beauty tainted by human flesh and colouring and all that mortal rubbish, but absolute beauty, divine and constant?" (211d–e)

Diotima impresses on Socrates the astounding value of seeing beauty itself—a vision that has infinitely greater value than any earthly sight. And, of course, many Christian priests and pastors through the history of the Christian tradition have followed the rhetoric of the priestess: the imagery of a series of steps or a ladder has been a popular one. Indeed, the anagogical drive (the upward thrust) of the Christian faith provides indispensable support for the doctrine of the beatific vision. The glory of the beatific vision atop

---

18. Cf. Adrian Pabst, *Metaphysics: The Creation of Hierarchy* (Grand Rapids: Eerdmans, 2012), 32.

the ladder makes eminently worthwhile the renunciation of earthly beauty. Renunciation and self-discipline—even a certain contempt for this-worldly, material things (*contemptus mundi*)—follow invariably once a person has made true beauty his final aim.

The Three Allegories of Plato's *Republic*: From the Cave to the Sun

The contrast between the unreal shadows of this-worldly objects and the true reality represented by the light of the sun is the focus of a series of three well-known allegories in Plato's *Republic*: the allegories of the sun, the divided line, and the cave. The three follow one another in succession as Socrates engages Glaucon, Plato's elder brother, in dialogue.[19] In the first dialogue, Socrates compares Goodness to the sun. He explains to Glaucon the analogy between the triad of sun, vision, and eye, on the one hand, and Goodness, reason, and soul, on the other hand. Socrates observes that eyes see much better when objects are illuminated by the sun than when the moon and the stars shine on them. Similarly, the soul possesses reason when it is "lit up by truth and reality," whereas the soul is instead reduced to shifting opinions "when its object is permeated with darkness."[20] Further, just as the sun is the cause of light and vision, so too the idea of the Good (τὸ ἀγαθόν) is the cause of knowledge and truth (508e). Moreover, just as light and vision are merely *like* the sun rather than being the sun itself, so too knowledge and truth are *like* the Good and are not the Good itself (508e–509a). Finally, much as the sun provides not only visibility but also growth and nurture, so the Good is not only the cause of the knowledge of objects but is also the cause of their existence and essence, while the Good itself "surpasses being in majesty and might" (509b).

It is no coincidence that Plato chooses the sun as the object of comparison to explain the nature of Goodness. Knowledge, for Plato, is the result of illumination; it is participation in the "light" of Goodness. Socrates's comment that truth and reality "shine resplendent" is an indication that the two terms of the analogy, Goodness and the sun, are closely interwoven (508d). It is also important that Socrates carefully distinguishes between Goodness on

---

19. John Ferguson presents a helpful elucidation of how the three analogies relate to each other, as well as of the influence of Parmenides on the analogy of the cave ("Sun, Line, and Cave Again," *ClQ* 13 [1963]: 188–93).

20. *Rep.* 508d. Hereafter, references from this work will be given in parentheses in the text; quotations come from Plato, *Republic*, trans. and ed. Robin Waterfield (Oxford: Oxford University Press, 1998).

the one hand, and knowledge and truth on the other hand. As an eternal idea or Form, Goodness appears to be in a class of its own. Knowledge and truth do not quite reach the level of Goodness. Finally, Socrates makes clear that we ought to shy away from sensible observation, which gives us access merely to the world of becoming—the region that is "mingled with darkness" (508d). Instead, the soul needs to look toward the intelligible world of the Forms, where "truth and reality shine resplendent."

The second analogy, that of the divided line, focuses more directly on the distinction between the visible and the intelligible world. In the analogy, Socrates asks Glaucon to imagine "a line cut into two unequal sections and, following the same proportion, subdivide both the section of the visible realm and that of the intelligible realm" (509d), so that the following picture emerges:

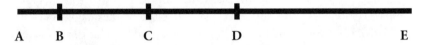

A   B   C   D   E

Figure 1. The Divided Line

In this divided line, AC represents the visible world while CE signifies the intelligible world. We may skip the details of Socrates's explanation—since they do not pertain directly to the topic of beatific vision—but it is important to note that the four segments of the divided line represent stages in the soul's access to reality. They represent four affections of the soul: conjecture (εἰκασία), which concerns shadows and reflections of the visible world (AB); belief (πίστις), which pertains to visible objects themselves (BC); understanding (διάνοια), which refers to the world of mathematical Forms accessed by means of visible objects and hypotheses (CD); and knowledge (νόησις), which, since it is purely abstract, comes closest to the first principle of the Good (DE) (511d–e). Plato's analogy of the divided line tells us both that sensible reality is indispensable in order to arrive at the intelligible world, and that when we reach the idea of the Good, we arrive at true sight. This highest insight is, in Plato's framework, knowledge (νόησις), which is located beyond the rest of the Forms. It is not ordinary, rational understanding (διάνοια), but knowledge (νόησις), that introduces us to Goodness itself. On this score, the Christian tradition would frequently make use of Plato's insights. Theologians would often maintain that neither the senses nor rational, discursive thought gives experiential union with God. It has often been thought that, beyond the senses and understanding, it is the mind (νόησις) in which the light of God manifests itself to the saints.

Figure 2. The Cave
Drawing courtesy of Alec Arnold

Building on the previous two allegories, Socrates next presents his famous allegory of the cave. Here Plato compares philosophical education to the release of prisoners from an underground cavernous cell. Having been tied up facing the wall of the cave since childhood, the prisoners hear sounds echoing off the prison wall and see shadows cast in front of them on the wall. These sounds and shadows are produced by people situated behind the prisoners, who hold up, behind the prisoners' backs, artifacts, human statuettes, and animal models, over the top of a low wall. With a fire burning close to the entrance of the cave, the various objects cast their shadows on the wall of the cave. The prisoners, unaware of anything that goes on behind them, believe that these shadows are the true reality.

Socrates asks us to imagine that one of the prisoners is set free and is told to look toward the firelight. Since "he's too dazzled to be capable of making out the objects whose shadows he'd formerly been looking at" (*Rep.* 515c), the prisoner is convinced that the shadows on the wall contain more reality than the objects he now sees, and so he runs back to join the other prisoners (515d–e). If, next, he would be "dragged forcibly" out into the sunlight

(515e), he would be unable to see anything, "because his eyes would be over-whelmed by the sun's beams" (516a).[21] It is only after getting used to his new situation that he would be able to appreciate reality for what it truly is: "And at last, I imagine, he'd be able to discern and feast his eyes on the sun—not the displaced image of the sun in water or elsewhere, but the sun on its own, in its proper place" (516b).

Andrew Louth articulates the educational process that Plato depicts here by speaking of two stages of ascent. The first step is that of awakening: "a realization that we are immersed in what only appears to be reality, that our knowledge is mere opinion (*doxa*)." The second stage is "a process of detachment from false reality and attachment to true reality, a process of *paideia*, of education, or correction."[22] It is a philosophical process of trying "to live now a life we can only really live beyond death."[23] This process is one of moral as well as intellectual purification, which has as its aim the vision of "something of unbelievable beauty."[24] Indescribable in its nature, this beauty, Louth points out, is so glorious that it transcends even the realm of the Forms.[25] Again, theologians in the later Christian tradition, linking the ineffability of beauty in Plato with Saint Paul's intimation that, caught up into Paradise, he "heard things that cannot be told" (2 Cor. 12:4), would often maintain that the ecstatic experience of the vision of God—which some perhaps experience already in this life—is not subject to the rational intellect and hence is beyond articulation in words.

Unfortunately, any subsequent return to the cave would make the erst-while prisoner a distinct outsider to the rest of the group. He would make a fool of himself: "Wouldn't they say that he'd come back from his upward journey with his eyes ruined, and that it wasn't even worth trying to go up there? And wouldn't they—if they could—grab hold of anyone who tried to set them free and take them up there, and kill him?" (*Rep.* 517a). Clearly, Socrates wants us to think through the implications of looking at beauty or at Goodness as the "Form of Forms."[26] Looking at the sun

21. Rachel Barney makes clear that when Socrates speaks of being "dragged forcibly" into the sunlight, we should understand this compulsion not as an external force of violence but as an expression of erotic attraction ("*Eros* and Necessity in the Ascent from the Cave," *AncPhil* 28 [2008]: 357–72).
22. Louth, *Origins*, 6.
23. Louth, *Origins*, 7.
24. Plato, *Symp.* 210e.
25. Louth, *Origins*, 11.
26. I purposely refer to Goodness (and beauty) as the "Form of Forms." This language

is like looking at Goodness itself, as we saw also in connection with the earlier allegory of the sun. Sadly, Socrates, the philosopher who has seen the intelligible sun of Goodness in all its brightness, will end up paying for it with his life.

Gazing beyond the Rim: The Winged Soul in Plato's *Phaedrus*

The myth of the winged soul in the *Phaedrus* makes particularly clear that whereas in Christian theology θεωρία often describes contemplation of God, for Plato this vision is not a seeing of God. The reason is that Plato's hierarchy is different from that of the Christian tradition. As a result, for Plato the ascent has a different aim. On Plato's understanding, it is not God (or the gods) for whom we aim as the object of our vision. In fact, according to Plato—for whom the gods rank lower than the Forms in the hierarchy of the universe—the gods themselves engage in the pursuit of the vision of the Forms as their ultimate telos.

After he has explained in the *Phaedrus* why the soul is immortal, Plato discusses the character of the preincarnate soul by means of the allegory of a charioteer and his team of two horses. The allegory—regularly appropriated in the Christian tradition—depicts a tripartite soul, with reason (τὸ λογιστικόν) as the charioteer in control of the passions (πάθη) as two horses: the spirited or irascible aspect of the soul (τὸ θυμοειδές) as the white, noble horse on the right, and the appetitive or desiring aspect of the soul (τὸ ἐπιθυμητικόν) as the black, ugly horse on the left.[27] Inter-

---

recurs in the later tradition, for example, in Nicholas of Cusa. As we will see, also in Cusa, the language alludes to that which lies beyond the senses and discursive knowledge.

27. *Phaedr.* 253d–e. Hereafter, references from this work will be given in parentheses in the text; quotations come from Plato, *Phaedrus*, trans. and ed. Robin Waterfield (Oxford: Oxford University Press, 2000). Plato doesn't explicitly identify the charioteer and the two horses by referring to them as the three parts of the soul. In the *Republic*, however, he explains the three parts of the soul in detail. There he also links them with the four natural virtues: wisdom (σοφία) having to do with the rational aspect; courage (ἀνδρεία) with the spirited part; temperance (σωφροσύνη) with the appetitive part; and justice (δικαιοσύνη) with the harmonious ordering of the three parts of the soul. See especially *Rep.* 580d–581e. Cf. Eric Voegelin, *Plato* (1957; reprint, Columbia: University of Missouri Press, 2000), 108–11. J. Warren Smith presents a different interpretation, according to which the black horse denotes the appetitive faculty in its sensual orientation and the white horse that same desiring faculty, but as well trained and guided by reason (*Passion and Paradise: Human and Divine Emotion in the Thought of Gregory of Nyssa* [New York: Herder and Herder/Crossroad, 2004], 56–58).

estingly, the souls' chariots are accompanied by the chariots of Zeus and of the other gods, riding through the heavens. Since the souls' chariots have black horses to contend with, it is much more difficult for them than for the chariots of the gods to reach the top of heaven's vault (247b). Plato then describes the experience of the gods standing at heaven's outer rim, gazing (θεωροῦσι) outward from heaven while the planetary spheres revolve:

> This region is filled with true being. True being has no colour or form; it is intangible, and visible only to intelligence, the soul's guide. True being is the province of everything that counts as true knowledge. So since the mind is nourished by intelligence and pure knowledge (as is the mind of every soul which is concerned to receive its proper food), it is pleased to be at last in a position to see true being and in gazing on the truth it is fed and feels comfortable, until the revolution carries it around to the same place again. In the course of its circuit it observes justice as it really is, self-control, knowledge—not the kind of knowledge that is involved with change and differs according to which of the various existing things (to use the term "existence" in its everyday sense) it makes its object, but the kind of knowledge whose object is things as they really are. And once it has feasted its gaze in the same way on everything else that really is, it sinks back into the inside of heaven and returns home. (247c–e)

Plato's description of what we might term a contemplative vision depicts not a vision *of* the gods (with the gods as the object of the vision) but a vision *by* the gods (with the gods as the subject of the vision).[28] They gaze on the truth, as well as on justice, self-control, and knowledge. In other words, they behold the eternal Forms or ideas, which Plato locates at the top of the hierarchical ladder.

Even a god can experience this contemplative vision only for a short while; then it "sinks back into the inside of heaven." The transient character of the ecstatic vision—the inability to hold on to it—is not just something that the gods of Plato's *Phaedrus* experience. As we will see, Saint Augustine laments the brevity of his mystical experiences of God in his *Confessions*, and both Western and Eastern theologians have recognized that any anticipation

---

28. For Plato's use of the verb θεορέω (to behold) and the noun θεωρία (contemplation), see Gerald A. Press, *Plato: A Guide for the Perplexed* (London: Continuum, 2007), 160.

of the beatific vision here on earth is at best momentary. The fullness of the vision of God—often simply referred to as the "beatific vision"—is reserved for the hereafter. In his earlier writings (notably the *Phaedo* and the *Republic*), Plato may have held a similar view, but in the *Phaedrus* he no longer seems to have supported the possibility of human souls gazing eternally on the Forms.[29] Since for Plato's *Phaedrus* even the gods cannot reach beyond heaven's outer rim for any extended period of time, it would seem out of place to speculate about human beings forever gazing on the eternal Forms.

As I have already mentioned, for the chariots of human souls in their original, preincarnate state, the journey is much more difficult than for the divine chariots. Some of these human souls set out to follow one of the gods, trying to resemble it as best they can,[30] and they "raise the heads of their charioteers into the region outside" (*Phaedr.* 248a). Others "poke their heads through from time to time, but sink back down in between, and so they see some things, but miss others," depending on how their horses behave. The rest of the souls "all long for the upper region and follow after, but they cannot break through, and they are carried around under the surface, trampling and bumping into one another as one tries to overtake another" (248a). Plato's vivid description makes clear that it is difficult for human souls—even in their preincarnate state—to attain to a vision of the eternal Forms: even those who are successful only manage to a certain degree, and more or less briefly.

At one point, Socrates comments that the human charioteers are inspired by the memory of the god that they attempt to follow, "and, in so far as possible (καθ' ὅσον δυνατὸν) for a mortal man to partake of a god, they derive their way of life and the things they do from him" (253a).[31] Many later Christian deliberations on the beatific vision would focus on how it is possible for created beings to see the creator. Responses to this dilemma

29. Richard Bett points out that in the *Phaedrus*, "the end-point of the soul's progress is not changeless and eternal contemplation of the Forms, but an eternal traversing of the heavens, punctuated by contemplation of the Forms at intervals" ("Immortality and the Nature of the Soul in the *Phaedrus*," *Phronesis* 31 [1986]: 20). Further, while Plato still maintains his earlier division between Being and Becoming (articulated in the *Phaedo* and the *Republic*), the myth of the winged soul does not present the soul's true nature as changeless ("Immortality," 21).

30. Divinization or imitation of the gods is an important theme already in Plato. See *Theaet.* 172c–177b; *Tim.* 90b–d. Cf. Julio Annas, *Platonic Ethics Old and New* (Ithaca, NY: Cornell University Press, 1999), 52–71; John M. Armstrong, "After the Ascent: Plato on Becoming Like God," *OSAP* 26 (2004): 171–83.

31. Also in *Theaet.* 176b, Plato speaks of becoming like God "so far as this is possible" (κατὰ τὸ δυνατόν). Cf. Louth, *Origins*, 14.

have varied—with the East typically limiting human participation in God to the divine energies and the West explaining that the vision of the divine essence will not entail a comprehension of it. Regardless of the approach taken, almost invariably theologians would be mindful of the Platonic caveat of seeing God only "in so far as possible," thereby acknowledging that the beatific vision does not cancel out the creator-creature divide.

Plato points out that it is crucial for human souls to be diligent in following after the divine chariots toward the edge of heaven. A soul that "catches even a glimpse of the truth" outside heaven will have its wings strengthened and will be able to remain free from injury until the next revolution (248c). In contrast, failure to sustain the contemplative vision leads to damaged or lost wings and thus to a fall into earthly embodiment.[32] After ten thousand years—and several judgments and reincarnations—hopefully the wings will have grown back and the soul can return to its original, preincarnate place in heaven (248c–249b).

While in their incarnate state, some—most notably philosophers—have a "recollection" (ἀνάμνησις) of their vision of the Forms. The soul of the philosopher experiences a kind of madness, "which occurs when someone sees beauty here on earth and is reminded of true beauty. His wings begin to grow and he wants to take to the air on his new plumage, but he cannot; like a bird he looks upwards, and because he ignores what is down here, he is accused of behaving like a madman" (249d). Socrates speaks of the lover of beauty as being "possessed" by (μετέχων, literally, "partaking of") madness (249e). The recognition that earthly realities—such as justice and self-control—have a "likeness" (ὁμοίωμα) to eternal Forms (250a) drives the soul's desire to recover its vision of the Forms themselves.

Socrates explains to Phaedrus the process of the return, speaking of the philosopher's desire of a boy's physical beauty. Gazing on his beauty—and being tormented by desire for the boy's presence day and night—makes the soul's wings grow again (251c–e). The charioteer "sees the light of his beloved's eyes," and the black horse "prances and lunges forward violently" (254a), tempting the philosopher to sleep with the boy. Coming close to the face of the beloved, the philosopher is struck by its beauty. "At this sight," comments Socrates, "the charioteer's memory is taken back to the nature of

---

32. Socrates lists nine categories of incarnate people, with philosophers at the top (since they have seen the most) and tyrants at the bottom (*Phaedr.* 248d–e). For a defense of the view that Socrates describes an original fall of souls into embodied existence, see D. D. McGibben, "The Fall of the Soul in Plato's *Phaedrus*," *ClQ* 14 (1964): 56–63.

true beauty" (254b), and, terrified by the vision, the soul pulls back the reins. Again the undisciplined horse drags the charioteer and the white horse near the beautiful boy; and again the same process unfolds. If despite the violent temptation no physical contact ensues, the philosopher and the boy end up living a harmonious life of self-control and restraint (256a–b), and upon their death they will soar with their wings restored (256b). And even if they do end up consummating their relationship, Socrates adds, they may be able to overcome this momentary weakness through a life of friendship and so eventually regain their wings (256b–e).

Plato's myth of the winged soul describes a process of *exitus* and *reditus*, of emanation and return, where both origin and destiny are characterized by a contemplation of sorts—a vision of eternal Forms—even if, in the *Phaedrus*, Plato does not expect that the experience of contemplation can be sustained for long. What is more, although the vision of the Forms is reserved for the end of the journey (and perhaps for certain ecstatic experiences), there is also a kind of vision that accompanies one throughout the journey itself. This vision is of physical beauty only, and it is marked by deep ambiguity. On the one hand, it is an indispensable reminder of the eternal beauty of the Forms beyond the vault of heaven: without seeing the boy's physical beauty, the philosopher's soul cannot regain its wings. On the other hand, the experience of physical attraction needs to be resisted; its purpose is to remind the soul of the vision that it experienced before the fall into a material body. The Christian doctrine of the beatific vision has benefited tremendously from this tension in Plato's attitude toward material beauty. Although the human gaze cannot and must not bypass the beauty of the created order, Christians believe that vision becomes happy vision—beatific vision—only when it rests its gaze on God in Christ.

Plotinus on Virtue as the Way to Beauty

Contemplation of beauty also lies at the heart of the philosophy of Plotinus (ca. AD 204–270). The third-century philosopher, who hailed from Egypt and spent much of his adult life teaching in Rome, regarded the cosmos, and human beings in particular, as animated by a longing to contemplate true Beauty and thus to return to the source of all that exists. Every action is for Plotinus in some way a reaching out for vision. Even animals, plants, and the earth itself, maintains Plotinus, "aspire to contemplation, and direct their gaze to this end" (though "different things contemplate and attain their end in different ways").[33] Pierre Hadot explains that for Plotinus the ultimate principle, the Good, is a continuous act of self-contemplation, an act that envelops everything else that we may say about reality.[34] Vision is the origin, the drive, and the aim of life. Plotinus's understanding of contemplation is therefore linked up closely with his overall philosophical system.

It is not my purpose, however, to deal with Plotinus's philosophy as a whole. I will limit myself to aspects of his thought that relate to what the Christian tradition knows as the beatific vision. Plotinus's treatise *On Beauty* (*Enneads* 1.6) may be a good place to begin,[35] since for Plotinus it is beauty (τὸ καλόν) that attracts us, and it is beauty that is our goal: "No eye ever saw the sun without becoming sun-like, nor can a soul see beauty without becoming beautiful. You must become first of all godlike and all beautiful if you intend to see God and beauty" (1.6.9). Plotinus here couches the divinization theme—becoming "godlike"—in the language of becoming "sun-like" or "beautiful," both of which are obviously Platonic in background. For Plotinus, to see God and beauty we must become like them.

Plotinus rejects the Stoic definition of beauty as "good proportion (συμμετρία) of the parts to each other and to the whole, with the addition of good colour" (1.6.1). This definition cannot be right, he argues, because it would mean that individual parts of a whole are themselves not beautiful. The definition also excludes objects devoid of parts, such as color, sunlight, gold, lightning, and stars. Furthermore, it is difficult to see how on such a definition we can speak of proportionality in connection with beautiful conduct, laws, and areas of knowledge. Even the soul's virtue would be denied beauty if we were to take "good proportion" as the definition. And most importantly, asks Plotinus, "what [on this theory] will the beauty of the intellect alone by itself be?" (1.6.1).

This final question reveals Plotinus's deepest motivation in rejecting "good proportion" as the definition of beauty: it neglects the participatory character of beauty. The reason that objects of sense perception strike us as beautiful is that we recognize in them the Form (τὸ εἶδος) of beauty. "We

---

33. *Enn.* 3.8.1. Hereafter, references from this work will be given in parentheses in the text; quotations come from Plotinus, *Enneads*, trans. and ed. A. H. Armstrong, 6 vols., LCL 440–445 (Cambridge, MA: Harvard University Press, 1966–1988).

34. Pierre Hadot, *Plotinus, or, The Simplicity of Vision*, trans. Michael Chase (Chicago: University of Chicago Press, 1993), 63. Hadot refers here to *Enn.* 6.8.16.

35. Cf. the helpful discussion of this treatise (as well as other sections of the *Enneads* dealing with beauty) in Dominic J. O'Meara, *Plotinus: An Introduction to the* Enneads (Oxford: Clarendon, 1993), 88–110.

maintain," insists Plotinus, "that the things in this world are beautiful by participating in form (μετοχῇ εἴδους)." Beauty, therefore, "rests upon the material thing when it has been brought into unity, and gives itself to parts and wholes alike" (1.6.2). The implication, for Plotinus, is that sense perception (αἴσθησις) recognizes it when the Form of beauty masters the shapeless nature of bodies and gathers them into unity (1.6.3). This means that it is possible genuinely to recognize beauty in material objects, since they are literally in-formed by the Form of beauty.

Plotinus then raises the question of how we can leave sense perception behind and "go up" to "contemplate" the "beauties beyond" (1.6.4). The answer, Plotinus was convinced, has to do with virtue, since virtue is beautiful. When people recognize the beauty of virtue, they are "delighted and overwhelmed and excited" since now they grasp true beauty. Plotinus describes the experience in erotic terms: "These experiences must occur whenever there is contact with any sort of beautiful thing, wonder and a shock of delight and longing and passion and a happy excitement. One can have these experiences by contact with invisible beauties, and souls do have them, practically all, but particularly those who are more passionately in love (ἐρωτικώτεραι) with the invisible, just as with bodies all see them, but all are not stung as sharply, but some, who are called lovers (ἐρᾶν), are most of all" (1.6.4). Virtuous living—which Plotinus describes in terms of "greatness of soul, a righteous life, a pure morality, courage with its noble look, and dignity and modesty" (1.6.5)—evokes in the soul recognition of the Form of true beauty and stirs in it a wild, erotic exultation. By contrast, an "ugly soul"—one that is "dissolute and unjust, full of all lusts, and all disturbance, sunk in fears by its cowardice and jealousies by its pettiness . . . living a life which consists of bodily sensations and finding delight in its ugliness"—is dragged into the dark "towards the objects of sense" (1.6.5).

Distinguishing between virtues and vices, Plotinus is sharply critical of preoccupation with the body and with the material world in general. This does not mean, however, that the body itself is evil. His antignostic rhetoric, especially in section 2.9 of the *Enneads*, makes clear that he repudiates the gnostic disgust with embodiment. Indeed, John Deck describes Plotinus's view by commenting: "The sensible world is beautiful. . . . To criticize it, as the Gnostics do, is to expect it to be the intelligible world—this is foolish, it is only an imitation."[36] Deck then quotes the following passage from Ploti-

---

36. John N. Deck, *Nature, Contemplation, and the One: A Study in the Philosophy of Plotinus* (Toronto: University of Toronto Press, 1967), 76–77. Deck refers here to *Enn.* 5.8.8.

nus: "Surely, what other fairer image of the intelligible world could there be? For what other fire could be a better image of the intelligible fire than the fire here? Or what other earth could be better than this, after the intelligible earth? And what sphere could be more exact or more dignified or better ordered in its circuit [than the sphere of this universe] after the self-enclosed circle there of the intelligible universe? And what other sun could there be which ranked after the intelligible sun and before this visible sun here?" (*Enn.* 2.9.4 [brackets in original]). Thus, although the sensible world of matter is nonbeing, and as such ought not to be the focus of our desires, this does not mean we may despise it. Deck suggests that "Plotinus is not saying that there is no being in the sensible world—the intelligible world *is* the being of the sensible world." Rather, explains Deck, according to Plotinus, there is no being in creation "*qua* sensible."[37] For Plotinus, the sensible world has being inasmuch as it participates in a higher, intellectual reality, and it is this participation that gives the material world its significance.

The "ugly soul" goes wrong, then, by turning to the lesser, material body to find fulfillment in the pleasures that it offers.[38] We get to "see" the Form of beauty when we turn away from objects of sense perception, when the soul is "separated from the lusts which it has through the body with which it consorted too much" (*Enn.* 1.6.5). When virtuous living thus purifies a soul, it is raised to the level of Intellect (νοῦς), and as a result it increases in beauty. Plotinus concludes: "For this reason it is right to say that the soul's becoming something good and beautiful is its being made like to God, because from Him come beauty and all else which falls to the lot of real beings" (1.6.6). Virtuous living makes the soul beautiful, like God. The vision of true beauty becomes possible, for Plotinus, when through virtue we are raised to the level of Intellect.

At this point, the soul is not yet on the level of God himself; the soul is simply elevated beyond the senses to the realm of the invisible Forms, one of

---

37. Deck, *Nature, Contemplation, and the One*, 77. Lloyd P. Gerson goes even further, insisting: "Even if matter is absolutely deprived of form and has a tenuous hold on being, it is not nothing, and so it is not deprived entirely of the One" (*Plotinus: The Arguments of the Philosophers*, ed. Ted Honderich [New York: Routledge, 1994], 113). Compare, however, Dennis O'Brien's linking of matter with evil in Plotinus ("Plotinus on Matter and Evil," in *The Cambridge Companion to Plotinus*, ed. Lloyd P. Gerson [Cambridge: Cambridge University Press, 1996], 171–95).

38. Although at times I adopt Armstrong's translation of σῶμα with "body," in our context this term often has the broader meaning of "object," that is, anything available to sense perception.

which is beauty. But the soul continues to press on, in the hope of reaching this God, whom Plotinus also calls the One (τὸ ἕν) or the Good (τἀγαθόν). Beauty continues to allure the soul, even when it has reached the stage of Intellect, for beauty is located not just at the intellectual level of the Forms but also reaches beyond them. The soul is restless until it reaches beyond the invisible Forms and comes to beauty itself, and thus to the One or the Good.

Beauty, therefore, is for Plotinus at or near the apex of the hierarchical ladder, so much so that at times he almost seems to identify beauty with the Good. He maintains, for example, that one may speak of the Good as "the primary beauty" (τὸ πρῶτον καλόν) (1.6.9). The reason for this near identification of the two, explains Plotinus, is that Goodness "holds beauty as a screen before it." It is right, therefore, to "place the Good and the primal beauty on the same level" (1.6.9).

Plotinus nonetheless does not quite equate beauty with the Good. At the very end of his treatise *On Beauty*, he explains that "the place of the Forms is the intelligible beauty, but the Good is That which is beyond, the 'spring and origin' of beauty" (1.6.9). Thus, the Good is beyond intelligible beauty. The reason for this is that we can recognize the Form of beauty, whereas the utter unity or simplicity of the Good places it radically beyond our ken: "For when you think of him as Intellect or God, he is more; and when you unify him in your thought, here also the degree of unity by which he transcends your thought is more than you imagined it to be; for he is by himself without any incidental attributes" (6.9.6). The terms "Intellect" and "God" shortchange the sublime character of this original source of everything that exists. This God is not *a* being among other beings. Preceding everything that exists, even the being of the Forms, this source of everything "is not one of all things, but is before all things" (3.8.9). So, whether we speak of the First (τὸ πρῶτον) or of the Good (or perhaps of beauty), we must recognize that the One is utterly beyond our naming, and as such eludes our knowledge. This primary Good, the Alone (τὸ μόνον), is therefore really the Beyond-Good (τὸ ὑπεράγαθον) (6.9.6).

Plotinus is thus ultimately an apophatic philosopher. The language of "Intellect" and "God" does not properly describe Goodness as the source of all things. And even when we have recourse to language such as the One or the Good, our attempt at naming ends in failure. This explains why in the end Plotinus reaches for the term "Beyond-Good" (τὸ ὑπεράγαθον). The expression is grounded in the acknowledgment that our straightforward descriptions of God—whether positive or negative—do not properly identify the ineffable One. Christian theologians have regularly drawn on this kind of Plotinian discourse, often indirectly via the sixth-century Syrian monk Dionysius. In this way, they attempted to safeguard the utter transcendence of God and also acknowledged that there is no natural access to God and that the vision of God is instead the result of a supernatural experience.[39]

Toward the Vision: Upward and Inward

Plotinus describes the journey of the soul toward contemplation by means of two spatial metaphors, that of upward ascent and that of a move inward.[40] Describing the Good as beautiful, Plotinus comments that

> the attainment of it is for those who go up to the higher world (ἀναβαίνουσι πρὸς τὸ ἄνω) and are converted and strip off what we put on in our descent . . . until, passing in the ascent all that is alien to the God, one sees with one's self alone That alone, simple, single and pure, from which all depends and to which all look and are and live and think: for it is cause of life and mind and being. If anyone sees it, what passion will he feel, what longing in his desire to be united with it, what a shock of delight! The man who has not seen it may desire it as good, but he who has seen it glories in its beauty and is full of wonder and delight, enduring a shock which causes no hurt, loving with true passion and piercing longing. (*Enn.* 1.6.7)

Again, Plotinus uses erotic language to describe the ascent. At this point, however, the soul doesn't just see the Form of beauty in beautiful objects or beautiful virtues. Moving higher than the level of Intellect, the soul appears to be gazing on the Good itself—"That alone, simple, single and pure." Further, the vision does not appear to lead to satiation of desire. To the contrary, when one sees this ultimate reality itself, this merely serves further to inflame one's passion, desire, and longing. As we will see, the Christian tradition has not been unanimous in its appraisal of the Plotinian heritage at this point. Some theologians, such as Gregory of Nyssa, Gregory Palamas, and Jonathan Edwards, have followed Plotinus by pointing out that the infinity of God requires that even once we have obtained the beatific vision, the desire for God will still continue on—and in this book I align myself with this position.

---

39. See my discussion of Bonaventure and Nicholas of Cusa in chap. 7.

40. Cf. Louth's comment: "For Plotinus, the higher is not the more remote; the higher is the more inward: one climbs up by climbing in, as it were" (*Origins*, 40).

Others, however, most notably in the Thomist tradition, have highlighted the rest that results from the beatific vision of God.

Plotinus casts the attainment of union with the Good in terms of vision of "primary" (πρῶτον) beauty, and he goes on to describe what is at stake in attaining this vision: "Here the greatest, ultimate contest is set before our souls; all our toil and trouble is for this, not to be left without a share in the best of visions. The man who attains this is blessed in seeing that 'blessed sight' (ὄψιν μακαρίαν), and he who fails to attain it has failed utterly" (1.6.7). Plotinus's language of "blessed sight" is to my knowledge the first occurrence of the term in the tradition that leads up to the Christian doctrine of the beatific vision. As we have already seen, Plotinus alludes to this vision also by speaking of union with God, of becoming godlike, and of erotic longing for the Good.

The second spatial metaphor Plotinus uses is that of a move inward. When he asks how we can possibly behold "inconceivable" beauty, he advises: "Let him who can, follow and come within, and leave outside the sight of his eyes and not turn back to the bodily splendours which he saw before. When he sees the beauty in bodies he must not run after them; we must know that they are images, traces, shadows, and hurry away to that which they image" (1.6.8). By turning within, we, like Odysseus, will set out on our journey home. "Let us fly to our dear country," comments Plotinus, with a quotation from Homer's *Iliad*.[41] He then continues: "Our country from which we came is there, our Father is there. How shall we travel to it, where is our way of escape (φυγή)? We cannot get there on foot; for our feet only carry us everywhere in this world, from one country to another. You must not get ready a carriage, either, or a boat. Let all these things go, and do not look. Shut your eyes (μύσαντα ὄψιν), and change to and wake another way of seeing (ὄψιν ἄλλην), which everyone has but few use" (1.6.8).[42] The passage is important for several reasons. First, for Plotinus the end goal of the journey is our "homeland" (πατρίς), where our "Father" (πατήρ) resides. God—also named Goodness or Beauty in the wider context of this passage—is both our origin and our destiny. The "blessed sight," we could say, constitutes a return to the point of origin. Much like Plato, Plotinus works with a schema of emanation and return.[43]

---

41. The quotation is from *Iliad* 2.140.

42. The same move inward is implied in Plotinus's depiction of the soul as moving in a circle, thus turning inward via Intellect to the One (*Enn.* 6.9.8).

43. Although it is not inappropriate to speak of emanation in connection with Plotinus

Second, Plotinus recommends that we shut our eyes and wake "another way of seeing." Plotinus asks his reader to leave sense perception behind and to rely on a way of seeing that belongs to the realm of Intellect instead. This injunction anticipates the doctrine of the spiritual senses, popular throughout much of the Christian tradition.[44] For Plotinus, "blessed sight" is in no way physical sight.[45] With the "blessed sight" the soul has moved from the senses to Intellect. The intellectual or noetic sight that results is contemplation, in which the mind's eye rests in the utter simplicity of true beauty and Goodness.

Another Kind of Vision

The language of vision in Plotinus's notion of "blessed sight" is not as straightforward as it may seem. We have already noted that it is not ordinary, physical sight. But this is not the only qualification we need to make. Although it is true that he believed that the soul sees by way of an intellectual vision, the term "vision" as a metaphor falls drastically short of capturing what the soul experiences. In the last section of *On Beauty*, Plotinus asks the sensible question: "And what does this inner sight see?" (1.6.9). In answering this question, he again focuses on moral formation. He urges his reader to cut and polish his moral character as one would a statue. When, as a result, finally "the divine glory of virtue shines out on you," so that there is nothing to be seen but "true light, not measured by dimensions . . . then you have become sight; you can trust yourself then; you have already ascended and need no one to show you; concentrate your gaze and see" (1.6.9). *Seeing* beauty is identical, for Plotinus—as it is typically also within later Christian Platonism—with the process of *becoming* beautiful. He captures this sentiment by following up with the comment with which we began our exploration of Plotinus: "No eye ever saw the sun without becoming sun-like, nor can a soul see beauty without becoming beautiful. You must become first of all godlike and all beautiful if you intend to see God and beauty" (1.6.9). Seeing

---

(and he does use the language of "flowing" [ῥέω] at times), Gerson points out that for Plotinus the One does not act by necessity, as constrained from the outside (*Plotinus*, 26–33).

44. See Paul L. Gavrilyuk and Sarah Coakley, eds., *The Spiritual Senses: Perceiving God in Western Christianity* (Cambridge: Cambridge University Press, 2012).

45. Although much of the Christian tradition follows Plotinus in excluding physical sight from the beatific vision, I will suggest a different approach in chap. 13.

beauty makes one beautiful, since virtue constitutes one's participation in beauty and Goodness.

This equation of seeing beauty and becoming beautiful means that, for Plotinus, this "other way of seeing" (ὄψις ἄλλη) is not really vision in any ordinary sense of the term. It is not just that there is no physical component, but also that we cannot properly distinguish or parse out the distinct aspects that are ordinarily involved in vision. With ordinary sight, we can distinguish the eye, the object, and the light that allows the eye to see the object (5.7.5). Distinguishing these components makes sense only, however, in situations where sensible objects are involved. But these distinctions fail to apply once the soul moves higher up and reaches the level of Intellect or perhaps even sees Goodness itself. There is, for Plotinus, no way properly to distinguish the eye, the object, and the means of vision once the soul moves into the realms of Intellect and of the Good. We may want to speak of "blessed sight" to describe our union with the Good, but the analogy of sight has obvious limitations. In Plotinus's "blessed sight" (as well as in the Christian beatific vision), it is impossible to disentangle the various components that we ordinarily associate with vision.

John Phillips helpfully describes what Plotinus believed goes on when the soul leaves physical sight behind.[46] Physical sight, says Phillips, is followed first by "intellectual vision" and then by "supraintellectual vision." At the stage of intellectual vision, explains Phillips, the soul leaves behind discursive reason. This does not mean, however, that the soul has now reached the pure simplicity of the One or the Good. After all, there is more than one intelligible Form; with the intelligible Forms we still have multiplicity. Subject and object, therefore, are still distinct from each other. At this level of Intellect, the soul is only partway in its attempt to leave multiplicity behind. Phillips explains that despite this multiplicity of the Forms, "both Intellect and the intellectual soul can 'see' them, as it were, at one glance by an intuitive power analogous to the eye's ability to form a comprehensive image of a face from its discrete features."[47] The soul has this ability to see with "one glance" because at the intellectual level perception is timeless, and all intelligible objects are present to the mind's eye at once.

At the next stage, that of supraintellectual vision, the very distinction between subject and object disappears. This is in line with Plotinus's earlier-noted comment that here "you have become sight" (*Enn.* 1.6.9). At this level,

---

46. John F. Phillips, "Plotinus and the 'Eye' of the Intellect," *Dionysius* 14 (1990): 79–103.
47. Phillips, "Plotinus," 84.

the Good or the One gives itself to the mind (νοῦς) or to Intellect as the power by which to see. For Intellect to reach up and "see" the One, it needs to transcend itself—hence the phrase "supraintellectual vision." Phillips explains that Intellect's desire is ultimately to contemplate the One in isolation, and he adds:

> To attain this higher and simpler intuition requires that Intellect transcend itself by going beyond νόησις [intellectual perception]. That this is an entirely different and unique mode of vision is clear from Plotinus' assertion that we cannot perceive what transcends us by applying our minds to it . . . , since νόησις only leads us to Being and the Forms: "rather, Intellect must, so to speak, turn back and, facing both directions, release itself to what is behind it and there, if it wishes to see that [*sc.* The One/Good], it must not be all Intellect" [*Enn.* 3.8.9]. Intellect thus "sees" the One, not in the manner of the noetic ἀθρόα ἐπιβολή [comprehensive look] by a focusing of its "eye" in active concentration, but by self-abandonment and cessation of all intellectual activity.[48]

Plotinus, in other words, postulates the abandonment not only of the senses and of rational, discursive thought, but also of the world of Forms and of noetic perception.

The "vision" of Goodness or Beauty that emerges here is, therefore, not vision in any ordinary sense of the term at all. The reason is that at this point every distinction between the eye, the light as the medium of vision, and the object of one's vision has disappeared. Moreover, since the soul has already left behind rational, discursive modes of thinking in the previous stage—that of intellectual vision—it has become quite impossible to use human reason and discourse adequately to describe this supraintellectual "vision." The reality that the soul encounters at this level far outstrips the abilities of human reason. The language of "vision" is borrowed from the lower levels of the senses and of rational thought. Plotinus comments that perhaps this experience "was not a contemplation but another kind of seeing (ἄλλος τρόπος τοῦ ἰδεῖν), a being out of oneself and simplifying and giving oneself over and pressing towards contact and rest" (*Enn.* 6.9.11). At the level of the One, the discourse of sight is wholly inadequate: the "blessed sight" of beauty itself is an utterly ineffable experience (as, *mutatis mutandis*, it had been for Plato).[49]

48. Phillips, "Plotinus," 89. Only the second set of brackets is in the original.
49. Much as with Plato, so with Plotinus we are reminded of Saint Paul's report that, caught

As a result, Plotinus repeatedly uses language that erases the distinction between subject (the eye), the object (the One), and the medium of light. Commenting that ultimately the soul wants to leave behind even Intellect itself, Plotinus explains that the soul at that point arrives at contemplation of the One, "and then, as he looks and does not take his eyes away, by the continuity of his contemplation he no longer sees a sight, but mingles his seeing with what he contemplates, so that what was seen before has now become sight in him, and he forgets all other objects of contemplation" (6.7.35). The object and the act of seeing are one at this stage. One paragraph later, Plotinus adds that "whoever has become at once contemplator of himself and all the rest and object of his contemplation . . . no longer looks at it from outside—when he has become this he is near, and that Good is next above him, and already close by, shining upon all the intelligible world. . . . The vision fills his eyes with light and does not make him see something else by it, but the light itself is what he sees" (6.7.36). In the moment of final ascent the transformation of the soul has rendered it so "godlike" that it is no longer possible to distinguish the contemplating soul from the Good or from the light that enables the soul to see the Good.[50] The soul is so united to the "object" of its vision that there is no need any longer for a light to mediate between the eye and the object of one's vision.

It is precisely at this climactic point of Plotinus's philosophy that the Christian tradition has been most reluctant to follow him. After all, it is not only *difficult* at this point to distinguish the subject that sees from the object of his sight, but Plotinus so emphasizes the union of the soul with the One that the two can no longer be distinguished. The Christian tradition, alert to the creator-creature distinction, would diverge from Plotinus at this point, while accepting at the same time that Scripture promises a genuine union between God and his people. Some, therefore, have distinguished in God between his essence and energies, insisting that human participation reaches only the divine energies (Gregory Palamas), while others have posited a created light of glory (*lumen gloriae*) that mediates the beatific vision of God (Thomas Aquinas). Both approaches attempt, each in its own way, to walk

---

up in Paradise, "he heard things that cannot be told, which man may not utter" (2 Cor. 12:4). The similarity between the Plotinian and Pauline approaches at this point would influence many later Christian theologians.

50. For similar expressions that blur subject, object, and light of vision, see *Enn.* 6.9.3. Cf. Louth, *Origins*, 50. These passages make it difficult to accept Phillips's judgment that even in the supraintellectual vision the "νοῦς confronts its Principle as something other than itself" ("Plotinus," 99).

the fine line between pantheist identification of creator and creature, on the one hand, and a deist-type of separation between the two, on the other hand.

Conclusion

Experiences of noetic self-transcendence are rare while we are on earth in the body. Plotinus was convinced that our embodied condition makes it particularly difficult to reach the "blessed sight."[51] Moreover, as we have already seen, he was also convinced that when through union with Intellect the soul leaves the material world behind, the Good is still beyond the soul's reach because of the ineffable transcendence of the One or the Good. As a result, for Plotinus moments of rapturous union with the One and of the vision of its beauty remain just that—brief instances, which the soul cannot endure for any length of time. In his treatise *On the Good or the One*, Plotinus explains that the soul finds itself "utterly unable to comprehend" the One, since, unlike the finite soul, the One is in no way bounded. As a result, after a momentary vision, the soul "slides away and is afraid that it may have nothing at all. Therefore it gets tired of this sort of thing, and often gladly comes down and falls away from all this, till it comes to the perceptible and rests there as if on solid ground" (*Enn.* 6.9.3). The "blessed sight" is not something that Plotinus thought we are able to sustain for long.

Porphyry, in *The Life of Plotinus*, explains that on four occasions while he was with Plotinus, his mentor attained the goal of being united to "the God who is over all things."[52] Plotinus himself recounts these experiences as follows: "Often I have woken up out of the body to my self and have entered into myself, going out from all other things; I have seen a beauty wonderfully great and felt assurance that then most of all I belonged to the better part; I have actually lived the best life and come to identity with the divine." Immediately, however, Plotinus acknowledges the inevitable descent: "Then after that rest in the divine, when I have come down from Intellect to discursive reasoning, I am puzzled how I ever came down, and how my soul has come to be in the body" (*Enn.* 4.8.1). To be sure, Plotinus knows the answer to his own question: since we have not yet "totally come

---

51. As will become clear especially in the last two chapters of this book, I do not think that the body itself is an obstacle to the beatific vision—though its fallen condition renders it difficult for us to see God.

52. Porphyry, *On the Life of Plotinus and the Order of His Books*, in Plotinus, *Enn.* 1:71.

out of this world," the soul cannot remain continuously in the world of the divine (6.9.10).

I have already noted in connection with Plato's myth of the winged soul that Christians have followed him in the claim that in this life any ecstatic experience of union with God will be brief. Plotinus agreed with this, but unlike Plato in the *Phaedrus*, he holds out hope for a permanent vision beyond these fleeting experiences of "blessed vision": "There will be a time," comments Plotinus, "when the vision will be continuous, since there will no longer be any hindrance by the body" (6.9.10). Plotinus, so it seems, regarded the ecstatic, momentary visions we may experience in this life as fleeting anticipations of a vision that will last forever. With this, he adumbrated in a remarkable way the Christian teaching of the beatific vision.

For Plotinus, however, this future hope remains disembodied in character. On this point Christianity could not possibly follow Neoplatonism. One of the challenges facing Christian theologians would be how to give expression to their faith in the beatific vision without gainsaying either the incarnation or the bodily resurrection. On a Christian understanding, the incarnate Christ can never be bypassed, not even in the beatific vision— although Christians have often struggled with how to give expression to this fundamental conviction. Thus, the heritage of Plato and Plotinus not only deeply shaped the Christian hope of seeing God face-to-face, but it also forced theologians to develop a uniquely Christian articulation of their belief.

CHAPTER 3

PROGRESS AND VISION

Gregory of Nyssa's Unending Search

A Spiritual Quest

Engagement with the fourth-century Cappadocian mystical theologian Gregory of Nyssa (ca. 335–ca. 394) is particularly germane as we try to retrieve the theme of the beatific vision. The beatific vision was of great significance to the bishop of Nyssa, who repeatedly reflected on it, often in passing, and on three occasions at some length. His sixth homily on the Beatitudes (probably written in the mid to late 370s), as well as his *Life of Moses* and his *Homilies on the Song of Songs* (both of which probably stem from the 390s),[1] deal extensively with the beatific vision. Furthermore, Gregory was a theologian for whom Christian doctrine, biblical interpretation, pastoral theology, and personal ascetic practices were closely linked. In each of these areas, his anagogical (or upward-leading) approach to theology inspired in him a desire to move from this-worldly, earthly realities to otherworldly, heavenly ones. The doctrine of the beatific vision fits neatly with Gregory's view of biblical interpretation as an upward move from history to spirit, with his desire to prepare his congregation for eternal life, and with his conviction that a life of almsgiving, care for the sick, and bodily renunciation is indispensable in reaching the aim of the Christian life.

For Gregory, therefore, the beatific vision was not a doctrine about which to speculate abstractly. Instead, he regarded it as the very aim of the Christian life—and hence, also of his own personal journey. Gregory looked forward

---

1. On internal grounds, it seems to me that *The Life of Moses* was written before the *Homilies on the Song of Songs*. See Hans Boersma, *Embodiment and Virtue in Gregory of Nyssa: An Anagogical Approach* (Oxford: Oxford University Press, 2013), 231n95.

concretely to experiencing the beatific vision at the point of death; this vision constituted the aim for which he strove throughout his life, and as such it determined his overall outlook on life. Gregory, we could say, was someone who made it the purpose of his existence to seek the face of God. The aim of the spiritual journey here on earth was, for Gregory, identical to the telos of seeking God in the hereafter. This concord between the destiny of the heavenly future and the aim of everyday spirituality means that the quest to see God lies at the heart of Gregory's mystical-theological approach. For him, God makes himself visible to saintly believers in their spiritual lives by means of theophanies, in anticipation of the beatific vision in the hereafter. Gregory's reflections on the beatific vision draw, therefore, on the spiritual, theophanic visions that saints such as Moses, Paul, and John (as well as the bride of the Song of Songs) experienced during their earthly lives. Saint Gregory worked on the assumption that we are to pursue the vision of God in this life, and that the resulting theophanies give us a foretaste of the reality of the beatific vision in the hereafter.

In what follows, then, I will highlight some of the characteristics of Gregory's doctrine of the beatific vision, based as it is on his insights in the biblical text.[2] I will argue that, for Saint Gregory, human souls find their telos when in union with Christ they become ever purer, in an ever-increasing growth in the beatific vision. Gregory was a theologian always in search of Christ, and though he was convinced that he had indeed found him, his desire to see Christ impelled him to seek still further. For Gregory this theological longing was grounded in his understanding of the beatific vision: the eschatological future of perpetual progress (*epektasis*) within the life of Christ means that already in this life Gregory set his desire on seeking the face of God in Jesus

---

2. To be sure, Gregory does not see biblical exegesis as being at odds with philosophical reflection. I do not have the space here to discuss in detail Gregory's reliance on Platonic philosophy and how this relates to the biblical character of his approach. Suffice it to say that I believe Gregory to be primarily a biblical theologian. Jaroslav Pelikan strikes the right balance when he comments that the Cappadocians "stood squarely in the tradition of Classical Greek culture, and each was at the same time intensely critical of that tradition" (*Christianity and Classical Culture: The Metamorphosis of Natural Theology in the Christian Encounter with Hellenism* [New Haven: Yale University Press, 1993], 9). To my mind, then, it is a gross exaggeration to state with Harold Fredrik Cherniss that, "but for some few orthodox dogmas which he could not circumvent, Gregory has merely applied Christian names to Plato's doctrine and called it Christian theology" (*The Platonism of Gregory of Nyssa* [Berkeley: University of California Press, 1930], 62). At the same time, Jean Daniélou may unduly minimize the importance to Gregory of a Platonic metaphysic (*Platonisme et théologie mystique: Doctrine spirituelle de Saint Grégoire de Nysse*, rev. ed., Théologie 2 [Paris: Aubier, 1944], 8–9).

Christ. For Gregory, then, the soul's true end—depicted under the biblical images of the pure in heart, Moses, and the bride—can be realized in the soul's mystical vision of God in Christ, prior to the eschatological beatific vision. At the same time, Gregory was convinced that, in an important sense, this end always remains elusive, since the soul will always keep searching for greater fulfillment of its desire. The reason for this is that seeing God implies at the same time a nonseeing, since, on Gregory's understanding, the soul can never (not even in the hereafter) attain to the very nature or essence of the infinite God.

Homilies on the Beatitudes: Obstacles to Purity

Gregory first extensively discusses the beatific vision in his *Homilies on the Beatitudes*. Anticipating the approach of many others in the later tradition, Gregory begins by positing the obvious paradox that the canonical witness presents: on the one hand, John, Paul, and Moses all rule out the possibility of seeing God (John 1:18; 1 Tim. 6:16; Exod. 33:20);[3] on the other hand, none of these three saints "failed to achieve that sublime blessedness which comes as a result of seeing God."[4] This paradox is closely linked to two obstacles that may prevent us from seeing God. The first has to do with the nature of God. The promise held out by the sixth beatitude—that the pure in heart shall see God—"exceeds the utmost limit (ὅρον) of blessedness" (*Beat.* 138.9–10). Gregory maintains that the divine nature "transcends all conceptual comprehension" (140.16–17). God's nature is beyond human limits, so that the only way to speak of the divine nature is by using apophatic negations: God is inaccessible, unapproachable, incomprehensible, and untraceable (140.17, 19, 20). The second obstacle concerns the lack of purity on the part of human beings. Gregory is keenly aware of the passions that stand in the way of the purity required to see God. Worrying about the "intractable difficulty" that the passions pose (144.16), Saint Gregory exclaims, "What sort of Jacob's ladder (Gen 28,12) is to be found, what sort of fiery chariot like the one which carried up the prophet Elijah to heaven (2 Kings/4 Kingdoms 2,11), by which our heart might be lifted up to the marvels above, and shake off this earthly

3. *Beat.* 137.13–22. Hereafter, references from this work will be given in parentheses in the text; quotations come from *Gregory of Nyssa: Homilies on the Beatitudes; An English Version with Supporting Studies*, trans. Stuart George Hall, ed. Hubertus R. Drobner and Albert Viciano (Leiden: Brill, 2000).

4. Gregory appeals to 2 Tim. 4:8, John 13:25, and Exod. 33:17.

burden?" (144.22–26).[5] Gregory makes clear to his readers that the Lord's promise faces tremendous hurdles.

Both the depth of the dominical saying and the intractable challenge that it poses to the spiritual quest make Gregory's mind "spin," "whirl," and "reel" (137.10; 137.25; 138.26).[6] In fact, he begins his homily by speaking of the vertiginous experience of looking down from a mountaintop into a deep sea: "People who look down from some high peak on a vast sea below, probably feel what my mind has felt, looking out from the sublime words of the Lord as from a mountain-top at the inexhaustible depth of their meaning. It is the same as in many seaside places, where you may see a mountain cut in half, sliced sheer on the seaward side from top to bottom, at whose upper end a projecting peak leans out towards the deep. As a person might feel who from such a view-point looked down from the great height on the sea at the bottom, so my mind spins now, sent reeling by this great saying of the Lord" (136.26–137.11). By comparing the impact that the sixth beatitude has on him to an experience of vertigo, Nyssen indicates that the Lord's saying about the pure in heart involves paradoxes and difficulties of such magnitude that they make us incapable of explaining the saying.[7] Gregory is alluding to an experience of rapture or ecstasy that takes him beyond the powers of sense and discursive reasoning.[8]

The paradox and obstacles surrounding the beatific vision do not render Gregory silent or agnostic on the topic. Both the paradox of seeing the invisible God and the obstacles that impede the vision can be subjected to rational analysis. Gregory takes several steps toward a resolution of the difficulties. With regard to the problem of divine incomprehensibility, he notes that it is possible—even for the "wise of the world"—to move from God's energies or operations to the divine operator (142.2–4). In particular, God's operations teach us about his transcendent wisdom, goodness, power, purity, and immutability (141.8–142.4). Gregory here distinguishes between

---

5. Within the context of the struggle against the passions, it is hard to imagine that the mention of Elijah's chariot does not at the same time call to Gregory's mind Plato's allegory of the chariot, which he relates in *Phaedr.* 246a–254e.

6. In each case, Gregory uses forms of the verb ἰλιγγιάω or of the noun ἴλιγγος.

7. Gregory uses the imagery of vertigo to describe the move beyond rational knowledge also in his seventh homily on Ecclesiastes. See *Eccl.* 413.5–414.9.

8. It does not seem to me that Gregory's rhetorical reference to his experience of vertigo implies that he actually had a mystical experience during the writing or preaching of his sermon. More likely, he playfully suits the rhetoric of the homily's opening paragraph to the theme of the sermon.

God's nature (φύσις) or being (οὐσία) and his energies (ἐνεργείαι). This distinction—which as a result of the fourteenth-century hesychast controversy has taken on particular prominence in Orthodox theology—helps Gregory affirm both that God *cannot* be seen (in his essence or being) and that he *can* be seen (in his operations). "He who is by nature invisible," affirms Gregory, "becomes visible in his operations (ἐνεργείαις), being seen in certain cases by the properties he possesses" (141.25–27). As a result of this distinction, the paradox becomes a little less intolerable; it is apparently possible for us to see God in creation, while he remains invisible inasmuch as he transcends the created order.

Saint Gregory explains that the *visio Dei* also becomes a reality when we wash away the accumulated filth of sin "by scrupulous living" (143.11–12) or when, as a whetstone strips off rust from iron, our heart recovers its original likeness to its archetype (143.13–20). This means that it is possible to see God's beauty in ourselves as in a mirror.[9] The result is that, "even though you are too feeble to understand the unapproachable light, yet if you go right back to the grace of the image which was built into you from the first, you possess in yourselves what you seek. Godhead is purity, absence of passion, and separation from every evil. If these are in you, God is certainly in you" (143.27–144.4). Gregory thus "resolves" the paradox of seeing the invisible God by limiting in two ways what it is that we see of God: we observe only his operations—not his nature—in creation (with the physical eyes), and we see merely a reflection of God's nature in the mirror of our lives (with the "eye of the soul").[10] Both of these limitations to the *visio Dei* imply that something

---

9. Cf. the comment of Edwart Baert: "Thus, the reappearance of the image of God, which is a return to the original state, is also a vision of God in the mirror of the pure soul" ("Le Thème de la vision de Dieu chez S. Justin, Clément d'Alexandrie et S. Grégoire de Nysse," *FZPhTh* 12 [1965]: 492 [translation mine]). For discussion of Gregory's use of the "mirror" metaphor in his *Homilies on the Song of Songs*, see Boersma, *Embodiment and Virtue*, 99. Cf., more extensively, Daniélou, *Platonisme*, 210–22.

10. At the same time, as we will see, for Gregory the "resolution" does not really remove the paradox, which remains as a result of his doctrine of perpetual progress (*epektasis*).

For discussion on Gregory of Nyssa's approach to the spiritual senses, see Boersma, *Embodiment and Virtue*, 93–100; Sarah Coakley, "Gregory of Nyssa," in *The Spiritual Senses: Perceiving God in Western Christianity*, ed. Paul L. Gavrilyuk and Sarah Coakley (Cambridge: Cambridge University Press, 2012), 36–55. Arguing that the later Gregory turned against his own earlier Platonic body-soul dualism, Coakley argues that Gregory turned from a "disjunctive" to a "conjunctive" approach, according to which sense perception itself can become spiritual perception. This interpretation overlooks that when Gregory wants us to use the senses to arrive at the reality that surpasses them, this "use" of the senses typically takes the form of a renunciation of

remains inaccessible to human sight: in the first instance, we do not see the nature or being of God, and in the second instance, we see his light only inasmuch as the soul reflects it. To be sure, we should not conclude that this means human beings do not really see God, for by witnessing the operations of God or the likeness of the archetype, we really do see God himself. After all, by drawing rational conclusions about God's operations we do get to see God in some way: "Each sublime idea brings God into view," comments Gregory (141.17–18). And he encourages his listeners to recover their likeness to the archetype, for, he says to them, the result will be that "you possess in yourself what you seek. . . . God is certainly in you" (144.2–4).

It should be clear that for Gregory everyday spirituality—seeing what God is like by looking at the world around us and observing with the "eye of the soul" "the luminous outpoured rays of the divine nature" in our hearts (144.8–9; 144.12)—is intrinsically linked to the beatific vision. Seeing God is not just something for the eschaton. Already today we get to contemplate in some derived fashion the light of God's being. What is more, for Gregory, earthly anticipations of the beatific vision take the form not just of ecstatic, theophanic experiences—though, as we will see, he does discuss them. Much more mundanely, however, we already experience the *visio Dei* in a real sense when we see traces of God in the way he works in the world and in the reflection of his purity in our own lives.

In none of this exposition has Gregory actually "solved" the paradox of seeing the invisible God. What he *has* done is to delineate, as it were, certain aspects of God's presence in the world (in his operations and in human purity) that make him visible, while limiting the invisibility of God to those inner aspects of God's being that are beyond ordinary human observation. Meanwhile, one of the two obstacles to the vision of God remains more or less intact; the requirement of "purity of heart" (and so our vision of God in ourselves as in a mirror) may hardly seem attainable. God's character is perfect purity, and a mere mirroring of this purity would hardly seem to be the kind of purity required for the vision of God. Regardless of Gregory's attempts thus far at securing the human vision of God, he has not yet fully addressed the gap separating the creature from the creator. Nor would it be out of place for his audience still to have questions about their ability to attain to the "purity of heart" that allows for the vision of God.

---

the senses. Coakley underestimates the (Christian Platonist) emphasis on ascent and anagogy throughout Gregory's writings, even in his later mystical commentaries (though it is true that these tend to be more thoroughly christological than some of his earlier works).

As we will see shortly, Gregory was keenly aware of the difficulty of attaining genuine "purity of heart." Nevertheless, in this homily on the sixth beatitude he never fully resolves this second obstacle to the vision of God—the lack of human purity vis-à-vis the holiness of God. Nyssen simply insists that the dominical saying is not only a warning but also a promise, which as such is attainable (145.20–146.2). Purity of heart cannot be out of reach, Gregory explains. He references the Lord's sharpening of the Old Testament law in the remainder of the Sermon on the Mount (Matt. 5:17–28), and he insists that we find in this teaching a "sharp-edged word like a plough digging out the roots of sins from the bottom of our heart," identifying Christ's words as "instruction which leads us to our goal" (147.15–16, 19–20). Gregory merely reinforces the urgency of Christ's demand as he insists that purity of heart is within our reach. We cannot but wonder how Gregory's audience would have responded to their preacher's optimistic assessment of their ability to achieve the goal of purity. After all, the passage concludes with the demand to "be perfect, as your heavenly Father is perfect" (Matt. 5:48). Christ's "instruction" regarding this perfection may not at all imply that people in fact have the ability to follow up on it. Purity may still be out of reach.

Gregory was quite aware of the exegetical and doctrinal difficulty he faced at this point: if perfection is unattainable, this means that purity is out of reach. And if purity is wishful thinking, then we will never see the face of God. In this particular sermon, Gregory leaves the issue unresolved. At the end, he simply places before his congregation the choice of either a life of virtue that takes on the shape of the Divinity or a life of vice taking on the form of the Adversary (148.3–8). He even adds that it is up to us which one to choose, since "there is offered to us the power to go either way by our own freedom of choice" (148.15–16).[11] This ending of the sermon seems rather unsatisfying, as it leaves Nyssen's congregation with a demand for purity that appears for all intents and purposes impossible to fulfill. Possibly, Gregory leaves the question of the attainability of purity unresolved for homiletical reasons—either so that he can end the sermon with a stern warning, or so that he doesn't have to start up a lengthy new discussion of what it means to attain perfection or purity. Whatever his reason for ending the sermon the way he does, Gregory clearly leaves the onus of purity resting firmly on the shoulders of his listeners.

11. While it is tempting perhaps to accuse Gregory of Pelagianism at this point, his overall theology (and particularly his christological understanding of participation) should caution us in this regard. See Boersma, *Embodiment and Virtue*, 211–50.

The Life of Moses: Vision as Perpetual Desire

Both in his book *On Perfection* and in his two masterful mystical treatises on Moses and on the Song of Songs, Gregory does develop a carefully considered christological response to this same issue.[12] Toward the end of his life, he resolved the issue of the apparent impossibility of perfection (and, by implication, also of purity) by redefining it in terms of infinite progress toward perfection as it exists in God. Thus, he writes in *On Perfection*: "For this is truly perfection: never to stop growing towards what is better and never placing any limit on perfection."[13] Gregory gives a similar definition in *The Life of Moses*, when he comments that "the perfection of human nature consists perhaps in its very growth in goodness."[14] Gregory speaks here of perfection as unending growth or progress in the life of God (*epektasis*), which is an important theme in the mystical works written toward the end of his life. Nyssen takes the concept from Philippians 3:13–14, where Saint Paul writes, "Brothers, I do not consider that I have made it my own. But one thing I do: forgetting what lies behind and straining forward (ἐπεκτεινόμενος) to what lies ahead, I press on toward the goal for the prize of the upward call of God in Christ Jesus." For Gregory, ever-increasing growth in purity and perfection is possible, explains Lucas Mateo-Seco, "because one already participates in a real manner in this good; an infinite growth is possible because this good is inexhaustible."[15] It is the infinite

12. Opinions differ as to the dating of *On Perfection*. Considering the less developed solution to the problem of perfection in this work (as compared to *The Life of Moses* and the *Homilies on the Song of Songs*), I am inclined to go with Gerhard May's dating of 370–378 for *On Perfection* (rather than accept Daniélou's suggestion of a later date). Cf. Jean Daniélou, "La Chronologie des œuvres de Grégoire de Nysse," *SP* 7 (1966): 168; Gerhard May, "Die Chronologie des Lebens und der Werke des Gregor von Nyssa," in *Écriture et culture philosophique dans la pensée de Grégoire de Nysse: Actes du colloque de Chevetogne (22–26 septembre 1969)*, ed. Marguerite Harl (Leiden: Brill, 1971), 56.

13. *Perf.* 214.4–6 (FC 58:122).

14. *Vit. Moys.* 1.10.5–6. ET used throughout: *The Life of Moses*, trans. and ed. Abraham J. Malherbe and Everett Ferguson (New York: Paulist, 1978). For detailed discussion of Gregory's unfolding of the notion of perfection, see Boersma, *Embodiment and Virtue*, 225, 227, 230–34, 237–38.

15. Lucas F. Mateo-Seco, "Epektasis—Ἐπέκτασις," in *The Brill Dictionary of Gregory of Nyssa*, ed. Lucas Francisco Mateo-Seco and Giulio Maspero, trans. Seth Cherney (Leiden: Brill, 2010), 265. For further discussion on the notion of *epektasis* in Gregory, see Daniélou, *Platonisme*, 291–307; Everett Ferguson, "God's Infinity and Man's Mutability: Perpetual Progress according to Gregory of Nyssa," *GOTR* 18 (1973): 59–78; Ronald E. Heine, *Perfection in the Virtuous Life: A Study in the Relationship between Edification and Polemical Theology in Gregory of Nyssa's De*

goodness of God that secures for Gregory the notion of perpetual progress in the life of God.

Gregory closely links his notion of *epektasis* to that of participation (μετοχή or μετουσία), which is common in the Platonic tradition. Gregory holds that created beings (especially created intelligibles) participate in the being of God, particularly through the life of virtue. He regards this as participation in the energies of God (as opposed to his nature or essence).[16] Since God is infinite, human progress must likewise be infinite, maintains Gregory.[17] David L. Balás, in his excellent study on participation in Saint Gregory, comments that "participation is, according to Gregory's conception, intimately connected with change, even continuous change."[18] Gregory's notion that participation allows for continuous (eternal) growth is an answer to the problem that a more static view of the beatific vision would seem to entail: If the vision of God simply satisfies human desire, would this satiety (κόρος) not lead to weariness with regard to the experience of God in the hereafter, and hence possibly to another fall, a recurring lapse from this beatific experience? That this was a genuine theological conundrum is clear from Origen's speculations on the topic of satiety, and it is likely in response to this Origenist problem that Gregory posited the notion of *epektasis*.[19]

Vita Moysis (Cambridge, MA: Philadelphia Patristic Foundation, 1975), 63–114; Everett Ferguson, "Progress in Perfection: Gregory of Nyssa's *Vita Moysis*," *SP* 14 (1976): 307–14; Albert-Kees Geljon, "Divine Infinity in Gregory of Nyssa and Philo of Alexandria," *VC* 59 (2005): 152–77.

16. Cf. David L. Balás, Μετουσια Θεου: *Man's Participation in God's Perfections according to Saint Gregory of Nyssa* (Rome: Herder, 1966), 128; Paulos Mar Gregorios, *Cosmic Man: The Divine Presence; The Theology of St. Gregory of Nyssa (ca 330 to 395 A.D.)* (New York: Paragon, 1988), 110–23; Elie D. Moutsoulas, "'Essence' et 'énergies' de Dieu selon St. Grégoire de Nysse," *SP* 18 (1989): 517–28; Verna E. F. Harrison, *Grace and Human Freedom according to St. Gregory of Nyssa* (Lewiston, NY: Edwin Mellen, 1992), 24–60, 88–131; Giulio Maspero, *Trinity and Man: Gregory of Nyssa's* Ad Ablabium (Leiden: Brill, 2007), 27–52; Alexis Torrance, "Precedents for Palamas' Essence-Energies Theology in the Cappadocian Fathers," *VC* 63 (2009): 47–70.

17. Gregory may not have been entirely consistent in denying human access to the divine essence. He comments, for example, that "we have a faint and slight apprehension of the divine Nature (θείας φύσεως) through reasoning, but we still gather knowledge enough for our slight capacity through the words which are reverently used of it" (*Eun.* 2.130.21–130.26, in *Gregory of Nyssa: Contra Eunomium II*, ed. Lenka Karfíková, Scot Douglass, and Johannes Zachhuber, VCSup 82 [Leiden: Brill, 2007], 87). See also Gregory's comments below (n. 23, as well as the quotation that immediately follows it), where he appears to affirm human participation in the divine essence or being. Cf. Torstein Theodor Tollefsen, *Activity and Participation in Late Antique and Early Christian Thought* (Oxford: Oxford University Press, 2012), 77.

18. Balás, Μετουσια Θεου, 136.

19. Cf. Marguerite Harl, "Recherches sur l'originisme d'Origène: La 'satiété' (κόρος) de la

Nyssen's combination of the themes of purity (or perfection), participation, and *epektasis* is of great significance for the way he articulates the
doctrine of the beatific vision, both in *The Life of Moses* and in the *Homilies on the Song of Songs.*[20] Following Jean Daniélou, scholars have tended
to analyze *The Life of Moses* in terms of the three theophanies that Moses
experiences: God appears to him in the burning bush (Exod. 3:1–6), in the
darkness of Mount Sinai (Exod. 20:21), and by the cleft in the rock (Exod.
33:21–22). The three stages have been characterized as a move from light, via
the cloud, into darkness.[21] In actual fact, however, Nyssen's understanding
of Moses's progress does not proceed quite this neatly by way of three distinct stages. Gregory does indeed trace Moses's ascent by following the three
theophanies in the book of Exodus. But when we analyze what distinguishes
them, it becomes clear that the notion of *epektasis* radically blurs the lines
between the second and the third "stages" of the ascent. There is only one
genuine marker in the ascent; it falls, as we will see, between the first and
second theophanies. The result is that there are really only two major stages
in the ascent of the soul.

At the burning bush—in its material form a witness to the incarnation[22]—
Moses comes to recognize that neither sense perception nor understanding
gives true access to Being: "It seems to me that at the time the great Moses
was instructed in the theophany he came to know that none of those things
which are apprehended by sense perception and contemplated by the understanding really subsists, but that the transcendent essence and cause (οὐσίας
καὶ αἰτίας) of the universe, on which everything depends, alone subsists."[23]
Nyssen then distinguishes between created realities, which exist by way of

---

contemplation comme motif de la chute des âmes," *SP* 8 (1966): 373–405; Heine, *Perfection*,
71–97.

20. Lucas F. Mateo-Seco observes that Gregory refers to 1 Cor. 13:12 (which speaks of the
beatific vision) in *The Life of Moses* "precisely when he speaks of the infinity of God and, as
a consequence, when he affirms the existence of progression towards infinity in the contemplation of God, that is, when he presents his thought on what scholars of Saint Gregory of
Nyssa usually call *epektasis*" ("1 Cor 13, 12 in Gregory of Nyssa's Theological Thinking," *SP* 32
[1997]: 153–62).

21. Cf. Daniélou, *Platonisme*, 17–23. I (mistakenly) follow this approach in Hans Boersma,
Heavenly Participation: The Weaving of a Sacramental Tapestry (Grand Rapids: Eerdmans,
2011), 160–61.

22. Nyssen mentions a number of ways in which he believes this passage of Exod. 3 speaks
of the incarnation. See Boersma, *Embodiment and Virtue*, 241.

23. *Vit. Moys.* 2.24.1–5. Hereafter, references from this work will be given in parentheses
in the text.

participation in Being, and immutable Being itself, which is "participated in by all but not lessened by their participation—this is truly real Being (τὸ ὄντως ὄν)" (2.25.8–10).

The second theophany leads Moses into the cloud on the mountain (Exod. 20:21). This theophany is a vision of God in darkness, and the reason for this is that Moses comes to see that "knowledge of the divine essence (θείας οὐσίας) is unattainable" (2.163.11–12) and that God is "beyond all knowledge and comprehension" (2.164.4). Here, Moses "slips into the inner sanctuary (ἄδυτον) of divine knowledge" and enters into the "tabernacle not made with hands" (2.167.1; cf. Heb. 9:11). Gregory identifies this heavenly tabernacle with Christ, uncreated in his preexistence (2.174.9–10), and he speaks of the incarnate Christ (as well as of his church) as the earthly tabernacle (2.174.5–6; 2.184.3).[24]

Having arrived at the "inner sanctuary" already in the cloud (the second stage), Moses's further ascent cannot possibly be an advance to a distinctly different stage. The first theophany taught him that created being exists only by way of participation, and the second theophany made clear that the Being of God is beyond knowledge. At this point Moses (as well as Gregory himself) faces a dilemma. On the one hand, there can be no knowledge of God that reaches beyond the "inner sanctuary." On the other hand, Moses has not yet arrived at the destiny of his ascent; at the very apex of his journey—the inner sanctuary itself—he appears to realize that he will never come to know the Being of God. And so, even though he has already seen God "face to face" (Exod. 33:11), Moses still asks God to show him his glory (33:18; *Vit. Moys.* 2.219.4–9)—which then leads to the third theophany, where Moses is allowed to see God's back from within a cleft of the rock—a divine manifestation that Saint Gregory again explains christologically, with Christ being identified as the rock (2.244.8). For Gregory, Christ is never left behind; the human person finds his identity always and only in him.

It is at this point that Gregory embarks on a detailed discussion of *epektasis* (2.219.1–2.555.5). Even though Moses has already come to Christ as the tabernacle and the inner sanctuary in the cloud, further progress still appears possible. But it is progress that takes place after the senses and the understanding have long been left behind (in the first two theophanies).

---

24. I have emphasized the christological character of Moses's entry into the tabernacle in Boersma, *Embodiment and Virtue*, 240–45. For a similar analysis, see Nathan Eubank, "Ineffably Effable: The Pinnacle of Mystical Ascent in Gregory of Nyssa's *De vita Moysis*," *IJST* 16 (2014): 25–41.

Everything that needs to be abandoned has already been let go by the time Moses experiences the third theophany. Already in the second theophany, he has achieved the experience of mystical ecstasy, the sense of vertigo, which comes from leaving behind every this-worldly apprehension of God. The reason Moses can nonetheless ascend still higher is that his entrance into the "inner sanctuary" does not mean the arrival at a point of static rest. Moses recognizes that even his "face-to-face" encounter with God (Exod. 33:11) beyond sense and understanding does not give him access to God's "true Being" (ὡς ἐκεῖνός ἐστι) (2.230.5–6). Moses still wants to see God "not in mirrors and reflections, but face to face" (2.232.2–4).

The reason for Moses's continued desire to see God face-to-face is that "the Divine is by its very nature infinite, enclosed by no boundary" (2.236.1–2). So, even though Moses has in fact had the rapturous experience of seeing God in the cloud, this does not satiate his desire: "The munificence of God assented to the fulfillment of his desire, but did not promise any cessation or satiety of the desire" (2.232.6–8). Therefore, just as "purity of heart" (human perfection) means "never to stop growing towards what is better and never placing any limit on perfection,"[25] so the beatific vision—which itself is true purity or perfection—always progresses. Nyssen comments, therefore, that "the true sight of God consists in this, that the one who looks up to God never ceases in that desire" (*Vit. Moys.* 2.233.3–5). And he adds a little later: "This truly is the vision of God: never to be satisfied in the desire to see him" (2.239.1–2). Gregory's definition of the *visio Dei* is nearly identical to his definition of purity. The pursuit of both elements of the dominical saying—purity and the vision of God—is driven by never-ending desire.

At this point, Gregory has provided a theological as well a pastoral response to the seemingly intolerable burden that the conclusion of his sixth homily on the Beatitudes imposed on his audience. Recognizing that the promise of the beatific vision seems out of reach because of a lack of purity, he ended that sermon simply by impressing on his hearers all the more strictly the demand for purity. In *The Life of Moses*, however, Gregory takes a different approach. He recognizes that our growth in purity—or, we could also say, our participation in Christ—leaves much to be desired. Regardless of how far we may have ascended in terms of purity, the Christian life is never one of absolute achievement; it always remains one of progress. That progress, in fact, is what now comes to define the life of purity for Gregory. And he recognizes that even when Moses reaches the peak of his theophanic

25. *Perf.* 214.4–6 (FC 122).

experiences, or when we ourselves reach our heavenly future and see God face-to-face, growth in God—in and through Christ—will still continue. For Gregory, seeing God kindles a desire to see ever more of him, so that the beatific vision implies a perpetual desire to see God—so much so that Gregory even defines the vision itself as the never-ending desire to see the face of God.

Homilies on the Song of Songs: Seeing More and More of Christ

Saint Gregory's *Homilies on the Song of Songs* similarly approaches the vision of God by interweaving the themes of purity (often discussed as virtue), participation, and *epektasis*. Again, while much of the metaphysical structure is Platonic, Gregory refuses to separate the beatific vision from Christology. Christ is always the object of our vision. When the bride comments, "Behold, you are beautiful, my kinsman, and glorious, in the shadow by our bed" (Song 1:16),[26] Gregory takes this to mean that she praises Christ's nobility, compared to which everything else—human approval, glory, celebrity, and worldly power—pales:

> For these things are tinged with a show of nobility for those whose attention is focused on sense perception, but they are not what they are reckoned to be. For how should something be noble when it lacks entire reality? That which is honored in this world, after all, has its being only in the heads of the people who make the judgment, but you are truly beautiful—not only beautiful (καλός), but the very essence of the Beautiful (αὐτὴ τοῦ καλοῦ ἡ οὐσία), existing forever as such, being at every moment what you are, neither blooming when the appropriate time comes, nor putting off your bloom at the right time, but stretching your springtime splendor out to match the everlastingness of your life—you whose name is love of humankind.[27]

For Gregory, Christ is not only "beautiful" (καλὸς) but also "the very essence of the Beautiful" (αὐτὴ τοῦ καλοῦ ἡ οὐσία). On Nyssen's understanding,

26. In this chapter, I take biblical translations of the Song of Songs from *Gregory of Nyssa: Homilies on the Song of Songs*, trans. and ed. Richard A. Norris, Writings from the Greco-Roman World 13 (Atlanta: Society of Biblical Literature, 2012).

27. *Cant.* 106.15–107.5. Hereafter, references from this work will be given in parentheses in the text; quotations come from *Gregory of Nyssa: Homilies on the Song of Songs*, trans. and ed. Norris.

Christ is the very definition of beauty, which means that he always equates the vision of God's beauty with the vision of the beauty of Christ.

Much as in *The Life of Moses*, so also in these homilies, the incarnation is the central event that makes God visible to the human eye. After the bride has already accomplished a number of ascents, Gregory notes in homily 5 that none of this can yet be characterized as "contemplation," properly speaking. Commenting on Song 2:8—"The voice of my kinsman: Behold, he comes leaping over the mountains, bounding over the hills"—Nyssen remarks that "all these ascents are described not in terms of contemplation or clear grasp of the Truth, but by reference to the 'voice' of the One who is desired, and the characteristics of a voice are identified by hearing, not known and rejoiced in by understanding" (*Cant.* 138.9–13). In the words "Behold, he comes," Gregory reads a reference to prophetic announcements of God's manifestation in the flesh, and he quotes from "the prophet: 'As we have heard, so also we have seen' (Ps 47:9). *The voice of my beloved*: this is what we have heard. *Behold, he is coming*: this is what the eyes see" (*Cant.* 140.14–17). The prophets announce the coming of Christ; the incarnation makes him visible to the eye.

In line with this, when in the next verse the kinsman stands behind the wall, "leaning through the windows, peering through the lattices" (Song 2:9), Gregory interprets this as a reference to the Law and the Prophets, which offer only marginal illumination.[28] The "anagogical sense of the words," he maintains, shows us that

> the Word follows a certain path and a certain sequence in adapting human nature to God. First of all he shines upon it by means of the prophets and the law's injunctions. (This is our interpretation: the windows are the prophets, who bring in the light, while the lattices are the network of the law's injunctions. Through both of them the beam of the true Light steals into the interior.) After that, however, comes the Light's perfect illumination, when, by its mingling with our nature, the true Light shows itself to those who are in darkness and the shadow of death. (144.19–145.9)

Although the Law and the Prophets do carry some borrowed light from the true Light, it really is the Light's perfect illumination in the incarnation that enables us to see. So, it is when the bride comes to "the shelter of the rock" and asks the groom, "Show me your face" (Song 2:14), that she recognizes the presence of Christ. Gregory imagines the bride speaking as follows:

28. Cf. Boersma, *Embodiment and Virtue*, 83.

"Speak to me no longer by way of the enigmas of the prophets and the law, but show me yourself clearly so that I may see. In that way I can leave the outworks of the law behind and come to be within the rock of the gospel" (163.16–20).

The encounter with Christ, therefore, fulfills the desire to see God face-to-face. The Law no longer prevents the bride from "union with the one she desires" (168.11–12). When the bride comments, "My kinsman is mine and I am his; he feeds his flock among the lilies, until the day dawns and the shadows depart" (Song 2:16–17), Gregory offers the following paraphrase: "'I have seen,' she says, 'the One who is eternally what he is face to face. I have seen him rising up in human form on my account out of the synagogue my sister, and I am resting in him and am becoming a member of his household'" (168.15–18). The bride sees God face-to-face in Christ.

Similarly, when, much later, in homily 15, Nyssen reflects at length on the mystery of the incarnation, he refers to the union between the groom and the bride ("I am for my kinsman, and my kinsman is for me"; Song 6:3). Gregory insists that "through these words we learn that the purified soul is to have nothing within her save God and is to look upon nothing else. Rather must she so cleanse herself of every material concern and thought that she is entirely, in her whole being, transposed into the intelligible and immaterial realm and make of herself a supremely vivid image of the prototypical Beauty" (439.6–11). This transposition of the soul into the intelligible realm implies that "she is conformed to Christ, that she has recovered her very own beauty" (439.17–18). Just as a mirror shows the exact imprint of the face it reflects, so the soul "has graven into herself the pure look of the inviolate beauty" (440.6–7). Accordingly, the mirror of the soul boasts of being shaped by the beauty of Christ: "Since I focus upon the face of my kinsman with my entire being, the entire beauty of his form is seen in me" (440.8–10).

Gregory adds to this christological *visio Dei* the notion that it is fueled by a never-ending, epektatic desire. Gregory's homilies on the Song of Songs do not develop this theme in the same programmatic way that *The Life of Moses* does, probably because the Song lacks the textual scaffolding of the three theophanies of the book of Exodus from which to construct the increasing progression of epektatic growth in the life of God. But that it is more difficult to trace the *epektasis* textually in the Song of Songs does not mean that Saint Gregory fails to develop the theme. When in his first homily he reflects on the Song's opening words ("Let him kiss me with the kisses of his mouth"), Nyssen refers back to the "bride Moses" loving the bridegroom in the same way as does the Song's virgin, and he explains:

Through the face-to-face converse accorded him by God (as the Scripture testifies [cf. Num. 12:8]), he became more intensely desirous of such kisses after these theophanies, praying to see the Object of his yearning as if he had never glimpsed him. In the same way, none of the others in whom the divine yearning was deeply lodged ever came to a point of rest in their desire. And just as now the soul that is joined to God is not satiated by her enjoyment of him, so too the more abundantly she is filled up with his beauty, the more vehemently her longings abound. (31.10–32.8 [brackets in original])

Rather than satisfying his desire for God, Moses's face-to-face contact with God intensifies his longings.

Gregory argues that the Song of Songs reflects this same epektatic pattern. The various segments of the Song replicate the soul's ordered ascent into the life of God. Thus, at the beginning of homily 5, Nyssen explains that the Song evokes both desire (ἐπιθυμία) and despair (ἀπογνώσις) at the same time: "For how is it possible to be without grief when one considers that the purified soul—even though through love she has been exalted toward participation in the Good by a whole series of ascents—does not yet seem, as the apostle says [Phil. 3:13], to have laid hold on what she seeks?" (137.8–12). And so, as he reflects on "the ascents already accomplished," Gregory mentions that he had earlier thought he would be able to "pronounce the soul blessed on account of her progress toward the heights" (137.13–14); but he then makes the distinction between merely hearing the "voice" of the beloved and "contemplating" the bridegroom himself, which I discussed above (138.8–141.5). Contemplation of the groom is the point in the epektatic ascent at which one moves beyond just hearing his voice.

In the next sermon the bride journeys toward even "better things," as she becomes "more clear-sighted and discerns the glory of the Word" (176.11–12). She reaches such perfection that she even instructs others about "eagerness for the same goal" (177.15). But this still does not imply the end of the journey: "Who, then, would not say that a soul exalted to such a degree had come to the highest peak of perfection? Nevertheless the limit that defines the things that have already been accomplished becomes the starting point of her being led to realities that transcend them" (177.17–178.1). Then—and here Gregory refers to the groom appearing to the bride in the form of a gazelle and a fawn (Song 2:9)—as an additional step, the bride begins "to see the One whom she desires when he appears to her in a form other than his own" (178.3–4). Coming ever closer to perfection, she "prays to see the very countenance of the One who addresses her, and she receives from him a word that no longer comes by way of intermediaries" (178.17–19). The bride directly contemplates God in Jesus Christ.

When in Song 2:16 the bride exclaims, "My kinsman is mine and I am his," it is clear to Gregory that at this point "the two actors move into one another. God comes into the soul, and correspondingly the soul is brought into God" (179.6–7). Again, Gregory uses this new stage of the bride's ascent as an occasion to reflect on the perpetual character of her progress: "She seems to attain the hope of the very highest good. For what is higher than to be in the One who is the object of desire and to receive the object of desire within oneself? But in this situation too she bewails the fact that she is needy for the Good. As one who does not yet have what is present to her desire, she is perplexed and dissatisfied, and she broadcasts this perplexity of her soul in her story, describing in her account how she found the one she sought" (179.12–19). Gregory concludes from the bride's "perplexity" that the limitless greatness of the divine nature (φύσις) means that "no measure of knowledge sets bounds to a seeker's looking" (180.1–3).[29] In fact, concludes Nyssen, "the intelligence that makes its course upward by seeking into what lies beyond it is so constituted that every fulfillment of knowledge that human nature can attain becomes the starting point of desire for things yet more exalted" (180.4–7).

It is only after the bride has departed from the watchmen making their rounds in the city, having asked them where the groom might be (Song 3:3), that she finds her lover and brings him into her mother's chamber (3:4). Saint Gregory has the bride explain that, no sooner had I "departed from the whole created order and passed by everything in the creation that is intelligible and left behind every conceptual approach, than I found the Beloved by faith, and holding on by faith's grasp to the one I have found, I will not let go until he is within my *chamber*" (*Cant.* 183.5–10).[30] The chamber, explains Gregory, is the heart, where God comes to live to return it to its original condition at the time of creation (183.10–13).

When he arrives at homily 8, Nyssen perceives that the ascent has still not come to a halt, as he reads the following words in Song 4:8: "Come away

29. Gregory repeatedly denies that God is subject to "limit" (πέρας) and boundary (ὅρος), thereby alluding to the infinity of God.

30. For Gregory, faith allows one to move past the limits of the senses and of discursive knowledge to union with God in Christ (and so to the beatific vision). See Martin Laird, *Gregory of Nyssa and the Grasp of Faith: Union, Knowledge, and Divine Presence* (Oxford: Oxford University Press, 2004), 100–107.

from frankincense, my bride, come away from frankincense. You shall come and pass through from the beginning of faith, from the peak of Sanir and Hermon, from the lions' dens, from the mountains of the leopards." The bride's ever-continuing movement reminds Gregory that Saint Paul reflects on his own *epektasis* to a still higher ascent (Phil. 3:13) *after* he has already been in the "third heaven" (2 Cor. 12:2) (*Cant.* 245.11–22). Our capacity to see God increases continuously, maintains Gregory. Yet, "the infinity and incomprehensibility of the Godhead remains beyond all direct apprehension" (246.8–10). Gregory again asserts that "the outer limit of what has been discovered becomes the starting point of a search after more exalted things" (247.11–12), while "the desire of the soul that is ascending never rests content with what has been known" (247.14–15). Nyssen then discusses the particularities of Song 4:8 by explaining that the bride has already accompanied the bridegroom to the "mountain of myrrh" (249.12–13)—which is a reference to being buried with Christ by baptism into death (Rom. 6:4)—and that she has come with him also to the "hill of frankincense" (249.14) (having risen with him to new life and to communion with the Godhead). Now, maintains Gregory, she is prepared through "unending growth" for yet greater heights (252.11–12).

Finally, in homily 12 Saint Gregory draws attention to the apparent incongruity between Song 5:3 ("I have removed my tunic. How shall I put it on?") and 5:7 ("the watchmen of the walls took my veil away from me"). How is it possible, Gregory asks, that the watchmen take the veil away from the bride when she has already been "stripped of all covering" (*Cant.* 360.2)? Nyssen sees here yet another reference to *epektasis*: the bride has so increased in purity, he explains, "that by comparison with the purity that now becomes hers she does not seem to have taken off that clothing but again, even after that former stripping, finds something on her to be taken off" (360.7–10). To Nyssen, the bride here faces the same situation in which Moses found himself when he asked God to show him his glory (Exod. 33:18) even though he had already seen him face-to-face (33:11).[31] The ascent into the life of God—which both for Moses and for the bride means union with Christ—is never-ending or epektatic growth in the divine life, spurred on by a desire that never comes to a point of rest. Christ, for Nyssen, is a never-ending source of enjoyment; he therefore continuously increases our longing to be found in him.[32]

31. Cf. Boersma, *Embodiment and Virtue*, 91–92, 237.
32. In the three writings that I have analyzed, Gregory does not clarify explicitly how he

Conclusion

Gregory's search for the vision of God in Christ continues to have a great deal to commend it. First, Gregory was someone for whom this-worldly realities—accessible to the senses and the intellect—are unable to fulfill our deepest desires. To be sure, his sixth homily on the Beatitudes makes clear that sensible and intellectual apprehension in this world already involves some incipient vision of God. But Gregory regarded purity of heart as central to attaining the beatific vision, since it is through growth in purity that we come to participate in the purity of God. It is growth in purity, then, that allows us to participate in the life of God and so in the beauty of Christ.

Second, Gregory recognized the correspondence between divine infinity and the insatiability of human desire, so that a proper Christian spirituality holds out the hope of a vision that does not culminate in a static point but ever continues and increases in relation to the ultimate object of this vision. When, in his two climactic mystical exegetical works, Nyssen reflects on what makes one most genuinely a human person, he turns to Moses and to the bride of the Song of Songs. Through the purity of their lives, they arrive at astounding theophanies. United to Christ, they see God. For Gregory, the epektatic character of this journey into the "inner sanctuary" (ἄδυτον) means that we should not think that this vision fully resolves the paradox of the dominical saying that the pure in heart shall see God. For Gregory, they both shall and shall not see God. If perfection or purity means "never to stop growing towards what is better and never placing any limit on perfection,"[33] and if "the true sight of God consists in this, that the one who looks up to God never ceases in that desire,"[34] then what makes the beatific vision glorious is that the soul revels with increasing intensity and intimacy in the infinite, ever-greater gift-giving of the invisible God who in Christ has made himself visible.

Whether we describe this epektatic participation in the life of God as participation in his essence or in his energies is perhaps not the crucial issue.

---

sees the relationship of the divine essence, the divine energies, and Christ. On the one hand, Nyssen seems to identify Christ with the divine essence or being itself. On the other hand, he asserts that we do participate (epektatically) in Christ, and in his other writings, he identifies Christ repeatedly with virtue, with perfection, with virginity, with wisdom, and so on, which seems to imply a close link between Christ and the energies of God. Gregory is not overly precise in his vocabulary.

33. *Perf.* 214.5–6.
34. *Vit. Moys.* 233.3–7.

Gregory does affirm the distinction, but we have also seen that he is not fully consistent, since at times he affirms that we participate in the very being or essence of God. Such inconsistency is perhaps not so surprising: it would seem odd if participation in the inner sanctuary—Christ himself—would not entail participation in the very being or nature of God. It seems to me, at least, that when we are united to Christ, we thereby share in the very being of God, which is why in this book I am suggesting that *all* participation in God is (in varying degrees) participation in his nature. The essence-energies distinction itself, therefore, is far from crucial. (Some articulations of it may even imply a division in God, which would be incompatible with divine simplicity.) Much more important, it seems to me, is that we affirm with Gregory that we can always enter more deeply into the infinite being and love of God (so that we don't lapse into a pantheistic assimilation of creator and creature) and that this sharing in the divine life is nothing but a deeper union with Christ.

Third, and more than anything else, Saint Gregory makes us aware that human beings cannot find their true identity, and therefore cannot flourish, when they exclude serious reflection on the transcendent purpose of the human person. Human personhood is defined by its telos. As human beings—both individually and in our common life together—we attain our identity (and so become fully human) only to the degree that we explicitly aim for the supernatural goal of the beatific vision, which God places before us as our true fulfillment. The reductionism inherent in modernity's abandonment of the beatific vision is, therefore, much more serious than may at first appear. It means a turning away from the infinite God who gives all good things in the vision of Christ in favor of a reorientation of the human gaze toward this-worldly goods. The loss of the beatific vision as the purpose of human existence leads to a "spirituality" in which nothing exceeds any longer the ebb and flow of this-worldly human desires. Gregory knew human nature well enough to recognize that our desires are infinite. When such infinite desire is directed away from its proper telos of the vision of God in Christ, the objects of desire inevitably end up holding their immanent sway over human existence in frightening ways, holding us in a form of bondage that, ironically, we have willed into existence by our own misshapen desires. We are perhaps more than ever in need, therefore, of the witness of Saint Gregory of Nyssa: only when with Gregory we redirect our gaze upon God in Christ can we find our true identity and aim.

CHAPTER 4

ANTICIPATION AND VISION

Augustine on Theophanies and Ecstasy

Sign and Reality: Sacramental Entwining?

How are we to conceive of the relationship between the pilgrimage and its destination? Is the eschatological *visio Dei* so unique that nothing in this life adumbrates it? Or does the glory of the eschaton cast its rays back onto our often mundane, terrestrial life? Do we see God only in the hereafter, or do we see him in some way already today? Is it possible, in other words, to point to certain sacraments (*sacramenta*) that allow us to share, in preliminary fashion, already today, in the reality (*res*) of the vision that God has in store for us? Saint Augustine faced these questions in two theological contexts. First, theophanies—appearances of God, especially in the Old Testament—raised the question of the relationship between God himself and these visible manifestations. Had God himself actually appeared to some of the saints already here on earth? Second, the possibility of ecstatic or mystical experiences raised the same issue, only from a different angle: Is it proper for believers to expect such experiences as part of their journey of faith? Can one hope to be joined to God in a beatific manner already in this life? In other words, does faith merge into sight already today? Or is mystical contemplation strictly reserved for the hereafter, when faith will give way to sight (2 Cor. 5:7)?

Augustine dealt extensively with both of these topics, exploring deeply the question of whether the vision of God as an eschatological reality enters into our everyday lives here and now. To be sure, Augustine himself does not use the sacramental discourse of sign (*signum*) and reality (*res*) to speak about the relationship between theophanies and mystical experiences, on the one hand, and the eschatological beatific vision on the other hand. Nonetheless, his views on the relationship between sign and reality correlate directly to the way in which he treats theophanies and ecstatic experiences. It will prove helpful, therefore, to ask whether the African bishop saw these experiences as in some way participating (sacramentally) in the beatific vision.

Augustine's understanding of the relationship between sign (*signum*) and reality (*res*) is much debated. Some interpret him as sharply separating the two, so that earthly and heavenly things have no inherent connection to one another. Referring to the "powerlessness" of external things for Augustine, Phillip Cary maintains that the bishop of Hippo invented "expressionist semiotics," which stems from the bishop's Platonist dualism, and he maintains that in Augustine's understanding, "words are external signs and . . . they get their significance by expressing things that belong to the deeper ontological level that belong to the soul or inner self."[1] For Augustine, Cary claims, outward signs do not actually give us the inward goods that they signify, and so he argues that with Augustine's "inward turn" the bishop "offers the West an alternative to finding the grace of God in external things such as the word of the Gospel and the sacraments of the church, not to mention the flesh of Christ."[2] The problem, according to Cary, is Augustine's nonsacramental expressionist semiotics, according to which "we learn nothing from words." "When combined with Augustine's new, systematic distinction between inner and outer, the legacy this leaves modernity is our taken-for-granted sense that external things are superficial, incapable of revealing inner depths."[3] The result, according to Cary, is a "two-track approach" to the sacrament, based on the Platonic distinction between body and soul.[4]

By contrast, Michael Cameron has argued that although the early Augustine may have stressed the arbitrariness and disjunction of the sign-thing relation, this disjunctive (or indicative) approach gave way in the 390s to a conjunctive (or mediative) approach in *Against Adimantus* (*Contra Adimantum*; 394) and *On Christian Teaching* (*De doctrina Christiana*; 396).[5] Cameron explains that in Augustine's understanding, literal signs use letters (*litterae*) to suggest actual things (the letters w-o-o-d pointing to actual trees), while these actual things in turn can serve as signs for other things.

---

1. Phillip Cary, *Outward Signs: The Powerlessness of External Things in Augustine's Thought* (Oxford: Oxford University Press, 2008), 17 (emphasis omitted).

2. Cary, *Outward Signs*, 4.

3. Cary, *Outward Signs*, 88.

4. Cary, *Outward Signs*, 163.

5. Michael Cameron, *Christ Meets Me Everywhere: Augustine's Early Figurative Exegesis* (New York: Oxford University Press, 2012), 231–38. Cf. Corine Boersma, "A Comparative Analysis of Sacramentality in Augustine and Dionysius" (MA thesis, Regent College, 2016), 14–22.

(E.g., the wood that Moses used to sweeten the bitter waters in the wilderness [Exod. 15:25] recalls the wood of the cross [1 Pet. 2:24].)[6] Signs can thus be literal and figurative at the same time. Cameron points out that for Augustine, the spiritual or figurative sense was not a later, external addition to the text but was actually present in it. When Paul interprets the incident at Massah and Meribah (Exod. 17:1–7; 1 Cor. 10:1–11), he comments that the Israelites "drank from the spiritual Rock that followed them, and the Rock was Christ" (1 Cor. 10:4). Saint Augustine points out that "Paul did not say, 'the rock signifies Christ,' but rather, 'the rock was Christ.'"[7] According to Cameron, therefore, the bishop of Hippo believed that the spiritual sense was already present in the text of Exodus: "The rock functionally 'became' Christ for the Israelites, for he gave himself to them through it."[8] Augustine, concludes Cameron, "insisted not only on the *congruence* of sign and reality but also on their sacramental *interdependence*."[9]

At stake in this disagreement about (the lack of) sacramentality in Augustine is not just the technical question of how we should interpret Augustine's own theology. If his theology is largely nonsacramental—and if this is exemplified in a strict separation between life here on earth lived by faith and the future eschatological life in heaven lived by sight—then it becomes tempting to point to the bishop of Hippo as the deepest theological cause of the rise of secularism in the West. The strict separation between heaven and earth, as well as between nature and the supernatural, which over time has led to an independent, autonomous natural realm, may in that case find its origin in the great progenitor of Western culture, Saint Augustine.[10] The rise of a "purely natural" order (*pura natura*), though strictly an invention of the sixteenth century, may then be traced back to the father of Western theology himself.[11]

We may be tempted, then, to turn away from Augustine and look to the Greek fathers instead, for a more sacramental approach to reality. After all,

---

6. Cameron, *Christ Meets Me Everywhere*, 231–32.

7. Augustine, *Contra Adimantum* 12.5, as quoted in Cameron, *Christ Meets Me Everywhere*, 235.

8. Cameron, *Christ Meets Me Everywhere*, 235.

9. Cameron, *Christ Meets Me Everywhere*, 234.

10. For a repudiation of this view, see Michael Hanby, *Augustine and Modernity* (London: Routledge, 2003).

11. For discussion of the historical development of "pure nature," see Louis Dupré, *Passage to Modernity: An Essay in the Hermeneutics of Nature and Culture* (New Haven: Yale University Press, 1993), 167–81.

as we saw in the previous chapter, theologians such as Gregory of Nyssa put the notion of "participation" front and center in their theology. And, one might argue, it is only the East that has maintained a proper sense of sacramentality, a genuine awareness that nature and the supernatural are closely linked, so that only the Eastern mind-set makes it truly possible to anticipate the heavenly future already in this life. Thus, one might conclude that the reason modernity did not affect the East as it did the West is that Orthodoxy never bought into the Western treatment of the natural order as autonomous and instead regarded it as inherently oriented toward the beatific vision as its telos—the result being that one could expect this telos to be anticipated in some significant fashion already in this life.

This chapter is meant as a test case. I will look at Saint Augustine's doctrine of the beatific vision through the lens of the question of sacramentality and ask the question: Did the African bishop *separate* sign and reality, or did he discern a sacramental *entwining* of the two, whereby the sign participates in the reality? I am inclined to the latter view: Augustine was genuinely sacramental in his approach to the beatific vision. He held that God really does manifest himself in Old Testament theophanies and that mystical contemplation is a realistic possibility for Christians today. To be sure, Augustine was cautious and modest in affirming eschatological anticipations of the beatific vision—and it is easy to see why later Western thinkers would draw on Saint Augustine in separating the eschatological beatific vision more radically from our temporal experience of faith. Nonetheless, the bishop of Hippo was convinced that in some preliminary fashion we share already today in the reality of the eschatological beatific vision. One of the implications of this conclusion is that the difference between East and West may not be quite as stark or obvious as it is sometimes thought to be.

The Backdrop of Omnipresence and Participation

By the time Saint Augustine arrives at his discussion of Old Testament theophanies in book 2 of *De Trinitate*, likely written in the second decade of the fifth century,[12] he has already discussed several important matters pertaining to the Trinity in the previous book. Most notably, for our purposes, he has argued at some length that Father, Son, and Spirit are consubstantial,

12. For the dating of *The Trinity*, see Lewis Ayres, *Augustine and the Trinity* (Cambridge: Cambridge University Press, 2010), 118–20.

coeternal, and coequal, and that they work inseparably, so that whatever one of the three persons does, the others do as well.[13] The bishop of Hippo links the principles of coequality and inseparability to the beatific vision as the final end or purpose of humanity. He interprets the well-known passage of 1 Corinthians 15:24–28—which speaks of the Son delivering the kingdom to the Father and becoming subject to the Father—as a reference to the beatific vision: "The fact is that the *man Christ Jesus, mediator of God and men* (1 Tm 2:5), now reigning for all *the just* who *live by faith* (Hb 2:4), is going to bring them to direct sight of God, to the *face to face* vision, as the apostle calls it (1 Cor 13:12), that is what is meant by *When he hands the kingdom over to God and the Father*, as though to say 'When he brings believers to a direct contemplation of God and the Father'" (*Trin.* 1.8.16).[14] According to Augustine, on the last day the Son will deliver the kingdom—that is to say, the believers—to the Father so that they may contemplate his substance.

Since, however, the Son is in the Father and the Father in the Son, to see the one is to see the other also (John 14:9–11) (*Trin.* 1.8.17). As Augustine puts it: "Whether we hear then 'Show us the Son,' or whether we hear 'Show us the Father,' it comes to the same thing" (1.8.17). It is crucial for Augustine that we distinguish between the Son in the form of God and the Son in the form of a servant. Some biblical texts have to be read by the "form-of-God rule," others by the "form-of-a-servant rule" (2.2.4). It is according to the latter that we must understand that the Son will be subjected to the Father (1 Cor. 15:28): "So inasmuch as he is God he will jointly with the Father have us as subjects; inasmuch as he is priest he will jointly with us be subject to him" (1.10.20). The upshot is a Trinitarian-shaped understanding of the beatific vision: seeing the Father means at one and the same time seeing the Son and the Spirit. It is the shared substance of God that Augustine believes we will see in the hereafter: "His essential goodness, in the last resort, is attained in that sight or vision in which God is manifested to the pure of heart—*How good is the God of Israel to the upright of heart* (Ps. 73:1)!"[15]

---

13. *Trin.* 1.4.7–1.6.13. Hereafter, references from this work will be given in parentheses in the text; quotations come from WSA I/5.

14. As an illuminating aside, Saint Gregory of Nyssa presents a nearly identical interpretation of this passage in *In Illud: Tunc et ipse Filius.* See Hans Boersma, *Embodiment and Virtue in Gregory of Nyssa: An Anagogical Approach* (Oxford: Oxford University Press, 2013), 188–97.

15. "Secundum illam uisionem bonus est secundum quam uisionem deus apparet mundis corde, quoniam: quam bonus deus israhel rectis corde!" (*Trin.* 1.13.31 [WSA I/5:94]). In the same section Augustine reiterates that in the eschaton we will see the "one God, therefore, Father Son and Holy Spirit, whose manifestation will mean nothing but a joy which will not

On this basis of an intertwined understanding of the Trinity and the beatific vision, Augustine then turns to the topic of theophanies in book 2. He
realizes that he faces the profound question of how the eternal light of the
triune God relates to seeing God within the economy of salvation. Crucially,
the bishop begins by asserting God's omnipresence in the world, which he
deduces from a variety of biblical passages (Jer. 23:24; Wis. 8:1; Ps. 139:7–8).
These make clear, according to Augustine, that both the Son and the Spirit
are present everywhere in the created order (*Trin.* 2.5.7). When the Son and
the Spirit were sent into the world in the incarnation and at Pentecost, they
were sent to a place where they were already present. And so Augustine
asks: "If then both Son and Holy Spirit are sent to where they already are,
the question arises what can really be meant by this sending of the Son or
of the Holy Spirit—the Father alone is nowhere said to have been sent"
(2.5.8). Again the bishop reiterates here the inseparability of the activities
of the three persons: one may even say that the Son was sent not just by the
Father, but also by himself, since the Father sent him by his Word (2.5.9). If
each of the three persons is omnipresent and if they are inseparable in their
economic actions, then—so Augustine was convinced—it must be erroneous to claim with the Homoians that only the (subordinate) Son becomes
visible in the theophanies while the Father remains invisible throughout.
The omnipresence of God also means—and this is the crucial point—that we
cannot interpret Augustine's theology of theophanies as one in which God
in a strictly extraneous fashion controls "purely natural" objects devoid of
his presence.[16] Such a separation between God and theophanies would run
counter to Augustine's emphatic acknowledgment of divine omnipresence.

Moreover, since the Word eternally contains in himself the entire economy of salvation—"there was timelessly contained the time in which that
Wisdom was to appear in the flesh"—Saint Augustine argues that the moment of the incarnation itself was already contained eternally in the Word
of God (2.5.9). Augustine was enough of a Platonist to be convinced that
all of history, as well as every created object that plays a role in time, par-

be taken away from the just" (1.13.31 [WSA I/5:94]). He also comments: "For that sight of God
in which we shall behold his unchanging substance (*substantiam*), invisible to human eyes and
promised only to the saints . . . this sight alone is our supreme good" (1.13.31 [WSA I/5:95–96]).

16. *Pace* Bogdan G. Bucur, "Theophanies and Vision of God in Augustine's *De Trinitate*:
An Eastern Orthodox Perspective," *SVTQ* 52 (2008): 67–93. I am indebted to Joshua Schendel
for pointing me to the significance of Augustine's comments on omnipresence for how we
interpret his understanding of theophanies.

ticipates in the eternal Mind or Word of God.[17] If all of time is contained in the eternal Word of God, this means that the temporal sending of the Son is also contained in the eternal Word. Within such a participatory metaphysic, it would make no sense to separate the Old Testament theophanies from the eternal Word of God—or, according to Augustine at least, from the other persons of the Trinity and from the substance of God. To be sure, as we will see, Augustine repeatedly and strongly asserts that in the theophanies, the Old Testament saints do not see the very substance of God. We may well ask how this relates to the bishop's conviction that the divine substance is present everywhere and that all things participate in the Word. But regardless of how we may deal with this dilemma, it should be clear that Augustine's theology of theophanies is not one that radically separates God from creation. Augustine's metaphysic would demand that in a theophany one has some kind of vision of God himself. Put differently, Augustine's universe is by no means a disenchanted, secular one, where one is deprived of the vision of God.

Trinitarian and Christological Controversies

Augustine discusses Old Testament theophanies against the backdrop of earlier controversies on the nature of the Trinity in the third century. Modalist or monarchian Christologies had highlighted the unity of the Godhead, insisting that this one God reveals himself at different times in different "modes," as Father, as Son, or as Spirit. Praxeas, for example, argued that the Father and the Son are one and the same person. This involved the claim that not just the Father but also the Son is invisible. In response to this focus on divine unity, both Tertullian in Africa and Novatian in Rome argued for a clear distinction between Father and Son, and they appealed for this to the Old Testament theophanies.[18] These indicate, according to Tertullian, in his

17. In question 46 of *Eighty-Three Different Questions* (388/396), Augustine advocates the Christian Platonist notion that individual things are created according to eternal ideas (*ideae*), forms (*formae*), species (*species*), or principles (*rationes*), which in turn are contained in the divine Mind (or Word). Augustine comments that these Platonic ideas "are themselves true because they are eternal and because they remain ever the same and unchangeable. It is by participation (*participatione*) in these that whatever is exists in whatever manner it does exist" (in FC 70:81]).

18. I do not discuss Novatian here. See further Michel René Barnes, "The Visible Christ and the Invisible Trinity: Mt. 5:8 in Augustine's Theology of 400," *ModTh* 19 (2003): 340–42; Kari

book *Against Praxeas* (ca. 210), that while the Son is (in some way) visible, the Father remains invisible.[19]

Tertullian takes his starting point in what may seem like a paradox in Scripture: On the one hand, God says to Moses, "Man shall not see me and live" (Exod. 33:20). On the other hand, "God has been seen by many persons, and yet . . . no one who saw Him died (at the sight)."[20] The African theologian resolves this dilemma by referring the former statement to the Father and the latter claim to the Son, thereby dividing rather sharply the invisible Father from the visible Son: "It will therefore follow, that by Him who is invisible we must understand the Father in the fulness of His majesty, while we recognise the Son as visible by reason of the dispensation of His derived existence; even as it is not permitted us to contemplate the sun, in the full amount of his substance which is in the heavens, but we can only endure with our eyes a ray, by reason of the tempered condition of this portion which is projected from him to the earth."[21] Though Tertullian does acknowledge that in himself the Son, as God, is invisible just like the Father, he nonetheless insists that in the Old Testament the Son appeared in visions and dreams, enigmatically (cf. Num. 12:6–8), so that the prophets saw him through a glass, darkly or enigmatically (cf. 1 Cor. 13:12). Tertullian concludes that "in early times it was always in a glass, (as it were,) and an enigma, in vision and dream, that God, I mean the Son of God, appeared—to the prophets and the patriarchs, as also to Moses indeed himself."[22] Tertullian had a strictly christological reading of the theophanies, which he grounded in the distinction between Father and Son.

Such christological readings of the theophanies predominated in the pre-Nicene church. Kari Kloos points out that Justin, Irenaeus, Tertullian, Novatian, Hilary, and Ambrose all interpreted the theophanies as manifestations of the Son of God—through what she calls "literal christological readings":

Kloos, *Christ, Creation, and the Vision of God: Augustine's Transformation of Early Christian Theophany Interpretation*, Ancient Christianity 7 (Leiden: Brill, 2011), 32–44.

19. Ernest Evans discusses the monarchian controversy and Tertullian's role in it in the introduction to *Tertullian's Treatise against Praxeas* (London: SPCK, 1948), 6–22. For discussion of Tertullian's interpretation of theophanies, see Kloos, *Christ, Creation, and the Vision of God*, 57–62; Gerald P. Boersma, *Augustine's Early Theology of Image: A Study in the Development of Pro-Nicene Theology* (New York: Oxford University Press, 2016), 22–25.

20. *Adv. Prax.* 14 (*ANF* 3:609).

21. *Adv. Prax.* 14 (*ANF* 3:609).

22. *Adv. Prax.* 14 (*ANF* 3:609). Tertullian interprets God speaking with Moses "mouth to mouth" (Num. 12:8) as a promise that was fulfilled in the transfiguration.

"Between the second and fourth centuries, nearly all Christian interpreters of the theophany narratives claim that the Son appeared and was seen in them. This 'literal christological reading'—positing not that Christ was symbolized or prefigured in the narratives, but that he actually appeared—pervades interpretations by early Christian authors of various christological and theological views."[23] Christological readings of the theophany narratives served to counter modalism by underscoring the distinct personhood of each of the three persons of the Trinity. Such interpretations also reconciled the biblical claim of divine invisibility with accounts in which God does become visible: the invisibility of God refers to the Father, the visibility to the Son. Finally, this approach underscored the sacramental unity of Old and New Testaments: Christ was seen as really present in the narratives of the Old Testament.[24]

The problem with these christological readings of the theophany narratives is that though they helped defeat modalist theologies in the late second and third centuries, they were less effective in upholding pro-Nicene theology in the face of Homoian threats in the next two centuries. The Homoians argued for a subordinate status of the Son, insisting that he is merely *like* (ὅμοιος) the Father. As such, they claimed that, unlike the Father, the Son is both visible and changeable.[25] In making this claim, they were able to build on the antimodalist theologies of Tertullian, Novatian, and others. After all, not only had these church fathers clearly distinguished between Father and Son, but they had also held to the visibility of the Son (as distinct from the Father), which suggested to the Homoians that the Son was subordinate to the Father.

As a result, the fourth-century theologians Hilary of Poitiers and Ambrose of Milan became more circumspect in their handling of the theophany narratives. While the antimodalist discourse of Justin and Novatian had emphasized the distinction between Father and Son, Hilary in contrast high-

23. Kloos, *Christ, Creation, and the Vision of God*, 2. Bucur argues that christological readings of the theophany narratives have their origin in the YHWH Christology of Mark's Gospel ("Theophanies and Vision of God," 72).

24. Bucur rightly comments that this christological exegesis shows that "we are reading Scriptures in light of Christ as much as we are reading Christ in light of the Scriptures. It is only in light of what is known and remembered—the God who did great deeds, to whom we are committed in faith—that one is able to recognize in the Crucified One the King of Israel and ruler of the whole world, glorified and reigning from Zion" ("Theophanies and Vision of God," 73).

25. Cf. Augustine's sharp critique of this division between Father and Son in *Trin.* 2.9.15.

lighted their unity and so their coequality. As Kloos puts it, "Hilary avoids any claim distinguishing the Father and the Son's qualities, instead emphasizing difference in activity or office: the Father commands and the Son executes in the world. Yet these different actions are inherently connected for Hilary, so that the Father and Son are inseparably united in all of their actions in the world."[26] Ambrose went even further than Hilary. Hilary continued to read the theophanies christologically, despite the Homoians using such exegesis for their own subordinationist ends.[27] But Ambrose, in the face of the Homoian threat, highlighted perhaps even more emphatically the equality of the divine persons and the unity of their works: while he generally maintained a christological reading of the Old Testament theophanies, in good part he departed from such a reading in connection with the crucial passage of the Mamre theophany in Genesis 18. Because Abraham saw three persons but worshiped only one (Gen. 18:3), Ambrose interpreted this as "symbolic of the distinction of Trinitarian persons and of the unity of the divine nature."[28] Ambrose, more than any of his predecessors, highlighted the unity of the Trinity's actions in the world.[29] Clearly, the bishop of Milan had become apprehensive of how a christological interpretation might be used to shore up a subordinationist Christology.

Against this backdrop of Old Testament theophany interpretations, Saint Augustine developed his own exegesis of the relevant passages and articulated his Trinitarian theology in book 2 of *De Trinitate*. The bishop's overriding concern was to undercut the Homoian allegation that the Son is visible in his own substance, whereas the Father remains invisible (1 Tim. 1:17).[30]

26. Kloos, *Christ, Creation, and the Vision of God*, 87. See also Boersma, *Augustine's Early Theology of Image*, 31–36.

27. Kloos explains that Hilary does qualify the christological exegesis of the theophany narratives to some extent, as Hilary also insists that "Christ does not need to be explicitly described in each narrative; the more important revelation is the collective pattern of God's visible manifestation to patriarchs and matriarchs, culminating in God the Son's visible manifestation as the Word made flesh" (*Christ, Creation, and the Vision of God*, 88). As we will see, this approach adumbrates Ambrose's and especially Augustine's pro-Nicene theophany interpretations.

28. Kloos, *Christ, Creation, and the Vision of God*, 93. I discuss Origen's and John Chrysostom's christological readings of the Mamre theophany (Gen. 18) in *Scripture as Real Presence: Sacramental Exegesis in the Early Church* (Grand Rapids: Baker Academic, 2017), 56–80.

29. For discussion of the circumstances surrounding Ambrose's *De fide*, see D. H. Williams, "Polemics and Politics in Ambrose of Milan's *De Fide*," *JTS* 46 (1995): 519–31.

30. *Trin.* 2.9.14–2.9.15. Hereafter, references from this work will be given in parentheses

Augustine directly charges his opponents with holding that the Son of God appeared before the incarnation, in many forms, so that "it follows both that he is visible in himself, because his substance (*substantia*) was apparent to mortal eyes even before he took flesh; and that he is mortal insofar as he is changeable" (2.9.15). Augustine responds by reiterating throughout his discussion that in the theophanies, people do not get to see, with bodily eyes, the substance (*substantia*) of God (2.14.24; 2.15.25, 26; 2.18.34, 35), God "as he is in himself" (*proprie sicuti est*) (2.17.32), or his essence (*essentia*) (2.18.35)—whether we understand the theophany to refer to the Father, the Son, or the Holy Spirit. The substance of God cannot be seen with bodily eyes.

Creature Control and Sacramental Presence

If God is not seen in his own substance, then what are the theophanies about? Does God—any of the three persons—actually appear? And if so, how? At the outset of his discussion, Saint Augustine highlights the unique character of the incarnation. Only in the incarnation does the Word actually assume flesh. So when the Spirit appears as a dove (Matt. 3:16), as a gust of wind (Acts 2:2), or as tongues of fire (Acts 2:3), these are not incarnations:

> Not thus, therefore, was a creature taken (*assumpta creatura*) by the Holy Spirit to appear under, in the way that that flesh, that human form, was taken (*assumpta*) of the virgin Mary. The Spirit did not make the dove blessed, or the violent gust, or the fire; he did not join them to himself and his person to be held in an everlasting (*in aeternum*) union. Nor on the other hand is the Spirit of a mutable and changing nature, so that instead of these manifestations being wrought out of created things, he should turn or change himself into this and that, as water turns into ice. But these phenomena appeared, as and when they were required to, *creation serving the creator (creatura seruiente creatori)* (Wis 16:24), and being changed and transmuted at the bidding of him who abides unchanging in himself, in order to signify and show (*significandum et demonstrandum*) him, as it was proper for him to be signified and shown (*significari et demonstrari*) to mortal men. (2.6.11)

---

in the text; quotations come from WSA I/5. Cf. the discussion in Paul A. Patterson, *Visions of Christ: The Anthropomorphite Controversy of 399 CE*, Studies and Texts in Antiquity and Christianity 68 (Tübingen: Mohr Siebeck, 2012), 78–80.

The Spirit, maintains Augustine, did not assume a creaturely form as the Word assumed human form, and the implication is that dove, wind, and fire were evanescent phenomena: they came and went, and the Spirit never united himself to them in any abiding sense (*in aeternum*). In other words, God signified or showed the Spirit's presence by means of creatures—creation serving the creator.

Augustine patterns the functioning of Old Testament theophanies on the Holy Spirit's association with dove, wind, and fire. Theophanies, like the sending of the Spirit, must be distinguished from the incarnation. Repeatedly, Augustine speaks of God showing himself "through some created bodily substance (*corpoream creaturam*)" (2.9.16), so that "all these occurrences consisted of created things serving the creator (*creatura seruiente creatori*) [Wis. 16:24] and impressing themselves on the senses of men as the divine arrangements required" (2.15.25). In line with this, Augustine maintains that perhaps it was the Father who appeared to Abraham and Moses "by means of some changeable and visible creature under his control (*per subiectam sibi commutabilem atque uisibilem creaturam*)" (2.10.17). Likewise, at the burning bush (Exod. 3:1–6), either an angel appeared to Moses, or "some created thing" (*aliquid creaturae*) was being "requisitioned to appear visibly for the business of the moment, and to produce audible voices which would convey the presence of the Lord by creature control (*per subiectam creaturam*)" (2.13.23). Also, in connection with the pillar of cloud and the pillar of fire, "God did not appear to mortal eyes in his own substance, but by creature control (*per subiectam creaturam*), and a physical creature at that" (2.14.24). At the conclusion of book 2, after commenting that the substance or essence of God cannot be physically seen, the bishop of Hippo suggests again that "we must believe that by creature control (*per subiectam uero creaturam*) the Father, as well as the Son and the Holy Spirit, could offer the senses of mortal men a token representation of himself in bodily guise or likeness" (2.18.35). According to Augustine, God used created things to appear in theophanies.

Saint Augustine thus counters the Homoian position—that the Son is visible in his own substance—with the notion that one or more of the divine persons appeared by means of angels or by creatures that God had under his control. This may suggest that God himself remained radically separate from the creatures at his disposal and may thus seem to imply a nonsacramental view of the theophanies—which in turn may seem to presage Western secularism, along with a view of the beatific vision that radically separates faith (today) and sight (in the eschaton). Basil Studer argues such a nonsacramental interpretation of Augustine, claiming that he followed Ambrose in strictly separating the divine substance from the creaturely form. Studer suggests that Augustine "turns against the opinion that God would have built that manifestation from his own nature and should therefore be considered as changeable in his substance. He therefore wants to treat the appearance of God as completely distinct from his nature, exclude any inner connection between the two."[31] Bogdan Bucur, too, suggests that Augustine "solves the paradoxical coexistence of what is visible and what is invisible in the theophany by severing the ontological link between the two, so that the *species* [the creature] is no longer 'owned' by the subject of the *natura* [God himself]."[32] Since God simply produces certain visible effects by means of creatures at his disposal—*per subiectam creaturam*—he does so, on this interpretation, without himself being present.

It seems to me, however, that this reading fails to pay sufficient attention to what Augustine believed God's use of creatures actually accomplishes. John Panteleimon Manoussakis points to Augustine's use of the term "sacraments" (*sacramenta*) at the end of book 2, and he suggests that Augustine's view is genuinely sacramental: "Are the earthquakes, the light, the fire, and the rest signs—that is, mere signifiers of God? Augustine's answer is clearly negative. They are more than signs. They are 'sacraments.' As neither the oil of unction nor the water of the holy water—not to mention the bread and the wine of the Eucharist—are mere 'signs' or 'symbols' of God but they effect God's grace, so too those theophanic phenomena of the Old Testament are neither mere signs nor symbols but efficacious *indications* in which He Who is indicated makes Himself present therein."[33] On Manoussakis's view, Augustine believed God was actually present in theophanic appearances.

Manoussakis is right, I think, to suggest that Augustine's view is sacramental.[34] We have already seen that Augustine argued that the divine

31. Basil Studer, *Zur Theophanie-Exegese Augustins: Untersuchung zu einem Ambrosius-Zitat in der Schrift* De videndo Deo (*ep. 147*), SA 59 (Rome: Herder, 1971), 97 (translation mine). As we will see below, Studer is right in his first claim: God's nature is not changeable according to Augustine. This does not mean, however, that he radically separates the divine nature from the theophanies.

32. Bucur, "Theophanies and Vision of God," 76. See also Barnes, "The Visible Christ," 342–46.

33. John Panteleimon Manoussakis, "Theophany and Indication: Reconciling Augustinian and Palamite Aesthetics," *ModTh* 26 (2010): 80. Manoussakis borrows the term "indication" (*Verflechtung*) from Husserl, Merleau-Ponty, and Balthasar, arguing that indications are signals or symbols that the living God is present in the event (80–81).

34. To be sure, the analogy with ecclesial sacraments is one that we need to treat with

substance is omnipresent, and his participatory metaphysic would be incompatible with a strict separation between sign and reality. We need to note carefully what precisely Augustine argues regarding the relationship between the divine substance and the theophanies. Though he repeatedly and strongly insists that in the theophanies no one *saw* the substance of God, he nowhere actually suggests that the divine substance was therefore *absent* from the theophanies. The fine point, which is often overlooked, is that Augustine merely argues that when one physically sees a theophany, one does not thereby observe the divine substance *with bodily eyes*. Augustine, we need to recall, was arguing against the Homoian notion that the substance of the Son became visible to bodily eyes. (This, at least, as we have seen, is what he accused them of.) To conclude from this that for Augustine the divine substance was in no way present in the theophany would be to jump to conclusions.[35]

It seems to me undeniable that Augustine links the theophanies with divine presence, and in that sense, his view may be called sacramental.[36] To describe God's relationship with created means in theophanic appearances, Augustine typically uses verbs such as "show" (*demonstrare*), "signify" (*significare*), "appear" (*apparere*), and "manifest" (*ostendere*). While the first two of these verbs may seem to distance God from the theophany, this is not what Augustine means to convey. It is God (Father, Son, and/or Holy Spirit) himself who "appears" or is "manifested" in the theophany. Thus, although God "has never shown himself to bodily eyes," there is one exception (*nisi*)

---

caution: we certainly should not try to squeeze Augustine's understanding of theophanies into the precise parameters of any particular tradition of sacramental theology as it has developed over the centuries, whether East or West. Augustine's notion of sacramental presence probably falls short of the way it is typically understood today both in Orthodoxy and in Catholicism.

35. Cf. Michael Hanby's response to Colin Gunton's charge that on Augustine's take, God is not substantially involved in the theophanies: "But this is exactly the wrong conclusion. In asserting that 'it is through the creature,' and not 'in his own substance' (*per suam substantiam*) that God creates sensible effects, Augustine is not denying that 'it is by means of the Word' that the Word itself is prefigured. These are not mutually exclusive alternatives, and no attentive reader of the *Confessions* could arrive at that conclusion. Instead, he is noting, first, a perfectly orthodox distinction between those theophanies which signal Christ's advent and the hypostatic union itself and, secondly, that the substance of God is never 'visible' apart from the mediation of creatures, be they material or intellectual, the definitive instance of which is Jesus himself. The conclusion *affirms* the need for the incarnation" (*Augustine and Modernity*, 15).

36. Kloos also suggests that Augustine moved toward an understanding of "theophanies as visible signs that make present what they signify" (*Christ, Creation, and the Vision of God*, 182). She comments that for Augustine, "God is seen in the theophanies as a thought is expressed by words, inseparably and inexhaustibly joined to the sign without being reducible to it" (187).

to this rule: when he shows himself "through some created bodily substance at the service of his power" (*Trin.* 2.9.16). Augustine makes clear that it is "the Father who appeared to Abraham and Moses . . . by means of some changeable and visible creature under his control" (2.10.17). When he sums up his argument by saying that different theophanies may have manifested different persons of the Trinity, he comments that it is "impossible without rashness to say that God the Father never appeared to the patriarchs or prophets under visible forms" (2.17.32). Again, the bishop reiterates that these are not manifestations of God "as he is in himself" (*proprie sicuti est*) but "in a symbolic manner" (*significatiue*) (2.17.32). Also, at one point Augustine speaks of the "presence" (*praesentia*) of God in the theophanies: the voice from the burning bush may have come from "some created thing" appearing visibly to "convey the presence of the Lord by creature control as needed" (2.13.23). For Augustine, God himself was present by means of a creature.

None of this is to suggest that Augustine goes out of his way to emphasize God's identification with the creaturely manifestations of his presence. The reason is likely a polemical one: he denies that God's own substance takes visible form. While the Homoians maintain that in the theophanies the person of the Son himself—that is to say, his own substance—is actually seen, with bodily eyes, Augustine argues that *none* of the three persons becomes visible in his own substance, even though sometimes all three of them, and at other times one or two of them, are said to be present in the narrative. Thus, while it may seem at times as though Augustine holds to a nonsacramental view of the theophanies, in reality he merely denies that the divine substance was ever seen with bodily eyes: God's substance remains invisible. Augustine is merely saying that when God appears, he does so by means of a creature—his own substance is not seen.[37]

---

37. Manoussakis, who rightly interprets Augustine's theology of theophanies as sacramental, suggests that when Augustine speaks of *creatura*, "his concern might not have been that of clarifying whether the theophanies were created or uncreated at all, but rather of affirming their reality, therefore a translation of *creatura* that might be closer to the intentions of the Saint would be 'real'; in other words, a palpable, experience-able event that was addressed to our physical being and not only *ad mente*" ("Theophany and Indication," 79). I am sympathetic to the overall drift of Manoussakis's argument, but I think here he overlooks the fact that Augustine juxtaposes the *creaturely* character of the theophany with the divine *substance* being physically seen in them. Augustine is simply saying that what is seen is not God's substance but a creaturely reality. Again—and here I am in agreement with Manoussakis—Augustine does not deny thereby that God makes himself present in the theophany.

We may wish for Saint Augustine to have been more explicit on several fronts. Augustine highlights that Moses saw a created bush and Abraham three human visitors, and that neither saw the divine substance with bodily eyes. Still, we may ask: Since *God* appeared by means of these creaturely modes—so that, as Augustine himself acknowledges, we can speak of the "presence of the Lord"—can we also say that the *substance* of God was present? Augustine does not actually say whether or not he thinks this is the case. He is content simply to refute the notion that God's substance is visible to bodily eyes. This raises the question: When he claims that God *appears* or *manifests* himself, does Augustine mean that God's substance is present, but is just not seen with the eyes of the body? One alternative would be to suggest—along with the fourteenth-century theologian Gregory Palamas—that it is not the essence but only the energies of God that are present to varying degrees in the theophanies. Given that Augustine does not work with the essence-energies distinction, however, he likely means the former: when God appears, his substance is really present, but he does not make himself *seen* with the physical eye. Had Augustine been more emphatic that despite being *invisible* in his substance God was nonetheless *present* in his substance, the sacramentality of his view would have been much more obvious. As it is, Augustine avoided saying explicitly that God's substance was present in the theophanies—likely the result of the Homoian insistence on the visibility of the Son. It is easy to see how later interpreters (including several contemporary scholars) ended up misreading Augustine's silence as indicative of a nonsacramental ontology. Still, it would hardly be just to lay the blame for modernity's separation of the divine substance from created reality at the feet of the fifth-century bishop of Hippo.[38]

A related question concerns the mode of the divine presence. If God *really* appeared by means of creatures (*per subiectam creaturam*), this raises the kind of issue that typically comes to the fore in connection with eucharistic theology: What kind of real presence do we have in the theophanies? Augustine never deals with this issue head-on. He appears satisfied to refute the Homoian claim that the Son is visible in himself (or in his substance)—something the African bishop counters by saying that none of the three persons is visible in his substance. It seems that Augustine deliberately avoided

---

38. In the thirteenth century, Thomas Aquinas would still argue that the divine substance *is* present to all created beings, though he qualifies this by saying that the divine essence does not take the place of the creature's essence. Instead, claims Aquinas, "His substance is present to all things as the cause of their being" (*ST* I, q. 8, a. 3). Using the language of causality, Aquinas tried to retain a participatory ontology (claiming that God's substance is present to creation) while avoiding a lapse into pantheism.

speculating *how* it is that the theophanies manifested God. Obviously, he does not say that the created objects were somehow transformed (or transubstantiated) into God (or into any of the three persons); the theophanies took the form of angels, human beings, or other objects, and Augustine's anti-Homoian rhetoric serves precisely to assert the genuinely creaturely mode of the theophanies. Nonetheless, a close identification obtains between God and the creature that he takes in his service.[39] God really does appear by means of theophanies. The manifestation is a real manifestation, the presence a real presence. For Augustine, to see a theophany is to experience the presence of God in sacramental form. Augustine, therefore, interpreted theophanies as preliminary adumbrations of the beatific vision itself.

To be sure, we should not equate theophanies with mystical contemplation, let alone with the beatific vision itself. The person experiencing a theophany is not taken out of the body; nor are the bodily senses rendered inoperative. Augustine highlighted the ordinary, physical character of seeing created realities in theophanies, at one point challenging the Homoian reading of the Mamre theophany (Gen. 18)—that the Son of God appeared here in human flesh—rhetorically asking the question: "I could still ask them how they would account for his *being found in the condition of a man* (Phil 2:7)—having his feet washed, sitting down to human victuals—before he took flesh. How could all this happen while he was still in the form of God, *not thinking it robbery to be equal to God* (Phil 2:6)?"[40] Abraham washing his visitors' feet and arranging a meal for them make clear that the theophany took place in an ordinary, physical setting. Thus, while according to Augustine God was sacramentally *present* in theophanies, he believed that the sacramental form also precludes us from saying that the theophanies were *identical* to the face-to-face vision that God promises with regard to the beatific vision itself (cf. 1 Cor. 13:12).

Moses's Desire for the Substance of God

Augustine was convinced, however, that the saints here below sometimes move beyond the limited and circumscribed sacramental forms of experi-

---

39. Augustine acknowledges that "the dove is called the Spirit" and that fire is also referred to as Spirit (Acts 2:3). Still, he then adds, "This is to indicate that it is the Spirit who was manifested by that fire, as by that dove. Yet we cannot say of the Holy Spirit that he is God and dove, or God and fire, as we say of the Son that he is God and man" (*Trin.* 2.6.11).

40. *Trin.* 2.11.20.

encing God's presence. He believed that on some occasions, created reality becomes diaphanous, the line between sacrament and reality becomes very thin, and we experience something like the beatific vision. Though Augustine was cautious about the possibility of leaving the *sacramentum* behind, he nonetheless believed that biblical figures such as Moses and Paul had entered "heaven of heaven" itself and had seen God; and at several points in his life Saint Augustine himself had mystical experiences in which he contemplated the very presence of God. As David Meconi puts it: "The reality of heaven (*res*) is available even now to those who have hope (*spes*)."[41]

At the end of his treatment of theophanies in book 2 of *De Trinitate*, Augustine discusses Moses's request that the Lord show himself openly, so that he might see God's majesty (Exod. 33:13, 18).[42] Augustine notes that we have been told just a few verses earlier that the Lord has *already* spoken with Moses "face to face, as a man speaks to his friend" (33:11). Augustine points out that Moses's renewed request to see God can only mean that in the earlier face-to-face encounters Moses had not seen God's substance; otherwise this new request to see God's majesty would be nonsensical: "How then, please, are we to suppose that in all that had happened up till now God appeared in his own substance, which is why these wretched people [i.e., the Homoians] believe the Son of God is not just visible by means of created things but in himself . . . ?" (*Trin.* 2.16.27). Augustine concludes from this that all Moses's previous encounters with the Lord had merely been "physical" (*corporaliter*)—here we undoubtedly need to think of theophanic appearances by means of creatures (*per subiectam creaturam*)—while Moses is now asking for a "spiritual vision of God," asking God, in effect, "Show me your substance." Augustine concludes, however, that "this favor was not granted to him, however much he longed for it" (2.16.27). Moses did not get to see the divine substance.

The bishop of Hippo reiterates his reluctance to acknowledge that Moses saw God's substance—even with spiritual rather than physical eyes—in epistle 147 (*De videndo Dei*), a letter to the aristocrat Paulina, likely written in 413.[43] Here as elsewhere, the bishop is primarily wary of the anthropo-

---

41. David Vincent Meconi, "Heaven and the *Ecclesia Perfecta* in Augustine," in *The Cambridge Companion to Augustine*, ed. David Vincent Meconi and Eleonore Stump (Cambridge: Cambridge University Press, 2014), 268.

42. Cf. the discussion in Ayres, *Augustine and the Trinity*, 159–70.

43. Cf. Ferdinand Cavallera, "La Vision corporelle de Dieu d'après Saint Augustin," *BLE* 7 (1915–1916): 460–71; Studer, *Zur Theophanie-Exegese Augustins*; Frederik Van Fleteren, "Vi-

morphite notion that it is possible to see God with bodily eyes.[44] Just as in *De Trinitate*, Augustine insists here too that God in himself is invisible to the eyes of the body. But he goes beyond just claiming that we cannot see God's substance with physical eyes. He comments that "we do not see God with the eyes of the body, as we see either heavenly or earthly bodies, *or with the gaze of the mind*," with which we see (or know) things such as that we live, that we wish to see God, that we seek this, or that we know and do not know certain things.[45] The overall claim, therefore, is that in this life we do not see God's substance either with eyes of the body or with eyes of the mind. Thus, the bishop insists, those things that we do not see by either bodily or mental vision, but that Scripture (or some other authority) nonetheless claims to be true, we must take on faith rather than by sight (*Ep.* 147.1.4–2.7). The resurrection, for instance, is something we take on faith, since no one saw Christ rise from the dead (4.11). Nonetheless, claims Augustine, we can use the term "knowledge" to speak of such faith, since the apostle John does write: "We *know* that, when he shall appear, we will be like him, because we shall see him as he is" (1 John 3:2) (5.12 [emphasis changed]). John *knows* of a future event, says Augustine, not "by seeing but by believing" (5.12).

Accordingly, Augustine treats the Old Testament theophanies in this epistle much as he does in *De Trinitate*, insisting that "no one has seen that fullness of divinity that dwells in God" (6.18). Pious persons, such as Moses, are not content with gazing "upon that form in which he appears when he wills" and instead burn "to gaze upon that substance by which he is what he is" (8.20). Comments Augustine:

> The saintly Moses, his faithful servant, revealed the flame of this desire of his when he said to God, with whom he was speaking face to face like a friend, *If I have found favor before you, show yourself to me* (Ex 33:13 LXX). What, then, does this mean? Was that not God? If it was not God, Moses would not say to him, *Show me yourself*, but, "Show me God," and yet, if he looked upon his nature and substance (*naturam substantiam que*), he would have much less reason to say, *Show me yourself*. God was (*ipse . . . erat*), therefore, in that form in which he had willed to appear (*in ea specie, qua apparere uoluerat*), but he did not appear in his own nature (*in natura*

---

44. On this issue, see also *Ep.* 148.

45. *Ep.* 147.1.3 (emphasis added). Hereafter, references from this work will be given in parentheses in the text; quotations come from WSA II/2.

dendo Deo, De," in *Augustine through the Ages: An Encyclopedia*, ed. Allan D. Fitzgerald (Grand Rapids: Eerdmans, 1999), 869.

propria), which Moses longed to see. That vision is, of course, promised to the saints in the next life. Hence, the reply given to Moses is true, that *no one can see the face of God and live* (Ex 33:20), that is, no one can, while living in this life, see him as he is (*sicuti est*). (8.20)

Perhaps even more clearly than in *De Trinitate*, Augustine makes clear here that it is God himself who appeared to Moses (and others) in theophanies (*ipse . . . erat*), though he adds that God did not appear in his own nature. Regardless of the kind of questions that this raises—most obviously the question: What does it mean for God to appear if he does not appear in his own nature?[46]—the notion that God himself was present (*ipse . . . erat*) in the theophany underscores our earlier finding that Augustine held to a sacramental understanding of the theophanies.

The bishop reiterates, however, that when Moses asked to see more than just a created form, so as to behold spiritually the substance of God (Exod. 33:18), God turned him down. Augustine makes clear that to see God in his own nature is a promise reserved for the future:

Many have seen him but have seen what was chosen by his will, not what was fashioned from his nature. And if one correctly understands it, this is what John said, *Beloved, we are now the children of God, and it has not yet appeared what we shall be. We know that, when he appears, we shall be like him because we shall see him as he is (sicut est)* (1 Jn 3:2), not as human beings saw him when God willed and in the form in which he willed, not in the nature in which he was in himself hidden, even when he was seen, but as he is (*sicut est*). (8.20)

The bishop of Hippo maintains that God cannot be seen as he is (*sicut est*) until the eschaton, according to the promise of 1 John 3:2.[47]

---

46. I suspect that when Augustine says that God "did not appear in his own nature," he means to say that despite his request Moses did not actually get to see the very substance of God spiritually, even though God in his own substance was present. (Moses was simply limited to seeing God's back and wasn't allowed to *see* the face of God, though it was obviously present.)

47. Augustine does maintain that Moses had some kind of spiritual vision, though he does not make clear what it is that Moses saw of God if it was not his substance. Augustine generally moves rather quickly to an allegorical reading of the episode, interpreting Moses as a figure of the Jewish people, who after the resurrection came to believe in Christ. God's promise to Moses that he would be able to see God's back from the cleft of the rock (Exod. 33:21–23) means,

Augustine's treatment of Moses so far may seem to intimate that the sight of God as he is (*sicut est*) is restricted to the eschatological future. Remarkably, however, Augustine does acknowledge—even in his letter to Paulina—that both Moses and the apostle Paul did in fact see God's substance. In chapter 31 of this letter Augustine raises the following issue: "Next, one can ask how the very substance of God could be seen by certain people still situated in this life because of what was said to Moses, *No one can see my face and live* (Ex 33:20), unless the human mind can be taken up by God (*diuinitus rapi*) from this life to the life of the angels before it is released from the flesh by this common death" (*Ep.* 147.13.31). Augustine appears to acknowledge here that the human mind can be "taken up by God from this life" and see the divine substance even before death. This is in fact what happened to the apostle Paul, claims Augustine, referring to 2 Corinthians 12:2–4. He maintains that Saint Paul's experience does not contradict Exodus 33:20 ("No man can see my face and live") because Paul's mind was in fact "withdrawn from this life," so that he experienced a kind of death (*Ep.* 147.13.31).

With regard to Moses, Augustine acknowledges that Numbers 12 leaves little doubt that Moses did see God's very nature, since the text contrasts the Lord making himself known to some in a vision and a dream with the Lord speaking to Moses "in plain sight, not through an enigma"—and, Augustine comments, "he also added, *And he saw the glory of the Lord* (Nm 12:8)" (13.32). Faced with the biblical text, Augustine acknowledges here that God granted Moses an exception (*exceptum*) because of his faithfulness, which had made him "worthy at that time of that contemplation (*contemplatione dignum*), that is, so that, just as he desired, he saw God as he is (*sicuti est*), which is the same contemplation that is promised to all his children in the end" (13.32). At this point, Augustine seems to have forgotten that earlier in the same letter he had explicitly denied that Moses saw the divine substance.

Augustine comes back to Moses's vision of God in his book *On the Literal Interpretation of Genesis*, probably completed by 415, where he again speaks of Moses's yearning to see God "in His divine essence (*substantia*) without the medium of any bodily creature that might be presented to the senses of

---

according to Augustine, that after the pascha of Christ (God passing by the cleft), many Israelites (Moses) would be able to see God's back (the flesh or humanity of Christ) in the catholic church (the rock), and so come to believe in his divinity (the face of God). See Augustine, *Trin.* 2.17.28–31 (WSA I/5:121–24); *Ep.* 174.13.32 (WSA II/2:335–36); *Gen. litt.* 12.27.55 (ACW 42:218).

mortal flesh."[48] Again Augustine refers to Numbers 12:6–8, and he acknowledges that this is "not to be understood as referring to a bodily substance made present to the senses of the flesh."[49] Moses must have died to the bodily senses, claims Augustine, because no one can see God and live: "This vision is granted only to him who in some way dies to this life, whether he quits the body entirely or is turned away and carried out of the bodily senses, so that he really knows not (to use the words of St. Paul) whether he is in the body or out of the body when he is carried off to this vision (2 Cor 12:2)."[50] Thus, both here and in *Epistle* 147, Augustine reconciles the biblical tension between not being able to see God and live (Exod. 33:20) and the examples of Moses and Paul seeing God (Num. 12:6–8; 2 Cor. 12:2–4) by explaining that in some way these saints did actually die: they were removed from the life of the bodily senses.[51]

Contemplation in *The Greatness of the Soul*

Saint Augustine wavered back and forth on the question of whether Moses saw God, and when he does acknowledge that in some exceptional cases God allowed saints (such as Moses and Paul) to see the divine substance, he expresses himself cautiously. Still, from early on the African bishop was convinced that such mystical experiences do actually happen, and this belief was grounded, it seems, in personal experience. Augustine claims on several occasions to have experienced an ecstatic vision of God.[52] The desire to reach

48. *Gen. litt.* 12.27.55 (ACW 42:217).

49. *Gen. litt.* 12.27.55 (ACW 42:218).

50. *Gen. litt.* 12.27.55 (ACW 42:219). Ronald J. Teske rightly comments: "In *De Genesi ad litteram* XII and *Epistula CXLVII*, Augustine clearly claims that both Moses and Paul enjoyed prior to death, though in a state like death, a vision of the divine substance and of the glory of God" ("St. Augustine and the Vision of God," in *Augustine: Mystic and Mystagogue*, ed. Frederick Van Fleteren, Joseph C. Schnaubelt, and Joseph Reino [New York: Peter Lang, 1994], 298).

51. Book 12 of *The Literal Meaning of Genesis* is structured around Saint Paul's ecstatic experience. I will not analyze Augustine's accounts of Paul's experience, except to say that they cohere with his interpretation of Moses's vision of the divine substance: Paul did see the divine substance, according to Augustine, as he was removed from the bodily senses.

52. John J. O'Meara rejects the use of the term "ecstasy" for Augustine's experiences because the characteristic signs of mystical states are allegedly absent and the experiences are described much later, in language borrowed in part from Neoplatonism (*The Young Augustine: The Growth of St. Augustine's Mind up to His Conversion*, 2nd ed. [New York:

beyond the sensible world and attain an ecstatic experience was initially fueled in the year 386 by his reading of Plotinus and Porphyry, the so-called books of the Platonists (*libri platonicorum*).[53] They encouraged Augustine to turn inward. As he puts it in his *Confessions*:

> I entered and with my soul's eye, such as it was, saw above that same eye of my soul the immutable light higher than my mind—not the light of every day, obvious to anyone, nor a larger version of the same kind which would, as it were, have given out a much brighter light and filled everything with its magnitude. It was not that light, but a different thing, utterly different from all our kinds of light. It transcended my mind, not in the way that oil floats on water, nor as heaven is above earth. It was superior because it made me, and I was inferior because I was made by it.[54]

Augustine writes here, more than a decade after the event, that by turning inward he actually saw with his soul's eye the light that created him.[55] To be sure, he immediately adds that he was unable to endure the light, and so the experience was just momentary: "And you gave a shock to the weakness of my sight by the strong radiance of your rays, and I trembled with love and awe. And I found myself far from you 'in the region of dissimilarity.'"[56] Both the transient character of the experience and the language Augustine employs are indebted to discourse of the Platonic tradition.[57] Still, as John Peter Kenney points out, Augustine believed that

---

Alba, 2000], 208). I am not sure everyone agrees on what precisely the "characteristic signs" of mystical states are. Augustine himself clearly thought he was experiencing a "death" of the bodily senses and was being "rapt" from this life, much like Moses and Paul had been. Moreover, Augustine speaks of Paul's mystical experience (2 Cor. 12:2–4) as an "ecstasy" (*extasis*), which he defines as follows: "But when the attention of the mind is completely carried off and turned away from the senses of the body, then there is rather the state called ecstasy (*extasis*). Then any bodies that are present are not seen at all, though the eyes may be wide open; and no sounds at all are heard. The whole soul is intent upon images of bodies present to spiritual vision or upon incorporeal realities present to intellectual vision without benefit of bodily images" (*Gen. litt.* 12.25 [ACW 42:194]).

53. *Conf.* 7.9.13. For discussion of the "books of the Platonists," see Carol Harrison, *Rethinking Augustine's Early Theology: An Argument for Continuity* (Oxford: Oxford University Press, 2006), 27–30.

54. *Conf.* 7.10.16; quotations come from Augustine, *Confessions*, trans. Henry Chadwick (Oxford: Oxford University Press, 1991), 123.

55. Augustine wrote his *Confessions* between 397 and 401.

56. *Conf.* 7.10.16.

57. For Plato's and Plotinus's views on the transience of ecstatic vision, see above,

already at this stage, while still in Milan, he had discovered the God of the Scriptures through interior contemplation.[58] After all, Augustine goes on to write that he "heard as it were your voice from on high: 'I am the food of the fully grown; grow and you will feed on me. And you will not change me into you like the food your flesh eats, but you will be changed into me.'"[59] The books of the Platonists enabled Augustine to transcend his mind and see the light that created him.

Augustine's *Greatness of the Soul*, written in 387 or 388, only one or two years after his reading of the Platonists and shortly after his baptism, presents his first articulation of an ascent to God as a Christian. He describes here seven levels (*gradus*) of the soul's greatness: (1) animation (*animatio*), which is vegetative life; (2) sensation (*sensus*), which is the sensitive life shared with animals; (3) art (*ars*), which concerns human creative and cultural achievements; (4) virtue (*virtus*), which has to do with moral purification; (5) tranquillity (*tranquillitas*), which gives joy and confidence; (6) entrance (*ingressio*), where the soul has an ardent desire to understand truth and perfection; and (7) contemplation (*contemplatio*), the very vision and contemplation of truth.[60]

The element of moral purification plays an important role as a condition for reaching the soul's ultimate aim. In the fourth level, the soul is engaged in a "strenuous effort," and "the annoyances and allurements of this world engage it in a mighty struggle, bitterly contested."[61] Once "free from all corruption and purified of all its stains," the soul rejoices and with confidence advances toward God.[62] In discussing the sixth level, Augustine again cautions that without purification one cannot sustain gazing into the light: "Those who wish to do this before they are cleansed and healed recoil so in the presence of that light."[63] With an appeal to David's prayer for God to create a clean heart in him and to renew a right spirit in his bowels (Ps. 50:12 [51:10]), Augustine insists, "This spirit is not really 'renewed' in anyone unless

---

chap. 2. The expression "region of dissimilarity" (*regio dissimilitudinis*) goes back via Plotinus (*Enn.* 1.8.13) to Plato (*Pol.* 273d).

58. John Peter Kenney, *Contemplation and Classical Christianity: A Study in Augustine* (Oxford: Oxford University Press, 2013), 86. Cf. also Frederick Van Fleteren's comment that "this 'unchangeable light' is God himself" ("Mysticism in the *Confessiones*—a Controversy Revisited," in Van Fleteren, Schnaubelt, and Reino, *Augustine: Mystic and Mystagogue*, 312).

59. *Conf.* 7.10.16.

60. I adopt the designations of the seven levels from Kenney, *Contemplation and Classical Christianity*, 97–100.

61. *Quant. an.* 33.73 (ACW 9:102).

62. *Quant. an.* 33.74 (ACW 9:103).

63. *Quant. an.* 33.75 (ACW 9:103).

his heart is first made clean, that is to say, unless he first controls his thoughts and drains off from them all the dregs of attachment to corruptible things."[64] For Augustine, then, it is purification—an exercise of great struggle as well as of divine grace—that leads the soul to the seventh and last level, where "we no longer have a level (*gradus*) but in reality a home (*mansio*) at which one arrives via those levels."[65]

Some interpret the description here as the rather optimistic view of a young Christian Platonist about his ability to reach the *visio Dei* already in this life: on the sixth level the soul arrives at its "highest vision,"[66] while on the seventh it reaches its actual home (*mansio*), interpreted as the abiding enjoyment of the peace of God.[67] On this reading, Augustine would later have abandoned his early optimistic view that a permanent vision of God is possible already in this life.[68] I am not convinced that Augustine is quite as optimistic in *The Greatness of the Soul* as is sometimes suggested. The word "home" (*mansio*) does not necessarily imply permanent presence; it may simply indicate the place where Augustine is convinced the soul ultimately belongs: even if it casts only a _brief_ glance into the place where God dwells, the soul has nonetheless seen its home. Also, Augustine says that "great and peerless souls" have actually arrived at this seventh level. Whether he is thinking here of Saint Paul (2 Cor. 12:2–4), of Plato, or of Plotinus, it does not ultimately matter: none of the three write of occupying one's final home in any permanent sense already during this life.[69] Finally, while it is true

64. *Quant. an.* 33.75 (ACW 9:104).

65. Augustine's turning to the humility of Christ made him increasingly aware of the need for divine grace in the process of purification, which later led to the Pelagian controversies. Nonetheless, Augustine always kept insisting that only the "pure in heart" will see God. In the opening paragraphs of *De Trinitate*, he comments that "it is necessary for our minds to be purified before that inexpressible reality can be inexpressibly seen by them; and in order to make us fit and capable of grasping it, we are led along more endurable routes, nurtured on faith as long as we have not yet been endowed with that necessary purification" (*Trin.* 1.1.3).

66. *Quant. an.* 33.75 (ACW 9:103).

67. Van Fleteren suggests that the difference between the sixth and seventh levels "is merely that, in the first, the soul casts its gaze, whereas in the second, the soul sees the vision permanently" ("Mysticism in the *Confessiones*," 311). See also Kenney, *Contemplation and Classical Christianity*, 100–101.

68. Frederick Van Fleteren, "Augustine and the Possibility of the Vision of God in This Life," in *SMC*, vol. 11, ed. John R. Sommerfeldt and Thomas H. Seiler (Kalamazoo, MI: Medieval Institute/Western Michigan University, 1977), 9–16.

69. Since both Plato and Plotinus believed that an ecstatic vision could only be transient in character, Augustine's repudiation in *Agreement among the Evangelists* (written in 400) of the notion that one can "cling constantly and unchangeably" to the light of immutable truth

that Augustine describes both the sixth and the seventh levels in terms of "vision"—so that one may be tempted to speak of the final level as *permanent* vision—still, he describes the vision of the penultimate level as the "ardent desire (*appetitio*) to understand truth and perfection."[70] I suspect that Augustine regarded the sixth level as the moment of entry into the state of ecstasy, while treating the seventh level as "the very vision and contemplation of truth" itself,[71] without implying anything about its duration. Although he believed it was possible for great souls to reach the vision of God already in this life, Augustine made clear that it would be preceded by a difficult moral struggle and could not be sustained for long.

The Firstfruits of the Spirit

Perhaps the most important reason to doubt that Augustine believed one could have a permanent vision of God in this life is that his own experience was different. He explains this particularly clearly in his second recounting in the *Confessions* of the ascent he experienced the year before his conversion: "I was caught up to you by your beauty and quickly torn away from you by my weight. With a groan I crashed (*ruebam*) into inferior things. This weight was my sexual habit. But with me there remained a memory of you. I was in no kind of doubt to whom I should attach myself, but was not yet in a state to be able to do that."[72] Augustine describes his ascent "step by step" from bodies to the soul, from there to its inward force, and then via the power of reasoning and intelligence to the light itself, so that "in the flash of a trembling glance it attained to that which is" (7.17.23). Nonetheless, Augustine laments the minimal success he had: the vision of the light was just a fleeting experience. The reason, according to Augustine, was his lack of virtue.

To be sure, by identifying with the humility of the mediator, Jesus Christ, Augustine overcame at least some of the limitations that had continually

---

is in line with the Platonic tradition and does not evidence a change in position on his part (*Cons.* 4.10.20 [WSA I/15:331]); *pace* Van Fleteren, "Augustine and the Possibility of the Vision of God," 16).

70. *Quant. an.* 33.75 (ACW 9:103).

71. *Quant. an.* 33.76 (ACW 9:104).

72. *Conf.* 7.17.23. Cf. the description in the next paragraph: "But I did not possess the strength to keep my vision fixed. My weakness reasserted itself, and I returned to my customary condition" (*Conf.* 7.17.23). Hereafter, references from this work will be given in parentheses in the text.

bothered him prior to his conversion and baptism. Or, at the very least, he gained a different perspective on them:

> I sought a way to obtain strength enough to enjoy you; but I did not find it until I embraced "the mediator between God and man, the man Christ Jesus" (1 Tim. 2:5), "who is above all things, God blessed for ever" (Rom. 9:5). He called and said "I am the way and the truth and the life" (John 14:6). The food which I was too weak to accept he mingled with flesh, in that "The Word was made flesh" (John 1:14), so that our infant condition might come to suck milk from your wisdom by which you created all things. To possess my God, the humble Jesus, I was not yet humble enough. I did not know what his weakness was meant to teach. (7.18.24)

Augustine's problem, he came to acknowledge, had been that he had failed to note the profound difference the incarnation made; he used to think of Christ "only as a man of excellent wisdom which none could equal" (7.19.25). In his pride he had thought he could follow Christ as a superb human example, failing to recognize his humility in becoming incarnate. And so, Augustine writes, "I prattled on as if I were an expert," getting "puffed up with knowledge (1 Cor. 8: 1)" (7.20.26). "Where was the charity," Augustine asks himself, "which builds on the foundation of humility which is Christ Jesus? When would the Platonist books have taught me that?" (7.20.26).[73] Although these books had led Augustine part of the way, even allowing him to experience the light of the transcendent God, in the end they disappointed him because of their failure to acknowledge that it is only by sharing in the humility of the incarnate Christ that we find true stability in the light of God.[74]

The experience of ecstasy that Augustine, together with his mother Monica, had shortly after his baptism in 387 is therefore all the more significant; now it was the young Augustine, converted to the humility of Christ, who had an experience similar to the ones described in book 7, yet this time informed by his conversion. In book 9 of the *Confessions* Augustine depicts the scene of Monica and himself "leaning out of a window overlooking a

73. Augustine elsewhere attacks the pride of Platonists such as Porphyry, who thought they could purify themselves by their own power and so reach the light of truth (*Trin.* 4.15.20). Frederick Van Fleteren explains that Augustine has Porphyry in mind here ("Mysticism in the *Confessiones*," 320–21).

74. Cf. John Peter Kenney's comment: "Platonists style themselves, in Augustine's view, as wise in their own estimation, an act of spiritual presumption based on mistaken pride (*superbia*) in their cognitive accomplishments" (*Contemplation and Classical Christianity*, 91).

garden" in the port city of Ostia (9.10.23). The two had an intimate discussion about eternal life, which led to the conclusion "that the pleasure of the bodily senses, however delightful in the radiant light of this physical world, is seen by comparison with the life of eternity to be not even worth considering" (9.10.24). "Step by step," comments Augustine, the two "climbed beyond all corporeal objects and the heaven itself," "ascending even further" through their dialogue, and so, he comments, "we entered into our own minds" (9.10.24). The result, Augustine reports, is that they were able

> to attain to the region of inexhaustible abundance (*regionem ubertatis in-deficientis*) where you feed Israel eternally with truth for food. There life is the wisdom by which all creatures come into being, both things which were and which will be. But wisdom itself is not brought into being but is as it was and always will be. Furthermore, in this wisdom there is no past and future, but only being, since it is eternal. For to exist in the past or in the future is no property of the eternal. And while we talked and panted after it, we touched it in some small degree by a moment of total concentration of the heart. And we sighed and left behind us (*reliquimus*) the "firstfruits of the Spirit" (Rom. 8:23) bound to that higher world, as we returned (*remeavimus*) to the noise of our human speech where a sentence has both a beginning and an ending. But what is to be compared with your word, Lord of our lives? It dwells in you without growing old and gives renewal to all things. (9.10.24)

Augustine makes clear that Monica and he moved from time to eternity. After all, they entered the "region of inexhaustible abundance," where wisdom dwells eternally, without past or future. They moved beyond the world of sacramental signs, of past and future, as they reached the eschatological reality of the "firstfruits of the Spirit."

We need not exaggerate the differences between Augustine's prebaptismal and postbaptismal mystical experiences: both left the mind behind; both reached the transcendent light of God; both were evanescent;[75] and for both

---

75. To be sure, Augustine does use somewhat different language with regard to the postbaptismal vision. This time he does not describe the brevity of the experience with the language of "crashing" (*ruebam*) back into inferior things as a result of weakness or his sexual habit. He simply writes that his mother and he "left behind" (*reliquimus*) the firstfruits of the Spirit and "returned" (*remeavimus*) to the noise of human speech. He does, however, add the rueful comment: "If only it could last, and other visions of a vastly inferior kind could be withdrawn!" (*Conf.* 9.10.25). And in book 10, he remarks: "And sometimes you cause me to enter into an

Augustine uses language reminiscent of Plotinus.[76] Indeed, seeing as in both cases Augustine left behind past and future, and along with it the discursive character of human language, he could say little, if anything, about how the vision at Ostia was different from the earlier ones; both experiences of the light were strictly apophatic. Nonetheless, in book 9 the *interpretation* of the experience has become christological and eschatological. By the time he came to Ostia, Augustine had arrived at a different perspective and had come to interpret his experience in the light of the humility of Christ and thus as an entry into the wisdom of God.

Accordingly, Kenney points out that when Augustine speaks of encountering eternal wisdom in Ostia, he links it with "heaven of heaven" (*caelum caeli*) itself—which he interprets to be the house of God, the place of eternal, created wisdom.[77] The reference to the "firstfruits of the Spirit" makes clear, Kenney rightly argues, that in Ostia Augustine came to view entry into this house of God as an initial sharing in the eschatological *visio Dei*: "Everlasting life for created souls will be a state of continuous contemplation of the eternal wisdom. The soul will enter into the joy of its Lord and be absorbed in divine contemplation without confusion, distraction, or cessation. And in Book XII that is the nature and condition of the *caelum caeli*. What Monica and Augustine enter spiritually in the ascension at Ostia is the house of God, the *caelum caeli*, the heavenly place where collective souls exercise continuous contemplation."[78] By entering into the "heaven of heaven," there to

extraordinary depth of feeling marked by a strange sweetness. If it were brought to perfection in me, it would be an experience quite beyond anything in this life. But I fall back into my usual ways under my miserable burdens. I am reabsorbed by my habitual practices. I am held in their grip. I weep profusely, but still I am held. Such is the strength of the burden of habit" (10.40.65). Cf. also *Trin.* 8.2.3.

76. The description in *Conf.* 9.10.24 is somewhat similar to that of Plotinus in *Enn.* 5.1.3.4–6. This does not mean that Augustine treated the experience of Monica and himself as equivalent to that of Plotinus: his reservations with regard to the pride of the Platonists are already clear at this point. The similarity simply means that he believes that the "books of the Platonists" had some usefulness in leading him toward his uniquely Christian view of the contemplation of eternal wisdom.

77. The "heaven of heaven" plays an important role in book 12 of the *Confessions*. See Kenney, *Contemplation and Classical Christianity*, 137–51. This *caelum caeli* is, as Kenney puts it, "the first product of creation . . . uniquely representative of God's perfection at the level of finite experience" (138), and as such it participates in God's eternity (139; cf. *Conf.* 12.9.9). Thus, the "*caelum caeli* is for Augustine the unseen place for which we hope (Rom. 8:23); it is where the souls hope to dwell forever in the presence of that eternal wisdom that they have now reached" (Kenney, 148).

78. Kenney, *Contemplation and Classical Christianity*, 149.

contemplate the wisdom of God, Augustine believed he had left behind the temporal world of sign and sacrament and had already come to anticipate the unmediated vision of God.

Even the language of anticipation may not quite adequately capture what Augustine believed he experienced. After all, he thought that Moses, Paul, and even he himself had actually come to share in the eschatological reality to come. Manoussakis puts it well when he comments that in Christ's transfiguration "the eschaton is not anticipated, if by this we mean simply 'expected,' but rather must be revealed—as if the veil of time is momentarily lifted so as to allow us to take a peek at the kingdom behind it, which we, from this side of the veil, await but which itself already exists and unfolds."[79] In line with this, Augustine came to regard the Ostia vision as an initial participation in the eschatological beatific vision, in which the sacramental reality of the eschaton—the vision of eternal wisdom in "heaven of heaven"—has already been reached, even if only momentarily.

Conclusion

Augustine's theology of theophanies, mysticism, and the beatific vision may not be easy to pin down. This is partly due to the occasional nature of his writing; we always need to keep in mind the historical backdrop that gave rise to his theological articulations. The Homoian context sheds much light on the contrast that Augustine posits between God's own substance and the creaturely objects involved in Old Testament theophanies.[80] By highlighting this historical context, we can begin to appreciate that when the bishop of Hippo denies that Old Testament saints saw the substance of God in the theophanies, he in no way intended to deny that God himself was present in them—even though Augustine may have been reticent unambiguously or explicitly to affirm this in light of the Homoian threat and did not go out of his way to articulate *how* exactly he understood the divine presence in theophanic appearances. Augustine's theology of theophanies is sacramental: he believed God was genuinely present in these appearances.

79. Manoussakis, "Theophany and Indication," 86.
80. Though my interpretation differs on points from that of Michel René Barnes, he rightly highlights the anti-Homoian polemic as key to interpreting the first books of *De Trinitate* ("Exegesis and Polemic in Augustine's *De Trinitate* I," *AugStud* 30 [1999]: 43–59; Barnes, "The Visible Christ and the Invisible Trinity").

Not only that, but Augustine also believed that there are occasions on which the veil is lifted and God is not just present by means of signs seen with bodily eyes but is seen in his own substance with spiritual eyes. Though he hesitated to acknowledge this with regard to Moses's vision of God from the cleft of the rock (Exod. 33:18–23), the bishop did so in several other places, and he granted the same with regard to Saint Paul's being caught up into Paradise (2 Cor. 12:4–6). Augustine's own experiences of leaving behind "human speech where a sentence has both a beginning and an ending" were no doubt instrumental in his recognition that on occasion we can see the light of the beatific vision shining upon the saints already today.

The purpose of this chapter is not to hold up Augustine's understanding of theophanies and ecstatic experience as normative in every respect—though I believe there is a great deal to be gained from his perspective. My aim is simply to point out that the bishop of Hippo did not separate faith from sight in any simplistic fashion and instead insisted that we already see God in some significant ways today, both in and through created signs such as theophanies and more directly in mystical experiences. The bishop of Hippo, therefore, can function as a resource, for both Eastern and Western theologies, in countering the modern preoccupation with purely temporal, natural realities.[81] For Saint Augustine, God's self-manifestation already in this life was an incentive to direct his gaze toward the eternal vision of the triune God.

81. To be sure, Augustine's discourse of seeing the *substantia* of God in the beatific vision—which stamps much of later Western theology—is at odds with Orthodox theology. I do not mean to paper over differences between East and West. My point is simply that Augustine's theology of the beatific vision should not be read through the lens of the modern separation of nature and the supernatural, and that his sense of continuity between vision in this life and in the eschaton has ecumenical import.

PART 2

BEATIFIC VISION IN
MEDIEVAL THOUGHT

CHAPTER 5

TRANSFIGURATION AND VISION

Thomas Aquinas and Gregory Palamas

Transfiguration and Modernity

Beginning with the earliest Christian theologians, the Synoptic Gospel accounts of the transfiguration (Matt. 17:1–9; Mark 9:2–8; Luke 9:28–36) were linked to several central Christian truths. In particular, the conviction that the transfiguration revealed God's glory in Christ and his eschatological kingdom was important for the early church,[1] and so Christology and eschatology played key roles in most theological reflections on the transfiguration. The transfiguration appeared to render both Christ's divinity and the eschaton present to the three disciples. The event served not as a symbol pointing away from itself to the glory of God and to a future kingdom that he would bring about, but it was a sacrament that rendered God himself and his future kingdom really present to the disciples on Mount Tabor. Thus, although in some respects the future kingdom may remain veiled, many have looked to the transfiguration narrative for an account in which God appeared in such a way as to reveal himself most fully and gloriously in Jesus Christ, and in

---

1. John Anthony McGuckin traces patristic reflections on the transfiguration in Eastern and Western fathers, beginning with Irenaeus in the late second century (*The Transfiguration of Christ in Scripture and Tradition* [Lewiston, NY: Edwin Mellen, 1986]). McGuckin highlights three themes as central in the patristic interpretive tradition of the transfiguration: (1) transfiguration as theophany; (2) transfiguration as soteriological event; and (3) transfiguration as epiphany of the New Age (99–128). Cf. also the patristic overviews in Kenneth Stevenson, "From Origen to Gregory of Palamas: Greek Expositions of the Transfiguration," *BBGG*, ser. 3, vol. 4 (2007): 197–212; and Christopher Veniamin, "The Transfiguration of Christ in Greek Patristic Literature: From Irenaeus of Lyons to Gregory Palamas" (PhD diss., University of Oxford, 1991).

so doing transformed or deified the disciples, drawing them into his beatify-ing light and thus into his eternal kingdom.[2] What is more, the theophanic character of the transfiguration rendered it transformative in character, not only for the three disciples at Mount Tabor but also for later Christians. As a result, for centuries, the transfiguration was the subject of meditation, reflection, and debate throughout the Eastern and Western traditions.

Modern exegesis (particularly in its historical-critical gestalt) has often failed to accord the transfiguration narrative the significance it had for the earlier tradition.[3] Though the reasons for this are multiple and complex, at the heart of this neglect of the transfiguration lies the nominalist rejection of the sacramental ontology of the earlier tradition.[4] The anagogical (vertical) and eschatological (horizontal) orientation of much of the earlier Christian tradition predisposed people to see in the transfiguration both the presence of God himself and the arrival of the future kingdom (which were ultimately simply two ways of saying one and the same thing). By contrast, in the mod-ern period we have come to treat history as simply the unfolding of events determined by this-worldly cause and effect and as a result have discounted eternity and eschaton as meaningful horizons that shape our everyday lives.[5]

---

2. Cory J. Hayes, in his dissertation on Gregory Palamas, helpfully puts it as follows: "The Transfiguration is a theophany with three interrelated facets. First, as 'His Father's glory,' it is a supernatural revelation or disclosure of God, in Christ, by which he shows himself to the apos-tles. Second, this disclosure of the divine is simultaneously a revelation of 'His own kingdom.' The revelation has an eschatological character in that it is a preview or anticipation of ultimate human destiny in God that is yet to be fully realized in 'the manifestation to come.' Third, it is only by the 'power of the divine Spirit' that the apostles were able to 'behold what is invisible'" ("*Deus in se et Deus pro nobis*: The Transfiguration in the Theology of Gregory Palamas and Its Importance for Catholic Theology" [PhD diss., Duquesne University, 2015], 11). In other words, according to Hayes, the manifestation or theophany of the transfiguration involves the three aspects of revelation, eschatology, and deification. Hayes speaks here particularly of Gregory Palamas's understanding of the transfiguration, but his description has broader applicability, both with regard to the fathers and (as I hope to make clear) with regard to Western theology.

3. Cf. the comment of Dorothy Lee: "For the most part, post-Enlightenment biblical scholars have shown little interest in the transfiguration, minimizing its theological status" (*Transfiguration*, New Century Theology [London: Continuum, 2004], 1–2). Perhaps dogmatic theology is in an even worse position than biblical exegesis. I know of no dogmatic handbook that treats the transfiguration at any length.

4. For discussion of the development and impact of nominalist metaphysics, see Hans Boersma, *Heavenly Participation: The Weaving of a Sacramental Tapestry* (Grand Rapids: Eerdmans, 2011).

5. To be sure, New Testament exegetes have arrived at an array of interpretations of the transfiguration. Some, following Rudolf Bultmann's suggestion, regard it as a resurrection

The metaphysic of modernity cannot account for the presence of the eternal Word of God in human form or, for that matter, for the presence of the eschaton in this world. The plausibility of both depends on a sacramental view of reality with its recognition that divine and future realities are present in and thus impinge on this-worldly events.

As a noteworthy aside, New Testament scholar N. T. Wright has recently called for a more robust recognition of God's presence in our world, and he is convinced that the transfiguration narrative is instructive in this regard. Wright maintains that the Spirit of God is "really present" in this world,[6] and that what we see in the transfiguration narrative is that God's purpose with the world "had taken human form and that the person concerned was going about doing the things that spoke of God's kingdom coming on earth as in heaven, of God's space and human space coming together at last, of God's time and human time meeting and merging for a short, intense period."[7] Wright quotes the story of Nicholas Motovilov visiting staretz Seraphim of Sarov (1754–1833) and being engulfed in the light that suffused the monk.[8] Wright suggests that this story, as well as the transfiguration narrative, shows

---

account that has been reconfigured so as to fit into Jesus's life. See Bultmann, *The History of the Synoptic Tradition*, trans. John Marsh (Oxford: Blackwell, 1963), 259. Cf. the discussion in Craig A. Evans, *Mark 8:27–16:20*, Word Biblical Commentary 34B (Nashville: Nelson, 2001), 33–34. M. Eugene Boring, for instance, claims that Mark's narrative is "a retrojection of post-Easter faith onto a pre-Easter screen" (*Mark: A Commentary*, NTL [Louisville: Westminster John Knox, 2006], 261). Of course, those who hold that the narrative presents the eschatological glory of Christ still face the question of the precise ontological status of the event: Is it simply a literary allusion to the eschaton (perhaps by means of typological echoes from various Old Testament passages), or did heaven and earth actually intersect on the mount of transfiguration? Luke Timothy Johnson largely remains at the literary level as he speaks of "the symbolism of cloud and light and voice and mountain" in Luke's Gospel (*The Gospel of Luke*, Sacra Pagina Series 3 [Collegeville, MN: Glazier/Liturgical Press, 1991], 155). Morna D. Hooker professes that she is not sure about the event's ontological status: "It seems likely that an historical 'happening' of some kind has been interpreted with the aid of Old Testament allusions" (*A Commentary on the Gospel according to St. Mark*, Black's New Testament Commentaries [London: A. & C. Black, 1991], 214).

6. N. T. Wright, *Simply Jesus: A New Vision of Who He Was, What He Did, Why It Matters* (London: SPCK, 2011), 141.

7. Wright, *Simply Jesus*, 140.

8. Wright, *Simply Jesus*, 141. Wright suggests that the story of Seraphim of Sarov reminds us that the transfiguration "is not, as it stands, a 'proof' of his [i.e., Christ's] 'divinity,'" since Moses and Elijah were also transfigured (141). As we will see, however, for the earlier tradition, the transfiguration of Christian believers was regarded as participation in the divinity of Jesus, and their transfiguration was thus predicated on his. Chalcedonian Christology is therefore central to stories such as that of Seraphim of Sarov.

us that Jesus is "the place where God's world and ours meet, where God's time and ours meet." Thus, we have here "a new set of signposts, Jesus-shaped signposts" of the coming new creation.[9] In all, Wright is much closer to the earlier tradition of interpretation than many other contemporary exegetes.

By claiming that modernity has undermined the sacramental ontology of the earlier period, I am implying that the premodern tradition, including much of the Western tradition, was sacramental in outlook. As we saw in the previous chapter, this claim is not uncontested. It has at times been argued that the West, beginning with Augustine, failed to regard earthly and temporal realities through a sacramental lens. Beginning with the bishop of Hippo, so it is sometimes maintained, Old Testament theophanies began to be treated not as the real (or sacramental) presence of the Son of God in time and space but as mere symbols of a God who uses human creatures to teach us about himself, while he does not in any metaphysically significant way identify with these creatures. The latter thus end up having a "purely natural" status, shorn of divine character. By separating created "likenesses" (*similitudines*) from supernatural realities, the Augustinian tradition is thus seen as paving the way for the nonsacramental metaphysic of modernity, in which nature and the supernatural are ontologically separate from one another.

This genealogical account typically treats Thomas Aquinas (1224/25–1274) as simply following the path set out by Saint Augustine. The Angelic Doctor allegedly regarded Old Testament theophanies and the transfiguration merely as creaturely symbols rather than as the actual presence of God. The truth of the matter seems to me more nuanced, which I will make clear through a comparison of Thomas Aquinas and Gregory Palamas (1296–1359). It is not the case that only Palamas (and perhaps, by implication, Orthodoxy more broadly) was sacramental in his reading of the transfiguration, so that we would find in Aquinas (and in Western theology more generally) a nonsacramental account. The first two parts of this chapter are devoted to making the case that Aquinas's and Palamas's interpretations of the transfiguration are remarkably similar, and that both recognized the real presence of the divinity of Christ and the genuine arrival of the eschaton on Mount Tabor.[10]

9. Wright, *Simply Jesus*, 142.

10. Hayes overstates the differences between Aquinas and Palamas. Hayes argues that for Palamas "the Transfiguration as revelatory theophany can be considered as a kind of hyper-sacrament. I say 'hyper' sacrament, because in the case of the Transfiguration, *signum* (the humanity of Christ) does not veil *res significata* (his divinity) as it communicates it. Rather, the Transfiguration represents *signum* becoming completely transparent to *res significata*"

I do not mean artificially to harmonize the accounts of Aquinas and Palamas. Aspects of their interpretations of the transfiguration narrative differ, and these dissimilarities do suggest that Palamas was the more sacramental of the two theologians. But again, these interpretive differences are relatively minor. The two theologians disagreed most sharply not in the way they understood the transfiguration itself but in the way it functioned in terms of spiritual theology. And, as we will see in the third part of this chapter, it is here that the divergence between them most clearly comes to the fore. It is in his underlying spiritual theology that we can indeed detect in Aquinas the beginnings of a separation between this life and the next, and between nature and the supernatural. Whereas Palamas regarded the disciples' participation in the divine energies on Mount Tabor as paradigmatic for how later Christians may experience the divine life, for Aquinas the most important role of the transfiguration is the encouragement it proffers in the face of persecution and martyrdom. In short, it is not that Aquinas had a nonsacramental understanding of the transfiguration itself; it is precisely because he *did* recognize the presence of the divine light of the eschaton in the transfiguration that he wanted to guard against the expectation that the disciples' extraordinary experience can also become ours. Saint Thomas operated with a much sharper distinction between the pilgrimage of *viatores* (grounded in faith) and the eschatological rest of *comprehensores* (the beatific vision of the divine essence) than did Gregory Palamas. As a result, although Saint Thomas did recognize the sacramental character of the transfiguration, this did not translate (as it did for Palamas) into something we may call "transfiguration spirituality."

Before comparing the two theologians, we need greater specificity in what constitutes a sacramental reading of the transfiguration narrative. The remainder of this chapter will be structured around three elements. I will argue that the first two characteristics of sacramentality can be observed both in Aquinas and in Palamas, while the third is present only in Palamas.

First, then, for a sacramental understanding, the transfiguration is a theophany (θεοφάνεια), perhaps *the* theophany, of God's presence in the world. Whereas the Old Testament presents numerous accounts of theophanies— invariably interpreted by the pre-Nicene tradition as manifestations of the

---

("*Deus in se et Deus pro nobis*," 91). By contrast, maintains Hayes, "for Thomas, the *claritas* of Christ is a created, corporeal effect of Christ's beatific vision that is, in principle, visible to the normal visual faculties, in a way similar to the corporeal light of the sun" ("*Deus in se et Deus pro nobis*," 197). As we will see, the contrast is somewhat more nuanced than these descriptions may suggest.

preincarnate Son of God—on Mount Tabor the disciples have access to the glory of the divine nature of the Son of God. The transfiguration is, therefore, a theophany of unprecedented glory, as the divinity of the eternal Son of God is revealed to the disciples in the brightness of the light. A sacramental reading thus affirms that in seeing Christ the disciples see God himself.

Second, if it is true that the disciples see the divinity of the Son of God, this can only mean that the kingdom of God has arrived on Mount Tabor. Their vision of the divinity of the Son places them in the eschatological kingdom. A sacramental understanding of the transfiguration takes seriously, therefore, that the kingdom of God is truly made present to the experience of the disciples. Christ is, as Origen recognized, the αὐτοβασιλεία, the kingdom itself.[11] Where the Son of God is present, the kingdom too has arrived in its glory.

These two characteristics focus on the sacramental reality (of Christ's divinity and of the eschaton) being really present in the experience of the disciples. But perhaps a third needs to be added to this, although this move will likely not go unchallenged. On my understanding, a sacramental reading of the transfiguration implies not only that the reality of Christ became present to the disciples on Mount Tabor (so that already *in via* they experienced a foretaste of the beatific vision), but it also means that the theophanic character of the transfiguration continues in the church today and abides into eternity. That is to say, God always and forever manifests himself in and through the humanity of Jesus Christ. A sacramental ontology means that the transfiguration continues to be the central paradigm for Christian spirituality both today (*in via*) and in the future (*in patria*), so that in the hereafter we will see Christ's divinity in and through his humanity in the beatific vision. The human nature of Christ—our (transformed, deified) flesh in heaven—is forever the transparent window on the infinite God. It is at this point that Aquinas and Palamas diverge most clearly.

The Glory of God in Christ

Saint Thomas Aquinas discussed the transfiguration on four different occasions.[12] He first elaborated on it in the mid-1250s, in his *Commentary on the*

---

11. Origen, *Spirit and Fire: A Thematic Anthology of His Writings*, ed. Hans Urs von Balthasar, trans. Robert J. Daly (Washington, DC: Catholic University of America Press, 1984), 362.

12. See Édouard Divry, *La Transfiguration selon l'Orient et l'Occident: Grégoire Palamas–*

Sentences (*Scriptum super Sententiis III*). Here he deals with the questions of whether the clarity of Christ's transfigured body was real or imaginary (Aquinas defending the former), and whether it was glorious (which Aquinas affirms).[13] He again turned to the transfiguration when he wrote his *Commentary on the Four Gospels*, also known as the *Catena aurea*, in the mid-1260s, at the request of Pope Urban IV. Here he collected numerous patristic commentaries, both Western and Eastern, on the Gospels, which significantly deepened his theological reflection on the transfiguration. During his second period of teaching at the University of Paris, Aquinas discussed the transfiguration a third time, now in his *Commentary on the Gospel of Matthew* (*Super Evangelium S. Matthaei Lectura*; 1269–1270). Aquinas works his way through the details of the text as he explains that the transfiguration narrative reveals the future glory as the end of evangelical teaching.[14] Finally, the *Summa theologiae* discusses the transfiguration in *pars* III, question 45, where Aquinas raises four questions: (1) whether it was fitting that Christ should be transfigured (article 1); (2) whether the clarity of the transfiguration was the clarity of glory (article 2); (3) whether the witnesses of the transfiguration were fittingly chosen (article 3); and (4) whether the testimony of the Father's voice, saying, "This is My beloved Son," was fittingly added (article 4).

The Angelic Doctor repeatedly reflects on the close link between the human and divine natures of Christ. The disciples see in the transfiguration not just a human being, but in some way they see the splendor of God himself. To be sure, in the *Commentary on the Sentences*, Aquinas still attributes the glorious clarity of Christ's body to a miraculous intervention of God that is extraneous in character. Christ, Aquinas claims here, did not have the clarity of glory as habitually inhering in him; instead, this clarity came to

---

Thomas d'Aquin vers un dénouement œcuménique, Croire et Savoir 54 (Paris: Téqui, 2009), 251–65; Aaron Canty, *Light and Glory: The Transfiguration of Christ in Early Franciscan and Dominican Theology* (Washington, DC: Catholic University of America Press, 2011), 196–244.

13. *Sent.* III, d. 16, a. 1–2; quotations come from Thomas Aquinas, *Scriptum super Sententiis: An Index of Authorities Cited*, ed. Charles H. Lohr (Avebury, NY: Fordham University Press, 1980), unless otherwise noted.

14. *Super Matth.* 17, lect. 1, n. 1417; the translation cited in this chapter is Thomas Aquinas, *Commentary on the Gospel of Matthew*, trans. Jeremy Holmes, ed. Aquinas Institute, Biblical Commentaries 34 (Lander, WY: Aquinas Institute for the Study of Sacred Doctrine, 2013). Cf. the helpful discussion in Jeremy Holmes, "Aquinas' *Lectura in Matthaeum*," in *Aquinas on Scripture: An Introduction to His Biblical Commentaries*, ed. Thomas G. Weinandy, Daniel A. Keating, and John P. Yokum (London: T. & T. Clark, 2005), 73–97.

him supernaturally, as a divine miracle.[15] Aquinas comments: "It must be said, therefore, that this brightness did not come from a certain property of a glorified body, existing in the body of Christ, but was brought into the body of Christ in a miraculous and divine manner."[16] In this early understanding of Aquinas, the clarity of Christ's body was the result of an extraneous (miraculous) act of God.

It may well have been his reading of the church fathers that changed Aquinas's opinion on this. The church fathers typically had not appealed to a miraculous act of God to explain the glorious light of Christ's body. Instead, they had mostly appealed to the hypostatic union for an explanation. John McGuckin puts it as follows:

> Undoubtedly the major tenet of the Patristic exegesis of the Transfiguration is the interpretation of the epiphany as a manifestation by Jesus to the disciples of his own divine status. . . . What the Fathers, Greek and Latin, all concur in finding here . . . is an *essential glorification*—or the glory of his very being as the eternal Logos. Such a glory, being eternal, is unaffected by the unfolding stages of the economy and proper to him alone. This is the Christological vision that stands behind nearly every single Patristic commentator who treats the text. The wonderful epiphany of Jesus radiant on the mountain is seen not as a glory flowing to Jesus from without, but as a glory streaming from within.[17]

According to McGuckin, then, Eastern and Western fathers were united in treating the transfiguration as the manifestation to the disciples of Jesus's divine nature.[18] This observation is important, especially since in a number of other respects McGuckin notes important divergences between East and West about the transfiguration. It appears to have been the unanimous patristic consensus that in the transfiguration it is not Christ but the disciples

15. This is not to say that in his later understanding Aquinas no longer thought of the transfiguration as miraculous. As we will see, he changed his mind on the extraneous character of the clarity of Christ's body.

16. *Sent.* III, d. 16, a. 2 (translation mine).

17. McGuckin, *Transfiguration*, 110 (bold changed to italics).

18. McGuckin refers to Clement, Origen, Gregory Nazianzen, Pseudo-Augustine, Leo the Great, Chrysostom, Hilary, Jerome, Proclos of Constantinople, Pseudo-Athanasius, Anastasius of Sinai, Maximus the Confessor, John of Damascus, and Gregory Palamas (*Transfiguration*, 110–13).

who were changed, so that they were able to see the light of the eternal Son of God.

As Thomas Aquinas studied the church fathers on the transfiguration in preparation for the *Catena aurea*, this patristic consensus regarding the source of the clarity of Christ's body could hardly have escaped him. With regard to Saint Luke's account of the transfiguration, it is particularly noteworthy that Aquinas presents a lengthy quotation from the *Oration on the Transfiguration* of John of Damascus (ca. 675–ca. 749):

> Moses indeed was arrayed with a glory, which came from without (*extrinsecus*); our Lord, with that which proceeded from the inherent brightness of Divine glory (*ex innato gloriae divinae fulgore*). (Exod. 34:29.) For since in the hypostatical union there is one and the same glory of the Word and the flesh, He is transfigured not as receiving what He was not, but manifesting to His disciples, what He was. Hence, according to Matthew, it is said, that He was transfigured before them, and that His face shone as the sun; (Mat. 17:2.) for what the sun is in things of sense, God is in spiritual things.[19]

John of Damascus explains the clarity of Christ's body as proceeding not "from without" (*extrinsecus*) but "from the inherent brightness (*innato . . . fulgore*) of Divine glory." The Damascene's appeal to the hypostatic union makes explicit that he considered Chalcedonian Christology to be required for a proper understanding of the transfiguration.[20] It is likely the church fathers, and perhaps most notably Saint John of Damascus, who alerted Aquinas to the possibility that the clarity of Christ's body was not simply the outcome of an external miraculous intervention of God.

Aquinas does, however, chart his own distinct path when he works out the connection between the divinity and the humanity of Christ. He does not simply follow John of Damascus by claiming that the clarity of Christ's body derives from his divinity. Instead, both in his *Commentary on the Gospel of Matthew* and in the *Summa theologiae*, Aquinas draws attention to the distinct role of Christ's soul, which sees his divine nature. Aquinas holds that from the moment of conception, Christ had the beatific vision of the essence

19. CA 3.319–20, in Thomas Aquinas, *Catena Aurea: Commentary on the Four Gospels, Collected out of the Works of the Fathers*, trans. John Henry Newman, 4 vols. (Oxford: Parker, 1841–1845).

20. For Aquinas's reliance on John of Damascus, see also Canty, *Light and Glory*, 211–13; Marcus Plested, *Orthodox Readings of Aquinas* (Oxford: Oxford University Press, 2012), 81–82.

of God.[21] To be sure, according to Aquinas, Christ was also *viator* or pilgrim: he was subject to suffering, and his body was mortal.[22] But in one important respect Christ was never a pilgrim; he was *comprehensor* from the outset in the sense that his soul always had the perfect beatifying vision of God. In fact, Aquinas claims that Christ's soul saw the divine essence more clearly than any other creature:

> Now the soul of Christ, since it is united to the Word in person, is more closely joined to the Word of God than any other creature. Hence it more fully receives the light in which God is seen by the Word Himself than any other creature. And therefore more perfectly than the rest of creatures it sees the First Truth itself, which is the Essence of God; hence it is written (Jo. i. 14): *And we saw His glory, the glory as it were of the Only-begotten of the Father, full* not only *of grace* but also *of truth.*[23]

Much like John of Damascus, Aquinas has recourse to the hypostatic union to explain that Christ was able to see God.

Aquinas's position, however, is more developed than that of the Damascene. Aquinas specifically highlights that it is Christ's *soul* that is united to the Word. He then explains that it is through being united to the Word that Christ's soul can see the essence of God. In other words, *Christ's* vision of the divine essence is dependent upon the *Word's* vision of the divine essence.[24]

21. For a defense of Aquinas's position, see Simon Francis Gaine, *Did the Savior See the Father? Christ, Salvation, and the Vision of God* (London: Bloomsbury T. & T. Clark, 2015). Aquinas may have thought that John of Damascus was closer to him than he actually was, since he writes, "As Damascene says (*De Fide Orthod.* iii.), *the human mind of Christ did not need to mount to God, since it was ever united to God both by personal being and by the blessed vision*" (*ST* III, q. 21, a. 1; quotations in this chapter come from Thomas Aquinas, *Summa Theologica*, trans. Fathers of the English Dominican Province, 5 vols. [1948; reprint, Notre Dame: Christian Classics, 1981]). I owe this insight to correspondence with Simon Gaine, OP.

22. Aquinas comments: "Now before His passion Christ's mind saw God fully, and thus He had beatitude as far as it regards what is proper to the soul; but beatitude was wanting with regard to all else, since His soul was passible, and His body both passible and mortal, as is clear from the above (A. 4; Q. 14, AA. 1, 2). Hence He was at once comprehensor, inasmuch as He had the beatitude proper to the soul, and at the same time wayfarer, inasmuch as He was tending to beatitude, as regards what was wanting to His beatitude" (*ST* III, q. 15, a. 10). For Aquinas, the mortality of the body (as well as the soul's passibility) implies that in an important respect Christ was a pilgrim here on earth.

23. *ST* III, q. 10, a. 4.

24. While Aquinas maintains here that Christ's soul sees the "essence" of God, John of Damascus did not speak of a vision of the divine essence.

When Aquinas says that Christ's soul receives "the light in which God is seen" (*luminis in quo Deus videtur*), he has in mind the light of glory (*lumen gloriae*), which he maintains is the light that God supernaturally bestows to enable people to see his essence.[25] As created medium, the light of glory is not something *by which* (*quo*) we see (as a created intelligible species), nor is it something *in which* (*in quo*) we see (as an image that leads to the thing represented), but it is instead something *under which* (*sub quo*) we see (as something perfecting the sight to see, as bodily light perfects bodily vision).[26] Thus, for Aquinas it is by means of the created light of glory that Christ's soul has always had the beatific vision of the divine essence.

Aquinas's expositions on the transfiguration in his *Commentary on the Gospel of Matthew* and in the *Summa theologiae* are in line with his overall understanding of Christ's beatific vision. When the Gospel of Matthew writes that Christ's "face shone like the sun," Aquinas comments: "Here he revealed the future glory, where bodies will be brilliant and splendid. And this brilliance was not from the essence [of his body], but from the brilliance of the interior soul (*ex claritate interioris animae*), full of charity; *then will your light break forth as the morning*, and there follows *and the glory of the Lord will gather you up* (Isa 58:8). Hence there was a certain splendor in his body. For Christ's soul was seeing God, and beyond all brilliance, from the beginning of his conception; *and we saw his glory* (John 1:14)."[27] Here the Angelic Doctor reiterates his position that Christ's soul had the beatific vision "from the beginning of his conception," which means that the soul passed on this clarity to his body in the transfiguration.[28]

When in the *Summa* Aquinas asks whether the clarity of Christ's body in the transfiguration was the clarity of glory, he answers mostly in the affirmative,[29] and he appeals to two authorities, Augustine and John of Damascus: "For the clarity of the glorified body is derived from that of the soul, as Au-

25. *ST* I, q. 12, a. 5.

26. *ST* Suppl., q. 92, a. 1, resp. 15.

27. *Super Matth.* 17, lect. 1, n. 1424.

28. Aaron Canty notes the absence of Greek authorities in Aquinas's *Commentary on the Gospel of Matthew* (*Light and Glory*, 222). Whatever the reason for this, it is clear that Aquinas is in line with the earlier tradition (including John of Damascus) in linking the clarity of Christ's body with his divinity; at the same time, he goes beyond this tradition by highlighting the specific role of the beatific vision of Christ's soul in transmitting this clarity to the body.

29. To be precise, Aquinas comments: "The clarity which Christ assumed in His transfiguration was the clarity of glory as to its essence, but not as to its mode of being (*quantum ad modum essendi*)" (*ST* III, q. 45, a. 2).

gustine says (*Ep. ad Diosc.* cxviii). And in like manner the clarity of Christ's body in His transfiguration was derived from His Godhead, as Damascene says (*Orat. de Transfig.*) and from the glory of His soul."[30] Here Aquinas appeals to John of Damascus (whom he had also quoted in the *Catena aurea*) to make the traditional appeal to the hypostatic union in explaining the nature of the light of the transfiguration. In addition, he appeals to Augustine for his insistence that the clarity came from Christ's divinity to his body through the mediation of the soul.[31] Because Christ's soul was glorified (i.e., had the beatific vision), his body was able to share in its clarity.[32]

Aquinas argues that Christ's body shared in this clarity of glory (*claritas gloriae*) in a manner that befit its bodily character. Speaking of the resurrection body of the saints, Aquinas comments that its "clarity will be caused by an overflow (*redundantia*) of glory from the soul into the body. For what is received into something is not received in the mode of what flows in, but in the mode of what receives it; and thus the clarity that is in the soul as something spiritual is received into the body as something corporeal (*ut corporalis*)."[33] Christ's body shared in the soul's clarity of glory in a corporeal manner. Accordingly, Aquinas suggests that the clarity that Christ had in the transfiguration "was seen by the non-glorified eyes of the disciples. Therefore, also the clarity of the glorified body will be visible to non-glorified eyes."[34] We may reasonably conclude that Thomas Aquinas regarded the clarity of Christ's body as corporeal in nature—even though it came to his body from his divinity by means of his soul.[35]

---

30. *ST* III, q. 45, a. 2.

31. Cf. Canty, *Light and Glory*, 243–44.

32. Augustine, in *Ep.* 118, to Dioscorus (AD 410), does not speak of Christ's beatific vision (which Augustine did not explicitly teach). Instead, the bishop of Hippo refers to the blessedness of the saints in the resurrection, which he claims will flow from their souls to their bodies: "But the perfect health of the body is that final immortality of the whole human being. For God made the soul with so powerful a nature that from its full happiness, which is promised to the saints in the end of time, there will also overflow into the inferior nature, that is, into the body, not the happiness that is proper to one who enjoys and understands, but the fullness of health, that is, the strength of incorruptibility" (*Ep.* 118.3.14 [WSA II/2:112–13]). Aquinas applies this Augustinian view of the relationship between soul and body in the resurrection to Christ in the transfiguration. (For a few passages in Augustine that may allude to something like the beatific vision in Christ, see Gaine, *Did the Savior See?*, 54–59.)

33. *Sent.* IV, d. 44, q. 2, a. 4, qc. 1.

34. *Sent.* IV. d. 44, q. 2, a. 4, qc. 2. Aquinas also comments here that "the clarity of the glorified body can naturally (*naturaliter*) be seen by a non-glorified eye." Cf. Hayes, "*Deus in se et Deus pro nobis*," 193.

35. Cf. Édouard Divry's comment: "Thomist realism affirms, in addition, in a manner that

Aquinas does not treat the clarity of Christ's body as something *different* from the clarity of his soul: *one and the same clarity* was present in both.[36] It is just the *mode* of clarity that was different in his body than in his soul. For Aquinas, Christ's body participated, albeit indirectly, in the clarity that his soul had as it beatifically gazed on the divine essence. Saint Thomas does *not* speak of two different kinds of clarity, the one of the soul, the other of the body. This means that he does not treat the clarity of Christ's transfigured body as merely an extraneous, created *symbol*, meant to *remind* one of the uncreated light of God (which, as we will see shortly, is the position held by Palamas's opponent, Barlaam). To be sure, Aquinas regarded the clarity of the light of transfiguration merely as a bodily (and, in that sense, created) participation in the light of God's own glory.[37] But it is participation in divine glory all the same. The body of Christ was truly divinized because the glory of the beatific vision of his soul overflowed into his body and thereby transformed also his body. Aquinas, therefore, does not posit a sharp disjunction between the clarity of Christ's own beatific vision (in which Christ sees the essence of God) and the bodily light that the disciples saw in the transfiguration. Aquinas appears intent, at least at this point, to keep heaven and earth, nature and the supernatural, close together.

Aquinas thus had the following theological construction in mind: (1) The Word perceives the divine essence: God's own light. (2) By virtue of the hypostatic union, Christ's soul had the beatific vision of this same light, in a creaturely (though spiritual) mode. (3) This same clarity over-

---

is shocking to Easterners, that the light seen at Tabor does not differ from the mode of natural light, in that it is materially visible" (*Transfiguration*, 297).

36. Aquinas posits a similar link between the divine and the human when he insists that, notwithstanding the gift of a created habit of grace, it is the Holy Spirit himself who indwells the believer and divinizes him (*ST* I, q. 43, a. 3; I–II, q. 3, a. 1; I–II, q. 110, a. 3; I–II, q. 114, a. 3; III, q. 1, a. 2). Cf. Bruce D. Marshall, "Action and Person: Do Palamas and Aquinas Agree about the Spirit?" *SVTQ* 39 (1995): 387–90.

37. Marcus Plested seems to me not quite correct when he states: "Thomas does not address the question of the Transfiguration in terms of a choice between created and uncreated light, still less in terms of an essence-energies distinction" (*Orthodox Readings of Aquinas*, 80). Aquinas treats the light of Christ's body as a corporeal (and hence created) sharing in the clarity of God's own light. Since the disciples saw Christ's divinity via his humanity, one would have to conclude that it was a (bodily) vision of the divine essence. Aquinas does not spell out this last point and unfortunately does not elaborate. For a helpful articulation of the difference between Aquinas and Palamas on the *visio Dei* in general (particularly the question of whether God's essence or his energies are seen), see Nicholas J. Healy, *The Eschatology of Hans Urs von Balthasar: Being as Communion* (Oxford: Oxford University Press, 2005), 163–76.

flowed into Christ's body, in a bodily mode. This last point gives rise to an important objection: as we just saw, Aquinas believed that the disciples' vision of the clarity of glory *in a bodily manner* implies that they could see this clarity of glory with nonglorified, natural eyes. This would seem difficult to accept from an Eastern perspective. Indeed, Gregory Palamas might well retort—and, it seems to me, with good justification—that a vision of glorious clarity requires at least a supernatural transformation of the bodily eyes.

Still, because he insists that it is the divine clarity of glory itself that overflows via the soul into Christ's body, Aquinas's understanding of the transfiguration is not as removed from that of Palamas as it may seem. Both Palamas's *Triads in Defense of the Holy Hesychasts* (dating from the late 1330s) and his two homilies on the transfiguration (homilies 34 and 35, which stem from the 1350s) focus on the transfiguration in defense of the *uncreated* character of God's energies—including the light of the transfiguration.[38] For Aquinas too the light was the divine light of glory itself—even if the disciples shared in it in a bodily (and hence created) manner, so that it was visible to natural eyes. This latter point would have been troubling to Palamas, but we should not forget that both theologians treated the transfiguration as a display of the light of God's glory. Whatever one may think of Aquinas's construct, he did not interpret the light as just an extraneous symbol of divine glory.

It is this latter point—a purely symbolic interpretation of the transfiguration—that lay at the heart of Palamas's controversy with the Italian humanist monk Barlaam of Calabria (ca. 1290–1348). The latter's interpretation of the transfiguration light as just a natural symbol of God's own glory undermined, according to Palamas, the sacramental character of the transfiguration.[39] Numerous quotations illustrate that it is Barlaam's symbolism at which Palamas took aim:

38. For the dating of the *Triads* and the homilies I rely on Brian E. Daley, ed., *Light on the Mountain: Greek Patristic and Byzantine Homilies on the Transfiguration of the Lord* (Crestwood, NY: St. Vladimir's Seminary Press, 2013), 352.

39. A. N. Williams rightly comments: "The light at the Transfiguration is *sacramental* in Gregory's view; it not only designates the was and will be of divine action but also creates a space in which human history and destiny unite to hallow the present. The vision revealed to the apostles on Tabor was not a *symbolic* light that appears and then disappears; rather, it possesses the value of the second coming of Christ ([*Triads*] I.3.26)" (*The Ground of Union: Deification in Aquinas and Palamas* [New York: Oxford University Press, 1999], 116 [emphasis added]).

This hypostatic light, seen spiritually by the saints, they know by experience to exist, as they tell us, and to exist not symbolically only (μὴ συμβολικὸν τοιοῦτον).[40]

But the enemies of such an illumination and such a light also claim that all the lights which God has manifested to the saints are only symbolic apparitions (συμβολικὰ εἶναι φάσματα), allusions to immaterial and intelligible realities. . . . Shall we say that this light, the beauty of the eternal Age to Come, is only a symbol, an illusion, something without true existence (σύμβολον καὶ φάσμα καὶ ἀνυπόστατον)? Certainly not, as long as we remain lovers of this light. (2.3.20)

Why in the Age to Come should we have more symbols (σύμβολα) of this kind, more mirrors, more enigmas? Will the vision face-to-face remain still in the realm of hope? For indeed if even in heaven there are still to be symbols (σύμβολα), mirrors, enigmas, then we have been deceived in our hopes, deluded by sophistry; thinking that the promise will make us acquire the true divinity, we do not even gain a vision of divinity. A sensible light replaces this, whose nature is entirely foreign to God! How can this light be a symbol (σύμβολον), and if it is, how can it be called divinity? For the drawing of a man is not humanity, nor is the symbol (σύμβολον) of an angel the nature of an angel. (3.1.11)

What saint has ever said that this light was a created symbol (σύμβολον κτιστὸν)? Gregory the Theologian says, "It was as light that the divinity was manifested to the disciples on the Mountain." So, if the light was not really the true divinity, but its created symbol (κτιστὸν σύμβολον), one would have to say, not that the divinity manifested was light, but that light caused the divinity to appear. (3.1.12)

This mysterious light, inaccessible, immaterial, uncreated, deifying, eternal, this radiance of the Divine Nature, this glory of the divinity, this beauty of the heavenly kingdom, is at once accessible to sense perception and yet transcends it. Does such a reality really seem to you to be a symbol alien to divinity, sensible, created (ἀλλότριόν . . . θεότητος,

---

40. *Triads* 2.3.8. Hereafter, references from this work will be given in parentheses in the text; quotations come from Gregory Palamas, *The Triads*, trans. Nicholas Gendle, ed. John Meyendorff (New York: Paulist, 1983).

αἰσθητόν τε καὶ κτιστὸν σύμβολον) and "visible through the medium of air"? (3.1.22)

So the man who has seen God by means not of an alien symbol but by a natural symbol (οὐκ ἀλλοτρίῳ, ἀλλα φυσικῷ συμβόλῳ), has truly seen Him in a spiritual way. I do not consider as a natural symbol (φυσικὸν ... σύμβολον) of God what is only an ordinary symbol (τοῦτ᾽ αὐτὸ μόνον σύμβολον), visible or audible by the senses as such, and activitated through the medium of the air. When, however, the seeing eye does not see as an ordinary eye, but as an eye opened by the power of the Spirit, it does not see God by means of an alien symbol (ἀλλοτρίῳ συμβόλῳ); and it is then we can speak of sense-perception transcending the senses. (3.1.35)[41]

Repeatedly, Saint Gregory Palamas assails the idea that the saints' vision of the light would be strictly symbolic. He associates this notion with imaginary existence, with mere allusion to intelligible realities, with purely human knowledge, and so with separation from the divine light of Christ. By attacking Barlaam's interpretation of the light as merely symbolic, Palamas was essentially accusing his theology of being nonsacramental in character.

Gregory was primarily an experiential theologian.[42] He objected particularly to Barlaam's insistence that the only knowledge we have comes from sensible perception, so that it would only be by rational reflection upon objects perceived by the senses that we can have any knowledge of God. "Barlaam," explains John Meyendorff, "in defending his nominalist positions, denied the possibility here below of attaining a supernatural knowledge of God, as distinct from analogical knowledge 'starting from the creatures.'"[43] Barlaam,

41. Meyendorff explains that for Palamas a *natural* symbol of God is "connatural and coexistent with God, analogous to the inseparable relationship between the sun and its rays. Symbols *not* participating in the nature of what they symbolise either have an independent existence from that symbolised (e.g., Moses and providence), or exist only notionally, as an illustration (e.g., a conflagration as symbol of a military onslaught)" (*Triads*, 139n34). For additional references to the light as merely symbolic, see *Triads* 1.3.5; 2.3.37; 3.1.14, 17, 19.

42. Cf. Joost Van Rossum's comment, "Palamas' theology has to be seen first of all as a 'theology of experience,' rather than as a philosophical theology or a 'system'" ("Deification in Palamas and Aquinas," *SVTQ* 47 [2003]: 368).

43. John Meyendorff, *A Study of Gregory Palamas*, trans. George Lawrence (Crestwood, NY: St. Vladimir's Seminary Press, 1998), 157. Cf. Anita Strezova's comment: "Barlaam insisted on the existence of uncreated divine ideas in the essence of God, reflected in created images, and on the analogical method of arriving at knowledge of God based on the existence of those

so it appears, believed that it was impossible to move beyond the senses and intellectual knowledge to an experiential vision of the Taboric light. As a result, he sharply attacked the hesychast practices of the Athonite monks, such as the Jesus prayer and the bodily postures associated with it, most notably the incessant "navel gazing" of the *omphalopsychoi* (literally, navel people).[44] For Barlaam, therefore, the Palamites were akin to the fourth-century Messalians, who had believed it was possible to see God with natural, bodily eyes.[45]

Barlaam's accusation of Messalianism was, in an important sense, misplaced. Palamas reiterated time and again that the senses are unable to see the divine light. In homily 34, in which Gregory sets out to prove that the light of the transfiguration was uncreated light, he states plainly: "Those who are not aware of this light and who now blaspheme against it think that the chosen apostles saw the light of the Lord's transfiguration with their created faculty of sight (αἰσθητικῇ τε καὶ κτισῇ δυνάμει), and in this way they endeavour to bring down to the level of a created object (κτίσμα) not just that light—God's power and kingdom—but even the power of the Holy Spirit, by which divine things are revealed to the worthy."[46] Gregory follows these comments with the following:

> There are people in our own times, who boast of pagan Greek learning and the wisdom of this world, and who completely disobey spiritual men in matters of the Spirit, and choose to oppose them. When they hear that the light of the Lord's transfiguration on the mountain was seen by the eyes of the apostles, they immediately reduce it to visible, created light (τὸ αἰσθητὸν . . . καὶ κτιστόν). They drag down that immaterial, never-

ideas and their reflections" ("Doctrinal Positions of Barlaam of Calabria and Gregory Palamas during the Byzantine Hesychast Controversy," *SVTQ* 58 [2014]: 181–82).

44. Cf. Russel Murray, "Mirror of Experience: Palamas and Bonaventure on the Experience of God—a Contribution to Orthodox–Roman Catholic Dialogue," *JES* 44 (2009): 436n11. Cf. also Meyendorff, introduction to *Triads*, 16. Meyendorff explains that most of Palamas's works do not mention this breathing method, and that "he only talked about it in order to defend it against Barlaam" (*Study of Gregory Palamas*, 140).

45. Norman Russell, *The Doctrine of Deification in the Greek Patristic Tradition* (Oxford: Oxford University Press, 2004), 304; Strezova, "Doctrinal Positions," 196, 231. Palamas wanted nothing to do with the Messalians: "God's essence is absolutely indivisible and incomprehensible, and no other being can receive it, either to a greater or lesser extent. Only the accursed Messalians think otherwise, supposing that God's essence can be seen by those among them who are worthy" (*Hom.* 35.17, in *The Homilies*, trans. and ed. Christopher Veniamin [Waymart, PA: Mount Thabor Publishing, 2009], 280; for the Greek text of Palamas's *Homilies* 34 and 35, see PG 151:432–50).

46. *Hom.* 34.8; quotations from Gregory's *Homilies* are from the Veniamin translation.

setting, pre-eternal light, which surpasses not only our senses (αἴσθησιν) but also our minds (νοῦν), because they themselves are at a low level, and are incapable of conceiving anything higher than earthly things. Nevertheless, He who shone with this light proved in advance that it was uncreated (ἄκτιστον) by referring to it as the kingdom of God.[47]

For Palamas, because the light of the transfiguration is truly divine—one of God's eternal energies—it must be uncreated and as such inaccessible to the senses.

The antihesychites, who at some point appear to have been persuaded by the Palamites that the light of Christ is uncreated, began to insist that if it is uncreated, it must be the divine essence itself. They concluded from this that on Mount Tabor the disciples had seen the divine essence. As a result, they now maintained that the light of the transfiguration was not a created light but was the divine essence.[48] In homily 35, therefore, Saint Gregory sets out to argue that the Taboric light is an uncreated energy, but not the divine essence itself. And he reproaches his opponents with the very same accusation they hurled at him, namely, that it is possible to see God with visible eyes: "They say that the light is not the divine glory, nor the kingdom of God, His beauty, His grace, or His radiance, as we have been taught by God and the theologians, but affirm instead that what they formerly claimed was visible and created is God's essence."[49] Palamas is insistent that although it is possible to participate in the energies of God and to see the light of the transfiguration (since the energies are in no way separate from God himself), this vision does not access the essence of God, which is unparticipable and as such expresses God's transcendence.

According to Saint Gregory Palamas, then, the light of the transfiguration is neither naturally accessible to the physical eyes nor arrived at by rational abstraction. Palamas keeps insisting that both the senses and the intellect are unable to grasp this glorious light: "This is why their vision is not a sensation (αἴσθησις), since they do not receive it through the senses (αἰσθητηρίων); nor is it intellection (νόησις), since they do not find it through thought (λογισμῶν) or the knowledge (γνώσεως) that comes thereby, but after the cessation of all mental activity (νοερᾶς ἐνεργείας)."[50] For Palamas, the light of the transfig-

47. *Hom.* 34.12.

48. I am following here the suggestion of Christopher Veniamin, in Gregory Palamas, *The Homilies*, 595n545.

49. *Hom.* 35.14.

50. *Triads* 1.3.18. Cf. 1.3.17: "And what am I to say of this union, when the brief vision itself is manifested only to chosen disciples, disengaged by ecstasy from all perception of the senses

uration is accessible only through supernatural grace, which transforms the human person so that he is able to participate in the divine energies.[51]

This sight of the light of the transfiguration thus depends, according to Palamas, on a transformation of the physical senses. "The initiated disciples of the Lord," comments Palamas, "'passed,' as we have been taught, 'from flesh to spirit' by the transformation of their senses (τῇ ἐναλλαγῇ τῶν αἰσθήσεων), which the Spirit wrought in them, and so they saw that ineffable light, when and as much as the Holy Spirit's power granted them to do."[52] In line with the earlier tradition, Palamas maintains that it is not as though the light is something that Christ did not have before ("Perish the blasphemous thought!"),[53] and so Palamas argues that nothing changed in Christ but that he "was revealed to His disciples as He was, opening their eyes and giving sight to the blind. Take note that eyes with natural vision (οἱ κατὰ φύσιν ὁρῶντες ὀφθαλμοί) are blind to that light. It is invisible, and those who behold it do so not simply with their bodily eyes, but with eyes transformed (μετασκευασθεῖσι) by the power of the Holy Spirit."[54] Only transformed eyes are able to see the light of transfiguration that is always already present in the incarnate Lord.

Palamas insists, therefore, that the light of the transfiguration is "the light of the Godhead."[55] Referring to the light of the new Jerusalem in Revelation 21:23—"The glory of God gives it light, and its lamp is the Lamb"—Palamas comments that John here "is also pointing us towards Jesus divinely trans-

---

or intellect (αἰσθητῆς καὶ νοερᾶς), admitted to the true vision because they have ceased to see, and endowed with supernatural senses (ὑπὲρ φύσιν τὴν αἴσθησιν) by their submission to unknowing?" And cf. 3.2.14: "There exists, then, an eternal light, other than the divine essence; it is not itself an essence—far from it!—but an energy of the Superessential. This light without beginning or end is neither sensible (αἰσθητόν) nor intelligible (νοητὸν), in the proper sense. It is spiritual and divine, distinct from all creatures in its transcendence; and what is neither sensible (αἰσθητόν) nor intelligible (νοητόν) does not fall within the scope of the senses as such (αἰσθήσει ἢ αἰσθήσει), nor of the intellectual faculty considered in itself (νοερᾷ δυνάμει καθ᾽ αὐτήν)."

51. Cf. Meyendorff, introduction to *Triads*, 13–15.
52. *Hom.* 34.8.
53. *Hom.* 34.13.
54. *Hom.* 34.13. Cf. *Triads* 3.1.22: "The disciples would not even have seen the symbol (σύμβολον), had they not first received eyes they did not possess before. As John of Damascus puts it, 'From being blind men, they began to see,' and to contemplate this uncreated light. The light, then, became accessible to their eyes, but to eyes which saw in a way superior to that of natural sight (ὑπὲρ ὀφθαλμοὺς), and had acquired the spiritual power of the spiritual light." Palamas also speaks of "sense-perception transcending the senses" (αἴσθησιν ὑπὲρ αἴσθησίν) (*Triads* 3.1.35).
55. *Triads* 3.1.22.

figured on Tabor, whose light is His body, and who, instead of daylight, has the glory of divinity revealed on the mountain to those who came up with Him."[56] Since there will be no need for a candle or a light in that future city, and there will be no night there (Rev. 22:5), Palamas rhetorically asks: "What light is this, in which there is no variableness, nor shadow of turning? (Jas. 1:17). What is this unchangeable and never-setting light? Is it not the divine light?"[57] To see this divine light, the natural vision of physical eyes is for Palamas obviously inadequate, and so the senses need to be transformed, so that we can "look with our inner eyes (τοῖς ἔνδον ὀφθαλμοῖς) at this great spectacle."[58]

Since Palamas believed that neither the senses nor the intellect is able to grasp the eternal light of God, spiritual vision did *not* mean for him simply a move from sensible to intellectual apprehension. Rather, he believed that the senses are actually *transformed* (a move from physical to spiritual eyes).[59] The eyes themselves continue to function throughout this process, according to Palamas. Thus, he could use language that seemed as though the vision of the disciples on the mountain had been ordinary, physical perception. The disciples, claims Palamas in his *Triads*, "saw the same grace of the Spirit which would later dwell in them; for there is only one grace of the Father, Son and Spirit, and they saw it with their corporeal eyes (σωματικοῖς εἶδον ὀφθαλμοῖς), but with eyes that had been opened so that, instead of being blind, they could see."[60] A little later, he describes spiritual vision as follows:

> Do you not understand that the men who are united to God and dei-fied, who fix their eyes in a divine manner on Him, do not see as we do? Miraculously, they see with a sense that exceeds the senses, with a mind that exceeds the mind, for the power of the spirit penetrates their human faculties (ταῖς ἀνθρωπίναις ἕξεσιν ἐγγινομένης), and allows them to see things which are beyond us. In speaking of a vision through the senses (τῇ αἰσθήσει), then, we must add that this transcends the senses (ὑπὲρ αἴσθησιν), in order to show clearly that it is not only supernatural, but goes beyond all expression.[61]

56. *Hom.* 34.15.
57. *Hom.* 34.15.
58. *Hom.* 35.18.
59. For discussion of Palamas's reliance here on the earlier patristic tradition, particularly Maximus the Confessor, see Hayes, "*Deus in se et Deus pro nobis*," 129–32.
60. *Triads* 3.3.9.
61. *Triads* 3.3.10.

It is easy to see why Barlaam would accuse the hesychasts of the Messalian notion that it is possible to see God with the physical eyes. For Palamas, the spiritual vision of the light was actually a vision "through the senses," so that the disciples saw the light "with their corporeal eyes." Crucially, however, Palamas maintained that when people have this corporeal yet spiritual vision, the Spirit of God "penetrates their human faculties" so as to transform them, so that this spiritual vision "through the senses" also "transcends the senses." And, what is more, not only does this spiritual vision exceed the senses, but it also "exceeds the mind." Both the senses and the intellect are valued—but the Spirit uses both so as to transcend both.[62]

Both Aquinas (in his later writings) and Palamas linked the disciples' vision of the light to the hypostatic union. Thus, both followed the patristic insight that Christ's body shone with a light that was his by virtue of this union. By no means, therefore, was it Aquinas's view that the light was a mere symbol, as Barlaam would have it. The reason, for Aquinas, why Christ's body could shine with the clarity of glory is that Christ's soul had the beatific vision (and thus the vision of the divine essence) from the moment of conception. Palamas grounded the same claim—that Christ's light in the transfiguration was the result of the hypostatic union—more immediately in the union between the divinity and the humanity of Christ. Christ's whole being (body and soul) was always already transformed by the light of the Godhead. Both Aquinas and Palamas, therefore, acknowledged the divine character of the light. We could say that both were sacramental at least in the sense that they closely linked the light of the transfiguration to the divinity of Christ. Christology (the hypostatic union) prevented both of them from separating Christ's divine glory from the light that the disciples saw on Mount Tabor. Both would reject as Nestorian a view that treats the transfiguration light as purely natural, unconnected to the Word of God. Both were convinced that Christ's divinity was really present on the mount of transfiguration.

It is true, however, that Aquinas highlighted the corporeal mode in which Christ receives this light, and he went so far as to suggest that anyone would have been able to see the clarity of Christ's transfigured body with natural eyes. This placed Aquinas in an awkward position: seeing as he did not distinguish between essence and energies, he effectively ended up arguing that

62. Cf. John Meyendorff's comment: "This completeness of the human being includes body as well as senses. From this results that astounding mystery of which the Transfiguration of Christ described in the Bible is an example; the vision of an uncreated light by created eyes" (*Study of Gregory Palamas*, 173). For the related point that bodily life is important in Palamas's conception of the human person and in his soteriology, see *Study of Gregory Palamas*, 142–46.

the disciples saw the glory of Christ's divinity—the divine essence—with natural eyes in a corporeal mode.[63] Palamas, by contrast, maintained that although the disciples never attained to the divine essence itself, the Spirit's transformation of the disciples' eyes and mind allowed them to look directly at the eternal light of God's glory and so participate in the divine energies.

The Glory of the Kingdom in Christ

Just as Aquinas and Palamas were both convinced that the clarity of Christ's body resulted from the hypostatic union of Christ, so both maintained that this same clarity was a witness to the real presence of the eschaton. It seems, however, that Palamas did greater justice to this eschatological in-breaking than did Aquinas, primarily because Palamas linked the transfiguration narrative with contemporary Christian experience in a way that Aquinas simply did not.

Throughout his writings, Aquinas draws attention to the real presence of the eschaton in the transfiguration. Already in his *Commentary on the Sentences* he highlights that it is the purpose of the narrative to teach us about the eschatological character of the body. The clarity of Christ's transformed body and the resurrection body are related as figure and reality. The clarity of Christ's transfigured body, claims Aquinas, is a figure (*figura*) of the future clarity of the saints.[64] Aquinas explicitly maintains that the clarity of Christ's transfigured body was glorious (*gloriosa*). Reflecting on Philippians 3:21—which says that Christ "will transform our lowly body to be like his glorious body"—he quotes a gloss (a marginal annotation) according to which "we will be assimilated to the clarity which he had in the transfiguration," and he adds: "But we will be assimilated to glorious clarity. Therefore, he then had glorious clarity."[65] Even though Christ's body was

---

63. To be sure, Aquinas never explicitly states that the disciples saw the divine essence (in a corporeal mode). Still, as we have seen, for Aquinas the light of Christ's divine nature was mediated via Christ's fully beatified soul to his body, and Aquinas does maintain that the disciples saw the very clarity of glory as a result of the hypostatic union. Because Aquinas does not distinguish between essence and energies, any sight of Christ's divinity via his humanity would have to imply a vision also of the divine essence. It is not clear to me how Aquinas would be able to make an argument for his position that the disciples were able to see the clarity of glory in a corporeal mode of being (cf. *ST* III, q. 45, a. 2).

64. *Sent.* III, d. 16, a. 1.

65. *Sent.* III, d. 16, a. 2 (translation mine).

subject to punishment, it nonetheless manifested the glory of the resurrection: "Non-glorious clarity does not show forth the glory of the resurrection. But Christ was transfigured precisely to show forth the glory of the resurrection, as has been said. Therefore, the clarity was glorious."[66] And in his *Commentary on the Gospel of Matthew*, Aquinas suggests again that in the transfiguration Christ "revealed the future glory, where bodies will be brilliant and splendid."[67]

To be sure, Aquinas does qualify, in two ways, this general claim that the clarity of Christ's transfigured body was the same as that of the resurrection bodies of the saints.[68] First, he suggests in a variety of ways that the clarity of glory was not, as it were, a permanent characteristic of Christ's body. Aquinas is distinctly uncomfortable with the claim—which he erroneously thinks stems from Hugh of Saint Victor—that the four so-called eschatological gifts (*dotes*) of resurrection bodies would also have been present as gifts in Christ's earthly body. According to Hugh, Christ assumed these four eschatological gifts at various stages during his life: subtlety (*subtilitas*) when he came out of the Virgin's womb; agility (*agilitas*) when he walked on the waves of the sea; clarity (*claritas*) in the resurrection; and impassibility (*impassibilitas*) when he gave his body to the disciples to eat without it being divided.[69] In his *Commentary on the Sentences*, Aquinas says that although Hugh may have claimed that Christ assumed these properties or gifts, in Christ they were not, properly speaking, present as gifts (*dotes*).

Christ, after all, had a passible body, and it would seem out of place for these eschatological gifts to be permanently present in a passible body. Aquinas insists, therefore, that during Christ's life on earth, his body did not yet have the qualities or habits (*qualitates sive habitus*) of a glorious body. Instead, he only had the acts (*actus*) of the four above-mentioned properties, and he had them "not as proceeding from something inherent (*ex aliquo inhaerente*) but supernaturally, by way of divine miracle."[70] In his *Commentary on the Gospel of Matthew*, Aquinas is even more categorical. Whereas some maintain that Christ had the four gifts, the Angelic Doctor counters this by saying: "I do not believe this, because a gift is a certain property of

66. *Sent.* III, d. 16, a. 2 (translation mine).

67. *Super Matth.* 17, lect. 1, n. 1424.

68. For these same two caveats, see Canty, *Light and Glory*, 205–8; Hayes, "*Deus in se et Deus pro nobis*," 170–72.

69. *Sent.* III, d. 16, a. 2.

70. *Sent.* III, d. 16, a. 2. As we have already seen, Aquinas later changed his mind on this, connecting Christ's bodily clarity to his divinity.

glory itself."[71] The clarity of Christ's body in the transfiguration was the result of "divine power" (*ex virtute divina*). Christ's body simply had "a certain likeness" (*aliquam similitudinem*) to a glorious body.[72]

In the *Summa theologiae*, Aquinas again explains that the clarity of glory was not present in Christ's transfigured body in the same way it will be in resurrection bodies in the future. The reason is that the clarity of the soul overflows into the body in different ways: "In Christ's transfiguration clarity overflowed (*derivate est*) from His Godhead and from His soul into His body, not as an immanent quality (*per modum qualitatis immanentis*) affecting His very body, but rather after the manner of a transient passion (*per modum passionis transeuntis*), as when the air is lit up by the sun. Consequently, the refulgence, which appeared in Christ's body then, was miraculous."[73] Although Aquinas does insist that the clarity of glory was present in the transfiguration, it was present merely as a "transient passion" rather than as an "immanent quality."[74]

Aquinas's second caveat is that he believes the intensity of clarity will be greater in resurrection bodies than it was in Christ's transfigured body. On the one hand, since Christ's soul was truly glorified in its beatific vision, the clarity of Christ's transfigured body was of the same kind as that of the saints' resurrection bodies. On the other hand, the latter will be more perfect than was the former.[75] Aquinas uses the act-habit distinction to argue that the act of Christ's transfigured body was only "similar in splendor" (*splendoris similis*) to resurrection bodies, which will have this same glory in a habitual fashion.[76]

---

71. *Super Matth.* 17, lect. 1, n. 1426.

72. *Super Matth.* 17, lect. 1, n. 1426. Cf. Canty, *Light and Glory*, 219.

73. *ST* III, q. 45, a. 2.

74. Cf. Canty, *Light and Glory*, 238. One may wonder how the presence of clarity can merely be an "act" or a "transient passion" if this clarity derives directly from the beatific vision that, on Aquinas's understanding, Christ had from the moment of conception. Aquinas's solution in *ST* III, q. 45, a. 2 is to say that by way of a divine dispensation, God prevented the clarity of the beatific vision to shine through in Christ's body (except, that is to say, at the time of the transfiguration). Cf. Canty, 219, 232–33, 244. Aquinas's conception of the transfiguration light as an exception to an exception may seem overly ingenious, but it does flow logically from his overall argument.

75. *Sent.* III, d. 16, a. 2. Cf. Canty, *Light and Glory*, 207. At this point we see an obvious difference between Aquinas and Palamas. Palamas, who believed that the disciples saw the very energies of the Godhead at Tabor, would never claim that the resurrection bodies of the saints will outshine Christ's body at the transfiguration.

76. *Sent.* III, d. 16, a. 2.

Notwithstanding these two caveats, it is clear that for Aquinas the light that shone from Christ's body is not different in kind from the light that will be the property of the resurrection bodies. In a real (though limited) way, Christ's transfigured body shared in the glory of the eschaton. As such, Aquinas's view is genuinely sacramental: the transfiguration did not just point to the resurrection but was actually a sharing in the same light that will one day be the property of the saints. The eschaton was thus really present on the mount of transfiguration.

Gregory Palamas describes the eschatological character of the transfiguration in a remarkably similar way. When in homily 34 he notes that in Luke the transfiguration took place "eight days after these sayings" (Luke 9:28), whereas according to Matthew it happened "after six days" (Matt. 17:1), Palamas not only gives an ordinary, commonsense explanation ("Luke is including the day on which the words were uttered and the day when the Lord was transfigured"),[77] but he also reflects on the mystical meaning of the eighth day as a reference to the eschaton: "The great vision of the light of the Lord's transfiguration is the mystery of the eighth day, that is, of the age to come, which is manifested after this world, which was made in six days, has ceased, and the sixfold action of our senses has been transcended. We have five senses, but if you add speech it brings the number of ways in which our senses work to six. The kingdom of God promised to those who are worthy surpasses not only our senses but also our words."[78] For Palamas, the transfiguration introduces us to the mystery of the eighth day—a common trope among patristic and Eastern theologians.[79]

Palamas treats the transfiguration, therefore, as the fulfillment of Jesus's promise that "some standing here . . . will not taste death until they see the kingdom of God after it has come with power" (Mark 9:1).[80] This power, explains Palamas, is the power of the Spirit, and it is only for those "who have stood with the Lord, those who have been established in His faith, men like Peter, James and John."[81] According to Palamas, therefore, one obvious reason that the light of the transfiguration cannot be ordinary (created) light is that the kingdom of

77. *Hom.* 34.5.
78. *Hom.* 34.6.
79. See Jean Daniélou, "La Typologie de la semaine au IVe siècle," *RSR* 35 (1948): 382–411; Jean Daniélou, *The Bible and the Liturgy*, Liturgical Studies 3 (Notre Dame: University of Notre Dame Press, 1956), 262–86; Hans Boersma, *Scripture as Real Presence: Sacramental Exegesis in the Early Church* (Grand Rapids: Baker Academic, 2017), 288–90.
80. *Hom.* 34.7.
81. *Hom.* 34.7.

God—which is what the transfiguration is—doesn't have ordinary light: "How could ordinary light be the glory and the kingdom of the Father and the Spirit? How could Christ come in that sort of glory and kingdom in the age to come, when there will be no need for air, light, place or anything of the sort, but God, according to the apostle, will be everything for us? (*cf.* 1 Cor. 15:28). Clearly, if He will be everything for us, He will also be our light."[82] The transfiguration, Cory Hayes rightly comments, was for Palamas "an anticipation and model of both the form and content of the Second Coming of Christ and the restoration of all things."[83] Palamas had a remarkably realized eschatology when it comes to the transfiguration. The light that the disciples saw on the mountain made the eschatological kingdom part of their real-life experience; the kingdom was really present on Mount Tabor.

The only limit that Palamas placed on the eschatological character of the kingdom is that it was not yet *fully* present in the transfiguration. Peter, in asking for three tabernacles to be built, did not know what he was saying (cf. Mark 9:6). Comments Palamas: "The time for all things to be restored had not yet come, but even when it does, we shall not need tents made by hand."[84] It appears that for Palamas, although the disciples truly participated in the eschatological light of glory, their participation in this uncreated light would be deepened after the second coming.[85] Moreover, since Palamas, unlike Aquinas, was convinced that the divine essence eternally remains beyond human reach, he also held to the notion of eternal progress (*epektasis*): the saints' participation in the energy of uncreated light would progress eternally.[86] "Always," writes Palamas, the recipient of the vision "is being borne on to further progress (ἐπὶ τὰ πρόσω) and experiencing even more resplendent contemplation. He understands then that this vision is infinite because it *is* a vision of the Infinite, and because he does not see the limit of that brilliance; but, all the more, he sees how feeble is his capacity to receive the light."[87] The infinity

82. *Hom.* 34.15.

83. Hayes summarizes the difference between the transfiguration and the eschaton as follows: "For Palamas, the difference between the Kingdom as presently manifested in the Transfiguration and the Kingdom of the 'manifestation to come' is one of degree (a matter of less versus more) and mode (a matter of partial versus full)" (*"Deus in se et Deus pro nobis,"* 32).

84. *Hom.* 35.9. Cf. Hayes, *"Deus in se et Deus pro nobis,"* 33.

85. Hayes, *"Deus in se et Deus pro nobis,"* 31.

86. Palamas's notion of eternal progress (*epektasis*) is similar to Gregory of Nyssa's understanding of it as discussed above, chap. 3, section entitled *"The Life of Moses*: Vision as Perpetual Desire."

87. *Triads* 1.3.22. Cf. 2.3.35: "This contemplation has a beginning, and something follows on from this beginning, more or less dark or clear; but there is never an end, since its progress (πρόοδος) is infinite, just as is the ravishment in revelation."

of God implies that although at the transfiguration the disciples truly saw the eschatological light and truly participated in the energies of God (as do many of the saints today), they will forever make further progress in their deification or participation in God.

In some ways, the approaches of Aquinas and Palamas are similar. Both saw the transfiguration as a proleptic anticipation of the eschatological kingdom. Both were convinced that the kingdom of God is truly revealed and really present on the mount of transfiguration, and as a result both regarded the clarity or the light of Christ's transfigured body as the very presence of the glory of the eschaton. The caveats that both theologians registered are also similar. According to Aquinas, the glory of the transfiguration was transient, and it was less perfect than the glory of the resurrection bodies will be. In Palamas's view, the fullness of the kingdom has not yet arrived, and the disciples' vision of the Taboric light was an experience that will be eternally deepened by their eternal progress into the life of God.

At the same time, it seems to me that it was not quite as easy for Aquinas as it was for Palamas to articulate *how* the disciples participated in the eschatological kingdom at the transfiguration. Palamas regarded the vision of the transfiguration and the beatific vision after the resurrection as a continuum—because, both now and in the hereafter, the believers participate in the divine energies (though they will do so much more intensely in the age to come). The disciples could share in these energies because their bodily eyes as well as their intellects were transformed or transfigured to comport with the eschatological reality of Christ's glory. Aquinas, by contrast, maintained that the disciples saw the glory of Christ's divine nature (indirectly, via the hypostatic union and Christ's own beatific vision of the divine essence), while at the same time he claimed that the disciples saw this light in a bodily manner, with ordinary physical eyes. That is to say, for Aquinas, the disciples did not experience a transformation of the senses and the intellect. Aquinas does not make clear how it would have been possible for the disciples to see the very clarity of glory in an ordinary bodily manner. It is fair to conclude that Gregory Palamas displays a consistency of approach that in some ways is lacking in Thomas Aquinas.

Christian Spirituality and Beatific Vision

It is the *spirituality* of the transfiguration that particularly sets Aquinas and Palamas apart from each other. Saint Thomas saw the function of the transfiguration primarily in historical terms as an encouragement for the disciples. He suggests in the *Summa*: "Our Lord, after foretelling His Passion to His disciples, had exhorted them to follow the path of His sufferings (Matthew 16:21–24). Now in order that anyone go straight along a road, he must have some knowledge of the end: thus an archer will not shoot the arrow straight unless he first see the target."[88] The purpose of the transfiguration, for Aquinas, was to prepare the disciples—and, presumably, later Christians as well—for martyrdom. Indeed, as Aaron Canty comments: "The transfiguration, as a manifestation of glory, acts as a beacon on their earthly sojourn so they can see beyond their looming martyrdom to the fullness of the kingdom of God beyond it."[89] For Aquinas, upon receiving a foretaste of the eschatological kingdom, the disciples were adequately prepared to follow their Lord on the difficult pilgrimage of suffering and death.

Aquinas, therefore, gives no indication that the Taboric light is something that Christians can expect to experience on their own faith journey. Presumably the reason is that the Angelic Doctor tends to emphasize that we live by faith, not by sight (cf. 2 Cor. 5:7). In this life, we participate in the divine light by the light of grace (*lumen gratiae*), in the hereafter by the light of glory (*lumen gloriae*).[90] For Aquinas, to say that the transfiguration glory can be ours today would be to claim that the resurrection glory is ours already today—as if we were no longer on pilgrimage and no longer needed to live by the light of faith. It is precisely because Aquinas treats the transfiguration as a unique participation in the eschaton that he wants us to be careful how we appropriate the narrative to our lives. Ironically, it is thus his sacramental understanding of the transfiguration—his acknowledgment of the real presence of the eschaton—that prevents him from translating it into a transfiguration spirituality for present-day *viatores*. For Aquinas, the eternal light of the Word was really present to the disciples' vision; and the eschaton too became really present to their experience. Aquinas did not believe that ordinary believers can expect such an experience today. To him,

88. *ST* III, q. 45, a. 1.
89. Canty, *Light and Glory*, 228.
90. Aquinas makes clear that the object of faith is not something seen. Instead, he claims, "Faith implies assent of the intellect to that which is believed" (*ST* II-II, q. 1, a. 4). To be sure, he does add that "the light of faith makes us see what we believe" (II-II, q. 1, a. 4). Nonetheless, the *lumen gratiae* pertains to faith and to this life, whereas the *lumen gloriae* pertains to the beatific vision and to the hereafter. Accordingly, for Aquinas, Jesus did not have faith, since he always had the sight of the beatific vision (*ST* III, q. 9, a. 2). See also the discussion in David L. Whidden, "The Theology of Light in Thomas Aquinas" (PhD diss., Southern Methodist University, 2011).

the transfiguration experience was so full of the splendor of the eschaton that one dare not appropriate it to one's ordinary, everyday spirituality.[91]

It is well known that Aquinas acknowledges that Moses and Paul, too, experienced a unique vision of God (cf. Num. 12:8; 2 Cor. 12:1–4). In fact, in Aquinas's understanding they were raptured so as to see the essence of God.[92] Their experience was—in Aquinas's view at least—even more glorious than the transfiguration: the disciples saw with bodily eyes, whereas Moses and Paul experienced a spiritual ecstasy as they were raptured into the third heaven.[93] The disciples saw a body that shared in the overflow of the soul's clarity, whereas Moses and Paul had a direct vision of the essence of God. Nonetheless, the differences between the vision of the disciples and that of Moses and Paul were by no means absolute for Aquinas. Both experiences made the eschaton present to the experience of believers. Indeed, Aquinas uses similar language to describe both kinds of vision.[94] He was inclined to restrict both kinds of experiences to a select few. Therefore, just as he refused to accept that the experiences of Moses and Paul were broadly accessible, so too did he decline to develop a transfiguration spirituality.

It hardly needs elaboration that Saint Gregory Palamas's spirituality was different in this regard. For him the transfiguration narrative was not primarily a historical event encouraging the disciples on their road to martyrdom. Instead, it was first of all a narrative that illustrates that worthy saints—both then and now—can come to share in the uncreated light of the resurrection.[95] For Palamas, in other words, the narrative encourages one to be transformed by the deifying light of Jesus Christ. As a result, Palamas effortlessly moves

---

91. Joost Van Rossum rightly comments: "In Thomas Aquinas, it is impossible to assume the possibility of such a realistic transfiguration of the human being during this earthly life as it was experienced by the hesychasts, because for him it would imply pantheism" ("Deification in Palamas and Aquinas," 380–81). Van Rossum overstates his case, however, when he adds: "For Thomas, the divine and the human have to be kept neatly distinct in order to prevent a pantheistic concept of deification" (381). Aquinas's teaching of deification means that he is closer to Palamas than Van Rossum is prepared to acknowledge. Cf. n. 36 above.

92. *ST* I, q. 12, a. 11; II-II, q. 175, a. 3.

93. *ST* II-II, q. 175, a. 4. Aquinas also makes very clear that Paul's rapture to the third heaven was not "the vision of something corporeal" (II-II, q. 175, a. 3).

94. Aquinas explains that Paul's rapture too was a "transitory passion" (*passio transeuns*), so that he was not blessed in a habitual fashion (*habitualiter*) but merely had the act (*actus*) of the blessed (*ST* II-II, q. 175, a. 3).

95. The manner in which, for Palamas, Christians are enabled to share in the light of transfiguration lies beyond the scope of this chapter. Suffice it to say that his writings frequently highlight both prayer and obedience.

from the transfiguration narrative to the experiences of believers and back.[96] At one point, he asks rhetorically, since the Son of God united himself to our nature and has become a single body with us, "how should he not commune worthily with the divine ray of His Body which is within us, lightening their souls, as He illumined the very bodies of the disciples on Mount Thabor? For, on the day of Transfiguration, that Body, source of the Light of grace, was not yet united with our bodies; it illuminated from the outside (ἔξωθεν) those who worthily approached it, and sent the illumination into the soul by the intermediary of the physical eyes; but now, since it is mingled with us and exists in us, it illuminates the soul from within (ἔνδοθεν)."[97] According to Palamas, the only difference between the experience of the disciples and our experience is that for them the light came from the outside, whereas for us it comes from within. One and the same light (the result of the hypostatic union) deified the three disciples and illuminates later believers.[98] As Cory Hayes puts it: "The grace that made the ineffable light of the Godhead visible to the apostles on Tabor is not [an] isolated event, but it serves as a marker in salvation history that stands as a scriptural proof that the vision of God is an integral part of Christian mystical experience. The Transfiguration is then the paradigm of mystical experience and of the essence of the Christian life which is the person being made gradually more and more God-like by deification."[99] For Palamas, the disciples' vision on Mount Tabor serves as the benchmark of an authentic transfiguration spirituality.

The result is that the lines between faith and vision became much more fluid for Palamas than they were for Aquinas. Using language that Palamas himself did not employ, we could say that for him the beatific vision begins already today. Already we can experience the light that transcends the senses and the intellect, inasmuch as Christ, through the Spirit, indwells us already today. As a result, the beatific vision becomes a reality whenever Christ ap-

---

96. Cf. A. N. Williams's comment that for Palamas "the Transfiguration is understood not only as an historic event, but one that announces a dramatic change in the manner in which humanity will encounter God" (*The Ground of Union*, 112; cf. 173).

97. *Triads* 1.3.38. Cf. Meyendorff, *Study of Gregory Palamas*, 151.

98. Cf. *Triads* 1.3.43: "Is it not clear that the divine light is always one and the same (ἕν καὶ τὸ αὐτό), whether it be that which the Apostles saw on Tabor, or that which purified spirits now see, or that of the very reality of eternal blessedness to come? That is why the great Basil called the light which blazed on Tabor at the Transfiguration of our Lord, a prelude to the glory of Christ in his second coming." Translation taken from Meyendorff, *Study of Gregory Palamas*, 194.

99. Hayes, "*Deus in se et Deus pro nobis*," 39.

pears to his saints—whether that is in the theophanies of the Old Testament, in the transfiguration in the Gospels, in the spiritual experiences of today's believers, or in the final vision of Christ in the eschaton. The sacramental perspective that characterized Palamas's theology of the transfiguration shaped therefore also his understanding of the Christian life.

For Palamas, whenever God makes himself visible, he does so in Jesus Christ. This means that the beatific vision not only begins, in a real sense, already today, but is also thoroughly Christ-centered. Hayes rightly suggests that for Palamas the transfiguration "is both the fulfillment and cause of all previous theophanies in the economy of salvation."[100] Old Testament theophanies, therefore, were patterned on the transfiguration and as such were already revelations of the eternal Son of God. Palamas saw this christological character of theophanies continuing into the hereafter and thus as characterizing the beatific vision itself. Comments Hayes: "The Transfiguration is that *toward which* Old Testament theophanies point because the theophany of the eschaton is that *to which* the Transfiguration points."[101] For Palamas, in other words, the eschatological beatific vision will be theophanic in character: it is by seeing Jesus Christ in his hypostatic union that we will see God to the extent that he enables us to participate in his divine energies.[102]

These differences between Aquinas and Palamas lead to different understandings of the beatific vision and, it seems to me, to a christological deficit in Aquinas's theology of the beatific vision. To be sure, not all agree on this latter point. Simon Gaine has recently argued that if Aquinas had been able to finish the third part of the *Summa*, his discussion of the beatific vision would have been christological in character, insofar as Christology is the focus of the *tertia pars*.[103] Gaine acknowledges that Aquinas holds that in the eschaton Christ's humanity will no longer be the medium for human contact with God. But according to Gaine, this does not detract from the Christ-centered character of the beatific vision in Aquinas. After all, argues Gaine, for Aquinas the vision of the essence of God includes, as a secondary object of knowledge, the saving role of Christ's humanity.[104]

100. Hayes, *"Deus in se et Deus pro nobis,"* 151.

101. Hayes, *"Deus in se et Deus pro nobis,"* 151.

102. Cf. Meyendorff, *Study of Gregory Palamas*, 177–84; Williams, *The Ground of Union*, 116–19.

103. Simon Francis Gaine, "Thomas Aquinas and John Owen on the Beatific Vision: A Reply to Suzanne McDonald," *NB* 97 (2016): 434–35.

104. Gaine, "Thomas Aquinas and John Owen," 436.

Moreover, Gaine suggests that although Aquinas did not view Christ as the medium through whom we see God, he did regard Christ as the "place" from which we will be able to see the essence of God directly. So, although Christ's humanity will no longer be the *means* of vision, the union between the head and the members implies that it is nonetheless *in Christ* that we will see the essence of God. "The point is," writes Gaine, "that this light of glory, like grace, is mediated to the members of the Body by the Head, the light of glory of the saints being a participation in the light of glory enjoyed by the Head. In other words, the saints' beatific vision is a participation in Christ's own beatific vision."[105] Gaine is right to suggest that for Aquinas Christ enjoys the light of glory. (In fact, he had this beatific vision from the moment of conception, according to Aquinas.)[106] It is also true that Aquinas insists that the incarnation was necessary (as being the most fitting means of our salvation) in part because it is by Christ's taking on our humanity that we can come to share in the divine nature.[107] What Aquinas does *not* suggest, however, is that it is by participating in *Christ's* beatific vision that *we* will have the beatific vision. To be sure, such a view may be consonant with Aquinas's overall position, but he does not spell this out anywhere. And it seems likely that had this been his actual position, he would explicitly have mentioned it at some point in his relatively prolific writing both on the beatific vision in general and on Christ's own beatific vision.

But let's suppose that Aquinas *did* actually believe that it is by participating in Christ's beatific vision that the saints will have theirs too. While such a view would indeed be quite christological, it is still not quite the same as that of Gregory Palamas. For Palamas, it is by seeing Christ's humanity, body and soul, in a suprasensible and supraintellectual manner, that we also see his divinity. (The notion of Christ having the beatific vision remains beyond the scope of Palamas's considerations.) In other words, it is by a transformation of both the eyes and the intellect that the saints will be able to see the light of Christ's human nature—and it is through their vision of his human nature that they will also be able to see his divine nature. Put differently, the beatific vision, for Palamas, is theophanic in character. His distinction between essence and energies means that we will *never* see the essence of

105. Gaine, "Thomas Aquinas and John Owen," 439.

106. Gaine appeals rightly to *ST* III, q. 9, a. 2, although here Aquinas speaks of the beatific vision that Christ had from the moment of the incarnation. Aquinas does not specifically deal here with the eschaton.

107. Gaine mentions *ST* III, q. 1, a. 2, and I suspect he has in mind Aquinas's notion that through the incarnation we participate in Christ's divinity.

God. We will always only see the divinized Christ, and it is in seeing his body and soul—with our eyes and intellect transformed—that we will see God inasmuch as we can ever see him. Even if Aquinas did hold that the saints see God by participating in Christ's beatific vision, this would still not mean that he also believed that it is *in our vision of Christ* that we will see God in the eschaton. For Aquinas, the theophanic character of God's revelation makes way for a vision of the essence of God; for Palamas, the theophanic character of God's revelation reaches its climax in the transfiguration—in *the vision of the glory of the incarnate Christ*. From a Palamite perspective, the Thomist position can only be regarded as insufficiently christological: for Aquinas, the beatific vision is not the vision of Christ but the vision of the essence of God.

Conclusion

The similarities between Aquinas's and Palamas's interpretations of the trans-figuration are not just minor points, which we can ignore as of little consequence once we notice the rather different spiritual theologies at play in the two interpretations. To be sure, it is highly significant that both Aquinas and Palamas had a sacramental reading of the transfiguration. Both turned to the patristic consensus regarding the hypostatic union so as to insist that the divine clarity of glory was really present on Mount Tabor. Both were convinced that the clarity of Christ's body was not simply a onetime miraculous display of light; for both, the light came not from the outside but from the inside, and as such was a display of the divinity of Christ. (As we have seen, the two theologians present different rationales for the disciples' ability to see this divine light.) Nonetheless, their shared commitment to the hypostatic union as the theological underpinning for the light of the transfiguration is important; neither treats the transfiguration merely as symbolic or as an accidental transformation that takes place from the outside. For both Aquinas and Palamas, it was possible to recognize the divine presence in human form in the transfiguration.

Furthermore, when Aquinas and Palamas claim that the transfiguration was a pledge—an initial realization—of the eschatological kingdom, they suggest that the kingdom was sacramentally present to the disciples' eyes. Again, it is not as though the two approaches are identical. Aquinas distinguished the disciples' sight of Christ's transfigured body from the glory of the beatific vision by explaining that the former was merely a transient passion, and that the light was only similar in splendor to the eschatological clarity of glory. Palamas dealt with the difference between the light of the transfiguration and our future sharing in the divine light by appealing to eternal progress (*epektasis*): our vision of the theophanic appearance of God in Christ progresses eternally, so that it will simply be deepened in the hereafter. Despite this difference between the two theologians, it seems to me highly significant that both maintained that the eschaton can truly break into our time and space, and that it did so for the disciples on Mount Tabor. Inasmuch as they held to the possibility of the future becoming really present in the here and now, both theologians repudiated what Meyendorff terms Barlaam's "nominalist" perspective—a purely symbolic understanding of the transfiguration, in which Mount Tabor would remain hermetically sealed off from heavenly and future glory. Both Aquinas and Palamas offer a healthy antidote to a modern, strictly chronological perspective on time.

Still, we should not ignore the differences. The main difference, in my understanding, is not the way the two theologians articulate their views on the theophanies per se (though, as we have seen, in some ways Palamas held to a more robustly sacramental reading of the transfiguration narratives). The most significant difference has to do with the functioning of the transfiguration in terms of contemporary Christian spirituality. By focusing his exegesis on Christ's preparation of the disciples (and later readers) for the way of martyrdom, Aquinas appears to suggest that the disciples' transfiguration experience was a one-off event, which we should not expect to be repeated. Aquinas did not extend his sacramental understanding of the transfiguration to the spiritual lives of contemporary believers—and it is here that we can see in the Angelic Doctor a harbinger of the later separation of nature and the supernatural.

For Palamas, by contrast, the transfiguration lies at the heart of his understanding of sanctification and deification. It is when we enter more deeply into the life of God and so see Christ's glory that we ourselves participate in the transfiguration theophany. Palamas, in other words, held open the prospect for contemporary Christians to participate, already during their earthly pilgrimage, in the divine, eschatological light of the transfiguration—thereby already experiencing the real presence of the beatific vision of Christ today.

CHAPTER 6

MYSTICAL UNION AND VISION

Symeon the New Theologian and John of the Cross

Theologies of Light and Darkness

Saint Symeon the New Theologian (949–1022) is known as a theologian of light; he reveled in relating his personal visions of the divine light. By contrast, Saint John of the Cross (1542–1591) spoke of the dark night of the soul; reduced to nothing, he failed to see the object of his desire. At a basic level, it may seem obvious that the two types of spirituality represented by these two mystics are incompatible. This was the conclusion, for instance, that Vladimir Lossky drew from his reflections on John of the Cross: "States of dryness, of the dark night of the soul, do not have the same meaning in the spirituality of the Eastern Church, as they have in the West. A person who enters into a closer and closer union with God, cannot remain outside the light. If he finds himself plunged in darkness, it is either because his nature is darkened by sin, or else because God is testing him to increase his ardour."[1] Lossky's theological project of establishing a neo-patristic synthesis was not always friendly to Western doctrine and spirituality.[2] Recent Orthodox readings of John of the Cross have been much more positive about the spirituality of the Carmelite monk, however, and in the process they have (sometimes

1. Vladimir Lossky, *The Mystical Theology of the Eastern Church* (1957; reprint, Cambridge: Clarke, 2005), 225. Lossky goes on to quote Symeon the New Theologian at some length, after which he concludes: "Two different dogmatic conceptions correspond to two different experiences, to two ways of sanctification which scarcely resemble one another" (226).

2. See Aristotle Papanikolaou, "Personhood and Its Exponents in Twentieth-Century Orthodox Theology," in *The Cambridge Companion to Orthodox Christian Theology*, ed. Mary B. Cunningham and Elizabeth Theokritoff (Cambridge: Cambridge University Press, 2008), 232–45.

sharply) criticized Lossky's interpretation of John.[3] These reassessments of John's theology serve the important interest of rapprochement between East and West, something to which I am deeply sympathetic.

This chapter will discuss the compatibility of Symeon's theology of light and John's theology of darkness. My reading of the two has brought me to the conclusion that although they share similar concerns, we should not elide the differences: it is with good reason that Symeon is known as the theologian of light and John as the theologian of darkness. Indeed, I cannot help but think that these differences do bring to the fore broader theological differences between East and West. John's darkness of the cross is predicated on a disjunction between nature and the supernatural, and between mystical union and beatific vision. As a result he has difficulty acknowledging the real presence of the eschatological kingdom in our lives today. Despite certain problems in Symeon's approach, his underlying emphasis on continuity between vision in this life and the next offers a more sacramental way of understanding the beatific vision than does John's sharp differentiation between mystical union in this life and the beatific vision in the next.

I will not argue that John of the Cross entirely fails to acknowledge that already today we have a preliminary advance on the gift of the beatific vision. His spirituality of the dark night of the soul is far too Dionysian (and hence much too paradoxical in character) to allow for such a one-dimensional conclusion. Still, it is fair to say that John's focus is on the abandonment of the cross, whereas Symeon highlights the new life of the resurrection. Without in any way desiring to reignite theological skirmishes between East and West, we may nonetheless have to recognize that Symeon and John do, in some ways, represent typically Eastern and Western theological emphases, respectively. Indeed, perhaps a Western acknowledgment that Symeon offers a certain corrective to John's approach may itself present an ecumenical opening of sorts.

In what follows, I will first give a fairly straightforward exposition of Symeon's theology of light and of John's theology of darkness. Seeing as I cannot possibly do justice to the complete oeuvre of either theologian, I have chosen to focus especially on those passages in Symeon's *Catechetical Discourses* where he relates his personal visions of the light and on those

---

3. Andrew Louth, "Patristic Mysticism and St. John of the Cross," in *The Origins of the Christian Mystical Tradition: From Plato to Denys* (Oxford: Oxford University Press, 1981), 179–90; and David Bentley Hart, "The Bright Morning of the Soul: John of the Cross on Theosis," *ProEccl* 12 (2003): 324–44.

sections in John's *Ascent of Mount Carmel* where he focuses particularly on the dark night of the soul.[4] This will be followed by a comparative analysis of their thought, from which I will conclude that, important similarities notwithstanding, John's theology fails properly to acknowledge the sacramental link between nature and the supernatural and between mystical union and the beatific vision.

Symeon's Visions of Light

Symeon the New Theologian is remarkably direct and experiential in his approach. He relates at some length his personal visions of the light and gives a rather detailed account of the spiritual and emotional experiences that surrounded the events. "No Christian writer before Symeon, not even Saint Augustine," writes George Maloney, "opened his own interior experience of Jesus Christ and the indwelling Trinity to a reading audience as does Symeon."[5] An affective and personal style marks Symeon's writings, and as a result a fairly distinct picture emerges, not only of how he *understood* the theology of light, but also of how he *experienced* the light.

Symeon's overt attention to his subjective spiritual experiences caused him a great deal of grief. By drawing attention to them and insisting that they were normative also for others, Symeon provoked a reaction among the monks at Saint Mamas, who launched a revolt against his leadership (ca. 995–998).[6] Traces of conflict shine through in Symeon's *Catechetical Discourses*, written while he was an abbot at Saint Mamas (ca. 980–998). Faced with the accusation that none of the fathers of the church had made the kind of prideful claims that Symeon seemed to make for himself, the abbot lashes out: "My good man, you deceive yourself! On the contrary, the apostles and

4. I have also collated material from some of their other writings, where this was necessary to avoid a one-sided picture of either theologian.

5. George Maloney, introduction to *The Discourses*, by Symeon the New Theologian, trans. C. J. de Catanzaro (Mahwah, NJ: Paulist, 1980), 13. Cf. Robert Penkett's comment: "Few other Orthodox writers come so close to Augustine (354–430) in the West in their autobiographical style and few other works come so close to his *Confessions* for the wealth of spiritual and theological reflection on what the writer himself had seen and experienced" ("Symeon the New Theologian's Visions of the Godhead," *Phronema* 15 [2000]: 99).

6. See Niketas Stethatos, *The Life of Saint Symeon the New Theologian*, trans. Richard P. H. Greenfield, Dumbarton Oaks Medieval Library 20 (Cambridge, MA: Harvard University Press, 2013), chaps. 38–41 (pp. 82–89). See also Maloney, introduction to *The Discourses*, 9.

the fathers have spoken things that are in harmony with my words, and even go beyond them. . . . If we disclose the truth by speaking of it, they immediately condemn us for being proud and ignore what the holy apostles said. But what did they say? 'We have the mind of Christ' *(1 Cor. 2:6)*. I would say to them, is this, in your judgment, an excess of pride?"[7] Symeon's forceful character, combined with his bold claims of having experienced visions of light, caused sharp dissent within his monastic community.

Symeon could not possibly yield to his opponents. The visions he saw throughout much of his life were only too real, and to him they were incontrovertible evidence of the Spirit's working in him—and hence of the spiritual authority that he had by rights within the monastic community.[8] The first vision occurred when, around age twenty, Symeon worked at the imperial court in Constantinople.[9] Using the stage name of "George," Symeon recounts how in his midteens he had met the famous monk Symeon the Studite, who had given him a book by Mark the Hermit to read.[10] As a result,

7. Symeon, *Discourses* 34.7; quotations come from Symeon the New Theologian, *The Discourses*, trans. C. J. de Catanzaro (New York: Paulist, 1980), here 352–53. For the Greek text, I have consulted Symeon the New Theologian, *Catéchèses*, trans. Joseph Paramelle, ed. Basile Krivochéine, 3 vols., Sources Chrétiennes 96, 104, 113 (Paris: Cerf, 1963–1965).

8. John Anthony McGuckin highlights the relationship between the visions and Symeon's attempts to shore up his authority: "Like all autobiographies it has the double role of articulating to the protagonist himself what was going on in his life, and also of presenting this tale to the reader as part of an elaborate nexus of argument designed to command the reader's allegiance to the spiritual authority the protagonist now claims to exemplify" ("The Luminous Vision in Eleventh-Century Byzantium: Interpreting the Biblical and Theological Paradigms of St. Symeon the New Theologian," in *Work and Worship at Theotokos Evergetis, 1050–1200: Papers of the Fourth Belfast Byzantine International Colloquium, Portaferry, Co. Down, 14–17 September 1995*, ed. Margaret Mullet and Anthony Kirby, Belfast Byzantine Texts and Translations 6.2 [Belfast: Belfast Byzantine Enterprises, 1997], 122).

9. I follow the traditional account of three distinct visions. This chronology is based on Niketas Stethatos, Symeon's follower and biographer (and also adopted by George Maloney, introduction to *The Discourses*, 28–30, and Penkett, "Symeon the New Theologian's Visions of the Godhead"). I do not, however, mean to imply that in every detail this accurately captures the historical chronology of events. It is impossible to trace to what extent the various accounts in the *Discourses* conflate the visionary events. Undoubtedly, McGuckin is right to insist that Symeon's accounts of the epiphanic events are "far from autobiographical in any simple or naive sense of simply 'recounting what happened to him.' Here is a man who was trained rhetorically . . . and who uses his technique and his knowledge (particularly of the scriptures) to telling effect in the process of constructing his religious autobiography" ("Luminous Vision," 121–22).

10. Symeon, *Discourses* 22.2. Hereafter, references from this work will be given in parentheses in the text.

the young Symeon carefully began to follow the commandments, in the hope of experiencing the working of the Holy Spirit. Symeon was "wounded by love and desire for Him," and he began to pray more fervently, tears welling up every evening from his eyes, as he prayed to the Mother of God "with groans and tears" (22.3).

In this state of ardent spiritual anticipation, Symeon experienced his first vision of the light around the year 969:

> One day, as he stood and recited, "God, have mercy upon me, a sinner" *(Lk. 18:13),* uttering it with his mind rather than his mouth, suddenly a flood of divine radiance appeared from above and filled all the room. As this happened the young man lost all awareness [of his surroundings] and forgot that he was in a house or that he was under a roof. He saw nothing but light all around him and did not know if he was standing on the ground. He was not afraid of falling; he was not concerned with the wor[l]d, nor did anything pertaining to men and corporeal beings enter into his mind. Instead, he was wholly in the presence of immaterial light and seemed to himself to have turned into light. Oblivious of all the world he was filled with tears and with ineffable joy and gladness. His mind then ascended and beheld yet another light, which was clearer than that which was close at hand. In a wonderful manner there appeared to him, standing close to that light, the saint of whom we have spoken, the old man equal to angels, who had given him the commandment and the book. . . . Once this vision was over and the young man, as he told me, had come to himself, he was moved with joy and amazement. He wept with all his heart, and sweetness accompanied his tears. Finally he fell on his bed. (22.4 [first set of brackets in original])

Symeon seems to have seen the light in two subsequent stages. Initially light flooded the room, so that he lost awareness of where he was. With the light transforming him (as he "seemed to himself to have turned into light"), his mind then ascended and saw another, even brighter light. Beside it stood his much-revered spiritual father, Symeon the Studite.[11] The vision then ended, with Symeon weeping with joy for what he had just experienced.[12]

---

11. Symeon the Studite was still alive at the time of the vision, since he did not pass away till much later, in 986 or 987. This makes sense of the parallel account in Symeon, *Discourses* 35.5.

12. Symeon seems to refer to this first visionary experience also in *Hymn* 25 (Symeon the New Theologian, *Hymns of Divine Love*, trans. and ed. George A. Maloney [Denville, NJ: Dimension, 1975], 135-38).

Symeon remained in the court for another seven years, a period on which he reflects negatively: "I fell back into my former sins or worse" (35.6).[13] When he entered the Studion monastery in 976, he soon had his second vision of light.[14] After spending a day in the city with his elderly namesake, he returned to the monastery in the evening. Despite his reluctance, at the urging of his spiritual father, Symeon ate and drank. He recounts that, more than ever, he was "burning with ardor": "With keenness of mind I called to mind in a single instant all my sins and was flooded with tears" (16.2). Though convinced he was "unworthy," he placed his trust in God's grace and left for his cell, where he began to cite the Trisagion.[15] Immediately, the vision of light followed:

> At once I was so greatly moved to tears and loving desire for God that I would be unable to describe in words the joy and delight I then felt. I fell prostrate on the ground, and at once I saw, and behold, a great light was immaterially shining on me and seized hold of my whole mind and soul, that I was struck with amazement at the unexpected marvel and I was, as it were, in ecstasy (ἐν ἐκστάσει). Moreover I forgot the place where I stood, who I was, and where, and could only cry out, "Lord, have mercy," so that when I came to myself I discovered that I was reciting this. (16.2)

Confessing that he did not know whether he was in or outside the body (cf. 2 Cor. 12:2), Symeon reports that he conversed with the Light, which expelled from him "all material denseness and bodily heaviness" that made his members "sluggish and numb." It seemed, adds Symeon, "as though I was stripping myself of the garment of corruption" (16.3). Once the light faded, however, Symeon was in "grief" and "vehement pain" (16.4).

Symeon reports that the light that enveloped him was "like a star," or "radiant like the sun," and that he saw "all creation encompassed by it" (16.5). The light also communicated with him: "I am hemmed in by roof and walls, yet it opens the heavens to me. I lift up my eyes sensibly to contemplate the things that are on high, and I see all things as they were before. I marvel at what has happened, and I hear a voice speaking to me secretly from on high, 'These things are but symbols and preliminaries (αἰνίγματά . . . καί προοίμια), for you will not see that

13. Cf. McGuckin, "Luminous Vision," 109.

14. Niketas Stethatos treats the vision of chapter 16 as a separate event, though John Mc-Guckin thinks it is the same as the final vision, recounted in 36.11 ("Luminous Vision," 115).

15. The Orthodox Trisagion—"Holy God, Holy Mighty, Holy Immortal, have mercy upon us"—is based on the seraphim's song of Isa. 6:3.

which is perfect (τέλειον) as long as you are clothed in flesh. But return to your-self and see that you do nothing that deprives you of the things that are above'" (16.5).[16] As a result of the event, Symeon encourages his readers to "acquire a contrite heart, a soul humbled in mind, and a heart that by means of tears and repentance is pure from every stain and defilement of sin," so that "even here and now we may see and enjoy the ineffable blessings of the divine light, if not perfectly, at least in part, and to the extent to which we are able" (16.5).

The third vision took place when Symeon was at Saint Mamas, where he served as abbot for many years, starting around 980. We again read that the vision was preceded by a moral lapse: Symeon had cast himself "into the pit and mud of the abyss *(Ps. 69:3)* of shameful thoughts and deeds" (36.2).[17] Symeon confesses, "Often as I groped for the spring in order to find the water I scratched the earth and stirred up the dust and, since I could not see at all, I bathed my face with mud as though it were water, and thought that I was wash-ing it perfectly clean" (36.4). God's grace, however, overcame his resistance: "Thou didst grasp the hair of my head and forcibly drag me up from thence" (36.3). "Thou camest to me and laidest hold of my head and so didst dip it into the waters and so madest me see more clearly the light of Thy countenance *(cf. Ps. 4:7, 89:16)*" (36.6). God began to cleanse Symeon's face with water, so that he learned to see again: "I saw the lightnings that were flashing about me and the rays of Thy countenance mingled with the waters, and I was struck with amazement as I saw that I was being washed with luminous water" (36.7).

At one point, God drew Symeon into heaven for an hour: "As Thou didst return into heaven Thou didst take me and bring me with Thee. 'Whether in the body or out of the body I do not know' *(2 Cor. 12:2)*. Thou alone knowest, for this was Thy doing!" (36.8). Explaining that what he saw was "a light like a sun without form," Symeon acknowledges that he still did not know who God was, and because of this concealment of God, he kept seeking him: "I longed to see Thy form and consciously to know who Thou wert. Therefore I

16. Cf. Basil Krivochéine's comment about Symeon: "The vision and the union with God begin here on earth. They are given their fulness, however, in the age to come, after the res-urrection" (*In the Light of Christ: Saint Symeon the New Theologian (949–1022); Life—Spiri-tuality—Doctrine*, trans. Anthony P. Gythiel [Crestwood, NY: St. Vladimir's Seminary Press, 1986], 204).

17. These moral lapses—whatever they may have been—need not necessarily have occurred during Symeon's time at Saint Mamas. It is quite possible that also here he conflates the various visionary experiences. In this paragraph and the next two, I recapitulate the gradually evolving events leading up to the third vision in front of the icon of the Theotokos. Cf. McGuckin, "Luminous Vision," 111–12.

continually wept because of the great vehemence and the fire of my love for Thee" (36.8). God repeatedly showed himself to Symeon in hidden fashion, "so that I could not see Thee at all, yet I saw Thy lightning flashes and the brightness of Thy countenance, as aforetime in the waters" (36.9). God continued to cleanse Symeon's mind, "increasing its vision," so that in the end, "Thou who art unmoved didst seem to come, and didst appear to become greater and to take form" (36.9). In this way, God finally became visible to Symeon, and the saint confesses, "Thou . . . didst grant me to see the outline of Thy form beyond shape. At that time Thou tookest me out of the world,"[18] and it seemed clearer than ever before to Symeon that he was indeed out of the body (cf. 2 Cor. 12:2). At this point, Symeon heard the voice of God, and they conversed together as friends. The Lord reminded Symeon that his experience was not yet the eschatological beatific vision itself: "Compared with the blessings to come, this is like a description of heaven on paper held in the hand; for to the extent that this would be inferior to the reality, the glory that will be revealed *(Rom. 8:18)* is incomparably greater than that which you have now seen" (36.10).

As his mind returned to the body, Symeon first wept for joy but then "again fell into sorrow and so I longed to see Thee again" (36.11). Turning to venerate the icon of the Theotokos, Symeon was transfigured more fully than ever before: "Thou Thyself didst appear to me within my poor heart, as though Thou hadst transformed it into light; and then I knew that I have Thee consciously within me. From then onwards I loved Thee, not by recollection of Thee and that which surrounds Thee, nor for the memory of such things, but I in very truth believed that I had Thee, substantial love, within me. For Thou, O God, truly art love *(1 John 4:8, 16)*" (36.11). This time, as Robert Penkett rightly points out, the vision was the result not of the Studite's intercession, but of that of Mary, the Mother of God.[19] And, most significantly, this time Symeon did not have an out-of-body ecstatic experience; instead, God in Christ came to indwell him permanently.

Vision as Union with Christ

This final point—that it is in Christ that God kept appearing to Symeon and then indwelling him—needs to be underscored. For Symeon, the light

---

18. Regarding Symeon's comment that God granted him sight of God's form, Krivochéine comments: "While remaining without form, the Godhead assumes a form in an inconceivable manner and localizes Himself in Symeon's heart" (*In the Light*, 206).

19. Penkett, "Symeon the New Theologian's Visions," 107.

is always the light of Christ.[20] At one point a voice speaks to Symeon from the light: "I am God who have become man for your sake. Because you have sought me with all your soul, behold, from now on you will be My brother *(cf. Mt. 12:50; Mk. 3:35; Lk. 8:21)*, My fellow heir *(cf. Rom. 8:17)*, and My friend *(cf. Jn. 15:14–15)*" (35.10).[21] For Symeon, visions of light occur only inasmuch as the mystic is united to Christ. Thus, Symeon depicts himself as the bride of the Song of Songs, who pursues the groom and who moans and cries when her lover draws away:

> He approached near to me.
> On seeing Him I jumped to my feet
> and I threw myself forward to grasp Him
> and He immediately fled.
> I ran vigorously
> and often, as I ran,
> I succeeded in grasping the fringe of His garment.
> He stopped a bit.
> I was greatly filled with joy;
> and He took off
> and I again in pursuit.
> So He would disappear, then return.
> He would hide, then appear.[22]

Symeon compares his visions of the light—and its withdrawal and subsequent return—to the bride's relationship with the groom. The goal of Symeon's pursuit is always union with Christ.

In this union with Christ, the believer joins him in his suffering, death, and resurrection: "I say and will not cease to say that those who have failed to imitate Christ's sufferings through penitence and obedience and have not become partakers of His death . . . will neither become partakers of His spiritual resurrection nor receive the Holy Spirit" (*Discourses* 6.10).[23] Saint Symeon speaks movingly of the need to follow Christ's example and so to participate in his suffering and death:

20. Cf. Krivochéine, *In the Light*, 239: "For Symeon, Christ is everything." Krivochéine devotes an entire chapter to the centrality of Christ in Symeon's visions (239–58).

21. Twice in his visions, Symeon addresses God as the "God free from pride" (*Discourses* 35.8) or "without pride" (36.6). Cf. Krivochéine, *In the Light*, 241–42.

22. Symeon, *Hymn* 29, in *Hymns of Divine Love*, 154. Cf. Krivochéine, *In the Light*, 244.

23. Cf. Krivochéine, *In the Light*, 243.

Behold, you walk on your way together; someone meets you on the way of life, he slaps your Master in the face, and so he does to you. Your Master does not talk back, do you resist? . . . How will you be a partaker (συγκοινωνὸς) in His glory *(1 Pet. 5:1)* when you refuse to be a partaker (συγκοινωνὸς) of His shameful death? Indeed it is in vain that you have left the world behind, when you are unwilling, as He commanded you, to take up your cross . . . which means that you cheerfully endure the assault of all trials. So you have been abandoned on the way of life and have been miserably separated from your most gentle Master and your God! (27.11)[24]

For Symeon, it is only by sharing in Christ's death that we will also join him in his resurrection.

This union with Christ directly implies, according to Symeon, that we come to see his divine light. In *Catechetical Discourses* 13 ("Of Christ's Resurrection"), Symeon makes clear that Christ's resurrection was not merely a historical event:

That most sacred formula which is daily on our lips does not say, "Having *believed* in Christ's resurrection," but, "Having *beheld* Christ's resurrection, let us worship the Holy One, the Lord Jesus, who alone is without sin." How then does the Holy Spirit urge us to say, "Having *beheld* Christ's resurrection," which we have not seen, as though we had seen it, when Christ has risen once for all a thousand years ago, and even then without anybody's seeing it? Surely Holy Scripture does not wish us to lie? Far from it! Rather, it urges us to speak the truth, that the resurrection of Christ takes place in each of us who believes, and that not once, but every hour, so to speak, when Christ the Master arises in us, resplendent in array *(cf. Ps. 93:1)* and flashing with the lightnings of incorruption and Deity. (13.4)

For Symeon, Christ's resurrection is a matter of sight, not just of faith. The reason is that the resurrection took place not just "a thousand years ago," but it happens "every hour" in the believer. Symeon thus maintains that those who see Christ really have come to participate in the eschatological life of resurrection.[25] Easter, claims Symeon, "happens daily and eternally in those

24. Cf. Krivochéine, *In the Light*, 243–44.

25. Cf. Demetri Stathopoulos's comment, "Through the shining of the Divine Light, the eschatological fulfillment is constantly present. Although man is confined within the limitations of his earthly existence, yet he has begun already to live in the age to come" ("The Divine Light in the Poetry of St. Symeon the New Theologian (949–1025)," *GOTR* 19 [1974]: 107).

who know its mystery" (13.1). The resurrection "takes place mystically in us at all times" (13.2). By sharing in Christ's resurrection and seeing his divinity, we ourselves come to participate in the divine nature.[26]

The overall picture that emerges is that of a wonderful exchange (*admirabile commercium*) between Christ and the believer: "Once He has appropriated what is ours, that which He works in us He attributes to Himself" (13.3). Christ, explains Symeon, "unites Himself to our souls and raises them up, though they were undoubtedly dead, and then grants to him who has thus been raised with Christ that he may see the glory of His mystical resurrection" (13.2). Before this union with Christ, one is worse than blind, because a blind person at least *feels* it when he hits his foot against a stone. "But in spiritual things, unless the mind comes to the contemplation of the things that are above thought, it does not perceive the mystical activity" (13.3).[27] Only if we are united to Christ and his resurrection is it possible to see him in his glory: "Those to whom Christ has given light as He has risen, to them He has appeared spiritually, He has been shown to their spiritual eyes" (13.4). Symeon concludes his discourse with an exhortation to obey the commandments—a feature that permeates his writings. Since faith and works invariably go together, we are to keep the commandments, so that Christ may make his home with us (cf. John 14:21, 23). In this way, by his coming, Christ will "raise from the dead him who has attained faith and give him life, and grant him to see Him who has risen in him and who has raised him up" (13.5). Only if we persevere in keeping God's commandments

26. Symeon repeatedly insists that he not only *saw* the light but also *became* light, so that his vision of God was a deifying vision. He writes, for instance: "God is light *(1 John 1:5)*, and to those who have entered into union with Him He imparts of His own brightness to the extent that they have been purified" (*Discourses* 15.3). By being conformed to the light, the visionary becomes "god by adoption" (15.3), which renders him "a blessed member of the blessed God" (35.3). Krivochéine comments that for Symeon, "deification is the result of union with Christ who acts together with the Father and the Holy Spirit" (*In the Light*, 384). See also Norman Russell, *The Doctrine of Deification in the Greek Patristic Tradition* (Oxford: Oxford University Press, 2004), 301–3.

27. In what follows, I will critique John of the Cross's bifurcation between nature and the supernatural. Symeon's comment that before union with Christ one is worse than blind makes clear that also his theology is marked by at least some degree of duality. Cf. Ivana Noble's comment that "Symeon's accounts of experiences are underpinned by the way in which he opposes the secular and the sacred, the world and God" ("Religious Experience—Reality or Illusion: Insights from Symeon the New Theologian and Ignatius of Loyola," in *Encountering Transcendence: Contributions to the Theology of Christian Religious Experience*, ed. Lieven Boeve, Hans Geybels, and Stijn van den Bossche, Annua Nuntia Lovaniensia 53 [Leuven: Peeters, 2005], 389).

can we expect to see the light of Christ: "So I urge you, let us keep God's commandments with all our might, so that we may . . . enjoy both present and future blessings, that is, the very vision of Christ" (13.5). For Symeon, keeping the commandments will purify us, so that we will truly be united to Christ and be able to see him.[28]

Ascending the Mount: John's Sketch and Poem

The Carmelite friar and priest John of the Cross wrote *The Ascent of Mount Carmel* in the early 1580s, several years after he had escaped from prison in Toledo (1578). In this treatise, the Spanish mystic presents a lengthy account of the Christian pilgrimage. He based his work on a "Sketch of the Mount"[29] and fashioned it as a commentary on his poem "The Dark Night."[30] Since both the sketch and the poem give clear insight into Saint John's theology and spirituality, I will briefly present them before discussing *The Ascent of Mount Carmel* itself in more detail. John placed a copy of the sketch at the beginning of the *Ascent* and provided each of the Carmelite nuns in Beas with a copy of it.[31] At the bottom of the sketch, John presents a poem, which gives instructions for how to climb the mountain:

Para venir a gustarlo todo	To reach satisfaction in all
no quieras tener gusto en nada	desire satisfaction in nothing.
para venir a saberlo todo	To come to the knowledge of all
no quieras saber algo en nada	desire the knowledge of nothing.
para venir a poseerlo todo	To come to possess all

---

28. The emphasis on observing the commandments as a condition for receiving the light is pervasive in Symeon. However, he also speaks of God's light coming to him despite his unworthiness and moral lapses. McGuckin, therefore, suggests that for Symeon, "vision does not necessarily occur 'after' the necessary degrees of repentance, as it does in the classic Christian mystical schemes of Purgative, Illuminative, then Unitive mystical *askesis*. Rather, the unmerited luminous visitation merciful in its essence, elicits repentance and causes purification in its very advent" ("Luminous Vision," 121).

29. See figures 3 and 4 (placed at the end of this chapter), taken from *The Collected Works of Saint John of the Cross*, trans. Kieran Kavanaugh and Otilio Rodriguez, rev. ed. (Washington, DC: ICS, 1991), 110–11. The sketch is also reproduced in Kieran Kavanaugh, *John of the Cross: Doctor of Light and Love* (New York: Crossroad, 1999), 34–35.

30. Kavanaugh, *John of the Cross*, 143.

31. Kavanaugh, "Introduction to *The Ascent of Mount Carmel*," in *The Collected Works of Saint John of the Cross*, 101.

no quieras poseer algo en nada	desire the possession of nothing.
para venir a serlo todo	To arrive at being all
no quieras ser algo en nada.	desire to be nothing.

Para venir a lo que gustas	To come to enjoy what you have not
has de ir por donde	you must go by a way in which you
no gustas	enjoy not.
para venir a lo que no sabes	To come to the knowledge you have not
has de ir por donde	you must go by a way in which you
no sabes	know not.
para venir a poseer lo que no posees	To come to the possession you have not
has de ir por donde	you must go by a way in which you
no posees	possess not.
para venir a lo que no eres	To come to be what you are not
has de ir por donde	you must go by a way in which you
no eres.	are not.

Cuando reparas en algo	When you delay in something
dejas de arrojarte al todo	you cease to rush toward the all.
para venir del todo al todo	To go from the all to the all
has de dejarte del todo en todo	you must deny yourself of all in all.
y cuando lo vengas del	And when you come to the
todo a tener	possession of the all
has de tenerlo sin	you must possess it without
nada querer.	wanting anything.

En esta desnudez halla el	In this nakedness the spirit
espíritu su descanso, porque no	finds its quietude and rest, for in
comunicando nada,	coveting nothing,
nada le fatiga hacia	nothing tires it
arriba, y nada	by pulling it up, and nothing
le oprime	oppresses it
hacia abajo, porque está en	by pushing it down, because it is in
el centro de su humildad.	the center of its humility.

The poem exudes self-denial and asceticism. Every object of one's desire must be renounced: nothing (*nada*) must be pursued, neither satisfaction nor knowledge nor possessions. Thus, the paths of enjoyment, knowledge, and possession must be eschewed and traded for the path of nonbeing (*no eres*). Any delay means defeat; only complete self-denial will do, and once the pilgrim has reached the "all" (*todo*), the pilgrim must possess it without possessiveness—without in any way desiring it. Only in the humility of "nakedness" (*desnudez*) can the spirit find rest. Paradoxically, so it seems, it is in nothingness (*nada*) that one gains all (*todo*).

The sketch itself reinforces this staunch asceticism with a sevenfold claim that the path onto Mount Carmel is the path of "nothing" (*nada*). Even at the top of the mountain, "nothing" is to be found. Along the way, the traveler puts away all desire, for both earthly and heavenly goods, possessions, joy, consolation, and rest. John's attitude regarding these benefits is unequivocal: (1) the more he desired to seek (or possess) them, the less he had; and (2) now that he least (or no longer) desires them, he has them all. It is, therefore, in abandoning all for the sake of nothing that one gains all. The virtues accompanying the upward pilgrimage—piety, charity, fortitude, justice, peace, joy, happiness, and delight—culminate in wisdom at the top of the mountain. John reminds his readers in the sketch's margin that neither suffering nor glory matters to him in any way. At the top of the mountain of perfection, a circle-shaped sentence reads, "I brought you into the land of Carmel to eat its fruit and its good things, (Jer. 2,7)"; and inside the circle, John comments: "Only the honor and glory of God dwells on this mount."

John's poem "The Dark Night" (1578 or 1579), which lies at the back of the treatise *The Ascent of Mount Carmel*, makes clear that the path of renunciation is a path leading into a dark night. The *nada* of Mount Carmel is at the same time a *noche oscura*:

Noche Oscura	**The Dark Night**
Canciones de el alma que se goza de haber llegado al alto estado de la perfección, que es la unión con Dios, por el camino de la negación espiritual.	Songs of the soul that rejoices in having reached the high state of perfection, which is union with God, by the path of spiritual negation.
1. En una noche oscura, con ansias, en amores inflamada ¡oh dichosa ventura!, salí sin ser notada estando ya mi casa sosegada.	One dark night, fired with love's urgent longings —ah, the sheer grace!— I went out unseen, my house being now all stilled.

2. A oscuras y segura,
   por la secreta escala disfrazada,
   ¡oh dichosa ventura!,
   a oscuras y en celada,
   estando ya mi casa sosegada.

   In darkness, and secure,
   by the secret ladder, disguised,
   —ah, the sheer grace!—
   in darkness and concealment,
   my house being now all stilled.

3. En la noche dichosa
   en secreto, que nadie me veía,
   ni yo miraba cosa,
   sin otra luz y guía
   sino la que en el corazón ardía.

   On that glad night
   in secret, for no one saw me,
   nor did I look at anything
   with no other light or guide
   than the one that burned in my heart.

4. Aquésta me guiaba
   más cierto que la luz del mediodía,
   adónde me esperaba
   quien yo bien me sabía,
   en parte donde nadie parecía.

   This guided me
   more surely than the light of noon
   to where he was awaiting me
   —him I knew so well—
   there in a place where no one
      appeared.

5. ¡Oh noche que guiaste!
   ¡Oh noche amable más que
      el alborada!
   ¡Oh noche que juntaste
   Amado con amada,
   amada en el Amado transformada!

   O guiding night!
   O night more lovely than
      the dawn!
   O night that has united
   the Lover with his beloved,
   transforming the beloved in her Lover.

6. En mi pecho florido,
   que entero para él sólo se guardaba,
   allí quedó dormido,
   y yo le regalaba,
   y el ventalle de cedros aire daba.

   Upon my flowering breast,
   which I kept wholly for him alone,
   there he lay sleeping,
   and I caressing him
   there in a breeze from the fanning
      cedars.

7. El aire de la almena,
   cuando yo sus cabellos esparcía,
   con su mano serena
   en mi cuello hería
   y todos mis sentidos suspendía.

   When the breeze blew from the turret,
   as I parted his hair,
   it wounded my neck
   with its gentle hand,
   suspending all my senses.

8. Quedéme y olvidéme,	I abandoned and forgot myself,
el rostro recliné sobre el Amado,	laying my face on my Beloved;
cesó todo y	all things ceased;
dejéme,	I went out from myself,
dejando mi cuidado	leaving my cares
entre las azucenas olvidado.	forgotten among the lilies.[32]

The poem is a retrospective reflection on the dark night, as the soul has already reached the state of perfect union with God. The passionate ardor with which Saint John speaks of the "dark night" (*noche oscura*) shows that it is fundamentally something to be grateful for and to rejoice in. The dark night is a "glad night" (*noche dichosa*) and a "guiding night" (*noche que guiaste*). The darkness of the night has allowed the poet to go out "unseen" (*sin ser notada*). The darkness is hardly an obstacle, seeing as the light burning in his heart was a guide better than the "light of noon" (*la luz del mediodía*). Indeed, this night is "more lovely than the dawn" (*amable más que el alborada*).

It is precisely in the darkness of the night that the union between bride and groom is consummated. Saint John omits any sense of deprivation, abandonment, dryness, or terror, for which the dark night of the soul is usually known. To be sure, as we will see, these elements do form an integral part of John's overall understanding of the dark night. But from the perspective of the perfect union between God and the soul, all this seems forgotten. Instead, the poem's numerous echoes of the Song of Songs transform darkness from something negative into a positive feature.[33] It is the night that has "united" (*juntaste*) the lover with his beloved and that has "transformed" (*transformada*) her into him.[34] The poem's last three stanzas dwell at length on the evocative erotic images of the allegory of the Song to describe the deifying union between lover and beloved in the dark night of the soul.

---

32. *The Collected Works of Saint John of the Cross*, 50–52.

33. Cf. Adam Johnson, "The Crucified Bridegroom: Christ's Atoning Death in St. John of the Cross and Spiritual Formation Today," *ProEccl* 21 (2012): 392–408.

34. Cristóbal Serrán-Pagán y Fuentes comments: "Paradoxically, the Sanjuanist dark night is a glad night because the lover and the beloved are united and transformed by love in the night" ("Mystical Vision and Prophetic Voice in St. John of the Cross: Towards a Mystical Theology of Final Integration" [PhD diss., Biola University, 2003], 137).

Dark Nights of the Soul

As John analyzes the journey to the summit of Mount Carmel, he explains that the one dark night can be broken down into three nights (or three aspects).[35] Here Saint John essentially follows the Dionysian division of the pilgrimage into the three aspects of purgation, illumination, and union.[36] The first step concerns the point of departure, where "individuals must deprive themselves of their appetites for worldly possessions" (1.2.1). John refers to this as the "night of the senses" (*noche del sentido*), since at this stage the sensible appetites must be purged (1.2.5; cf. 1.1.4). The second step has to do with faith, since the intellect experiences the light of faith as a dark night (1.2.1). Finally, the third night pertains to God as the point of arrival: "God is also a dark night to the soul in this life" (1.2.1).[37] Saint John explains that the three so-called nights are actually three parts of one night: "The first part, the night of the senses, resembles early evening, that time of twilight when things begin to fade from sight. The second part, faith, is completely dark, like midnight. The third part, representing God, is like the very early dawn just before the break of day" (1.2.5).

John deals with the role of faith—the second night—particularly in book 2, and in what follows I will highlight some of the key themes that he brings to the fore here. Throughout, he discusses faith as the "secret ladder" mentioned in the second stanza of "The Dark Night." The reason that the secret ladder represents faith is that "all the rungs or articles of faith are secret to and hidden from both the senses and the intellect" (2.1.1). The poem describes the house as "being now all stilled," "because once the soul attains union with God, the natural faculties and the impulses and anxieties of the spiritual part remain at rest" (2.1.2). By this time, the night of the senses—the topic of the first stanza—has long passed. We now enter the "night of the spirit" (*noche del espíritu*) (2.12.1), where it is no longer the senses but instead the "spiritual faculties and gratifications and

---

35. *Ascent* 1.2.1. Hereafter, references to *The Ascent of Mount Carmel* will be given in parentheses in the text; quotations come from *The Collected Works of Saint John of the Cross*. For the Spanish edition, I have consulted Juan de la Cruz, *Obras completes*, ed. José Vincente Rodríguez and Frederico Ruiz Salvador, 3rd ed. (Madrid: Editorial de Espiritualidad, 1988).

36. One chapter earlier (in *Ascent* 1.1), John had presented a different breakdown, speaking of a night of the senses and a night of the spirit, and insisting that both have an active and a passive aspect: both human effort and the work of God are at play in the purification of the senses and of the spirit.

37. Later, John explains that the new daylight must be compared to God: "For when these three parts of the night—which are night to the soul from a natural viewpoint—have passed, God supernaturally illumines the soul with a ray of his divine light. This light is the principle of the perfect union that follows after the third night" (2.2.1).

appetites" that must be negated (2.1.2). This self-denial will lead the soul to union with her beloved. This darkness of the spirit is much more intense than the earlier darkness of the senses, since now the "spiritual night, which is faith, removes everything, both in the intellect and in the senses" (2.1.3). Now the dark night blinds the light of reason (2.2.2). The resulting experience is one of spiritual dryness, in which the soul loses all sense of God's nearness and may despair because of her own sin and spiritual emptiness.[38]

In this darkness of the spirit, the believer comes to share in the suffering and death of Christ. Saint John reflects on this by way of a meditative excursus on Matthew 7:14, "*Quam angusta porta et arcta via est quae ducit ad vitam! Et pauci sunt qui inveniunt eam* (How narrow is the gate and constricting the way that leads to life! And few there are who find it)" (2.7.2). John wants his readers to note especially the hyperbolic word *quam* (how): "This is like saying: Indeed the gate is very narrow, more so than you think." The "gate of Christ," explains John, is the "night of sense." It involves leaving behind "all sensible and temporal objects" (2.7.2). When Jesus next speaks of a "constricting" way, he has in mind obstacles that concern the spiritual or rational part of the soul (2.7.3). This is the night of the spirit, and John warns his readers not to be content too quickly with the success of their renunciation (2.7.5). On the narrow road, "there is room only for self-denial (as our Savior asserts) and the cross" (2.7.7).

Progress on the "constricted way" (*arcta via*) is entirely dependent on *imitatio Christi*: "I would not consider any spirituality worthwhile that wants to walk in sweetness and ease and run from the imitation of Christ," writes John (2.7.8). As he outlines what this imitation entails, he insists that Christ not only died to the "sensitive part"—having no place to lay his head (cf. Matt. 8:20) and dying a natural death (2.7.10)—but he was also "annihilated (*aniquilado*) in his soul," as the Father left him "without any consolation or relief" (cf. Matt. 27:46) (2.7.11). Indeed, Christ was "reduced to nothing (*resuelto . . . en nada*), so as to pay the debt fully and bring people to union with God." The purpose of Christ's complete self-emptying is that in their "annihilation" (*aniquilare*), believers too may be "reduced to nothing" (*resuelto en nada*) and so achieve spiritual union with God. For John, it makes no sense for believers to pursue "consolations, delights, and spiritual feelings," when they really only can achieve spiritual union with God "in the living

---

38. John H. Coe mentions "spiritual dryness, distance from God, frustration, sense of moral failure, loneliness, spiritual impotence, and confusion over allegiance to the world, self, or God" ("Musings on the Dark Night of the Soul: Insights from St. John of the Cross on a Developmental Spirituality," *JPT* 28 [2000]: 302).

death of the cross, sensory and spiritual, exterior and interior" (2.7.11). To be sure, the dark night of the soul is not simply the same as the darkness that Christ himself experienced. For believers, the darkness is merely purgative in character, cleansing them of sin and so preparing them for union with God.[39] Indeed, it is because Christ obtained our redemption on the cross that John can describe the dark night in his poem as a "glad night" (*noche dichosa*) and as a "guiding night" (*noche que guiaste*).

Saint John draws on the Dionysian paradox of "luminous darkness" in discussing the nature of faith and the dark night of the spirit. He explains that just as the sun obscures other lights and "overwhelms, blinds, and deprives" the eyes of vision, so the light of faith "suppresses and overwhelms" the light of the intellect (2.3.1). The reason that faith blinds the soul is that "it informs us of matters we have never seen or known, either in themselves or in their likenesses. In fact, nothing like them exists" (2.3.3). Faith, therefore, is a dark night with respect to the understanding. At the same time, faith does provide its own light: "The more darkness it [i.e., faith] brings on them, the more light it sheds" (2.3.4). After all, when the Israelites came to the Red Sea, a dark cloud illuminated the night (Exod. 14:20). A person in darkness can only receive enlightenment from another darkness, claims Saint John with an appeal to Psalm 18:3 (19:2; "Day to day pours out speech, / and night to night reveals knowledge"). He then adds:

> Expressed more clearly, this means: The day, which is God (in bliss where it is day), communicates and pronounces the Word, his Son, to the angels and blessed souls, who are now day; and this he does that they may have knowledge and enjoyment of him. And the night, which is the faith, present in the Church Militant where it is still night, manifests knowledge to the Church and, consequently, to every soul. This knowledge is night to souls because they do not yet possess the clear beatific wisdom, and because faith blinds them as to their own natural light. (2.3.5)

Here John explains that the knowledge of faith is night, not only because it is *dark* in comparison to the beatific vision faith, but also because the light of faith is so *bright* that it blinds the natural understanding. This blinding character of faith reminds John of the Dionysian paradox of darkness and light.

We may want to inquire more deeply, however, into the question of how Saint John understands the relationship between faith and reason, or be-

---

39. Cf. Johnson, "The Crucified Bridegroom," 399.

tween natural understanding and the supernatural gift of faith. He sharply distinguishes between what he terms "substantial union" (*unión sustancial*) and "union of likeness" (*unión de semejanza*) (2.5.3). The former is a natural union, and in that sense everyone is united to God, since God dwells substantially in every soul: "This union between God and creatures always exists. By it he conserves their being so that if the union should end they would immediately be annihilated and cease to exist." The latter is a supernatural union, which occurs only where there is a "likeness of love" (*semejanza de amor*) (2.5.3). This latter union or likeness allows for degrees, since it is "to the soul that is more advanced in love, more conformed to the divine will" that God communicates himself more (2.5.4). The rebirth that the Holy Spirit works renders people more like God in purity. In this way, claims John, "pure transformation can be effected—although not essentially—through the participation of union (*participación de unión*)" (2.5.5). The result is that the soul becomes "God by participation" (*Dios por participación*) (2.5.7). The gift of faith results in "union of likeness" and so in divinization.

This rebirth of the Holy Spirit, effecting a transition from nature to grace—or from "substantial union" to "union of likeness"—implies, for John, a radical renunciation, not only of the intellect but also of the other faculties of the soul. The requirement that the soul must be blinded means that people can no longer be attached "to any understanding, feeling, imagining, opinion, desire, or way of their own" (2.4.4). "They must," insists John with Dionysian flair, "pass beyond everything to unknowing (*sobre todo se ha de pasar al no saber*)" (2.4.4).[40] The reason for this is the utter dissimilarity between creator and creature: there is no proportionality between the human intellect and God.[41] This rejection of the traditional doctrine

40. John was heir to a tradition of affective Franciscan spirituality that traced its roots to Dionysius. Luis Girón-Negrón explains that the *recogidos* movement in early sixteenth-century Spain advocated an affective spirituality that drew on the sixth-century Syrian monk in promoting a radically apophatic mysticism ("Dionysian Thought in Sixteenth-Century Spanish Mystical Theology," *ModTh* 24 [2008]: 693–706). John thus turned to Dionysius's apophatic path of unknowing to advocate a strict renunciation of intellect, memory, and will. For additional historical background, see David B. Perrin, "The Unique Contribution of John of the Cross to the Western Mystical Tradition," *ScEs* 51 (1999): 199–230.

41. John writes, for example, that "among all creatures, both superior and inferior, none bears a likeness to God's being or unites proximately with him. Although truly, as theologians say, all creatures carry with them a certain relation (*certa relación*) to God and a trace of him (greater or less according to the perfection of their being), yet God has no relation (*ningún respecto*) or essential likeness (*semejanza esencial*) to them. Rather the difference that lies between his divine being and their being is infinite. Consequently, intellectual comprehension of

of analogy pertains also to the intellect, since the intellect works through sensible observation or images presented to the faculties of the imagination and of fantasy.[42] Dionysius, Baruch, Aristotle, and Paul all agree, according to Saint John, on this radical equivocity between God and the intellect.[43] The soul "must strip itself of everything pertaining to creatures and of its actions and abilities (of its understanding, satisfaction, and feeling)" (2.5.4). Each of the faculties—understanding, memory, and will—must enter into the spiritual night. This purgation implies not a transformation of the faculties but requires their complete abandonment and rejection in the darkness of the night. The faculties must be fully emptied out. Relating understanding, memory, and will to the virtues of faith, hope, and love, respectively, Saint

---

God through heavenly or earthly creatures is impossible; there is no proportion of likeness (*no hay proporción de semejanza*)" (*Ascent* 2.8.3). Similarly, John suggests, "Everything the intellect can understand, the will enjoy, and the imagination picture is most unlike and disproportioned (*muy disímil y desproporcionado*) to God" (2.8.5).

42. I cannot agree, therefore, with Karol Wojtyła's suggestion that John of the Cross does teach the analogy of being. In his analysis of *Ascent* 2.8, Wojtyla argues that John merely rejects a likeness between creator and creature with regard to essence: "No creature, even the most perfect, considered in its essence, can be compared to the divine essence" (*Faith according to St. John of the Cross*, trans. Jordan Aumann [San Francisco: Ignatius, 1981], 40). Wojtyla suggests that despite positing an infinite difference in essence between creator and creature, John's approach is basically that of the Fourth Lateran Council and of Thomas Aquinas (40–41). But this ignores that John nowhere positively acknowledges *any* proportional similitude between creator and creature. He only and insistently drives home the difference between creator and creature. Hans Urs von Balthasar also wrongly suggests that John of the Cross does teach the analogy of being (*The Glory of the Lord: A Theological Aesthetics*, vol. 3, *Lay Styles*, trans. Andrew Louth et al., ed. John Riches [1986; reprint, San Francisco: Ignatius, 2004], 140, 149).

43. John explains (in *Ascent* 2.8.6) that contemplation is called "mystical theology," which is secret to the intellect, so that Dionysius refers to it as a "ray of darkness" (cf. *MT* 1000A, in *Pseudo-Dionysius: The Complete Works*, trans. Colm Luibheid, ed. Paul Rorem [Mahwah, NJ: Paulist, 1987], p. 135); the prophet Baruch explains that no one knows the way of wisdom or can think of her paths (Bar. 3:23); Aristotle maintains "that just as the sun is total darkness to the eyes of a bat, so the brightest light in God is total darkness to our intellect" (cf. *Metaph.* 2.1); and Paul also teaches that "what is highest in God is least known by humans" (cf. Rom. 11:33). John's use of these sources is at best one-sided. Aristotle famously discussed the analogy of being in *Metaph.* 4.2 (1003a33–b5), an important source for Aquinas's later articulation of it. Moreover, John's appropriation of Dionysius's apophaticism ignores that for Dionysius, the way of negation is based on a prior affirmation of creation as analogous to God. He comments, for instance, "We use whatever appropriate symbols we can for the things of God. With these analogies we are raised upward toward the truth of the mind's vision, a truth which is simple and one" (*DN* 592C, in *Pseudo-Dionysius: The Complete Works*, 53). Cf. Alec Andreas Arnold, "Christ and Our Perception of Beauty: The Theological Aesthetics of Dionysius the Areopagite and Hans Urs von Balthasar" (ThM thesis, Regent College, 2015), 13–45.

John comments: "These virtues, as we said, void the faculties: Faith causes darkness and a void of understanding in the intellect, hope begets an emptiness of possessions in the memory, and charity produces the nakedness and emptiness of affection and joy in all that is not God" (2.6.2).[44] It is hard to avoid the conclusion that for John, grace comes close to destroying, rather than perfecting, nature.[45]

Imaginative Visions

Because of the radical character of the dark night of the spirit, John was deeply suspicious of spiritual experiences that aim to alleviate this darkness. Genuine spirituality, he claims, does not seek "sweetness and delightful communications" from God. "A genuine spirit," he continues, "seeks rather the distasteful in God than the delectable, leans more toward suffering than toward consolation, more toward going without everything for God than toward possession, and toward dryness and affliction than toward sweet consolation" (2.7.5). The Christian journey "does not consist in consolations, delights, and spiritual feelings, but in the living death of the cross, sensory and spiritual, exterior and interior" (2.7.11). Rather than use the exterior senses, supernaturally induced "imaginative visions" (*visiones imaginarias*) present images to the intellect by means of the faculty of fantasy (2.16.2), and John cautions that both God and the devil can use this faculty to present visions to the soul (2.16.3–4). People should "neither feed upon nor encumber themselves" with such visions, regardless of whether they have divine or diabolical origin (2.16.6).

The most basic reason for John's caution is not even that the devil's schemes can deceive people.[46] Instead, the foundational theological rationale has to do with the simplicity of God, which transcends the forms and images of visions: "God's wisdom, to which the intellect must be united, has neither mode nor manner, neither does it have limits nor does it pertain to distinct and particular knowledge, because it is totally pure and simple"

---

44. John expounds at some length on the emptying of each of the faculties (*Ascent* 2.6.2–4).

45. For more positive assessments of Saint John of the Cross on this point, see Denys Turner, *The Darkness of God: Negativity in Christian Mysticism* (Cambridge: Cambridge University Press, 1995), 246; and Hart, "Bright Morning," 339–40.

46. John dwells at length on the dangers surrounding imaginative visions and explains that it is easy to be misled by them, even when they are divine in origin (*Ascent* 2.18–19).

(2.16.7).[47] Scripture, after all, makes clear that at Mount Sinai the Israelites "saw absolutely no form in God" (cf. Deut. 4:12) and "did not see God in any image" when he spoke to them from the midst of the fire (cf. Deut. 4:15) (*Ascent* 2.16.8). Similarly, explains John, Moses did "not see God through comparisons, likenesses, and figures" (cf. Num. 12:6–8) (2.16.9). Peter, although he did see Christ's glory in the transfiguration, did not want his readers to rely on this and instead pointed them to the "words of the prophets bearing testimony to Christ which you must make good use of, as a candle shining in a dark place" (cf. 2 Pet. 1:19) (2.16.15). Significantly, the Carmelite mystic adds the comment: "Manifestly, in this high state of union God does not communicate himself to the soul—nor is this possible—through the disguise of any imaginative vision, likeness, or figure, but mouth to mouth: the pure and naked essence (*esencia pura y desnuda*) of God (the mouth of God in love) with the pure and naked essence (*esencia pura y desnuda*) of the soul (the mouth of the soul in the love of God)" (2.16.9). One only reaches this "essential union" (*unión esencial*) of love by renouncing and avoiding all "imaginative visions, forms, figures, or particular ideas" (2.16.10). Thus, according to John, Scripture shows that God's simplicity makes it impossible to be united with him through imaginative visions.

The pursuit of visions and revelations bothers John particularly because he is convinced that such a quest bypasses God's ultimate self-disclosure in Christ: "Those who now desire to question God or receive some vision or revelation are guilty not only of foolish behaviour but also of offending him by not fixing their eyes entirely on Christ and by living with the desire for some other novelty" (2.22.5). God can only respond to such people by insisting: "If I have already told you all things in my Word, my Son, and if I have no other word, what answer or revelation can I now make that would surpass this? Fasten your eyes on him alone because in him I have spoken and revealed all and in him you will discover even more than you ask for and desire. . . . For he is my entire locution and response, vision and revelation, which I have already spoken, answered, manifested, and revealed to you by giving him to you as a brother, companion, master, ransom, and reward." John appeals to the Father's words spoken at Mount Tabor: "This is my beloved Son, with whom I am well pleased; listen to him" (Matt. 17:5). Desiring visions or revelations would be like demanding a second incarnation, claims

---

47. Cf. the discussion on divine simplicity (including insightful reflections on *Ascent* 2.16.6–7) in A. N. Williams, "The Doctrine of God in San Juan de la Cruz," *ModTh* 30 (2014): 504–7.

John (2.22.5). He was convinced that the unsurpassable character of God's revelation in Christ should caution us against the consolation of visions or revelations.

To be sure, John did not categorically reject all imaginary visions. God gives them to whomever he wants, whenever he wants, and human beings are passive in this process (2.16.11). It is just that we are not to *seek* such visions, since they involve multiple particular images, which are presented to the intellect. But that God does give such visions to people as an integral part of their spiritual journey is something John does not want to gainsay: God first perfects the corporeal senses (using sermons, masses, holy objects, physical renunciation) (2.17.4). He then gives supernatural communications (visions of saints or holy things, sweet odors, locutions, and the like). God also perfects the interior bodily senses of the natural use of the imagination and fantasy (through "considerations, meditations, and holy reasonings"). Most notably, God further enlightens people by means of "supernatural imaginative visions from which the spirit profits notably" (2.17.4). God does use imaginative visions in the process of bringing the soul to union with him.

Even such supernatural visions, however, are only sacramental means. Such images "are like curtains and veils covering the spiritual goods they contain" (2.16.11). We ought not to focus on sensible, exterior means. God gives them "so that by means of the rind (*corteza*) of those sensible things, in themselves good, the spirit, making progress in particular acts and re-ceiving morsels of spiritual communication, may form a habit in spiritual things and reach the actual substance (*sustancia*) of spirit foreign to all sense" (2.17.5). Appealing to 1 Corinthians 13:11 ("When I was a child, I spoke like a child, I thought like a child, I reasoned like a child. When I became a man, I gave up childish ways"), Saint John cautions against attachment to sensible things: "In their attachment to the rind (*corteza*) of sense (the child), they will never reach the substance (*sustancia*) of spirit (the perfect person)" (2.17.6). So, whereas the Lord uses outward means such as visions because they befit human nature, we should not be satisfied with such "morsels for the senses" (cf. Ps. 147:17).

Saint John summarizes his position by commenting: "Individuals must not fix the eyes of their souls on that rind (*corteza*) of the figure and object supernaturally accorded to the exterior senses, such as locutions and words to the sense of hearing; visions of saints and beautifully resplendent lights to the sense of sight; fragrance to the sense of smell; delicious and sweet tastes to the palate; and other delights, usually derived from the spirit, to the sense of touch, as is more commonly the case with spiritual persons.

Neither must they place their eyes on interior imaginative visions. They must instead renounce all these things" (2.17.9). John's overriding concern is that by focusing on the outward sacrament (*sacramentum*) the soul will miss out on the inward reality (*res*). By renouncing the multiplicity of the outward sacrament of the senses, the intellect enters into darkness, and only so will it attain to the inward reality of the light of divine simplicity.[48]

Finally, and perhaps most significantly for our chapter, John straight-forwardly rejects the possibility of seeing the essence of God in this life. When he speaks of spiritual visions of incorporeal substances (angels and souls), he comments simply that they do not occur in this life in the mortal body (2.24.2). He then discusses the possibility of seeing the divine essence, and he reminds his readers that Scripture links the vision of God's essence with death: Moses was told that no one could see God and live (Exod. 33:20); the Israelites were afraid they would die if they were to see God (Exod. 20:19); Manoah, Samson's father, feared death because he thought he and his wife had seen God (Judg. 13:22) (*Ascent* 2.24.2). John then comments, taking a page out of Aquinas's book of idioms, that such visions "do not occur in this life, unless in some rare cases and in a transient way (*por vía de paso*)" (2.24.3).[49] He refers to the "substantial visions" of Paul (2 Cor. 12:2–4), of Moses (Exod. 33:22), and of Elijah (1 Kings 19:11–13) as examples of visions that, "even though transitory, occur rarely or hardly ever, and to only a few" (2.24.3). The vision of the essence of God is something almost strictly reserved for the hereafter.[50] In

48. Notwithstanding his rejection of the *analogia entis*, therefore, one could say that for John a proportional relationship does obtain between God and faith. Once through faith the human faculties have completely emptied out the multiplicity of their contents, they are then fitted for divine union with the God who is utterly simple. Wojtyla suggests, therefore, that faith "is the *proportionate* means of union, and therefore it possesses an *essential likeness* to God" (*Faith*, 42). I agree with Wojtyla's description of the role of faith, but we should keep in mind that Saint John does not use the language of "proportionality" or "essential likeness" to describe the union with God atop Mount Carmel.

49. John's discussion at this point relies at least partially on Thomas Aquinas's *Quodlibetum* I, q. 1, which John references explicitly in the previous paragraph (*Ascent* 2.24.1). Aquinas, in *Quodlibet* I, q. 1, asks whether Saint Benedict saw the divine essence when in a vision he saw the entire world. Aquinas answers negatively on the grounds that we cannot see the divine essence as long as we are tied to our mortal bodies.

50. David Bentley Hart argues that although John of the Cross did not make the Palamite distinction between essence and energies, nonetheless "his use of terms such as 'power,' 'glory,' 'fire,' 'light,' 'will,' and 'action' describes a general demarcation between what can properly be said of active union and what cannot (i.e., 'coessentiality')" ("Bright Morning," 338). On my reading, John is closer to Thomas than to Palamas. John suggests that whereas in this life it

this life, we must be content with the darkness of the light of faith, which God gives to those who seek union with him.

Conclusion

Symeon the New Theologian and John of the Cross are not each other's polar opposite. Both were affective theologians for whom the experience of faith—or the absence of such experience—was of utmost importance. Although John of the Cross was much more of a dogmatic theologian than Symeon, for both mystics the soul's relationship with God was paramount in the articulation of the faith. And although it is true that Symeon is often autobiographical whereas John usually takes on a more didactic mode, this does not gainsay that for both theology was mystagogical in character.

Moreover, the pilgrimage of faith looks in many ways similar for Symeon and John. Renunciation—at least with regard to the senses—was important to both (though John highlights it much more than does Symeon). Both were deeply aware of their unworthiness before God and of the need for repentance and purgation. Both aimed at union with God and regarded deification as the ultimate aim of the spiritual journey. Both had recourse to the bridal mysticism of the Song of Songs in their descriptions of the quest for mystical union. Both were aware that all sorts of obstacles lie strewn across the road toward union and that the dangers of self-deception are numerous and severe. Perhaps Symeon is more prickly and sharp in his comments about this, but likely this is mostly a consequence of the stiff opposition he faced from some of his monks. Both spiritual masters had a keen eye for the spiritual dangers on the journey and aimed to lead their readers to union with God in Christ.

We must also do justice to some of the ways in which Symeon was actually a theologian of *darkness* and John a theologian of *light*. Symeon often lamented the absence of Christ; he shed tears of grief over the departure of the light; and he acknowledged that he backslid even after having seen the glory of the Lord.[51] Also, as we have noted, it was important for Symeon not only to participate in Christ's resurrection but also to share in his suffering and death. Conversely, although John quotes Dionysius only four times, he

---

is impossible to see the divine essence in mystical union, in the beatific vision we *will* attain to the essence of God.

51. Hart rightly observes: "Symeon the New Theologian may have given voice principally, in his poetry, to his ecstasies, but his treatises leave no doubt that between his episodes of spiritual exaltation lay prolonged intervals of despondency and misery" ("Bright Morning," 326).

was deeply shaped by the apophatic mysticism of the sixth-century monk. For John, the torment and affliction of the dark night of the soul stem precisely from the soul's inability to endure the light.[52] He saw darkness not *just* as darkness, and he did not *only* associate it with the cross. It may only be one aspect of the soul's dark night, but we do need to do justice to its Dionysian, paradoxical character as a blinding light.

All that being said, the two theologians differed considerably in their respective evaluations of visionary experiences. Symeon relentlessly focused on light, deeply desired the positive experience that this light offers, and insisted that the ability to see it constitutes the sine qua non of Christian experience. Without it, Symeon opined, one really ought to question the genuine character of one's repentance and faith. John, by contrast, warned in no uncertain terms against the dangers of "imaginative visions" and other spiritual experiences. For John, they cannot possibly constitute the ultimate aim of the Christian pilgrimage, and they may well imply a not-so-subtle focus on oneself rather than on Christ. Thus, where Symeon pulls us into the light of the risen Lord, John demands that we take refuge in the darkness of the cross. Where Symeon looked for the consolation of encounters with Christ, John was convinced that such visions actually run the danger of bypassing him. Where for Symeon visions of Christ were indispensable evidence of the gifting of the Spirit, John believed they may indicate a desire for self-gratification. At this basic level of the desirability of "imaginative visions," the two theologies are simply incompatible.

The difference between the two cannot easily be downplayed. For Symeon, the insistence on seeing the light of Christ stems directly from his conviction that the real presence of the eschatological kingdom of light pervades the lives of believers already today. Symeon—much like other theologians of the East—treats the epiphanies of light as an initial (we could say, sacramental) pledge of the much greater glory yet to come. Jesus himself reminds Symeon in his second vision, "These things are but symbols and preliminaries, for

---

52. John comments, for instance: "When the divine light of contemplation strikes a soul not yet entirely illumined, it causes spiritual darkness, for it not only surpasses the act of natural understanding, but it also deprives the soul of this act and darkens it. This is why St. Dionysius and other mystical theologians call this infused contemplation a 'ray of darkness'—that is, for the soul not yet illumined and purged. For this great supernatural light overwhelms the intellect and deprives it of its natural vigor" (*Dark Night* 2.5.3, in *The Collected Works of Saint John of the Cross*, 402). Cf. *Dark Night* 2.5.5 (pp. 402–3); 2.12.5 (p. 423); 2.17.2 (p. 436). Cf. also Girón-Negrón, "Dionysian Thought," 700–702; and Andrew Louth, *The Origins of the Christian Mystical Tradition: From Plato to Denys* (Oxford: Oxford University Press, 1981), 184–85.

you will not see that which is perfect as long as you are clothed in flesh."[53] Because John was convinced—and in this he is a typical representative of Western theology—that in the hereafter we will see the essence of God, he posits much more of a disjunction between today's darkness of the cross and the light of glory to come. John's Dionysian paradox of the blinding light may soften the contrast between the two theologians, but it hardly removes it.

The Byzantine mystic seems to me least attractive when he chides those who have not (yet) seen a vision of light and do not regard it as a core Christian experience. But perhaps we ought not to dismiss Symeon's harsh words altogether: they may contain an important element of truth. After all, one important corollary of his theology of light is the recognition that the eschatological light of glory is, in some way, already present in our lives today. John of the Cross, it seems to me, insufficiently acknowledged this sacramental presence of the eschaton in our lives.[54] Dark nights of the soul do occur, but they are not the be-all and end-all of Christian spirituality. Perhaps, therefore, John unduly downplayed the connection between the transfiguration light (as a this-worldly possibility) and the beatific vision of the eschaton.

Given his Dionysian proclivities, it seems odd that John would so sharply distinguish the dark night of the soul from the eschatological beatific vision. After all, the Dionysian aspect of his thought implies that the blinding, divine light reaches people already today—not just Moses, Elijah, and Paul. It was the aim of John's spiritual direction to lead every one of his readers into the dark night of the soul. One would think that this implies that the eschaton *does* cast its rays into our lives and so becomes sacramentally present to us. But John's sharp distinction between mystical union (the Dionysian dark night) and beatific vision (the eschatological sight of God's essence) prevented him from treating the former as a genuine pledge of the latter. And so we must ask the question: If it is the light of God that already today casts one into apophatic darkness, then how can it be that the glorious vision of the divine essence is reserved for the beatific vision in the hereafter? John's approach to seeing the essence of God does not fit the broader Dionysian contours of his understanding of the dark night. For consistency's sake, John

53. Symeon, *Discourses* 16.5. Recall also Jesus's comment to Symeon that his vision was "like a description of heaven on paper held in the hand" (*Discourses* 36.10). See above, p. 170.

54. As we have seen, Saint John does use sacramental-like discourse by arguing that we must leave behind the rind (*corteza*) of sense for the sake of the substance (*sustancia*) of the spirit. But the substance of which he speaks here is that of mystical union with God, something he explicitly distinguishes from seeing the essence of God in the hereafter.

would have done well to abandon the less fortunate binaries that characterize his theology, namely, that of nature and the supernatural as well as that
of mystical union and the beatific vision. A dogmatic implication, I think,
would be that we correct the inadequacies of John's legacy in this regard. Already today, we participate in some way in the very telos of our lives, namely,
the vision of God in Christ. A robust acknowledgment in this regard would
lead to a more sacramental understanding of the beatific vision than John of
the Cross presented. In the process, we would bridge the East-West divide
on a key point of spiritual theology.

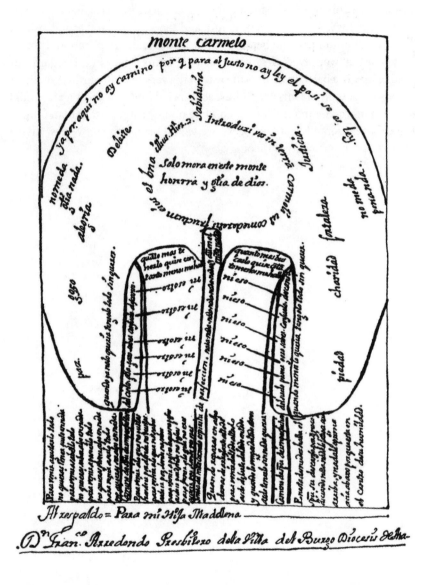

Figure 3. Sketch of Mount Carmel by St. John of the Cross.
From *John of the Cross: Selected Writings*, ed. Kieran Kavanaugh (Classics of Western Spirituality series, ed. Dr. John Farina). Reprinted by kind permission of Paulist Press.

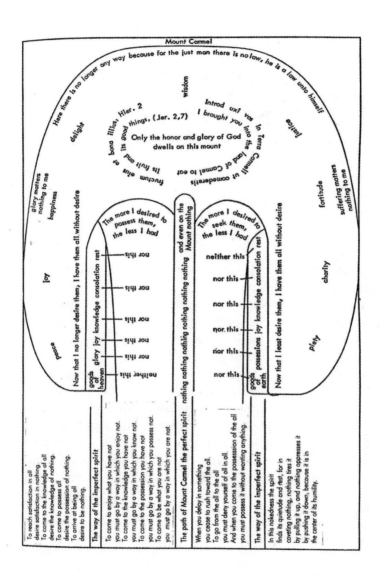

Figure 4. English translation of terms used in St. John's original drawing.
From *John of the Cross: Selected Writings*, ed. Kieran Kavanaugh (Classics of Western Spirituality series, ed. Dr. John Farina). Reprinted by kind permission of Paulist Press.

CHAPTER 7

FACULTIES AND VISION

Bonaventure and Nicholas of Cusa

Joining Knowledge and Love

The question of how knowledge and love relate to one another, and how they in turn relate to Christ as the central object of the Christian faith, has occupied theologians throughout the centuries. They have often ranked knowledge and love, intellect and will, in order of priority. Either one or the other has to take the lead, so it would appear. Most often perhaps, theologians have sided with the intellect as being first in line. Many representatives of both East and West have maintained that it is only possible to will something if one has already made an intellectual judgment that the object of the will is in fact a good that is worthy of one's pursuit. This intellectualist position, flourishing particularly within Christian Platonism, has typically resulted in a doctrine of the beatific vision that equates the *visio Dei* with knowledge of God, so that the enjoyment (*fruitio*) of this vision, as an act of the will, is regarded as a second step, something that follows the beatific vision itself.[1]

---

1. Thomas Aquinas is the most obvious example in this regard. He treats the beatific vision as an act of the speculative intellect. With an appeal to Saint Augustine, Aquinas maintains that "the essence of happiness consists in an act of the intellect: but the delight that results from happiness pertains to the will" (*ST* I-II, q. 3, a. 4, in *Summa Theologica*, trans. Fathers of the English Dominican Province, 5 vols. [1948; reprint, Notre Dame: Christian Classics, 1981]). The Angelic Doctor rejects the notion that delight ranks before vision, insisting instead that the sight of God causes delight, so that the will subsequently experiences the delight of rest (*ST* I-II, q. 4, a. 1). Aquinas also maintains that this delight ranks below happiness, since the cause (vision) is greater than the effect (delight). He maintains that the will does not seek the good of happiness for the sake of repose. Accordingly, delight is a perfection that comes along with vision but not a perfection that makes the vision perfect in its own species (*ST* I-II, q. 4, a. 2).

By contrast, a voluntarist approach tends to emphasize that the human person is driven by desire and that it is the yearning of the will (*voluntas*) that inclines the intellect to follow it.[2] Voluntarism, which has increasingly come to dominate philosophy and theology since the late Middle Ages, maintains that it is love, not knowledge, that ultimately yields the vision of God, and focuses on the joy that one gains from being in eternal fellowship with God.[3]

In this chapter, I will argue that the very distinction between knowledge and love dissolves in the deifying union of the pilgrim with Jesus Christ. Union with Christ in his death and resurrection involves a meeting of time and eternity, of nature and the supernatural. To insist that it is either knowledge or love that yields the beatific vision is to try and capture the ineffable mystery through rational means. To be sure, in many respects I consider myself an intellectualist rather than a voluntarist; it seems to me that the Christian Platonist tradition is right to maintain that love implies knowledge, and that we can only desire something of which we have prior knowledge.[4]

---

2. Severin Valentinov Kitanov points out that a "voluntarist psychology" entered the mainstream theological tradition in the West particularly in the wake of the famous condemnation of Aristotelianism by Bishop Stephen Tempier in 1277 (*Beatific Enjoyment in Medieval Scholastic Debates* [Lanham, MD: Lexington, 2014], 74–75).

3. The term "beatific vision" is more naturally associated with knowledge (which has to do with illumination and insight) than with love (which may express that a person is *beatus* or happy but does not speak directly of vision). It is not surprising, considering the voluntarist frame of much contemporary thought, that the doctrine of the beatific vision has experienced a decline in the modern period.

4. For Plato, desire follows the good as one perceives it. In the *Symposium*, Socrates pointedly rejects Agathon's suggestion that Love is the greatest among the gods. He explains that the priestess Diotima has taught him that Love is merely an intermediary daemon, which always desires the permanent possession of goodness for itself (*Symp.* 206a). In the course of the dialogue between Socrates and Diotima, the latter suggests that Love is an intermediary between ignorance and knowledge, "because knowledge is one of the most attractive things there is, and attractive things are Love's province. Love is bound, therefore, to love knowledge, and anyone who loves knowledge is bound to fall between knowledge and ignorance" (*Symp.* 204b, in *Symposium*, trans. and ed. Robin Waterfield [Oxford: Oxford University Press, 1994]). According to Plato, then, love has knowledge (of the good) for its object. To be sure, desire is a tremendously important category for Plato. This is clear in particular from the myth of the winged soul in the *Phaedrus*, where he dwells at length on the physical attraction between a lover and a beautiful boy (*Phaedr.* 250c–257a). Plato makes clear, however, that erotic desire ought not to be in the driver's seat. The appetitive or desiring aspect of the soul (τὸ ἐπιθυμητικόν) is the black horse, which must be guided and controlled—along with the white horse, the spirited or irascible aspect of the soul (τὸ θυμοειδές)—by the charioteer of reason (τὸ λογιστικόν). The charioteer guides the horses in the right direction when he aims for the top of heaven's vault and there gazes upon what Plato calls the truth or true being (*Phaedr.* 247c–d).

My only caveat with regard to this general rule is that it does not pertain to God himself (in whom knowledge and love are one and the same) or to our deifying participation in Christ (which is identical to eternal life, where the categories of *before* and *after* simply do not pertain in any straightforward, temporal sense). Therefore, when it comes to deification and the beatific vision of God in the hereafter, we should not presume that it is possible to distinguish, let alone prioritize, the intellective and desiring faculties.

This chapter looks at the relationship between knowledge and love through the lens of two medieval treatises: the *Itinerarium mentis in Deum* (*The Soul's Journey into God*), written by Bonaventure of Bagnoregio, the well-known minister general of the Franciscan Order; and *De visione Dei* (*On the Vision of God*), a treatise by the German theologian, canon lawyer, and cardinal Nicholas of Cusa. The two writings are separated by nearly two hundred years—Bonaventure wrote *The Soul's Journey into God* in 1259, while Cusa's *On the Vision of God* stems from 1453. Nonetheless, we may profitably compare the two. Both treatises rely heavily on the mystical theology of Dionysius, the well-known sixth-century monk, who both Bonaventure and Cusa thought was Saint Paul's convert mentioned in Acts 17.[5] Bonaventure, however, stands at the early stages of what Bernard McGinn has called *affective Dionysianism*, while Cusa wrote *On the Vision of God* specifically to counter the separation of intellect and will, and may be interpreted as a

---

Plotinus similarly subjects the desire of the will to the good perceived in the object of knowledge: "Shall we then hand over the decision to desire . . . to the soul and, trusting in this soul's experience, maintain that what is desired by this is good, and not enquire why it desires? And shall we produce demonstrations of what each and every thing is, but commit the good to desire? But we see many absurdities in this" (*Enn.* 6.7.19; quotations come from Plotinus, *Enneads*, trans. and ed. A. H. Armstrong, 6 vols., LCL 440–45 [Cambridge, MA: Harvard University Press, 1966–1988]). A little further down, Plotinus asks: "Is the Good good, and does it have that name, because it is desirable for one, but because it is this for all we say that it is the Good?" Plotinus responds that "surely the object of desire itself must have such a nature that it is right to call it this" (6.7.24). Likewise, he suggests: "The Good, therefore, must be desirable, but must not become good by being desirable, but become desirable by being good" (6.7.25).

5. William J. Hoye rightly comments that both Bonaventure and Nicholas of Cusa cite Dionysius as normative. He adds, "A copy of the writing of Bonaventure [i.e., the *Itinerarium*] was in Cusa's possession since he was a student" ("Die Vereinigung mit dem gänzlich Unerkannten nach Bonaventura, Nikolaus von Kues und Thomas von Aquin," in *Die Dionysius-Rezeption im Mittelalter. Internationales Kolloquium in Sofia vom 8. bis 11. April 1999 unter der Schirmherrschaft der Société internationale pour l'étude de la philosophie médiévale*, ed. Tzorcho Boiadjiev, Georgi Kapriev, and Andreas Speer, Rencontres de Philosophie Médiévale 9 [Turnhout, Belgium: Brepols, 2000], 485 [translation mine]).

sample of what McGinn terms *intellective Dionysianism.*[6] Both theologians developed their understanding of the beatific vision under the influence of Dionysius, with Bonaventure taking the Eastern theologian in a more Franciscan (voluntarist) direction and Nicholas reading him more in line with Dominican (intellectualist) thought.

My interest in comparing these two theologians is twofold. First, I am deeply committed to keeping faith and reason, knowledge and love, together. The separation of the two, as the result of an ever-increasing emphasis on the will and on human desire in the modern period, has been the object of incisive critiques,[7] and I share the suspicion regarding the contemporary reification of the will. The virtual loss of the beatific vision as a topos in theology seems unavoidable once human desire takes the driver's seat and is allowed to determine the telos of human existence. The contemporary neglect of the beatific vision should, therefore, be a red flag: it signifies the high degree of accommodation in contemporary theology to the uninhibited voluntarism of Western society. The consequences of this shift may be unintended, but they are both real and serious; a culture that takes the dictates of desire as the starting point and guide for what constitutes the good life cannot but end in a violent clash of diverging wills.

Now, it will hardly do to caricature Bonaventure and Cusa by turning the former into the Franciscan villain of desire and lionizing the latter as the Dominican defender of the intellect. Both recognize that faith and reason are intimately intertwined, and so we should resist a reading of Bonaventure simply through the lens of the late modern abdication of human rationality. Nonetheless, Bonaventure's affective Dionysianism stretches the link between knowledge and love to the breaking point, as he consistently opposes desire to knowledge. By contrast, for Cusa's intellective Dionysianism, the dialectic between positive and negative discourse

---

6. Bernard McGinn, *The Flowering of Mysticism: Men and Women in the New Mysticism—1200–1350,* vol. 3 of *The Presence of God: A History of Western Christian Mysticism* (New York: Crossroad Herder, 1998), 79; Bernard McGinn, *The Harvest of Mysticism in Medieval Germany,* vol. 4 of *The Presence of God: A History of Western Christian Mysticism* (New York: Herder and Herder, 2005), 449.

7. See John Milbank, *Theology and Social Theory: Beyond Secular Reason,* 2nd ed. (Malden, MA: Wiley-Blackwell, 2006); Louis Dupré, *Passage to Modernity: An Essay in the Hermeneutics of Nature and Culture* (New Haven: Yale University Press, 1993); Brad S. Gregory, *The Unintended Reformation: How a Religious Revolution Secularized Society* (Cambridge, MA: Belknap Press of Harvard University Press, 2012); Thomas Pfau, *Minding the Modern: Human Agency, Intellectual Traditions, and Responsible Knowledge* (Notre Dame: University of Notre Dame Press, 2015).

puts a limit on the role of the intellect, since both kataphatic and apophatic discourse end with the mystical experience of God. In other words, though Cusa emphasizes the intellect, he refuses to speculate as to which of the two faculties yields the beatific vision.

Second, with Dionysian thought patterns pervading both theologians' work, the questions that loom for both is whether and how they can do justice to the role of Christ. Dionysius is the theologian of negation, paradox, and ignorance; and with the dark clouds of Dionysian apophaticism, an actual vision of God may seem almost impossible. The chasm between human knowledge and the incomprehensible God may seem to place the beatific vision out of reach. We must ask, therefore, whether we can combine Dionysian apophaticism with a positive focus on Jesus Christ as we encounter him in the Scriptures. Or does the "ignorance" to which Dionysius guides his readers inevitably downplay divine revelation and, in particular, the centrality of Christ? In short, the significance in Dionysius of the metaphor of the cloud—focusing on human ignorance alongside the paradoxical language of "luminous darkness"—may tempt us to think of God's positive self-revelation in Christ as a mere stepping-stone to the insight that God lies beyond such limited expressions of the divine. On such an understanding, Christ may still mediate—he is still a stepping-stone—but his purpose would be to point to an (apophatic) reality beyond himself. Christ, we could say, would still be a sign—perhaps even a sacrament—but the reality to which he points would forever lie beyond our visionary reach.

Such a treatment of Christ and of the beatific vision is by no means imaginary. The Neoplatonist tradition that helped shape the Dionysian approach to the beatific vision is thoroughly apophatic. For Plotinus the unity or simplicity of the Good places it radically beyond our ken: "For when you think of him as Intellect or God, he is more; and when you unify him in your thought, here also the degree of unity by which he transcends your thought is more than you imagined it to be; for he is by himself without any incidental attributes."[8] Terms such as "Intellect" (νοῦς) and "God" (θεός) shortchange the sublime character of this "point" of origin. After all, for Plotinus the Good (τἀγαθόν) or the One (τὸ ἕν) is not *a* being among other beings. Preceding everything that exists, even the Being of the Forms, the source of everything is prior to all things, so that "all things will be other than it, and it will be other than all things."[9] So, whether we speak of the First (τὸ

8. *Enn.* 6.9.6.
9. *Enn.* 3.8.9.

πρῶτον) or of the Good (or perhaps of Beauty), we must recognize that the One is utterly beyond our naming, and as such eludes our knowledge.[10] This primary Good, the Alone, (τὸ μόνον) is, therefore, really the Beyond-Good (τὸ ὑπεράγαθον).[11]

Beauty—while Plotinus is full of praise for it—does not quite express the utter transcendence of the One: Beauty is too closely linked with the matter it in-forms for Plotinus simply to equate it with the Good.[12] Unlike Beauty, the ineffable One remains beyond the reach of the Forms.[13] Even the Good does not quite capture the monadic character of the One, since the lower level of Intellect (νοῦς) can participate in the Good. And so Plotinus reaches for the term "Beyond-Good" to highlight the utter transcendence of the One. The Plotinian ὑπεράγαθον seems far removed from the specific and particular contours of a faith that is centered on the incarnate Christ.

Much of the Plotinian account as I have just sketched it is echoed in Dionysius and in the tradition that built on him. An important exception, however, is precisely Plotinus's ὑπεράγαθον, which the tradition reconfigures in the light of the Christian faith. Dionysius starts off his *Mystical Theology* with the exclamation: "Trinity!! Higher than any being, any divinity, any goodness!"[14] Though Dionysius does not elaborate on the Trinitarian character of the God he claims is beyond both affirmation and negation, he nonetheless goes beyond Plotinus by identifying the ὑπεράγαθον with the Trinity—and by starting off his treatise by personally addressing this triune God.

Certainly, Dionysius is a genuine heir to Plotinus's thought. He maintains that neither affirmations nor denials properly identify the Trinity, since both positive and negative language remain tethered to this-worldly conceptualities. Neither of the two kinds of discourse properly grasps God. Indeed, as Dionysius puts it:

---

10. Andrew Louth comments that for Plotinus the One is "absolutely simple, beyond any duality whatsoever, and of which, therefore, nothing can be said. It is the One, because beyond duality; it is the Good, because it has no need of anything else. It is the source of all, it is beyond being. Nothing can be affirmed truly of the One" (*The Origins of the Christian Mystical Tradition: From Plato to Denys* [Oxford: Oxford University Press, 1981], 38).

11. *Enn.* 6.9.6.

12. *Enn.* 5.5.12.

13. See Dominic J. O'Meara, *Plotinus: An Introduction to the* Enneads (Oxford: Clarendon, 1993), 97–99.

14. *MT* 997A. Hereafter, references from this work will be given in parentheses in the text; quotations come from *Pseudo-Dionysius: The Complete Works*, trans. Colm Luibheid, ed. Paul Rorem (Mahwah, NJ: Paulist, 1987).

The fact is that the more we take flight upward, the more our words are confined to the ideas we are capable of forming; so that now as we plunge into that darkness which is beyond intellect, we shall find ourselves not simply running short of words but actually speechless and unknowing. . . . My argument now rises from what is below up to the transcendent, and the more it climbs, the more language falters, and when it has passed up and beyond the ascent, it will turn silent completely, since it will finally be at one with him who is indescribable. (1033B–C)

The Syrian monk wants to reach beyond both positive and negative naming of God, so as to "deny that which is beyond every denial" (1033C).

In important ways, this theological approach simply continues the trajectory set up by Plotinus. Nonetheless, Dionysius introduces an important modification of the Neoplatonist philosopher. The reason for the darkness and the silence at the summit of Dionysius's ascent is that the Trinity is a mystery that lies beyond human discourse. Nothing we say, whether positive or negative, can possibly capture what the Trinity is like. We only properly understand Dionysius's mysticism if we keep in mind that the "darkness of unknowing" (1001A) has reference to the triune God, who alone is "higher than any being, any divinity, any goodness" (997A). In fairness, we may well ask how we can make sense of the doctrine of the Trinity within the context of the darkness of unknowing. Still, it is as a Christian theologian, with a firm faith in the doctrine of the Trinity, that Dionysius sets out in search of the one who is "beyond all being and knowledge" (997B). As we will see, Bonaventure and Cusa follow this Dionysian approach, each in his own creative way. Though they appropriate Dionysius in rather different ways, both Bonaventure and Cusa combine their Dionysian theologies with a deep, personal faith in Jesus Christ, which shapes the way they speak of their beatific experiences of God.

Bonaventure, *The Soul's Journey into God*

Saint Bonaventure (1217–1274) developed at some length the Trinitarian theology that remained largely implicit in Dionysius. What is more, the Franciscan mystic gave the Dionysian approach to the beatific vision a remarkably christological (even crucicentric) turn—and he did so in a treatise that was meant to focus the reader's desires on Christ. As is well known, *The Soul's Journey into God*—which Bonaventure wrote in 1259, two years after being appointed minister general of the Franciscan Order—was deeply shaped by his visit to Mount La Verna in Tuscany, where Francis had received his vision of the six-winged seraph thirty-five years earlier. The seraph of Francis's vision, which had taken the form of the crucified Christ, had left behind stigmata in Francis's hands and feet, and a wound in his side. Francis's vision—and his emphasis on the suffering Jesus—profoundly affected Bonaventure's theological approach. In the latter's understanding of the *visio Dei*, therefore, the Eastern mysticism of Dionysius joined with the Western influence of the Augustinian (and particularly the Franciscan) tradition.

The pervasive character of its Christology is perhaps the most appealing aspect of *The Soul's Journey into God*. William Harmless comments, "It is hard to name a mystical theology more self-consciously Christ-centered than Bonaventure's. He often speaks of Christ as the *medium*, Latin for 'middle' or 'center.'"[15] Denys Turner concurs: "The central theological vision is Christological. It is with Christ that the *Itinerarium* begins and ends. It is Christ who is the means. It is Christ who is the meaning."[16] Indeed, we could say that Christ is the sacramental hinge through which the world both comes from God and returns to him. Bonaventure puts it as follows:

> Since God is the Beginning and the End of all things, it is necessary to posit within God an intermediate person of the *divine nature*, so that there may be one person who only produces, another who is only produced, but an intermediary who both produces and is produced. It is also necessary to posit an intermediary (*medium*) in the *going forth* (*in egressu*) and in the *return* (*regressu*) of things: in the *going forth*, a center which will be closer to the productive principle [i.e., the Father]; in the *return*, a medium which will be close to the one returning. Therefore, as creatures went forth (*exierunt*) from God by the Word of God, so for a perfect return (*reditum*), it was necessary that the Mediator *between God and humanity* be not only God but also human so that this mediator might lead humanity back to God.[17]

15. William Harmless, "Mystic as Cartographer: Bonaventure," in *Mystics* (New York: Oxford University Press, 2008), 102.

16. Denys Turner, "Hierarchy Interiorised: Bonaventure's *Itinerarium Mentis in Deum*," in *The Darkness of God: Negativity in Christian Mysticism* (Cambridge: Cambridge University Press, 1995), 117.

17. *Red. art.* 23 (in vol. 1 of *Works of Saint Bonaventure*, trans. and ed. Zachary Hayes [Saint Bonaventure, NY: Franciscan Institute, 1996], 59).

For Bonaventure, Christ is the medium both in the Trinitarian life and in the creation and salvation of humanity. The *exitus* as well as the *reditus* of creation take place in and through him.[18]

Much more than Dionysius, Bonaventure focuses on the crucified Christ, through whom alone it is possible to reach ecstatic contemplation. Bonaventure takes the six wings of the seraph of Francis's vision as "a symbol of six stages of illumination which begin with creatures and lead to God to whom no one has access properly except through the Crucified."[19] The six steps of illumination proceed by way of three main approaches. The journey outward takes place through contemplation (*speculatio*) of God both through (*per*) and then also in (*in*) the vestiges of the sensible world. Next, the journey inward involves contemplation of God through and in the image imprinted on human beings. Finally, the journey upward is a contemplation of the Being (unity) and Goodness (Trinity) of God himself. While in the first two steps the senses (*sensus*) and the imagination (*imaginatio*) are involved, the next two steps require first reason (*ratio*) and then understanding (*intellectus*), while in the last two steps the mind uses its intelligence (*intelligentia*) and so arrives at the mind's summit (*apex mentis*). Having reached this sixth step, the mind comes to the seventh and final point, where ecstasy finally finds peace and rest.[20]

Contemplation is not reserved just for the final stage. It is true that that is where understanding comes to rest (*requies*) and where the affections pass over into God. Nonetheless, the Seraphic Doctor applies the language of contemplation (*speculatio*) to each of the seven stages. *Visio Dei* begins with sense perception. Bonaventure speaks not only of seeing God *through* the created order, but also *in* it. God can be contemplated "not only *through* them [i.e., sensible things], but also *in* them in as far as God is present in them by essence, power, and presence" (*Itin.* 2.1). Vision of sensible objects already implies vision of God. Turner points to Bonaventure's use of *per* and *in* by suggesting that the preposition *per* suggests simply "simulacra

---

18. Paul Rorem shows that Bonaventure renders Dionysius's notion of anagogical "uplifting" with the Latin term *reductio* ("Dionysian Uplifting (Anagogy) in Bonaventure's *Reductio*," *FcS* 70 [2012]: 183–88).

19. *Itin.* prol. 3. Hereafter, references to *Itinerarium mentis in Deum* (*The Soul's Journey into God*) will be given in parentheses in the text; quotations come from vol. 2 of *Works of St. Bonaventure*, trans. Zachary Hayes, ed. Philotheus Boehner (Saint Bonaventure, NY: Franciscan Institute, 2002).

20. Helpful charts of the various steps can be found in McGinn, *The Flowering of Mysticism*, 107; and Harmless, "Mystic as Carthographer," 89.

which reveal God," while *in* suggests realities that "not only reveal God but make God present."[21] In other words, when we see God *in* the vestiges in the world and *in* human beings as his image, we see him as sacramentally present in them.

We recognize this presence of God, Bonaventure claims, when we link bodily vision with the eternal generation of the Son. Just as a sensible object impresses a likeness of itself (in the form of a species) on our minds, so the Father, the eternal light, generates the eternal likeness of his Son (2.7). Thus, our perception of sensible objects can lead to conclusions about the relationship between Father and Son: just as there is beauty, sweetness, and wholesomeness in the likeness of the species formed in our minds, so there is beauty, sweetness, and wholesomeness to be found in the eternal likeness of the Son (2.8). What is more, because making judgments about sensible things (through abstraction) only makes sense if we follow infallible laws, these laws must be changeless, incorruptible, and eternal. In other words, they are uncreated, "existing eternally in the eternal Art from which, and through which, and in accordance with which all beautiful things are formed" (2.9). It is the "eternal Art"—the eternal Word conceived by the Father—that is the eternal measure for the judgments we make in sense perception. Put differently, Bonaventure describes sensible things as "shadows, echoes, and pictures" of God's eternal Art (2.11). All creatures, therefore, are "divinely given signs" that can lift us from sensible to intelligible things, "from signs to that which is signified" (2.11).

Thus, even the simple act of seeing created objects with physical eyes is, for Bonaventure, a form of contemplation. Physical sight has this contemplative character because the eternal generation of the Son is the pattern of all human perception and because the eternal Word of God is the standard or rule by which we make sense of sensible objects. Bonaventure sees God as present in the created world around us. In other words, contemplation for Bonaventure is what Eastern theologians would have called θεωρία φυσική (natural contemplation). Within the physical realm, we see the presence of God—the "eternal Art" of the Father.[22] Beatific vision has its origin in physical perception of created things.

21. Turner, "Hierarchy Interiorised," 109.

22. For the implications of natural contemplation with respect to environmental philosophy, see Bruce V. Foltz's reflections on Maximus the Confessor in "Seeing Nature: *Theōria Physikē* in the Thought of St. Maximos the Confessor," in *The Noetics of Nature: Environmental Philosophy and the Holy Beauty of the Visible* (New York: Fordham University Press, 2014), 158–74.

Bonaventure arrives at the heart of his discussion when he deals with the fourth step. Here he moves from the natural to the supernatural image—or, as he calls it elsewhere, from the image to the likeness.[23] He points to the incarnation as key to our ability to see God as sacramentally present within ourselves as his image, and he maintains that "our soul would not be able to be lifted up perfectly from sensible realities to see itself and the eternal truth within itself unless the truth, assuming a human form in Christ, should become a ladder to repair the first ladder that had been broken in Adam" (*Itin.* 4.2). It is only through the mediation of Christ (*mediante Christo*) that the soul enters into the enjoyment of the truth of paradise and can eat from Christ as the tree of life (4.2). Through the infusion of the virtues of faith, hope, and love—each of them centered on Jesus Christ as the "supreme hierarch" who "purges, illumines and perfects" us (4.5)—the mind "returns to its interior where it sees God in the *splendor of the Saints* [Ps. 109 (110):3]" (4.6).

In the sixth stage, the soul marvels at the paradoxical nature of the triune God. This contemplation causes Bonaventure also to gaze upon the miracle of the hypostatic union. The mind reaches as it were the sixth day of creation, seeing "humanity made in the image of God" in Jesus Christ (6.7). Here the mind arrives at its summit, the *apex mentis*, since now it contemplates our humanity "ineffably united in Christ," as it sees at the same time "the first and the last, the highest and the lowest, the circumference and the center, the *Alpha* and the *Omega* [Rev. 1:8], the caused and the cause, the creator and the creature, that is, the *book written within and without* [Ezek. 2:9 (10)]" (6.7).

Much of the journey is christologically anchored. The mind contemplates the Son of God in the vestiges of God in creation, in the image of God as it is reformed by grace, and especially at the summit as the mind contemplates the triune character of God and the hypostatic union. All of this, however, is in an important sense mere preparation. The senses, the understanding, and even the mind itself—that to which the East typically refers as the *nous*—can guide a person only up to a point. In the end, the beatific vision of God takes place only if and when the mind is transcended in a moment of ecstasy. At this crucial moment of mystical transport (*excessus mysticus*), the mind transcends even itself (7.1). Bonaventure's description of this moment of "passing" into God in step seven of the *Itinerarium* is stunning for its combination of devotion to the cross of Christ (the most emphatically kataphatic element of the Christian faith) and an embrace of the Dionysian discourse of silence and darkness (the most radical apophaticism imaginable). For Bonaventure,

23. See Turner, "Hierarchy Interiorised," 111.

the two fit hand in glove because it is in the cross, in dying with Christ, that all sense perception and intellectual activity are left behind (7.4). The person who experiences this, claims Bonaventure, "celebrates the Pasch, that is, the Passover, with Christ (pascha, *hoc est transitum, cum eo facit*)" (7.2). At this point, the believer enters along with Christ into paradise (Luke 23:43) and there tastes the hidden manna (Rev. 2:17). Since, however, both perception and intellect have been left behind, Bonaventure describes paradise itself by quoting the opening paragraph of Dionysius's *Mystical Theology*, with its language of "dazzling darkness" that teaches "in the total obscurity that is super-manifest" (*Itin.* 7.5).

Bonaventure thus takes quite literally the notion that "man shall not see me and live" (Exod. 33:20). It is only when we lose our life by dying with Christ that we are able to see the Father, claims the Seraphic Doctor (*Itin.* 7.6).[24] At the end of his treatise, therefore, he exhorts his readers: "Let us die, then, and enter into this darkness. Let us silence all our cares, desires, and imaginings. Let us pass over (*transeamus*) with the crucified Christ *from this world to the Father* [John 13:1], so that when the Father has been shown to us, we may say with Philip: *It is enough for us* [John 14:8]" (7.6). As Bonaventure was surely aware, Jesus responded to Philip's request that he might see the Father by pointing to himself: "Whoever has seen me has seen the Father. How can you say, 'Show us the Father'?" (John 14:9). Bonaventure's claim is that, by seeing Jesus—and, more particularly, by contemplating his crucifixion and his death—we pass over to the *visio beatifica* of the Father himself.

As we will see, Bonaventure regarded desire as the crucial element in moving along on the six steps toward the cross. We should be cautious, however, not to caricature the *Itinerarium* as a sample of thoroughgoing voluntarism. Bonaventure's rhetoric never simply repudiates the intellect.[25] In fact,

---

24. Bonaventure's exegesis goes back to Augustine, who presents two possible explanations for the reason that no one can see God's face and live. The second option Augustine presents is that "even now in this life, to the extent that we perceive in a spiritual way the Wisdom of God *through which all things were made* (Jn 1:3), we die to fleshly, materialistic attachments; and reckoning this world to be dead to us we ourselves die to this world and say what the apostle said, *The world has been crucified to me and I to the world* (Gal 6:14). Of this sort of death he says elsewhere, *But if you are dead with Christ, why do you lay down laws as though you were still living on this world* (Col 2:20)?" (*Trin.* 2.17.28, in *The Trinity*, trans. Edmund Hill, ed. John E. Rotelle, 2nd ed., WSA I/5 [Hyde Park, NY: New City Press, 2012]).

25. Zachary Hayes summarizes Bonaventure well: "For Bonaventure, the important issue is, above all, knowledge integrated into the spiritual journey toward love; love of God and love of one's fellow human beings. It is clear that Bonaventure had a high regard for the intellectual life, but he never envisioned knowledge independently of the only goal that the human person

he considered the understanding to be indispensable on the journey toward ecstasy. As we have already seen, the six steps of the ascent correspond to the six levels of the powers of the soul, which enable us to move from the temporal to the eternal. Bonaventure refers to them as "sense, imagination, reason, understanding, intelligence, and the high point of the mind, or the spark of conscience" (*Itin.* 1.6). The mind's journey into God, therefore, is mostly one in which the intellect is very much engaged. It is a journey of faith seeking understanding. Bonaventure does not simply separate faith and reason or knowledge and love.

Nonetheless, the predominant role of the affections in *The Soul's Journey into God* is evident from the outset. As he describes his retreat to Mount La Verna, Bonaventure relates that he sought "ecstatic peace" (*Itin.* prol. 1) with a "panting spirit" (*anhelo spiritu*) (prol. 2 [translation altered]). He makes clear that ecstasies of the mind come only to a person of desires (*vir desideriorum*) (prol. 3). Bonaventure therefore leads his readers to "groans of prayer" (prol. 4). Throughout the treatise he warns against learning bereft of devotion and of knowledge apart from love: "Do not think that reading is sufficient without unction, speculation without devotion, investigation without admiration, circumspection without exultation, industry without piety, knowledge without charity, intelligence without humility, study without divine grace, the mirror without the inspiration of divine wisdom" (prol. 4). Seeing that only humility and piety constitute the proper disposition for divine grace, Bonaventure asks the reader to pay attention "more to the stimulation of affect (*exercitio affectus*) than to the instruction of the intellect (*eruditio intellectus*)" (prol. 5). Bonaventure's polemic against what today we would call a purely academic approach to matters of faith is prominent, and he combines it with a strong emphasis on love, piety, and the affections.

Bonaventure's voluntarism comes to the fore particularly when, in the final chapter, he quotes at length the opening section of Dionysius's *Mystical Theology* (*Itin.* 7.5). The Franciscan theologian places the quotation within the context of a plea to give up all "intellectual activities" so that our affection (*affectus*) may be transformed into God, for which we need "the fire of the Holy Spirit" (7.4). Bonaventure insists that "little importance should be given to investigation and much to unction; little to speech but much to interior joy; little to words or writing and all to the gift of God, namely the Holy Spirit" (7.5). After the lengthy quotation of Dionysius that speaks of

---

finally has: loving union with God" (introduction to *On the Reduction of the Arts to Theology*, by Bonaventure, in *Works of Saint Bonaventure*, 1:9).

ascent to the "super-essential radiance of the divine darkness," Bonaventure immediately returns to his stock-in-trade, insisting that there is only one way to enter into this "dazzling darkness" (7.5), and that is by means of desire rather than understanding: "Now if you ask how all these things are to come about, ask grace, not doctrine; desire, not intellect; the groaning of prayer and not studious reading; the Spouse, not the master; God, not a human being; darkness, not clarity; not light, but the fire that inflames totally and carries one into God through spiritual fervor and with the most burning affections" (7.6).[26] Bonaventure's concluding appeal to Dionysius serves to underscore the intellect's subservience to the will and to human desire: it is the will's desire that properly prepares one for the journey, and it is the affections at the summit of the mind (*apex mentis*) that in the end carry one into God.[27]

In one respect, Bonaventure's appeal to Dionysius is quite apropos. The Eastern mystic recognized the limits of the intellect, and he therefore employed paradoxes to describe the moment of ecstasy, thus indicating the intellect's inability properly to name God. But Dionysius did not suggest that the affections could enter the one place from which the intellect was barred.[28]

26. Joseph Ratzinger writes that Bonaventure would have been inclined to this preference of love over sight "by reason of his Franciscan view which attributed a higher value to the *affectus* rather than to the *intellectus*" (*The Theology of History in St. Bonaventure*, trans. Zachary Hayes [Chicago: Franciscan Herald Press, 1989], 90).

27. Lydia Schumacher has argued that Bonaventure's essentialist (as opposed to Augustine's merely participatory) metaphysic implies an epistemology according to which the human mind can see created objects exactly as they are in the mind of God (*Divine Illumination: The History and Future of Augustine's Theory of Knowledge* [Malden, MA: Wiley-Blackwell, 2011], 143–45). Thus, simply by turning inward, the human mind can find the divine Being as it is manifested subjectively in the mind. This subjective turn, argues Schumacher, takes place when one loves as Christ loved, humbly and sacrificially. This leads to an abandonment of the intellect: "Bonaventure concludes that the one who is truly consumed with love for Christ is bound to transcend the realm of knowable entities in an ultimate experience of self-abandonment that entails ecstatic union with the love of God. . . . This conception of the apex of the ascent to God stands in striking contrast to that of Augustine, for whom human 'transcendence' in this life does not entail a literal leap beyond the realm of reason, much less the obliteration of the self" (Schumacher, 150).

28. Bernard McGinn comments that the affective Dionysianism of a later Franciscan, Thomas Gallus, "is based upon a misreading, though one not without foundation in the *corpus dionysiacum*. There is little language about love in Dionysius's account of the ascent to God; but a noted text about the transcendental and cosmic nature of love (*erōs*) in the fourth chapter of the *Divine Names* . . . provided him with at least some basis for his interpretation" (*The Flowering of Mysticism*, 81). Cf. Bernard McGinn, "God as Eros: Metaphysical Foundations of

Ironically, it seems to me, Bonaventure's strong favoring of the affections is predicated on an underlying, hidden rationalist assumption, namely, that it is one of the human faculties—either the intellect or the affections—that carries us into God. I remain unconvinced that our entry into the life of God can be thus explained. Given divine simplicity, knowledge and love are one in God.[29] The beatific vision—as well as ecstatic raptures that adumbrate this vision—cannot be an experience in which either knowledge or love takes the lead. If even momentarily one of the two were left behind, the ecstatic experience could hardly end up being a participation in the knowledge and the love of God. It seems more fitting to me to refuse to opt between intellectualism and voluntarism when it comes to the mind's ecstatic entry into the life of God.

Nicholas of Cusa, *On the Vision of God*

Nearly two hundred years after Bonaventure's celebrated treatise, the mystical German theologian and canon lawyer Nicholas of Cusa (1401–1464) wrote his treatise on the beatific vision. Like Bonaventure's *Itinerarium*, Cusa's *On the Vision of God* (1453) was deeply shaped by Dionysius's *Mystical Theology*. However, whereas the Franciscan theologian had embraced a more affective Dionysian approach, Cusa's Dionysian mysticism was more intellectual in character, as is evident particularly from the influence of John Scotus Eriugena (ca. 815–ca. 877) and Meister Eckhart (1260–1328) on Cusa's writings.[30]

Christian Mysticism," in *New Perspectives on Historical Theology: Essays in Memory of John Meyendorff*, ed. Bradley Nassif (Grand Rapids: Eerdmans, 1995), 189–209.

29. Cf. *SCG* 1.45.1–7; 1.73.1–5; Michael M. Waddell, "Aquinas on the Light of Glory," *Tópicos* 40 (2011): 126–27.

30. Cf. Louis Dupré, "The Mystical Theology of Nicholas of Cusa's *De visione Dei*," in *Nicholas of Cusa on Christ and the Church: Essays in Memory of Chandler McCuskey Brooks for the American Cusanus Society*, ed. Gerald Christianson and Thomas M. Izbicki (Leiden: Brill, 1996), 208–12; Bernard McGinn, "Seeing and Not Seeing: Nicholas of Cusa's *De visione Dei* in the History of Western Mysticism," in *Cusanus: The Legacy of Learned Ignorance*, ed. Peter Casarella (Washington, DC: Catholic University of America Press, 2006), 34–37. Nicholas (unpersuasively) denied that Eckhart positively influenced his thinking. See Meredith Ziebart, "Laying Siege to the Wall of Paradise: The Fifteenth-Century Tegernsee Dispute over Mystical Theology and Nicholas of Cusa's Strong Defense of Reason," *JMRCul* 41 (2015): 46, 61n31. Cf. Stefanie Frost, *Nikolaus und Meister Eckhart: Rezeption im Spiegel der Marginalien zum Opus tripartitum Meister Eckharts*, Beiträge zur Geschichte der Philosophie und Theologie des Mittelalters, n.s., 69 (Münster: Aschendorff, 2006).

Still, neither his speculative bent nor his Neoplatonic inclinations elim- inated the role of the affections in Cusa's theology. The cardinal's *On the Vision of God* is a deeply devotional treatise.[31] His purpose with the book was to lead the Benedictine monks of Tegernsee (in today's Bavaria) "ex- perientially (*experimentaliter*) into the most sacred darkness" so that they might end up "feeling the presence" of God's light and might have a fore- taste, a "delicious sampling," of the feast of eternal happiness (pref. 1). The devotional character of Cusa's work becomes evident especially when, after dealing with a few prolegomena, the author asks his brother contemplatives to take their place in front of the "icon of God"—a depiction of the face of Christ—which he has given to them along with the treatise itself (pref. 2).[32] The German cardinal then leads the monks in prayer: "Lord, in this image of you I now behold your providence by a certain sensible experience. For if you do not abandon me, the vilest of all, you will never abandon anyone" (4.9). The remainder of the treatise, while it certainly includes deep theo- logical speculation, is written entirely in the form of a prayer, in which the Benedictine monks, still standing in front of the icon, conclude with the plea, "Draw me, Lord, for no one may come to you unless drawn by you, so that drawn to you, I may be made absolute from this world and may be joined to you, the absolute God, in the eternity of the glorious life. Amen" (25.120). Cusa's book, then, is a mystagogical treatise that aims to lead its readers into an experience of the vision of God.

Much of the so-called Tegernsee Debate, which raged from 1452 until 1460, concerned the question of whether or not the intellect plays an integral role in the journey toward the vision of God.[33] The abbot of the Tegern-

---

31. Cusa aims to uplift his readers "through a certain devotional exercise, to mystical theol- ogy" (*DVD* pref. 4, in *Nicholas of Cusa: Selected Spiritual Writings*, trans. and ed. H. Lawrence Bond [Mahwah, NJ: Paulist, 1997], 237]). Cusa's Latin works can be accessed online: www .cusanus-portal.de. Hereafter, references to *De visione Dei* (*On the Vision of God*) will be given in parentheses in the text; quotations come from *Nicholas of Cusa: Selected Spiritual Writings*.

32. Cusa writes that the icon of the face of Christ is similar to the one painted by Rogier van der Weyden (ca. 1399–1464) and similar also to the image of the Veronika in his Koblenz chapel (*DVD* pref. 2; cf. Johannes Hoff, *The Analogical Turn: Rethinking Modernity with Nicholas of Cusa* [Grand Rapids: Eerdmans, 2013], 27–29). Jean-Luc Marion argues convincingly that the icon in question depicts the face of Christ himself ("Voir, se voir vu: L'Apport de Nicolas de Cues dans le *De visione Dei*," *BLE* 117, no. 2 [April 2016]: 14–15). For further discussion on the role of the icon, see chap. 13 below, section entitled "Pedagogy and Providence in Nicholas of Cusa and Jonathan Edwards."

33. My discussion of the historical background relies especially on Bernard McGinn, *Har- vest of Mysticism*, 448–56; Jacob Holsinger Sherman, *Partakers of the Divine: Contemplation*

see monastery, Kaspar Ayndorffer, posed the question to Cusa by asking "whether without intellectual knowledge, or even any prior or accompanying thinking, a devout soul can attain God by *affectus* alone, or through the highest point of mind that they call *synderesis* [conscience] and to be immediately moved or carried up into him."[34] Within this late medieval debate, Cusa, as a representative of the so-called *via antiqua*, took the more traditional, Thomist approach: love must be informed by knowledge of the good. The Carthusian prior Vincent of Aggsbach, a defender of the *via moderna* of Thomas Gallus and Hugh of Balma, attacked Cusa for his Thomist intellectualism, his reliance on Aristotelian philosophy, and his overall academic approach to theology. Vincent's nominalist inclinations led him to accept a separation of knowledge and love, and he interpreted Dionysius's mysticism as affective in character. According to Vincent, one could reach the mind's summit (*apex mentis*) simply through love, without reliance on the intellect. He argued against the notion that "wisdom (*sapientia*) is consummated in affection only after having passed through a cognitive stage."[35]

Cusa, without denying the significant role that love and desire play in the mystical journey, maintained that nonetheless the intellect is integral to it.[36] Though the journey begins in a context of faith—a group of Benedictine monks standing in front of an icon, engaged in an exercise of prayer—the intellect is involved throughout: the icon demands intellectual reflection; the prayer it evokes engages the mind; and the monks embark on a rational discussion with each other about what they have seen. By emphasizing the interconnectedness of reason and faith, of the intellect and the will, the cardinal made clear that the path of love does not bypass the realities it encounters in time and space; the community of faith, the material object of

---

and the Practice of Philosophy (Minneapolis: Fortress, 2014), 170–73; Ziebart, "Laying Siege to the Wall of Paradise."

34. As quoted in McGinn, *Harvest of Mysticism*, 452.

35. Ziebart, "Laying Siege," 53. M. Führer argues that Cusa's *On the Vision of God* is a response to the subject-object crisis that entered the Middle Ages around the year 1100, and which can be seen in Anselm's lament in his *Proslogion* that he doesn't intuitively or directly experience what he has come to know of God by rational argument ("The Consolation of Contemplation in Nicholas of Cusa's *De visione Dei*," in Christianson and Izbicki, *Nicholas of Cusa on Christ and the Church*, 224–28).

36. William J. Hoye comments: "For Bonaventure, union with the unknown takes place on the other side of the intellectual faculty. This union is, according to him, 'unknowing' in the sense that it is affective. But such a limitation of the intellect could hardly satisfy Nicholas of Cusa, who used the expression 'mystical theology' to signify the highest step of his thinking" ("Vereinigung," 489 [translation mine]).

an icon, and the rational praxis of faith are all means that the intellect uses on its pilgrimage. In that sense, we may characterize Cusa's approach to the beatific vision as a sacramental one: the path to God was not mired, from the outset, in irrationality, let alone absurdity.[37]

Nicholas's high view of the intellect is unmistakable once he begins to reflect on what is implied in the mutual gaze between the figure of the icon and the monks in front of it. Although he physically sees God's face represented in the icon in contracted or limited form, Nicholas makes clear that God's true face is "absolute from every contraction [or limitation]. It has neither quality nor quantity, nor is it of time and place, for it is the absolute form, which is the face of faces" (*DVD* 6.17). We do not see God's face with "eyes of flesh," therefore, but with the "eyes of the mind and the intellect." Nonetheless, God's face is not separate from the world around us. Instead, God's absolute face, the "face of faces" (6.17)—which Cusa also terms "contraction of contractions" (2.7), "essence of essences" (9.34), and "form of . . . forms" (14.60)—can be seen in every particular face, since God's sight (his essence) "penetrates all things" (9.35). Since God is present in all things, when we look at the world around us, even at ourselves, we see God.[38] For Cusa, we know the God we love from our surroundings. It is our increasing intellectual acquaintance with the presence of God in the world that stimulates our desire for him. Meredith Ziebart is right, therefore, to suggest: "Contemplation of the icon gives rise to the realization of the priority of both the object of desire and, necessarily, some knowledge thereof, without which there would have been no turning in love towards it in the first place."[39] The intellect plays an important role for Cusa in the journey toward the *visio Dei*.

Despite the significance of sense perception and intellectual apprehension of eternal forms, neither the senses by themselves nor the intellect by itself

37. Johannes Hoff comments that "Cusa's *vera icona* lacks the characteristics of an art image" and instead "has the character of a liturgical image that can be approached *simultaneously* from a plurality of *embodied viewpoints* like a sacramental threshold that mediates between the earthly liturgical gathering of the church and the fullness of the divine glory without blurring the difference between the human and the divine" (*The Analogical Turn*, 32).

38. Cusa comments: "Whoever, therefore, merits to see your face sees all things openly and nothing remains hidden to this person. Whoever has you, O Lord, knows all things and has all things. . . . And how will you give yourself to me if you do not at the same time give me heaven and earth and all that are in them? And, even more, how will you give me yourself if you do not also give me myself?" (*DVD* 7.25). These kinds of comments, betraying Eckhart's influence, do not quite imply pantheism, but Cusa does push to the limit the identification of God with the believer, and vice versa.

39. Ziebart, "Laying Siege," 52.

gives us the vision of God that we long for. Only a vision of the "essence of essences" itself can satisfy this desire—and neither the senses nor the intellect is able to mount up to this "form of forms." Wherever the intellect may guide us, its object of knowledge is not truly God himself. This means, claims Cusa, that we need to "ascend above every end, every limit, and every finite thing," which involves intellectual ignorance and obscurity: "The intellect, therefore, must become ignorant and established in darkness if it wishes to see you. But what, my God, is intellect in ignorance if not learned ignorance? . . . The intellect knows that it is ignorant of you because it knows that you can be known only if the unknowable could be known, and the invisible seen, and the inaccessible reached" (*DVD* 13.52). Cusa's expression "learned ignorance" (*docta ignorantia*) is one of many paradoxical phrases that indicate that the wayfarer has arrived at the limit of his epistemic abilities.[40]

At this point, Cusa arrives at the wall that separates earthly life from heavenly paradise. He refers to it as the "wall of paradise" (*murus paradisi*). This wall contains the "coincidence of opposites" (*coincidentia oppositorum*), such as ignorance and knowledge, possibility and necessity, darkness and light, visibility and invisibility, potency and act, movement and rest, time and eternity, plurality and unity: "I have discovered that the place where you are found unveiled is girded about with the coincidence of contradictories. This is the wall of paradise, and it is there in paradise that you reside. The wall's gate is guarded by the highest spirit of reason, and unless it is overpowered, the way in will not lie open" (*DVD* 9.37). Discursive reason plays an invaluable role in the pilgrim's journey. At the gate of paradise, however, it inevitably runs up against the wall of contradictories. For Nicholas, the intellectual pursuit of faith ends at this wall. It is precisely this insight, that the intellect falls short and cannot take us to the paradise of our desire, that, so to speak, puts the pilgrim up against the wall and then takes him inside paradise. It is, therefore, the surrender of the intellect to silence that allows one to overpower the wall and enter paradise.[41]

The cardinal devotes a remarkably long section (chaps. 17–25) to what he sees behind the wall, inside paradise. Surprisingly perhaps, he speaks

40. As Clyde L. Miller summarizes Cusa at this point: "That God's infinity is seen to be beyond the limits of *ratio* helps us learn to acknowledge the confounding of reason in the face of contrariety and confront our ignorance of the divine. Only when discursive and dialectical reason are set aside can God's gift of vision occur" ("The Icon and the Wall: *Visio* and *Ratio* in Nicholas of Cusa's *De visione Dei,*" PACPhA 64 [1990]: 95–96).

41. Whereas in his earlier work, *On Learned Ignorance* (1440), Cusa had identified God with the coincidence of opposites, in *The Vision of God* he maintains that God lies beyond the wall of opposites (McGinn, *Harvest of Mysticism*, 448).

here at some length of the Trinity and of Christ. In Augustinian fashion he describes God as "infinitely lovable," and he comments: "You, therefore, my God, who are love, are the loving love, the lovable love, and the love which is the bond of loving love and lovable love" (17.71). God is the triune God of love, in whom the human intellect perceives absolute, uncontracted love, which Nicholas describes as "loving love" (Father), "lovable love" (Son), and the "bond of loving love" (Holy Spirit). The cardinal does not explain how it is possible to see this triune love inside the wall of paradise. We already know that the intellect cannot grasp this mystery, for "the wall shuts out the power of every intellect" (17.75). The eye may look into paradise, but it can "neither name nor understand" what it sees (17.75). Nonetheless, when Nicholas is "drawn away from the sweetness of this vision," he has a recollection of the triune love of God, which he hopes is reproduced in his own being (17.76).

The final chapters, 21–25, form the most significant part of the treatise. Here the cardinal addresses Jesus, whom he sees on the other side of the wall, in paradise: "O good Jesus, you are the Tree of Life in the paradise of delights. For none can be fed by that desirable life except from your fruit. You are, O Jesus, the fruit prohibited to all the children of Adam who, expelled from paradise, seek their means of living in the earth in which they toil" (21.92). Happiness thus comes from being united to Jesus. "Have mercy, O Jesus," exclaims Cusa, "and grant me to see you without veil, and my soul is saved!" (21.93). Since Jesus is both true God and true man, it is when we see the human Jesus that God gives himself to us to see: "You, O God, who are Goodness itself, could not satisfy your infinite mercy and generosity without giving us yourself! Nor could this be done more fittingly, in a way more possible for our receiving than that you took our nature, for we could not approach yours. Thus, you have come to us and are called Jesus, the ever blessed Savior" (23.106). The reason, according to Nicholas, that it is the intellect that takes us to the wall of paradise and subsequently allows us to see God is that the paradisal Word can be found within the intellect.[42]

Nicholas's descriptions of the *visio Dei* behind the wall of paradise are nothing short of remarkable. One would think that, having arrived at the wall of coincidences, the cardinal would lapse into Dionysian silence. But this is by no means the case. Instead, he embarks on an extended discussion of the Trinity and the person of Christ. Although he displays a keen

42. At the same time, Cusa is quick to add that it is by faith that the intellect approaches the Word, and he even acknowledges that it is love that unites the intellect to the Word (*DVD* 24.113).

awareness that these are mysteries to be adored, not intellectual puzzles to be solved, it is nonetheless emphatically the triune God of love and Christ as the tree of life whom we encounter beyond the wall in paradise.

What are we to make of this obviously kataphatic teaching regarding the Trinity and Christ as the object of the *visio Dei*? How is it possible for the positive contents of the Christian faith to feature so prominently even after the intellect has been left behind in the wall of paradise?[43] Dionysius, who is constantly in the background of Cusa's theology, recognized that the dialectic between affirmations and denials only takes us so far: by negating a positive statement one still claims to know something particular about God. For instance, to say that God is "not wise" is still to remain within the orbit of ordinary human discourse. God is truly known only when the mind transcends this dialectic and moves beyond itself. For Dionysius, "the most divine knowledge of God, that which comes through unknowing, is achieved in a union far beyond mind, *when mind turns away from all things, even from itself.*"[44] This is why Dionysius ended up calling the God beyond Being "Holy of Holies," "King of Kings," "Lord of lords," and "God of gods,"[45] and, ultimately, the "Perfect" and the "One."[46] By contrast, perhaps, Cusa's thick descriptions of the Trinity and of Christ hardly give the impression of someone whose mind has turned away from itself in true Dionysian fashion. It seems as though, for Cusa, the basic truths of the Christian faith are illuminated once the Dionysian dialectic has brought one past the wall of paradise.

Cusa does not give us a rationale for this approach. Surely, he must have been aware that the lengthy final section of his treatise transgresses the Dionysian dialectic.[47] Still, we must keep in mind that even Dionysius had started *Mystical Theology* with the exclamation, "Trinity!! Higher than any being, any divinity, any goodness!"[48] True, his brief treatise presents no further discussion either of the Trinity or of Christ. The conclusion of the trea-

---

43. Peter Casarella discusses the relationship between apophaticism and the name of Jesus in Cusa's book *On Learned Ignorance* and in sermon 20 ("*His Name Is Jesus*: Negative Theology and Christology in Two Writings of Nicholas of Cusa from 1440," in Christianson and Izbicki, *Nicholas of Cusa on Christ and the Church*, 281–307).

44. DN 872A, in *Pseudo-Dionysius: The Complete Works*, 109 (emphasis added).

45. DN 969A.

46. DN 977B–980C.

47. Cf. Hoff's comment: "Following Dionysius, Cusa had no misgivings about 'Despoiling the Hellenes,' but he never lost sight of the ultimate aim of his exercise: to obtain a hearing for the biblical calling upon the 'name of Jesus'" (*The Analogical Turn*, 14).

48. MT 997A.

tise simply states that both assertion and denial fall short of articulating who God is.[49] Nonetheless, the exclamation that begins Dionysius's exposition reverberates throughout, and Cusa could rightly have appealed to Dionysius for his claim that the God beyond the wall of paradise is none other than the triune God whom we see in Jesus Christ.[50] Cusa, I suspect (like Dionysius before him), recognized that the symbols of the Christian faith—the triune God as revealed in Christ—are in line with the ineffable vision of God beyond the wall of paradise.[51] Put differently, neither Dionysius nor Nicholas of Cusa intended to unsettle the contents of the Christian faith with their radical apophaticism. They took both the kataphatic and the apophatic stages of the wayfarer's journey with utter seriousness. And however different the reality of the beatific vision might be from this-worldly intellectual apprehensions of God, for Cusa (and, I suspect, also for Dionysius) this did not unsettle God's self-revelation in Jesus Christ.[52]

Both Dionysius and Cusa were cognizant of Saint Paul's comment that when he was caught up into paradise, "he heard things that cannot be told, which man may not utter" (2 Cor. 12:4).[53] Both theologians emphasized the ineffable character of Paul's experience. But they were also aware of the obligation that contemplation must in turn give way to action, and that contemplation comes with the task of sharing from the riches of one's experience, however inexpressible it may have been[54]—hence Cusa's treatise for

49. *MT* 1048B.

50. Moreover, also in *The Divine Names*, when at the end Dionysius describes God as "One," he repeatedly brings up the Trinity. The One is not found beyond the Trinity: "We use the names Trinity and Unity for that which is in fact beyond every name, calling it the transcendent being above every being" (*DN* 981A [p. 129]).

51. Clyde Miller grasps this point well when he writes: "Apart from Jesus there is no symbolic or conceptual measure or proportion on the basis of which we can obtain some cognitive purchase on what transcends the finite. The first part of *De visione Dei* points to the God who lies beyond these human limits, a God at best glimpsed in a darkling vision when reason and discourse are left behind. What remains in the second part are the *symbola fidei*—the mysteries of Trinity and Incarnation revealed to the eyes of faith" ("Icon and the Wall," 98).

52. Something similar is at work, I think, in Eph. 3, where Paul prays that "Christ may dwell in your hearts through faith—that you, being rooted and grounded in love, may have strength to comprehend with all the saints what is the breadth and length and height and depth, and to know the love of Christ that surpasses knowledge, that you may be filled with all the fullness of God" (3:17-19). On the one hand, the love of Christ "surpasses knowledge" (ὑπερβάλλουσαν τῆς γνώσεως). On the other hand, the saints are encouraged to "comprehend" (καταλαβέσθαι) the breadth, length, height, and depth of precisely this love of Christ.

53. Nicholas of Cusa quotes this passage in *DVD* 17.79.

54. Gregory of Nyssa's theology follows a similar pattern. See Martin Laird, "Apophasis

the Benedictine brothers at Tegernsee. The only way to share the fruits of contemplation was by returning to the positive language of the Scriptures and to the basic dogmas of the church: God is who he has revealed himself to be in Christ.

Conclusion

We cannot ignore the differences between the affective and intellective strands of Dionysian mysticism. For Bonaventure, renunciation of the intellect drives the pilgrimage, and it is affective desire that ultimately outstrips the intellect and so leads to the vision of God. For Cusa, it is the intellectual pursuit—and, notably, ultimately its failure as it culminates in the wall of contradictories—that allows one to enter paradise and partake of the fruit of the tree of life. Of course, both theologians offer carefully nuanced discussions of how one arrives at the beatific vision. Bonaventure does not disdain sense perception and the role of the intellect, while Cusa's mystagogy appeals to love and to the affections. At the end of the day, however, Bonaventure seems to have a hard time keeping love and knowledge together; already the pilgrimage itself is mostly sustained by desire, so that one wonders whether the minister general downplays perhaps unduly the intellectual apprehension of the mysteries of faith. Nicholas of Cusa, rightly it seems to me, keeps knowledge and love together, every step of the way; the pilgrim always already has in mind the object of his desire, and the desire is always driven by the particularities of the Christian faith.

It will be clear by now that, regardless of their differences, both Bonaventure and Cusa combined their Dionysian mysticism with a deep, personal faith in Jesus Christ. For Bonaventure, it is by identifying with Christ in his death on the cross that the pilgrim passes over from the world of sense perception and intellectual apprehension into paradise, where we see God. Nicholas of Cusa speaks of Jesus as the tree of paradise, whose hypostatic union "resolves" the problem of intellectual contradictions in the wall of paradise—though it does so in an ineffable manner, which is beyond intellectual comprehension.

Bonaventure is certainly right to ask us to identify with the suffering Lord. It is through participation in the suffering and death of Christ that

---

and Logophasis in Gregory of Nyssa's *Commentarius in Canticum Canticorum*," *SP* 37 (2001): 126–32.

we share in his resurrection and so experience the divinizing vision of God. The New Testament scholar Michael J. Gorman has recently argued that Saint Paul's central message can be captured with the phrase "You shall be cruciform, for I am cruciform."[55] Human holiness, according to Gorman, is a participation in the holiness of Christ.[56] As such, holiness allows us to share in Christ's kenotic life and death, and thus in the Trinitarian divine life. Gorman summarizes this "Christification" or deification as follows: "Theosis is transformative participation in the kenotic, cruciform character and life of God through Spirit-enabled conformity to the incarnate, crucified, and resurrected/glorified Christ, who is the image of God."[57] Thus, we come to share in the life of God by participating in the suffering of Christ. Bonaventure takes a similar approach. The attraction of his theology lies in the central role that our identification with the suffering and death of Christ plays in his theology. The only way to arrive at the deifying vision of God is through the darkness and death of the cross.

Nonetheless, there is a subtle difference here between Bonaventure and Cusa. While the Seraphic Doctor does well to insist that the intellect cannot experience the *transitus* to the vision of the Father without the darkness of the intellect, he appears to assume that the affections are able to bypass this renunciation. Bonaventure maintains that it is when one is inflamed with "spiritual fervor" and "the most burning affections" that one is able to pass over with the crucified Christ so as to see the Father.[58] To be sure, Bonaventure makes clear that God's grace drives the affections and that it is "Christ who starts the fire."[59] He clearly maintains that it is thanks to God's initiative that we are able finally to see him. Still, we must ask the question, why is the intellect stymied in its upward thrust by the encounter of the cross, while desire can move on without such self-denial? Doesn't Bonaventure's privileging of desire at least run the danger of assuming that there is something in the human person that does not need to undergo the purging of the cross? It seems to me that the *entire* person—both the intellect *and* the affections—experiences the deifying vision of God by the cruciform identification with Christ of which Bonaventure speaks. No aspect of the soul—including the affections—can avoid the renunciation of the cross.

55. Michael J. Gorman, *Inhabiting the Cruciform God: Kenosis, Justification, and Theosis in Paul's Narrative Soteriology* (Grand Rapids: Eerdmans, 2009), 105–28.

56. Gorman, *Inhabiting the Cruciform God*, 112.

57. Gorman, *Inhabiting the Cruciform God*, 125 (italics omitted).

58. *Itin.* 7.6.

59. *Itin.* 7.6.

Perhaps we must rethink one of the central assumptions in the voluntarist-intellectualist debate, namely, that it is either the will or the intellect that allows for ecstatic rapture and for beatific vision. When we are united with Christ, entering into his suffering and death allows us in turn to experience also his resurrection. This participation in Christ cannot be parsed out by prioritizing either knowledge or love. Precisely because union with Christ constitutes the movement from this-worldly life into an eschatological mode of existence, it is impossible for the one faculty to precede the other. Prioritizing between intellect and will is no longer possible and no longer has any meaning in the mystery of the deifying union with Christ. It is because knowledge and love are one in God that they are united also in the deified believer. To claim that it is either the one or the other that enables us to see God is to lapse into a rationalist reification of the faculties that tries to explain how it is possible for the human eye to see the face of God. Where the light of God's face meets the human gaze, all distinctions between knowledge and love are overcome.

CHAPTER 8

SPEECH AND VISION

Dante's Transhumanizing Journey

Legomena and *Phenomena*

Each of the five senses plays a unique role in bringing us nearer to God by
accessing the world around us. The physical, sensory capacities of hearing,
vision, smell, taste, and touch are all intimately linked to religious experience. Inasmuch as the natural world around us is a self-manifestation of
God, he uses every one of the physical senses to draw us into his presence.
This book deals with vision, in particular, and natural contemplation (θεωρία
φυσική) includes vision as one important means through which God draws
us into his presence.[1] But the fertile Christian tradition of the spiritual senses
reminds us that none of the five senses by itself fully explores how God reveals himself to us and how we draw near to him.[2] Each of the senses plays
a unique role in our relationship to God, and only when we reflect on them
together do we get a robust picture of how the senses are meant to function
in relation to God.

Particularly significant throughout the Scriptures and the Christian tradition is the notion of hearing or listening in response to divine speech.[3] In

1. The Greek term for contemplation (θεωρία) is itself derived from the verb "to gaze at,
behold" (θεάομαι). Cf. *TDNT* 5:318. For the notion of natural contemplation, see Bruce V. Foltz,
The Noetics of Nature: Environmental Philosophy and the Holy Beauty of the Visible (New York:
Fordham University Press, 2014); Norman Wirzba, "Christian *Theoria Physike*: On Learning
to See Creation," *ModTh* 32 (2016): 211–30.

2. For the history of the doctrine of the spiritual senses, see Paul L. Gavrilyuk and Sarah
Coakley, eds., *The Spiritual Senses: Perceiving God in Western Christianity* (Cambridge: Cambridge University Press, 2012).

3. Cf. the wonderful classic by Klaus Bockmuehl, *Listening to the God Who Speaks: Re-*

Genesis 1 God *speaks* the world into being, and John's Gospel makes clear that God does so through his eternal Word: "In the beginning was the Word, and the Word was with God, and the Word was God. He was in the beginning with God. All things were made through him, and without him was not any thing made that was made" (John 1:1–3). Creation is the result of God's speaking, so that it is in and through the Word that created realities arrive at their true identity. This centrality of speaking and listening in the Scriptures explains the key role that the Shema has played both in the Jewish and in the Christian tradition: "Hear, O Israel: The LORD our God, the LORD is one. You shall love the LORD your God with all your heart and with all your soul and with all your might. And these words that I command you today shall be on your heart" (Deut. 6:4–6). The book of Revelation depicts Christ as the beginning and the end of revelatory speech. He is "the Alpha and the Omega, the first and the last, the beginning and the end" (Rev. 22:13; cf. 21:6). It is through the law in the Old Testament and through the proclamation of the gospel in the New that God gathers for himself a people who obediently follow Christ as their creator and redeemer.

The Protestant emphasis on proclamation has traditionally highlighted God's speech (and the human response of obedient listening), and at times it has done so in contrast with a Catholic (and perhaps Orthodox) emphasis on vision—in the adoration of the sacrament, in bowing before images, and in praying with icons.[4] Lutheran theologian Robert W. Jenson sharply contrasts speech and vision when he writes:

> Western intellectual history has for the most part continued the Greek tradition for which "to be" meant to have form and so to appear and be seen, whether with the body's or the mind's eye. But there plainly is another possibility: that to be is to be *heard of*; and it is this interpretation that is demanded by the doctrine of creation. Within such an interpretation, instead of apprehending immediately encountered realities as "phenomena," "things that appear," we will apprehend them as "*legomena*," "things that are spoken of." Things are as we hear of them, from third parties or themselves.[5]

---

flections on God's Guidance from Scripture and the Lives of God's People, ed. Kathryn Yanni (Colorado Springs: Helmers and Howard, 1990).

4. Cf. J. M. F. Heath, *Paul's Visual Piety: The Metamorphosis of the Beholder* (Oxford: Oxford University Press, 2013), 21–28.

5. Robert W. Jenson, *Systematic Theology*, vol. 2, *The Works of God* (New York: Oxford University Press, 1999), 35–36; quotation marks after *legomena* missing in original.

As this chapter will make clear, I believe that Jenson's contrast between *phenomena* and *legomena* is overdrawn,[6] and it is in part the aim of this chapter to uphold the merit of a certain prioritizing of vision over speech through a study of Dante's *Paradiso*. Nonetheless, we begin this exploration of vision in Dante with the caveat—an important one, as we will see, also for Dante himself—that speech has a distinct role to play within the journey of salvation. It is the Logos, the eternal Word of God become flesh, who addresses us in the human words of Scripture and in ecclesial proclamation, and who makes us more than human by uniting us with himself in the incarnation.[7]

"To soar beyond the human cannot be described / in words"

The early fourteenth-century *Paradiso*, written by Dante Alighieri (1265–1321), embarks on a remarkable project: it describes Dante's journey of salvation as he soars through the heavens and is increasingly transformed into the living light of the triune God.[8] The end of his pilgrimage is nothing less than "transhumanizing"—*trasumanar*, to use Dante's own Italian neologism:

Trasumanar significar *per verba* non si poria; però l'essemplo basti a cui esperïenza grazia serba.	To soar beyond the human cannot be described in words. Let the example be enough to one for whom grace holds this experience in store.[9]

6. For a better approach, see the Reformed theologian G. C. Berkouwer, who in his treatment of the *visio Dei* denies that there would be "an anthropological division between hearing and seeing (as if man did have direct access to God via hearing)," though he acknowledges that the divine word "indicates what is prevalent in the relationship—the divine initiative: His voice, His word, which makes known His will (cf. Num. 7:89; Deut. 4:12, 15)" (*The Return of Christ*, trans. James Van Oosterom, ed. Marlin J. Van Elderen [Grand Rapids: Eerdmans, 1972], 363).

7. Origen famously spoke of three "incarnations" of the eternal Word: in the Virgin Mary, in Scripture, and in our own souls. See Hans Boersma, *Scripture as Real Presence: Sacramental Exegesis in the Early Church* (Grand Rapids: Baker Academic, 2017), 111–18.

8. I don't make a judgment on whether or not Dante the poet has actually experienced a mystical vision. The point is that as a poet, he takes the standpoint of someone who has had such an experience (as is clear especially from canto 33), and in line with a long tradition of mystical literature he now describes both the ascent and the final mystical experience itself. To do this, he invents his journey through the spheres as a literary conceit.

9. *Par.* 1.70–72. Hereafter, references from this work will be given in parentheses in the text; quotations come from Dante, *Paradiso*, trans. Jean Hollander and Robert Hollander, ed. Robert Hollander (New York: Doubleday, 2007).

It seems fitting that the first neologism of the *Paradiso* is the term *trasu-manar*.[10] This marks a humble acknowledgment that the words (*verba*) at the poet's disposal are inadequate to his task, namely, to describe the saints' beatific vision of God and his own experience of being raptured into the divine presence. The language available to Dante is incommensurate with the glory of which he must speak, and hence he expresses the purpose of his pilgrimage through a neologism that alludes at one and the same time to the suprahuman goal of the journey and the suprahuman task of the poet. As I hope to make clear in this chapter, Dante's pilgrimage to the beatific vision in the *Paradiso* is also a journey of deification— an ascent that reaches beyond the natural limits of humanity[11]—and, as such, it leads him to a realm beyond language. In deification, speech gives way to vision.

Language, for Dante, serves a provisional role, which we may call "sacramental." As such, it is an indispensable means through which he arrives at his supernatural end of seeing God face-to-face. The sacramental reality itself, however, is better expressed through the metaphor of vision than that of speech. In the end, the sacramental gift (*sacramentum*) of language makes way for the reality (*res*) of vision in the contemplative union with God. Dante succinctly describes this sacramental transition from language to vision in the highest heaven, the Empyrean itself:

Da quinci innanzi il mio veder fu maggio	From that time on my power exceeded
che 'l parlar mostra, ch'a tal vista cede,	that of speech, which fails at such a vision,
e cede la memoria a tanto oltraggio.	as memory fails at such abundance.

(*Par.* 33.55–57)

10. Cf. the reflections on this neologism, as well as that of "imparadise" (*'mparadisa*) in *Par.* 28.3 and of "entrine" (*s'interna*) in *Par.* 28.120 in Peter O'Leary, "Imparadising, Transhumanizing, Intrining: Dante's Celestial Vision," *Postmed* 6 (2015): 154–64. Dante coins several other, related neologisms. He speaks of a seraph who "ingods" (*s'india*) himself (*Par.* 4.28); of Folco of Marseille's sight being "in-Himmed" (*s'inluia*) (9.73); of Peter Damian being "inwombed" (*m'inventro*) in the radiance of light (21.84); and of the seraphim being "intruthed" (*s'invera*) by the blazing point of light (28.39).

11. While Dante does not use language of "divinization" much, his neologisms make clear that this is what he has in mind. He also speaks of Richard of Saint Victor being in contemplation as "more than human" (*più che viro*) (*Par.* 10.132). Most importantly, Dante's own transformation into light, which I will discuss below, only makes sense as a process of being deified in and by the light of glory.

At the culmination of the process of *trasumanar*, Dante gazes directly into the light of God's being, and words cannot tell what he experiences at this point. His speech "fails at such a vision."

Dante repeatedly reminds his reader of the inadequacy and provisional character of language. When he arrives in the Starry Sphere, Dante meets Adam, who mentions that he has regained the immediacy of knowledge, which he had lost in the Fall:

Indi spirò: "Sanz' essermi proferta da te, la voglia tua discerno meglio che tu qualunque cosa t'è più certa;	Then it breathed forth: "Without your telling me, I can discern your wishes even better than you can picture anything you know as certain.
perch' io la veggio nel verace speglio che fa di sé pareglio a l'altre cose, e nulla face lui di sé pareglio."	For I can see them in that truthful mirror which makes itself reflective of all else but which can be reflected nowhere else."

(26.103–8)

In heaven, language is no longer needed. Adam has access to Dante's thoughts and wishes in a direct fashion ("Without your telling me"). The reason is that Dante's thoughts are reflected in "that truthful mirror" of the mind of God itself.[12] Adam's beatific vision means that he sees all created realities—including the very thoughts of his earthly visitor—at once in the mind of God.[13]

When, in the final canto, Dante himself sees the vision of God, he too comes to know in an immediate fashion all of created reality in the mind of God:

Oh abbondante grazia ond' io presunsi ficcar lo viso per la luce etterna, tanto che la veduta consunsi!	O plenitude of grace, by which I could presume to fix my eyes upon eternal Light until my sight was spent on it!

---

12. Robert Hollander explains that the term *pareglio* is probably a substantive, meaning "parhelion" or "mock-sun," so that a *pareglio* is a reflection of the sun (in Dante, *Paradiso*, 721). In other words, Adam can see Dante's thoughts reflected in the "mock-sun" of God's mind.

13. The notion that saints and angels can see people's thoughts in the divine mind is also expressed in *Par.* 9.21; 11.19–21; 15.55; 20.79–80; 22.35–36; 26.95–96, 103–4.

Nel suo profondo vidi che s'interna,	In its depth I saw contained,
legato con amore in un volume,	by love into a single volume bound,
ciò che per l'universo si squaderna:	the pages scattered through the universe:

sustanze e accidenti e lor costume	substances, accidents, and the interplay between them,
quasi conflati insieme, per tal modo	as though they were conflated in such ways
che ciò ch'i' dico è un semplice lume.	that what I tell is but a simple light.

(33.82–90)

In the depth of the eternal light of God, Dante sees the multiplicity of the scattered pages of creation joined in the unity of a single volume. The many words of time are united in the one eternal Word. Dante is now able to read creation (and, presumably, also history) as a single volume because the many words of the pages of the book of creation are no longer scattered through the universe: they are bound together in the mind of God.[14] In the beatific vision, the reading of individual, scattered pages gives way to a united vision of all created things in God.[15] Such unified apprehension is possible for Dante because, seeing as he has fixed his eyes (*ficcar lo visio*) upon the eternal Light, speech now yields to vision.

Dante's experience is that of Saint Paul in 2 Corinthians 12:3–4, where he says that, "caught up into paradise," "he heard things that cannot be told, which man may not utter."[16] Dante patterns his *peregrinatio* among the saints

---

14. Dante's reference to scattered pages being bound by love into a single volume is likely a double entendre. It is a reference to providence in general (all of time being united in the eternal Word), but it is also a humble acknowledgment on Dante's part that God's providence in Christ extends to Dante's poem, as its many pages are taken up into one volume by "the truthful Author" (*verace autore*) (*Par.* 26.40) in whom all things hold together (cf. Col. 1:17). Dante's poetry thus has its anchor in the eternal Word, the "alpha and omega" (*Alfa e O*) (*Par.* 26.17), who in himself holds "the boundaries of the letters of the alphabet which can be combined in and produce all possible words" (Giuseppe Mazzotta, *Dante, Poet of the Desert: History and Allegory in the Divine Comedy* [Princeton: Princeton University Press, 1987], 11). I am grateful to Dominic Manganiello for personal email correspondence on this point.

15. "Dante," comments Christian Moevs, "has experienced the revelation that all perceivers and things perceived ultimately are the qualified projections or reflections of one limitless and dimensionless reality" (*The Metaphysics of Dante's Comedy* [Oxford: Oxford University Press, 2005], 78).

16. Dante alludes to 2 Cor. 12:2 ("whether in the body or out of the body I do not know") when he writes:

in the spheres of paradise and his subsequent lightning-bolt experience on Paul's *raptus*. This means that Dante not only enjoys the bliss of the vision of God, but also faces the Pauline dilemma of how to put into words this ineffable experience. This dilemma becomes increasingly pressing in the poem, as Dante moves up through the planetary spheres and arrives finally at the highest sphere (the Primum Mobile) and then, beyond the spheres, at the Empyrean itself.

"For this reason Scripture condescends"

The difficulty that Dante the poet encounters is how to describe the reality (*res*) of heaven, where saints enjoy the beatific vision, while both he and his readers remain tethered to sacramental means (*sacramenta*). This dilemma is particularly poignant since Dante the pilgrim undertakes his journey as an embodied human being, whereas the souls he meets en route in the planetary spheres are disembodied and behold the divine essence in this state. Although Dante makes his way step by step through the nine heavenly spheres (beginning with the moon and ending with the final sphere of the Primum Mobile), the saints he meets in each successive sphere are actually already in the highest heaven itself. They are not in the spheres at all; all along, they have had their place within the Empyrean rose.[17] Having gone to heaven and back in Pauline fashion, Dante faces the difficult task of reducing the reality (*res*) he has seen to a linguistic sacrament (*sacramentum*), and he does this by inventing a pilgrimage through the heavens and by pretending that

---

S'i' era sol di me quel che creasti
novellamente, amor che 'l ciel
  governi,
tu 'l sai, che col tuo lume mi levasti.

Whether I was there in that part only which you
created last is known to you alone, O Love who
  rule
the heavens and drew me up there with your
  light. (*Par.* 1.73–75)

17. Jeffrey Burton Russell puts it as follows: "Theologically speaking, God, heaven, and the blest are not on the planets or in the spheres at all, but beyond them in the empyrean, beyond the cosmos itself in the highest heaven. Dante the poet pretends that to greet him the blest descend from the empyrean to spheres appropriate to their lives: warriors descend to Mars, contemplatives to the sun" ("The Heavenly Paradise," in *A History of Heaven: The Singing Silence* [Princeton: Princeton University Press, 1997], 166). See also Erich Auerbach, *Dante: Poet of the Secular World*, trans. Ralph Manheim (1929; rev. ed., New York: New York Review of Books, 2007), 116.

the blessed have their place in their various spheres. Dante employs poetic license that enables him to describe in some way the reality of paradise.

When Dante arrives at the moon, he does not immediately realize that the saints do not really have an abiding place there. Beatrice needs to correct his Platonic notion that at death the souls return to their own stars (*Par.* 4.22–24). She emphatically warns Dante that he should not think in an earthly manner about what he sees in the spheres:

"D'i Serafin colui che più s'india,	"Not the Seraph that most ingods himself,
Moïsè, Samuel, e quel Giovanni	not Moses, Samuel, or whichever John you please—
che prender vuoli, io dico, non Maria,	none of these, I say, not even Mary,
non hanno in altro cielo i loro scanni	have their seats in another heaven
che questi spirti che mo t'appariro,	than do these spirits you have just nowseen,
né hanno a l'esser lor più o meno anni;	nor does their bliss last fewer years or more.
ma tutti fanno bello il primo giro,	No, all adorn the highest circle—
e differentemente han dolce vita	but they enjoy sweet life in differing measure
per sentir più e men l'etterno spiro.	as they feel less or more of God's eternal breath.
Qui si mostraro, non perché sortita	Those souls put themselves on here
sia questa spera lor, ma per far segno	not because they are allotted to this sphere
de la celestïal c'ha men salita.	but as a sign of less exalted rank in Heaven.
Così parlar conviensi al vostro ingegno,	It is necessary thus to address your faculties,
però che solo da sensato apprende	since only in perceiving through the senses can they grasp
ciò che fa poscia d'intelletto degno."	that which they then make fit for intellect."

(4.28–42)

Beatrice makes explicit that the angels and the blessed "adorn the highest circle," that they are not really "allotted to this sphere," and that their distribution across the various spheres in the narrative is a symbolic description of the reality that the saints occupy varying ranks in heaven itself.[18] In other words, the fictive positioning of saints throughout the planetary spheres is necessary because embodied human beings such as Dante depend on sensible observation and because poetic discourse relies on the temporal cosmos in which such sensible observation takes place. The reality (*res*) to which the journey through paradise refers is, on Dante's understanding, purely intellectual. The entire poetic narrative of the *Paradiso* thus takes the form of poetic accommodation.

As a result, Dante regards his poetic task as analogous to God's accommodation to human limitations in Scripture. After she has confided to Dante that the saints he sees in the moon are not really there at all—since they are already with God in the Empyrean—Beatrice tells him in canto 4 that the journey through paradise is an accommodation to the senses:

"Per questo la Scrittura condescende a vostra facultate, e piedi e mano attribuisce a Dio e altro intende;	"For this reason Scripture condescends to your capacity when it attributes hands and feet to God, but has another meaning,
e Santa Chiesa con aspetto umano Gabrïel Michel vi rappresenta, e l'altro che Tobia rifece sano."	and for your sake Holy Church portrays Gabriel and Michael with the faces of men and that other angel who made Tobit well again."

(4.43–48)

The entire account of Dante soaring through the heavens with Beatrice condescends to the circumstances of the readers, who can only grasp the reality of the intellectual Empyrean through material images and multiple words—in other words, through sacramental means. As Jeffrey Russell puts

---

18. When Dante arrives in the Starry Sphere, the entire church triumphant welcomes him, having come down from the Empyrean to greet him (*Par.* 23.19–23). Robert Hollander points out that, by implication, "Dante has seen some of these souls before. If all of them now descend, their number includes all the souls since Piccarda whom he has already seen in the various seven previous heavens" (in Dante, *Paradiso*, 635). Thus, Dante sees some of the saints three times: he meets some of them in one of the lower spheres of paradise, he encounters them again in the Starry Sphere, and they eternally have their place in the rose in the Empyrean itself.

it: "Dante the poet, knowing that what he has seen is beyond human language, must accommodate his readers as God accommodates him, using language, and even pressing through it with neologisms, in order to describe what is beyond description."[19] By presenting a lengthy, drawn-out account of his journey through paradise, Dante condescends to his readers, using human words that express the inexpressible.

"Who, filled with longing, / finds satisfaction in his hope"

It is perhaps tempting to take Dante's account of the heavenly spheres more literally. On such a reading, we might take the distribution of the blessed across the heavenly spheres as depicting their continuing postmortem pilgrimage: after having gone through purgatory, the blessed would then continue to move up through varying degrees of increasing happiness toward the final face-to-face vision of God. The end of purgatory, on such a reading, would not immediately lead to the beatific vision of the divine essence in heaven. Instead, there really would be varying degrees of happiness between purgatory and the final vision of God. In other words, Dante would allow for progress in the process of deification even after the blessed have moved from purgatory into heaven.

Although such a reading of the *Paradiso* is incorrect, it would fit with earlier theological understandings of the hereafter. The saints in heaven, so it was commonly thought, do not yet have as clear and direct a vision of God as one day they will; on the day of judgment, when body and soul will be reunited, the saints will have a clearer vision of God than they do in the intermediate state.[20] This notion of a graduated perfection of the vision of God became the subject of intense controversy a decade after Dante's death, in the 1330s. Pope John XXII (1316–1334) wrote on this topic in 1331, in his book *On the Glory of the Souls* (*De gloria animarum*), which he followed up with four sermons, claiming that it is only at the last judgment that faith will make way for sight and that only then will the saints see Christ not just in his humanity but also

---

19. Russell, "The Heavenly Paradise," 165.

20. Nicholas Constas makes clear that patristic and Byzantine theologians treated the intermediate state as an (often dream-like) state of further preparation for the eschaton, and he comments: "The Byzantines believed that only in the clarifying light of the eschaton would the authentically and abidingly human appear in definitive relief and resolution" ("'To Sleep, Perchance to Dream': The Middle State of Souls in Patristic and Byzantine Literature," *DOP* 55 [2001]: 119). I am indebted to Sarah Coakley for drawing my attention to this article.

in his divinity.[21] Pope John retracted his views on his deathbed, and they were formally banned by his successor, Benedict XII, when in 1336 he published the constitution *Benedictus Deus*. Here the pope claimed that "the divine essence immediately manifests itself to them [i.e., the saints], plainly, clearly and openly, and in this vision they enjoy the divine essence."[22] *Benedictus Deus* decisively precluded a graduated progression toward the beatific vision.

The views of Pope John XXII, for which he appealed to Augustine and Bernard of Clairvaux, may have been suppressed in the 1330s, but they did echo earlier, patristic positions on the beatific vision. As we saw earlier, in the early church, a number of theologians—most famously Saint Gregory of Nyssa—held to the notion of *epektasis*, a perpetual progress of the saints into the infinite life of God.[23] In comparison to this patristic (and later Orthodox) notion, Pope John XXII's views were rather tepid. After all, belief in *epektasis* had a number of theological corollaries, none of which John XXII was willing to adopt as his own: (1) *Epektasis* meant an eternal "journey" ever more deeply into the life of God, continuously spurred on by the will (perhaps a desiring will). (2) Inasmuch as eternal progress was grounded in the infinity of God, it meant an increase in the blessed's vision of God, not only from the time they entered heaven until the last judgement, but also thereafter. (3) This doctrine of eternal progress typically implied a christological (theophanic) understanding of the beatific vision patterned on the transfiguration: the saints would never see God directly but would only ever see him in and through Christ. And (4) all of this precluded an eternal resting in the divine essence, since God's essence remained forever out of reach. Pope John XXII held none of these implications of the doctrine of eternal progress. He restricted himself to the assertion that the immediate, intuitive vision of the divine essence does not happen right after death (for the saints) or right after purgatory (for the rest of us), but is deferred till the final

21. For the sermons and the controversy, see Marc Dykmans, *Les Sermons de Jean XXII sur la vision béatifique*, Miscellanea Historiae Pontificiae 34 (Rome: Presses de l'Université Grégorienne, 1973); John E. Weakland, "Pope John XXII and the Beatific Vision Controversy," *AnM* 9 (1968): 76–84; F. A. van Liere, "Johannes XXII en het conflict over de visio beatifica," *NedTT* 44 (1990): 208–22; Christian Trottmann, *La Vision béatifique des disputes scolastiques à sa définition par Benoît XII*, Bibliothèque des écoles françaises d'Athènes et de Rome 289 (Rome: École française de Rome, 1995); William Duba, "The Beatific Vision in the *Sentences* Commentary of Gerald Odonis," *Vivarium* 47 (2009): 348–63.

22. Pope Benedict XII, "Benedictus Deus," January 29, 1336, in Xavier LeBachelet, "Benoît XII," in *Dictionnaire de Théologie Catholique*, vol. 2, pt. 1, cols. 657–58 (Paris: Letouzey et Ané, 1932), http://www.papalencyclicals.net/Ben12/B12bdeus.htm.

23. For the term *epektasis*, see above, chap. 3, section entitled "*The Life of Moses*: Vision as Perpetual Desire."

judgment. Nonetheless, it is clear that his understanding of the intermediate state contained vestiges of the earlier position.

Dante's depiction of paradise does evince similarities with these earlier views, but we would misread the *Paradiso* if we interpreted the presence of the saints in the various heavenly spheres as Dante incorporating either an earlier patristic understanding of *epektasis* or the position that would be condemned in 1336. To be sure, Dante's journey through the heavens is driven by desire, and various saints he meets along the way also express their longing for the light of God. Based on this, Lino Pertile does read the *Paradiso* as reflecting a doctrine of *epektasis*.[24] He turns to canto 23, where Dante in the Starry Sphere sees Beatrice, who with longing seeks out "the region of the sky / in which the sun reveals less haste" ("la plaga / sotto la quale il sol mostra men fretta") (23.12). Beatrice is like a bird perched on her nest with her brood,

che, per veder li aspetti disïati	who in her longing to look upon their eyes and beaks
e per trovar lo cibo onde li pasca,	and to find the food to nourish them—
in che gravi labor li sono aggrati,	a task, though difficult, that gives her joy—
previene il tempo in su aperta frasca,	now, on an open bough, anticipates that time
e con ardente affetto il sole aspetta,	and, in her ardent expectation of the sun,
fiso guardando pur che l'alba nasca.	watches intently for the dawn to break.

$$(23.4-9)$$

Beatrice's longing for Christ's appearance arouses a similar desire in Dante himself:

sì che, veggendola io sospesa e vaga,	I, therefore, seeing her suspended, wistful,
fecimi qual è quei che disïando	became as one who, filled with longing,
altro vorria, e sperando s'appaga.	finds satisfaction in his hope.

$$(23.13-15)^{25}$$

24. Lino Pertile, "A Desire of Paradise and a Paradise of Desire: Dante and Mysticism," in *Dante: Contemporary Perspectives*, ed. Amilcare A. Iannucci (Toronto: University of Toronto Press, 1997), 148–63.

25. The language of "desire," found here in *Par.* 23.4 and 23.14, recurs a little later in 23.39 and 23.105.

Even though Dante does not see the object of his desire, he is nonetheless satisfied. By interpreting this satisfaction of longing as a continuation of hope, he appears to make desire the engine of continuing progress. Understandably, therefore, Pertile comments: "What the poet describes is not Paradise as timeless fruition, but a Paradise of desire, a Paradise in time, where desire is at the same time constantly present and constantly satisfied by the certainty of fulfillment."[26] Dante, according to Pertile, travels through a paradisal cosmos of desire.

Dante's depiction of *epektasis*, argues Pertile, makes him disagree with Thomas Aquinas (as well as contradict his own earlier understanding in the *Convivio*).[27] For Aquinas, the soul achieves rest precisely by acquiring the happiness of seeing the essence of God,[28] whereas for Dante (at least on Pertile's understanding), happiness means to find satisfaction in the ever-progressing desire for more of God. By depicting Dante as being in line with the earlier patristic tradition, Pertile concludes that this puts him on a different theological trajectory than that of Aquinas.[29]

Pertile rightly points out the dynamic process of Dante's journey and the key role that desire plays within this process. It is also true, at least in some sense, that paradise itself becomes a place of desire for Dante. Both Dante himself and the blessed express their longing throughout the *Comedy*'s third cantica. Indeed, we may go so far as to echo Pertile's suggestion that "it is because Dante imagines and structures it in terms of a tension between desire and fulfilment that his Paradise becomes poetically

---

26. Pertile, "Desire of Paradise," 149.

27. Pertile, "Desire of Paradise," 153.

28. *ST* I-II, q. 3, aa. 4, 8.

29. This is not the place to ferret out Dante's Thomistic and/or Franciscan proclivities, but broadly speaking, his theological paradigm fits better with a Thomist than with a Franciscan theological perspective—though Francis de Capitain went too far in describing the *Divine Comedy* as "the *Summa* in verse" ("Dante's Conception of the Beatific Vision," *ACQR* 27 [1902]: 418). In a number of instances, Dante puts forward positions that do not cohere with those of the Angelic Doctor. Kenelm Foster explains that Dante (1) rejects Aquinas's simultaneous creation of matter and form, insisting that God first created prime matter; (2) has a more substantial role than Aquinas for angels in the formation of the sublunary world by means of the heavenly bodies; (3) holds to a different understanding of the body-soul relationship and the process of human generation than Aquinas; (4) posits two final ends for human beings, corresponding to man's mortal and immortal natures, whereas Aquinas speaks of one, supernatural end; and (5) hardly works with the distinction between essence and existence (*The Two Dantes and Other Studies* [Berkeley: University of California Press, 1977], 57, 60–61).

representable and *Paradiso* works as poetry. The presence of desire in the pilgrim allows the poet to describe his ascent as a dynamic progression."[30] Dante's use of language does give a sense of dynamic progression, which in turn also allows for desire to play a continuing role in the various celestial spheres.

None of this means, however, that Dante regards desire as literally unending. Instead, he affirms that the natural desire for ultimate truth brings satisfaction and rest—and as such an end to all desire. When on the moon he has listened to Beatrice, Dante exclaims in response:

"Io veggio ben che già mai non si sazia	"I now see clearly that our intellect
nostro intelletto, se 'l ver non lo illustra	cannot be satisfied until that truth enlighten it
di fuor dal qual nessun vero si spazia.	beyond whose boundary no further truth extends.
Posasi in esso, come fera in lustra,	In that truth, like a wild beast in its den, it rests
tosto che giunto l'ha; e giugner puollo:	once it has made its way there—and it can do that,
se non, ciascun disio sarebbe *frustra*."	or else its every wish would be in vain."
	(4.124–29)[31]

For Dante, all truths lead to the one, ultimate truth, which allows for the intellect to be satisfied (*sazia*) and to rest (*posasi*).

Similarly, when on Saturn he asks Benedict of Nursia to see him with his face unveiled—that is to say, the monk's bodily appearance—Benedict rebukes him, since such vision is not possible at this stage:

Ond' elli: "Frate, il tuo alto disio	And he: "Brother, your lofty wish
s'adempierà in su l'ultima spera,	shall find fulfillment in the highest sphere,
ove s'adempion tutti li altri e 'l mio.	where all desires are fulfilled, and mine as well.

---

30. Pertile, "Desire of Paradise," 156.

31. Cf. the discussion of this passage in Christopher Ryan, *Dante and Aquinas: A Study of Nature and Grace in the Comedy*, ed. John Took (London: Ubiquity Press, 2013), 118–20.

Ivi è perfetta, matura e intera	There only all we long for is perfected,
ciascuna disïanza; in quella sola	ripe, and entire. It is there alone
è ogne parte là ove sempr' era."	each element remains forever in its
	place."

(22.61–66)

In the seventh sphere, Dante cannot yet see Benedict's unveiled face. Benedict claims unequivocally that this desire (*disio*) of Dante—along with every other desire—will be fulfilled only in the highest sphere, the Empyrean itself.

When Bernard leads Dante into the Empyrean and prays to Mary on his behalf, the role of desire comes to an end:

E io ch'al fine di tutt' i disii	And, as I neared the end of all desire,
appropinquava, si com' io dovea,	I extended to its limit, as was right,
l'ardor del desiderio in me finii.	the ardor of the longing in my soul.

(33.46–48)

Here, in the Empyrean, in the presence of God, Dante reaches the end of his desires. The term "end" (*fine*) should be understood teleologically as the purpose at which desire aims: God is the end or aim of all Dante's desire. At the same time, the word "end" also implies that when desire has reached its purpose, it ceases.[32] Presumably, Dante means to say that once the ardor of his soul reaches its climactic end, it has reached its conclusion and gives way to final rest.

Dante, therefore, does not retrieve earlier eschatological views of *epektasis*. To be sure, the desire to see the light of God is an important factor in Dante's journey through paradise. But we would lapse into literalism if we took these expressions of longing—on the part of the blessed and of Dante himself—as reflecting an actual progression of the saints in eternity. The entire journey through paradise—including Dante's encounters with the blessed in the various spheres—is an expression of condescension or accommodation to Dante's readers.[33] His descriptions of *epektasis* are part and

---

32. Dante gives no indication that he thinks desire continues within the presence of God, and my overall interpretation pleads against taking the word "end" here as allowing for desire to continue. For a different interpretation, see Hollander, in Dante, *Paradiso*, 923.

33. Cf. John Freccero's comment: "Insofar as the *Paradiso* exists at all . . . it is an accommodation, a compromise short of silence. . . . The prodigious achievement of the poet is that he manages . . . to represent non-representation without falling either into unintelligibility or into silence. Within the story, this accommodation takes the form of a 'command performance' of all of the souls of the blessed for the exclusive benefit of the pilgrim" ("An Introduction to the *Paradiso*," in *Dante: The Poetics of Conversion*, ed. Rachel Jacoff [Cambridge, MA: Harvard

parcel of this poetic accommodation. They are Dante's way of dealing with the dilemma of having to express in words something that language cannot properly convey. Put differently, for Dante, desire belongs to the penultimate reality of a world in which sacraments still have their place. My personal convictions line up more with the earlier view of Gregory of Nyssa than with Dante: Gregory's *epektasis* does greater justice to divine infinity (and to the creator-creature distinction) than Aquinas's and Dante's vision of the divine essence. The conclusion seems to me inescapable, however, that for Dante, once we arrive at the reality (*res*) of the beatific vision—that is to say, once we are face-to-face with God in the Empyrean—desire ceases, and we find satisfaction not in hope but in the divine essence of God himself as the object of our desire.[34]

University Press, 1986], 211). I thank Dominic Manganiello for drawing my attention to this passage.

34. In the final quatrain of the last canto, immediately after Dante has experienced the bolt of lightning by which he intuits truthfully the mystery of the incarnation, we read once more about Dante's desire:

A l'alta fantasia qui mancò possa;	Here my exalted vision lost its power.
ma già volgeva il mio disio	But now my will and my desire, like wheels
e 'l *velle*,	revolving
sì come rota ch'igualmente è mossa,	with an even motion, were turning with
l'amor che move il sole e l'altre stelle.	the Love that moves the sun and all the other
	stars.

(33.142–45)

It seems unlikely to me that this final stanza speaks of epektatic desire that continues once Dante has gained the beatific vision. Such a reading (1) does not properly explain how it is possible for the vision to have "lost its power," since presumably the beatific vision continues along with the will and with desire; (2) clashes with Dante's repeatedly expressed view that desire comes to an end in the beatific vision; and (3) makes it appear as though at this point Dante already joins the saints in heaven for the final beatific vision, which ignores that Dante came back to Earth to write his poem. In short, such a reading assumes, wrongly I think, that Dante actually joins the saints in the Empyrean in the everlasting beatific vision. Much more likely, since Dante patterns his experience on Paul's *raptus* of 2 Cor. 12:3–4, the poet describes here the lapse back into temporal reality after his mystical experience, in a manner rather similar to Augustine's descriptions of the same in his *Confessions* (cf. chap. 4 above, section entitled "The Firstfruits of the Spirit"). The description of Dante's will and desire as turning now with the Love that moves the sun and the stars likely depicts the continuing effects that his contemplative, mystical experience has in the day-to-day active life that follows it.

"Beatitude itself / is based upon the act of seeing"

This understanding of desire serving only a penultimate role fits with Dante's overall intellectualist understanding of the beatific vision.[35] Dante was convinced that the saints will see the essence of God and that this vision of the divine essence—rather than the subsequent enjoyment of it—constitutes true happiness. Tamara Pollack, in a careful study of Dante's doctrine of beatitude against the backdrop of medieval scholastic theology, makes clear that Dante treats vision as the formal cause of happiness. Vision—or knowledge—makes beatitude what it is. Pollack appeals to a well-known passage in canto 28. Speaking of the three highest ranks of angels penetrating the truth, Beatrice comments:

"e dei saper che tutti hanno diletto quanto la sua veduta si profonda nel vero in che si queta ogne intelletto.	"And you should know that all of them delight in measure of the depth to which their sight can penetrate the truth, where every intellect finds rest.
Quinci si può veder come si fonda l'esser beato ne l'atto che vede, non in quel ch'ama, che poscia seconda."	From this, it may be seen, beatitude itself is based upon the act of seeing, not on that of love, which follows after."

(28.106–11)

Not only does Beatrice reiterate that the intellect "finds rest" (*queta*) in truth itself, but she also explicitly affirms that happiness is based on the act of seeing and denies that this happiness would consist in the act of love. So, not only does the act of love *follow* that of vision as its consequence, but, more importantly, it is knowledge rather than love that constitutes happiness. Pollack comments: "In my opinion, it is clear from this passage that Dante intends the priority of vision to love in the stronger sense of that which is 'more principle'

---

35. Intellectualist views of the beatific vision equate the happiness (beatitude) of the vision with the intellectual act of apprehending the divine essence. Thomas Aquinas, for example, argues that "the essence of happiness consists in an act of the intellect: but the delight that results from happiness pertains to the will" (*ST* I-II, q. 3, a. 4). For Dante, desire (as an act of the will) leads to the happiness of the beatific vision, which is strictly an act of the intellect. For more on the relationship between intellect and will, see the discussion on Bonaventure and Nicholas of Cusa in the previous chapter.

[*sic*] and constitutes the unitive power of the soul, rather than in the weaker and generally uncontested sense of simple antecedence. . . . In sum, Dante, like William of Auxerre and Aquinas, conceives the highest power of the soul, by which the soul is capable of being joined directly to God, to be the intellect, and the essence of beatitude to consist in an act of vision."[36] It is precisely his intellectualist position—that is to say, his treatment of beatific vision as an act of the intellect rather than of the will—that allows Dante to say that desire comes to an end once the intellect has entered truth itself.

As a result, Dante, much like Thomas Aquinas, abandoned the earlier approach to the beatific vision as the ultimate theophany. For Dante, the intellect reaches truth itself—or, in theological terms, it attains to the essence of God. Pollack explains that the condemnations of 1241 and 1244—which banned the view that the angels and the blessed fail to see the divine essence—entrenched the rejection of the earlier theophanic understanding of the beatific vision. Pollack describes the condemned views as follows: "The position in question was inspired by an encounter with the apophatic theology of the later Greek fathers, with their emphasis on the inaccessible mystery, the transcendent unknowability of God, who becomes knowable to His creatures solely through His theophanies or manifestations."[37] In other words, according to the condemnations by the bishop of Paris, God is supremely knowable, so that in the hereafter the saints will see the divine essence itself. This face-to-face vision of God is made possible by the light of glory (*lumen gloriae*), which strengthens the intellect so that it can see the divine essence. Comments Pollack: "In the years following the condemnations, and chiefly through the influence of Albert the Great, the doctrine of the *lumen gloriae* ('light of glory') was elaborated, as the illuminating grace which strengthens the intellect so that it can see God. This was in effect the Greek idea of a vision through theophanies, redefined now as an inward, or immanent medium which transforms the soul into a divine image."[38] The light of glory thus took the place of theophanies as the interpretive principle for the doctrine of the beatific vision, enabling theologians to affirm that beatitude consists in seeing the divine essence.[39]

36. Tamara Pollack, "Light, Love and Joy in Dante's Doctrine of Beatitude," in *Reviewing Dante's Theology*, vol. 1, ed. Claire E. Honess and Matthew Treherne, Leeds Studies on Dante (Oxford: Lang, 2013), 294–95.

37. Pollack, "Light, Love and Joy," 304.

38. Pollack, "Light, Love and Joy," 304–5.

39. For further discussion of the decisions of 1241 and 1244, see H.-F. Dondaine, "L'Object et le 'medium' de la vision béatifique chez les théologiens du XIIIe siècle," *RTAM* 19 (1952): 60–99; Trottmann, *La Vision béatifique*, 115–208; and Tamara Pollack, "Light and Mirror in

Pollack points to Dante's encounter with the eleventh-century Benedictine monk and cardinal Peter Damian. When Dante asks Damian why he is the one sent to welcome Dante to Saturn, Damian comes up with a fascinating response that combines a strong claim to knowledge with a plea of ignorance:

posi rispuose l'amor che v'era dentro: "Luce divina sopra me s'appunta, penetrando per questa in ch'io m'inventro,	Then the love that was within it [i.e., the light] spoke: "Divine light focuses on me, piercing the radiance that holds me in its womb.
la cui virtù, col mio veder congiunta, mi leva sopra me tanto, ch'i' veggio la somma essenza de la quale è munta.	Its power conjoined with my own sight, raises me so far above myself that I can see the Highest Essence, the source from which it flows.
Quinci vien l'allegrezza ond' io fiammeggio; per ch'a la vista mia, quant' ella è chiara, la chiarità de la fiamma pareggio.	And this inflames the joy with which I burn: for, in the clarity of my sight, I match the clearness of my flame.
Ma quell' alma nel ciel che più si schiara, quel serafin che 'n Dio più l'occhio ha fisso, a la dimanda tua non satisfara,	Nonetheless, the most enlightened soul in Heaven, that seraph who fixes most his eye on God, could not produce an answer to your question,
però che sì s'innoltra ne lo abisso de l'etterno statuto quel che chiedi, che da ogne creata vista è scisso."	for what you ask is hidden in the depths of the abyss of God's eternal law, so that the sight of any being He created is cut off from it." (21.82–96)

Dante's *Paradiso*: Faith and Contemplation in the Lunar Heaven and the *Primo Mobile*" (PhD diss., Indiana University, 2008), 19–21.

The radiance that "enwombs" Peter Damian in the sphere of Saturn is pierced by the "divine light" (*luce divina*)—a reference to the scholastic notion of the light of glory (*lumen gloriae*). It is this light that raises Damian far above himself, enabling him to see the divine essence (*la somma essenza*).[40] With the benefit of heavenly hindsight, Damian makes clear that the thirteenth-century developments of the beatific vision have turned out to be correct: it is possible to see the divine essence thanks to the supernatural gift of the light of glory. As Pollack aptly summarizes: "Damian's statement in *Paradiso* is an impeccable definition according to the parameters established in 1241."[41]

At the same time, Damian states all this merely by way of preface. His main point is not positively to affirm what he knows (or to insist that he sees the divine essence), but to profess his ignorance. He is unable to answer Dante's question of why he, rather than someone else, has been sent to greet Dante in Saturn. The answer to this question lies "hidden in the depths of the abyss of God's eternal law," so that Damian is unable to see it. It seems as though Dante puts in poetic terms what Thomas Aquinas had articulated by means of the distinction between "attaining" (*attingere*) and "comprehending" (*comprehendere*) the essence of God.[42] By maintaining that, strictly speaking, comprehension of the divine essence is impossible, Aquinas safeguarded the creator-creature distinction along with the incomprehensibility of God.

In sum, while Dante was an affective poet, for whom desire plays an important role in the journey to the beatific vision, his theology is ultimately intellectualist in character. This explains why he does not treat desire as unending, and why, unlike earlier theologians, particularly in the East, he

40. Dante does not use the phrase "light of glory" specifically, but his description makes clear that this is what he has in mind:

"Its power conjoined with my own sight,
raises me so far above myself that I can see
the Highest Essence, the source from which it flows." (*Par.* 21.85–87)

41. Pollack, "Light, Love and Joy," 305. Similarly, in the Starry Sphere, Dante states in response to the apostle John that the mind of everyone who sees the truth must be moved by love

"To that essence (*l'essenza*), then, which holds such store of goodness
that every good outside of it is nothing
but a light reflected of its rays." (*Par.* 26.31–33)

42. *ST* I, q. 12, a. 7. Cf. *ST* I-II, q. 4, a. 3.

did not hold to an eternal progression of the soul into the divine life. For Dante, only once the mind comes to rest in the truth of God will the soul have reached the supernatural end of all desiring, namely, the essence of God. Dante would have considered anything that fell short of such a vision as a failure to overcome the limitations inherent in the sacramental means of grace.

"Speech, which fails at such a vision"

We have seen that Dante the poet deliberately uses language as a form of condescension or accommodation. In no way does he mean to suggest that the saints whom Dante the pilgrim encounters actually have their place in the various heavenly spheres, and in no way does he mean to suggest that, driven by desire, they continually progress more deeply into the infinite life of God. Throughout Dante's description of paradise, he wants us to remember that the saints have actually already reached their destination in heaven and that together with the angels they enjoy the beatific vision of God himself.

As much as possible, however, Dante wants to intimate to his readers what it is like to see God by means of a mystical rapture. But instead of positively describing this vision of God in words—something inherently impossible—Dante relativizes the role of language (and memory) in relation to vision. Now, an important caveat is in order: words do play an important function in Dante's journey. Although he admits poetic defeat already in the second tercet of the first canto—"He who comes down from there can neither know nor tell what he has seen"[43]—Dante insists that he will nevertheless attempt to describe what he saw:

Veramente quant' io del regno santo	Nevertheless, as much of the holy kingdom
ne la mia mente potei far tesoro,	as I could store as treasure in my mind
sarà ora materia del mio canto.	shall now become the subject of my song.
	(1.10–12)

In fact, not only does Dante make an *attempt* at articulating his mystical experience, but what he calls "the subject of my song" turns into no fewer than thirty-three cantos. Dante is hardly short of words in recounting what

---

43. "E vidi cose che ridire / né sa né può chi di là sù discende" (*Par.* 1.5–6).

he has seen in the "holy kingdom." He describes, at times in minute detail, the conversations with the various saints he meets along the way.

Indeed, Dante is under a prophetic burden to convey the heavenly realities to people on Earth. Several times, the saints he encounters on his heavenly journey impress on him the requirement to pass on what he has heard and seen. Peter, whom he meets in the Starry Sphere, tells Dante that the abuses of the papacy and the clergy are such that they will cause Providence to act soon. Peter then adds:

"e tu, figliuol, che per lo mortal pondo	"And you, my son, who for your mortal burden,
ancor giù tornerai, apri la bocca,	must return below, make sure they hear this
e non asconder quel ch'io non ascondo."	from your mouth, not hiding what I do not hide."
	(27.64–66)[44]

Dante the poet faces a prophetic task—as a result of his mystical rapture—which he takes seriously because it is supernaturally charged. The outcome is a lengthy cantica, in which it may almost seem as though Dante travels through a world where the sacramental means of language have not yet given way to the reality of the beatific vision.

In actuality, however, Dante's poetic discourse is ill-suited to the world of paradise. Dante addresses the issue immediately in the first canto:

Nel ciel che più de la sua luce prende	I was in that heaven which receives
fu' io, e vidi cose che ridire	more of His light. He who comes down from there
né sa né può chi di là sù discende;	can neither know nor tell what he has seen,
perché appressando sé al suo disire,	for, drawing near to its desire,
nostro intelletto si profonda tanto,	so deeply is our intellect immersed
che dietro la memoria non può ire.	that memory cannot follow after it.
	(1.4–9)

Dante alerts his reader here that the more deeply the human intellect enters the light that it desires, the more difficult it is for memory to follow. Similarly,

---

44. Cf. similar instructions to Dante in *Purg.* 32.103–5; 33.52–57; *Par.* 17.124–42.

upon entering the sun, Dante confesses that his poetic abilities do not match the brightness of its light:

Perch' io lo 'ngegno e l'arte e l'uso chiami,	Were I to call on genius, skill, and practice,
sì nol direi che mai s'imaginasse;	I could not ever tell how this might be imagined.
ma creder puossi e di veder si brami.	Enough if one believes and longs to see it.

(10.43–45)

When in the Starry Sphere a flame appears, which turns out to be the apostle Peter, it dances around Beatrice, and Dante apostrophizes:

e tre fiate intorno di Beatrice	Three times it circled Beatrice,
si volse con un canto tanto divo,	its song so filled with heavenly delight
che la mia fantasia nol mi ridice.	my phantasy cannot repeat it.

Però salta la penna e non lo scrivo:	And so my pen skips and I do not write it,
ché l'imagine nostra a cotai pieghe,	for our imagination is too crude, as is our speech,
non che 'l parlare, è troppo color vivo.	to paint the subtler colors of the folds of bliss.

(24.22–27)

Dante's powers of fantasy or imagination are simply no match for the lyrics of the Petrine song. As a result, his speech fails; Dante does not even make an attempt to relate the contents of the song he hears.

Once he has entered the Primum Mobile, Dante becomes increasingly preoccupied with the inadequacy of language to express the reality of the rapturous experience. The light of the Crystalline Sphere has so changed Beatrice that when Dante turns his eyes to gaze upon her, her beauty transcends his ability to take it in:

Da questo passo vinto mi concedo	I declare myself defeated at this point
più che già mai da punto di suo tema	more than any poet, whether comic or tragic,
soprato fosse comico o tragedo:	was ever thwarted by a topic in his theme,

ché, come sole in viso che più
trema,
così lo rimembrar del dolce riso
la mente mia da me medesmo
scema.

for, like sunlight striking on the weakest
eyes,
the memory of the sweetness of that smile
deprives me of my mental
powers.

(30.22–27)

The sweetness of Beatrice's smile is such that his mental powers fall short, and so Dante adds:

ma or convien che mio seguir desista
più dietro a sua bellezza,
poetando,
come a l'ultimo suo ciascuno artista.

But now I must desist in my pursuit,
no longer following her beauty in my
verse,
as every artist, having reached his limit,
must.

(30.31–33)

Dante gives up on his attempts to catch the beauty of Beatrice's smile in poetic discourse. The light of the Primum Mobile is such that he simply is not up to the task.

Once Dante has entered the Empyrean itself—and thus has moved into a purely intellectual realm[45]—speech entirely fails and is superseded by sight. Dante follows the instruction of Bernard (his new guide in the Empyrean) (31.58–60) to look upward, and as his sight rises ever higher and so increases in purity, Dante arrives at the acknowledgment that we have previously noted:

Da quinci innanzi il mio veder fu
maggio
che 'l parlar mostra, ch'a tal vista
cede,
e cede la memoria a tanto oltraggio.

From that time on my power
exceeded
that of speech, which fails at such a
vision,
as memory fails at such abundance.

Qual è colüi che sognando vede,
che dopo 'l sogno la passione
impressa

Just as the dreamer, after he awakens,
still stirred by feelings that the dream
evoked,

45. Pollack points out that by insisting that the Empyrean is purely intellectual and is, in fact, identical to beatitude itself, Dante rejects a common medieval understanding of the Empyrean as corporeal ("Light, Love and Joy," 265).

rimane, e l'altro a la mente non riede,	cannot bring the rest of it to mind,
cotal son io, ché quasi tutta cessa	such am I, my vision almost faded from my mind,
mia visïone, e ancor mi distilla	while in my heart there still endures
nel core il dolce che nacque da essa.	the sweetness that was born of it.

(33.55–63)

Dante's power of vision exceeds that of speech. As Philip McNair puts it: "Gazing upon the Ultimate Reality, his vision transcends his power of speech, for Dante-the-character sees more than Dante-the-poet can express."[46] Human discourse comes to an end in the actual experience of the vision of God in the conclusion of the *Paradiso*.[47] Thus, just after he has seen the three circles of the Trinity, Dante admits:

Oh quanto è corto il dire e come fioco	O how scant is speech, too weak to frame my thoughts.
al mio concetto! e questo, a quel ch'i' vidi,	Compared to what I still recall my words are faint—
è tanto, che non basta a dicer "poco."	to call them "little" is to praise them much.

(33.121–23)

Dante could not have been more emphatic in his insistence that language only has a penultimate role in the journey of salvation.

This restricted reach of language is closely linked to the limits of memory. In several of the above quotations Dante comments that he is unable to remember what he has seen. The power of memory seems to be discarded in paradise. Certainly the faults of sin are not remembered there (9.103–5). But also, Beatrice's beauty is such that it escapes Dante's memory (14.79–81; 30.25–27). Repeatedly, he confides to the reader his struggle to remember

---

46. Philip McNair, "Dante's Vision of God: An Exposition of *Paradiso* XXXIII," in *Essays in Honour of John Humphrey's Whitfield: Presented to Him on His Retirement from the Serena Chair of Italian at the University of Birmingham*, ed. H. C. Davis et al. (London: St. George's Press, 1975), 20.

47. Cf. *Par.* 33.106–7:

Omai sarà più corta mia favella,	Now my words will come far short
pur a quel ch'io ricordo, che d'un fante	of what I still remember, like a babe's
che bagni ancor la lingua a la mammella.	who at his mother's breast still wets his tongue.

and his failure to call to mind what he has seen (23.43–45, 49–51; 33.94–96). He dearly longs to remember something of what he has seen in the light of the Empyrean (33.67–69).

To be sure, Dante's memory functions better than his linguistic capacity. When the stars of the Milky Way seem to make the sign of a cross within Mars, Dante exclaims:

Qui vince la memoria mia lo 'ngegno;	Here my memory outstrips my skill;
ché quella croce lampeggiava Cristo,	for that cross so flamed forth Christ
sì ch'io non so trovare essempro degno.	that I can find no fit comparison.

$$(14.103–5)^{48}$$

Dante remembers his vision of the cross; it is just that he cannot find the words properly to give expression to his memory. Similarly, Dante explains that his sight of Beatrice's smile in the Primum Mobile has left an impression on him that endures, even though he cannot express it in words (30.25–27).[49] In some ways memory seems to outstrip language. Nonetheless, the overall picture that emerges from Dante's descriptions is that memory must disappear because only the vision of God remains—along with the love and joy that result from this vision. In the reality of this ultimate encounter with the light of God, Dante is so transformed—"transhumanized" into the divine life—that the sacramental gifts of language and memory yield to the reality of the vision of God.

"I grew more bold and thus sustained my gaze"

It is not enough to observe negatively that human language fails in the eternity of the Empyrean. We also need to ask: How is it that vision can go where speech cannot? Dante does *not* claim that vision has a natural ability to see something that human language is unable to express. Traveling ever closer to the source of light, Dante is frequently reminded that his ordinary visionary powers—much like human discourse—fall short. Dante often comments that his gaze cannot sustain the light that he sees (3.128–29; 4.139–42; 5.1–3, 133–39; 14.78; 21.7–12; 25.25–27, 136–39; 28.16–18; 30.79–81). Repeatedly it blinds him (10.64; 25.118–23; 26.1–15). At the same time, however, the light

---

48. See also *Par.* 33.106–7, quoted above in the previous footnote.
49. Cf. above, p. 242.

has transforming power: as he ascends to the moon and gazes on Beatrice, Dante is "changed within" (*dentro mi fei*) (1.67). It is precisely when the light overcomes the power of his sight that he is "transhumanized." At one point Beatrice tells Dante that when her light overcomes his power of sight, "this is the result / of perfect vision" ("ché ciò procede / da perfetto veder") (5.4–5).[50] Continually, Dante is by grace exposed to a vision that, at that point, is beyond his ability to endure. Repeatedly, therefore, he either is forced to turn away his gaze or is blinded by the light. Nonetheless, each time, these encounters with the light strengthen his vision, so that at the end of his journey he is able to look into the "living light" (*luce viva*) of the Empyrean (30.49).[51]

Dante emphasizes the rapidly transhumanizing or deifying effects of the light as he reflects on what transpires in the Empyrean. When Beatrice tells him that they have entered the Empyrean, Dante sees the light of heaven, which transforms him:

Non fur più tosto dentro a me venute	No sooner had these few words reached my mind
queste parole brievi, ch'io compresi	than I became aware of having risen
me sormontar di sopr' a mia virtute;	above and well beyond my powers,
e di novella vista mi raccesi	and such was the new vision kindled within me

50. Cf. 26.76–78:

così de li occhi miei ogne quisquilia	exactly thus did Beatrice drive away each mote
fugò Beatrice col raggio d'i suoi,	from my eyes with the radiance of her own,
che rifulgea da più di mille milia.	which could be seen a thousand miles away.

51. Blindness is, for Dante, not simply the opposite of vision. Instead, it is a means toward vision. Dante is blinded in his attempt to see the apostle John in the Starry Sphere, and so he is unable to see Beatrice as he looks back (25.118–39), but John soon reassures him that his blindness is but temporary:

"perché la donna che per questa dia	"for the lady who guides you through
regïon ti conduce, ha ne lo sguardo	this holy place possesses in her glance
la virtù ch'ebbe la man d'Anania."	the power the hand of Ananias had."
	(26.10–12)

By giving Beatrice the role of Ananias, John places Dante in the position of Paul—since according to Paul's conversion narrative in Acts 9:10–19, Ananias healed Paul of the blindness he experienced. Thus, the reference to Ananias reinforces the notion that Dante's blindness is an episode within the supernatural process of the healing of his vision.

tale, che nulla luce è tanto mera,	that there exists no light so vivid that my eyes
che li occhi miei non si fosser difesi.	could not have borne its brightness.

(30.55–60)

Dante wants us to take this last tercet seriously; at this point, his natural powers have been so strengthened that his "new vision" (*novella vista*) is able to endure any light whatsoever. His eyes have been transformed so that he sees the heaven of "pure light" (*pura luce*) (30.39), a "light intellectual" (*luce intellettüal*) (30.40), a "living light" (*luce viva*) (30.49).[52]

Notwithstanding the presence of the light of glory (*lumen gloriae*), at this point we are only in canto 30, and the next several cantos portray an ever greater effulgence of light, originating from a ray (*raggio*) that pours down from above and into which Dante's eyes are increasingly capable of gazing as he himself is being transformed into light. When he sees "light that flowed as flows a river" (*lume in forma di rivera*) (30.61)—a metaphor for the gathered heavenly saints—Beatrice encourages him to drink from these waters, though she recognizes that his vision is not yet strong enough for it (30.81). When Dante bends down to drink from the river's water—"to make still better mirrors of my eyes" ("per far migliori spegli / ancor de li occhi") (30.85–86)—his eyelids drink the water, and he recognizes the saints (30.94–96). Dante then familiarizes himself with the heavenly company of saints, now represented as the petals of a white rose.

At one point, Bernard, who has taken over from Beatrice as Dante's final guide, perfects his vision even more, advising him:

"vola con li occhi per questo giardino;	"Let your sight fly through this garden,
ché veder lui t'acconcerà lo sguardo più al montar per lo raggio divino."	for seeing it will help prepare your eyes to rise, along the beam of holy light."

(31.97–99)

Gazing upon the garden itself is not enough; seeing it is only a means of equipping Dante to move even higher along the "beam" (*raggio*) of holy light. Bernard insists that by gazing upon Mary's brightness in particular,

---

52. These three phrases all seem to me synonyms describing the light of glory (*lumen gloriae*), to which Dante referred as *luce divina* in *Par.* 21.83 (cf. above, n. 40). It is the light that flows from the divine essence and transforms Dante so as to enable him to see more clearly.

Dante's vision will be strengthened so as to enable him to endure the sight of Christ himself:

"Riguarda omai ne la faccia che a Cristo più si somiglia, ché la sua chiarezza sola ti può disporre a veder Cristo."	"Look now on the face that most resembles Christ, for nothing but its brightness can make you fit to look on Christ."

(32.85–87)

As Gabriel sings the *Ave Maria* and the angelic choir responds in sacred chant, their faces become ever more luminous (32.94–99). Once Bernard has explained to Dante the identity of some of the saints seated close to Mary in the rose, he tells Dante to take the next step in strengthening his vision:

"e drizzeremo li occhi al primo amore, sì che, guardando verso lui, penètri quant' è possibil per lo suo fulgore."	"And let us fix our eyes on Primal Love, so that, looking up toward Him, you penetrate, as far as may be done, His brilliance."

(32.142–44)

Following Bernard's fervent intercession of Mary (33.1–39), first the Virgin, and then also Dante, turn their eyes to God himself (33.43–45, 49–54).

As Dante rises higher through the ray (*raggio*) of light, the power of his sight finally surpasses that of his speech (33.55–56). Dante refuses to let go of his vision; he keeps looking up through the "living ray" (*vivo raggio*) (33.76–78) to God and so finally reaches the destiny of his vision:

E' mi ricorda ch'io fui più ardito per questo a sostener, tanto ch'i' giunsi l'aspetto mio col valore infinito.	And I remember that, on this account, I grew more bold and thus sustained my gaze until I reached the Goodness that is infinite.
Oh abbondante grazia ond' io presunsi ficcar lo viso per la luce etterna, tanto che la veduta vi consunsi!	O plenitude of grace, by which I could presume to fix my eyes upon eternal Light until my sight was spent on it!

(33.79–84)

His vision strengthened, so that he is able to fix his eyes on the "eternal Light" (*luce etterna*), Dante sees all the pages of the cosmos bound by love into a single volume (33.85–87). In this way, as we noted above, Dante recognizes the unity of the Word as encompassing the multiplicity of the cosmos.

Words cannot express what he remembers from seeing the eternal light of God, and Dante immediately adds that this "living light" (*vivo lume*) did not undergo change, "for It is always what It was before" ("che tal è sempre qual s'era davante") (33.111). Instead, Dante recognizes that he is the one who has been transformed, and that his vision has improved accordingly:

ma per la vista che s'avvalorava	but that my sight was gaining strenth, even as I gazed
in me guardando, una sola parvenza,	at that sole semblance and, as I changed,
mutandom' io, a me si travagliava.	it too was being, in my eyes, transformed.

(33.112–14)

Only now that Dante's subjective perception ("in my eyes") of the light has been sufficiently altered is Dante finally equipped to see the three circles of the triune God (33.115–20).

"Sending forth Its rays / It is the source of every good"

We need to delve yet more deeply into the reason that vision outstrips language in Dante's paradisal ascent. It goes without saying that Dante's natural vision is incapable of gazing upon the light of heaven. Dante may believe in a natural desire for final happiness, but he does not think that the supernatural end of the beatific vision is something one can reach by one's own natural powers. For Dante, it is grace (including merit) that supernaturally transforms a person, so that he is able to see God in the light that envelops him and that transforms Dante. So, it is not as though vision *naturally* can reach God in a way that language cannot. Whether we use the discourse of seeing or of hearing, God must supernaturally and graciously transform us.[53]

---

53. G. C. Berkouwer articulates this same insight well when he comments that "it will not do to describe the Hebrews as a people of the ear alone, as if their eyes did not need to be opened to all the works of God's hands and to God Himself in the appearance of His glory" (*The Return of Christ*, 364).

Nonetheless, both the Hellenic and the Christian traditions have often valued sight over speech. Plato observes in the *Timaeus*, "Vision, in my view, is the cause of the greatest benefit to us, inasmuch as none of the accounts now given concerning the Universe would ever have been given if men had not seen the stars or the sun or the heaven."[54] For Plato, vision is the greatest of the senses because it gives us knowledge of the universe. Vision thus connects us with the cosmos as a whole.[55] Saint Augustine followed Plato in this estimation of vision. Since Augustine believed knowledge is the result of illumination, he regarded vision as the most genuine way to arrive at knowledge. As Lise Gosseye puts it: "Since seeing, in Augustine's epistemology, is bound up with knowledge—just as faith is reached through hearing—the divine illumination that will help us to see more clearly will eventually aid us in knowing more fully."[56] As a result, Augustine writes, "Let us use for preference the evidence of the eyes; this is the most excellent of the body's senses, and for all its difference in kind has the greatest affinity to mental vision."[57] For Augustine, vision has a capacity to access reality that language lacks.

Augustine did not object to language per se. He had high regard for it. Language, however, was intimately tied up with sacramentality in Augustine's mind. Language is made up of many words, and as symbols their purpose is to draw us to the one Word. We are to move from multiplicity to unity. Words—particularly the Scriptures—lead us to the eternal Logos. For Augustine this meant both that words play an exalted role and that they have

54. *Tim.* 47a (in *Timaeus and Critias*, trans. Robin Waterfield, ed. Andrew Gregory [Oxford: Oxford University Press, 2008]). Plato also comments: "'Well, have you ever stopped to consider,' I asked, 'how generous the creator of the senses was when he created the domain of seeing and being seen?' . . . 'Nevertheless, there is no sense-organ which more closely resembles the sun, in my opinion, than the eye'" (*Rep.* 507c, 508b, in *Republic*, trans. and ed. Robin Waterfield [Oxford: Oxford University Press, 1998]). Similarly, Aristotle writes: "For it is not only with a view to action but also when we have no intention to do anything that we choose, so to speak, sight rather than all the others. And the reason for this is that sight is the sense that especially produces cognition in us and reveals many distinguishing features of things" (*Metaph.* 980a25–28, in *Metaphysics*, trans. and ed. Hugh Lawson-Tancred, rev. ed. [London: Penguin, 2004]).

55. Suzanne Conklin Akbari, "Illumination and Language," in *Seeing through the Veil: Optical Theory and Medieval Allegory* (Toronto: University of Toronto Press, 2004), 3.

56. Lise Gosseye, "Salutary Reading: Calvinist Humanism in Constantijn Huygens' *Ooghentroost*," in *The Turn of the Soul: Representations of Religious Conversion in Early Modern Art and Literature*, ed. Lieke Stelling, Harald Hendrix, and Todd Richardson, Intersections: Interdisciplinary Studies in Early Modern Culture 23 (Leiden: Brill, 2012), 236.

57. *Trin.* 11.1.1 (WSA I/5:304).

a limited function. On the one hand, words are indispensable as signs (*signa*) representing a reality (*res*) that is not immediately present to the mind. As such, signs helpfully put us in touch with the realities to which they refer.[58] Signs thus have a sacramental function: they mediate and make present to us realities outside ourselves, and without this it would be impossible to return to God.[59]

On the other hand, the mediatory or sacramental role of words also bespeaks their limitation. In fact, vision compares favorably to linguistic apprehension in at least three ways. First, the metaphor of vision is better suited than that of speech for the atemporal realm of the eschaton. As Augustine recognizes, here below we measure time, and we measure words, because of their temporal extension:

> By this method we measure poems by the number of lines, lines by the number of feet, feet by the number of syllables, and long vowels by short, not by the number of pages (for that would give us a measure of space, not of time). The criterion is the time words occupy in recitation, so that we say, "That is a long poem, for it consists of so many lines. The lines are long, for they consist of so many feet. The feet are long for they extend over so many syllables. The syllable is long, for it is double the length of a short one."[60]

The distension of language is fitting for our temporal world. For the eternal present of the life of God, however, ordinary language is unsuitable.

Whereas words take time, vision is instantaneous. When I listen to a lecture, it may perhaps take an hour to unfold and for me to grasp its central message. Slowly but surely, the various components of the argument unfold, and I string them together in my mind so as to come to an understanding of what the speaker is trying to explain. By contrast, when I see an object, I grasp it as a whole: the entire vista is displayed before my eyes, and I take in the sight all at once. To be sure, I may take some time to focus on particular aspects of the object, but this does not gainsay that I am able to take in the entire object in one grasp. On Dante's Augustinian understanding of heaven,

---

58. See particularly Augustine's famous discussion in *Doctr. chr.* 2.1.1–2.7.11.

59. Corine Boersma describes the sacramental function of linguistic signs in Augustine in "A Comparative Analysis of Sacramentality in Augustine and Dionysius" (MA thesis, Regent College, 2016).

60. *Conf.* 11.26.33, in *Confessions*, trans. Henry Chadwick (Oxford: Oxford University Press, 1991).

the metaphor of sight was more suitable for the atemporal reality of heaven than that of speech.

Margaret Miles notes two additional aspects of vision that render it more fitting than speech as a metaphor for our eschatological relationship with God. As she describes how Saint Augustine understands the "mechanics" of vision, Miles explains that according to his theory of illumination, rays of light shine from our eyes and touch whatever we see. This implies an active role for the person who sees. Vision is not the passive reception of a particular object by the eyes; rather, the soul is directed to the object, and so the viewer initiates the vision. Whereas vision is thus proactive, hearing is much more passive. It "is initiated by the object which imposes itself on the ear; the ear is helpless, while it is in the environs, not to hear a sound that strikes it."[61] Although Augustine was in many ways a theologian of the word and in no way despised the sacramental function of language, vision, for him, has the advantage that it requires an active role on the part of the viewer.

Finally, and most importantly, vision alludes to an immediacy in our relationship with God that speech does not convey. Miles explains that for Augustine, vision actually unites the viewer with the object. In fact, the viewer, the object, and the will that unites them become almost as one. Vision, therefore, says Miles, "is definitely, for Augustine, a two-way street: the soul forms images of sensible things 'out of its own substance' (*substantiae suae*), but the result is that the mind itself is formed by the very images it formulates and carries."[62] Vision attaches the soul to its object, so that the object shapes the soul.[63] Vision, we could say, entails immediacy between viewer and object, something that simply does not pertain in the same way between a listener and a speaker. Or, to put it differently, for Augustine vision reaches beyond the sacramental means (*signum*), as the soul's gaze directly unites her to the object (*res*) at which she aims. As such, spiritual vision is more apt than spiritual hearing as a metaphor for the divine-human relationship in the eschaton.

---

61. Margaret Miles, "Vision: The Eye of the Body and the Eye of the Mind in Saint Augustine's *De Trinitate* and *Confessions*," *JR* 63 (1983): 127.

62. Miles, "Vision," 128.

63. Miles, "Vision," 129.

Conclusion

Dante powerfully describes the increasing immediacy of his relationship with God. It will be clear at this point that, on Dante's understanding, the light of God cascades down from the Empyrean all the way to earthly reality. In some sense, all of created reality participates in the divine light. Dante begins his *Paradiso* with this acknowledgment:

La gloria di colui che tutto move	The glory of Him who moves all things
per l'universo penetra, e risplende	pervades the universe and shines
in una parte più e meno altrove.	in one part more and in another less.

(1.1–3)

In some sense, Dante (and we all) can see God throughout the universe, since it participates in his glory in varying degrees of intensity ("in one part more and in another less").[64] Dante's ascent through paradise is a journey in which God's grace—along with the mediation of Beatrice, Bernard, Mary, and numerous other saints—supernaturally strengthens Dante's ability to see God not just in the universe, but immediately, face-to-face.

When God "looks down" through the various realms of heaven all the way to Earth, he sends forth the rays of his light. God's good will determines what is just, explains the Eagle in Jupiter:

"Cotanto è giusto quanto a lei consuona:	"Only what accords with It is just: It is not drawn
nullo creato bene a sé la tira,	to a created good but, sending forth Its rays
ma essa, radïando, lui cagiona."	It is the source of every good."

(19.88–90)

God's will sends forth the rays of his light and thus determines what is good.

---

64. Cf. *Par.* 13.55–69. Cf. also this invitation that Dante extends to his readers:

Leva dunque, lettore, a l'alte rote	With me, then, reader, raise your eyes
meco la vista, dritto a quella parte	up to the lofty wheels, directly to that part
dove l'un moto e l'altro si percuote;	where the one motion and the other intersect,
e lì comincia a vagheggiar ne l'arte	and from that point begin to gaze in rapture
di quel maestro che dentro a sé l'ama,	at the Master's work. He so loves it in Himself
tanto che mai da lei l'occhio non parte.	that never does His eye depart from it. (10.7–12)

The same illumination affects also the angels, explains Beatrice. When she is with Dante in the Crystalline Sphere, she comments to him about the angels:

"La prima luce, che tutta la raia, per tanti modi in essa si recepe, quanti son li splendori a chi s'appaia."	"The Primal Light that irradiates them all is received by them in just as many ways as there are splendors joined with It."
	(29.136–38)

The "Primal Light" (*prima luce*) that irradiates the angels is the eternal light of glory. They, too, receive the light of God in varying degrees of splendor.

On Dante's understanding, then, it is by shining down—the divine *exitus*—that the light of God's truth, goodness, and beauty constitutes, in varying degrees, the truth, goodness, and beauty of created beings.[65] By looking up—the human *reditus*—and by gazing into this light of God ever more deeply, human beings learn, by God's supernatural grace, to sustain this light and so to move ever higher into its rays. Dogmatically, we could say that God's providential care (the light of his face) calls into being the contingent created order, which reaches its salvific telos through worship and adoration of this same creator God (seeking the light of God's face). Dante depicts the human return to God by describing his journey through the various heavenly spheres to the height of the Empyrean itself.[66] Dante enters ever more deeply into the rays of the divine light, until, finally, this light equips him to see the essence of God.[67] It is clear why, on his understanding, vision exceeds language: it is through our vision of God that he, as the object of our hope, enters us and transhumanizes us.

---

65. As Diego Fasolini puts it: "Dante-pilgrim, looking at God-as-light, interprets himself as a *person-stared-at-by-the-light*, as a *looking-individual-who-is-being-looked-at*, a *knowing-person-who-is-already-known*" ("'Illuminating' and 'Illuminated' Light: A Biblical-Theological Interpretation of God-as-Light in Canto XXXIII of Dante's *Paradiso*," *L&T* 19 [2005]: 297).

66. For a more detailed dogmatic sketch, see below, chap. 13, section entitled "Pedagogy and Providence in Nicholas of Cusa and Jonathan Edwards."

67. Although it is beyond the cope of this chapter, I would be remiss not to add that, for Dante, the incarnation forms the hinge between *exitus* and *reditus*. It is when he sees the second circle of the Trinity, "painted with our likeness" (*pinta de la nostra effige*; *Par.* 33.141–42). Despite the important place that Christ thus occupies in the final canto, my criticism of Aquinas also applies to Dante: for both, the beatific vision reaches beyond Christ to the essence of God.

PART 3

BEATIFIC VISION IN
PROTESTANT THOUGHT

CHAPTER 9

ACCOMMODATION AND VISION

John Calvin on Face-to-Face Vision of God

Calvin and the Beatific Vision?

Nowhere in his writings does John Calvin (1509–1564) provide any kind of extended discussion of the doctrine of the beatific vision. Unlike many in the earlier tradition, Calvin did not devote a treatise to the topic. Nor did he write the kind of devotional theology, common in the Middle Ages and revived in later Puritan thought, that dissected the spiritual steps leading up to the beatific vision. It is hardly surprising that no one has written on Calvin's understanding of the subject at any length, and we may be tempted to conclude, therefore, that he had little or nothing to say about it. We may well point to the reformer as a source of the declining centrality of the doctrine of the beatific vision and see his neglect as contributing to the declining otherworldliness of Western spirituality, inasmuch as it set in motion an overall cultural shift from otherworldly to this-worldly concerns.

Such an interpretation of Calvin's spiritual theology is not without warrant. I agree that the absence of any extended discussion of the beatific vision in Calvin's works may unwittingly have contributed to the eventual occlusion of transcendent ends and hence also to the secularization of Western culture. Charles Taylor points out that the "sanctification of ordinary life"—that is to say, the shift from transcendent to immanent ends—in Reformed Christianity had "a tremendous formative effect on our civilization,"[1] and it is fair to suggest that the Reformation was one link in a larger chain that eventually reduced the telos of humanity to immanent, this-worldly (mostly economic)

---

1. Charles Taylor, *A Secular Age* (Cambridge, MA: Belknap Press of Harvard University Press, 2007), 179.

flourishing.[2] I am largely sympathetic to genealogies of modernity that give the Reformation a place within the broader trajectory leading from late medieval nominalism to the secularism of modernity.[3] The marginalization (within some streams of the Reformation tradition) of the beatific vision as a dogmatic locus fits within this historical development.

But this narrative, no matter how legitimate, does not present the entire story. This book takes aim at the immanentizing tendencies of modernity, and in the current chapter (as well as the other chapters of part 3) I intend to look for resources within the Protestant Reformation that counter the reductionism of modernity's this-worldly horizons. Reformed theology did not simply abandon the doctrine of the beatific vision wholesale, and Calvin's theology was marked by an otherworldliness that we do well to retrieve. Specifically, we should not overlook the numerous places in his commentaries where he mentions the beatific vision. So far, most Calvin scholarship has argued that Calvin simply abandoned the traditional doctrine of the beatific vision.[4] This chapter will take issue with this view. Again, this is not to deny that, in some ways, Calvin represented a departure from medieval eschatology. The *place* that the beatific vision occupies within Calvin's overall theology is certainly modest, and this in itself is an observation worth pon-

---

2. James K. A. Smith helpfully summarizes Taylor's analysis, explaining how an eternal telos (including final judgment, beatific vision, etc.) gave way to "mundane" flourishing in this world. Smith summarizes the trend as follows: "Even our theism becomes humanized, immanentized, and the telos of God's providential concern is circumscribed within immanence. And this becomes true even of 'orthodox' folk: 'even people who held to orthodox beliefs were influenced by this humanizing trend; frequently the transcendent dimension of their faith became less central' ([*Secular Age*,] p. 222). Because eternity is eclipsed, the this-worldly is amplified and threatens to swallow all" (*How (Not) to Be Secular: Reading Charles Taylor* [Grand Rapids: Eerdmans, 2014], 49–50).

3. See also Louis Dupré, *Passage to Modernity: An Essay in the Hermeneutics of Nature and Culture* (New Haven: Yale University Press, 1993); Brad S. Gregory, *The Unintended Reformation: How a Religious Revolution Secularized Society* (Cambridge, MA: Belknap Press of Harvard University Press, 2012); Thomas Pfau, *Minding the Modern: Human Agency, Intellectual Traditions, and Responsible Knowledge* (Notre Dame: University of Notre Dame Press, 2015).

4. Richard A. Muller has suggested that the Reformed scholastics derived their theology of the beatific vision from the medieval scholastic systems because the reformers "did not discuss the topic" (*Post-Reformation Reformed Dogmatics: The Rise and Development of Reformed Orthodoxy, ca. 1520 to ca. 1725*, 4 vols. [Grand Rapids: Baker Academic, 2003], 1:260). Suzanne McDonald similarly comments that "Calvin has nothing directly to say about it in the *Institutes*" ("Beholding the Glory of God in the Face of Jesus Christ: John Owen and the 'Reforming' of the Beatific Vision," in *The Ashgate Research Companion to John Owen's Theology*, ed. Kelly M. Kapic and Mark Jones [Burlington, VT: Ashgate, 2012], 141n1).

dering. But equally worth pondering is the actual *content* of his understand-ing of the beatific vision as we find it in comments scattered throughout his commentaries. Calvin did treat the beatific vision as the end of the earthly pilgrimage, and his commentaries show that he reflected carefully on how to articulate this end theologically.

It will not do simply to point the finger of blame at Calvin. First, we should not confuse Calvin's own theology with the impact it may have had in later Reformed (and evangelical) thought. This chapter will make clear that although the beatific vision only had a small place in Calvin's *Institutes*, he was nonetheless convinced that only God himself constitutes our final end, so that only our vision of him yields true happiness.[5] What is more, as we will see, Calvin's commentaries give evidence of careful and creative thinking on the topic. It may well be true that later Reformed theologians did not typically turn to Calvin for an articulation of the beatific vision, but this is not because he did not hold to it. A much more likely explanation is that it takes a bit of investigative work to determine what Calvin's understanding of this particular doctrine was like: one has to scour his commentaries in some detail. Part of the purpose of this chapter is to do exactly that, and thereby to make clear that for Calvin we find our ultimate happiness in the beatific vision. For contemporary Reformed theologians to ignore or discount the beatific vision would be to depart from the reformer's attitude toward it.

Second, although Calvin himself may not have provided an extensive treatment of the beatific vision as such, this does not mean that the beatific vision is alien to the Reformed tradition as a whole. The subsequent chapters, in which I deal with John Donne, a number of Puritan authors, Jonathan Edwards, and Abraham Kuyper, make clear that the beatific vision played a prominent role in the dogmatic understanding of significant elements of the Reformed tradition. Nor are the theologians that I treat in part 3 anomalies. Numerous scholastic Reformed divines of the late sixteenth and seventeenth centuries turned to medieval theology to shore up support for the distinctive

---

5. Nicholas Wolterstorff wrongly suggests that "it is obvious that Calvin's formulation of the true goal of human existence as the acknowledgment of God in one's life constitutes a profound turn toward this world and a repudiation of avertive religion" (*Until Justice and Peace Embrace: The Kuyper Lectures for 1981 Delivered at the Free University of Amsterdam* [Grand Rapids: Eerdmans, 1983], 14). To some extent Calvin's theology does represent a "turn toward this world," but this chapter will make clear that for Calvin "the true goal of human existence" was not anything this-worldly but rather the eternal contemplation of God himself—in other words, "avertive" religion, in Wolterstorff's terminology.

teachings of the Calvinist Reformation.[6] As a result, they ended up with a renewed appreciation for the doctrine of the beatific vision. In their dogmatic theology, Reformed orthodox theologians would touch on the topic in the context of a variety of theological loci, particularly the nature of theology, the divine attributes (God's blessedness), and eschatology.[7]

Finally, though it is true that the beatific vision has suffered a decline within contemporary Reformed and evangelical theology, this problem is hardly unique to Calvinist thought. In the first chapter, I purposely pointed both to the Reformed theologian Herman Bavinck *and* to the Catholic theologian Hans Urs von Balthasar as having sidelined the doctrine of the beatific vision. Inasmuch as contemporary theology and Western culture shy away from any sort of *contemptus mundi* spirituality and instead immanentize human happiness, the doctrine of the beatific vision—with its unapologetic focus on God himself as our ultimate end—is bound to dissipate because it does not fit the overall theological orientation. This is a problem endemic to both contemporary Protestant and Catholic thought, regardless of what role the Reformation may historically have played in the process.[8]

None of this renders irrelevant the question of why Calvin did not treat the beatific vision at any length. I suspect a variety of factors are behind this lack of attention, but it is worth at least listening to Calvin's own comments on it. He mentions his uneasiness about unwarranted speculation as the reason for not discussing the doctrine in greater detail. In his discussion of

6. For Reformed scholasticism, see Muller, *Post-Reformation Reformed Dogmatics*. See also Willem J. van Asselt, *Introduction to Reformed Scholasticism*, trans. Albert Gootjes (Grand Rapids: Reformation Heritage, 2010); Herman J. Selderhuis, ed., *A Companion to Reformed Orthodoxy* (Leiden: Brill, 2013).

7. The understanding of the beatific vision among Reformed scholastics is a topic that needs further investigation. The doctrine is treated at some length by Franciscus Junius, Sibrandus Lubbertus, Amandus Polanus, Bartholomäus Keckermann, Antonius Walaeus, William Ames, Johannes Alsted, Johannes Wollebius, Franciscus Gomarus, Edward Leigh, Francis Turretin, Johannes Braunius, Petrus van Mastricht, and Hermann Witsius. I am much indebted to the doctoral research of Joshua Schendel (Saint Louis University) on this topic. For an initial exploration, which focuses on John Owen's use of Franciscus Junius, see Sebastian Rehnman, *Divine Discourse: The Theological Methodology of John Owen* (Grand Rapids: Baker Academic, 2002), 57–71.

8. To underscore this point, I mention the work of sociologist Christian Smith, who has pointed out that "moralistic therapeutic deism" is a religious approach widely shared among both Catholic and Protestant youth. See Christian Smith with Melinda Lundquist Denton, *Soul Searching: The Religious and Spiritual Lives of American Teenagers* (New York: Oxford University Press, 2005), and Christian Smith with Patricia Snell, *Souls in Transition: The Religious and Spiritual Lives of Emerging Adults* (New York: Oxford University Press, 2015).

the eschaton in the *Institutes*, Calvin reminds us that our mental capacity does not reach higher than the "very lowest roots" of the mystery of our eternal enjoyment of God.[9] He cautions that "we must all the more, then, keep sobriety (*sobrietas*), lest forgetful of our limitations we should soar aloft with the greater boldness, and be overcome by the brightness of the heavenly glory."[10] He warns against "trifling and harmful questions" about the future life and adds an entire section in which he explains his avoidance of "superfluous investigation of useless matters."[11] His commentaries are similarly marked by counsels against undue eschatological speculation.[12] Calvin desired to keep within the bounds of positive biblical revelation and typically hesitated to speculate about eschatological questions that Scripture does not explicitly address.

Pedagogical Accommodation

Scripture, of course, does address the topic of the beatific vision in numerous places, and Calvin, therefore, did not hesitate to deal with the subject per se—even if he cautioned against excessive theological speculation. As a result, Calvin repeatedly treats the topic in his commentaries. In fact, he does this so often that it is possible to delineate a fairly consistent dogmatic approach, which I will argue is pedagogical in character. For Calvin, God reveals himself sacramentally in Christ throughout salvation history so as to train us in our face-to-face vision of him, in order that after the resurrection we may be able to see the reality of the divine majesty (or essence) directly or openly.

Calvin's pedagogical approach comes to the fore when he makes the point that seeing God "face-to-face" allows for gradations. The vision of God becomes increasingly clear through salvation history. Or, we could also say, God trains his people in such a way that through the external *sacramenta* they are able to discern him ever more clearly. When Jacob fought with God at Peniel, the patriarch did not yet have the spiritual maturity to see the

9. *Inst.* 3.25.10; quotations come from John Calvin, *The Institutes of the Christian Religion*, trans. Ford Lewis Battles, ed. John T. McNeill, Library of Christian Classics 20 (Philadelphia: Westminster, 1960).

10. *Inst.* 3.25.10.

11. *Inst.* 3.25.11.

12. *Comm.* Exod. 33:18; *Comm.* Ezek. 1:25–26; *Comm.* 1 John 3:2. For references to the commentaries in this chapter, see *Calvin's Commentaries*, 45 vols. (Edinburgh: Calvin Translation Society, 1846–1851).

reality (*res*) of God's own presence—God's "majesty," as Calvin often calls it. The reason God refused to reveal his name to Jacob (Gen. 32:29), insists Calvin, is that Jacob was not yet ready for it: "The Lord manifested himself to them [i.e., 'the fathers'], by degrees (*gradatim*), until, at length, Christ the Sun of Righteousness arose, in whom perfect brightness shines forth. This is the reason why he rendered himself more conspicuous to Moses, who nevertheless was only permitted to behold his glory from behind: yet because he occupied an intermediate place between patriarchs and apostles, he is said, in comparison with them (*prae illis*), to have seen, face to face (*facie ad faciem*), the God who had been hidden from the fathers."[13] Calvin here uses the language of a "face-to-face" encounter not simply to denote the ultimate sacramental reality of the beatific vision (as in 1 Cor. 13:12), but to describe *any* kind of intimacy with God. For Calvin, anyone who relates to God in an intimate manner sees him face-to-face. This is very much a relative matter, allowing for varying degrees. Calvin maintains, therefore, that the "face-to-face" vision of God is something that increases in clarity through salvation history—from Jacob and the other patriarchs, via Moses, to the apostles.[14] Compared to the gospel light, the vision that Jacob and Moses had of God was only "like sparks, or obscure rays."[15] Speaking of the tabernacle's veil, Calvin comments that "in the light of the gospel, we behold 'face to face' (*facie ad faciem*) what was then shewn afar off to the ancient people under coverings. (2 Cor. iii. 14.)."[16] The face-to-face vision that the believers have today is much greater than Moses's was.[17]

13. *Comm.* Gen. 32:29. Cf. *Comm.* Exod. 33:20: "Long before the birth of Moses, Jacob had said, 'I have seen God face to face (*facie ad faciem*),' (Gen. xxxii. 30;) and to Moses, as I have lately shewn, a still clearer vision was vouchsafed. Now, however, he obtains something better and more excellent; and yet not so as perfectly to see God such as He is in Himself (*qualis in se est*), but so far as the human mind is capable of bearing. For, although the angels are said to see God's face in a more excellent manner than men, still they do not apprehend the immense perfection of His glory, whereby they would be absorbed. Justly, therefore, does God declare that He cannot be seen by a mortal man; for we shall not see Him as He is (*sicuti est*), until we shall be like Him. (1 John iii. 2.)." Cf. also *Comm.* Exod. 33:11.

14. Cf. Arnold Huijgen's comment: "So, though Moses holds the highest rank, Calvin does not unqualifiedly ascribe to Moses a face to face vision of God. It is only 'in comparison with them' (the fathers) that Moses received a face to face vision" (*Divine Accommodation in Calvin's Theology: Analysis and Assessment*, Reformed Historical Theology 16 [Göttingen: Vandenhoeck & Ruprecht, 2011], 217).

15. *Comm.* Gen. 32:30.

16. *Comm.* Exod. 26:31. Cf. *Comm.* Heb. 7:25.

17. In the concluding chapter, I will present a pedagogical approach to the beatific vision—based in part on this graduated, biblical use of the language of seeing God "face-to-face."

In line with this, Calvin comments in connection with John 1:18 ("No one has ever seen God; the only God, who is at the Father's side, he has made him known") that God is now "openly (*palam*) beheld in the face of Christ," and Calvin insists that in comparison to us, the fathers had "nothing more than little sparks of the true light." Calvin then adds: "If it be objected, that at that time also God was seen *face to face*, (Gen. xxxii. 30; Deut. xxxiv. 10,) I maintain that that sight is not at all to be compared with ours; but as God was accustomed at that time to exhibit himself obscurely, and, as it were, from a distance, those to whom he was more clearly revealed say that they *saw him face to face*. They say so with reference to their own time; but they *did not see God* in any other way than wrapped up in many folds of figures and ceremonies."[18] For Calvin, then, Jacob, Moses, the believers today—and, of course, the saints in the hereafter[19]—all see God face-to-face, but with increasing clarity.[20]

The reason that face-to-face vision allows for varying degrees of brilliance is simply this: God "assumes the face which we are able to bear (*faciem induit quam possimus ferre*)."[21] It is, to use Arnold Huijgen's phrase, "accommodation as pedagogy."[22] God relates to his people as father and as teacher, and this requires that he accommodate himself to them: "God's accommodation relates to changing times, and circumstances; thus, it also has a history itself, in which it progresses toward the pedagogical end of raising God's people to further knowledge of God."[23] God's pedagogical program, therefore, necessitated, according to Calvin, that God manifest himself through a veil (*velum*)—while at the same time God relates to his people within this teaching program with increasing familiarity and shows himself more and more clearly to them.[24]

18. *Comm.* John 1:18.

19. *Comm.* 1 Cor. 13:12: "The knowledge of God, which we now have from his word, is indeed certain and true, and has nothing in it that is confused, or perplexed, or dark, but is spoken of as comparatively *obscure*, because it comes far short of that clear manifestation to which we look forward; for then *we shall see face to face.*"

20. Cf. Randall C. Zachman, *Image and Word in the Theology of John Calvin* (Notre Dame: University of Notre Dame Press, 2007), 127.

21. *Comm.* Exod. 33:20.

22. Huijgen, *Divine Accommodation*, 155.

23. Huijgen, *Divine Accommodation*, 208. For Calvin's understanding of accommodation, see also Cornelis van der Kooi, *As in a Mirror: John Calvin and Karl Barth on Knowing God—a Diptych*, trans. Donald Mader, Studies in the History of Christian Traditions 120 (Leiden: Brill, 2005), 41–57.

24. One of the implications of Calvin's pedagogical accommodation is that Moses never

The veil—the various created realities *through* which people see God in salvation history—does not only inhibit the vision of God. While it does serve that purpose (so that God's people are not destroyed by the brilliance of the light), the veil is also the very thing that *enables* the vision of God. Only by providing his people with veils can God manifest himself to them and can they discern his presence. Signs (or sacraments) are a veiled representation of the very presence of God. As Ronald Wallace explains: "Where God gives a sign, there He comes Himself to be present with men. The sign is thus a veil behind which He conceals His presence on the scene of human affairs."[25] In other words, for Calvin, through signs (or veils) God both hides and reveals himself.

Jesus Christ, in his humanity, also functions as a veil that allows us to see God in an attenuated fashion. Referring to Jesus's fulfillment of Isaiah's prophecies, Calvin insists that "the glory of Christ's divinity ought not to be the less admired, because it appeared under a vail of infirmity. This is unquestionably the very object to which the Holy Spirit directed the eyes of the prophet."[26] Calvin similarly speaks of Christ's body or his visible appearance as the "veil" of his flesh.[27] Christ's glory or divinity was concealed under the "veil" of his flesh, but the veil was at the same time the means to reach God's majesty.[28] Wallace summarizes Calvin's approach well with the comment, "In the New Testament . . . the humanity is like a veil behind which God conceals His majesty in order to reveal Himself."[29]

God's veiled or sacramental manifestation of himself is a matter of pedagogical tact or wisdom. The reformer often insists that God accommodates himself to our infirmity, our capacity, or our ability to comprehend him. This is clear, for example, when God appeared to Moses at the burning bush as the "angel of the LORD" (Exod. 3:2): "It was necessary that he should assume (*induere*) a visible form, that he might be seen by Moses, not as he was in his essence (*essentia*), but as the infirmity (*infirmitas*) of the human mind could comprehend him. For thus we must believe that God, as often as he appeared of old to the holy patriarchs, descended in some way from

---

saw the divine essence: his vision—though "face-to-face"—was less brilliant than ours, and (on Calvin's understanding) we do not see God's essence today.

25. Ronald S. Wallace, *Calvin's Doctrine of the Word and Sacrament* (1953; reprint, Eugene, OR: Wipf and Stock, 1997), 75.

26. *Comm.* Matt. 12:17.

27. *Inst.* 2.13.2.

28. *Comm.* Isa. 52:14; *Comm.* Matt. 17:9.

29. Wallace, *Calvin's Doctrine*, 12–13.

his majesty, that he might reveal himself as far as was useful, and as far as their comprehension would admit."[30] God appeared to Moses as an angel, in visible form, because Moses was still unable to endure the brilliance of God's essence.[31] Similarly, when Scripture says that the seventy elders "saw the God of Israel" (24:10), Calvin comments that they saw him "not in all His reality and greatness, but in accordance with the dispensation which He thought best, and which he accommodated (*attemperauit*) to the capacity of man."[32] When God reveals himself to us in this life, he assumes the face we are able to bear—which is to say, he sacramentally accommodates himself to the infirmity of our creaturely and spiritual capacities.[33]

Christological Accommodation

Calvin interprets this divine accommodation consistently in a christological fashion. That is to say, we should not imagine that God first manifested his divinity through a variety of created means and only in the fullness of time through the humanity of Christ. For Calvin, Christ is not an afterthought.[34] Rather, throughout history God always accommodates himself

---

30. *Comm.* Exod. 3:2.

31. Later in the commentary, Calvin comments about God's accommodated revelation to Moses: "Although God revealed Himself to Moses in a peculiar manner, still He never appeared in the fulness of His glory, but only so far as man's infirmity could endure. For this expression [i.e., 'face to face'] contains an implied comparison, *i.e.*, that no man was ever equal to Moses, or arrived at such a pitch of dignity" (*Comm.* Exod. 33:11).

32. *Comm.* Exod. 24:9. For similar statements, see *Comm.* Isa. 6:1; *Comm.* Ezek. 1:25–26; *Comm.* 2 Cor. 3:18; *Comm.* Heb. 11:27; *Comm.* 1 John 3:2.

33. As is well known, Calvin often has recourse to the notion of "accommodation" to explain how the transcendent God can reveal himself to humanity. Arnold Huijgen explains that Calvin adopted the notion from John Chrysostom via Desiderius Erasmus ("Divine Accommodation in Calvin: Myth and Reality," in *The Myth of the Reformation*, ed. Peter Opitz, Refo500 Academic Studies 9 [Göttingen: Vandenhoeck & Ruprecht, 2013], 252–53). J. Todd Billings rightly connects the notion of accommodation to Calvin's understanding of seeing God in divine revelation (*Union with Christ: Reframing Theology and Ministry for the Church* [Grand Rapids: Baker Academic, 2011], 70–75).

34. To be sure, for Calvin the incarnation was occasioned by sin, and in that sense Calvin's Christology was infralapsarian. But, as Edwin Chr. van Driel points out, for Calvin the Word of God served as mediator of divine glory irrespective of the Fall, so that he was supralapsarian with regard to the broader notion of christological mediation. For Calvin, the divine Word was the "medium" between God and creatures from the very beginning ("'Too Lowly to Reach God without a Mediator': John Calvin's Supralapsarian Eschatological Narrative," *ModTh* 33 [2017]:

in Jesus Christ (or the Word of God). The entire pedagogical program is christological in character.[35] As Todd Billings puts it: "In so far as they [i.e., the Israelites] experienced this covenantal bond with God, they participated in the Mediator, Christ. For Christ 'was always the bond of union between God and man.' 'God has never manifested himself to men in any other way than through the Son,' for fellowship with God would be impossible apart from Christ as mediator."[36] For Calvin, Christ was the substance of the law, and the patriarchs were bound to God only through the Word.[37]

In line with this, Calvin interprets the Old Testament theophanies as manifestations of the preincarnate Word, the second person of the Trinity.[38] The "angel of the LORD" is a reference to Christ, insists Calvin, seeing as he is the head of the angels in his office as mediator, "which he figuratively (*figuram*) bore from the beginning."[39] Explains Calvin: "And Paul sufficiently expounds this mystery to us, when he plainly asserts that Christ was the leader of his people in the Desert. (1 Cor. x. 4.) Therefore, although at that time, properly speaking (*proprie loquendo*), he was not yet the messenger of his Father, still his predestinated appointment to the office even then had this effect, that he manifested himself to the patriarchs, and was known in this character. Nor, indeed, had the saints ever any communication with God except through the promised Mediator."[40] Similarly, although Calvin does not want to *limit* Isaiah's vision of the Lord (Isa. 6:1) to a vision of Christ, nonetheless he observes that John 12:41 ("Isaiah said these things because he saw his glory and spoke of him") says it was Christ—and rightly so, insists Calvin, because "God never revealed himself to the Fathers but in his eternal

---

275-92). In a similar vein, Kees van der Kooi rightly suggests: "The elevation of God above the transient world *always* makes a certain form of mediation necessary. Thus it is not in sin that the necessity of accommodation itself is found" (*As in a Mirror*, 42–43). At the same time, as we will see, Calvin's understanding of the beatific vision as a vision of the divine essence means that he believed this accommodation would come to an end at the second coming.

35. To be sure, as Edwin van Driel has rightly pointed out to me, we can only call Calvin's entire pedagogical program "christological" by interpreting that expression as including the Word's mediation apart from the incarnation.

36. J. Todd Billings, *Calvin, Participation, and the Gift: The Activity of Believers in Union with Christ* (Oxford: Oxford University Press, 2007), 159. Billings's two quotations are from *Inst.* 4.8.5 and *Comm. Gen.* 48:16, respectively.

37. *Inst.* 2.9.4; 2.10.7. Cf. Billings, *Calvin, Participation, and the Gift*, 160.

38. Cf. Huijgen's comment on Calvin's view: "So, every theophany, or presence of God, in the Old Testament took place through Christ the Mediator" (*Divine Accommodation*, 238).

39. *Comm. Exod.* 3:2.

40. *Comm. Exod.* 3:2. Cf. also *Comm. Exod.* 14:9.

Word and only begotten Son."[41] Even though Isaiah uses the general word אֲדֹנָי (Lord), Calvin argues that Christ's glory is intimated in this passage, for at the time Christ was the image of the invisible God (cf. Col. 1:15).[42]

Calvin maintains that, also today, we see God ever only in Christ. The reason our face-to-face vision of God today is clearer than that of anyone in the Old Testament—including Moses—is that the Word has now taken on human flesh. God has revealed himself to us in Christ. In John 1:18 ("No one has ever seen God; the only God, who is at the Father's side, he has made him known"), the Evangelist "magnifies the manifestation of God, which has been brought to us by the gospel, in which he distinguishes us from the fathers, and shows that we are superior to them; as also Paul explains more fully in the Third and Fourth chapters of the Second Epistle to the Corinthians. For he maintains that there is now no longer any vail, such as existed under the Law, but that God is openly (*palam*) beheld in the face of Christ."[43] Although the Father is invisible "in his naked majesty," "he is revealed to us in Christ alone, that we may behold him as in a mirror."[44] To be sure, the term "openly" (*palam*), like the expression "face-to-face" (*facie ad faciem*), allows for degrees; and, as we will see, even God's revelation in Christ is not ultimate for Calvin. Nonetheless, he considers the openness of God's revelation in Christ hitherto unprecedented. Indeed, "it is madness to wish to know anything besides Him [i.e., Christ]. For since the Father has manifested himself wholly in Him, that man wishes to be wise apart from God, who is not contented with Christ alone."[45]

Calvin's pedagogical approach comes to the fore also in his treatment of the intermediate state. He departs from the preceding Western tradition by

41. *Comm.* Isa. 6:1.

42. *Comm.* Isa. 6:1. Commenting on Ezek. 1:25–26, Calvin similarly argues from John 12:41 that both Isaiah and Ezekiel saw "an obscure glimpse" of "the mystery which was at length manifested in the person of Christ." Calvin clarifies, however, that the name Jehovah does not only have reference to Christ: "The whole essence of God is here comprehended." Still, when we speak of the person rather than of the essence, we should say that "the peculiar property of Christ is shown forth." Cf. John T. Slotemaker, ""*Fuisse in Forma Hominis*" Belongs to Christ Alone': John Calvin's Trinitarian Hermeneutics in His *Lectures on Ezekiel*," *SJT* 68 (2015): 421–36. Calvin's exegesis of theophanies as appearances of the preincarnate Christ in effect reverts back to a pre-Augustinian understanding. Cf. above, chap. 4, section entitled "Trinitarian and Christological Controversies."

43. *Comm.* John 1:18. Calvin comments elsewhere that inasmuch as Christ is our "wisdom" (1 Cor. 1:30), "the Father has fully revealed himself to us in him, that we may not desire to know any thing besides him" (*Comm.* 1 Cor. 1:30).

44. *Comm.* Col. 1:15.

45. *Comm.* Col. 2:3. Cf. *Comm.* Heb. 1:3.

linking the beatific vision exclusively to the fullness of the kingdom after the resurrection. That is to say, the blessed departed in the intermediate state do not yet enjoy the happiness of the beatific vision. In his earliest theological work, *Psychopannychia* (1534), Calvin defends—against Pope John XXII (1316–1334) and current-day Anabaptists—the position that the soul is a substance and that after bodily death it continues to live, endowed with sense and understanding.[46] Calvin maintains that death increases the peace of the believers, since at death they leave the warfare of the world behind. In their new place of peace, explains Calvin, "while wholly intent on beholding God, they have nothing better to which they can turn their eyes or direct their desire."[47] Calvin clarifies, however, that this postmortem vision of God does not yet proffer complete happiness. The *visio Dei* remains inchoate until the resurrection of the dead:

> Still, something is wanting which they [i.e., the blessed departed] desire to see, namely, the complete and perfect glory of God, to which they always aspire. Though there is no impatience in their desire, their rest is not yet full and perfect, since he is said to rest who is where he desires to be; and the measure of desire has no end till it has arrived where it was tending. But if the eyes of the elect look to the supreme glory of God as their final good, their desire is always moving onward till the glory of God is complete, and this completion awaits the judgment day. Then will be verified the saying, "I will be satisfied, when I awake, with beholding thy countenance." (Psalm xvii. 15).[48]

For Calvin, the beatific vision of God is our ultimate end; only God gives perfect rest and peace. At the same time, inasmuch as his glory remains incomplete until the resurrection, our desire for him must continue (though

---

46. John Calvin, *Psychopannychia*, in *Tracts*, trans. Henry Beveridge, vol. 3 (Edinburgh: Calvin Translation Society, 1851), 419–20. Calvin mistakenly thought that Pope John XXII had taught a soul sleep in the intermediate state (*Psychopannychia*, 415). In actual fact, Pope John XXII neither believed that souls are mortal nor that they will sleep in the intermediate state. Instead, he taught that after bodily death, the blessed souls merely see Christ's humanity, that they will see his divine nature only after the resurrection, and that their happiness is, therefore, incomplete until then. Joseph N. Tylenda's excellent article on this topic makes clear that Calvin probably accepted in good faith a common misconstrual of Pope John's teachings ("Calvin and the Avignon Sermons of John XXII," *ITQ* 41 [1974]: 44–45).

47. Calvin, *Psychopannychia*, 435–36.

48. Calvin, *Psychopannychia*, 436.

without sinful "impatience")[49] in the intermediate state.[50] Calvin's position—one that he retained in his subsequent career[51]—was that the believers will see God in the full glory of his kingdom only at the resurrection.

Provisional Accommodation

While he recognizes the importance of signs (or veils), Calvin often cautions his readers not to turn them into obstacles: they point beyond themselves. Already today, the strictly subsidiary role of these teaching tools is evident. The physical object of the tabernacle, for example, is a sign of something greater. Reflecting on Psalm 27:4—

> One thing have I asked of the LORD,
>   that will I seek after:
> that I may dwell in the house of the LORD
>   all the days of my life,
> to gaze upon the beauty of the LORD
>   and to inquire in his temple—

49. Calvin maintains that after death the souls are "in peace" (*Psychopannychia*, 467 [emphasis omitted]).

50. At one point, Calvin quotes Bernard of Clairvaux: "Bernard, professedly handling this question in two sermons delivered on the Feast of All Saints, teaches, that 'the souls of the saints, divested of their bodies, still stand in the courts of the Lord, admitted to rest but not yet to glory. Into that most blessed abode,' he says, 'they shall neither enter without us, nor without their own bodies'; that is, neither saints without other believers, nor spirits without flesh: and many other things to the same purpose" (*Psychopannychia*, 469). Tylenda points out that although Calvin did not realize it, his teaching on the intermediate state was almost identical to that of Pope John XXII, the very person he thought he was opposing in his treatise. Like John XXII, Calvin marshaled Bernard in support of his position ("Calvin and the Avignon Sermons," 46–47).

51. Calvin later comments: "Although full vision will be deferred until the day of Christ, a nearer view of God will begin to be enjoyed immediately after death, when our souls, set free from the body, will have no more need of the outward ministry, or other inferior helps" (*Comm.* 1 Cor. 13:12). In his *Institutes*, Calvin comments regarding the souls of the faithful departed: "Scripture goes no farther than to say that Christ is present with them, and receives them into paradise" (*Inst.* 3.25.6). Calvin insists here that Scripture defers the "crown of glory" until Christ's coming, and he states that "the souls of the pious, having ended the toil of their warfare, enter into blessed rest, where in glad expectation they await the enjoyment of promised glory, and so all things are held in suspense until Christ the Redeemer appear" (3.25.6).

Calvin raises a hypothetical objection to David's grief and affliction over being banished from the sanctuary: "'Surely,' some may say, 'he could have called on God beyond the precincts of the temple. Wherever he wandered as an exile, he carried with him the precious promise of God, so that he needed not to put so great a value upon the sight of the external edifice. He appears, by some gross imagination or other, to suppose that God could be enclosed by wood and stones.'"[52] Though he disagrees with this objection, Calvin does point away from the visible sanctuary to its eternal model: David's

> object was altogether different from a mere sight of the noble building and its ornaments, however costly. He speaks, indeed, of the beauty of the temple, but he places that beauty not so much in the goodliness that was to be seen by the eye, as in its being the celestial pattern which was shown to Moses, as it is written in Exod. xxv. 40, "And look that thou make them after this pattern which was showed thee in the mount." As the fashion of the temple was not framed according to the wisdom of man, but was an image of spiritual things, the prophet directed his eyes and all his affections to this object.[53]

For Calvin, we could say, the tabernacle was merely a *sacramentum*, and David contemplates, not this external beauty, but the spiritual *res* on which the outward tabernacle was patterned.[54]

Calvin's argument so far perhaps makes us wonder whether the visible tabernacle has any positive role to play. But he goes on to insist that church buildings—as well as the liturgical worship performed in them—do serve an important function, since God "preserves his people under a certain order," so that temples "still have their beauty" and should, therefore, draw our "affections and desires." Similarly, we dare not neglect "the Word, sacraments, public prayers, and other helps of the same kind," because God "manifests" (*repræsentat*) himself in them "as in a mirror or image."[55] All these divine means are for Calvin like "veils": though they hide God, they also render him present.[56] Just as the physical structure of the tabernacle was in some sense

52. *Comm.* Ps. 27:4.

53. *Comm.* Ps. 27:4.

54. Calvin is quick to add a polemical note against those "who wrest this place in favour of pictures and images, which, instead of deserving to be numbered among temple ornaments, are rather like dung and filth, defiling all the purity of holy things" (*Comm.* Ps. 27:4).

55. *Comm.* Ps. 27:4.

56. Zachman, in his extended discussion of how the various symbols of God's presence to

unimportant while nonetheless God used it to point David to its eternal pattern, so also God does not strictly identify with the sacramental means that he uses while they are nonetheless indispensable ordinances through which God draws us to himself.

In the eschaton, the subsidiary character of sacramental means will become more evident. Calvin maintains that at the conclusion of the pedagogical program—that is to say, at Christ's return—all teaching tools will be left behind. Or, to put it more theologically, sacramental means will give way to the reality at which they aim. Though we are not at that point yet, we do anticipate it: "We are far from having attained, as yet, the perfection of wisdom. That perfection, therefore, which will be in a manner a maturity of spiritual age, will put an end to education and its accompaniments."[57] All hierarchical structures and exercise of authority will cease at Christ's return. Any "distinction in ranks" or "orders of dignity," all "dominion" of angels, as well as the offices of "Bishops, teachers, and Prophets" will be terminated.[58] We could say that at the end of history, all *sacramenta* will give way to the *res* to which they have pointed and which, in a veiled manner, they have rendered present. Even Christ's rule, therefore, is merely temporary or provisional, and after the resurrection his mediation too will cease. His office as mediator will no longer be necessary to see God. The pedagogical training being completed, the saints will be able to see God directly in his majesty, *sicuti est* (cf. 1 John 3:2). In short, God's accommodation in Christ is only a temporary or provisional measure. We could say that as the great *sacramentum*, Christ as mediator has served as the ultimate sacramental ordinance whereby God has drawn us to himself. For Calvin, when the reality of the beatific vision comes about, such sacramental mediation will not be needed anymore.

Calvin dwells at some length on the provisionality of Christ's mediation in his reflections on 1 Corinthians 15:28—"When all things are subjected to him, then the Son himself will also be subjected to him who put all things in subjection under him, that God may be all in all." Both in the *Institutes* and in his commentary on the passage, Calvin explains that although it is true that the kingdom of the Son of God will not come to an end, Christ's role as mediator *will* end at the resurrection. This means that Christ's lordship is temporary; he will hand back to the Father his role as ruler of the world:

Israel function for Calvin, comments that "the tabernacle truly is the symbol of the presence of God, by means of which God may be truly said to dwell among God's people" (*Image and Word*, 211).

57. *Comm.* 1 Cor. 13:11.
58. *Comm.* 1 Cor. 15:24.

"When as partakers in heavenly glory we shall see God as he is, Christ, having then discharged the office of Mediator, will cease to be the ambassador of his Father, and will be satisfied with that glory which he enjoyed before the creation of the world."[59] Saint Paul's reference to the eschatological subjection of the Son, therefore, does not speak of his divinity (or, for that matter, of his humanity); according to Calvin, it has reference to his mediatorial office, including his lordship.[60] Christ's mediation will come to an end.

Christ's abdication of his mediatorial role in the resurrection has immediate implications for the beatific vision. Calvin maintains that "the vail being then removed, we shall openly (*palam*) behold God reigning in his majesty and Christ's humanity will then no longer be interposed to keep us back from a closer view of God."[61] Christ's lordship (or, as Calvin puts it in his commentary, his humanity) currently functions as a veil, and once it is removed, we will "enjoy the direct vision (*præsenti . . . aspectu*) of the Godhead."[62] Indeed, Christ's discharge of his office of mediator will allow us to "see God as he is." Christ's lordship, reiterates Calvin, functions "until such time as we should see his divine majesty face to face." "Then," Calvin continues, "he returns the lordship to his Father so that—far from diminishing his own majesty—it may shine all the more brightly. Then, also, God shall cease to be the Head of Christ, for Christ's own deity will shine of itself, although as yet it is covered by a veil."[63] In short, the ending of Christ's role as mediator will ultimately render the beatific vision of the divine essence possible.

Calvin does not go so far as to claim that Christ's human nature (or his embodiment) will disappear in the eschaton.[64] This would seem to be out of

---

59. *Inst.* 2.14.3. Cf. *Comm.* John 14:28: "In what manner, therefore, will he lay aside the kingdom? It is, because the Divinity (*divinitas*) which is now beheld in Christ's face alone, will then be openly visible in itself (*palam in se*). . . . He was not appointed to be our guide, merely to raise us to the sphere of the moon or of the sun, but to make us one with God the Father" (translation modified, HB).

60. Calvin insists that the key to understanding this Pauline passage is that "those things which apply to the office of the Mediator are not spoken simply either of the divine nature or of the human" (*Inst.* 2.14.3), and he argues, therefore: "The name 'Lord' exclusively belongs to the person of Christ only in so far as it represents a degree midway between God and us" (*Inst.* 2.14.3). In his commentary on 1 Cor. 15:27, Calvin focuses less on Christ's mediatorship, and more directly on his two natures, insisting that Christ "will transfer it [i.e., the kingdom] in a manner (*quodammodo*) from his humanity to his glorious divinity."

61. *Comm.* 1 Cor. 15:27.

62. *Inst.* 2.14.3.

63. *Inst.* 2.14.3.

64. Heinrich Quistorp has argued that, for Calvin, after the resurrection, Christ's human-

line with his general insistence on an embodied resurrection.[65] What Calvin does suggest is that all accommodated access to God will come to an end at the resurrection, and that as a result the incarnate Christ will no longer mediate our vision of God. Calvin maintains this not only in his comments on 1 Corinthians 15:27–28, but also elsewhere. Inasmuch as we are still away from the Lord (cf. 2 Cor. 5:6), we do not see him face-to-face today. That is to say, insists Calvin, at this time "God is not openly (*palam*) beheld by us."[66] Calvin repeatedly compares this relative darkness of our faith with the immediacy of the beatific vision of God in the future. Calvin refers to this future vision as "God's own immediate presence."[67] He insists that God will then "openly (*palam*) show himself to us."[68] This will be a "full vision," which is to say that "we shall see God—not in his image, but in himself, so that there will be, in a manner, a mutual view."[69]

Calvin hardly ever uses the technical theological language of seeing the essence (*essentia*) of God in the eschaton. As far as I know, the only exception occurs in his discussion of seeing God "as he is" (1 John 3:2). He comments there: "When the Apostle says, that we shall see him as he is, he intimates a new and an ineffable manner of seeing him, which we enjoy not now; for as long as we walk by faith, as Paul teaches us, we are absent from him. And when he appeared to the fathers, it was not in his own essence (*in sua essentia*), but was ever seen under symbols (*sub symbolis*). Hence the majesty of God, now hid, will then only be in itself seen, when the veil of this mortal

---

ity "recedes" into the background (*Calvin's Doctrine of the Last Things*, trans. Harold Knight [London: Lutterworth, 1955], 169). This is true to some extent, particularly with regard to the commentary on 1 Cor. 15:27, but Calvin primarily has in mind Christ's role as mediator, so that when it comes to an end, Christ's humanity no longer functions as a veil that separates us from the divine essence. Building on Quistorp, Jürgen Moltmann overstates the case with the claim that Calvin had a "functional Christology" and that he believed Christ's human nature itself will come to an end on the last day—all this because for Calvin the incarnation was strictly occasioned by sin (*Crucified God: The Cross of Christ as the Foundation and Criticism of Christian Theology*, trans. John Bowden [Minneapolis: Fortress, 1993], 257–58). For further discussion of this issue, see Richard A. Muller, "Christ in the Eschaton: Calvin and Moltmann on the Duration of the *Munus Regium*," *HTR* 74 (1981): 31–59; Billings, *Union with Christ*, 82–83.

65. For Calvin's emphasis on bodily resurrection, see *Inst.* 3.25.7–8. Cf. the discussion in Quistorp, *Calvin's Doctrine*, 133–43.

66. *Comm.* 2 Cor. 5:7.

67. *Comm.* Ps. 17:15.

68. *Comm.* Ps. 27:8. We again see here that for Calvin to behold God "face-to-face" (*facie ad faciem*) or "openly" (*palam*) is a matter of degrees.

69. *Comm.* 1 Cor. 13:12.

and corruptible nature shall be removed."[70] Calvin states here rather unambiguously that we will see the divine essence (the majesty of God) after the resurrection. It seems clear, then, that Calvin—along with the mainstream Western tradition since the high Middle Ages—believed that the object of the beatific vision is the divine essence. This also sheds light on the debate on whether or not Calvin held to deification.[71] Since he believed that in the eschaton we will see the essence of God—without the mediation of Christ— the conclusion seems inevitable that Calvin also anticipated a deifying union with God (or the Father) himself.[72]

For the most part, Calvin avoids the explicit language of seeing the divine essence and of deification, quite possibly so as not to give the impression that the creator-creature distinction will disappear.[73] Thus, in the same commentary on 1 John 3:2, Calvin warns his readers not to overstate matters: "The perfection of glory will not be so great in us, that our seeing will enable us to comprehend (*comprehendat*) all that God is; for the distance between us and him will be even then very great."[74] The Genevan reformer is in line here

70. *Comm.* 1 John 3:2.

71. In recent debate about deification in Calvin, some have defended the position that he upholds the teaching: Carl Mosser, "The Greatest Possible Blessing: Calvin and Deification," *SJT* 55 (2002): 36–57; Julie Canlis, "Calvin, Osiander and Participation in God," *IJST* 6 (2004): 169–84; J. Todd Billings, "United to God through Christ: Assessing Calvin on the Question of Deification," *HTR* 98 (2005): 315–34; Van Driel, "Too Lowly to Reach God," 275–92. Others reject the presence of deification in Calvin: Jonathan Slater, "Salvation as Participation in the Humanity of the Mediator in Calvin's *Institutes of the Christian Religion*: A Reply to Carl Mosser," *SJT* 58 (2005): 39–58; Bruce L. McCormack, "Union with Christ in Calvin's Theology: Grounds for a Divinization Theory?," in *Tributes to John Calvin: A Celebration of His Quincentenary*, ed. David W. Hall (Phillipsburg, NJ: Presbyterian and Reformed, 2010), 504–29. Mediating positions are taken by Yang-Ho Lee, "Calvin on Deification: A Reply to Carl Mosser and Jonathan Slater," *SJT* 63 (2010): 272–84; A. J. Ollerton, "*Quasi Deificari*: Deification in the Theology of John Calvin," *WTJ* 73 (2011): 237–54.

72. This comes to the fore most famously in *Comm.* 2 Pet. 1:4, where Calvin comments that "the end of the gospel is, to render us eventually conformable to God, and, if we may so speak, to deify us (*quasi deificari*)." Calvin similarly insists that Christ became our mediator in order to "join us to God" (*Inst.* 1.13.24); that Christ gathers believers into "participation in the Father" (*Inst.* 1.13.26); that the perfection of human happiness is "to be united with God" (*Inst.* 1.15.6); that Christ leads us to a "firm union with God" (*Inst.* 2.15.5); and that Christ descended to us "that he might unite us to God" (*Comm.* John 14:28; cf. *Comm.* Jer. 31:34; *Comm.* 1 John 4:15). Cf. Van Driel, "Too Lowly to Reach God," 290n65.

73. When he does use the language of deification, Calvin immediately adds, "The word nature is not here essence but quality," and he warns against "fanatics who imagine that we thus pass over into the nature of God, so that his swallows up our nature" (*Comm.* 2 Pet. 1:4).

74. *Comm.* 1 John 3:2.

with the traditional caution regarding our ability to comprehend God, and it may well be that this same theological motivation made him generally shy away also from the language of seeing the divine essence (*essentia*)—though in the latter case, he avoided language that *was*, of course, commonly accepted in the Western tradition. Still, regardless of the language employed, the *content* of Calvin's doctrine of the beatific vision is, at this point, fully in line with that of the mainstream Western tradition: since Christ will no longer interpose as mediator, in the eschaton we will have direct vision of the essence of God.

Conclusion

Calvin's eschatology is strictly theocentric. He looked forward to the beatific vision as the final end of human life and was convinced that human happiness consists in being united to God. One may well ask why the reformer mostly restricted his reflections on the beatific vision to his biblical commentaries, only dealing with the topic when the biblical text demanded it from him. Calvin's own appeal to *sobrietas* seems to me insufficient justification for such a limitation on discussing the beatific vision. Sobriety and epistemic humility ought to mark all dogmatic reflection, not just reflection on the beatific vision.[75] There is no reason sobriety and extended theological discussion cannot go hand in hand. If, as Calvin was convinced, the beatific vision is the final human telos, then certainly it ought to take pride of place in a dogmatic exposition of the Christian faith. I do not, therefore, mean to excuse the relative absence of the beatific vision from the *Institutes*. Nonetheless, by myopically focusing on this problem, we may lose sight of important aspects of Calvin's eschatology, which only come to light when we carefully investigate also his biblical commentaries. They bring to the fore his firm conviction that the beatific vision constitutes our ultimate end, and a complete picture of Calvin's eschatology must do justice to his deeply held beliefs on this matter.

This is all the more important since Calvin's exegetical comments about the beatific vision display remarkable theological acumen. Though he does

---

75. To be sure, Calvin himself was keenly aware of this, as is witnessed, for instance, in his repeated cautions against the "labyrinths" of the divine mysteries, particularly that of predestination. See Richard A. Muller, *The Unaccommodated Calvin: Studies in the Foundation of a Theological Tradition* (New York: Oxford University Press, 2000), 81–85.

not usually mention the work of previous theologians on the beatific vision, he clearly works within the parameters of the broader theological tradition, which is particularly evident with regard to his views on the object of the beatific vision. His opinion that we will see the majesty (or essence) of God is in line with the broad consensus of Western medieval Christianity. At the same time, Calvin's cautious vocabulary (especially with regard to the term *essentia*) means that he did not simply parrot past articulations of the doctrine. Furthermore, the way he navigates questions surrounding the presence of God in and through "signs" and "veils" indicates his keen awareness that the telos of the future vision is in some manner already present in salvation history. Put differently, Calvin's doctrine of the beatific vision was in line with the earlier sacramental understanding of it. For Calvin, God manifests himself throughout history, and we anticipate the beatific vision whenever and wherever we discern his presence today.

Calvin's use of the terms "face-to-face" (*facie ad faciem*) and "openly" (*palam*) is particularly fascinating. For Calvin, face-to-face vision of God was not simply a synonym for beatific vision. Instead, he understood face-to-face vision of God as an expression of familiar intimacy between God and human beings, something that allows for degrees of intensity. Thus, Calvin's use of the language of *facie ad faciem* and of *palam* highlights salvation history and divine pedagogy. Apart from Irenaeus in the second century, no theologian has tied the vision of God so closely to a divine pedagogical program as Calvin.[76] In some ways, this caused him to depart from the earlier tradition. Divine pedagogy not only meant a stronger emphasis on salvation history than was common in the patristic era and the medieval tradition, but it also led to a different exegesis of certain biblical narratives. Since he rigorously stuck to his conviction that, as part of his teaching program, God gradually lifted the veil over time, Calvin could no longer accept the notion—nearly unanimously agreed upon in the earlier Western tradition—that Moses saw the essence of God. Calvin was convinced that Moses's "face-to-face" vision wasn't anything like the "face-to-face" vision under the new covenant as Saint Paul describes it in 2 Corinthians 3 and 4, and Calvin treated the latter, in turn, as far inferior to the "face-to-face" vision of God in the eschaton.

Calvin's independent mind also shows in his willingness to move away from settled opinion so as to retrieve earlier viewpoints that he considered more acceptable. One such instance is his treatment of the intermediate

76. For discussion of Irenaeus's treatment, see chap. 13, section entitled "Pedagogy and Salvation History."

state. Although he did not discuss the topic in detail in his later theological writings, he appears to have remained true to his early conviction, expressed in the *Psychopannychia*, that the vision of God in the intermediate state is inferior to that of the saints after the resurrection. The teaching of Thomas Aquinas and of Pope Benedict XII's 1336 *Benedictus Deus* had cemented the theological position that immediately after death, the souls of the saints have an immediate, intuitive view of the divine essence. Calvin, however, charted a different path, appealing to earlier theologians, including Bernard of Clairvaux. By claiming that even after death the vision of God is subject to gradation, Calvin returned at least partially to earlier patristic (and Eastern) views, which had emphasized that after death the soul continues to desire a clearer vision of God.

Similarly, Calvin's insistence that the Old Testament theophanies were manifestations of the eternal Son of God, and as such prefigured the incarnation, represented a notable retrieval of a much earlier tradition. Ever since Augustine's *De Trinitate*, this viewpoint had been rejected for fear of subordinationism.[77] Though Calvin was by no means subordinationist in his Christology, he was convinced that when God stoops down into history, he always does so in Christ. This return to a pre-Nicene reading of the theophanies seems to me an important moment in the history of exegesis. Calvin's view that all revelation of God in history is christological not only injected an important anti-Marcionite element in his reading of Scripture, but it also served to underscore the sacramental presence of Christ in the Old Testament. Calvin, we could say, acknowledged the sacramental presence of Christ as hidden within the Old Testament Scriptures—an important antidote to any separation between nature and the supernatural, since it tells us that historical realities can only properly be understood in the light of Christ.

To be sure, Calvin did not extend his christological treatment as far as he might have. In particular, he adopted the medieval consensus that the eschatological promise of seeing God face-to-face, as he is (cf. 1 Cor. 13:12; 1 John 3:2), entails a vision of the divine majesty *in se*. For Calvin, this implied that all mediation will come to an end and that in the eschaton we will no longer see God in Christ. Fortunately, as we will see in subsequent chapters, Puritan theologians such as Isaac Ambrose, Thomas Watson, and John Owen did not follow Calvin in this, and also Jonathan Edwards had a more consistently christological approach to the beatific vision. It is hard to escape the conclusion that for Calvin, the humanity of Christ fails to have

---

77. See chap. 4, section entitled "Trinitarian and Christological Controversies."

a meaningful role in the eschaton. By separating the vision of the divine essence from the vision of Christ's humanity, Calvin ended up with a challenging dilemma, namely, how to maintain the creator-creature distinction in the light of our ability to see the divine essence itself. It seems to me that a rejection of (christological) accommodation in the eschaton makes it difficult to articulate this distinction convincingly. Even on this score, however, we should recall that Calvin maintained remarkable *sobrietas*, not in the least in terms of the vocabulary that he employed to describe our final telos. Though he was convinced that we will see the essence of God and that we will be deified in the process, Calvin's language always demonstrated deep respect for the transcendence of God.

CHAPTER 10

MODERNITY AND VISION

*John Donne's Restoration of
"Commerce twixt heauen and earth"*

Donne's Rejection of Pure Nature

The English poet and preacher John Donne (1572–1631) lived through a time of great social and cultural upheaval. Religious divisions had torn the church apart in the sixteenth century, and Stuart England continued to suffer the aftereffects as the Church of England's establishment attempted to chart a *via media* between Catholics and nonconformists. Francis Bacon's new philosophy—perhaps most famously articulated in his 1520 *Novum Organum*—turned to empirical investigation as the foundation for modern science, an approach that to many seemed to exclude questions of purpose and instead focused on human mastery of the natural world. In line with Bacon's approach, William Gilbert attacked Aristotelian philosophy and replaced scholastic methodology with experimental science. Elsewhere in Europe, Galileo Galilei's and Johannes Kepler's discoveries of new stars and planets—as well as their support of Copernicus's observation that the sun is at the center of the universe—had shaken the world of science. Meanwhile Niccolò Machiavelli's pragmatist political philosophy had undermined traditional notions of the common good, and his book *The Prince* (published after his death in 1532) appeared to alter the moral foundation of good and evil itself.

Each of these developments in the areas of religion, science, and politics centered on the relationship between heaven and earth. The sacramental system of medieval Catholicism gave way to a Protestant approach in which the Word was at the center of spiritual experience. Whereas in the Ptolemaic cosmos the planetary spheres influenced life on Earth, circling around it in true harmony, the discovery of a dazzling, new array of planets and stars seemed to imply that the harmony was gone and that Earth could no longer depend on the nurturing impact of its surrounding spheres. In the political sphere, not only was the divine right of kings under attack, but it seemed that political theorists were willing to entertain the thought that political authority comes from below rather than from above. In each of these areas, heaven and earth were increasingly treated as separate realms. Though it would take some time before these developments climaxed in eighteenth-century Deist thought, Donne's friendship with the Herbert family brought him in close contact with Edward Herbert, whose 1624 book *De veritate* (*On Truth*) signaled the beginning of the end of revealed religion.[1]

As we will see, Donne's writings—his poems as well as his sermons—reveal deep suspicion of the ever-widening chasm between heaven and earth in early seventeenth-century England. Donne was troubled by the metaphysic of pure nature—an approach to the natural world that removed from consideration any and all teleological concerns—that underpinned the religious, scientific, and political developments of modernity.[2] Increasingly, so it seemed to him, the early modern period distorted the sense of sight by separating empirical observation through the physical senses from their ultimate goal, namely, the beatific vision of God.[3] This was a particularly serious problem for Donne, since he followed Saint Augustine in treating sight as the noblest of the senses.[4] Donne was convinced that by limiting

1. Donne famously wrote Edward Herbert a poem, "To Sir Edward Herbert, at Julyers" (1610).

2. The notion of "pure nature" (*pura natura*)—the idea of a world whose natural ends are separate from the supernatural end of the beatific vision—came into prominence around the time of John Donne through the work of the Spanish scholastic theologian Francisco Suárez. See Henri de Lubac, *Augustinianism and Modern Theology* (New York: Crossroad/Herder and Herder, 2000), 145–81. See also Louis Dupré, *Passage to Modernity: An Essay in the Hermeneutics of Nature and Culture* (New Haven: Yale University Press, 1993), 174–81.

3. Charles Monroe Coffin depicts Donne as troubled by a "new world," which Coffin describes as "a sundered universe anticipating a complete dualism of mind and matter such as Descartes elaborated" (*John Donne and the New Philosophy*, Columbia University Studies in English and Comparative Literature 126 [New York: Columbia University Press, 1937], 22). Convinced that the new philosophy had introduced a "cleavage between the realms of the physical and metaphysical," Donne believed the medieval intimacy with the divine world was disintegrating, so that he was left with "a welter of facts and experiences over which men wield their dissecting knives and measuring sticks and at which they look through their optic glasses," while "the old correspondence of heaven and earth is broken, and beauty's elements, harmony and color, are spent" (Coffin, 285).

4. See, for instance, Donne, *FirAn* 353; *Sermons* 9.16.352; 7.13.346; 8.9.221 (*The Sermons of John Donne*, ed. George R. Potter and Evelyn M. Simpson, 10 vols. [Berkeley: University of California Press, 1953–1962]; the location numbers represent the volume, sermon, and page

their scope of vision to this-worldly empirical data, people were shielding their world from its heavenly horizons.

In his poetry, therefore, Donne reintroduced his contemporaries to the traditional themes of contempt of the world (*contemptus mundi*) and the art of dying (*ars moriendi*), warning them that by paying undue attention to the present world, they would end up excluding God from their daily affairs while banishing the supernatural to a separate realm upstairs. The result could only be a separation between heaven and earth, and between nature and the supernatural. Furthermore, in his sermons on the beatific vision, Donne proposed a sacramental, participatory understanding of reality, in which heaven and earth are closely linked, and he highlighted the sacramental connection between the vision of God in this world and in the next. In short, Donne turned to the doctrine of the beatific vision to counter what he regarded as the dreariness of a purely natural, material world—and, most importantly, to reorient his contemporaries toward God as their only true, final end.

The Anniversaries: "'Tis all in pieces, all cohærance gone"

Few poems may seem as ill conceived as Donne's *Anniversaries*. The two lengthy poems certainly do justice to their author's reputation as a metaphysical poet. The two *Anniversaries*—written in 1611 and 1612, respectively, in commemoration of the death in 1610 of the daughter of his wealthy patron, Sir Robert Drury, Elizabeth, at the young age of fourteen—are so obviously exaggerated in their praise of the young Elizabeth, a girl whom Donne had never met, that to take them at face value, without any metaphysical import, would seem to render them preposterous. The well-known dramatist and poet Ben Jonson, a contemporary of Donne, famously commented that "Dones Anniversarie was profane and full of Blasphemies: that . . . if it had been written of the Virgin Marie, it had been something."[5] Jonson was likely not alone in his scathing verdict.

Had the poems been strictly about Elizabeth Drury, Jonson's judgment would have been quite justified. Throughout both *The First Anniuersarie* and

---

number, respectively). Cf. Edward W. Tayler, *Donne's Idea of a Woman: Structure and Meaning in* The Anniversaries (New York: Columbia University Press, 1991), 40–42.

5. This oft-quoted statement comes from William Drummond's report of a conversation he had with Ben Jonson. See R. F. Patterson, ed., *Ben Jonson's Conversations with William Drummond of Hawthornden* (London: Blackie, 1923), 5.

The Second Anniuersarie, Donne's praise of the young girl is so exaggerated as to appear patently ludicrous. Elizabeth is a "Queene" (*FirAn* 7),[6] a "blessed maid" (*FirAn* 443), "fil'd with grace" (*SecAn* 465). She is the one

> of whom th'Auncients seem'd to prophesie,
> When they call'd vertues by the name of shee. (*FirAn* 175–76)

As the model of virtue, she so kept God's image in her heart that "what decay was growen, / Was her first Parents fault, and not her own" (*SecAn* 458). Her beauty was such that she was the "measure of all Symmetree" (*FirAn* 310). Indeed, her "rich beauty lent / Mintage to others beauties" (*SecAn* 223–24). She

> could not lacke, what ere this world could giue,
> Because shee was the forme, that made it liue. (*SecAn* 71–72)

These are but some of the numerous examples of the lavish praise that Donne heaps on the young Elizabeth. One wonders how the poems were received by Sir Robert. He must have found it hard to recognize his daughter in the hyperbole that his protégé had penned.

The poems, however, are not just about Elizabeth Drury. Donne himself responded to Ben Jonson's criticism by commenting that they described "the Idea of a Woman, and not as she was."[7] The poems never mention Elizabeth by name, and it is precisely the nameless character of the woman whose loss he laments that Donne draws to the fore in *The First Anniuersarie*:

> Thou hast forgot thy name, thou hadst; thou wast
> Nothing but she, and her thou hast o'repast.
> For as a child kept from the Font, vntill
> A Prince, expected long, come to fulfill
> The Ceremonies, thou vnnam'd hadst laid,
> Had not her comming, thee her Palace made:
> Her name defin'd thee, gave thee forme and frame,
> And thou forgetst to celebrate thy name. (31–38)

---

6. Throughout, I quote from the original 1611 and 1612 editions of *FirAn* and *SecAn*, as reproduced in *The Variorum Edition of the Poetry of John Donne*, vol. 6, *The Anniversaries and the Epicedes and Obsequies*, ed. Paul A. Parrish (Bloomington: Indiana University Press, 1995), 5–37. References have been placed in the text.

7. Patterson, *Ben Jonson's Conversations*, 5.

Donne tells his readers directly that they themselves are "the Idea of a Woman" ("thou wast / Nothing but she"; "Her name defin'd thee"). The readers are like matter that, in Aristotelian fashion, must be imbued with form to assume its identity. Elizabeth's coming did exactly this: her name gave "forme and frame" to his contemporaries. Or, again, they are like a child that has to wait for the arrival of a prince before it can be named at baptism. When Elizabeth (the prince) arrived, she gave them their name—which was the same as hers ("Her name defin'd thee"). Thus, Donne's contemporaries became the palace in which Elizabeth lived. In short, Donne's readers took their name and identity from Elizabeth. Their forgetfulness of their own name and identity ("Thou hast forgot thy name") is thus the same as the forgetfulness of the name and identity of the idealized woman who is the subject of Donne's hyperbolic praise.

To be sure, at some level *The Anniversaries* do speak of Elizabeth Drury: they do commemorate, at Sir Robert Drury's request, his daughter's passing. Nonetheless, at a deeper level, we must, as Peter Rudnytsky puts it, "resist the temptation to identify the nameless 'she' of the poems with *any* specific personage."[8] The real question, therefore, is why Donne felt the need to present "the Idea of a Woman" and why he placed his hearers in the position of having forgotten their true selves. The answer to this question is best given, perhaps, in Donne's description of Elizabeth as "Shee, who in th'Art of knowing Heauen, was growen / Here vpon Earth," to the greatest perfection (*SecAn* 311–12), and in his acknowledgment that "shee to Heauen is gone,"

> Who made this world in some proportion
> A heauuen, and here, became vnto us all,
> Ioye, (as our ioyes admit) essentiall. (*SecAn* 467–70)

Elizabeth acquired here on earth the art of knowing heaven and made this world like heaven itself. Throughout *The Anniversaries*, Donne is preoccupied with the relationship between heaven and earth. Convinced that the modern world has torn asunder heaven and earth, he wants to help his readers restore the "commerce twixt heauen and earth" (*FirAn* 399), and Elizabeth becomes his "cipher" for a proper conception of the relationship between the two.[9] Rudnytsky puts it well when he comments,

8. Peter L. Rudnytsky, "'The Sight of God': Donne's Poetics of Transcendence," *TSLL* 24 (1982): 195.

9. Tayler explains that the mind (or, in Donne's metaphor, the watchtower) "stands for

"What in *The first Anniversary* had been lamented as the breakdown of 'this commerce twixt heaven and earth' is rectified in *The second Anniversary* when the soul 'Dispatches in a minute all the way / Twixt heaven and earth' (ll. 188–89)."[10]

In the lengthy subtitle of *The First Anniuersarie*, Donne calls his poem *An Anatomie of the World. Wherein the frailtie and the decay of this whole World is represented.* Somewhat macabre perhaps, Donne takes Elizabeth Drury's death as the occasion to perform an anatomy, not on her body, but on the world—which not only has forgotten its identity but has languished and died along with Elizabeth, and to which he repeatedly refers as a "carcasse" (*FirAn* 439; *SecAn* 55–56, 60).[11] After performing his anatomy, Donne announces in *The Second Anniuersarie*'s subtitle that here he is going to outline *The Progres of the Soule*, as he considers *the incommodities of the Soule in this life and her exaltation in the next.* He enjoins the reader,

> Forget this rotten world; And vnto thee,
> Let thine owne times as an old story be. (*SecAn* 49–50)

He repeats the sentiment a few lines later:

> Forget this world, and scarse think of it so,
> As of old cloaths, cast of a yeare agoe. (*SecAn* 61–62)

---

the height of earthly knowledge, but also it mediates, in the manner habitual with Western philosophy, heaven and earth" (*Donne's Idea of a Woman*, 65). By speaking of Elizabeth as a "cipher," I do not mean to imply that Donne treats the link between Elizabeth and what she represents as tenuous or arbitrary. Tayler rightly argues that for Donne, Elizabeth is not a "symbol" of something entirely unrelated; rather, by attending to her actual person by means of the senses, both poet and reader are able to attain to (and become one with) her real form or essence by means of intellectual abstraction. It is in this sense that Tayler identifies the "idea" represented by Elizabeth as "the 'richness' of prelapsarian innocence and virtue" (65). One may still legitimately question how appropriate such a treatment of Elizabeth is as a commemoration of her death; I am not attempting here to defend Donne's metaphysical conceit so much as simply to draw attention to it.

10. Rudnystky, "The Sight of God," 200. My reading of Donne's *Anniversaries* is much indebted to Rudnytsky's insightful article.

11. Similarly, Donne speaks of a

> Sicke world, yea dead, yea putrified, since shee
> Thy'ntrinsique Balme, and thy preseruatiue,
> Can neuer be renew'd, thou neuer liue. (*FirAn* 56–58)

Donne encourages us instead:

> Look vpward; that's towards her, whose happy state
> We now lament not, but congratulate. (*SecAn* 65–66)

Whereas the *Anatomie* lays bare the split between earth and heaven, the *Progres* aims to heal the partition. Or, to put it in sacramental terms, the *Anatomie* analyzes the divorce between sacrament (*sacramentum*) and reality (*res*), while the *Progres* points to a restoration of a sacramental universe.[12]

It would be a mistake to look for scientific precision in the way Donne performs his anatomy. His poetic sensibilities do not allow for such exactitude. Instead, Donne intends to evoke a sense of dread, which he broadly links to seventeenth-century philosophical and scientific developments—focusing on empirical investigation while losing epistemic confidence—and to a loss of virtue in society. All this is captured in the repeated lament, "Shee, shee is dead; shee's dead" (*FirAn* 183, 237, 325, 369, 427). Elizabeth's death stands for the religious, philosophical, scientific, and social disintegration that Donne believed he was witnessing all around him.[13]

Donne humorously refers to shortening life spans and decreasing physical statures—"We're scarse our Fathers shadowes cast at noon" (*FirAn* 144)—as witnessing to the decline of the times. The underlying problem is that the "new Philosophy cals all in doubt" (*FirAn* 205), as astronomers find new planets and put into question the traditional understanding of the movements of the spheres. The result, claims Donne, is a fragmenting world:

> And freely men confesse, that this world's spent,
> When in the Planets, and the Firmament
> They seeke so many new; they see that this
> Is crumbled out againe to his Atomis.
> 'Tis all in pieces, all cohærance gone;

12. Catherine Gimelli Martin has argued that, with the loss of the medieval sacramental world, Donne searched for a *via media*. While acknowledging that Donne was a Protestant at heart, Martin maintains that Donne's struggle with the desacralizing of nature leads him to search for Protestant alternatives to the loss of medieval forms of mediation. Elizabeth Drury thus becomes a way to mediate between heaven and earth ("Unmeete Contraryes: The Reformed Subject and the Triangulation of Religious Desire in Donne's *Anniversaries* and *Holy Sonnets*," in *John Donne and the Protestant Reformation: New Perspectives*, ed. Mary Arshagouni Papazian [Detroit: Wayne State University Press, 2003], 193–220).

13. Cf. Rudnytsky, "The Sight of God," 186.

All iust supply, and all Relation:
Prince, Subiect, Father, Sonne, are things forgot,
For euery man alone thinkes he hath got
To be a Phœnix, and that there can bee
None of that kinde, of which he is, but hee. (*FirAn* 209–18)

The "new Philosophy" of Francis Bacon and others may lead to new discoveries, but Donne was convinced that this scientific method was predicated on the atomizing of the natural world.[14] As astronomers discover new planets, our own world fragments, "crumbled out againe to his Atomis."[15] The nominalist denial of universals implies a disregard for real relations among people and things. Just as the natural world is dissected into its individual parts, so relations among people are ignored, while everyone thinks of himself as a solitary phoenix, rising from the ashes of the past.

Throughout *The Anniversaries*, Donne is particularly concerned with developments in astronomy, since the harmonious order of the old cosmology had assumed that heavenly spheres influence the earthly affairs of humanity. The problem, according to Donne, is that the adherents to the "new Philosophy" do not have powers comparable to those that the stars used to have:

What Artist now dares boast that he can bring
Heauen hither, or constellate any thing,
So as the influence of those starres may bee
Imprisond in an Herbe, or Charme, or Tree
And doe by touch, all which those starres could doe?
The art is lost, and correspondence too.
For heauen giues little, and the earth takes lesse,
And man least knowes their trade, and purposes.
If this commerce twixt heauen and earth were not
Embarr'd, and all this trafique quite forgot,

14. For extensive discussion of secondary literature on Donne's attitude toward the "new Philosophy," see Parrish, *Variorum Edition*, 403–11.

15. Donne was widely read in the field of astronomy and was particularly familiar with the work of Kepler, Galileo, and Gilbert. See Coffin, *John Donne and the New Philosophy*, 88–159. Donne's deep ambivalence toward the new philosophy does not mean he simply rejected the heliocentrism of the Copernican revolution. He recognized its irreversibility but was troubled by its implications. See also Alyia Shahnoor Ameen, "The Response of John Donne to the New Philosophy," *ASA University Review* 5 (2011): 285–95.

Shee, for whose losse wee haue lamented thus,
Would worke more fully'and pow'rfully on vs. (*FirAn* 391–402)

Whereas the stars had once seemed to influence the natural world from afar, the "touch" of empirical research can no longer "bring / Heauen hither." The loss of correspondence between heaven and earth is captured succinctly by Donne's indictment that as a result of recent astronomical developments, "heauen gives little, and the earth takes lesse." Heaven and earth have become disjointed.[16]

Donne was troubled that contemporary science had overreached in its attempt to control the heavens. As a result, the spheres of the cosmos lost their proportionality and thus also the beauty of their harmony. The reason is that it no longer appeared that the spheres traveled by way of the circular journeys Ptolemy had conceived. Even the sun now appeared surrounded by other stars, which "watch his steps" (*FirAn* 265), so that he is no longer able to "Perfit a Circle" (*FirAn* 269). A similar lack of proportionality haunts all the stars:

So, of the stares which boast that they do runne
In Circle still, none ends where he begunne. (*FirAn* 275–76)

The problem, insists Donne, is with our attempt to dominate the cosmos:

For of Meridians, and Parallels,
Man hath weau'd out a net, and this net throwne
Vpon the Heauens, and now they are his owne.
Loth to goe vp the hill, or labor thus
To goe to heauen, we make heauen come to vs. (*FirAn* 278–82)

Donne was deeply suspicious of the "net throwne / Vpon the Heauens." He was convinced that the result would not be true "commerce" between heaven

---

16. Barbara Kiefer Lewalski comments: "Clearly, even while they coexist, the order of grace can have comparatively little influence upon the order of nature as such, because of the breakdown of correspondence, and even the limited influence she was able to exercise was deprived of permanent effect when she proved to be subject to the death pervading all nature" (*Donne's* Anniversaries *and the Poetry of Praise: The Creation of a Symbolic Mode* [Princeton: Princeton University Press, 1973], 261).

and earth, but instead a fragmented cosmos in which heaven is subjected to human control.[17]

The modern world may deny the reality of universal forms, but they do exist—at least on Donne's understanding. It is Elizabeth Drury who personifies the form of forms. We already saw that "Her name defin'd thee, gave thee forme and frame" (*FirAn* 37). Without this form providing order in society, everything must fall apart:

> Shee, after whom, what forme soe're we see
> Is discord, and rude incongruitee
> Shee, shee is dead, she's dead; when thou knowest this
> Thou knowst how vgly a monster this world is. (*FirAn* 323–26)

Compared to Elizabeth, every other form is mere "discord," "rude incongruitee." Indeed, her beauty was the cause of every other beauty:

> Who could not lacke, what ere this world could giue,
> Because shee was the forme, that made it liue. (*SecAn* 71–72)[18]

Seeing as forms do exist—and, in particular, seeing as Elizabeth continues to live in heaven—all is not lost, according to Donne. Though the world may be a "carcasse," Elizabeth has left behind the "memory" (*FirAn* 74) of a better time:

> Her Ghost doth walke; that is, a glimmering light,
> A faint weake loue of vertue and of good. (*FirAn* 70–71)

And so from the matter of the dead carcass of this world a new one may yet be produced (*FirAn* 75–77). In fact, the new world may turn out even better than the old one, whose death is the subject of Donne's lament:

17. Cf. Rudnytsky's comment that "Donne's 'poetics of transcendence' was essentially a rearguard holding action attempting to recover the grounds of religious belief in the face of the advances of science" ("The Sight of God," 197).

18. Cf. *SecAn* 223–24:

> Shee whose rich beauty lent
> Mintage to others beauties, for they went
> But for so much, as they were like to her.

This new world may be safer, being told
The dangers and disease of the old. (*FirAn* 87–88)[19]

Donne believed that the virtues of the old world might yet again flourish in the new.

Donne's poems would be doomed to failure had Elizabeth simply gone to heaven and left a dead carcass behind. The reality is that the eternal forms of beauty and virtue still inform the world, though few may discern or follow them. Donne turns to Moses for poetic inspiration, as he addresses a largely skeptical audience. God spoke

To Moses, to deliuer vnto all,
That song: because he knew they would let fall,
The Law, the Prophets, and the History,
But keepe the song still in their memory. (*FirAn* 463–66)

Donne's contemporaries were no different from the Israelites. Knowing that God's people would abandon the Scriptures—"The Law, the Prophets, and the History"—Moses had given them a song (Deut. 32:1–43) in which he bemoaned their faithlessness and yet also held out hope for a new future.[20] By placing himself in the position of Moses, Donne looked forward to a time when heaven and earth would be reconnected.

In *Progres*, Donne set himself the task of showing how the disjunction between heaven and earth may be overcome and a sacramental understanding of the cosmos be regained. His recipe was relatively simple and, in its simplicity, is likely as offensive today as it must have been to the adherents of the "new Philosophy" of his own day: Donne proposed a combination of contempt of the world (*contemptus mundi*) and the art of dying (*ars moriendi*). We have already seen that Donne suggests that we "Forget this rotten world" (*SecAn* 49). He is unflinching in his disregard of earthly matters:

19. Later in the *Anatomie*, therefore, Donne comments that "herbes and roots by dying, lose not all," and he then exclaims:

But they, yea Ashes too, are medicinall,
Death could not quench her vertue so, but that
It would be (if not follow'd) wondred at. (*FirAn* 403–6)

20. Cf. P. G. Stanwood, "'Essentiall Joye' in Donne's *Anniversaries*," *TSLL* 13 (1971): 230.

What fragmentary rubbidge this world is
Thou knowest and that it is not worth a thought. (*SecAn* 83–84)

Donne refers to the body as a prison (*SecAn* 173), with the earth being "prisons prison" (*SecAn* 250), a "liuing Tombe" (*SecAn* 252).[21] Both
physical beauty and honor are ephemeral, maintains Donne—the former
because it does not last ("You both are fluid, chang'd since yesterday"
[*SecAn* 393]), and the latter because "all honors from inferiors flow" (*Sec-
An* 407). All this, insists Donne, yields but "casuall happinesse" (*SecAn*
412).

To be sure, Donne's contempt for the world was by no means absolute.
Both Felicia McDuffie and Ramie Targoff have drawn attention to the pervasive and positive role that the body plays in Donne's theology.[22] Targoff,
in her reading of *The Anniversaries*, makes clear that Donne treats body
and soul as belonging together. She shows that in *The Second Anniuersarie*
the soul experiences great difficulty as it parts ways with the body.[23] The
reason is that for Donne, their separation is unnatural. Targoff concludes
that it is the "central paradox" of *The Second Anniuersarie* that "despite the
poem's saturation in *contemptus mundi* and *vanitas* traditions . . . Donne
chooses not to represent the soul as joyfully anticipating its liberation from
the flesh."[24] The body's death is not *simply* a blessing resulting from the
soul's release.[25]

Donne does, however, try to steer his readers away from earthly to heavenly concerns. Repeatedly he calls upon them to go up to heaven:

Vp vp, my drowsie soule, where thy new eare
Shall in the Angels songs no discord heare. (*SecAn* 339–40)

21. Donne makes an exception for Elizabeth's body: "Shee, whose faire body no such prison
was" (*SecAn* 221).

22. Felicia Wright McDuffie, *"To Our Bodies Turn We Then": Body as Word and Sacrament
in the Works of John Donne* (New York: Continuum, 2005); Ramie Targoff, *John Donne, Body
and Soul* (Chicago: University of Chicago Press, 2008).

23. Targoff comments: "The soul's attachment to the body is the real, if undeclared subject
of *The Second Anniversarie*; that attachment also represents one of Donne's least recognized,
but most important, contributions to early modern poetry" (*John Donne*, 90).

24. Targoff, *John Donne*, 103. Targoff rightly draws attention to this paradox in Donne's
approach, though I am less than convinced that it is unique to Donne.

25. Targoff, *John Donne*, 81.

The upward call turns to a crescendo as Donne encourages his soul to turn to the heavenly company:

> Vp to those Patriarckes, which did longer sit,
> Expecting Christ, then they'haue enioy'd him yet.
> Vp to those Prophets, which now gladly see
>
> Their Prophecies growen to be Historee.
> Vp to th'Apostles, who did brauely runne,
> All the sunnes course, with more light then the Sunne.
> Vp to those Martyrs, who did calmely bleed
> Oyle to th'Apostles lamps, dew to their seed.
> Vp to those Virgins, who thought that almost
> They made ioyntenants with the Holy Ghost,
> If they to any should his Temple giue. (*SecAn* 345–55)

Donne's spirituality was unmistakably anagogical or upward-looking: the soul must turn up toward the heavenly company.

Death, therefore, is something to be welcomed. Life here on earth is not inconsequential or insignificant, but its main purpose lies beyond itself, since it is a preparation for death:

> Thinke then, My soule, that death is but a Groome,
> Which brings a Taper to the outward romme,
> Whence thou spiest first a little glimmering light,
> And after brings it nearer to thy sight:
> For such approches doth Heauen make in death. (*SecAn* 85–89)

Donne imagines death as a groom, entering the room with a candle in hand, lighting up the heavenly chamber for the soul. Donne follows this up with a lengthy word of admonition to his soul, telling her she should imagine lying on her deathbed, preparing for her departure (*SecAn* 85–120).

Donne's appropriation of the *contemptus mundi* and *ars moriendi* traditions is not meant to convey that earthly matters are of no concern per se. We have already seen that the driving force behind *The Anniversaries* is Donne's attempt to restore "commerce twixt heaven and earth" and that he assails modern empiricism for its dualistic separation of the two. The reason for these traditional theological motifs is, quite simply, that the human telos does not lie in temporary matters. Put in terms derived from sacramental theology, while outward sacraments may be indispensable, Donne aimed to prepare his readers for the inward reality itself; and he was convinced that only in this way would they arrive also at a proper perspective on earthly matters.

Life's telos, on Donne's understanding, is the beatific vision. Comparing the "accidentall ioyes" that we have here to the "essentiall ioy" that will be ours in heaven, Donne calls the soul to its final end of the beatific vision:

> Then, soule, to thy first pitch worke vp againe;
> Know that all lines which circles doe containe,
> For once that they the center touch, do touch
> Twice the circumference; and be thou such.
> Double on Heauen, thy thoughts on Earth emploid;
> All will not serue; Onely who haue enioyd
> The sight of God, in fulnesse, can thinke it;
> For it is both the obiect, and the wit.
> This is essentiall ioye, where neither hee
> Can suffer Diminution, nor wee;
> Tis such a full, and such a filling good;
> Had th'Angels once look'd on him, they had stood. (*SecAn* 435–46)

A diameter crosses the circle's center only once, whereas it traverses the circumference twice. For Donne this serves as a helpful analogy for how we should treat earthly versus heavenly concerns: "Double on Heauen, thy thoughts on Earth emploid." The ineffable reality of the beatific vision, in which object and wit coincide, is "essentiall ioye."[26] Whereas modern empiricism has distorted the circular harmony of the cosmos, the perfect circle of heaven does exist—and, what is more, it is our goal to join it. There was for Donne no better way to prepare for the beatific vision than to double one's thoughts on heaven already today.

On Donne's understanding, there is a sense in which everyone—even a modern empiricist—is anagogical (upward-leading) in perspective:

> They who did labour Babels tower t'erect,
> Might haue considerd, that for that effect,

26. Ever concerned to join heaven and earth closely together, Donne makes clear that there are accidental joys in heaven ("accidental ioyes in Heauen doe grow" [*SecAn* 382]), and that essential joys can be found even on earth (since Elizabeth "A heauen, and here, became vnto vs all, / Ioye, (as our ioyes admit) essentiall" [*SecAn* 469–70]). For detailed discussion of Donne's distinction between accidental and essential joys, see Stanwood, "Essentiall Joye."

All this whole solid Earth could not allow
Nor furnish forth Materials enow;
And that his Center, to raise such a place
Was far too little, to haue beene the Base;
No more affoords this world, foundatione
To erect true ioye, were all the meanes in one. (*SecAn* 417–24)

Modernity's attempt to build its own tower of Babel (Gen. 11:1–9)—the anagogical project par excellence—is doomed to failure, according to Donne, because the earth does not have sufficient resources and provides too small a foundation for such a tower. Earthly goods, therefore, are insufficient to "erect true ioye."

Donne reminds us that human ascent is predicated on divine descent:

This man, whom God did wooe, and loth t'attend
Till man came vp, did downe to man descend,
This man, so great, that all that is, is his,
Oh what a trifle, and poore thing he is! (*FirAn* 167–70)

God did not wait "Till man came vp" but instead "did downe to man descend." Donne's oblique reference to the incarnation intimates his rejection of any and all autonomous attempts to reach heaven by force.[27] Only because of the humiliation of God can there be a divinization of man.[28]

The ultimate proof that *contemptus mundi* and *ars moriendi* offer the proper antidote to the "new Philosophy" is the instantaneous commerce that is realized between heaven and earth at the point of death. Donne goes out of his way to emphasize the speed of the soul's entry into heaven. Whereas our "slow-pac'd soule" (*SecAn* 185), tied to a body, traverses perhaps twenty or thirty miles a day, it

Dispatches in a minute all the way,
Twixt Heauen, and Earth. (*SecAn* 188–89)

The soul does not tarry at any of the planets—whether the moon, Venus, Mercury, the sun, or Mars (*SecAn* 189–204):[29]

27. Donne does admit that one "may pretend a conquest, since / Heauen was content to suffer violence" (*SecAn* 151–52; cf. Matt. 11:12), but for Donne this "violence" is based on the incarnation, and it can only lead one into heaven through death (*SecAn* 156).

28. Cf. Donne's exhortation, "Be more then man, or thou'rt lesse then an Ant" (*FirAn* 190).

29. Donne's polemic against Dante's *Paradiso* is palpable at this point, considering the long

But ere shee can consider how shee went,
At once is at, and through the Firmament. (*SecAn* 205–6)

Heaven, therefore, is not some physically distant place. The instantaneous flight of the soul from here to there makes clear that we enter a different dimension altogether. Donne concludes, therefore, that death is the true answer to modernity's problem, since it is through death that heaven and earth are reconnected:

As doth the Pith, which, least our Bodies slacke,
Strings fast the little bones of necke, and backe;
So by the soule doth death string Heauen and Earth,
For when our soule enioyes this her third birth,
(Creation gaue her one, a second, grace,)
Heauen is as neare, and present to her face,
As colours are, and obiects, in a roome
Where darknesse was before, when Tapers come. (*SecAn* 211–18)

Death strings heaven and earth together by means of the soul's instantaneous ascent from the latter to the former.

One may object to Donne's *Anniversaries* that their otherworldly spirituality is hardly an answer to the epistemological problem of modernity—the nominalist disconnect between heaven and earth. Put differently, one may ask, is Donne's traditional Christian handling of the motifs of *contemptus mundi* and *ars moriendi* anything but a nostalgic escape from the hard, incontrovertible facts that the Baconian method has unveiled to us? Even if one were sympathetic, that is, to Donne's accusations against the modern age in the *Anatomie*, does his description of "the Progres of the Soule" provide in any way an antidote? To some extent, these objections make a valid point: for all its problems, the Baconian method has wrested numerous truths (and goods) from nature, which we would not otherwise have had at our disposal. Nature, after all, does have a relative autonomy.

I am not sure, however, that Donne would deny any of this. He does not dispute that the "new Philosophy" yields new, factual knowledge. But he is

---

duration of Beatrice and Dante's journey through the heavenly spheres. In a fascinating article, Raymond-Jean Frontain discusses Donne's *Anniversaries* as "a Reformed alternative to Dante's *Paradiso*" ("Donne's Protestant *Paradiso*: The Johannine Vision of the *Second Anniversary*," in Papazian, *John Donne and the Protestant Reformation*, 113).

not interested in purely natural knowledge, since such knowledge—which deliberately omits all questions of finality—cannot address the question of how to reach the beatific vision or how to connect heaven and earth. Whereas the Baconian project sets out by excluding the question of purpose, it is precisely with the purpose of existence that Donne begins. His project takes its starting point in the telos of human existence, the vision of God, in which "the obiect, and the wit" coincide. A clash with the "new Philosophy" was inevitable: by leaving out the question of purpose, the modern age ended up fragmenting and isolating earthly realities. Though traumatized by this instability of the modern, experimental age, Donne offered a timeless theological response: only the beatific vision truly restores the "commerce twixt heauen and earth."

Goodfriday, 1613: "To See God dye"

Donne's poem *Goodfriday, 1613. Riding Westward* may seem much less successful than *The Anniversaries*. Whereas the latter holds out hope that the beatific vision may bridge the gap between heaven and earth, the distance only seems to widen in *Goodfriday, 1613*. The poet, riding off into the sunset, is incapable of turning east, to face the one who offers healing on the cross, and the poem ends with a plea that seems to admit defeat:

> Restore thine Image, so much, by thy grace,
> That thou may'st know mee, and I'll turne my face. (41–42)[30]

The rider wishes he could turn around, but he is incapable of doing so—dependent as he is upon the prior grace of God. Donne's journey from London to the Montgomery Castle in Wales (where he was planning to visit the family home of the Herberts)[31] turns into a metaphor for his inability to turn to God. Accordingly, Theresa DiPasquale has suggested that "the speaker can never quite bring himself to surrender entirely to grace or to rely on God instead of the 'opus operatum' of his own poetic work."[32] The moving

30. Throughout this section, I quote from the poem as found in *John Donne: Selections from Divine Poems, Sermons, Devotions, and Prayers*, ed. John Booty (Mahwah, NJ: Paulist, 1990), 100–101. Line numbers have been placed in the text.

31. For detailed (revisionary) discussion of Donne's itinerary, see Margaret Maurer and Dennis Flynn, "The Text of *Goodf* and John Donne's Itinerary in April 1613," *TC* 8 (2013): 50–94.

32. Theresa M. DiPasquale, *Literature and Sacrament: The Sacred and the Secular in John*

portrayal of the crucifixion scene in the middle sonnet notwithstanding, at the end Donne still rides westward, his back to the cross.

This reading of Donne's poem is not actually wrong. Donne did struggle to align himself with the grace of God, and his troubled mind was perhaps not atypical of the Calvinist spirituality that Donne represents. Certainly, the poem ends with a prayer that in an important sense still awaits a divine response. Nonetheless, I want to suggest that the rider's inability to turn his horse so as to look upon the cross lies encapsulated within the wider compass of God's cosmic grace in Christ. Put differently, Donne's point in the poem is that although he may be unable to look upon Christ as he would wish, nevertheless he casts himself at the mercy of Christ's vision of him (rather than his own vision of Christ), grounded as the latter is within the cosmic reach of God's power and love.

From the beginning of the poem, Donne places his spiritual struggles in a wider, cosmic context:

Let mans Soule be a Spheare, and then, in this,
The intelligence that moves, devotion is,
And as the other Spheares, by being growne
Subject to forraigne motions, lose their owne,
And being by others hurried every day,
Scarce in a yeare their natural forme obey:
Pleasure or businesse, so, our Soules admit
For their first mover, and are whirld by it. (1–8)

As in *The Anniversaries*, so here the planets of Donne's cosmos have strayed from their path. And the cosmic spheres are not the only ones to be hurried along by "forraigne motions."[33] Even on this Good Friday, the soul is lacking in devotion. As one of the spheres, she fails to obey her "natural forme" and instead is "whirld" by pleasure or business as her first mover.[34] Donne's

---

Donne, Medieval and Renaissance Literary Studies (Pittsburgh: Duquesne University Press, 1999), 119.

33. Helen Gardner explains that in a Ptolemaic universe, the planets' natural motion was from west to east, but that the Primum Mobile daily turned around their direction. Other forces too could deflect the proper movements of the spheres (*John Donne: The Divine Poems*, ed. Helen Gardner, 2nd ed. [Oxford: Clarendon, 1978], 98).

34. Cf. Marian F. Sia and Santiago Sia, *From Suffering to God: Exploring Our Images of God in the Light of Suffering* (New York: St. Martin's Press, 1994), 41. Robert H. Ray comments that just as an angel or intelligence was believed to govern the motions of the spheres, so "Donne

metaphysical conceit treats the soul as a metaphor for a cosmic sphere, and the consequence is deeply troubling to Donne:

> Hence is't, that I am carried towards the West
> This day, when my Soules forme bends towards the East. (9–10)

His soul's natural inclination may be to go east, but his passions (spiritually) and his horse (physically) fail to follow: they carry him west. The image of the horse carrying Donne westward despite his soul's natural inclination to go east underlines Donne's helplessness: he may be the rider, but he is hardly in control.

The center of the forty-two-line poem, however, makes clear that even though the instability of souls and spheres may steer them off course, nonetheless the cross contains and so redeems even cosmic waywardness:

> Could I behold those hands which span the Poles,
> And tune all spheares at once, peirc'd with those holes? (21–22)

Donne uses the image of Christ's outstretched arms to depict him as the cosmic redeemer. His pierced hands extend not only east and west, but—and here the poet deliberately skews the traditional image—they also "span the Poles" and so reach north and south as well. Donne may well have had in mind the patristic understanding of the cross as representing the "breadth, and length, and depth, and height" (Eph. 3:18) of Christ's love, a love that encompasses the farthest reaches of the universe.[35] His hands, encompassing the cosmos, tune it—and in the process undoubtedly tune Donne's soul as well.[36] However great the threat of cosmic and personal disharmony, for Donne it is always already encapsulated by the greater harmony of Christ's redemptive love.

Not only does Donne portray the cross as correcting any and all misdirection of the planets, he also presents Christ as one of them. As he laments his soul being carried toward the west despite its natural, eastward inclination, Donne adds:

---

sees 'devotion' as the intelligence that governs man's soul's motion" (*A John Donne Companion* [1990; reprint, New York: Routledge, 2014], 147).

35. This interpretation of Eph. 3:18 goes back to Irenaeus, *Dem.* 34 (ACW 16:69–70). Cf. also Justin Martyr, *First Apology* 60. Throughout this chapter, I quote from the King James Version.

36. For the link between the harmony of the universe and of the soul in patristic thought, see Hans Boersma, *Scripture as Real Presence: Sacramental Exegesis in the Early Church* (Grand Rapids: Baker Academic, 2017), 131–58.

> There I should see a Sunne, by rising set,
> And by that setting endlesse day beget;
> But that Christ on this Crosse, did rise and fall,
> Sinne had eternally benighted all. (11–14)

By speaking of the sun's rising, Donne intends to convey a triple entendre. Interpreting the sun as the Son of God—an early Christian interpretation facilitated in English by verbal similarity between "sun" and "Son"—allows Donne to compare Christ's being raised upon the cross to the rising of the sun. Next, the poem speaks of the sun rising and setting—Christ's elevation to the cross led to his death—and links this rising and setting to his begetting an endless day. The subtle but daring sexual imagery is difficult to ignore: Christ's death is the nuptial act that gives birth to an endless day. Indeed, the very intimacy implied in this rising and setting renders it unseemly for Donne to watch:

> Yet dare I'almost be glad, I do not see
> That spectacle of too much weight for me. (15–16)[37]

Regardless of his inability to look on, however, a new day has risen through the rising and setting of the sun, and so the crucifixion puts on dramatic display Christ's redemptive act as a cosmic event.

Donne has no doubt that it is the shocking, cosmic reality of the cross that caused the earth to quake and the sun to hide (cf. Matt. 27:45; 28:2). In some of the most memorable lines of the poem, Donne writes:

> Who sees Gods face, that is selfe life, must dye;
> What a death were it then to see God dye?
> It made his owne Lieutenant Nature shrinke,
> It made his footstoole crack, and the Sunne winke. (17–20)

Donne reminds his readers of the great conundrum of the beatific vision, namely, that the very goal of human existence seems outside our reach: "There shall no man see me, and live" (Exod. 33:20). Donne puts the paradox starkly: the sight of life causes death. If we thought, however, that God's invisibility was simply due to divine transcendence (1 Tim. 1:17; 6:16), Donne clarifies that one thing is even more profoundly invisible than the life of God, namely, his death: "What a death were it then to see God dye?" The earth

---

37. Cf. DiPasquale, *Literature and Sacrament*, 123.

splits and the sun hides at such a sight. The death of God, Donne boldly suggests, makes the cosmic spheres quiver in fear. Their wayward deviations fail to have the final say. As cosmic event, the death of God trumps all.

Donne also reminds himself that his westward look is neither first nor last. To be sure, he does question his ability to look upon Christ, both inasmuch as he is the crucified ("pierc'd with those holes") and as he is humbled in the incarnation ("Humbled below us"). Donne lacks the courage to look upon the flesh and blood of his Savior:

> Could I behold that endlesse height which is
> Zenith to us, and our Antipodes,
> Humbled below us? or that blood which is
> The seat of all our Soules, if not of his,
> Made durt of dust, or that flesh which was worne
> By God, for his apparell, rag'd, and torne? (23–28)

The blood dripping from Christ's body on the cross turns dust into dirt—not only the dust at the foot of the cross, but also the dust of Christ's own body (cf. Gen. 2:7)—while the flesh that God has worn is "rag'd, and torne." Donne is afraid to look either on Christ's flesh or on his blood.

It can hardly escape Donne's reader that the blood that is shed and the flesh that is torn are the realities made present in the Eucharist.[38] And so, after confessing that he dares not even look upon the Virgin Mary ("If on these things I durst not looke, durst I / Upon his miserable mother cast mine eye, / Who was Gods partner here, and furnish'd thus / Halfe of that Sacrifice, which ransom'd us?" [29–32]),[39] Donne speaks of the presence of these sacrificial realities in his memory (cf. Luke 22:19; 1 Cor. 11:24), thereby reinforcing the eucharistic cast of this segment of the poem:

> Though these things, as I ride, be from mine eye
> They'are present yet unto my memory,
> For that looks towards them; and thou look'st towards mee,
> O Saviour, as thou hang'st upon the tree. (33–36)

38. Cf. Theresa DiPasquale's comment: "These lines [i.e., 23–28] reflect upon an essentially sacramental mystery, pondering not only the hypostatic union of God and Man in Christ, but the substance of Eucharist, Jesus's Blood and Body, which is the point of sacramental contact between the human and the divine" (*Literature and Sacrament*, 124).

39. As an aside, we should note that Donne's depiction of Mary as coredemptrix stands out within early seventeenth-century Protestant thought.

Donne may not dare to face the cross directly by turning in an eastern direction so as to shorten the distance between himself and the cross, but he does acknowledge the presence of Christ in his memory: in faith, he does look upon Christ, and it is in this memorial gaze that Donne discovers that all along his Savior has also been looking at him. The reciprocity of sight expressed in line 35—"For that looks towards them; and thou look'st towards mee"—transcends whatever hesitation or fear Donne may express throughout the poem. His eucharistic sharing in Christ—"This do in remembrance of me"—is the moment of the mutuality of the gaze between Donne and his Savior. The memorial of flesh and blood reveals that, all along, Christ has had his sight upon the lonely rider.

In light of this climactic moment of mutual sight, the remainder of the poem turns into a prayer ("O Saviour"). In the final sestet, Donne opens himself up in penitence to the Lord, knowing that his Savior looks at him:

I turne my backe to thee, but to receive
Corrections, till thy mercies bid thee leave.
O thinke mee worth thine anger, punish mee,
Burne off my rusts, and my deformity,
Restore thine Image, so much, by thy grace,
That thou may'st know mee, and I'll turne my face. (37–42)

No longer is the westward rider a wayward rider. No longer is it "Pleasure or businesse" that is the first mover of his soul. In and through meeting his Savior's gaze in the eucharistic "memory" of faith, Donne is transformed. He therefore turns his back to Christ for "Corrections," thereby identifying himself with his Savior, by whose "stripes" we are healed (Isa. 53:5).[40] He pleads with the crucified Lord for purgation—not shying away from words such as "anger," "punish," and "Burne"—since it is only in this way that his soul will be restored to its proper image.

Donne places himself at the mercy of the Savior's pierced hands, knowing that only Christ's disciplining will purify him and lead him to the final goal of the vision of God: "That thou may'st know mee, and I'll turne my face." This expression of hope cannot but conjure up Saint Paul's confident expression of hope: "Now I know in part; but then shall I know even as also I am known" (1 Cor. 13:12). Donne asks his Savior to prepare him for the

40. Both the Geneva Bible and the King James Version translate the Hebrew word *burah* with "stripe."

face-to-face vision of the eschaton. For Donne, knowledge and vision were undoubtedly identical, and so for Christ to know him was also for Christ to see him. Thus, despite Donne's westward ride, Christ prepares him for the beatific vision: through Christ's continuous "knowing" of him—punishing and purging the westward rider—he prepares Donne for the time when he will finally be able to turn around and face east, seeing his Savior in face-to-face, beatific vision. Even Christ's "Corrections" aim at restoring the "commerce twixt heauen and earth."

The ending is nothing short of remarkable. First, we can only properly interpret this ending when we read it against the backdrop of the poem as a whole. *Goodfriday, 1613* is filled with hope and anticipation of a face-to-face vision between Donne and his Savior. Christ's redemption as a cosmological event outperforms and corrects any and all cosmological disturbances, including those of Donne's soul. Moreover, Christ's westward gaze from the cross captures Donne's eyes, even though he has his back turned to his Lord; the first mutual gaze is not that mentioned by way of eschatological hope at the poem's end but that experienced in the memorial celebration of the Eucharist. Both cosmologically and sacramentally, Donne's westward ride is simply no match for the crucifixion: Christ will know him, and he will turn his face.

Second, the beauty of the poem's ending is that it focuses squarely on the crucified Lord as the object of the beatific vision. We already noted that for Donne, "to see God dye" was more terrifying than to see "God's face, that is selfe life." The crucifixion—the death of God on the cross—was an event literally of cosmological proportions, and the vision of God dying more disturbing than the vision of his life. Donne reiterates this Christ-focused approach to the beatific vision in his concluding line. His great eschatological hope—as, at least, he poetically expresses it here[41]—is for him and his Savior to see one another. "I'll turne my face" is the poem's hopeful final clause. Donne points himself and his readers to the eschatological hope of seeing the one who looks as though he had been slain (Rev. 5:6). For Donne's *Goodfriday, 1613*, it is when we "see God dye"—a sight both terrifying and beatifying at the same time—that the distance between rider and cross is bridged and the "commerce twixt heauen and earth" restored.

---

41. As will become clear later in the chapter, Donne's sermons hold out a vision of the divine essence. His dogmatic understanding of the beatific vision thus follows more traditional Thomist lines than his devotional poem would seem to indicate.

Sermons: "his eye . . . turnes us into himselfe"

Nearly two years after writing his poem *Goodfriday, 1613*, Donne was ordained a priest in the Church of England. Though in some ways his role changed dramatically—particularly after he was appointed dean of Saint Paul's Cathedral in London in 1621—Donne nonetheless emphasized similar themes in his preaching as he had in his poetry, and his preaching style reflected his poetic background. David Edwards comments: "Of course Dr Donne the preacher had Jack Donne the poet inside him and he could not stop being witty. . . . He had been called to preach the Gospel but he pointed out that when the holy apostles had been called to stop being fishermen, 'they did but leave their nets, they did not burne them.'"[42] Donne put the rhetorical skills he had acquired through his many years of writing poetry in the service of preaching the gospel.[43]

It was not only his writing abilities, however, that marked continuity between Donne the poet and Donne the preacher. More fundamentally, he considered his basic task unchanged; it is just that he had become convinced that preaching could be more effective in this regard than poetry.[44] The remainder of this chapter will make clear that when Donne articulated his understanding of the beatific vision in his preaching, he continued to intimate to his congregation his desire for a reintegration of heaven and earth. We can see this attempt at restoring a more sacramental understanding of the nature-supernatural relationship in (1) Donne's emphasis on God's vision as both providential and deifying (in a sermon on Ps. 32:8); (2) his participatory ontology; and (3) his emphasis on the continuity between vision of God in this life and in the next (points 2 and 3 in a sermon on 1 Cor. 13:12)—even though his Thomist conviction that we will see the essence of God serves as a countervailing force in this regard.

42. David L. Edwards, *John Donne: Man of Flesh and Spirit* (London: Continuum, 2001), 117. The quotation is from *Sermons* 2.13.285; quotations come from *The Sermons of John Donne*, ed. Potter and Simpson.

43. Jeanne Shami comments that his rhetorical skill was "probably the most impressive feature of Donne's Sermons" ("The Sermon," in *The Oxford Handbook of John Donne*, ed. Jeanne Shami, Dennis Flynn, and M. Thomas Hester [Oxford: Oxford University Press, 2011], 332).

44. Jeanne Shami points out that for Donne, poetry was to preaching as the apocryphal books are to the canonical books. Both, he insisted, "can be used for the 'edification' of their audiences, for the finding of forceful illustrations. But only the 'canonical' books can be used for 'foundation,' for the solid and unquestionable bases of truth" ("Anatomy and Progress: The Drama of Conversion in Donne's Men of a 'Middle Nature,'" *UTQ* 53 [1984]: 222). Shami discusses the complex nature of Donne's vocational choice in "Donne's Decision to Take Orders," in Shami, Flynn, and Hester, *Oxford Handbook of John Donne*, 523–36.

Jeanne Shami points out that much like *The Anniversaries*, Donne's series of eight sermons on Psalm 32, probably preached in the winter of 1624–1625, aimed at reestablishing "commerce" between heaven and earth.[45] This group of sermons, argues Shami, "follows a pattern similar to that already observed in the *Anniversaries*, showing the drama of a sinner's gradual awakening from lethargy, his sense of God's heavy hand upon him, his growing sense of his responsibility and potential, and his decision to celebrate the newly established commerce between himself and God with joy and confidence."[46] Tracing the eight sermons on the famous penitential psalm, Shami shows that they gradually move from an "anatomy" of one's spiritual state to a description of the soul's "progress" toward a heavenly life already lived here on earth. Donne's desire to reestablish "commerce twixt heauen and earth" continued to be his aim, also in this sermon series.

The sixth sermon of the series is of particular significance. Here, Donne reflects on the psalmist's words, "I will instruct thee, and teach thee in the way which thou shalt goe, I will guide thee with mine eye" (Ps 32:8).[47] The last clause of the verse especially caught Donne's attention, as it reiterated for him the significance of God's vision of us preceding our vision of him— which, as we have seen, also plays a key role in *Goodfriday, 1613*. In his sermon on Psalm 32:8, much as in his earlier poem, Donne makes clear that it is vision that reconnects heaven and earth, and, significantly in Donne's view, it is a vision that begins with God's vision of us.

Donne starts out his sermon by explaining that David provides instruction in matters of faith (*de credendis*), of action (*de agendis*), and of hope (*de sperandis*).[48] When he raises the question of what the psalmist's "way" (*de via*) is and what is to be done in it (*in via*), Donne explains that God has his eye on our ways: "He sees all our wayes; *All my wayes are before thee*, sayes *David* [Ps. 119:168]. And he sees them not so as though they belonged not to him, for he considers them, *Does not he behold all my wayes, and tell all my steps?* [Job 31:4] He sees them, and sees our irremediable danger in

45. Shami, "Anatomy and Progress," 229.

46. Shami, "Anatomy and Progress," 230.

47. I am using Donne's own quotations from the King James Version. While using the KJV, Donne was a careful philologist in his own right, who did his own careful text-critical and linguistic study of the Hebrew text. See Chanita Goodblatt, "The Penitential Psalm 32: The Sacred Philology of Sin," in *The Christian Hebraism of John Donne* (Pittsburgh: Duquesne University Press, 2010), 77–107.

48. *Sermons* 9.16.352. Hereafter, references from this work will be given in parentheses in the text.

them; *Formido, & fovea, & laqueus, Fear, and a pit, and snares are upon thee* [Isa. 24:17]" (9.16.362). Any discussion of morality is predicated, according to Donne, on the acknowledgment that God looks down at our ways.

This divine vision leads Donne to the question of how we, in turn, may recognize it. He points to Exodus 33, where God's promise that he will send an angel ahead of the people (Exod. 23:20) is no longer good enough for Moses: "God had told him of an Angel, but that satisfied not *Moses*; He must have something shewed to him, he must see his guide." At Moses's plea that God show him his glory (Exod. 33:18), God heeds his request: "Shall we see any thing? They did see that Pillar in which God was, and that presence, that Pillar shewed the way. To us the Church is that Pillar; in that, God shewes us our way" (9.16.362). By way of verbal association, Donne moves from God's presence in the pillar of cloud and the pillar of fire (Exod. 13:21–22) to the church as the pillar of truth (1 Tim. 3:15), since he is convinced that God is present in both Old and New Testament pillars and leads his people along the way by means of both.

After providing additional moral exhortations to continue walking in God's way, Donne arrives at "the last words of the Text, *Firmabo super te oculos meos*, I will settle my providence, fixe mine eye upon thee, *I will guide thee with mine eye*" (9.16.366). Donne reinforces this identification of God's eye with his gracious and powerful providence in a variety of ways.[49] After a brief warning that we should not confuse hope with presumption, he turns to the narrative of Peter's repentance as an example:

> Wee heare of no blowes, wee heare of no chiding from him towards *Peter*, but all that is said, is, *The Lord turned back and looked upon Peter* [Luke 22:61], and then he remembered his case; The eye of the Lord lightned his darknesse; The eye of the Lord thawed those three crusts of Ice, which were growne over his heart, in his three denials of his Master. A Candle wakes some men, as well as a noyse; The eye of the Lord works upon a good soule, as much as his hand, and hee is as much affected with this consideration, The Lord sees me, as with this, The Lord strikes me. (*Sermons* 9.16.366)

Reflecting on the power of the eye, Donne cannot help but think of Pliny's natural history, where he has read of turtles who, according to some, "cherish

---

49. Jeffrey Johnson collates a number of examples where Donne highlights the theme of vision and speaks of God's eyesight in particular (*The Theology of John Donne* [Cambridge: Brewer, 1999], 66–67).

their eggs by gazing at them with their eyes."[50] The observation leads Donne to interject: "What cannot the eye of God produce and hatch in us?"

Donne goes on to suggest that when God looks on us, it is by way of approval (*visio approbationis*): "*This land doth the Lord thy God care for, and the eyes of the Lord are always upon it, from the beginning of the yeare, even to the end thereof*" (Deut. 11:12) (9.16.366). Indeed, writes Donne, the eye of the Lord radiates light, as it "makes midnight noone, and S. *Lucies* day S. *Barnabies*; it makes *Capricorne Cancer*, and the Winters the Summers Solstice" (9.16.367).[51] Scripture often speaks of God's eye as an indication of approval, insists Donne, quoting various biblical passages (Ezra 5:5; Ps. 32:8; Gen. 1:31). Donne goes so far as to distinguish between God's *face* (as his ordinance for the church in general) and his *eye* as his "personall providence" to the believers, that is to say, "that blessed Spirit of his, by whose operation he makes that grace, which does evermore accompany his Ordinances, effectuall upon us" (9.16.367).[52] Thus, by the light that radiates from God's eye—his Holy Spirit—he guides and cares for his people.

Donne expounds specifically on two effects that God's providential eye has, namely, conversion and union. In conversion, God's "eye turns ours to looke upon him." Donne has the divine eye and the human eye calling out to each other: "Behold," God's eye exclaims, using the text of the sermon, "*the eye of the Lord is upon all them that feare him.*" "Behold," the human eye calls back with "cheerefull readinesse," "*as the eye of a servant lookes to the hand of his Master, so our eyes waite upon the Lord our God, till he have mercy upon us* [Ps. 123:2]" (9.16.367). Donne takes the picture of a portrait

---

50. Pliny, *Natural History*, vol. 3, trans. H. Rackham (1940; reprint, London: Heinemann, 1967), 9.12.37 (p. 189). Donne writes: "Wee reade in a Naturall story of some creatures, *Qui solo oculorum aspectu fovent ova*, which hatch their egges onely by looking upon them" (*Sermons* 9.16.366). Donne likely refers to the story from memory. He does not mention that it concerns turtles, and the Latin (presumably designed to make the audience think that he is quoting) deviates significantly from Pliny's original. Elsewhere, Donne compares the warmth of the Lord's eye to the "eye of the Ostrich," which "is said to hatch her young ones, without sitting" (*Sermons* 7.5.152). Here Donne seems to mix up Pliny's discussions of ostriches and of turtles.

51. In the Julian calendar, still in effect in England in Donne's day, Saint Lucy's Day coincided with the winter solstice as the shortest day of the year (December 13), associated with the astrological sign of the Capricorn. Saint Barnabas Day coincided with the summer solstice as the longest day of the year (June 11) and was associated with the Cancer sign.

52. Jeffrey Johnson, in his reflections on this sermon, comments: "It is the Holy Spirit who for Donne fosters . . . the commerce between the earthly community, especially in the Church, and the heavenly community" (*Theology of John Donne*, 87).

as an example of this mutual gaze: "And then, when, as a well made Picture doth alwaies looke upon him, that looks upon it, this Image of God in our soule, is turned to him, by his turning to it, it is impossible we should doe any foule, any uncomely thing in his presence" (9.16.368).[53] Inasmuch as God has turned the soul to look to him, the life of the convert will inescapably reflect being in his presence.[54]

To underscore that one's turning of the eye toward God implies the turning of one's whole life, Donne draws upon Psalm 25:15 ("Mine eyes are ever toward the Lord; For he shall pluck my feet out of the net"), as he pulls his listeners along with rhetorical prowess:

Upon those words of *David, Mine eyes are ever towards the Lord, Quasi diceretur, quid agitur de pedibus?* as though it were objected, Is all thy care of thine eyes? What becomes of thy feete? *Non attendis ad eos?* Doest thou looke to thy steps, To thy life, as well as to thy faith, To please God, as well as to know God? And hee answers in the words which follow, *Ipse evellet,* As for my feet, God shall order, that is, assist me in ordering them; If his eye be upon me, and mine upon him, (O blessed reflexion! O happy reciprocation! O powerful correspondence!) *Ipse evellet, He will plucke my feet out of the net,* though I be almost ensnared, almost entangled, he will snatch me out of the fire, deliver me from the tentation. (9.16.368)

According to Donne, looking away from one's feet to the Lord is no reason for concern about where one will step: when one's eyes return the gaze of the Lord in contemplation, it is impossible for the life of action to remain out of sync. Moral transformation invariably follows conversion.

The second consequence of God's guiding gaze is even more marvelous, according to Donne: union with God. God's keeping us as the "apple of his eye" (Ps. 17:8; cf. Deut. 32:10; Zech. 2:8) means that we become part of him

---

53. Although Donne likely did not have Nicholas of Cusa in mind, his *De visione Dei* (1454) had similarly taken Christ's gaze from the icon upon each of the monks as an indication of divine providence. See chap. 13, section entitled "Pedagogy and Providence in Nicholas of Cusa and Jonathan Edwards."

54. As a moderate Calvinist, Donne consistently highlights both the priority of the divine initiative in conversion and the demand that human beings turn to God in conversion. Donne's Calvinism is discussed in Daniel W. Doerksen, "Polemist or Pastor? Donne and Moderate Calvinist Conformity," in Papazian, *John Donne and the Protestant Reformation*, 12–34, and Jeanne Shami, "'Speaking Openly and Speaking First': John Donne, the Synod of Dort, and the Early Stuart Church," in Papazian, *John Donne and the Protestant Reformation*, 35–65.

(9.16.368). If conversion means that God's eye "turnes us *to* himselfe," union implies that his eye "turnes us *into* himselfe" (9.16.368 [emphasis added]). This next step implies divinization, explains Donne, claiming that "we are not onely His, but He; To every Persecutor, in every one of our behalfe, he shall say, *Cur me?* Why persecutest thou me?" (Acts 9:4). Donne, an avid reader of Augustine, can hardly have been unaware of the church father's frequent use of this text to speak of the unity of Christ and his church.[55] For Donne, the ultimate consequence of the encounter between God's eye and the human eye is that God renders us divine.[56] In this way, Donne draws heaven and earth closely together: the metaphor of vision covers the entire journey of faith, beginning with God's providential vision of the believers' way, via their reciprocating his gaze in conversion and faith, to their final union with God in deification. For Donne, we may say, deification is the way in which heaven and earth are reunited.

Preparing a sermon on the traditional passage of 1 Corinthians 13:12 ("For now we see through a glasse darkly, but then face to face; now I know in part, but then I shall know, even as also I am knowne") gave Donne the opportunity to reflect more systematically on the beatific vision.[57] Indeed, no sermon gives as much insight in Donne's views on the beatific vision as this one, preached on Easter Day 1628. It is evident that he again attempts to inculcate a heavenly mind-set in his congregation, and he does so by emphatically drawing attention to the continuity between vision in this world and the next. Also in this sermon, therefore, Donne shows himself keen to reinvigorate the "commerce twixt heauen and earth," which, as we have seen, was the focus of his attention both in *The Anniversaries* and in *Goodfriday, 1613*.

Donne structures his sermon on Paul's famous text in organized fashion around four categories or steps: (1) sight of God here in a "glasse" or mirror (*in speculo*); (2) knowledge of God here, "darkly" or "in part" (*in ænigmate*); (3) sight of God in heaven, "face to face"; and (4) knowledge of God

---

55. Cf. Michael Fiedrowicz, general introduction to *Enarrat. Ps. 1–32* (WSA III/15:53–54). Katrin Ettenhuber discusses Donne's use of Augustine in his sermons on Ps. 32:8 and 1 Cor. 13:12, in "'The Evidence of Things Not Seen': Donne, Augustine, and the Beatific Vision," in *Donne's Augustine: Renaissance Cultures of Interpretation* (Oxford: Oxford University Press, 2011), 205–24.

56. Again, however, moral exhortation is never far from Donne's mind. He concludes with a warning that hope should not lead to presumption; hope properly is accompanied by fear, since God's face is against those who do evil (Ps. 34:16), and he may hide his face from us (Deut. 32:20) (*Sermons* 9.16.369).

57. Cf. the discussion of this sermon in Shami, "The Sermon," 339–42.

in heaven, "as I am knowne." This fourfold structure allows Donne to sketch the progress of the journey toward perfect sight and knowledge (though, as we will see, the tidy structure also comes with certain drawbacks). Donne distinguishes two kinds of sight and two kinds of knowledge, but his exposition makes clear that all four may be subsumed under the larger category of vision: for each of the four steps, Donne analyzes the kind of vision that is involved, discussing the place of vision, the medium in or through which we see, and the light by which we are able to see. Table 1 makes clear how Donne divides the various types of vision of God:

Table 1: Donne's Outline of 1 Corinthians 13:12

	Place	Medium	Light
Sight of God here	Whole world	Book of creatures	Light of nature
Knowledge of God here	Church	Ordinance of God	Light of faith
Sight of God in heaven	Heaven	Self-disclosure of God	Light of glory
Knowledge of God in heaven	God	God	God

As the last column makes clear, Donne superimposes his fourfold schema on Thomas Aquinas's threefold division of light into the light of nature (*lumen naturae*), the light of grace (*lumen fidei*), and the light of glory (*lumen gloriae*).[58] Because Donne bases himself on the biblical text, he posits four rather than three kinds of light.

As he speaks about the sight of God in the natural world, Donne's participatory ontology comes to the fore. Aquinas, explains Donne, calls the theater in which we see God "the whole world" (*Sermons* 8.9.223). With a lengthy appeal to Psalm 139, Donne argues that God is present everywhere in the world: "*David* compasses the world, and findes God every where, and sayes

---

58. In his sermon on Job 19:26 (May 1620), Donne has a brief excursus on 1 Cor. 13:12, where he distinguishes only three stages: (1) seeing God *per speculum*, which tells us from the creature that there is a creator; (2) seeing God *in aenigmate*, in the church and in the sacrament; and (3) seeing God himself, so that in the sight of him all our problems and riddles will be resolved (*Sermons* 3.3.111).

at last, *Whither shall I flie from thy presence? If I ascend up into heaven, thou art there*" (Ps. 139:7–8). God is present even in hell, as David makes clear in verse 8—though, Donne adds, God is present there "without any emanation of any beame of comfort." No matter how small or how great a creature, it proclaims its creator: "If every gnat that flies were an Arch-angell, all that could but tell me, that there is a God" (8.9.223). The one creature is no better a mirror than the next. Donne comments: "All things that are, are equally removed from being nothing; and whatsoever hath any beeing, is by that very beeing, a glasse in which we see God, who is the roote, and the fountaine, of all beeing. The whole frame of nature is the Theatre, the whole Volume of creatures is the glasse, and the light of nature, reason, is our light, which is another Circumstance" (8.9.224). For Donne, all creatures have their being from God as the fountain of being.

The natural light of reason, therefore, allows everyone to see God in the created order. Everyone is enlightened by this light, insists Donne, with an appeal to John 1:9—"That was the true light, that lighteth every man that commeth into the World" (8.9.224 [italics omitted])—and, in particular, with appeals to the interpretations of this passage by Chrysostom, Augustine, and Cyril (8.9.224–25). The result, according to Donne, is that "God affords no man the comfort, the false comford of Atheism: He will not allow a pretending Atheist the power to flatter himself, so far, as seriously to thinke there is no God. He must pull out his own eyes, and see no creature, before he can say, he sees no God; He must be no man, and quench his reasonable soule, before he can say to himselfe, there is no God" (8.9.225). The presence of God in the natural world implies, for Donne, the human ability rationally to conclude the existence of God.

Since the light of faith shines in the church through the medium of God's ordinances—Scripture, preaching, and sacraments—Donne impresses on his listeners the importance of the church. Although it may not be impossible to become a scholar without going to university, "the ordinary place for Degrees is the University, and the ordinary place for Illumination in the knowledge of God, is the Church" (8.9.226). Donne insists that one must listen to the church, therefore, and, as he fulminates against "private Conventicles, private Spirits, private Opinions," he warns that the church has the authority to excommunicate (8.9.227). Although the church is not above the Scriptures (8.9.228), the Scriptures do have their place within the church (8.9.227).

Since he regards the church as the place where we come to faith, Donne highlights preaching and the sacraments as the media through which we come to faith. He emphasizes that faith varies in degrees and that it is dark in comparison with the light of glory. The knowledge of faith "is but *In ænig-mate*, sayes our Text, *darkly*, obscurely; Clearly in respect of the naturall man but yet but obscurely in respect of that knowledge of God which we shall have in heaven; for, sayes the Apostle, *As long as we walk by faith, and not by sight, we are absent from the Lord* [2 Cor. 5:6–7]. Faith is a blessed presence, but compared with heavenly vision, it is but an absence" (8.9.229). Scripture prophesies, "*I will search Ierusalem with Candles*" (Zeph. 1:12), and since these words refer to "the best men in the Christian Church," it is clear that even in them some darkness will be found (8.9.230). And since the apostle writes, "*Now, after ye have knowen God, or rather are knowen of God*" (Gal. 4:9), we must conclude that "the best knowledge that we have of God here, even by faith, is rather that he knows us, then that we know him." Donne concludes, therefore, that faith is "infinitely" below the face-to-face vision that we will have in heaven (8.9.230).

As he discusses the sight of God in heaven, Donne explains that the place where this vision will occur is the "spheare" of heaven, which is uncreated, since the Son of God has been there in all eternity. "In that place," exclaims Donne, "where there are more Suns then there are Stars in the Firmament, (for all the Saints are Suns) And more light in another Sun, the Sun of righteousnesse, the Son of Glory, the Son of God, then in all of them, in that illustration, that emanation, that effusion of beams of glory, which began not to shine 6000. yeares ago, but 6000. millions of millions ago, had been 6000. millions of millions before that, in those eternall, in those uncreated heavens, shall we see God" (8.9.231). It is the light of the Son of God that eternally illuminates heaven, and it is there that we shall see God.

Donne is brief when it comes to the medium of our heavenly sight of God. He simply refers to it as "*Patefactio sui*, Gods laying himself open, his manifestation, his revelation, his evisceration, and embowelling of himselfe to us, there," and Donne makes clear that it involves a seeing of the essence of God (8.9.231).[59] Donne's discourse—remarkable for its brevity—appears ambiguous, perhaps even odd. He continues to speak of a "medium" when it comes to the vision of God's essence in heaven. When describing this medium, however, he does not refer to Christ—which, as we will see in our

---

59. Also in his Candlemas sermon (probably from 1627) on Matt. 5:8, Donne writes that "the seeing of God principally intended in this place, is that *Visio beatifica*, to see God so, as that that very seeing makes the seer Blessed, They are Blessed therefore, because they see him; And that is *Videre essentiam*, to see the very Essence and nature of God" (*Sermons* 7.13.341). Donne appeals to 1 Cor. 13:12 and 1 John 3:2. Donne held that believers will see the divine essence immediately upon death (*John Donne*, ed. Gardner, 114–17).

next chapters, is what some of the Puritans and Jonathan Edwards did—but simply to God's *patefactio sui*—his self-disclosure. To be sure, Donne has already spoken eloquently about the eternal light of Christ in heaven, but that was in his discussion of the *place* of the vision. He does not speak of Christ also being the *medium* of the vision.

Perhaps Donne does mean that God's self-disclosure in heaven is the shining of the Sun of Righteousness, who eternally shines in heaven, but he does not say so explicitly, and his suggestion that we will see the essence of God would seem to militate against it. Indeed, we may wonder why Donne speaks of a medium for seeing God in the first place, since he thinks of God's self-manifestation as the direct communication of his essence to us. Perhaps the demands of Donne's overall schema—place, medium, and light in each stage—force his hand, as it were, and maybe he does not want us to take the language of "medium" at face value. In any case, a medium seems redundant or out of place if we see God's essence immediately in heaven.

If by the light of reason we see God in nature and by the light of faith we see him in Scripture and in the sacraments, it is the light of glory that enables us to see God's self-disclosure in heaven. Donne does not discuss whether this light is created or uncreated; nor does he elaborate on its relation to Christ. He does, however, give it the highest of praise: "To this light of glory, the light of honour is but a glow-worm; and majesty it self but a twilight; The Cherubim and Seraphim are but Candles; and that Gospel it self, which the Apostle calls the glorious Gospel, but a Star of the least magnitude" (8.9.232–33). Donne confesses that he "cannot tell, what to call this light" by which we will see God (8.9.233).[60]

Perhaps the most remarkable feature of Donne's sermon is his imposition of a fourfold structure upon Aquinas's threefold pattern (the light of nature, of faith, and of glory). He outdoes Aquinas by insisting that beyond the third stage of the face-to-face vision of God in heaven—which, as we have seen, includes the vision of the divine essence—there is more to come: "I shall not only *see God face to face*, but I shall *know* him, (which, as you have seen all the way, is above sight) and *know him, even as also I am knowne*" (8.9.233). In this fourth stage, as table 1 makes clear, God is place, medium, and light, all in one. Donne supports this with a reference to 1 Corinthians 15:28, in-

---

60. Some reticence may well be appropriate before the mystery of the vision of God, but Donne's lack of specificity with regard to the light of glory seems less than felicitous: one cannot help but wonder whether it is the essence of God, or the eternal light of the Son of God, or perhaps a created gift that God will give the soul in heaven.

sisting that then *"God shall be all in all."* At that point, there will be no more
ordinances, since God himself will be "Service, and Musique, and Psalme,
and Sermon, and Sacrament, and all. *Erit vita de verbo sine verbo*; We shall
live upon the word, and heare never a word; live upon him, who being the
word, was made flesh, the eternall Son of God." Donne cautions that seeing
God (who himself sees all things) does not imply that we too will see all
things—"for then we should see the thoughts of men"—but it does mean that
we will see everything in which we have put our faith here on earth (8.9.233).

The knowledge of God in heaven will not be a bodily vision of the humanity of Christ, cautions Donne.[61] We will see God "as he is" (*sicuti est*),
according to 1 John 3:2 (8.9.234). Only on earth did God at times assume
"materiall things to appeare in" (8.9.234). "But," explains Donne, "in heaven
there is no materiall thing to be assumed, and if God be seen face to face
there, he is seen in his Essence" (8.9.235). To be sure, Donne immediately
acknowledges that the divine-human distinction will remain, as he insists,
along with Aquinas, that we will not *comprehend* the divine essence: "A comprehensive knowledge of God it cannot be; To comprehend is to know a
thing as well as that thing can be known; and we can never know God so,
but that he will know himselfe better. . . . But it is *Nota similitudinis, non
æqualitatis*; as God knowes me, so I shall know God; but I shall not know
God so, as God knowes me. It is not *quantum*, but *sicut*; not as much, but as
truly; as the fire does as truly shine, as the Sun shines, though it shine not out
so farre, nor to so many purposes" (8.9.235).[62] We may not ever comprehend
the divine essence, but Donne does suggest that even our continuous seeing
and knowing of God in heaven will in turn be surpassed by something even
greater: "And as this seeing, and this knowing of God crownes all other joyes,
and glories, even in heaven, so this very crown is crowned; There growes
from this a higher glory, which is, *participes erimus Divinæ naturæ*, (words,
of which *Luther* says, that both Testaments afford none equall to them)
That we shall be made partakers of the Divine nature [2 Pet. 1:4]; Immortal
as the Father, righteous as the Son, and full of all comfort as the Holy Ghost"

61. In his sermons on Job 19:26 and on Matt. 5:8, Donne insists emphatically on bodily
resurrection (*Sermons* 3.3.112 and 7.13.342–46). He follows Saint Thomas (*ST* I-II, q. 4, a. 5) in
insisting that the soul will rejoice at being joined again by the body (*Sermons* 3.3.112). Donne
denies, however, that we will see God with bodily eyes, appealing in the latter sermon especially
to Augustine's famous *Ep.* 148 to Fortunatian.

62. Aquinas expresses a similar reservation about comprehending the divine essence in
ST I, q. 12, a. 7; I-II, q. 4, a. 3.

(8.9.236). Here, as in *Goodfriday, 1613* and his sermon on Psalm 32:8, Donne treats deification as the crown of the beatifying journey.[63]

Conclusion

Donne's schema of four types of vision and knowledge may not be without its problems, but it does serve to underscore the continuity of vision (and knowledge) in this life and the next. Donne's sermon on 1 Corinthians 13:12 evidences a participatory ontology, and the preacher is at pains to point out that we are being prepared for the climactic beatific vision through a long life of seeing God in creation (by the light of nature) and in the church (by the light of faith). The presence of vision links these various stages together. As a result, Donne can make a comment such as the following: "This day, this whole Scripture is fulfilled in your eares [cf. Luke 4:21]; for now, (now in this Preaching) you have some sight, and then, (Then when that day comes, which (in the first roote thereof) we celebrate this day) you shall have a perfect sight of all" (*Sermons* 8.9.219–20). The Sunday worship celebrates that we already participate in the vision of God. Similarly, in his sermon on Matthew 5:8, Donne comments:

> This world and the next world, are not, to the pure in heart, two houses, but two roomes, a Gallery to passe thorough, and a Lodging to rest in, in the same House, which are both under one roofe, Christ Jesus; The Militant and the Triumphant, are not two Churches, but this the Porch, and that the Chancell of the same Church which are under one Head, Christ Jesus; so the Joy, and the sense of Salvation, which the pure in heart have here, is not a joy severed from the Joy of Heaven, but a Joy that begins in us here, and continues, and accompanies us thither, and there flowes on, and dilates

63. It is not difficult to be critical of elements of Donne's sermon on 1 Cor. 13:12, particularly the four stages of the vision of God. The distinction between the last two stages does not hold up well: it is hard to see how the "sight of God" is different from the "knowledge of God" in heaven. Donne maintains that in both the saints see God face-to-face, and that in both they see the essence of God; Donne gives at least partially identical descriptions of the final two stages, despite distinguishing the two. Similarly, it seems odd to suggest that divinization is a "higher glory" than seeing the essence of God. Perhaps we need to keep in mind that Donne the preacher always remained Donne the poet. The fourfold structure may have been irresistible to Donne in light of the symmetry it provides; and the notion that divinization would be a crown in addition to that of the beatific vision may be little more than a climactic rhetorical flourish.

it selfe to an infinite expansion, (so, as if you should touch one corne of powder in a traine, and that traine should carry fire into a whole City, from the beginning it was one and the same fire). (7.13.340)[64]

Seeing as the church militant and the church triumphant are one church, Donne was convinced that the vision and the joy of the pure in heart are one and the same in both.

To be sure, Donne does weaken this sense of continuity between the vision of God today and in the hereafter by insisting that in the hereafter we will see the divine essence, whereas in this life no one is able to see this. In this, Donne for the most part simply follows Thomas Aquinas.[65] This does imply an unfortunate disjunction between vision of God in this life and the next, and as such it stands in tension with Donne's thought elsewhere. In this respect, Donne's Thomism does not serve to advance his overall sacramental approach: the heavenly future remains, in some ways, unhelpfully separate from life here on earth.

Overall, however, Donne is at pains to highlight the continuity between vision in this life and the next, vision on earth and in heaven. This continuity is predicated on his participatory ontology, according to which God is present throughout the created order. As a result, the entire pilgrimage of the believer falls under the rubric of vision. The journey begins with God's providential eye watching over the path of the pilgrim. Through conversion and union the believer learns to reciprocate this vision of God, as the believer prepares here and now for the beatific vision of God in heaven. The deifying character of the beatific vision means, for Donne, that heaven and earth cannot remain separate. Donne's overall theology of the beatific vision, therefore—both in his poetry and in his sermons—evidences his ardent longing for the restoration of "commerce twixt heauen and earth."

64. Donne also comments: "The sight of God which we shall have in heaven, must have a *Diluculum*, a break of day here; If we will see his face there, we must see it in some beames here" (7.13.346).

65. Donne denies categorically that God's essence can be seen in this life, insisting that no one—not even Adam in paradise, Moses on Mount Sinai, the apostles on the mount of transfiguration, Paul in his rapture to the third heaven, or Augustine in his vision at Ostia—ever saw the divine essence while on earth (*Sermons* 8.9.231–32). Although he appeals to Aquinas, Donne actually goes beyond the Angelic Doctor in this regard (cf. *ST* I, q. 12, a. 11; II-II, q. 175, a. 3).

CHAPTER 11

CHRIST AND VISION

Puritan and Dutch Reformed Articulations
of the Beatific Vision

Puritanism and Neo-Calvinism

English Puritans and Dutch neo-Calvinists may not seem to have a great deal in common. It would be easy to pit the two streams of Reformed thought against each other: Puritans were inward-focused, neo-Calvinists outward-looking. Puritans dealt with the soul, neo-Calvinists with the body. Puritans centered on the contemplative life, neo-Calvinists on the active life. Puritans highlighted the difference between our earthly life and our heavenly future, neo-Calvinists the continuity between this life and the new heaven and new earth. We might be tempted to hypothesize, therefore, that while Puritans looked forward to the beatific vision, neo-Calvinists treated the teaching with suspicion. Now, these portrayals—as well as the hypothesis that stems from it—do have merit; nonetheless, I will argue in this chapter that the two streams of thought have more in common than we might perhaps expect.

It is true that within the Calvinist tradition, the doctrine of the beatific vision flourished nowhere quite like it did among the Puritans. They read and appropriated scholastic theology on the topic—both of the medieval and of the Calvinist variety. In addition, because of their practical and contemplative interests, they also turned to medieval mysticism and to contemporary Ignatian spirituality for inspiration about the doctrine.[1] As a result, Puritan theologians often discussed the beatific vision and closely tied it to their everyday spirituality, most notably practices of meditation and contemplation.[2] This approach placed a unique stamp on their understanding of the

---

1. In what follows, I will discuss both of these strands of influence in greater detail.

2. The Puritans discussed in this chapter were by no means the only ones treating the be-

beatific vision, and in particular it reinforced the Christ-centeredness of their understanding of it; since they meditated on Christ, his work, and his glory on a daily basis, it is hardly surprising that Christ was also central to their understanding of the ultimate vision of God. After all, daily meditation on Christ was simply preparation for heaven. As Isaac Ambrose put it: "Consider that *looking unto Jesus* is the work of heaven. . . . If then we like not this work, how will we live in heaven?"[3] Therefore, although the Puritans were by no means unique in recognizing that in the eschaton we will see God in Christ, it is perhaps true that the link between Christology and the beatific vision has nowhere been as sustained and profound as among the Puritans.

Abraham Kuyper's neo-Calvinist heirs have often been wary of the mystical piety associated with Puritanism and have tended to neglect the doctrine of the beatific vision.[4] In some sense, this is hardly surprising. Kuyper's theology, after all, took its starting point in his famous saying, "There is not a square inch in the whole domain of our human existence over which Christ, who is Sovereign over all, does not cry: 'Mine!'"[5] Kuyper's neo-Calvinism unambiguously asserted Christ's rule over every aspect of life and emboldened the Dutch common people (*kleine luyden*) at the turn of the twentieth century to get involved in social and cultural affairs, in politics and economic life, in the arts and the sciences.[6] Nonetheless, Kuyper also had a distinctly

---

atific vision. Tom Schwanda mentions in addition: Robert Bolton, *Mr. Boltons last and learned worke of the foure last things, death, iudgement, hell, and heauen. With an assise-sermon, and notes on Iustice Nicolls his funerall. Together with the life and death of the authour*, ed. Edward Bagshaw (London, 1632; STC [2nd ed.] 3242); John Howe, *The blessednesse of the righteous discoursed from Psal. 17, 15* (London, 1668; Wing H3015); and William Bates, *The four last things viz. death, judgment, heaven, hell, practically considered and applied in several discourses* (London, 1691; Wing B1105), 285–342. See Tom Schwanda, "The Saints' Desire and Delight to Be with Christ," in *Puritanism and Emotion in the Early Modern World*, ed. Alec Ryrie and Tom Schwanda (New York: Palgrave Macmillan, 2016), 78n55.

3. Isaac Ambrose, *Looking unto Jesus a view of the everlasting Gospel, or, the souls eying of Jesus as carrying on the great work of mans salvation from first to last* (London, 1658; Wing A2956), 1.3.7.

4. Herman Bavinck is the most obvious example. See chap. 1, section entitled "No 'Melting Union': Herman Bavinck."

5. Abraham Kuyper, "Sphere Sovereignty," in *Abraham Kuyper: A Centennial Reader*, ed. James D. Bratt (Grand Rapids: Eerdmans, 1998), 488.

6. For Kuyper's views on culture and on public theology, see John Bolt, *A Free Church, a Holy Nation: Abraham Kuyper's American Public Theology* (Grand Rapids: Eerdmans, 2001); Vincent E. Bacote, *The Spirit in Public Theology: Appropriating the Legacy of Abraham Kuyper* (Grand Rapids: Baker Academic, 2005).

mystical bent and, much like the earlier Puritans, consistently highlighted the beatific vision as the object of the saints' greatest desire.

This is not to say that the English Puritans and the Dutch theologian ended up with identical teachings regarding the beatific vision. Most notably, I will argue that the place of Christ in the beatific vision constitutes the main point of difference between the Puritans I will discuss—Isaac Ambrose, John Owen, Richard Baxter, and Thomas Watson—and Abraham Kuyper. Whereas these Puritans typically saw the beatific vision as an eternal vision of Christ, Kuyper restricted the saints' future communion with Christ to the intermediate state. And whereas the Puritans generally wanted little to do with the notion that at some point we will see the essence of God (or, when they did, they made sure that the link with Christ was obvious), Kuyper maintained that seeing God's essence will constitute the believers' ultimate bliss after the resurrection. As a result, the Puritans ended up with a more consistently "sacramental" approach to the beatific vision: the Puritans I discuss rejected any vision of God apart from his self-revelation in Jesus Christ—something that is particularly evident in connection with Isaac Ambrose and John Owen, as I will show in the next two sections of this chapter. They argued that both in our contemplation today and in the future vision of God, we see him always only in Christ. By contrast, Kuyper's spirituality—though in some ways very much focused on Christ—ended up with a disjunction between an indirect vision of God (by means of revelation) today and a direct vision of his essence in the eschaton.

Looking unto Jesus: Isaac Ambrose

When, in thanksgiving for being healed of a serious illness,[7] the Presbyterian vicar of Garstang, Isaac Ambrose (1604–1664), published his lengthy tome *Looking unto Jesus* (1658), he took his cue from Hebrews 12:2—"looking to Jesus, the founder and perfecter of our faith." Ambrose devoted his book to Christology, beginning with the eternal generation "of our Jesus" and our election in Christ in book 2, and concluding with his second coming in judgment in book 5. In his focus on seeing Christ, Ambrose by no means restricted himself to a treatment of the beatific vision in the eschaton. He

---

7. Ambrose, *Looking unto Jesus*, preface. Cf. Tom Schwanda, *Soul Recreation: The Contemplative-Mystical Piety of Puritanism* (Eugene, OR: Pickwick, 2012), 148. Schwanda's book is the best available introduction to Ambrose's mystical spirituality.

had a more immediate goal, namely, to encourage his readers to look away from all other objects in order to turn their eyes to Jesus instead.[8]

Nonetheless, the practice of "looking unto Jesus" reaches its climax in the hereafter. Only looking at Jesus makes one genuinely happy: "Come, let the proud man boast in his honour, and the mighty man in his valour, but let the Christian pronounce himself happy; onely happy, truly happy, fully happy in beholding Christ, having Christ, in *looking unto Jesus*."[9] Ambrose's reflections on the second coming conform to this overall christological perspective. He begins his lyrical description of the future meeting of Christ and his saints with the comments:

> They look, and gaze, and dart their beames: and reflect their glories on each other. Oh the communications! oh the darting of beames betwixt Christ and his Saints! look as when two admirable persons, two lovers meet together, their eyes sparkle, they look on, as if they would look through one another. And such is the effect of these looks. Did not *Moses* face shine when he had been with God? and shall not the faces of the elect glitter and shine when Christ also looks on them? nor stayes it there; but as they shine by Christ, so shall their shine reflect on Christ, and give a glory to Christ; and this I take it to be the meaning of the Apostle, *that when Christ shall come, he shall be glorified in his Saints* [cf. 2 Thess. 1:10]; not onely in himself, but in his Saints also; whose glory as it comes from him, so it redounds also to him, *for of him, and through him, and to him are all things* [cf. Rom. 11:36]. (5.1.4)

The mutual sight of Christ and his saints leads to a mutual glorification. The saints will be astonished to see "the beauty of God put forth in Christ," to see "the substantial reflection of the Fathers light and glory in Jesus Christ." The result, insists Ambrose, is that Christ and his saints will mutually rejoice and delight in one another (5.1.4).

This encounter between Christ and the saints will be followed, explains Ambrose, by the final judgment, after which the saints will march behind Christ and the angels into the empyreal heaven, at which point the earth will be set on fire, and the saints will come to dwell in new heavens and a new

---

8. Ambrose explains that in Heb. 12:2, the Greek for "looking unto"—ἀφορῶντες εἰς—contains two prepositions (ἀπό and εἰς), the one signifying "a turning of the eye from all other objects," the other "a fast fixing of the eye upon such an object" (*Looking unto Jesus* 1.2.1).

9. Ambrose, *Looking unto Jesus* 1.3.6. Hereafter, references from this work will be given in parentheses in the text.

earth (cf. 2 Pet. 3:13), which is the "heaven of heavens, and place of glory" (5.1.6–7). Christ will then present the elect to his Father, so that at this point his work as mediator is finished. Indeed, *all* work of mediation now comes to an end: "*In heaven there is no need of sun or moon*, that is, as some interpret, there is no need of preaching, or prophesying; of the Word or Sacraments, *for the Lambe is the light thereof* [cf. Rev. 21:23], Christ is the only means of all the communication that the Elect there shall have" (5.1.8). He will be subject to the Father (cf. 1 Cor. 15:28) in the sense that Christ will deliver up his kingdom to the Father and will no longer function as mediator: "At that day his Mediatourship shall cease; and by consequence in respect of his Mediatourship, or in respect of his humanity, he shall that day be subject to his Father" (5.1.8). Thus, Ambrose distinguishes between Christ's role as mediator (which will end at the second coming) and his function as "means of communication" (which will continue forever).

In his reflections on Paul's saying that "God may be all in all" (1 Cor. 15:28), Ambrose devotes an entire section to the saints' enjoyment of God—a discussion that focuses squarely on the divine essence (5.1.9). Ambrose insists that the Pauline passage speaks of "enjoying God immediately" rather than "by meanes." Ambrose also explains the famous texts of 1 Corinthians 13:12 and 1 John 3:2 as references to the direct sight of God: "We see him but in a glasse darkly; but when he shall be our *all in all*, we shall see him *face to face*, we shall then see God as he is clearly and immediately" (5.1.9 [emphasis added]). Not only will we enjoy him "immediately," but we will also enjoy him "fully": "Our enjoyment of God is but here in it's infancy, there it will be in it's full age; here it is in drops, there it will be in the ocean; here we see Gods back parts, and we can see no more, but there we shall see his face, not his second face (as some distinguish) which is his grace and favour enjoyed by faith, but his first face, which is his Divine essence enjoyed by sight. Yet I meane not so, as if the soul which is a creature could take in the whole essence of God which is incomprehensible; but the soul shall and must be so full of God, as that it shall not be able to receive, or desire one jot more" (5.1.9). The beatific vision, for Ambrose, is a vision of the divine essence itself, and the proviso that we will not be able to comprehend this essence inasmuch as it is infinite, is of course entirely traditional.

This may seem like a remarkably nonchristological approach. But Ambrose immediately corrects such an impression. Anticipating the objection that his treatment may seem insufficiently christological, he devotes the entire next section, 5.1.10, to the vision of Christ as the saints' "all in all." Here he explains that the vision of Christ after the resurrection will be one of Christ in his glorified humanity. In the eschaton, explains Ambrose, the "lustre of his Deity" will shine through in his humanity, so "that thereby our very bodily eyes may come to see God, as much as is possible for any creature to see him."[10] At the same time, the saints will also see Christ's "essential divine glory." Ambrose insists, however, that one must first die in order to see Christ's divinity (cf. Exod. 33:20): "No man in this life, he must first dye, and be changed, and then he shal have a peculiar revelation of the divine majesty; then he shall *see him as he is*; but how that is, I cannot tell." Therefore, although in the intermediate state the saints will "see the essential glory of Christ more immediately and fully" than they did on earth, "during the time of the last Judgment" the vision of Christ's divinity will be much more glorious, and after that the manifestations of Christ's glory will appear more brightly than ever before (5.1.10).

Ambrose does not claim to know how it is that the saints will see Christ's divine essence after the resurrection,[11] but he does discuss at some length what it means to see Christ's "face," that is to say, his divine essence. This sight of Christ's face involves, according to Ambrose, six distinct elements: seeing the eternal relations among the persons of the Trinity; seeing Christ as the first being or principle of all created good; seeing Christ in everything he has done from everlasting to everlasting; seeing Christ as having done all this specifically with a view to our happiness; seeing Christ, as he is, directly; and seeing Christ forever, without interruption (5.1.10). For Ambrose, therefore, the vision of God is never anything but a vision of Christ. Even when it comes to the vision of the divine essence, this is nothing but a vision of the essence of *Christ*. Ambrose thus refuses to think of the divine essence in abstraction from the person of Jesus Christ. As a result, he treats the beatific

10. Ambrose opines that this "ocular vision" of Christ's glorified humanity will be possible because (1) our eyes will be gloried; (2) they will act in a glorified body; and (3) they will be acted upon by a glorified spirit (5.1.10). Earlier, Ambrose had argued that "there may be some use" of ocular sight in heaven, referring not only to Job's claim that "*with these eyes I shall behold him*" (Job 19:27), but also to the key verses of 1 John 3:2 and 1 Cor. 13:12—which at that point he had interpreted as referring to a beatific, physical seeing of Jesus in heaven (*Looking unto Jesus* 1.3.1).

11. Ambrose mentions four possibilities, refusing to make a choice: (1) Christ's divinity will be known by means of his humanity; (2) Christ's divine essence will be represented by a distinct species, which the understanding will be able to see because the light of glory will elevate it; (3) Christ's divine essence will be seen directly (rather than by a distinct species) by means of the light of glory that will elevate the understanding; or (4) the divine essence of Christ will be immediately represented to the understanding, with divine grace enabling it to see (*Looking unto Jesus* 5.1.10).

vision as simply a vision of Christ. For Ambrose, happiness is found only in "looking unto Jesus," from beginning to end.

The Glorious Mystery of Christ: John Owen

The nonconformist theologian John Owen (1616–1683) set out to defend, as he put it in the subtitle of his 1679 book, *Christologia*, the "glorious mystery" of the person of Christ.[12] In particular, he intended to "declare his Excellency, to plead the cause of his Glory, to vindicate his Honour, and to witness him the only Rest and Reward of the Souls of men."[13] In the last two chapters of the book, Owen deals with Christ's present role in heaven, both his state of glory (chap. 19) and the exercise of his office (chap. 20). In some sense, then, the centrality of Christ in Owen's treatment of the beatific vision was guaranteed simply by the overall topic of the treatise, including the final two chapters.

Still, we should not fail to note *how*, according to Owen, Christ functions in relation to the beatific vision. First and foremost, he treats Christ as the object of the saints' vision in heaven, both immediately after death and after his second coming. Although this key insight needs further articulation (as well as nuancing), one cannot come away from reading the *Christologia* without getting the overwhelming impression that Owen holds out the vision of Christ as the prospect for the hereafter.[14] This is evident, for example, in the

---

12. John Owen, *Christologia, or, A declaration of the glorious mystery of the person of Christ, God and man with the infinite wisdom, love and power of God in the contrivance and constitution thereof . . .* (London, 1679; Wing O762). For discussion of Owen's Christology, see Alan Spence, *Incarnation and Inspiration: John Owen and the Coherence of Christology* (New York: T. & T. Clark, 2007). For Owen's overall theology, see Sebastian Rehnman, *Divine Discourse: The Theological Methodology of John Owen* (Grand Rapids: Baker Academic, 2002); Kelly M. Kapic, *Communion with God: The Divine and the Human in the Theology of John Owen* (Grand Rapids: Baker Academic, 2007); Carl R. Trueman, *John Owen: Reformed Catholic, Renaissance Man* (2007; reprint, New York: Routledge, 2016).

13. Owen, *Christologia*, preface. Hereafter, page references from this work will be given in parentheses in the text.

14. Cf. Kyle Strobel, "Jonathan Edwards' Reformed Doctrine of the Beatific Vision," in *Jonathan Edwards and Scotland*, ed. Kelly Van Andel, Adriaan C. Neele, and Kenneth P. Minkema (Edinburgh: Dunedin, 2011), 164–66; Suzanne McDonald, "Beholding the Glory of God in the Face of Jesus Christ: John Owen and the 'Reforming' of the Beatific Vision," in *The Ashgate Research Companion to John Owen's Theology*, ed. Kelly M. Kapic and Mark Jones (Burlington, VT: Ashgate, 2012), 141–58.

two definition-like descriptions that he gives of the beatific vision. He offers the first when he focuses in chapter 19 on the question of how Christ's human nature is glorified in heaven after his ascension. Owen begins by reiterating the traditional Chalcedonian conviction that Christ's human nature subsists within the person of the Son of God (319–20). Owen insists that when at death the saints join the heavenly worship, they see there the glory of this mystery of the incarnation in heaven: "The enjoyment of Heaven is usually called the *Beatifical Vision*. That is, such an intellectual present view, apprehension and sight of God and his Glory, especially as manifested in Christ, as will make us *blessed* unto eternity" (320). A "great part of our Blessedness" will consist in contemplating this mystery of the incarnation, maintains Owen (320). The focus of the beatific vision—which begins immediately after death—appears to be contemplation of the mystery of the incarnation.

Second, when in the next chapter Owen describes the worship that currently takes place among the saints in heaven, he states that although this worship is not carnal (as if heavenly worship conformed to the way we "frame *Images*" in our minds), it is also not merely mental (as if it consisted of the "silent thoughts of each individual person") (345): when Scripture speaks of voices, postures, and gestures in heaven, this describes something real, even if we don't quite know what it is. Owen summarizes the biblical depiction of worship in the heavenly temple, where Christ (in his human nature) is situated in front of God himself, who is seated on his throne, surrounded by angels and saints (346). Owen then speaks of the "*full clear apprehensions* which all the Blessed Ones have of the Glory of God in Christ, of the work and effects of his Wisdom and Grace towards Mankind" (347). Also in this brief description, Owen reiterates that the beatific vision is an apprehension of God's glory *in Christ*. This time he focuses not on the mystery of the incarnation per se, but on the saving work of Christ more broadly. Whether the object of the vision is the hypostatic union or Christ's work of mediation, it is clear that for Owen, the beatific vision that the saints already enjoy in heaven does not just consist of them looking at Jesus with the eyes of the soul. Instead, they contemplate God's salvation in Christ: his incarnation and subsequent work of redemption. On Owen's understanding, then, when believers die and join the heavenly assembly in worship, their contemplation of Christ constitutes the beatific vision.

Christ is also the object of the saints' contemplation after the resurrection. This is clear from Owen's posthumously published *Meditations and discourses on the glory of Christ* (1684).[15] Owen devotes the final three chapters of this

---

15. John Owen, *Meditations and discourses on the glory of Christ, in his person, office, and*

treatise to Paul's distinction between faith and sight (2 Cor. 5:7). Owen explains that faith ("in this Life") and sight ("in that which is to come") both have the glory of Christ as their object. Again, therefore, Owen makes clear from the outset that the beatific vision is a vision of Christ. He then discusses four differences between faith and sight. First, with reference to 1 Corinthians 13:12, faith sees Christ *"through or by a glass* in a Riddle, a parable, a dark saying" (174). This Pauline expression refers to the way in which Christ's glory comes to us in the gospel, namely, reflexively, obscurely, and in "dark sayings" (cf. Ps. 78:2) (174–76). By contrast, the vision "we shall have of the glory of Christ in Heaven, is *immediate, direct, intuitive,* and therefore *steady,* eaven and constant" (179). What is remarkable about this description of the vision of Christ after the resurrection is not just its christological contents, but also the adjectives Owen uses to describe it: "immediate," "direct," and "intuitive." These are the very adjectives traditionally used in Western theology to describe the vision that the blessed have of the essence of God. Owen here uses these same adjectives to describe the saints' vision of Christ instead—thereby reinforcing the impression that he replaces the vision of the divine essence with the vision of Christ in the hereafter.[16]

Second, whereas the sight that we have through the light of faith "is frequently *hindred* and *interrupted* in its operations" (199), the sight that we will have of "the Glory of Christ in Heaven" will be *"equal, stable, always the same, without interruption or diversion"* (228). Third, faith gathers the elements of Christ's glory *"one by one, in several parts and parcels* out of the Scripture" (234). God has, as it were, "distributed" the glory of Christ for us in his revelation, so that our minds would not be "overwhelmed" by it (235). This will change in our heavenly vision of Christ after the resurrection: "There, the whole Glory of Christ will be at *once* and *alwaies* represented

---

grace with the differences between faith and sight: applied unto the use of them that believe (London, 1684; Wing O769). Hereafter, page references from this work will be given in parentheses in the text.

16. This impression is reinforced when we read that, in the hereafter, sight is "an act of the internal power of our minds," whereby we shall be able to see Christ *"face to face, to see him as he is,* in a direct comprehension of his Glory" (*Meditations,* 230). Owen here applies the language of "direct comprehension" not to the divine essence (as traditionally had been done) but to the glory of Christ. In this regard, it is interesting that in the *Christologia* Owen discusses the question of whether "absolute comprehension" is possible. Whereas Thomas Aquinas deals with this question in connection with the vision of the divine essence (*ST* I, q. 12, a. 7; I-II, q. 4, a. 3), Owen speaks of it in connection with the mystery of the incarnation. Speaking of the glory of Christ (!), he suggests that although faith will be replaced by sight, "no finite creature can have an absolute comprehension of that which is infinite. We shall never search out the Almighty to perfection in any of his works of infinite Wisdom" (*Christologia,* 320).

unto us; and we shall be enabled in one act of the Light of Glory to comprehend it" (237). Again, Owen's modification of the earlier tradition is notable. Using the traditional, Thomistic distinction between "light of faith" and "light of glory," as well as the discourse of "comprehension," Owen applies it not to the essence of God but to the glory of Christ. The light of glory will allow us to comprehend (in some manner) the glory of Christ in a steady, uninterrupted manner.[17]

Finally, Owen argues that the effect of sight will be different from that of faith. He acknowledges that faith transforms us to some extent. The change it works, however, is only gradual and partial (242–44). By contrast, our vision in heaven will be "perfectly and absolutely *transforming*. It doth change us wholly into the Image of Christ. *When we shall see him, we shall be as he is, we shall be like him, because we shall see him*, 1 Joh. 3.2" (238). Interpreting 1 John 3:2 as a reference not to the essence of God but to Christ, Owen maintains that the absolute transformation affects both soul and body.[18] At death, the soul is immediately released from the "weakness, disability, darkness, uncertainties, and fears" that were caused by its union with the body (238). At the resurrection, the body, too, will be prepared for glory. It will "never more be a trouble, a burden unto the Soul, but an assistant in its Operations, and participant of its blessedness. Our eyes were made *to see our Redeemer*, and our other Sences to receive impressions from him, according unto their capacity" (241). In short, the transformation is absolute, both in the sense that after death the soul will be made perfect like Christ, and in the sense that at the resurrection the body will become a proper instrument for the physical beholding of Christ.[19]

---

17. Cf. the discussion on the light of glory in Owen, *Meditations*, 185–87. Owen does not explicitly say whether the light of glory will be implanted at death or at the resurrection. The Thomistic phrasing would suggest the former. However, on both occasions where he deals with it (*Meditations*, 185–87 and 237), the context for his language of the "light of glory" is the beatific vision after the resurrection, and Owen suggests that this light of glory is necessary for the immediate comprehension of Christ's glory—and he explicitly links the latter to the resurrection. Perhaps Owen fails to draw explicit attention to his linking of the light of glory with the resurrection because the earlier tradition had instead linked it with the separated souls' vision of God.

18. For Aquinas's interpretation of 1 John 3:2 as referring to the essence of God, see *ST* I, q. 12, a. 1; Suppl. 92.1. For a defense of Aquinas's reading of this biblical passage, see Simon Francis Gaine, *Did the Saviour See the Father? Christ, Salvation, and the Vision of God* (London: Bloomsbury T. & T. Clark, 2015), 26–29.

19. Owen concludes his reflections on the transforming nature of the vision of Christ's glory by explaining that it is "*beatifical*," that is to say, a vision that gives "perfect rest and blessedness" (*Meditations*, 244).

For Owen, then, the beatific vision—both immediately at death and after the resurrection—is, for all intents and purposes, a vision of Christ in his glory. After the resurrection, this vision, which involves a change from the light of faith to the light of glory, will be direct or immediate—we could also say, a comprehension of sorts (although after the resurrection of the body, it will include corporeal sight). In many respects Owen's approach is simply traditional, probably taken directly from Thomas Aquinas. The one major difference is that Owen uses this theological framework to speak of the saints' beatific vision of Christ (the glory of his incarnation and redemption)—rather than of the essence of God.[20] For Owen, the Johannine promise of seeing him "as he is" (*sicuti est*) does hold out the prospect of the beatific vision, but Owen reconfigures both this promise and the beatific vision itself so that they come to refer to the vision of Christ in glory.

Owen's Christ-centered understanding of the beatific vision raises the question of how he believed that in heaven both Christ and the saints relate to God the Father. Owen does not deal with the question at great length, but he does address it briefly in a couple of places. When, in his *Christologia*, he begins his discussion of Christ's present condition in glory, he first makes a caveat: Christ's mediatorial work, as it continues in heaven, will one day come to an end. Quoting 1 Corinthians 15:24–27, Owen explains that "at the end of this dispensation he [i.e., Christ] shall give up the Kingdom unto God, even the Father, or cease from the Administration of his Mediatorial Office & Power."[21] Christ's role as mediator was necessitated by sin, and so it will end once the enemy is completely subdued (315–16). Owen describes the future situation as follows: "Then will God be *all in all*. In his own immense Nature and Blessedness he shall not only be *All essentially* and *causally*, but *in All* also; he shall *immediately be All* in and unto us" (316). Owen goes on to say that we are not in a position to arrive at a good understanding of this today, so he will restrict himself to a discussion of the heavenly glory of Christ in his human nature (316–17).

At the very end of the *Christologia*, Owen briefly returns to the notion of an "immediate enjoyment of God," which the saints will have after Christ has given up the kingdom to the Father. Owen explains that one of the reasons God has ordered the continuation of Christ's mediatorial work in heaven

---

20. Owen had been trained in Aquinas (and scholasticism more broadly) under Thomas Barlow in Oxford (Rehnman, *Divine Discourse*, 31–39; Trueman, *John Owen*, 9–12).

21. Owen, *Christologia*, 315. Hereafter, page references from this work will be given in parentheses in the text.

after his ascension—even though full atonement has already been made—is that Christ's work offers encouragement to believers on earth (353–54, 366–67). By way of clarification, Owen suggests: "Were nothing proposed unto us but the *Immensity of the Divine Essence*, we should not know how to make our approaches unto it" (367). Thus, for the moment, Christ continues his work as mediator in heaven, while at the same time Owen reminds his readers of his earlier suggestion that this work will come to an end when Christ gives up the kingdom to the Father, at which point "all things issue in the immediate Enjoyment of God himself" (368).

Owen does, at this point, use the language of "immediate enjoyment" of God, and perhaps his comment about the "*Immensity of the Divine Essence*" is meant to suggest that one day we will see the divine essence itself. However, Owen immediately adds the important qualification that he is only talking here about Christ's *mediatory office* coming to an end, while three other christological elements will continue forever: (1) Christ in his human nature will always be the immediate head of the glorified creation; (2) Christ will forever be the means and way of communication between God and the saints; and (3) Christ in his human nature will be the eternal object of divine glory, praise, and worship—contemplation will lead to praise (368–69).[22] Regardless of the ambiguity, Owen did not think of heaven as a place in which we will leave Christ behind for the sake of the essence of God.

The second of the aforementioned elements is particularly intriguing: the notion that Christ will always be the means of communication between God and the saints. Although Owen is brief, it is nonetheless clear that—much like Isaac Ambrose—he distinguishes between Christ as mediator and Christ as means. Christ's mediatorial work will come to an end once sin is fully vanquished. Christ's office as mediator is strictly tied to a fallen, sinful state. But for Owen this does not mean that at the end we will see the Father apart from Christ. Whatever blessings God may communicate to us in eternity (after the resurrection), Owen is insistent that "they shall be all made in and through the Person of the Son and the humane Nature therein. That *Taber-*

---

22. Owen displays a similar ambiguity in *Meditations*, 192, where he writes: "THIS *beholding of the glory of Christ given him by his Father*, is indeed subordinate unto the ultimate vision of the essence of God. What that is we cannot well conceive; only we know that *the pure in heart shall see God*. But it hath such an immediate connexion with it, and a subordination unto it, as that without it we can never behold the face of God, as the objective blessedness of our souls. For he is and shall be to eternity, the only means of communication between God and the Church."

nacle shall never be folded up, never be laid aside as useless" (*Christologia*, 368).[23] Owen continues, as if anticipating objections:

> And if it be said, that I cannot declare the way and manner of the eternal Communications of God himself unto his Saints in Glory by Christ; I shall only say, that I cannot declare the way and manner of his Communications of himself in Grace by Christ unto the souls of men in this World, and yet I do believe it. How much more must we satisfy our selves with the evidence of Faith alone in those things, which as yet, are more incomprehensible. And our *adherence* unto God by Love and Delight shall alwaies be through Christ. For God will be conceived of unto Eternity, according to the manifestation that he hath made of himself, in him and no otherwise. (368–69)

Owen was convinced that we can never bypass Christ's human nature (his "*Tabernacle*") and that God will *only* ever be seen in Christ. It may be true that in one or two comments in his oeuvre, Owen sheds doubt on this christocentric approach; possibly he was unable to arrive at a conclusion that fully satisfied him. Nonetheless, the overwhelming impression Owen gives—both in the quotation above and in his overall treatment of the beatific vision— is that he believed the beatific vision is the eternal vision of God in Jesus Christ.[24]

"Contemplative-Mystical Piety" (1): Richard Baxter and Isaac Ambrose

The reason Puritan theologians such as Isaac Ambrose and John Owen focused persistently on Jesus Christ as the object of the beatific vision has everything to do with their spirituality; if Christ is the one in whom we believe today, he must also be the one we will see in the hereafter. Or, to put it in sacramental terms, the one we encounter in sacramental form here on earth

---

23. Suzanne McDonald rightly suggests that Owen "struggles" at this point ("Beholding the Glory of God," 150n27). Indeed, it is hardly possible that the saints will immediately see the divine essence *and* that they will see God in and through Christ.

24. Simon Francis Gaine ("Thomas Aquinas and John Owen on the Beatific Vision: A Reply to Suzanne McDonald," *NB* 97 [2016]: 436) downplays the difference between Aquinas and Owen by quoting Owen's comment that the vision of Christ is "subordinate" to the vision of God's essence (*Meditations*, 192). But this overlooks the unrelenting focus in Owen's writings on the believers' vision of Christ (rather than of God's essence) and unduly elevates one small comment by Owen that simply does not fit well into his overall thought.

is the same one we will see in reality in eternity. Even though they do not use explicitly sacramental language, time and again the Puritans reflect on the need to experience union with Christ already today. The logic is simple but compelling: If we have no vision of Christ whatsoever today, how can we possibly expect to see him in glory in the hereafter?

The Puritans therefore never treated the theology of the beatific vision as a purely intellectual matter. Rather, as the next two sections will make clear, for the Puritans this doctrine always served an experiential or mystagogical aim. Tom Schwanda helpfully refers to this as the "contemplative-mystical piety" of Puritanism. For Schwanda, this term denotes an attitude and awareness based on the grammar of gazing on the triune God that communicate a deep desire to live in conscious union and communion with God.[25] Schwanda rightly detects among the Puritans a combination of two elements: a grammar of vision and a desire for union with God. The eschatological goal of the beatific vision determines the mystical longing of the believer on earth. When the Puritans spoke of the outward life of holiness or of the inward life of the affections, it was almost invariably with a view to realizing, in some small measure, the future goal of the beatific vision and the enjoyment of God in Christ.

This affective piety is on display throughout *The saints everlasting rest* (1649), a large tome written by the famous Kidderminster preacher, Richard Baxter (1615–1691). The beatific vision is not the focus of the book, but Baxter does briefly address the topic as part of a broader attempt to impress both on himself and on his readers the importance of preparing for heaven through self-examination and practices of meditation.[26] J. I. Packer explains the far-reaching aim of Baxter's book as follows: "With this first book, *The Saints' Everlasting Rest*, which he began to write in order to direct his thoughts upward when he thought he was on his deathbed, he hit the ground running: not only because the book centres, fair and square, on that which was always central to the godliness that he lived and taught, namely the hope of glory strengthening the heart, but because the sublime rush of his rhetoric transcended anything that Puritan stylists had achieved up to that

---

25. Schwanda, *Soul Recreation*, 18.

26. For a contemporary edition of Baxter's autobiography, see *The Autobiography of Richard Baxter*, ed. J. M. Lloyd Thomas and N. H. Keeble, Everyman's University Library 863 (Totowa, NJ: Rowman and Littlefield, 1974). For Baxter's overall theology (in relation to that of John Owen), see Tim Cooper, *John Owen, Richard Baxter, and the Formation of Nonconformity* (Burlington, VT: Ashgate, 2011).

time (1649)."[27] Converted as a fifteen-year-old by reading Edmund Bunny's *Resolution*—a hugely popular 1584 revision by a Puritan pastor of a book published two years earlier by the Jesuit author Robert Parsons[28]—Baxter always remained convinced of the importance of the imagination and the affections for the contemplation of heaven. To what extent Bunny's *Resolution* formed the foundation for Baxter's later teaching regarding self-examination and meditation remains obscure, but it is clear that Baxter's spirituality was, in significant respects, similar to that of Ignatius of Loyola.[29]

Baxter's *The saints everlasting rest* deals with the future hope primarily under the rubric of rest rather than of vision. Still, the basic point is the same: God himself is the saints' final goal. Baxter defines "rest" as follows: "Rest is [The end and perfection of motion.] The saints Rest here in Question is [The most happy estate of a Christian, having obtained the end of his course]."[30] The only end that truly can give rest to the motion of a human being is God, so that "the first true saving Act, is to chuse God only for our End and Happiness" (1.3.2).[31] Baxter maintains that this perfection of happiness includes both body and soul. The body will share in the fruition of God, though Baxter casts suspicion on the notion that our changed bodily eyes will be equipped to see God (1.4.5). Throughout his book, the Kidderminster pastor focuses on intellectual contemplation instead.

27. J. I. Packer, *A Quest for Godliness: The Puritan Vision of the Christian Life* (Wheaton, IL: Crossway, 1990), 61.

28. For detailed discussion, see Robert McNulty, "The Protestant Version of Robert Parsons' *The First Book of the Christian Exercise*," *HLQ* 22 (1959): 271–300.

29. E. Glenn Hinson, noting the similarity between Ignatian spirituality and Baxter's approach to meditation, thinks it unlikely that Baxter would have read Ignatius's *Spiritual Exercises* and speculates that Jesuit and Puritan authors drew from the same medieval sources ("Ignatian and Puritan Prayer: Surprising Similarities; A Comparison of Ignatius Loyola and Richard Baxter on Meditation," *TMA* 20 [2007]: 89). Charles E. Hambrick-Stowe also observes that devotional manuals were common throughout Catholic and Protestant Europe and adds: "Far from inventing the genre, Puritan authors built on well-established traditions in Catholic spiritual writing, adapting classical practices and even pirating and protestantising Catholic materials" ("Practical Divinity and Spirituality," in *The Cambridge Companion to Puritanism*, ed. John Coffey and Paul C. H. Lim [Cambridge: Cambridge University Press, 2008], 196). Cf. also Schwanda, *Soul Recreation*, 130–31.

30. Richard Baxter, *The saints everlasting rest, or, A treatise of the blessed state of the saints in their enjoyment of God in glory . . .* (London, 1651; Wing B1384), 1.2.1 (brackets in original). Hereafter, references from this work will be given in parentheses in the text.

31. Cf. John Casey, *After Lives: A Guide to Heaven, Hell, and Purgatory* (New York: Oxford University Press, 2009), 313–14.

According to Baxter, the believing soul looks for the enjoyment of Christ. Already here on earth, the true believer aims to unite his understanding to divine truth. The genuinely contemplative person "sometimes hath felt more sweet embraces between his Soul and Jesus Christ, then all inferior Truth can afford" (1.4.6).[32] Baxter appeals to this contemplative person directly:

> Christian, doth thou not sometime, when, after long gazing heavenward, thou hast got a glimpse of Christ, dost thou not seem to have been with *Paul* in the third Heaven, whether in the body or out, and to have seen what is unutterable? Art thou not, with *Peter*, almost beyond thy self? ready to say, *Master, it's good to be here?* Oh that I might dwell in this Mount! Oh that I might ever see what I now see! Didst thou never look so long upon the Sun of God, till thine Eyes were dazzled with his astonishing glory? and did not the splendor of it make all things below seem black and dark to thee, when thou lookedst down again? (1.7.5)

Baxter maintains that contemplative practices rearrange the affections and desires in such a way that Christians become fitted for the glory of heaven. Such contemplative preparation may involve mystical experiences in which, along with Peter and Paul, believers get a taste of heavenly glory.

Thus, although Baxter holds out the heavenly rest and the beatific vision as the object of future hope, he closely joins this future prospect to contemplative practices. He urges his readers to use the senses as a means to reach heaven. This, after all, is what Scripture itself does: "And it is very considerable, how the holy Ghost doth condescend in the phrase of Scripture, in bringing things down to the reach of Sense; how he sets forth the excellencies of Spirituall things, in the words that are borrowed from the objects of Sense; how he describeth the glory of the new *Jerusalem*, in expressions that might take even with flesh it self" (4.11.1). For Baxter, descriptions taken from the senses are metaphors that take us to heaven itself.

The similarity to Ignatian spiritual practices is striking when Baxter urges his readers to meditate concretely on the realities of heaven and tells them: "But get the liveliest Picture of them in thy minde that possibly thou canst;

32. Baxter comments that he purposely leaves aside the question of the relationship between Christ's office as mediator and the vision of God after the resurrection (1.7.5). He highlights, however, the immediacy of our face-to-face vision of God: "We shall then have Communion without Sacraments, vvhen Christ shall drink vvith us of the fruit of the Vine nevv, that is, Refresh us with the comforting Wine of immediate fruition, in the Kingdom of his Father" (1.7.5).

meditate of them, as if thou were all the while beholding them, and as if thou were even hearing the *Hallelujahs*, while thou art thinking of them" (4.11.2). Baxter also tells his readers to "compare the objects of Sense with objects of Faith" (4.11.3). He begins with illicit pleasures—drunkenness, prostitution, gambling, and the like (4.11.3)—and keeps moving up the scale to ever-greater pleasures. Along the way, he asks his readers to compare the "delights above" with those of food and drink (4.11.4), natural knowledge (4.11.5), morality and natural affections (4.11.6), the works of creation (4.11.7), divine providence (4.11.8), particular mercies of God experienced in this life (4.11.9), divine ordinances (4.11.10), the various foretastes saints of the past have experienced of heaven (4.11.11),[33] the glories of the church and of Christ in his humiliation (4.11.12), the life of sanctification (4.11.13), and the foretastes that we ourselves may have of heaven today (4.11.14). None of these measure up to the glory and joy of heaven itself. Paradoxically, therefore, by focusing on the dissimilarities between earthly and heavenly glory, Baxter encourages contemplative practices that he hopes will enable his readers to participate in the glories of heaven already today.

Continuously, Baxter aims to narrow the gap that may separate him from heaven. He laments the many obstacles that stand in the way of meditation: "Awake then, O my drowsie Soul! who but an Owl or Mole would love this worlds uncomfortable darkness, when they are called forth to live in light?" (4.14.2). Having gone on at some length extolling the joys of contemplation, Baxter suddenly interrupts himself: "But alas, what a loss am I at in the midst of my contemplations! I thought my heart had all this while followed after, but I see it doth not." But he refuses to resign himself to this lapse: "Rather let me run back again, and look, and find, and chide this lazy loytering heart." Baxter turns to the Lord in incomprehension: "Lord, what's the matter that this work doth go on so heavily?" (4.14.2). He expresses frustration at his inability to rouse his soul properly to the contemplation of God. Speaking of his bodily life, Baxter comments: "This clod hath life to stir, but not to rise, Legs it hath, but wings it wanteth. As the feeble childe to the tender mother, it looketh up to thee, and stretcheth out the hands, and fain would have thee take it up. Though I cannot so freely say [My heart is with thee, my soul longeth after thee] yet I can say, I long of such a longing heart" (pt. 4, concl. [square brackets in original]). Desire is a crucial element in Baxter's

---

33. Baxter here reflects on the visions of Paul (2 Cor. 12:2–4), Peter (Matt. 17:4), Moses (Exod. 34:29–35), and John of Patmos. Baxter comments: "I confess these were all extraordinary foretastes, but little to the full Beatifical Vision" (*Saints everlasting rest* 4.11.11).

contemplative piety.[34] By no means ignorant of the chasm that often separates the believer here below from the glories above, Baxter was nonetheless convinced that if we acquaint ourselves with heaven today, we will be ready to live there in the future: "Fetch one walk daily in the New *Jerusalem!*" is one of Baxter's concluding pleas with his readers (pt. 4, concl.).[35] Or, as he also puts it, when a Christian is true to his profession, then "as *Moses* before he died, went up into Mount *Nebo*, to take a survey of the land of *Canaan*; so the Christian doth ascend this Mount of Contemplation, and take survey by Faith, of his Rest" (pt. 4, concl.).[36]

Isaac Ambrose's 1658 treatise, *Looking unto Jesus*, is equally contemplative in its focus on the reader's affections. As he moves through the various stages of Christ's saving work, Ambrose applies each of them to the believer by means of nine headings: knowing, considering, desiring, hoping, believing, loving, joying, praying, and conforming.[37] The nine aspects, therefore, reappear throughout the book, since they are ways in which the believer appropriates the various stages of Christ's redemptive work. The result of this setup is that Ambrose forces his readers constantly to ask how it is that they can "look unto" a particular aspect of Jesus's person and work. The vision of Jesus's redemption is always tied to our knowing it, our considering it, our desiring it, and so on.

After having discussed, for instance, the first eight modes of appropriating the mystery of the incarnation, Ambrose discusses our "conforming" to Christ's incarnation. He maintains that if we look to Christ in his incarnation, we will be transformed to become like him.[38] He works out in detail the various ways in which he believes this to be the case: As Christ was conceived in Mary's womb, so he must be conceived also in us (4.2.9). As Christ was sanctified in the Virgin's womb, so we must be sanctified in ourselves. As

---

34. Cf. Belden C. Lane's comment: "Desire, in Baxter's thinking, was absolutely fundamental to Puritan epistemology" ("Two Schools of Desire: Nature and Marriage in Seventeenth-Century Puritanism," *CH* 69 [2000]: 383).

35. Cf. Baxter's pithy word of encouragement: "Be sick of love now, that thou mayst be well of love there" (4.14.2).

36. For a similar passage reflecting on Moses—"who had a sight of *Canaan*, though he did not enter into it"—see Thomas Watson, *A body of practical divinity consisting of above one hundred seventy six sermons on the lesser catechism composed by the reverend assembly of divines at Westminster . . .* (London, 1692; Wing W1109), 486.

37. Schwanda points to Samuel Rutherford and Thomas Hooker as possible sources of Ambrose's ninefold classification (*Soul Recreation*, 49–50).

38. Ambrose, *Looking unto Jesus* 4.2.9. Hereafter, references from this work will be given in parentheses in the text.

Christ is by nature the Son of God, so we must by grace become sons of God. As Christ became the son of man, thereby humbling himself, so we should humble ourselves. And as the two natures of Christ were inseparably joined in one person, so our natures and persons must be "inseparably joyned and united to Christ, and thereby also to God," since our "spiritual and mystical union" with Christ is patterned on the "hypostatical union." Therefore, inasmuch as there is an "analogical proportion" between Christ and his saints, their lives are patterned on his (4.2.9). Christ's life becomes the matrix or framework that envelops the believer's life from beginning to end.

By no means is our appropriation of Christ's redemption a purely intellectual matter for Ambrose. Throughout the treatise, the twelfth-century mystic Saint Bernard of Clairvaux serves as the model for his contemplative piety.[39] At one point, Ambrose appeals to the Cistercian abbot with the words: "Consider that *looking unto Jesus* is the work of heaven; *it is begun in this life* (saith *Bernard*) *but it is perfected in that life to come*; not only Angels, but the Saints in glory do ever behold the face of God and Christ: if then we like not this work, how will we live in heaven? the dislike of this *duty* is a bar against our entrance; for the life of blessednesse is a life of vision, surely if we take no delight in this, heaven is no place for us" (1.3.7). Ambrose appreciates Bernard precisely because, like his medieval champion, he is convinced that when Christ comes to us in our contemplative practices, in some manner he renders the future present to our sight.

When he discusses the distinction between ocular and mental vision, Ambrose subdivides the latter into "notional and theoretical" vision, on the one hand, and "practical and experimental" vision, on the other hand (1.3.1). Whereas notional or theoretical looking is simply the "enlightning of our understandings," in practical or experimental looking we are affected by seeing spiritual things, so that "we desire, love, believe, joy, and embrace them." This is the look, according to Ambrose, that Paul longed for and that also Bernard preferred "above all looks." This knowledge is not a "swimming [superficial] knowledge of Christ, but an hearty feeling of Christs inward workings; it is not heady notions of Christ, but hearty motions towards Christ that are implied in this inward *looking*" (1.3.1). The reason, therefore, that Ambrose links the nine modes of appropriation to each stage of Christ's work of redemption is that these nine activities constitute our actual, experimental looking upon Jesus: "*Looking unto*, is the act; but how? it is such a *look* as includes all these acts, *knowing, considering, desiring, hoping, beleeving,*

39. Schwanda, *Soul Recreation*, 38–40.

loving, joying, enjoying of Jesus, and conforming to Jesus. It is such a look as stirs up affections in the heart, and the effects thereof in our life; it is such a *look* as leaves a quickening and enlivening upon the spirit; it is such a *look* as works us into a warme affection, raised resolution, an holy and upright conversation. Briefly, it is an inward, experimental *looking unto Jesus*" (1.3.2). By no means does Ambrose ignore "notional" or "theoretical" looking; his *Looking unto Jesus* gives evidence of familiarity not only with Bernard but also with Aquinas and other medieval authors. Ambrose's writing shows that he was a well-informed theologian and a careful thinker. Nonetheless, what really mattered to him was "practical" or "experimental" knowledge: the nine ways in which the believer is united to Jesus primarily have to do with one's affections and with the practice of holiness.

"Contemplative-Mystical Piety" (2): Thomas Watson and John Owen

Much like Baxter and Ambrose, so the Puritan preacher Thomas Watson (ca. 1620–1686) wanted to incite his readers' affections and desires. Watson—like Ambrose—was deeply influenced by Saint Bernard's bridal mysticism.[40] One can only truly appreciate Watson's affective piety, therefore, against the backdrop of Bernard and other medieval mystics. As Tom Schwanda puts it: "From the broader perspective of the history of emotions Watson's language resonates with the Roman Catholic mystical tradition."[41] As a result of his experiential mysticism, Watson linked up the doctrine of the beatific vision with the mystical and moral life of the Christian. He was keen to link the believer's life today with the future aim of seeing God.

In a sermon on Matthew 5:8 ("Blessed are the pure in heart, for they shall see God"), published in 1660 when he served as rector at Saint Stephen Walbrook in London, Watson directly links our purity with God's: "There is a *Primitive* Purity which is in God Originally and Essentially as light is in the Sun," and it is this purity of God that is the pattern of ours: "God is the Pattern and Prototype of all holinesse."[42] "Evangelical purity" results, according to Watson, when "grace is mingled with some sin" (223). Through this

---

40. Tom Schwanda, "'Sweetnesse in Communion with God': The Contemplative-Mystical Piety of Thomas Watson," *JHRP* 1, no. 2 (2015): 34–63.

41. Schwanda, "Saints' Desire," 77.

42. Thomas Watson, *The beatitudes: or A discourse upon part of Christs famous Sermon on the Mount . . .* (London, 1660; Wing [2nd ed.] W1107), 222. Hereafter, page references from this work will be given in parentheses in the text.

mingling of grace we come to share in God's holiness. Indeed, insists Watson, "God is in love with the pure heart, for he sees his own picture drawn there; Holinesse is a beame of God, it is the Angels glory" (227). Watson's sermon carefully dissects the heart, pointing out precisely what constitutes its purity (238–48).

This explanation of purity leads into a discussion of nine reasons why "heart-purity" is essential (248–53). One of them ties in directly to the sixth beatitude: "Heart purity makes way for heaven; the pure in heart *shall see God*" (252). Watson explains this as follows: "Happiness is nothing but the quintessence of holiness; purity of heart is heaven begun in a man" (252). In this way, Watson not only links purity with the beatific vision, but he actually claims that purity of heart constitutes the initial phase of beatitude. Also for Watson, therefore, we may say that the future reality is in some way already present today.

Regarding the beatific vision itself, Watson begins by presenting a brief outline. He describes the beatific vision as "the heaven of heaven" and treats it as "the quintessence of happiness" (259). The beatific vision will be partly intellectual (which allows separated souls to see God) and partly corporeal, in the sense that we will see Jesus Christ with corporeal eyes. Watson then briefly reflects on how it is possible to say with Job 19:26 that our own eyes will see God: "Put a back of steel to the glass, and you may see a face in it; so the humane nature of Christ is as it were a back of steel, through which we may see the glory of God [cf. 2 Cor. 4:6]" (260).[43] Watson appears to suggest that after the resurrection, Christ's human nature will turn the person of Christ into a mirror for us, in which we will see the glory of God himself.

Watson then presents in some detail nine "excellencies" that characterize the beatific vision (260–64). It will be transparent, transcendent, transforming, joyful, satisfying, unweariable, beneficial, perpetuated, and speedy. Part of the function of this list is simply to fill in particular details of what the beatific vision will be like. It becomes clear, for instance, that for Watson, as for Ambrose and Owen, Christ will be the means of our face-to-face vision of God.[44] It is also noteworthy that, on Watson's view, the saints will not partake of the divine essence;[45] the vision itself involves both the understanding

---

43. Watson repeats this in *A body of practical divinity*, 474.

44. Watson, *Beatitudes*, 260: "But through Christ we shall behold God in a very illustrious manner."

45. Watson, *Beatitudes*, 261–62: "The Saints by beholding the brightness of Gods glory, shall have a tincture of that glory upon them; not that they shall partake of Gods very *essence*; for

and the will;[46] and the saints' desire for God will be unending (seeing as the divine essence is infinite).[47]

More than simply trying to teach his readers, Watson's paean of praise on the beatific vision is designed to direct their imagination, and so to affect their desires and instill a longing to see God in Christ. To give but one example, Watson does not simply *explain* that the glory of the beatific vision will be transcendent, but he asks his readers to *imagine* it:

> Imagine what a blessed sight it will be to see Christ wearing the Robe of our humane nature, and to see that nature sitting in glory above the Angels. If God be so beautiful here in his Ordinances, Word, Prayer, Sacraments; if there be such excellency in him when we see him by the eye of faith through the prospective glass of a promise, O what will it be when we shall see him *face to face!* when Christ was transfigured on the Mount, he was full of glory, *Matth.* 17.2. If this *transfiguration* were so glorious, what will his *inauguration* be? what a glorious time will it be, when as it was said of *Mordecai*, we shall see him in the presence of his Father, *arrayed in royal apparel, and with a great Crown of gold upon his head,* Esth. 8.15. . . . There will be glory beyond *Hyperbole;* if the Sun were ten thousand times brighter than it is, it could not so much as shadow out this glory; in the heavenly Horizon we shall behold beauty in its first magnitude and highest elevation; there we shall *see the King in his glory* [Isa. 33:17]. All lights are but Eclipses, compared with that glorious Vision; *Appelles* pensil would blot, Angels tongues would but disparage it.[48]

---

as the iron in the fire becomes fire, yet remains iron still; so the Saints by beholding the lustre of Gods Majesty shall be glorious creatures, but yet creatures still."

46. After mentioning that Aquinas believed the *formalis ratio* of the beatific vision to be an act of the understanding (vision) while Ockham believed it to be an act of the will (fruition), Watson comments: "But certainly true blessedness comprehends both" (*Beatitudes*, 263).

47. Watson, *Beatitudes*, 263–64: "For the Divine Essence being infinite, there shall be every moment new and fresh delights springing forth from God into the glorified soul; the soul shall not so desire God, but it shall still be full; nor shall it be so full, but it shall still desire; so sweet will God be, that the more the Saints behold God, the more they will be ravished with desire and delight." Since Watson elsewhere quotes Gregory of Nyssa directly, it seems likely that he took his understanding of perpetual desire (*epektasis*) from Nyssen. Cf. above in chap. 3, section entitled "*The Life of Moses*: Vision as Perpetual Desire."

48. Watson, *Beatitudes*, 261. Apelles, the court painter of Emperors Philip and Alexander the Great in the fourth century BC, was the most famous painter of ancient Greece. For a very similar passage, see Watson, *Body of practical divinity*, 474.

This passage is worth quoting in full because it illustrates how Watson puts rhetoric in the service of his pastoral-theological aims. Through a series of comparisons—with the gospel promise, the transfiguration, and the sun— Watson encourages his readers to imagine an even greater glory. Thus, the imagination functions to lead the readers' minds and hearts upward toward the beatific vision itself—which, Watson assures his readers with his comment about "*Appelles* pensil" and "Angels tongues," will be ineffably glorious.

In John Owen, too, we see the immediate significance of the doctrine of the beatific vision for the piety and holiness of the believer—though, as the intellectual giant among the Puritans, Owen expressed the practical bent of his divinity in a more subdued manner than, say, Richard Baxter or Isaac Ambrose.[49] When in his *Christologia* (1679) Owen explains how Christ's glorified humanity differs in kind from the glory of the saints, he comments that all believers "are or should be conversant in their minds about these things, with longings, expectations and desires after nearer *Approaches* unto them, and enjoyments of them. And if we are not so, we are *earthly*, carnal and unspiritual. Yea the want of this frame, the neglect of this Duty, is the sole cause why many Professors are so *carnal* in their minds, and so worldly in their conversations."[50] For Owen, meditating on Christ's glory has everything to do with holy living.

We have already seen that Owen focuses the last three chapters of his *Meditations and discourses* (1684) on the differences between beholding Christ's glory by faith and by sight. The underlying assumption is that both faith and sight engage in some kind of beholding of Christ. Thus, Christ is already present to believers even if we only see him obscurely. Owen maintains that it is precisely the obscure character of our sight of Christ that drives us to him. Christ's position behind a wall, gazing at us through the windows and looking at us through the lattices (cf. Song 2:9), engenders in us a deep desire. The wall is our mortal state that must be demolished before we can see Christ "as he is."[51] Meanwhile, we see him through the "windows" of his ordinances. They are "full of refreshment unto the souls of them that do believe." But, adds Owen, this view is "imperfect, transient, and doth not abide: We are for the most part quickly left to bemoan what we

49. Cf. Packer's comment about Owen's writing style: "His studied unconcern about style in presenting his views, a conscientious protest against the self-conscious literary posturing of the age, conceals their common clarity and straightforwardness from superficial readers; but then, Owen did not write for superficial readers" (*A Quest for Godliness*, 193).

50. Owen, *Christologia*, 326.

51. Owen, *Meditations*, 177.

have lost." We also see Christ through the "lattices"—the preaching of the gospel—but no matter how believers are thus "ravished with the views" of "desirable beauties and glories" of Christ,[52] we still only see him "by parts, unsteadily and uneavenly."[53] The preaching of the Word and the celebration of the sacraments present us with a true vision of Christ—Christ is really present to the believer—but at the same time, these sightings of the beloved merely deepen the yearning for a steady and lasting vision of Christ.[54]

Beatitude and Glory in Abraham Kuyper

In significant respects, Abraham Kuyper (1837–1920), the progenitor of Dutch neo-Calvinism, introduces us to a markedly different theology and spirituality.[55] The prolific pastor, theologian, journalist, and prime minister gave rise to a tradition that focused less on the inner movements of the heart and more on Christian engagement with political, economic, and other cultural affairs. Neo-Calvinism is known for its robust embrace of the goodness of the created order and its claim that nothing in it escapes the sovereign rule of Jesus Christ. A neo-Calvinist worldview, therefore, is one that redeems all of life and claims it all for the service of Christ.[56] As we have seen in chapter 1, many within the neo-Calvinist tradition have concluded that all this active

52. Owen, *Meditations*, 177.

53. Owen, *Meditations*, 178.

54. Elsewhere, Owen distinguishes between three degrees in the manifestation of Christ's glory: (1) the *shadow*, under the law; (2) the *perfect image*, the complete revelation in a mirror; and (3) the *substance*, which is only in heaven (*Meditations*, 195). Owen immediately enjoins on his readers the duty "to breathe and pant after our deliverance from beholding it in the *Image* of it, that we may enjoy the *Substance* it self" (196).

55. Kuyper's works can be accessed online at kuyper.ptsem.edu. The best collection of Kuyper's key writings in English is *Abraham Kuyper: A Centennial Reader*, ed. James D. Bratt (Grand Rapids: Eerdmans, 1998). All translations of Kuyper are my own, unless otherwise indicated. For an excellent bibliography of Kuyper's writings, see Tjitze Kuipers, *Abraham Kuyper: An Annotated Bibliography, 1857–2010*, trans. Clifford Anderson with Dagmare Houniet, Brill's Series in Church History 55 (Leiden: Brill, 2011). A bibliography of secondary literature on Kuyper can be found online at kuyperbib.ptsem.edu.

56. Kuyper's understanding of a Christian "worldview" (*wereldbeschouwing*) has been hugely influential, not just in the Netherlands but also in North America, not least through his programmatic *Lectures on Calvinism: Six Lectures from the Stone Foundation Lectures Delivered at Princeton University*, 8th ed. (Grand Rapids: Eerdmans, 1987). Cf. Peter S. Heslam, *Creating a Christian Worldview: Abraham Kuyper's Lectures on Calvinism* (Grand Rapids: Eerdmans, 1998).

engagement makes little sense if it simply comes to a sudden halt at the eschaton and gives way to eternal contemplation of God in the beatific vision.

In some ways, these neo-Calvinist heirs rightly appeal to Kuyper's own theology. He does, in a number of places, highlight the this-worldly character of the new heavens and the new earth. The four volumes of *Van de voleinding* (*On the Consummation*) repeatedly denounce spiritualizing tendencies within the Christian tradition.[57] For Kuyper, the various elements of the created order—the natural world, the various spheres of life, and the numerous planets of the cosmos—are on a shared journey toward the final consummation.[58] Nonetheless, Kuyper also had a spiritual or mystical side, which permeates many of his theological writings, and particularly his meditations—something that scholars have only recently begun to explore in some depth.[59] Kuyper addresses the topic of the beatific vision throughout his writings, and its relative prominence makes clear that he had more than just a passing interest in the topic.

In the second part of this chapter, therefore, I want to draw attention to what we may call the "mystical" Kuyper. I hope to make clear that when we look beyond his political and cultural writings to his theology more broadly—both his dogmatic work and his numerous meditations[60]—the

57. Kuyper can at times be critical of the idea that in eternity we will only be singing psalms ("In het huis mijns Vaders zijn vele woningen," in *In Jezus ontslapen: Meditatiën* [Amsterdam: Höveker & Wormser, 1902], 36; *Dictaten Dogmatiek*, vol. 5, *Locus de Consummatione Saeculi*, 2nd ed. [1892; reprint, Kampen: Kok, 1913], 320). Nonetheless, direct worship of God is for Kuyper our ultimate goal. He comments, for instance, that the sound of musical instruments in our earthly worship penetrates the heavenly spheres, "where angels eternally pluck golden harps and everything flows into one ocean of worship around God's throne" ("Looft Hem met snarenspel en orgel," in *Nabij God te zijn*, 2 vols. [Kampen: Kok, 1908], 2:30).

58. Kuyper, *Van de voleinding*, ed. H. H. Kuyper, 4 vols. (Kampen: Kok, 1929–1931), 1:351–52.

59. Several scholars have analyzed Kuyper's two-volume set of meditations from 1908, *Nabij God te zijn* (*To Be Near unto God*): Kick Bras, *Een met de ene: Protestantse mystiek van Abraham Kuyper tot Maria de Groot* (Vught, Neth.: Skandalon, 2013), 17–42; Ad de Bruijne, "Midden in de wereld verliefd op God: Kuypers aanzet tot een neocalvinistische spiritualiteit," in *Godsvrucht in geschiedenis: Bundel ter gelegenheid van het afscheid van prof. dr. Frank van der Pol als hoogleraar aan de Theologische Universiteit Kampen*, ed. Erik A. de Boer and Harm J. Boiten (Heerenveen, Neth.: Groen, 2015), 441–53; George Harinck, "'Met de telephoon onzen God oproepen': Kuypers meditaties uit 1905 en 1906," in Boer and Boiten, *Godsvrucht in geschiedenis*, 454–65.

60. Kuyper deals with the beatific vision not only in his meditations but also in his dogmatic theology. Though he usually does not acknowledge his sources, his indebtedness to the Reformed scholastics with regard to the beatific vision is clear when he distinguishes pilgrim knowledge (*theologia stadii* or *viatorum*), the knowledge of Christ (*theologia unionis*), and

Kuyper who emerges is one who, along with the great tradition of the church, regarded the beatific vision as the ultimate goal of the Christian pilgrimage. For Kuyper, our future rests in nothing less than God himself. Part of the purpose of this section, therefore, is to retrieve a side of Kuyper that is regularly undervalued and is often simply unknown.

At the same time, we will see that Kuyper's doctrine of the beatific vision significantly diverged from that of the Puritans we have just looked at. On the one hand, Kuyper shared with the earlier Puritans the conviction that already today we may have a foretaste of the beatific vision. On the other hand, Kuyper posited a sharp disjunction between the beatitude (*zaligheid*) that the saints obtain immediately after death and the glory (*heerlijkheid*) that follows the resurrection of the body. The former is characterized by fellowship with Christ, the latter by the beatific vision of the eternal Being (*Eeuwige Wezen*) of God himself. The result is an unfortunate isolation of the beatific vision from Christology. Christ, for Kuyper, is not the one in whom (or even through whom) we will eternally see God.

For Kuyper, beatitude (*zaligheid*) concerns the saints' status (*staat*), while glory (*heerlijkheid*) has to do with their rank (*stand*).[61] Kuyper distinguishes the two by saying that we obtain beatitude at death, while glory—something far superior—will be ours only when Christ returns and our souls will be reunited with their bodies. Unfortunately, this distinction isn't always properly recognized. Kuyper chastises his church's confessional statement, the Heidelberg Catechism, because in speaking about the resurrection it "is completely silent about glory (*heerlijkheid*); the creedal contents are explained in a strictly spiritual manner and are limited to the beatitude (*zaligheid*) that follows immediately after death. Now, *beatitude* and *glory* are not the same. Beatitude concerns the spiritual life, while glory aims at the state of happiness that has been prepared for us in external matters. And so beatitude can be enjoyed immediately upon death, whereas glory can be enjoyed only after

---

the beatific knowledge of vision (*theologia visionis* or *patriae*) (*Dictaten Dogmatiek*, vol. 1, *Locus de Deo*, 2nd ed. [1891; reprint, Kampen: Kok, 1910], pt. 1.75–76; *Encyclopædie der heilige godgeleerdheid*, vol. 2 [Amsterdam: Wormser, 1894], 190–96). For discussion of this threefold division of theology in Reformed scholasticism, see Rehnman, *Divine Discourse*, 57–71.

61. Kuyper, *Dictaten Dogmatiek*, 5:316. The translation of the Dutch term *zaligheid* is difficult. I mostly translate it as "beatitude" because both the Dutch and the English words denote happiness and because of the direct connection of the term with the theology of the beatific vision. At the same time, Kuyper often associates *zaligheid*—or, at least, an undue focus on it—with a pietistic focus on being freed from sin, and the word "salvation" conveys this better than "beatitude."

the resurrection of the body."[62] According to Kuyper, the catechism should have focused not just on the spiritual beatitude (*zaligheid*) of the intermediate state, but also on the glory (*heerlijkheid*) of our earthly, embodied, and communal future after the second coming.[63] Instead of focusing only on our own beatitude—a rather self-interested, anthropocentric approach[64]—we should keep in mind first and foremost the honor and glory of God.

For Kuyper, then, the beatitude of separated souls is not yet *perfect* blessedness. He repeatedly draws his readers' attention to the souls under the altar, who continue to cry, "How long?" (Rev. 6:11).[65] They do not yet have perfect glory. Similarly, when he reflects on the Pauline contrast between today's partial knowledge and the perfection of the future (1 Cor. 13:9–10), Kuyper explains that we should not imagine that we will have this full knowledge immediately after death: "Paul does not say that τὸ ἐκ μέρους [the partial] will disappear at the point of death. No, it remains also after death; it continues until τὸ τέλειον [the perfect] comes. Then it will pass away."[66] The intermediate state is characterized, according to Kuyper, by a desire for greater glory and perfection. He concludes, therefore, that not only love but also hope will continue into eternal life—that is to say, until the resurrection, when those who now are blessed will be glorified.[67]

The change from beatitude to glory is more than simply the reunification of body and soul. After the resurrection, our communion with God will be direct, so that it will no longer be mediated through Christ: "Until the resurrection from the dead, the blessed in heaven do not have direct communion with the triune God, but only have communion through Christ, the

---

62. Kuyper, *Van de voleinding*, 1:220.

63. Cf. Kuyper, *Van de voleinding*, 1:309: "With reference to his kingdom, Jesus speaks of a meal in which he will drink the wine new. We consistently get the picture of a life that in no way is just spiritual or internal, but that will also be external and physical. We may even say that whatever has been revealed to us about the future glory has reference to things that will be observed outwardly in physical form. *Beatitude* is spiritual, but *glory* comes to human beings from the outside, so that there are two distinct elements. Israel's Messiah comes *for the world* and targets the entire world." Cf. 1:244–45; 3:28.

64. Kuyper, *Van de voleinding*, 1:246; 1:333.

65. E.g., Kuyper, "Overkleed te worden," in *In de schaduwe des doods: Meditatiën voor de krankenkamer en bij het sterfbed* (Amsterdam: Wormser, 1893), 285; "Nu ken ik ten dele," in *In Jezus ontslapen*, 174; *E voto Dordraceno: Toelichting op den Heidelbergschen Catechismus*, vol. 2 (Amsterdam: Wormser, 1893), 230.

66. Kuyper, *Dictaten Dogmatiek*, 5:318.

67. Kuyper, "Overkleed te worden," 285: "Therefore, not only *love*, but also *hope* accompanied them through death and the grave into eternity."

Mediator. According to 1 Corinthians 15:24–28, at the consummation of all things, Christ will cease to be viceroy and will deliver the kingdom to God the Father. Then also the Son himself will be subjected, to him who put all things in subjection under him. Then we will have direct communion with the triune God, 'that God (himself) may be all in all.'"[68] We have seen that Ambrose and Owen similarly used this passage to insist that Christ's role as mediator will come to an end at the second coming. But they both claimed that Christ continues forever as the "means" through whom the saints will see God. Kuyper does not make such a link between Christ and the beatific vision. Instead, after discussing the end of Christ's kingship, he speaks about the saints' eternal, direct communion with the "Eternal Being" (*het Eeuwige Wezen*) and of the vision and enjoyment of the triune God (*visio et fruitio Dei Triunius*).[69] According to Kuyper, therefore, the blessed will experience an increase in salvation at the resurrection, not only because body and soul will be reunited, but also because now, for the first time, they will see and enjoy God himself.

Kuyper's sharp distinction between beatitude (*zaligheid*) and glory (*heerlijkheid*) corresponds to a twofold longing of the believer: On the one hand, believers look forward to communion with Christ at the point of death. On the other hand, they anticipate his return and the subsequent beatific vision. So, believers first of all long to be with Jesus when they die—although Kuyper makes clear that this does not mean a *vision* of Jesus, since after death the souls will be separated from their bodies.[70] Rather, maintains Kuyper, those who have died have "active fellowship" with the mediator.[71] Thus, although they may not *see* Jesus in the intermediate state, they do have spiritual *fellowship* with him, and so for Kuyper it is entirely appropriate for the apostle Paul to long to be with Christ after death (cf. Phil. 1:23).

Furthermore, although we may not see Jesus right away after death, in his parousia we will see him, and at this time he will usher in the state of glory. In this sense, Kuyper claims that we *do* long for an actual vision of Jesus. In a meditation on 1 Corinthians 13:12 in his 1891 book *Voor een distel een mirt (A Myrtle for a Brier)*, Kuyper suggests that our longing reaches beyond the preached Word to Jesus himself. Kuyper alludes to an "immeasurable distance" (*onmetelijken afstand*) between the weak shining of the Word and the

68. Kuyper, *Dictaten Dogmatiek*, 5:315.

69. Kuyper, *Dictaten Dogmatiek*, 5:315.

70. Cf. Kuyper's comment: "After death, a soul in heaven cannot see Jesus, who has a body, but is able to have communion with him" (*Dictaten Dogmatiek*, 5:317).

71. Kuyper, *E voto Dordraceno*, 2:228.

full radiance of heaven itself,[72] and he compares the difference to the "juxta-position between a *portrait* and the *actual person* himself. . . . The continual gazing at the Word stimulates in your soul the longing for *Jesus himself.* Then you no longer want to *read* about Jesus, but you want to possess *Jesus* himself. Then you no longer find rest even in burning *faith*, but long to *behold.*"[73] Paradoxically, the Word feeds dissatisfaction with itself, because it fuels our longing to possess Jesus as the reality proclaimed by the Word.

Direct Knowledge of the Eternal Being

In a sense, it is odd, however, that Kuyper fuels his readers' desire to see Jesus, because after his return it is no longer Jesus but the essence of God that the saints will see and enjoy. On the last day, according to Kuyper, we will turn away from the mirror to the "actual being" (*wezen zelf*) of God's perfections.[74] Although Kuyper does not explain what he has in mind when he talks about seeing the "Eternal Being" (*Eeuwige Wezen*) of God, there is little doubt that he means seeing the divine essence. This is clear from his section on "the essence of God" in his discussion of the doctrine of God.[75] The section heading, "*De essentia Dei*," indicates that he treats the Dutch term *wezen* as the equivalent of the Latin *essentia*.[76] To see the Eternal Being (*Eeuwige Wezen*) means, therefore, to see the essence of God. On this point, Kuyper was in line with much of the Western tradition following Saint Augustine.

How did Kuyper think it possible for finite creatures to see the infinite being of God? In at least one place, the Dutch theologian makes clear that vision of the divine essence does not imply ability to "understand" God. As he discusses the Heidelberg Catechism's treatment of the doctrine of the Trinity, Kuyper cautions that the mystery of the Trinity is such that we cannot understand (*begrijpen*) even a part of it. He then distinguishes be-

---

72. Kuyper, "Door een spiegel in een duistere rede," in *Voor een distel een mirt: Geestelijke overdenkingen bij den Heiligen Doop, het doen van belijdenis en het toegaan tot het Heilig Avondmaal* (Amsterdam: Wormser, 1891), 9.

73. Kuyper, "Door een spiegel," 9–10.

74. Kuyper, "Nu ken ik ten deele," 178.

75. Kuyper, *Dictaten Dogmatiek*, vol. 1, pt. I.124–58.

76. It seems clear that Kuyper's general predilection for the terms "the Eternal One" (*de Eeuwige*) and "the Eternal Being" (*het Eeuwige Wezen*) explains the absence of the language of seeing the divine "essence," and so we may conclude that Kuyper held to the belief that after the resurrection we will see divine essence (which he equated with God's *Eeuwige Wezen*).

tween understanding (*begrijpen*) and knowing (*kennen*) God. Understanding the essence of God isn't possible even in the eschaton.[77] In eternal life we will *know* God; we will not *understand* him.[78] It is probably fair to say that Kuyper not only cautioned here against intellectualism in general, but also attempted to safeguard the creator-creature distinction. Claiming that in the hereafter we will be able to *understand* God—or, as others in the tradition would have put it, *comprehend* God—would put the creature in the place of the creator. Kuyper, therefore, did not mean to subvert divine transcendence when he suggested that beatific knowledge is knowledge of the divine essence.[79] Seeing or knowing the divine essence is not the same as understanding it.

We may not ever be able to understand God, but our beatific knowledge of him will, according to Kuyper, nonetheless be direct or immediate in character. Just as God always already knows our essence, so we will also come to know his. Paul makes clear that our future knowledge of God will be patterned on his knowledge of us: "Now I know in part; then I shall know fully, even as I have been fully known" (1 Cor. 13:12). For Kuyper, the change from seeing in a mirror dimly (and having partial knowledge) to knowing fully means that, even though our intellectual faculty remains the same, our earthly knowledge will be "destroyed" (*vernietigd*), so that the *mode* of our new knowledge will be quite different from our current mode of knowing.[80] Indeed, the manner of our knowing will undergo such a change that it will come to resemble God's way of knowing us. According to 1 Corinthians 13:12,

77. Kuyper, *E voto Dordraceno*, 1:145.

78. Kuyper's argument at this point runs into difficulties. In the second volume of his *Encyclopædie*, as he argues against a contemplative (defined as nonlogical) vision of God in the hereafter, Kuyper explicitly makes the point that our eschatological knowledge of God will be logical (since God is logical) and that there is only a gradual difference (*gradueel verschil*) between God's knowledge and ours (*Encyclopædie*, 2:194)! This eschatological logical knowledge that Kuyper claims we will have seems to be the same as the intellectual "understanding" that he denounces in his commentary on the Heidelberg Catechism.

79. Nonetheless, Kuyper again faces a problem. When he denies that we will ever *understand* God's essence, this raises the question: Will we be able fully to *know* his essence? Kuyper fails to explain how our beatific *knowledge* of God's essence respects his transcendence. Whereas Thomas Aquinas at least tries to explain this by distinguishing between attaining and comprehending the divine essence (*ST* I, q. 12, a. 7; I-II, q. 4, a. 3), Kuyper fails to qualify his suggestion that we will have direct knowledge of God's essence. To avoid a lapse into pantheism, Kuyper would at least have to put in place some sort of "safeguard," along the lines of Aquinas (or, even better in my view, he might interpret the vision of God's essence christologically).

80. Kuyper, *Dictaten Dogmatiek*, vol. 1, pt. III.11–12. Kuyper similarly maintains that our intellectual faculty will remain the same in *Encyclopædie*, 2:194.

"our intellectual faculty will know in a manner that approaches the way in which God's knowledge operates."[81]

Kuyper explains the Pauline image of the mirror by saying that in the eschaton we will turn around, away from the mirror, in order to face God himself: "It is not the case," says Kuyper, "that one intellectual faculty is removed while another comes about. Rather, the human being is turned around, with his back to the mirror and his face to the person."[82] As a result, we will see the Eternal Being directly or immediately. All mediation will disappear as we come to know the very essence of God.[83] Kuyper treats the beatific vision as a direct vision of the essence of God.

The result of this emphasis on immediacy is, unfortunately, that Kuyper disconnects Christ from the vision of God. Like Ambrose and Owen, he ties Christ's role as mediator—prophet, priest, and king—exclusively to our postlapsarian situation. The prophetic, priestly, and royal roles of Adam and Eve functioned *directly*, without mediation, claims Kuyper.[84] And once all sin has been left behind, our threefold office will again function directly, without mediation.[85] Comments Kuyper: "The blessed in their vision are not granted a knowledge acquired through means, but a knowledge reached without means—immediate knowledge, through seeing πρόσωπον πρὸς πρόσωπον [face-to-face], as the apostle puts it."[86] Unlike Ambrose and Owen, Kuyper does not distinguish between "mediation" and "means." Once Christ's role as mediator is finished, what results is direct access to God. For Kuyper, the beatific vision is a direct vision of the essence of God, which as such leaves the person of Christ behind.

Although the vision of God will be direct or immediate, this does not mean that Kuyper thinks it will be an intuitive, contemplative vision, which bypasses the senses. We have already seen that he doesn't think believers will see Christ after death, because the souls in that state are separate from their

81. Kuyper, *Dictaten Dogmatiek*, vol. 1, pt. III.12. Cf. vol. 1, pt. I.166.

82. Kuyper, *Dictaten Dogmatiek*, vol. 1, pt. III.12. For almost identical language (turning around from the mirror to the person), see *De gemeene gratie*, vol. 1 (Leiden: Donner, 1902), 480: "Nu ken ik ten deele," 178.

83. Cf. Kuyper, "Nu ken ik ten deele," 176.

84. Kuyper, *E voto Dordraceno*, 1:287.

85. Kuyper, *E voto Dordraceno*, 1:288. Kuyper appeals to 1 Cor. 13:12, John 16:26, and 1 Cor. 15:28. To be sure, in at least one place Kuyper suggests that in the future the Father will be shown to us "in Christ" ("Hetgeen onze oogen gezien hebben: Het sacrament en ons oog," in *Voor een distel een mirt*, 15).

86. Kuyper, *Dictaten Dogmatiek*, vol. 1, pt. I.76. Kuyper similarly speaks of direct knowledge in the eschaton in *Encyclopædie*, 2:194.

bodies; Kuyper never speaks of separated souls seeing God (say, with a spiritual vision). Kuyper does speak of postmortem *fellowship* of the separated souls with Christ, but he does not equate this fellowship with a *vision* of Christ (or of God). It appears as though for Kuyper there simply is no beatific vision of any kind for separated souls—at least, he never mentions any such vision.

Quite possibly the reason for this absence of vision among separated souls is Kuyper's suggestion that the beatific vision will be a vision of body and soul together. In at least one place in his *Dictaten Dogmatiek* (*Dogmatic Dictations*), Kuyper posits rather unambiguously (and in deviation from the Augustinian tradition) that this vision and enjoyment of God will be an act not only of the soul but also of the body: it will be an act of the entire person. Kuyper appeals to 1 John 3:2, which states that "we shall see him as he is," and he insists that this refers to "a direct seeing with the bodily eye—of course not apart from spiritual vision, for in the state of perfection, the action of the eye of the soul and of the body is one."[87] Kuyper reminds his readers that it is in this same way that Moses also saw God's back (Exod. 33:20–23). Although he immediately adds that God does not have a body, Kuyper nonetheless continues: "God descended on Horeb in a creaturely fashion, so that the outward grasp of the senses perceived that there was a sign of the *praesentia Dei*." In similar fashion, claims Kuyper, we will see the presence of God in the brilliance and majesty of the mediator at Christ's return.[88] To what extent Kuyper actually meant to insist on this bodily vision of God's essence remains unclear. To my knowledge, he does not refer to it anywhere else; nor does he explain *how* he believes physical and spiritual sight will be united in the beatific vision. Still, considering his criticisms of what he considered an undue focus on beatitude (*zaligheid*) in the tradition, I suspect that Kuyper may have had in mind a state of glory (*heerlijkheid*) in which body and soul will be reunited and in their glorified state will see the very essence of God.

"Mysticism of the Heart": Experiential Piety

As a Reformed theologian, Kuyper strongly objected to any and all bypassing of divine revelation—a problem that he observed especially in the Eastern

---

87. Kuyper, *Dictaten Dogmatiek*, 5:317.

88. Kuyper, *Dictaten Dogmatiek*, 5:317. Just two pages earlier, Kuyper had said that after the resurrection we no longer see God through the mediator. I suspect that Kuyper is not now suggesting that we *will* see God through the mediator, after all, but rather that we will be able to see the divine nature of Christ directly (both physically and spiritually)—though it remains odd that he speaks here of Christ as the mediator.

Church's isolation of the work of the Spirit from God's revelation in his Son[89] and in medieval practices of contemplation.[90] Whenever he discusses these issues, Kuyper is quick to remind his readers of the importance of revelation, objecting to any and all attempts to circumvent it: "Whether it's called meditation, contemplation, or whatever, it always makes an attempt to penetrate to the essence (*wezen*) of the majestic God apart from revealed means. It cannot accept that God is discovered only through the veil of revelation. It wants to push aside that veil, or that curtain, and it doesn't stop until it arrives at the fancy that it now possesses God, sees God, and enjoys God directly, immediately, without any intermediate operation."[91] Whereas Puritans such as Baxter, Ambrose, and Watson reappropriated medieval practices of meditation and contemplation, Kuyper treated them with suspicion, worried as he was about attempts to access God directly, apart from the divinely appointed means of revelation.

None of this is to say that Kuyper opposed mysticism as such. He distinguished between false mysticism (*mysticisme*) and true mysticism (*mystiek*).[92] Whereas he detected the former in Eastern Orthodoxy and medieval contemplative practices, he observed the latter in the Calvinist experiential mysticism that he had come to know in his first congregation in Beesd. As a result of his encounter with experiential Calvinism—as well as his intellectual appropriation of German Romanticism[93]—Kuyper became convinced

89. Kuyper, *Drie kleine vossen* (Kampen: Kok, 1901), 47–48. Cf. also the sharp comments on p. 74 against Russian "fanaticism" (*dweperijen*).

90. In his *Encyclopædie* (1:80–81), Kuyper has harsh words for Hugh of Saint Victor, who moves from *cogitatio*, via *meditatio*, to *contemplatio*, and who distinguishes between the "eye of the flesh" (*oculus carnis*), the "eye of the intellect" (*oculus rationis*), and the "eye of contemplation" (*oculus contemplationis*). Kuyper objects that in Hugh, the human *ratio* is transcended by contemplation as a higher form of the intellect (*kenvermogen*), so that contemplation takes over where reason leaves off.

91. Kuyper, *Drie kleine vossen*, 59.

92. Kuyper, *Drie kleine vossen*, 47. We should note that the term "mysticism" (*mysticisme*) always has a negative connotation for Kuyper. Since the English language does not have two distinct terms for *mystiek* and *mysticisme*, I have taken recourse to the expressions "true mysticism" and "false mysticism." Kuyper's 1901 book *Drie kleine vossen* deals with three dangers in the spiritual life: intellectualism (*intellectualisme*), mysticism (*mysticisme*), and activism (*practicisme*).

93. While Kuyper's spirituality was certainly shaped by the pious, experiential (*bevindelijke*) Calvinists of his congregation in Beesd (1863–1867), the legendary impact of a woman named Pietje Baltus has probably been exaggerated. We should not lose sight of the impact of German Romanticism and idealism through Kuyper's university training. See J. Vree, "More Pierson and Mesmer, and Less Pietje Baltus: Kuyper's Ideas on Church, State, Society and Culture

that intellectual knowledge (*kennen*) cannot replace spiritual aptitude (*kunnen*).[94] Genuine appropriation of the Scriptures yields "mysticism of the heart" (*mystiek van ons hart*).[95] Kuyper puts it as follows: "That Christ exists, who he was and is, what he did and suffered, how he now lives in heaven to pray for us—these are things that the Word, and only the Word, teaches you. But your personal bond with Christ, and his with you, this is caused, not by the Word but by mysticism of the heart. This is what Calvin called *unio mystica*, i.e., the mystical union and incorporation into Christ."[96] Kuyper, deeply influenced by the piety (*bevindelijkheid*) of experiential Calvinism, refused to let go of the subjective (*onderwerpelijk*), mystical element of the faith for the sake of the objective (*voorwerpelijk*) truths of the gospel. For Kuyper, the two elements invariably went hand in hand.[97]

Kuyper's spirituality, therefore, was characterized by a certain tension: On the one hand, he believed God does not allow us to bypass divine revelation in order to contemplate him directly. On the other hand, he cared deeply about a personal bond with God and about a mysticism of the heart. The tension becomes especially poignant as he discusses the particulars of experiential communion with God in his meditations. In the first meditation of his celebrated two-volume work *Nabij God te zijn* (*To Be Near unto God*) (1908),[98] Kuyper meditates on Psalm 73:28 ("But for me it is good to be near God"). He begins by distinguishing between "having a love for God" and "loving God."[99] It is only through "loving God" that we reach God himself and arrive at "fellowship" (*gemeenschap*) with the Eternal One—"hidden communion" (*verborgen omgang*) with God.[100] In "loving God," the being

---

during the First Years of His Ministry (1863–1866)," in *Kuyper Reconsidered: Aspects of His Life and Work*, ed. Cornelis van der Kooi and Jan de Bruijn, VU Studies on Protestant History 3 (Amsterdam: VU Uitgeverij, 1999), 299–310. See also James D. Bratt, *Abraham Kuyper: Modern Calvinist, Christian Democrat* (Grand Rapids: Eerdmans, 2013), 32–35.

94. Kuyper, *Drie kleine vossen*, 33.

95. Kuyper, *Drie kleine vossen*, 67.

96. Kuyper, *Drie kleine vossen*, 67–68.

97. Kuyper often purposely ties these two elements together. See, e.g., Kuyper, *Drie kleine vossen*, 29, 35–36, 67, 70.

98. This meditation has been republished in M. E. Brinkman and C. van der Kooi, eds., *Het calvinisme van Kuyper en Bavinck*, Sleutelteksten in godsdienst en theologie 22 (Zoetermeer, Neth.: Meinema, 1997), 31–35.

99. Kuyper, "Het is mij goed nabij God te wezen," in *Nabij God te zijn*, 2 vols. (Kampen: Kok, 1908), 1:1.

100. Kuyper, "Het is mij goed," 1:2.

of God becomes personal to us, so that we meet him and come to know him in intimate communion.[101]

This love of God, claims Kuyper, means that the eye sees him and the heart becomes aware of him, so that any and all separation from God falls away.[102] Kuyper expresses the mystical experience as follows:

> You can be "near" to God in one of two ways: either you feel drawn into the heavens, or God descends from those heavens and visits you where you are, in your desolation, your cross, or your joys, which you experienced. That "nearness" indicates that there is oh, so much that separates you from God—so much that yet again isolates you, so that you are lonely and feel abandoned, because your God has left you again or because you have moved away from God. But "nearness" also means that this makes you restless, that you can't handle it, so that everything draws you back again to him—until that which caused the separation, falls away again. Then there is a renewed encounter, then he comes *near* you again, then you know that you are *near* unto God yet again. Then that blessedness (*dat zalige*) is back again—that blessedness (*dat zalige*), which is better than anything else. Then it is *good* again, oh, so *good*, above all, to be *near* unto your God. It is only at certain moments that we enjoy this blessedness (*zaligheid*) here. But beyond this, what awaits you is the happy blessedness (*gelukzaligheid*) of eternal life, when that being "*near unto God*" will always be yours—forever with him in the Father's house.[103]

This description of the mystical life cannot but remind one of Augustine's account, in his *Confessions*, of his brief mystical experience in Ostia, which he was unable to sustain for long.[104] Kuyper seems to align himself with the African bishop: in this life, mystical anticipations of the beatific vision are only brief, since, after every experience, we fall back again into our ordinary lives. Kuyper suggests that to experience such nearness to God, while still on earth, places the believer in line with Jacob, Moses, David, and Paul.[105] Thus, although his language is tempered—perhaps because he had never experienced the vision of God directly himself—in his most mystical moments

---

101. Kuyper, "Het is mij goed," 1:2.
102. Kuyper, "Het is mij goed," 1:4.
103. Kuyper, "Het is mij goed," 1:4.
104. *Conf.* 9.10.23.
105. Kuyper, "Het is mij goed," 1:5.

Kuyper appears to intimate that believers may experience a direct, mystical encounter with God.

In line with this, several of Kuyper's meditations explicitly refer to personal, intimate contact with the Eternal Being (*Eeuwige Wezen*) of God. Kuyper speaks, for instance, of a "touch" (*aanraking*) between the soul and the Eternal Being.[106] God's work in one's heart, Kuyper continues, must be discerned, discovered, and even felt personally by means of a "spiritual, direct perception."[107] In this way, it is possible to know "directly from yourself" (*rechtstreeks uit u zelf*) that God exists.[108] When Kuyper reflects on Asaph's words in Psalm 73:23, "Nevertheless, I am continually with you," he makes the intriguing parenthetical comment: "As long as we exercise extreme care, one of the benefits of silent prayer may be that we lose ourselves in spiritual contemplation of the Infinite Being."[109] This seems like a fairly straightforward affirmation of mystical contemplation. Apparently, some people may already in this life experience immediate contact with the very being of God.[110] In his most mystical moments, it is hard to distinguish Kuyper's spirituality from the contemplative-mystical piety among the Puritans.

Clearly, there is some tension between Kuyper's mysticism and his sharp denunciations of meditation and contemplation. But the tension does not amount to a blatant contradiction. When Kuyper harps at ill-conceived attempts directly or immediately to reach the being (*wezen*) of God, the immediate object of his ire is the neglect of divine revelation—less so the desire for direct, intimate communion with God per se. Kuyper's mysticism does allow—even encourages—personal, intimate contact with the being of God already in this life. Certainly, he designed his meditations in an effort to help draw his readers into personal contact with God himself.

---

106. Kuyper, "Uw naam worde geheiligd," in *Nabij God te zijn*, 1:297.

107. Kuyper, "Uw naam worde geheiligd," 1:297.

108. Kuyper, "Uw naam worde geheiligd," 1:298. For this passage, see also Bruijne, "Midden in de wereld," 444–45.

109. Kuyper, "Ik zal dan gedurig bij U zijn," in *Nabij God te zijn*, 2:5.

110. Kuyper makes a similar suggestion when he discusses the inner-Trinitarian operations of the divine persons. He argues that this is a topic that is best approached, not by way of dogmatic reasoning, "but only by way of communion with the eternal Being along the mystical path of contemplation and meditation" (*Dictaten Dogmatiek*, vol. 2, *Locus de Creatione*, 2nd ed. [1891; reprint, Kampen: Kok, 1911], pt. I.15).

Conclusion

In some sense, Kuyper's theology of the beatific vision was fairly traditional: he treated the beatific vision as a direct encounter with the Eternal Being (*Eeuwige Wezen*) of God, with which he meant that we will see the essence of God—even though he does not use the traditional language of the essence of God. Kuyper also appears to have followed the broad tradition of Western thought in affirming that Moses and Paul saw the essence of God. Although sharply critical of Russian Orthodox mysticism as well as of Western medieval treatments of meditation and contemplation, Kuyper nonetheless did recognize the value of contemplation, particularly as he had witnessed it in the experiential piety (*bevindelijkheid*) of traditional Calvinism, an affective piety that was similar to the contemplative mysticism of Puritanism. Thus, there was much in the spirituality of the earlier tradition from which, in his more mystical moments, Kuyper was able to draw.

Kuyper was much too deeply grounded in the theological tradition and was far too careful a thinker simply to dismiss the earlier tradition's focus on the beatific vision as an otherworldly, Platonic holdover from another era. In many ways, recent neo-Calvinists have simply remade Kuyper in their own image by suggesting that he was mostly interested in this-worldly transformation and that he primarily had in mind cultural transformation also when he thought of the eschatological future. Kuyper's understanding of eschatology was much more in line with the great tradition of the church than is commonly recognized. As for the earlier tradition, so for Kuyper, God himself constitutes our final end. And if the end determines the means, then the beatific vision must give shape to our theology and spirituality.

At the same time, Kuyper's doctrine of the beatific vision was, in some ways, idiosyncratic. He was obviously displeased with the large role that beatitude (*zaligheid*)—the soul's salvation immediately after death—played in many people's everyday spirituality. Thus, whereas the Western tradition has typically maintained that the saints will obtain the beatific vision—direct, intuitive apprehension of the essence of God—immediately after death, Kuyper did not speak of *any* kind of vision in connection with the intermediate state. He thought it appropriate for believers to long for heavenly beatitude (*zaligheid*) after death, but for Kuyper this involved *communion* with Christ, not *vision* of Christ. He never used the language of vision to describe the soul's postmortem state of separation from the body. In Kuyper's account, the beatific vision is reserved for the resurrection life of glory (*heerlijkheid*).

Only then will we see the "Eternal Being" of God. Kuyper's denial of any kind of vision of God in the intermediate state put him at odds with the broad tradition of the church.

Kuyper's doctrine of the beatific vision does have elements that we may characterize as sacramental. In particular, by acknowledging a proper role for mysticism (*mystiek*) of the heart, Kuyper recognized that the reality of the eschatological beatific vision may be proleptically experienced already in this life. We could say that for Kuyper, the heavenly future becomes present already on earth. In this sense, we could almost say that Kuyper's discovery of the experiential (*bevindelijk*) mysticism of traditional Dutch Calvinism turned him into a Dutch Puritan. At the same time, it can hardly be denied that the Puritan authors we have discussed were far more attuned than Kuyper to the role of Christology in every phase of our postmortem existence. Theologians such as Ambrose, Watson, and Owen realized that if union with Christ is a foretaste of heaven, then it is impossible that in heaven the beatific vision leaves him behind: just as today our mysticism of the heart is christologically shaped—it is in and through union with Christ that we are united to God—so too in the end we are united to God only in and through Christ.

To be sure, Puritans such as Ambrose and Owen were entirely right to suggest, with an appeal to 1 Corinthians 15:24–28, that in the end Christ will give the kingdom to the Father, so that Christ's role as mediator will come to an end. And it is important to recognize that only in this world do sacraments serve to lead us to the beatific vision. Just as Christ will no longer be our mediator after the resurrection, so too his sacramental role will come to an end. This does not imply, however, that Christ himself will also be left behind: Christ is not only *sacramentum* but also *res*. The Puritans rightly argued, therefore, that the ultimate reality of seeing God face-to-face is nothing else than seeing Christ.

Puritan divines were often wary of asserting that in the eschaton we will see the essence of God. This is partly due to their recognition that the vision of God is always a vision of Christ. Ambrose, Watson, and Owen were all simply too christological in their approach to speak at length about seeing the divine essence. For the Puritans, unlike for Kuyper (and, it will be recalled, unlike for Calvin as well),[111] Christ is now and always the "means" of our vision of God. It seems to me that on this score the Puritans had a profound insight. When Christ surrenders his sacramental role, he does not

---

111. See chap. 9, section entitled "Provisional Accommodation."

disappear from view. Also in the eschaton, it is in seeing the person of Christ that we see God. The Puritan reluctance to acknowledge a beatific vision of the divine essence also has to do with their deep awareness of the continuing creator-creature distinction—something that comes through particularly in Watson's conviction that we will progress eternally into the infinite life of God. The acknowledgment that we will see God in and through Jesus Christ is thus at the same time a recognition that it is as finite creatures that we will partake of the infinite God.

CHAPTER 12

MEDIATION AND VISION

An Edwardsean Modification of Thomas Aquinas

Edwards as Neoplatonist

Few Protestant theologians have thought as carefully about the beatific vision as the New England pastor, philosopher, and theologian Jonathan Edwards (1703–1758). His understanding of the beatific vision marks a notable modification of views that became dominant in the Western Church through the rise of Aristotelian anthropology as articulated in the theology of Thomas Aquinas, as well as through the papal constitution *Benedictus Deus* of 1336— the latter the outcome of a sharp debate on the beatific vision. Edwards's account treats the resurrection of the body as significant, even indispensable, for the deifying vision of God.[1] It also regards Christ—the "grand medium" of the *visio Dei*—as the consummate theophanic appearance of God. And, finally, it takes seriously the infinite progress of the vision of God, beginning in this life, continuing in the intermediate state, and on into the eternity of the resurrection. In each of these ways, Edwards drew on the Neoplatonist metaphysic that he inherited from the Cambridge Platonists and so, indirectly, from the Eastern fathers.[2]

---

1. Although Edwards does not use the terms "deification" or "divinization," the theological notion as such is very much present in his thought. See Michael J. McClymond and Gerald R. McDermott, *The Theology of Jonathan Edwards* (New York: Oxford University Press, 2012), 410–23.

2. Previous scholarship has drawn attention to the similarities between Edwards and Maximus the Confessor as well as between Edwards and Gregory Palamas. See Michael Gibson, "The Beauty of the Redemption of the World: The Theological Aesthetics of Maximus the Confessor and Jonathan Edwards," *HTR* 101 (2008): 45–76; Michael J. McClymond, "Salvation as Divinization: Jonathan Edwards, Gregory Palamas and the Theological Uses of Neoplatonism,"

Edwards does not refer to his understanding of the beatific vision as sacramental in character. My designation of his position as sacramental in this chapter is nonetheless a helpful heuristic device, inasmuch as it points to Edwards's inclination to link heaven and earth, or nature and the supernatural, closely in his views on the beatific vision. Edwards's Neoplatonist proclivities are well known, and they are perhaps most obvious in his immaterialist or idealist metaphysic. For Edwards, there are no substances besides the one substance that only and truly exists, namely, God himself, the "being of beings" (*ens entium*).[3] On Edwards's understanding, only the idealist notion that "to be is to be perceived" (*esse est percipi*) sufficed properly to counter the baleful impact of the materialism of Thomas Hobbes and others, a materialism that implied an independent and autonomous realm of matter, independent from invisible, spiritual realities.[4] For Edwards, that is, God's vision causes created things to participate in his eternal being.[5] This sacramental ontology, according to which created things participate as sacraments in eternal realities, not only stamps Edwards's overall metaphysic but also carries over into his understanding of the beatific vision.

Beatific Vision and Embodiment

At first sight, the underlying assumption of this chapter may seem to be an unlikely one: How could Edwards's immaterialist metaphysic and his

---

in *Jonathan Edwards: Philosophical Theologian*, ed. Paul Helm and Oliver Crisp (Burlington, VT: Ashgate, 2003), 139–60. Moreover, as we will see in this chapter, Edwards's eschatology has notable similarities with that of Gregory of Nyssa.

3. Jonathan Edwards, "Of Atoms," in *WJE* 6:215. I expand in greater detail Edwards's immaterialism in chap. 13, section entitled "Pedagogy and Providence in Nicholas of Cusa and Jonathan Edwards."

4. For Hobbes's reliance on nominalist philosophy, see Hans Boersma, *Scripture as Real Presence: Sacramental Exegesis in the Early Church* (Grand Rapids: Baker Academic, 2017), 6–8. See also Matthew Levering, *Participatory Biblical Exegesis* (Notre Dame: University of Notre Dame Press, 2008), 108–18, and Scott W. Hahn and Benjamin Wiker, *Politicizing the Bible: The Roots of Historical Criticism and the Secularization of Scripture, 1300–1700* (New York: Herder and Herder/Crossroad, 2013), 285–393.

5. Oliver D. Crisp persuasively argues that Edwards's Neoplatonism implies that he was a panentheist, since "what he says amounts to something like the claim that the being of God includes and penetrates the whole universe, so that every part exists 'in' him in some sense, although his being is not exhausted by the creation" (*Jonathan Edwards on God and Creation* [New York: Oxford University Press, 2012], 142).

indebtedness to Christian Platonism possibly coincide with sacramental-ism? Wouldn't his immaterialist metaphysic and his Platonist inclinations be much more likely to undermine a sacramental metaphysic? If both the body with which we see and the objects of our sense perception exist strictly by virtue of God's own vision (*esse est percipi*), would it not be logical to think of eschatological bliss as the soul's continuous gaze on the essence of God—for which neither the body nor any extraneous created object is re-quired? Conversely, would we not be more likely to affirm the continuation of matter in the eschaton, both in terms of bodily resurrection and in terms of the continuation of material objects, if we affirmed the independence and significance of material existence? Is it not counterintuitive, therefore, to link Edwards's Neoplatonism with a robust affirmation of the bodily resurrection, with his notion that mediation will continue even with regard to the beatific vision, and with the idea that the progression of the vision of God already begins in this life (as well as in the Old Testament theophanic appearances of God) and will continue forever in the eschaton? Still, Edwards not only affirmed, but actually highlighted, each of these theologoumena. And it is my contention that these affirmations of mediation—and the overall sac-ramental mind-set that they imply—are in no way opposed to Edwards's Neoplatonist proclivities. Rather, in each of these instances, Edwards parts ways with a nonsacramental approach to the beatific vision, which I argue found its way into Western theology in part through the thirteenth-century appropriation of Aristotelianism.

Caroline Walker Bynum's excellent book *The Resurrection of the Body in Western Christianity, 200–1336*, has done much to debunk the all-too-common and all-too-facile accusation that the body-soul dualism of the Christian Platonist tradition led to a general disregard of the body. She makes clear that the Platonist hold on Christian theology during much of the history of the church did not, generally speaking, make people ignore or downplay the bodily resurrection.[6] On Bynum's understanding, the story, which she traces from its early beginnings all the way to the fourteenth cen-tury, must be told quite differently. Most of the Western tradition, she insists, showed deep "concern for material and structural continuity" between this

6. Similarly, Adrian Pabst argues that Platonism does not lead to a devaluing of created realities. The Platonic notion of "participation" (μέθεξις) implies a close link between visible and invisible realities (nature and the supernatural). A dualistic denigration of visible realities is unlikely to occur with a sacramental metaphysic in which nature and the supernatural are connected by way of participation. See Adrian Pabst, *Metaphysics: The Creation of Hierarchy* (Grand Rapids: Eerdmans, 2012).

life and the next.[7] She even speaks of "materialism," which she maintains characterized Western eschatology throughout the Middle Ages,[8] and which "expressed not body-soul dualism but rather a sense of self as psychosomatic unity."[9] According to Bynum, despite the common "suspicion of flesh and lust, Western Christianity did not hate or discount the body."[10] In short, Bynum's position—one that I would echo—is that Platonist metaphysics did not cause Christians to downplay the bodily resurrection.

At the same time, Bynum points to a rift that occurred in the development of the doctrine of the resurrection of the body, which she traces to Saint Thomas Aquinas in the thirteenth century, and which appears to have been cemented through the papal bull of 1336, *Benedictus Deus*. Thomas Aquinas located the eschatological continuity of personal identity in the soul rather than in the body. In Aquinas's Aristotelian hylomorphism, explains Bynum, it was the form (i.e., the soul) rather than the matter on which the form impressed itself (i.e., the body) that was the carrier of human identity and so made for personal continuity in the hereafter.[11] The implication of Aquinas's view of "formal identity" (the form being the carrier of identity) is that immediately upon entering the intermediate state, the soul of the saint achieves perfect beatific vision.[12] After all, if the body is not part of

---

7. Caroline Walker Bynum, *The Resurrection of the Body in Western Christianity, 200–1336*, Lectures on the History of Religions 15 (New York: Columbia University Press, 1995), 11.

8. Bynum uses the term "materialism" in a general sense, as an approach that affirms the embodied character of created reality. She does not use the term in a technical, metaphysical sense to denote the notion that only matter has genuine subsistence—a position that is diametrically opposed to the immaterialism or idealism (aligned with Platonic metaphysics) that Edwards espoused. The distinction between the general and technical uses of the term "materialism" is important for this chapter, since we will see that Edwards's eschatology was materialist in Bynum's general sense (strongly affirming the embodied character of the hereafter) while he was a philosophical idealist or immaterialist in the technical sense.

9. Bynum, *Resurrection*, 11.

10. Bynum, *Resurrection*, 11.

11. Bynum, *Resurrection*, 238–39. This is not to deny that in Aquinas's hylomorphism the human person properly consists of body (matter) and soul (form). It is just that Aquinas is less than clear on the requirement of continuity of numerically the same matter for the continuation of identity (*ST* I, q. 119, a. 1, resp. 5). To be sure, despite Aquinas's emphasis on "formal identity," his theology also contains aspects of a "material identity" view, according to which the very same matter of the present body will be taken up in the bodily resurrection. See Silas Langley, "Aquinas, Resurrection, and Material Continuity," *PACPhA* 75 (2001): 135–47; Antonia Fitzpatrick, "Bodily Identity in Scholastic Theology" (PhD diss., University College, London, 2013).

12. To be sure, Aquinas makes clear that soul and body belong together and that, as a

the identity of the human person, then the body's absence cannot hinder the perfection of the beatific vision.[13] Thus, in the *Summa contra Gentiles*, Aquinas comments that "the separation of the soul from the body makes it capable of the divine vision, and it was unable to arrive at this so long as it was united to the corruptible body. . . . Therefore, immediately after its separation from the body the man's soul receives its reward or punishment 'according as he hath done' in the body (see II Cor. 5:10)."[14] By placing the formal identity of the human person in the soul, Aquinas's anthropology dealt a blow to earlier, Platonic views of bodily resurrection, which typically had maintained that the intermediate state did not yet constitute the ultimate perfection of the beatific vision, since this consummate happiness would require the reunification of body and soul.[15]

Aquinas's hylomorphic account of the human person came in for sustained attack from more traditionalist theologians throughout the 1270s. These theologians—Henry of Ghent, William de la Mare, John Peckham, and others—were concerned that the body would get short shrift in the beatific vision if personal identity was linked strictly with the soul as the body's form.[16] In other words, traditionalist Christian Platonists objected to the emerging Aristotelian views by insisting on the significance of the body for the resurrection.[17] It is fair to say, however, that *Benedictus Deus*—Benedict

---

result, in some sense the soul experiences a lack of happiness in the intermediate state. See further below, n. 20.

13. Phillip Blond rightly comments that for Aquinas, matter itself was a bar to beatitude, a position that "derives from the Aristotelian cognitive legacy, where the end of man is commonly taken to be a purely intellectual contemplation of the first cause. And since intellectual cognition is defined by abstraction of universals from their individuation in matter, it follows that cognition of universals cannot take place if universal forms remain enmeshed in material nature. And if this is true for any sensible form, how much more true it is for God himself who as the form of all forms is the ultimate transcendent universal" ("The Beatific Vision of St. Thomas Aquinas," in *Encounter between Eastern Orthodoxy and Radical Orthodoxy: Transfiguring the World through the Word*, ed. Adrian Pabst and Christoph Schneider [Burlington, VT: Ashgate, 2009], 198).

14. *SCG* 4.91.2, in *Summa contra Gentiles*, trans. Anton C. Pegis et al., 5 vols. (1956; reprint, Notre Dame: University of Notre Dame Press, 1975). Cf. Bynum, *Resurrection*, 266–67.

15. I recognize that Aquinas was also deeply influenced by Platonic categories, which he inherited in part from Dionysius, and we do well to recognize the overall participatory metaphysic at work in Aquinas's theology. Still, the Aristotelian influence on his anthropology means a notable shift in terms of how theologians came to regard the body-soul relationship.

16. See Bynum, *Resurrection*, 271–78.

17. Bynum comments that the controversy surrounding the beatific vision in the early 1330s can "from one point of view be seen as a rearguard and unsuccessful action by the partisans of

XII's papal bull of 1336—vindicated the views that Aquinas and others had begun to introduce to Western eschatology. Contradicting the views expressed by Pope John XXII, the bull proclaimed by Benedict XII maintained that immediately after death, the souls of saints will see the divine essence *nude, clare, et aperte*, that this vision is true beatitude and rest (*requies*), and that the acts of faith and hope will therefore cease once the saints enjoy this beatific vision.[18] Embodiment did not appear necessary for the beatific vision, and the beatific vision of the divine essence was something that the separated souls of the saints attained all at once, immediately after death.[19] As a result, it became more difficult to argue that in the resurrection the *visio Dei* could advance to a state of greater happiness, beyond what the soul experienced in the intermediate state.[20] None of this is to suggest that either

---

the body. It was, however, in a deeper sense an indication of how far the separated soul had (as William of La Mare suggested) come to contain the particularity and capacity for experience earlier treatments had lodged in body. The soul that was defined in the bull *Benedictus Deus* of 1336 was not a self for which body is the completion or housing or garment, but a self of which body is the expression (*abundantia* or *refluentia*)" (*Resurrection*, 278).

    18. Pope Benedict XII, "Benedictus Deus," January 29, 1336, in Xavier LeBachelet, "Benoît XII," in *Dictionnaire de Théologie Catholique*, vol. 2, pt. 1 (Paris: Letouzey et Ané, 1932), cols. 657–58: "Ac post Domini nostri Jesu Christi passionem et mortem viderunt et vident divinam essentiam visione intuitiva et etiam faciali, nulla mediante creatura in ratione objecti visi se habente, sed divina essentia immediate se nude, clare et aperte eis ostendente, quodque sic videntes eadem divina essentia perfruuntur, necnon quod ex tali visione et fruitione eorum animae, qui jam decesserunt, sunt vere beatae et habent vitam et requiem aeternam, et etiam illorum, qui postea decedent, eamdem divinam videbunt essentiam ipsaque perfruentur ante judicium generale." Cf. Bynum, *Resurrection*, 285. For an English translation of *Benedictus Deus*, see http://www.papalencyclicals.net/Ben12/B12bdeus.htm.

    19. For discussion on Aquinas's views regarding the beatific vision and bodily resurrection, see Matthew Levering, *Jesus and the Demise of Death: Resurrection, Afterlife, and the Fate of the Christian* (Waco: Baylor University Press, 2012), 109–25.

    20. To be sure, *Benedictus Deus* did not pronounce on the vexed question of whether the bodily resurrection perhaps entailed an extensive or even intensive increase of the beatific vision. Aquinas, in his early commentary on Lombard's *Sentences*, still posited both, insisting on an intensive increase with the comment that "due to appetite for the body, the soul [in its separated state] is held back from passing into that highest good [of beatitude] with its whole intention" (*Sent.* IV, d. 49, q. 1, a. 4, qa. 1; Aquinas, *On Love and Charity: Readings from the* Commentary on the Sentences of Peter Lombard, trans. Peter A. Kwasniewski, Thomas Bolan, and Joseph Bolin, ed. Peter A. Kwasniewski [Washington, DC: Catholic University of America Press, 2008], 380). In the *Summa theologiae*, however, he reversed himself, rejecting an increase in intensity of the beatific vision: "The desire of the separated soul is entirely at rest, as regards the thing desired; since, to wit, it has that which suffices its appetite. But it is not wholly at rest, as regards the desirer, since it does not possess that good in every way that it would wish to possess it. Consequently, after the body has been resumed, Happiness

Aquinas or *Benedictus Deus* undermined the bodily resurrection. Obviously, neither did. Still, both articulated the doctrine of the beatific vision in such a way as to render a proper rationale for the bodily resurrection more difficult to sustain.

Edwards distinguishes carefully between the vision of God in the intermediate state and the vision of God that will follow the resurrection of the body. In a sermon on Romans 2:10 ("but glory and honor and peace for everyone who does good, the Jew first and also the Greek") dating from 1735, Edwards deals with each in turn.[21] Notably, with regard to the happiness of the saints "in their state of separation from their bodies,"[22] Edwards highlights the particularity of space and of bodies present in heaven: angels lead the souls of the faithful upon death (cf. Luke 16:22) through the aerial heavens and the starry heavens into the "third heaven" (2 Cor. 12:2), also called Paradise, or the new Jerusalem, which Edwards insists is an actual place (L 15r–16r) ("'tis absurd to suppose that that Heaven where the body of [Christ] is is not a Place") (L 15v). Christ is present here in his glorified body, as are several of the saints, such as Enoch (Gen. 5:24) and Elijah (2 Kings 2:1–12) (L 15v). At death, the saints are brought to Christ, who welcomes them "to the full Enjoym[ent] of his Love" (L 16v); he enters into conversation with them and also presents them to the Father. The picture Edwards evokes is vivid and, in many ways, physical. He even describes the bodiless saints as having the tears wiped from their eyes (Rev. 21:4) (L 17r) and as being "Clothed in white Robes & Palms in their Hands" (Rev. 7:9) (L 17v). It would be fair to say that Edwards's separated soul is, to use Carol Zaleski's phrase, a "somatomorphic soul"—a soul that takes on many of the char-

---

increases not in intensity, but in extent" (*ST* I-II, q. 4, a. 5; quotations come from Thomas Aquinas, *Summa Theologica*, trans. Fathers of the English Dominican Province, 5 vols. [1948; reprint, Notre Dame: Christian Classics, 1981]). See further, Peter Dillard, "Keeping the Vision: Aquinas and the Problem of Disembodied Beatitude," *NB* 93 (2012): 397–411; Blond, "Beatific Vision of St. Thomas Aquinas," 195–96.

21. For an insightful analysis of this sermon, see Kyle C. Strobel, *Jonathan Edwards's Theology: A Reinterpretation*, T. & T. Clark Studies in Systematic Theology 19 (London: T. & T. Clark, 2013), 137–43.

22. Edwards, sermon on Rom. 2:10 (December 17, 1735), L 14v. I am indebted to Ken Minkema, executive director of the Jonathan Edwards Center at Yale University, for providing me with a new transcription of the sermon, on which I rely throughout. Minor editing has been done to these quotations, using brackets and ellipses, for the sake of readability. The current online version of *WJE* 50 lacks L 11v–20v. Hereafter, references to this sermon will be given in parentheses in the text.

acteristics of embodied existence.[23] The souls will dwell "in habitations of sweet delight & Pleas[ure]," and they will contemplate God's love for them in Christ's work of redemption. What is more, they will "behold the beauty & Excellency of [Christ] ... & see face to face. & Know even as they are Known 1 Cor 13.12" (L 18r).

Although the beatific vision in the intermediate state is bodiless—since the souls are separated from their bodies—the place where the souls arrive is nonetheless an actual place (the third heaven located above the starry and the aerial heavens), and embodied beings (Christ, Enoch, and Elijah) live in this heavenly city. In a sense, Edwards is perhaps simply guided by the particulars of the biblical narrative.[24] Still, it is difficult to suppress the question of how such a vivid, embodied reading of the narrative fits with the souls being separated from the body. In all, Edwards has a remarkably "embodied" (or somatomorphic) understanding of the intermediate state.

Despite the glory that the saints encounter in the third heaven, this is still only a penultimate step to the ultimate happiness they will enjoy at the resurrection of the body. In the intermediate state the saints are in "a Joyf[ul] Expecta[tion] of their more ... full & Compleat blessedness at the Resurrection" (L 20r).[25] It is at the resurrection that the body will be reunited with the soul. But, cautions Edwards with an appeal to 1 Corinthians 15:42–44, "the body shall not Rise as it was afore there shall be a vast difference in it" (L 22v). This will no longer be a natural body; instead, it will be a spiritual body, with such glory that

> we now Cannot Concieve of. [I]t shall [not] be such a dull & heavy molded thing as it is Now[.] [I]t shall ... be active & vigorous as a flame of fire fit for the Use of a Glorified soul. [I]t will [be] No Clog [or] a hindrance to the soul is it ... now but an ... organ Every way fit for the Uses of a Glo[rified] spirit & it ... shall not be such a weak Infirm & frail thing as it is now for

23. Carol Zaleski points out that in the Middle Ages, in visions and otherworld journeys, the separated soul took on numerous corporeal characteristics (*Otherworld Journeys: Accounts of Near-Death Experience in Medieval and Modern Times* [New York: Oxford University Press, 1987], 51). See also Bynum, *Resurrection*, 279–317.

24. In particular, the observations that, already upon death, the saints have their tears wiped and are dressed in white robes are hard to take literally, considering that Edwards is speaking of separated souls.

25. This "Joyf[ul] Expecta[tion]" is not only the result of the soul's anticipation of reunification with the body. It also has to do with the fact that the history of the work of redemption unfolds for the separated souls as well as for those on earth.

tho tis sown in weakn[ess] it is Raised in Power[.] . . . [N]ow the body . . . stands in need of food . . . & sleep Continually to Revive it but it shall not be so then[.] [N]ow the body . . . is subj[ect] to . . . weariness & to diseases but it shall not be so then[.] [N]ow . . . if G[od] Lets in any Great matter of . . . divine Light into the soul[,] the body is Ready to sink under it but it shall not be so then[.] [T]he Glorious body then shall not fail or flagg at all . . . by the most Powerfull Exercises of mind[.] . . . [N]ow no man Can be G[od] & live but the body would Immediately sink & be dissolved but . . . the body shall not fail at all by the . . . Immediate beholding of G[od][.] . . . [N]ow the saints . . . Can bear but little[.] [W]hen G[od] a little discovers hims[elf] . . . as he doth sometimes the saints are forced to beseech G[od] either . . . to strengthen them to bear it or to hold his hand. [B]ut then the body shall be so . . . vigorous & spiritual that the Constant & Everlasting view of the Glo[ry] of G[od] . . . shall not in any wise overcome it or Cause it in the Least to fail. (L 22v–r)

Edwards highlights the dissimilarity between natural and spiritual bodies, insisting that the glory of the resurrection is such that we cannot properly imagine what the body will then be like.

Not only will the bodies of the saints be strong enough to endure the "Immediate beholding" of God, but they will also be raised in amazing beauty, insists Edwards (L 23v). Since they will be like Christ's glorious body (Phil. 3:21), they will have "the most Lovely Proportion of the . . . feature & parts of their Countenance & parts of their bodies," which will reflect the excellencies of their minds. Appealing to the shining of Moses's face and of the face of Christ in the transfiguration, Edwards argues that it is likely that we have to take the language of the righteous "shining" with light (Dan. 12:3; Matt. 13:43) literally, so that their bodies will actually be clothed with light (L 23v).

Following the final judgment, the saints, "with their Glorified bodies," will leave this world (L 27r). They will ascend to the highest heaven, which will then celebrate an even more joyful day than that of Christ's first ascension into heaven (L 27r–v). Edwards then explains how this is the moment of "ultimate & Consumate" happiness. He points to seven aspects that make this moment of happiness stand out beyond anything that came before— including the vision of the intermediate state. First, the reunification of body and soul means that the saints will be "happy in the . . . whole man." This unity of body and soul is "natural" to the human soul, maintains Edwards. Second, with every member of the body of Christ being in its perfect state, the church will be "Perfect and Compleat" (L 27v). As a result, Christ, "having his mystical body Compleat will Rejoice & all his saints will Rejoice with him. [Christ] will Rejoice in the Compleatness of his . . . Ch[urc]h & the Ch[urc]h will Rejoice in its own Compleatness" (L 28v). Third, the entire work of redemption will now have been completed, as Christ and the saints have now fully triumphed over their enemies. Fourth, it will now become clear how "all the wheels of Provid[ence]" have conspired together to bring about this final end, which will give great happiness to the saints (L 29r). Fifth, since this moment will initiate the marriage of the Lamb, the church will now appear as a bride for her husband, so that she will enjoy a "more Glo[rious] Union to [Christ] than Ever before," having prepared herself with her wedding gown (Rev. 19:7–9) (L 29v). Sixth, Christ will present his church to the Father (Heb. 2:13; 1 Cor. 15:24) as the fruits of his reign. And finally, Christ will deliver up the kingdom to the Father, and the glory of God and of his Son will be displayed "in a more abund[ant] manner than Ever before" (L 30v). In all this, Edwards goes out of his way to articulate the reasons why the saints in heaven will have greater happiness after the resurrection than before. One of the reasons—in fact, the first one Edwards mentions—is that body and soul will be reunited.[26] Each of the other reasons for the increase in happiness has to do with the fact that only now is God's plan of redemption in Christ complete. The saints, so it seems, will find happiness in the many ways in which God brings salvation to its climactic fullness. Edwards dwells at length on the great advance in happiness that the resurrection of the body brings about.

Beatific Vision and Christ

Edwards's teaching on the beatific vision stands out for its remarkable Christ-centeredness: Christ is the central object of the beatific vision. This viewpoint is not unique to Edwards. As we have seen, earlier theologians, such as Gregory of Nyssa, Bonaventure, and Nicholas of Cusa, had also focused on Christ as the one in whom God is seen in heaven. The Puritans of the seventeenth century had also presented christocentric treatments of the beatific vision. Still, Edwards links Christology to the beatific vision in a particularly promising fashion; by treating Christ as the "grand medium"

---

26. On this score, there is little difference between Edwards and Aquinas. Aquinas also affirms that the soul has "an aptitude and a natural inclination to be united to the body" (*ST* I, q. 76, a. 1).

of the beatific vision, the Northampton preacher reaffirmed the importance not only of eschatological bodily vision per se but also of bodily eyes seeing a bodily object—Jesus Christ.

When in 1730 Edwards preached on the sixth beatitude—"Blessed are the pure in heart, for they shall see God" (Matt. 5:8)—he began by commenting that here, as earlier at Mount Sinai, God himself is speaking. This appearance of God, however, is different from the one at Sinai: now God is incarnate, his face is freely beheld by all, the sound of his voice does not arouse terrors, and God makes a clearer and more perfect revelation of his mind than he once did to the people of Israel.[27] With these comments Edwards intimates that the vision of God is not just *mentioned* in the Beatitudes but actually *takes place* when Jesus preaches them. The disciples have a clearer vision of God by seeing Jesus on the mountain than did Moses when he saw God on Mount Sinai.

Edwards immediately continues to clarify what it means to see God. He seems initially to take a traditional Thomist approach, explaining that the sight of God is not a sight with bodily eyes. "[True] blessedness of the soul don't enter in at that door," explains Edwards,[28] and he appeals to biblical passages asserting the invisibility of God (Heb. 11:27; Col. 1:15; 1 Tim. 1:17).[29] Thomas Aquinas had similarly argued that it is "impossible for God to be seen by the sense of sight, or by any other sense, or faculty of the sensitive power."[30] Edwards goes on to state explicitly that when the saints and angels see God, this happens in a nonbodily way.[31] Edwards contrasts this non-bodily seeing of God with Old Testament theophanic manifestations, where God's people saw the "glory of the LORD" (Exod. 19:17–19; 33:9–10), where the seventy elders saw God in visible shape (Exod. 24:9–11), and where Moses saw the back parts of God (Exod. 33:18–23). With such visible appearances, God condescended "to the infant state of the church."[32]

Edwards reiterates his opinion that the beatific vision is spiritual rather than bodily sight in his 1735 sermon on Romans 2:10. He insists plainly that

---

27. Edwards, "Pure in Heart Blessed," *WJE* 17:59.

28. Edwards, "Pure in Heart Blessed," *WJE* 17:61 (brackets in original). Edwards explains a little later that the vision of God is "an intellectual view," in which God is "beheld with the understanding," and he links this to the fact that "the eye of the soul is vastly nobler than the eye of the body" (17:65).

29. Edwards, "Pure in Heart Blessed," *WJE* 17:61–62.

30. *ST* I, q. 12, a. 3.

31. Edwards, "Pure in Heart Blessed," *WJE* 17:62.

32. Edwards, "Pure in Heart Blessed," *WJE* 17:62.

"the Beatifical vision of J[ahweh] is not a sight with the Eyes of the Body but with the Eye of the soul."[33] Edwards links this spiritual vision with the well-known biblical texts of 1 John 3:2 and 1 Corinthians 13:12. It involves, he says, an "understanding of [Christ] as mediatour how he has undertaken from all Et[ernity]" to fulfill the covenant of redemption between the Father and the Son.[34] Edwards dwells at some length on the love and wisdom of God in his plan of salvation, which he has accomplished in Christ. The saints will see the beauty of Christ's work, as well as of his glorified human nature.[35] With this same vision of the eyes of the soul, the saints will see "the Glo[ry] of [Christ] in his Divine nature," and they will lovingly and freely converse with Christ in an intimate manner, as his friends.[36]

The vision of the eyes of the soul is, according to Edwards, an intellectual sight. Edwards can sound rather Thomistic as he highlights the intellectual character of the beatific vision. For example, he explains that the understanding is the "principal and leading faculty";[37] he equates the vision of the eyes of the soul with an "Intellectual view";[38] and he comments that it "is an intellectual view by which God is seen. God is a spiritual being, and he is beheld with the understanding."[39] Edwards usually highlights the place of the intellect and of understanding in the beatific vision when he contrasts the eyes of the body with the eyes of the soul; he is quick to equate the latter with intellectual sight.

Nonetheless, the intellectual character of the beatific vision was not as clear-cut for Edwards as it was for Aquinas. The latter identified happiness with the intellectual act of seeing God. "The essence of happiness," Saint Thomas explains, "consists in an act of the intellect: but the delight that results from happiness pertains to the will."[40] Edwards takes a rather different approach. This is especially notable in his sermon on Matthew 5:8. To be sure, also here Edwards is in some ways quite in line with Thomas. For example, Edwards emphasizes that the joy and delight of the beatific vision are of a kind "suitable to the nature of an intelligent creature,"[41] and he states:

33. Edwards, sermon on Rom. 2:10, L 41r.
34. Edwards, sermon on Rom. 2:10, L 38r.
35. Edwards, sermon on Rom. 2:10, L 38v.
36. Edwards, sermon on Rom. 2:10, L 39r.
37. Edwards, "Pure in Heart Blessed," *WJE* 17:72.
38. Edwards, sermon on Rom. 2:10, L 41r.
39. Edwards, "Pure in Heart Blessed," *WJE* 17:63.
40. *ST* I-II, q. 3, a. 4.
41. Edwards, "Pure in Heart Blessed," *WJE* 17:66.

"And the delight and joy the soul has in that sight is the highest excellency of the other faculty, viz. the will."[42] In other words, both faculties are operative, the intellect in seeing God and the will in enjoying him. Accordingly, Edwards comments that "the soul's seeing of God and having pleasure and joy in it is the greatest excellency of both the faculties." Here he links the sight of God to the intellect, and the resulting pleasure and joy to the will. In all this, Edwards hardly deviates from Aquinas.

Edwards then adds, however: "The happiness of seeing God is a pure sweet without any mixture. That pleasure has the best claim to be called man's true happiness that comes unmixed, that has no alloy. But so doth the joy of seeing God; it neither brings any bitterness, neither will it suffer any."[43] It is the "pleasure" or the "joy" of seeing God that Edwards here identifies as the soul's happiness. Similarly, he comments a little further that "pleasure may justly be looked upon as the true happiness of men."[44] For Edwards, it was not only the intellect's act of seeing God but also the will's pleasure or joy that follows it that constitutes happiness. On this point, Edwards was much less of an intellectualist than Thomas Aquinas.

We should also note the sheer weight that Edwards gives to the affective aspect of the beatific vision.[45] When he speaks of the happiness of the beatific vision, he notes that it is "capable of ravishing the soul above all other loves."[46] He dwells at length on the increase in joy that results from our beholding of God's happiness.[47] As he reflects on the affective character of the beatific vision, Edwards comments: "The pleasure of seeing God is so great and strong that it takes the full possession of the heart; it fills it brimful, so that there shall be no room for any sorrow, no room in any corner for anything of an adverse nature from joy. There is no darkness can bear such powerful light. It is impossible that they that see God face to

42. Edwards, "Pure in Heart Blessed," *WJE* 17:68.

43. Edwards, "Pure in Heart Blessed," *WJE* 17:68.

44. Edwards, "Pure in Heart Blessed," *WJE* 17:71.

45. Michael J. McClymond highlights the affective character of spiritual sight in Edwards in his fine essay, "Spiritual Perception in Jonathan Edwards," *JR* 77 (1997): 211–13.

46. Edwards, "Pure in Heart Blessed," *WJE* 17:67.

47. Edwards, "Pure in Heart Blessed," *WJE* 17:70. As he describes union with Christ in the afterlife, Edwards's affective language is pronounced. The union is one "of hearts and affections," in which "the heart shall be wholly and perfectly drawn" ("True Saints, When Absent from the Body, Are Present with the Lord," *WJE* 25:231). The saints will "swim in the ocean of love, and be eternally swallowed up in the infinitely bright, and infinitely mild and sweet beams of divine love" (25:233). This "stream of love" is "the stream of Christ's delights, the river of his infinite pleasure; which he will make his saints to drink of with him" (25:235).

face, that behold his glory and love so immediately as they do in heaven, should have any such thing as grief or pain in their hearts."[48] Edwards emphasized the affective aspect of the beatific vision much more than did Thomas Aquinas.

Edwards complements the intellectual vision of God not only by highlighting the affective aspect of the beatific vision, but also by insisting that the eyes of the body will have a role to play. According to Edwards, in the resurrection the saints will see Christ's body with their bodily eyes. Aquinas, though he of course acknowledges the bodily nature of Christ's resurrection body,[49] does not discuss in detail how the saints will see Christ in the resurrection. For the most part, he is content to make the traditional argument that they will see God's essence with the mind's eye.[50] Edwards comments on the saints' vision after the resurrection:

> [The saints] in heaven will behold an outward glory as they [behold] the human nature of Christ, which is united to the Godhead, as it is the body of that person that is God. And there will doubtless be appearances of a divine and inimitable glory and beauty in Christ's gloried body, which it will indeed be a ravishing and blessed sight to see.
>
> But the beauty of Christ's body that will be beheld with bodily eyes will be ravishing and delighting chiefly as it will express his spiritual glories. The majesty that will appear in Christ's body will express and show forth the spiritual greatness and majesty of the divine nature. The pureness and beauty of that light and glory will express the perfection of divine holiness. The sweetness and ravishing mildness of his countenance will express his divine and spiritual love and grace.
>
> Thus it was, when the three disciples beheld Christ at his transfiguration upon the mount. They beheld a wonderful, outward glory in Christ's body, an inexpressible beauty in his countenance; but that outward glory and beauty delighted them principally as it was an expression or signification of the divine excellencies of his mind, as we may see by their manner of speaking of it. It was the sweet mixture there was of majesty and grace in his countenance that ravished them.[51]

48. Edwards, "Pure in Heart Blessed," *WJE* 17:71.
49. *ST* III, q. 54.
50. *ST* I, q. 12, a. 3.
51. Edwards, "Pure in Heart Blessed," *WJE* 17:62–63 (brackets in original).

Although Edwards does not refer to it as "beatific vision," he nonetheless is remarkably insistent on a bodily vision that the saints will have of the body of Christ, and he compares this vision to that of the transfiguration.[52] The three disciples saw the "outward glory and beauty" of Christ's body, and they delighted in it because this bodily glory was an "expression or signification" of the divine excellencies of his mind.

Christ's glorified body is, according to Edwards, the carrier of divine glory and beauty, and it is because his human nature (his body) puts on display the glory of his divinity that the saints' sight of the body of the Savior is "ravishing and blessed." Edwards goes out of his way, in other words, to emphasize that in eternity the saints will have the ability to see bodily sights and that the very vision of the Godhead comes through the physical sight of the body of Christ. It is the union of the two natures that allows the saints to move from a bodily vision of Christ's humanity to an acknowledgment also of his divinity. Thus, the bodily vision of Christ's human nature will, in turn, put the saints in touch with the Godhead.[53]

All of this raises the question of the relationship between the "eyes of the body" and the "eyes of the soul," between physical and spiritual sight. Edwards does not directly address this question, but he does deal with it obliquely. On the one hand, he seems to suggest that the two are quite distinct. He explicitly separates them,[54] and he reserves the term "beatific vision" for sight with the eye of the soul. On the other hand, there is significant overlap between what the saints see of Christ with the eyes of the body and what they see of him with the eyes of the soul. It is with the eyes of the soul that the saints will see Christ's divine nature and will comprehend the glory of Christ's work of mediation. But when the eyes of the body see the body of Christ, they, too, will see the majesty of Christ's divinity shining through in his body.

Did Edwards perhaps think that the beatific vision (with spiritual eyes) is mediated through the bodily vision of Christ? Miscellany no. 777 ("Happi-

---

52. Cf. Edwards, sermon on Rom. 2:10, L 37v: "the Eye will never be Cloyed or Glutted in Beholding this Glo[rious] sight. [W]hen [Christ] was transfigured in the m[oun]t[ain] Peter was for making three Tabernacles."

53. Edwards goes on to claim that this intellectual sight—not achieved by "ratiocination" ("Pure in Heart Blessed," WJE 17:63–64)—will be "as clear and lively as seeing with bodily eyes" (17:65), and that this sight of the saints will allow them to converse with Christ "as sight of the bodily eye doth an earthly friend" (17:66).

54. This separation is particularly clear in the sermon on Rom. 2:10, where Edwards speaks of seeing Christ in a "twofold sense" (L 37r–v) and then discusses in turn the saints' sight of Christ with the "Eye of the Body" and their sight of him with the "Eye of the soul."

ness of Heaven Is Progressive"), which dates from the late 1730s, sheds light on this question. Edwards deals here in some detail with Christ's mediation of the beatific vision. He begins by observing that to have an "immediate and intuitive view" of someone's mind would imply an immediate perception of the ideas and operations of that person's mind. Such an immediate and intuitive view, therefore, would entail a "union of personality," so that for "all intents and purposes" the two would be one and the same individual person.[55] Interestingly, though Edwards does not mention either Thomas Aquinas or *Benedictus Deus*, they both insist on an "immediate" and "intuitive" vision of the divine essence in the intermediate state.[56] Edwards did not appropriate this understanding of the beatific vision, because he believed it does not allow for a proper distinction between God and the creature.

Edwards, therefore, took a different approach. The only creature that can have such an immediate sight of God, insists Edwards, is Jesus Christ, "who is in the bosom of God."[57] Only Christ knows God "immediately." Other human beings have access to God only by means of "manifestations or signs," and Jesus Christ is the "grand medium" of their knowledge of God (Matt. 11:27; John 1:18; 6:46).[58] The "signs" by which they are able to see or know God are (1) images (e.g., theophanies) and the man Jesus Christ; (2) words

55. Edwards, "Happiness of Heaven is Progressive," *WJE* 18:427.

56. In *ST* I, q. 12, a. 5, Aquinas explains that the *lumen gloriae* is a created light that perfects the intellect, so as to allow for the immediate vision of God: "Therefore it may be said that this light is to be described not as a medium in which God is seen, but as one by which he is seen; and such a medium does not take away the immediate vision of God." Aquinas insists that consummate human happiness means seeing God's essence because (1) Scripture teaches it (1 Cor. 13:12; 1 John 3:2; 1 Cor. 15:24; John 14:21); (2) God as pure act is supremely knowable; (3) beatitude is the use of the intellect as our highest function, and without seeing the divine essence, the intellect would not reach its highest function; (4) our natural desire for God as the first cause of everything we see cannot remain void; and (5) the intellect is proportionate to the vision of the divine essence, even though there is no strict proportion between the finite and the infinite (*ST* Suppl. q. 92, a. 1). For *Benedictus Deus*, see n. 18 above.

57. Edwards, "Happiness of Heaven is Progressive," *WJE* 18:428.

58. Edwards, "Happiness of Heaven is Progressive," *WJE* 18:428. Edwards uses the expression "grand medium" at least fifteen times in his writings to refer to Christ as the bond between God and the believer. Throughout this chaper, I speak of Edwards as affirming Christ's "mediation" of the beatific vision. I use this language because Edwards himself speaks of Christ as the "medium" of the beatific vision. We should note, however, that there is no material difference on this score between Edwards and the earlier Puritans. As we saw in the previous chapter, theologians such as Isaac Ambrose and John Owen denied Christ's continuing role as "mediator" while affirming that he continues forever as the "means" of our vision of God. Edwards agrees with his Puritan forebears that Christ's reconciling or mediating work is complete.

and declarations, either in the mind or in the Scriptures; (3) effects of God's works in creation and providence; and (4) a priori deductions from the necessity of God's existence and perfections.[59] In short, all knowledge of God is mediated knowledge, and Christ is the great mediator.

Edwards draws from this a startling conclusion with regard to the object of the beatific vision:

> Hence that BEATIFICAL VISION that the saints have of God in heaven, is in beholding the manifestations that he makes of himself in the work of redemption: for that arguing of the being and perfections of God that may be a priori, don't seem to be called seeing God in Scripture, but only that which is by [the] manifestations God makes of himself in his Son. All other ways of knowing God are by seeing him in Christ the Redeemer, the image of the invisible God, and in his works, or the effects of his perfections of his redemption, and the fruits of it (which effects are the principal manifestation or shining forth of his perfections); and in conversing with them by Christ, which conversation is chiefly about those things done and manifested in this work—if we may judge by the subject of God's conversation with his church—by his work in this world.[60]

Edwards insists that it is God's manifestation of himself in images, words, and effects (all centered on Christ—his person, his words, his work) that constitutes the beatific vision.[61] Whereas Aquinas claims that because "the Divine Essence cannot be seen by means of phantasms," the soul reaches happiness without the body,[62] for Edwards, some theophanic mediation—in the form of Christ's humanity—remains in the eschaton. Edwards appears to be following the christological approach of the earlier Puritans. Much like Isaac Ambrose and John Owen, Edwards believed that Christ forever is our means of communication with God. For Edwards, mediation is not just a this-worldly phenomenon. It also characterizes our relation to God in the hereafter.[63]

---

59. Edwards, "Happiness of Heaven is Progressive," *WJE* 18:428–29.

60. Edwards, "Happiness of Heaven is Progressive," *WJE* 18:431 (brackets in original).

61. Cf. Edwards's comment in "True Saints," *WJE* 25:230: "And when the souls of the saints leave their bodies, to go to be with Christ, they behold the marvellous glory of that great work of his, the work of redemption, and of the glorious way of salvation by him; which the angels desire to look into."

62. *ST* I-II, q. 4, a. 5.

63. See William M. Schweitzer, *God Is a Communicative Being: Divine Communicativeness*

Edwards takes a similar approach in the sermon he preached at the funeral of David Brainerd, the controversial "enthusiast" and missionary to the natives, who spent a year in Edwards's home before dying from tuberculosis in 1747. In this sermon on 2 Corinthians 5:8 ("True Saints, When Absent from the Body, Are Present with the Lord"), preached on October 12, Edwards claims that those who, like Brainerd, die in the Lord, "go to be with Christ" so as to "dwell in the immediate, full and constant sight of him." Christ is "the sun that enlightens the heavenly Jerusalem; by whose bright beams it is that the glory of God shines forth there, to the enlightening and making happy all the glorious inhabitants."[64] Again Edwards insists here on the invisibility of God, as a result of which "no one sees God the Father immediately."[65]

Edwards, therefore—quite unlike Aquinas—holds that in some sense there will never be an "immediate" vision of God or of the Father, never a vision of the "essence" of God.[66] For Edwards, such a vision of God would imply a natural, personal union of the believer with God, an erasing of the distinction between creator and creature. Only Christ, the only begotten Son of God, who is eternally in the bosom of the Father, has such a natural, personal union with God. For the believer, the *visio Dei* always remains mediated vision—mediated, that is, through Christ. Human beings, inasmuch as they are creatures, are dependent for their knowledge of God on created signs, and the great sign (the "grand medium," as Edwards calls him) is Christ himself.

The difference between Aquinas and Edwards is notable. For Aquinas, in heavenly happiness the senses belong to happiness only "consequently," with the bodily senses receiving a certain "overflow" from the soul.[67] While Edwards allows for bodily vision to *yield* spiritual vision, the most Aquinas is willing to grant the senses in heaven is that by way of consequence, they will *receive* an "overflow" from the soul. He does not connect bodily sight of Christ in heaven to the beatific vision.[68]

---

and Harmony in the Theology of Jonathan Edwards, T. & T. Clark Studies in Systematic Theology 14 (London: Bloomsbury, 2012), 136.

64. Edwards, "True Saints," *WJE* 25:229.

65. Edwards, "True Saints," *WJE* 25:230.

66. To be sure, as we will see below, Edwards does affirm that, in a different sense, the beatific vision will in fact be an "immediate" vision.

67. *ST* I-II, q. 3, a. 3; I-II, q. 4, a. 6.

68. At one point, Aquinas does mention a corporeal vision of Christ in the eschaton, and he compares it to the transfiguration, adding that "we will be intelligible participants by the

The mediation of Christ does not mean that Edwards places Christ as an eternal barrier between the saints and God. It is not as though God (the Father) is at a remove from the saints in heaven, with Christ as a third party situated in between God and the saints. The vision of Christ in the hereafter is not the vision of an object that is separate from the saint: Edwards has a deep sense of the saints' union with Christ. Edwards explains in his funeral sermon for David Brainerd that the souls, when absent from the body, will be "brought into a most perfect conformity to, and union with," Jesus Christ.[69] Since all "deformity, disagreement and sinful unlikeness" will be abolished, not the "least degree of obscurity" will remain before the light of Christ. Inasmuch, therefore, as the saints will see the "Sun of righteousness without a cloud," they themselves will "shine forth as the sun." At this point, explains Edwards, "the saints' union with Christ is perfected."[70] Edwards waxes eloquent on the perfection of this union:

> When the soul leaves the body, all these clogs and hindrances [of sin] shall be removed, every separating wall shall be broken down, and every impediment taken out of the way, and all distance shall cease; the heart shall be wholly and perfectly drawn, and most firmly and forever attached and bound to him, by a perfect view of his glory. And the vital union shall then be brought to perfection: the soul shall live perfectly in and upon Christ, being perfectly filled with his Spirit, and animated by his vital influences, living as it were only by Christ's life, without any remainder of spiritual death, or carnal life.[71]

The union of the saints with Christ will be perfected through the perfection of their holiness. This holiness of the saints will so join them to Christ that it is *in him* that they will see the glory of God.[72]

---

gift of the light of Christ himself which he will pour out in us according to the virtue of his own divinity" (*De divinis nominibus*, cap. 1, lect. 2, in Harry Clarke Marsh, "Cosmic Structure and the Knowledge of God: Thomas Aquinas' 'In Librum beati Dionysii de divinis nominibus expositio'" [PhD diss., Vanderbilt University, 1994], 287). As Cory J. Hayes points out, however, Aquinas does not identify this corporeal vision of Christ with the beatific vision itself ("*Deus in se et Deus pro nobis*: The Transfiguration in the Theology of Gregory Palamas and Its Importance for Catholic Theology" [PhD diss., Duquesne University, 2015], 195).

69. Edwards, "True Saints," *WJE* 25:231.

70. Edwards, "True Saints," *WJE* 25:231.

71. Edwards, "True Saints," *WJE* 25:231–32 (brackets in original).

72. Cf. Kyle C. Strobel's comment: "Our call is not simply to gaze on the beauty of Christ, to see Christ as beautiful, but to be caught up into this beauty itself—that our whole being would

Since in Christ humanity and divinity are joined together, by being perfectly united to Christ's humanity (in its holiness), the saints are also united to his divinity. This means that Edwards's vision of Christ is truly a *visio Dei*: the believer really does see God, but he sees him *in Christ*.[73] Christ may be the "grand medium" of the vision of God, but in the eschaton, this medium is no longer a sacrament.[74] That is to say, although knowledge of God is always mediated through Christ's humanity, in heaven the intimacy between Christ and the saints is such that in and through his humanity they now immediately discern his divinity as well as the glory of his redemption as the sacramental reality (*res*) to which they have been looking forward. The beatific vision is a vision of the real presence of God in Christ: the merging of sacrament and reality in him.

Edwards draws out this point explicitly toward the end of his funeral sermon, when he reflects on the implications of the participation of the heavenly saints with Christ. Here he insists that the Father's placement of the Son at his right hand in heaven means that the believers, too, are joined to the Father. Through their union with Christ, they "in some sort, partake of his child-like relation to the Father; and so are heirs with him of his happiness in the enjoyment of his Father, as seems to be intimated by the Apostle in Gal. 4:4–7. The spouse of Christ, by virtue of her espousals to that only begotten son of God, is as it were, a partaker of his filial relation to God, and becomes the 'King's daughter' (Ps. 45:13), and so partakes with her divine husband in his enjoyment of his Father and her Father, his God and her God."[75] The saints are Christ's bride, and as his bride, Edwards suggests, they are the Father's daughter-in-law and enjoy his presence accordingly.

---

consent to his, and that we would partake in his filial relationship with the Father" ("Theology in the Gaze of the Father: Retrieving Jonathan Edwards's Trinitarian Aesthetics," in *Advancing Trinitarian Theology: Explorations in Constructive Dogmatics*, ed. Oliver D. Crisp and Fred Sanders [Grand Rapids: Zondervan, 2014], 160–61).

73. See also Edwards, sermon on Rom. 2:10, L 44v–45r: "they being in [Christ] shall Partake of the . . . Love of G[od] the F[ather] to [Christ] and as the son . . . Knows the F[ather] so they shall Partake with him in his sight of G[od] as being as it were Parts of him as he is in the Bosom of the . . . F[ather] so are they in the Bosom of the F[ather] as he has Immense Joy in the Love of the F[ather] so have they Everyone of them in their measure the same Joy in the . . . Love of the F[ather]." Paul Ramsey rightly suggests, therefore, that in Edwards's view, "to see God immediately is to see him in Christ" ("Appendix III: Heaven Is a Progressive State," *WJE* 8:699–700).

74. Edwards simply uses the language of "medium." The discourse of sacramentality is my own.

75. Edwards, "True Saints," *WJE* 25:234.

Shifting images, Edwards depicts the love of the Father for the Son as a stream that through the Son reaches the believers, so that they get to drink of the same stream of love that flows from the Father to the Son: "The saints shall have pleasure, in partaking with Christ 'in his pleasure,' and shall see light 'in his light' [Ps. 36:9]. They shall partake with Christ of the same 'river of pleasure'; shall drink of the same water of life; and of the 'same new wine' in Christ's Father's kingdom (Matt. 26:29). . . . Christ, at his ascension into heaven, received everlasting pleasures at his Father's right hand, and in the enjoyment of his Father's love, as the reward of his own death, or obedience unto death."[76] Edwards preserves the invisibility of the Father, and he never ceases to insist on the mediating role of Christ as the "grand medium" of the *visio Dei*. Nonetheless, inasmuch as the believers' union with Christ is perfected in the resurrection, the beatific vision really is a vision also of God the Father.[77] And as a result, Edwards affirms that this beatific vision will be "immediate" in character.[78] This affirmation does not contradict his denial of immediacy elsewhere: when Edwards affirms the immediate vision of God, he means to say that there is no longer any barrier or wall between God and the saint. Union with Christ removes the distance between the two.[79]

As we have already seen, Edwards never spells out in detail how, in the beatific vision after the resurrection, physical and spiritual sight will relate to each other. Clearly, however, the vision of the bodily Christ with bodily eyes is of tremendous significance for Edwards: "we have no Reason to think that there is any such thing as Gods manifesting hims[elf] by any natu[ral] Glo[rious] appearance that is the symbol of his Pres[ence] in H[eaven] . . . any otherwise than by the Glorifi[ed] Body of [Christ]."[80] We may affirm,

---

76. Edwards, "True Saints," *WJE* 25:235.

77. Cf. Strobel's comment: "In the ages preceding consummation, the saints had a vision of the Father *by* Christ, where in eternity they have it *with* Christ" (*Jonathan Edwards's Theology*, 122).

78. Edwards, "Pure in Heart Blessed," *WJE* 17:64.

79. Cf. Edwards, sermon on Rom. 2:10, L 43r: "This shall be an Immediate sight. [I]t will be no apprehension of Gods excellency . . . [b]y arguing of it from his works. [N]either will It be . . . such a sp[iritual] . . . sight of G[od] as the saints have in this [world] seeing of him in his word . . . or making use of ordinances which is Called a seeing through a Glass darkly but then they shall see him F[ace] to F[ace] 1 Cor. 13. 12." William W. Wainwright comments that for Edwards, the mind's apprehension of spiritual beauty is immediate (i.e., noninferential): it doesn't depend on reasoning ("Jonathan Edwards," in *The Spiritual Senses: Perceiving God in Western Christianity*, ed. Paul L. Gavrilyuk and Sarah Coakley [Cambridge: Cambridge University Press, 2012], 235).

80. Edwards, sermon on Rom. 2:10, L 41v.

therefore, that Edwards thought that the beatific vision of God (with spiritual eyes) is mediated through the bodily vision of Christ. Edwards's lengthy reflections on Christ as the "grand medium," and his insistence that we see God in and through the human nature of Christ, suggest at the very least that bodily vision after the resurrection will be of an exalted character and will entail the perfection of spiritual insight. For Edwards, it is the sight of Christ's body with bodily eyes that enables the eyes of the soul to attain the beatific vision.[81]

To be sure, Edwards does not spell out how bodily sight of the bodily Christ marks an advance on the sight of the separated soul in the intermediate state. In that regard, he is no different from Saint Thomas. But Edwards does go far beyond Aquinas in integrating both bodily vision and union with Christ into his doctrine of the beatific vision. In that sense, Edwards's view seems to me sacramental in a way that Aquinas's is not. In the "grand medium" of the God-man, the saints are joined to God in the fullness of the light of his presence. The vision of God will always be mediated in and through Christ. Put differently, for Edwards all vision of God—even in the hereafter—is theophanic in character; vision of God will forever depend on God condescending to us in visible appearance, particularly in the incarnation of the Son of God in Jesus Christ.[82] Edwards, therefore, was unable to adopt Aquinas's language of the beatific vision as the direct sight of the essence of God. For Edwards, such language would imply that in the hereafter we bypass Christ, and it would violate the foundational principle that human beings depend on manifestations or signs, even after the resurrection.[83]

81. Thus, while the saints will physically see Christ, the beatific vision does not entail a physical seeing of the Father. As we see Christ (with bodily eyes), he becomes, as it were, the eye by which we will (spiritually) see the Father. I am indebted to Kyle Strobel for his insights in this regard.

82. Edwards comments that God used to show himself in the Old Testament in an "outward shape" or the "form of a man." These were divine self-manifestations of the second person of the Trinity, explains Edwards (sermon on Rom. 2:10, L 41v). But after the incarnation, there is no need for God to assume such outward forms or shapes. The church today lives in a more perfect state, claims Edwards: "but now [Christ] does Really subsist in a . . . Glorified B[ody] those outw[ard] symbols & appearances are done away as being needless & Imperfect. . . . This more Imperfect way theref[ore] is altogether needless in H[eaven] seeing . . . [Christ] there appears in a Glorified B[ody]" (L 42r–v).

83. Aquinas attempted to avoid erasing the creator-creature distinction by insisting that the intellect will not comprehend God. The creature does not know the infinity of God in an infinite mode (*ST* I, q. 12, a. 7; cf. *Sent.* IV, d. 49, q. 2, a. 3). As Nicholas J. Healy puts it: "The creature sees the whole of God, but does not wholly see God—*totus sed non totaliter*" (*The*

Beatific Vision and Progressive Happiness

The mediated character of all vision of God allows Edwards to posit a never-ending progression in the vision of God to ever-greater intimacy. For Edwards, the vision of God gradually increases in clarity both in redemptive history and in the saints' own lives, with conversion, death, and bodily resurrection serving as the main points of advancement—but with the increase in clarity and intimacy never ceasing. Already the Old Testament theophanies introduced a certain vision of God, and the bodily vision of Christ on earth (particularly the transfiguration), as well as visionary experiences of the saints in this life, are anticipations of the vision of God that we will enjoy in the hereafter. The result is a blurring of the line between faith and vision. We may not see "face-to-face" at the present time, but Edwards makes clear that the "knowledge of God in Christ of believers is the imperfect beginning of this heavenly sight"[84] and that holiness itself is "the imperfect beginning of a blessed-making sight of God."[85]

Already in this life, insists Edwards in his sermon on Romans 2:10, the faithful have the image of God stamped upon them. This renewal, he claims with an appeal to Colossians 3:10 and Ephesians 4:23–24, implies a new ability to see: they "have their Eyes opend," and their acquaintance with God changes their soul into the image of God's glory.[86] The result is that, through Christ's indwelling, their excellency begins to shine, "tho it be but as a spark"; yet it is something ten thousand times more excellent than any ruby, or the most precious pearl that ever was found on earth.[87] As Kyle Strobel rightly points out: "Faith and sight, rather than being contraries, are for Edwards united in a spiritual register."[88] Edwards does not contrast faith and hope (restricted to temporal existence) with love (as perduring into eternity).[89]

Eschatology of Hans Urs von Balthasar: Being as Communion [Oxford: Oxford University Press, 2005], 171).

84. Edwards, "Pure in Heart Blessed," *WJE* 17:75.

85. Edwards, "Pure in Heart Blessed," *WJE* 17:76.

86. Edwards, sermon on Rom. 2:10, L 2v.

87. Edwards, sermon on Rom. 2:10, L 3r.

88. Strobel, *Jonathan Edwards's Theology*, 153.

89. Ramsey comments that "Edwards did not share the view that in heaven faith disappears in sight (leaving only a formal faith) and hope ceases with its substantive realization (also only leaving its form), while love alone is the immediate activity of the soul enjoying all it sees of God and seeing all it wills or desires" ("Appendix III," 716). To be sure, to my knowledge Edwards does not use the term "hope" in the context of heaven. And he does comment about the intermediate state that "now shall faith be turnd into vision & hope into fruition" (sermon on

Nor does he distinguish between mediate knowledge (today) and immediate knowledge (in the hereafter).

Entirely in line with this, Edwards welcomes the possibility of the saints seeing God already in this life in special, ecstatic experiences, in which God

> sometimes is Pleased to . . . Remove the veil[,] to draw the . . . Curtain & Give the saints . . . sweet views[.] . . . [S]ometimes that is as it were a window or . . . Gap opend in Heaven . . . & [Christ] shews hims[elf] through the Lattice[.] [T]hey have sometimes . . . been . . . of sweet Light breaking forth from above into the soul. & G[od] . . . & the Redeemer sometimes Comes to them & makes friendly visits to them & manifests Hims[elf] to them. [S]ometimes the saints have times of Light & Gladness for some Considerable time together . . . at [other] times the views are more short.[90]

For Edwards, such visions are anticipations of the beatific vision. They come with great joy—concerning pardon of sin, God's excellency and love, and delight in doing what is good.[91] The result is a "peace that arises from light," along with a "sweet Repose" and satisfaction, as well as a pleasure that gives life and durable enjoyment, since it is like "the durable Light of the . . . stars or sun."[92] Such experiences make the soul shine like the face of Moses and of Stephen.[93] Thus, Edwards highlights emphatically that the vision of God is something that begins already here on earth.

Also on this score, there is a remarkable difference between Aquinas and Edwards. While Aquinas does acknowledge that at times saints experience an ecstatic rapture, these are rare, miraculous occurrences—experienced by saints such as Jacob, Moses, and Paul.[94] The general line, for Aquinas, is: "God cannot be seen in His essence by a mere human being, except he be separated from this mortal life."[95] The reason Aquinas gives for his reticence is precisely that (1) he treats the beatific vision as sight of the divine essence; and (2) the body does not facilitate but stands in the way of such a vision. Our soul, says Aquinas, "as long as we live in this life, has its being in cor-

---

Rom. 2:10, L 17r). Nonetheless, as we will see below, Edwards's overall view on the role of desire in the hereafter bears out the general assessments of Ramsey and Strobel (cf. below, n. 116).

90. Edwards, sermon on Rom. 2:10, L 6v–7r.

91. Edwards, sermon on Rom. 2:10, L 7r–v.

92. Edwards, sermon on Rom. 2:10, L 9r; L 10r.

93. Edwards, sermon on Rom. 2:10, L 10v.

94. *ST* I, q. 12, a. 11; II-II, q. 175, a. 3.

95. *ST* I, q. 12, a. 11.

poreal matter; hence naturally it knows only what has a form in matter, or what can be known by such a form. Now it is evident that the divine essence cannot be known through the nature of material things."[96] By contrast, for Edwards, the presence of the body does not cause a hindrance to visionary experiences.[97]

Thus, as is well known, at one point Edwards holds up the visionary experiences of his wife Sarah as an example of evangelical piety. Her soul, he writes, was "as it were perfectly overwhelmed, and swallowed up with light and love and a sweet solace, rest and joy of soul." Her experience would last "for five or six hours together, without any interruption," as her soul "seemed almost to leave the body."[98] Edwards concludes his account with the comment: "Now if such things are enthusiasm, and the fruits of a distempered brain, let my brain be evermore possessed of that happy distemper!"[99] For Edwards, visionary experiences such as Sarah's are to be expected as part of the progression toward the full vision of beatific bliss in the eschaton.

This continuous progress in vision means, as Edwards himself puts it, that happiness is "progressive."[100] For Edwards, this progression marks life after death and even life after the resurrection. He argued that if it is true that we see God in and through the work of Christ, then the more of that work is accomplished, the clearer the vision of God becomes. Accordingly, the church in heaven enjoyed an increase in glory when Israel was led out of Egypt and into Canaan, when David's throne was established, when the Jews returned from Babylonian exile, when Christ came to earth, when Constantine became emperor, and when the Protestant Reformation took place; and, Edwards asserts, particularly the arrival of the millennium will mark a period of great glory in heaven.[101] Each of these advancements of

---

96. *ST* I, q. 12, a. 11.

97. Cf. Phillip Blond's suggestion that, once we acknowledge that matter is not the reason we cannot see God, "there is no logical reason that such a displacement of finite knowing cannot take place in this life as indeed it does in certain mystical events" ("Beatific Vision of St. Thomas Aquinas," 199).

98. Edwards, *Some Thoughts Concerning the Revival, WJE* 4:332.

99. Edwards, *Some Thoughts Concerning the Revival, WJE* 4:341.

100. For an excellent account, see Ramsey, "Appendix III," 706–38.

101. Edwards, "Happiness of Heaven is Progressive," *WJE* 18:431–32. Robert W. Caldwell points out that Christ's ascension and the final consummation are the two main junctures that divide history according to Edwards: "Edwards often drew attention to two redemptive-historical events that are of such magnitude that heaven is dramatically transformed by them: the ascension of Christ and the final consummation of all things" ("A Brief History of Heaven in the Writings of Jonathan Edwards," *CTJ* 46 [2011]: 55). See also Strobel, *Jonathan Edwards's Theology*, 109.

the church on earth marked an increase in the joy of the saints in heaven, claims Edwards.[102] Because Edwards linked the heavenly saints' vision of God so closely to the earthly progress of Christ's work, history came to play an important role in Edwards's understanding of the beatific vision. For Edwards, the *visio Dei* is not an abstract beholding of the divine essence, but is in good part knowledge of, and subsequently also rejoicing in, Christ's work of redemption throughout history.[103] Because this history of redemption is progressive, the beatific vision must be progressive as well.

The question should perhaps be asked: Doesn't this continuous progress stand in the way of the achievement of eschatological perfection and rest? Edwards makes clear that this is not the case: the beatific vision will be "perfect."[104] The saints' vision of God in Christ will be "truly happifying."[105] The *visio Dei* will yield "pleasure" and "delight,"[106] which will be the soul's "highest perfection and excellency."[107] This happiness will be "pure sweet without any mixture,"[108] without any "bitterness,"[109] and the foremost reason for this is that the

> pleasure of seeing God is so great and strong that it takes the full possession of the heart; it fills it brimful, so that there shall be no room for any sorrow, no room in any corner for anything of an adverse nature from joy. . . . The pleasure will be so great as fully and perfectly to employ every faculty. The sight of God's glory and love will be so wonderful, so engaging to the mind, and shall keep all the powers of it in such strong attention, that the soul will be wholly possessed and taken up.[110]

---

102. Edwards, "Happiness of Heaven is Progressive," *WJE* 18:432. Cf. the comments in his sermon on Rom. 2:10, on the joy of the Old Testament saints at the coming of Christ into the world; of the apostles, Evangelists, and early Christians and martyrs, who saw the Christian faith established throughout the Roman Empire; as well as of the saints of former ages who rejoiced at the Reformation of Luther, Calvin, and others (L 19r–v).

103. Cf. Steven M. Studebaker and Robert W. Caldwell, *The Trinitarian Theology of Jonathan Edwards: Text, Context, and Application* (Burlington, VT: Ashgate, 2012), 216.

104. Edwards, sermon on Rom. 2:10, L 43r.

105. Edwards, "Pure in Heart Blessed," *WJE* 17:61 (emphasis omitted).

106. Edwards, "Pure in Heart Blessed," *WJE* 17:66–68.

107. Edwards, "Pure in Heart Blessed," *WJE* 17:68.

108. Edwards, "Pure in Heart Blessed," *WJE* 17:68.

109. Edwards, "Pure in Heart Blessed," *WJE* 17:69.

110. Edwards, "Pure in Heart Blessed," *WJE* 17:71.

The language seems unequivocal: according to Edwards, the saints in heaven will have "perfect sight," which will transform them "perfectly."

Still, Edwards carefully qualifies this affirmation of perfection by saying that it will be *"according to men's capacity*, a perfect sight," and he adds that it will not be comprehensive, as if our minds could comprehend God. The vision will simply be "perfect *in its kind,*" in that "it shall be perfectly certain, without any doubt or possibility of doubt."[111] Edwards's language here echoes that of Aquinas: he too is careful to acknowledge God's incomprehensibility.[112] But Aquinas is willing to say that there will nonetheless be some kind of comprehension in the eschaton. With an appeal to 1 Corinthians 9:24 and 2 Timothy 4:7–8, Aquinas insists that God can be comprehended in the sense that we can, as it were, reach or attain to him.[113] The reason Aquinas puts it this way is that for him the perfection of the beatific vision implies that it is a vision of the divine essence. So, we comprehend (in the sense of reaching) the essence of God.

Edwards is more cautious. The object of the vision is twofold: first, the object is everything in God that tends to "Excite & Inflame Love i. e. Every thing that is Lovely.—tends to . . . Exalt their Esteem & admira[tion] tends to win & Endear the Heart";[114] and second, the object of the vision is "Every thing in G[od] that Gratifies Love[.] [T]hey shall see in him . . . all that Love desires. Love desires the . . . Love of the . . . beloved so the saints in Gl[ory] shall see Gods Transcendent Love to them[.] G[od] will make . . . Ineffable manifeste of his Love to them. [T]hey shall see as much Love in G[od] towards them as they . . . desire[.] . . . [T]hey neither will nor . . . Can Crave any more."[115] For Edwards, the sight of God both excites love and gratifies love. With the former, Edwards comes close to affirming that desire for God will continue forever.[116] Aquinas was much more radical in excluding desire

111. Edwards, "Pure in Heart Blessed," *WJE* 17:71 (emphasis added).

112. Aquinas cautions that God cannot be comprehended if we mean by it an "inclusion of the comprehended in the comprehensor" (*ST* I-II, q. 4, a. 3).

113. Aquinas speaks of this comprehension as "holding of something already present and possessed: thus one who runs after another is said to comprehend him when he lays hold on him" (*ST* I-II, q. 4, a. 3).

114. Edwards, sermon on Rom. 2:10, L 43v.

115. Edwards, sermon on Rom. 2:10, L 44r.

116. In this particular sermon, he maintains that though desire will cease, the soul "shall be inflamed with love, and satisfied with pleasure," so that "the soul will desire no greater" (sermon on Rom. 2:10, L 44r). In Miscellany no. 822 (ca. 1740–1742), however, he cautiously suggests that perhaps desire is compatible with the perfection of the beatific vision. There will be "no uneasiness of craving," he suggests, "but not so as to leave no desire of increasing: for doubtless when they study and contemplate [it will be] with a desire of gaining knowledge, and

from eschatological happiness. "Man is not perfectly happy," insists Aquinas, "so long as something remains for him to desire and seek."[117] Because Aquinas believed that sight of the essence of God brings about the rest that we seek, desire must be excluded from heavenly happiness.

Edwards wants us to know that the end of history does not bring eternal boredom.[118] It is not as though, once we will have been satisfied with the sight of God in Christ, no further joys will await us. To be sure, the joy of the saints' sight of God is satisfying, "the fountain that supplies it being equal to man's desires and capacities."[119] The human soul, Edwards explains, is like a "vessel," which God, as the infinite fountain of joy, is able fill to the brim.[120] Because the fountain is infinite, the vessel cannot possibly contain all the water that streams from it. Edwards comments:

> The understanding may extend itself as far [as] it will; it doth but take its flight out into an endless expanse and dive into a bottomless ocean. It may discover more and more of the beauty and loveliness of God, but it never will exhaust the fountain. Man may as well swallow up the ocean as he can extend his faculties to the utmost of God's excellency. . . .

---

the satisfaction that arises from it; so we are told the angels desire to look into these things. But they shall have no uneasy desires. Their desires shall be no more than a suitable preparation for delight in their satisfaction" ("Degrees of Glory. Perfection of Happiness," *WJE* 18:533–34 [brackets in original]).

117. *ST* I-II, q. 3, a. 8. Aquinas seems to struggle at this point, since he does believe that in the intermediate state the soul desires the body to join it. He attempts to solve the dilemma by saying that the desire of the separated soul is at rest with regard to the thing desired, but not with regard to the desirer (*ST* I-II, q. 4, a. 5). Blond comments on Aquinas's ambivalence by commenting that for Aquinas, "though the soul is fully satisfied for itself it still experiences a lack in its other half. However the soul is either satisfied or it is not. Self-evidently Aquinas concedes that it is not—yet he argues that the separated soul is at rest, replete in its contemplation" ("Beatific Vision of St. Thomas Aquinas," 195).

118. "After they have had the pleasures of beholding the face of God millions of ages, it won't grow a dull story" (Edwards, "Pure in Heart Blessed," *WJE* 17:73). Cf. Caldwell's comment: "Edwards . . . argued that perfection is not a static state but admits degrees. One who is perfected merely has no sin or natural defect; she still retains the potentiality for growth and increase in holiness" ("Brief History of Heaven," 62).

119. Edwards, "Pure in Heart Blessed," *WJE* 17:72.

120. Edwards, "Pure in Heart Blessed," *WJE* 17:72. Cf. Amy Plantinga Pauw's comment: "As the saints continue to increase in knowledge and love of God, God receives more and more glory. This heavenly reciprocity will never cease, because the glory God deserves is infinite, and the capacity of the saints to perceive this glory and praise God for it is ever increasing" ("'Heaven Is a World of Love': Edwards on Heaven and the Trinity," *CTJ* 30 [1995]: 399).

How blessed therefore are they that do see God, that are come to this exhaustless fountain! They have obtained that delight that gives full satisfaction; being come to this pleasure, they neither do nor can desire any more. They can sit down fully contented, and take up with this enjoyment forever and ever, and desire no change. After they have had the pleasures of beholding the face of God millions of ages, it won't grow a dull story; the relish of this delight will be as exquisite as ever. There is enough still for the utmost employment of every faculty.[121]

Edwards was convinced that divine infinity (the "exhaustless fountain" of God) implies that the creature will draw from this wellspring of joy forever. As Robert Caldwell puts it: "Because God's infinite fullness shall never be exhaustively communicated to a finite creation, God shall never cease from communicating more and more of it to the creature."[122]

Edwards does not indicate the provenance of his metaphor of a vessel continuously being filled with water from the divine fountain, but it has a long history, going back to Gregory of Nyssa, who in turn had drawn it from Plato and Origen.[123] Origen speculated about a supratemporal fall of the soul because he believed that once the soul would reach the perfection of the vision of God, it would reach satiety (κόρος) and, unable to ascend higher, would fall away from this satisfying sight of God.[124] Gregory of Nyssa struggled with the same problematic, but rather than accept the notion of a supratemporal fall, he argued that the vessel of the soul would expand eternally, so as to be able to take in ever more of the perfection of God.[125] In other words, the finite vessel of the human soul would expand infinitely through its ever-transforming vision of God, which would amplify the soul's ability to see him.

Edwards does not appear to have taken his understanding of eternal progress directly from Gregory of Nyssa's notion of *epektasis*.[126] Nonetheless, the

121. Edwards, "Pure in Heart Blessed," *WJE* 17:72–73 (brackets in original).

122. Caldwell, "Brief History of Heaven," 54. Cf. also Ramsey's articulation of Edwards's logic: "If communicating his fullness was God's end in any of his works, that communication must be as infinite as that fullness is" ("Appendix III," 712).

123. See Verna E. F. Harrison, "Receptacle Imagery in St. Gregory of Nyssa's Anthropology," *SP* 22 (1989): 23–27.

124. See Marguerite Harl, "Recherches sur l'originisme d'Origène: La satiété (κόρος) de la contemplation comme motif de la chute des âmes," *SP* 8 (1966): 373–405.

125. See the discussion above, p. 83.

126. See Patricia Wilson-Kastner, "God's Infinity and His Relationship to Creation in the

Northampton pastor's idea that the saints can never "exhaust" the fountain, that beholding the face of God will never grow "dull" since God's fountain will always be equal to their desires and capacities, picks up on the theme of infinite progress in a way remarkably similar to Nyssen's articulation of it.[127] Along similar lines, Edwards suggests that in God's "Infinite Glory" there is enough "to Entertain . . . Contemplations forever & Ever without . . . ever being Glutted . . . & he is also an Infinite fount[ain] of Love. . . . [F]or G[od] is Love[,] yea . . . an Ocean of Love without shores & bottom."[128] By appropriating the patristic understanding of the beatific vision as eternally progressing, Edwards decisively rejected the high medieval consensus that we will one day attain to the very essence of God.

Conclusion

The discovery of Aristotle in the thirteenth century, it has often been noted, set the stage for a much greater focus on the created order. This is undoubtedly true, and there is no need here to revisit this observation. A greater focus on the created order, however, does not necessarily mean recognition of its sacramental character. It is the Platonic notion of participation (μέθεξις) that acknowledges the interconnectedness of nature and the supernatural and that enables Christian theology to articulate a sacramental ontology. It has been the argument of this chapter that Edwards built on these Platonic insights in his articulation of the doctrine of the beatific vision.

Concretely, this means that Edwards presented a Reformed articulation of this doctrine remarkably similar to premodern and Eastern expressions of it. On the one hand, an Edwardsean approach maintains that already the Old Testament theophanies, and already the rapturous visions of the saints today, are instances of a vision of God that genuinely anticipates the beatific vision that follows the bodily resurrection. So, there is genuine vision (not just

---

Theologies of Gregory of Nyssa and Jonathan Edwards," *Foundations* 21 (1978): 317. Sang Hyun Lee writes that "Edwards was . . . acquainted with the Eastern tradition through the writings of the Cambridge Platonist Ralph Cudworth and, indirectly, Gregory of Nyssa himself" ("Introduction," in Jonathan Edwards, *Writings on the Trinity, Grace, and Faith, WJE* 21:3). See also McClymond and McDermott, *Theology of Jonathan Edwards*, 413–14.

127. For Nyssen's understanding of *epektasis*, see chap. 3, section entitled "*The Life of Moses*: Vision as Perpetual Desire." For Gregory, *epektasis* is driven by ever-increasing desire. As we have seen, for Edwards the question of continuing desire is somewhat more complicated.

128. Edwards, sermon on Rom. 2:10, L 5v.

faith) on this side of the eschaton. On the other hand, an Edwardsean view also maintains that we will never have an immediate vision of the essence of God. If Christ is the "grand medium," this means that even the consummate vision of God is theophanic in character. So, while there is a beatific vision of God in the hereafter, as finite creatures we will always desire to see more of God's infinite glory in Christ.

Christ is always the "grand medium"—throughout redemptive history and into the eschaton, as well as throughout our lives and, again, into the eschaton. A sacramental understanding of the beatific vision acknowledges that everything we see with the eyes of the body today is a theophany of God in Jesus Christ, and that everything we will ever see with the eyes of the soul is also a theophany of God in Jesus Christ. This is perhaps the deepest insight of Edwards's theology of the beatific vision: the recognition that wherever we turn our eyes we see God in Jesus Christ.

PART 4

BEATIFIC VISION:
A DOGMATIC APPRAISAL

CHAPTER 13

PEDAGOGY AND VISION

Beatific Vision through Apprenticeship

God as Teacher

The Christian tradition offers a rich array of theological reflection on the beatific vision. Because most Christians have regarded it as the object of their ultimate hope, it has been the topic of thorough and sustained consideration. In the foregoing discussion of the history of the doctrine, I have paid particular attention to the relationship between the doctrine of the beatific vision and the sacramental ontology that undergirds it. Throughout, my working assumption has been that we need a properly conceived teleological metaphysic as the plausibility structure within which it makes sense to look forward to the beatific vision. That is to say, the sacramental presence of the final cause (the telos or purpose) within the nature of things allows us to sustain the eschatological hope of seeing God face-to-face in Jesus Christ.[1] Our hope of the beatific vision is grounded in present-day manifestations of God. When he appears to us today, we already see something of his eternal love in Jesus Christ, which in turn fuels our hope.[2] God's love is really, sacramentally, present to us in Christ. In this final chapter I will explain the dogmatic implications of such a teleological (sacramental) approach to the doctrine of the beatific vision. In dialogue with several of the key figures discussed earlier in the book, I will articulate some of the more noteworthy elements of a theology of the beatific vision.

1. Cf. my discussion in chap. 1, section entitled "Sacramental Teleology."
2. Pope Benedict XVI presents a beautiful meditative exposition on the real presence of hope in his 2007 encyclical *Spe salvi*. Cf. Hans Boersma, "The Real Presence of Hope and Love: The Christocentric Legacy of Pope Benedict XVI," *Books & Culture* 19, no. 5 (September/October 2013): 11–14.

Central to a constructive articulation of the doctrine of the beatific vision is the question: How are we to understand the journey from sacrament (*sacramentum*) to reality (*res*)? If our sacramental vision of God today is an anticipation of the ultimate beatific vision of God in the hereafter, how are we to understand the pilgrimage that takes us from here to there? In this chapter, I will offer some dogmatic reflections on this question. I take as my starting point the notion of God as teacher. Beginning with the second-century theologian Saint Irenaeus, Christian thinkers have spoken of God as teacher and of divine providence as pedagogy.[3] Now, I do not wish to absolutize this metaphor for the divine-human relationship. For one, we tend to think of a teacher primarily as someone who provides us with knowledge or information. Although knowledge is one important element of Irenaeus's understanding of divine pedagogy, it is by no means the be-all and end-all. He precisely criticizes his Gnostic opponents for reducing salvation to (self-) knowledge. An Irenaean understanding of God as teacher, therefore, treats the relationship more as that of a master to an apprentice. God "trains" us in order that we may become "skilled" in divine virtues—the Greek term ἀρετή combining our notions of "excellence" and "virtue"—and so become more like God.

We also want to be careful with the theme of pedagogy because the notion of God as teacher (or, for that matter, as master craftsman) may give the impression that God relates to us strictly from the outside, giving us knowledge or instructions that we must follow up in order to become skilled practitioners ourselves. With such an understanding, we would lapse into Pelagianism: the beatific vision would be the outcome of our own efforts to ascend the mountain to see God. But God's teaching program is much more intense than that of a coach who encourages us from the side. God comes to indwell us with his Holy Spirit and so to unite us to Christ. As the "inner teacher," therefore, God in Christ guides us along the process of salvation, to habituate us to his presence.[4] As we will see, one of Irenaeus's key insights is

---

3. Cf. my discussion of Irenaeus's focus on knowledge in Hans Boersma, *Violence, Hospitality, and the Cross: Reappropriating the Atonement Tradition* (Grand Rapids: Baker Academic, 2004), 127–28. Calvin's appropriation of the theme of divine pedagogy, like that of Irenaeus, was centered on the salvation-historical progress of revelation and the accompanying increase in vision. See chap. 9, section entitled "Pedagogical Accommodation."

4. Michael Cameron observes that in Augustine's *De magistro* (11.38), "Christ the inner teacher acquaints the soul with the realities behind all signs" ("Sign," in *Augustine through the Ages: An Encyclopedia*, ed. Allan D. Fitzgerald [Grand Rapids: Eerdmans, 1999], 794).

that, as teacher, God accustoms or habituates us to seeing him, which results in a vision that improves over time.

Divine pedagogy, as I develop it in this chapter, has at least four elements. First, it is predicated on God's continuous providential care. Sight is not something that we humans initiate in relation to God. God, according to Scripture, is the one who sees us first. God is light (1 Tim. 6:16; 1 John 1:5), and one way to speak of him as creator and sustainer of all is by using the metaphor of vision: God looks at this world, and the result is its continuing existence in his presence.[5] It is from the "Father of lights" that all good things come (James 1:17). Our vision of God is based on his vision of us—to speak with the psalmist, "in your light do we see light" (Ps. 36:9). As our inner teacher, God in Christ gives us the illumination that allows us to see him in the temple situated on his holy hill (Ps. 43:3). The temple continues to be the aim of those who look forward to the new Jerusalem, who will see a city in which God Almighty and the Lamb constitute the temple (Rev. 21:22). John then adds: "And the city has no need of sun or moon to shine on it, for the glory of God gives it light, and its lamp is the Lamb" (21:23). God's providential pedagogy brings us into the divine life, where we see by the light of God in Christ. In the next section of this chapter ("Pedagogy and Providence in Nicholas of Cusa and Jonathan Edwards") I will explicate in greater detail this grounding of the beatific vision in God's prior vision of us.

Second, divine pedagogy (and divine providence) implies a process with an end. If God apprentices us so that we learn to see him, then the entire journey toward the beatific vision is intrinsically related to the telos. It is fruitful to look at both the history of salvation (*historia salutis*) and one's personal pilgrimage (*ordo salutis*) as God training us for the beatific vision in the hereafter. We can see this apprenticeship in action throughout history, in God's revelation of himself in nature, in theophanies, in prophetic revelation, in Scripture, and most fully in Christ himself. Through each of these self-manifestations, God unveils himself so that we see something of his face. Irenaeus, whom I will discuss in the third section, was the first theologian to recognize that the entire history of salvation may be taken as God accustoming his people to the brilliance of his face. One implication of this approach is that the ancient Israelites' vision of God and the vision of God in the new

5. Scripture also uses the metaphor of speech for God's creative activity: "And God said . . ." (Gen. 1:3, 6, 9, 11, 14, 20, 24, 26); "By the word of the LORD the heavens were made, / and by the breath of his mouth all their host" (Ps. 33:6). I discuss the relationship between speech and vision in more detail in chap. 8.

Jerusalem cannot be separated. Though the two are by no means identical and must be distinguished, we dare not separate them; the latter is the final cause of the former and is, therefore, mystically or sacramentally present within it. So, although doctrinally we may reserve the language of "beatific vision" for the final cause itself—that is to say, for the vision of God in the hereafter—we should not erroneously conclude that the beatific vision is in a category all its own, separate from the earlier process of apprenticeship. The apprenticeship is already a participation in the life of God and, as such, already a vision of God.

To be sure, the various stages of apprenticeship genuinely differ from each other. God truly shows more of his character (his essence) in the incarnation than he did before. It is crucial to recognize the *sui generis* nature and the unsurpassability of the incarnation. The opening passage of the Epistle to the Hebrews reflects on the ontological singularity of the incarnation, insisting that "in these last days," God has spoken to us through his Son (Heb. 1:2). "He is," continues the book of Hebrews, "the radiance of the glory of God and the exact imprint of his nature, and he upholds the universe by the word of his power" (1:3). The entire epistle is a reflection on the qualitative progress and the definitive character that marks God's self-revelation in Christ.[6] The incarnation means that Christ *is* God in a way that the theophanies were not. In comparison to God's glory in Christ, they were only temporary and obscure sacramental manifestations of the character (or essence) of God.

Furthermore, Saint Paul intimates that our spiritual vision of Christ today is more glorious than that of Moses (2 Cor. 3:7–18); and in the divine pedagogy it really is to the disciples' (and our) advantage that Christ ascended, so that he could send the Helper (παράκλητος; John 16:7). The dispensation of Pentecost means genuine pedagogical progress inasmuch as the disciples could not yet bear Jesus's teachings (16:12), while the Spirit is the one who today guides us "into all the truth" (16:13) and reveals Christ to us in a manner that was impossible until then. Through the events surrounding pascha and Pentecost, God leads the believers to a level of clarity of spiritual insight in Christ's truth and love that they had previously been unable to reach. We see the same Christ today through faith that the disciples and others witnessed physically long ago. Still, our vision of him is the result of

---

6. Luke Timothy Johnson comments: "The special and superior character of God's speech in and through his Son Jesus is the main point of Hebrews' argument, together with the corollary that it requires a greater and better response of faith than that shown by 'the fathers'" (*Hebrews: A Commentary*, NTL [Louisville: Westminster John Knox, 2006], 65).

further spiritual progress. "Blessed are those who have not seen and yet have believed" (20:29), says Jesus to Thomas after he has put his finger and his hand in Christ's wounds. The spiritual vision of faith is of a greater, more glorious character than the disciples' vision of Christ on earth.

Similarly, the glory of the beatific vision—already now for the blessed in heaven and even more so after the resurrection for all the saints—will be a great improvement in vision compared to the vision of faith that we have today. Compared to earlier visions of God, ours today may be astonishingly glorious (particularly because God has now, irreversibly and unsurpassably, taken on human flesh in Christ), but it is still much inferior to the final beatific vision of God in Christ. "We walk by faith, not by sight," claims the apostle Paul (2 Cor. 5:7). To be sure, this is not an absolute statement. People saw God in all sorts of ways throughout the apprenticeship program. Even faith is a seeing of sorts. (The scholastic language of *lumen fidei* alongside *lumen gloriae* is but one indication of this.) But we will see the essence of God's truth and love in Christ much more gloriously in the hereafter than we do today.

Even so, it is less than helpful strictly to reserve the language of seeing the essence of God to the hereafter. This way of distinguishing between vision today and vision in the hereafter runs into several problems. It implies, on the one hand, that when (here on earth) revelation mediates the vision of God, this is not really vision of God himself—that is to say, it is not a vision of his essence. But if God's essence is his character of love, then to see him in and through various creaturely modes is truly to see him—his being or οὐσία, however imperfectly and incompletely. On the other hand, by reserving the vision of the divine essence to the hereafter, we may appear to suggest that at that point we will leave behind God's self-revelation in Christ—at least in the sense that in the eschaton we will no longer see God by seeing Christ. By contrast, in the pedagogical approach as I outline it here, God always and only reveals himself in Christ. That is to say, whenever we see God—whether in the Old Testament Scriptures or face-to-face in the eschaton—we see him inasmuch as we see Christ. This is not to gainsay the immediate or direct character of the beatific vision, since the hypostatic union means that when we see the human Jesus, we see the Son of God. Therefore, we see the very truth or essence of God's love when we look at Jesus.[7] Even in the eschaton,

---

7. The Orthodox Palamite approach maintains that (both now and in the hereafter) we participate only in the uncreated divine energies. Nikolaos Loudovikos explains that for Palamas, the essence-energies distinction "does not compromise either the divine unity or the

this sight is only a finite participation in the infinity of God's love in Christ. In the section entitled "Pedagogy and Salvation History," therefore, I will discuss the theology of divine vision in the book of Exodus and will explain how Irenaeus applied this graduated divine pedagogy to a theology of vision that covers the entirety of salvation history.

Third, God's pedagogy of vision centers on Christ. This is already clear from what I have said so far, but since it has been one of the key elements throughout this book, it is important to focus on this point as a distinct aspect of divine pedagogy. One of the reasons the doctrine of the beatific vision has come under suspicion in the modern period is that it is often assumed, a priori, that *visio Dei* simply means a direct, intuitive vision of the essence of God, which in turn leads to the conclusion that the beatific vision takes us beyond God's mediation of himself through Christ. As we have seen, however, many within the Christian tradition—theologians such as Gregory of Nyssa, Symeon the New Theologian, Gregory Palamas, Bonaventure, Nicholas of Cusa, a variety of Puritan theologians, as well as Jonathan Edwards—treated the beatific vision in a thoroughly christological fashion.[8] It seems to me that their christological unpacking of the doctrine is grounded squarely in the Scriptures themselves and that such a

---

divine simplicity, as it only means that, paradoxically, divinity is not exhaustively expressed in its communion with creation, although it is divinity in its totality that comes in communion with beings. Or, in other words, that God is always more than his essential expressions" ("Striving for Participation: Palamite Analogy as Dialogical Syn-Energy and Thomist Analogy as Emanational Similitude," in *Divine Essence and Divine Energies: Ecumenical Reflections on the Presence of God in Eastern Orthodoxy*, ed. Constantinos Athanasopoulos and Christoph Schneider [Cambridge: Clarke, 2013], 125). Loudovikos goes on to show that for Palamas, the divine essence expresses itself in the energies, so that in some sense for Palamas it is legitimate to say that we participate in the divine essence (125–26). Indeed, Loudovikos quotes Palamas as saying that in each energy, "God in his wholeness" is "present in his creatures, imparting himself to them and absolutely participated in, according to the image of the sunbeam, in a little part of which we can see the sun in its wholeness" (126). In short, it seems as though Palamas's essence-energies distinction simply serves (1) to acknowledge that human apprehension of God is never comprehensive; and (2) to distinguish between God's being and his operations, without in any way separating the two. All this seems helpful to me, though I still prefer the more unencumbered language of seeing God himself (his essence) in Christ. This is not because I think we grasp God comprehensively but because this language highlights that God's self-revelation in Christ truly reveals who he himself is.

8. This christological focus was in play also among numerous other medieval authors. See Boyd Taylor Coolman, "Spiritual and Sensuous: The Christian Doctrine of the Spiritual Senses of the Soul, Eschatologically Considered," in *Sensing Things Divine: Towards a Constructive Account of Spiritual Perception*, ed. Frederick D. Aquino and Paul L. Gavrilyuk (Oxford: Oxford University Press, forthcoming).

christological approach forms the sine qua non of a biblical articulation of the doctrine. God's pedagogy is one in which the master artisan communicates his own skill (or virtue). That is to say, he communicates himself. This can never be anything else than his self-communication in Christ. Therefore, an understanding of the beatific vision must begin and end with the hypostatic union of the incarnate Son of God. In the section "Pedagogy and Christology," therefore, I will turn to the Gospel of John as well as to several other key New Testament passages on the beatific vision (e.g., Matt. 5:8; 1 Cor. 13:12; 1 John 3:2) to discuss the relationship between Christ and the beatific vision in greater detail.

Finally, God's pedagogy is transformative. By habituating his people throughout history to an ever-greater vision of himself in Christ (and by training us personally to become more like Christ), God changes us. At some level, this insight is relatively straightforward: only "the pure in heart" will see God (Matt. 5:8), so that without holiness "no one will see the Lord" (Heb. 12:14). This is the reason Christians have always maintained that only by undergoing a final purgation will we be able to see the face of God in the hereafter. While Christian traditions differ on how to understand this final purgation, they are agreed that it is by changing or transforming us that God enables us to come into his presence after death.

The transformative nature of God's pedagogy, however, is unique, in that it transforms us into the divine light. We already saw that when God teaches us, he does not simply instruct us from the outside. Instead, he illumines us and so transfigures us to be like Christ. In him, therefore, we join the divine life, becoming sons and daughters of God (cf. Rom. 8:14–17; Gal. 4:4–7). This Christian teaching of divinization does not mean that we take the place of God—that would only be the case if we ended up with a comprehensive vision of God, something that no one in the tradition, either East or West, has been bold enough to claim. Almost all have recognized that the invisibility of God (Exod. 33:20; John 1:18; 1 Tim. 6:16) holds true also in the eschaton. Our divinization in the beatific vision does mean, however, that through God's unveiling of himself in Christ we are transformed into the likeness of the object of our vision—we are ontologically changed so as to become more like God in Christ.

The apostle Paul speaks of this deifying process when he comments, "We all, with unveiled face, beholding the glory of the Lord, are being transformed into the same image from one degree of glory to another" (2 Cor. 3:18). The light of God—which I take to be his personal presence in Christ through the Spirit—transforms us into itself. The glory of God becomes ours, so that, like God—and in the risen Christ—we take on incorruptibility and immortality (1 Cor. 15:53–54). So, to become "partakers of the divine nature" (θείας κοινωνοὶ φύσεως; 2 Pet. 1:4) means that we escape the "corruption" of the world as we share increasingly in the divine virtues. Saint Peter claims that God calls us to his own "glory and excellence" (δόξῃ καὶ ἀρετῇ; 1:3), and immediately after mentioning our participation in the divine nature and our escape from corruption, he spells out in detail how these "excellences" or "virtues" of the divine nature take shape in a human life of virtue (1:5–7).[9] Thus, while the beatific vision by no means erases the creator-creature distinction, it does imply participating in divine glory and excellence and, in that sense, sharing in the divine nature.[10]

In the section "Pedagogy and Transformation: Bodily Vision of God," I will use especially Gregory of Nyssa and Gregory Palamas to suggest that our divinization involves a transformation not only of the intellect but also of the body. It seems important that the apostle Paul speaks of our future sharing in the divine attribute of immortality, not in connection with our soul or our intellect—though this is certainly true as well—but with regard to the body (1 Cor. 15:53). This leads me to conjecture that a transformation of the body may lead to a vision of God through transfigured physical eyes, so that we can say with Job, "In my flesh I shall see God" (Job 19:26).[11] In light of the Christian tradition's general caution with regard to a physical vision of God, I offer this possibility with some trepidation and as a hypothesis. Nonetheless, it seems to me that perhaps immaterialism (advocated by both Gregory of Nyssa and Jonathan Edwards) may provide us with metaphysical building blocks that allow us to speak with integrity of a suprasensible and supraintellectual vision of God.

Pedagogy and Providence in Nicholas of Cusa and Jonathan Edwards

In 1454 the German theologian Nicholas of Cusa (1401–1464) sent a twofold gift of encouragement to the monks of the Benedictine community at

---

9. Cf. the nuanced discussion in James Starr, "Does 2 Peter 1:4 Speak of Deification?" in *Partakers of the Divine Nature: The History and Development of Deification in the Christian Traditions*, ed. Michael J. Christensen and Jeffery A. Wittung (Grand Rapids: Baker Academic, 2007), 81–92.

10. For more on the doctrine of deification, see Norman Russell, *The Doctrine of Deification in the Greek Patristic Tradition* (Oxford: Oxford University Press, 2006); Michael J. Gorman, *Inhabiting the Cruciform God: Kenosis, Justification, and Theosis in Paul's Narrative Soteriology* (Grand Rapids: Eerdmans, 2009).

11. This difficult verse can be interpreted in a variety of ways, and I am not suggesting that by itself it proves a bodily beatific vision. The various interpretive strategies of relating this verse to the beatific vision make for an interesting case study.

Tegernsee: a newly penned book of his, *De visione Dei*, along with an icon, likely of the face of Christ.[12] At the beginning of his treatise, Cusa asks the monks to engage in an experiment:

> I am sending, to your charity, a painting that I was able to acquire containing an all-seeing image, which I call an icon of God. Hang this up some place, perhaps on a north wall. And you brothers stand around it, equally distant from it, and gaze at it. And each of you will experience that from whatever place one observes it the face will seem to regard him alone. To a brother standing in the east, the face will look eastward; to one in the south, it will look southward; and to one in the west, westward. First, therefore, you will marvel at how it is possible that the face looks on all and each one of you at the same time. . . . Next, let the brother who was in the east place himself in the west, and he will experience the gaze as fastened on him there just as it was before in the east. Since he knows that the icon is fixed and unchanged, he will marvel at the beginning of its unchangeable gaze (*mutationem immutabilis visus*).[13]

Nicholas points out that no matter where a monk may place himself in relation to the icon, the face it depicts looks at him directly. Of course, as both Cusa and the Benedictine monks were aware, in reality the Christ figure would look not just on one individual but on every one of the monks at the same time, regardless of where they placed themselves before the icon.

It is with good reason that Nicholas of Cusa asked the monks of Tegernsee to subject themselves to the gaze of Christ. Nicholas was convinced that it is only God's gaze in Christ that calls creation into being and sustains it in its created form.[14] After a few introductory chapters, Nicholas turns his treatise

12. I discuss Cusa's understanding of the beatific vision in chap. 7.

13. *DVD* pref.; quotations in this section come from *Nicholas of Cusa: Selected Spiritual Writings*, trans. and ed. H. Lawrence Bond (Mahwah, NJ: Paulist, 1997), here 235–36.

14. Cusa's notion that divine vision (or knowledge) is the cause of creation is part of the mainstay of the Christian Platonist tradition. Augustine comments famously, "It is true of all his creatures, both spiritual and corporeal, that he does not know them because they are, but that they are because he knows them" (*Trin.* 15.13.22; quotation comes from Augustine, *The Trinity*, trans. Edmund Hill, ed. John E. Rotelle, 2nd ed., WSA I/5 [Hyde Park, NY: New City Press, 2012]). Thomas Aquinas quotes this passage and adds: "God causes things by His intellect, since His being is His act of understanding; and hence His knowledge must be the cause of things, in so far as His will is joined to it. Hence the knowledge of God as the cause of things is usually called the *knowledge of approbation*" (*ST* I, q. 14, a. 8; quotations come from

into the form of a prayer, and he addresses the God who looks on him (as well as on the monks of Tegernsee):

> Lord, in this image of you I now behold your providence (*providentiam*) by a certain sensible experience. For if you do not abandon me, the vilest of all, you will never abandon anyone. . . . By no imagining, Lord, do you allow me to conceive that you love anything other than me more than me, for it is I alone that your gaze does not abandon. And since the eye is there wherever love is (*ibi oculus ubi amor*), I experience that you love me because your eyes rest most attentively on me, your humble servant. Your seeing, Lord, is your loving (*videre tuum est amare*).[15]

Cusa is enthralled with God's vision of himself and of all reality. God's face is a face whose "eye reaches all things without turning" and in so doing loves all things.[16] This divine love causes Cusa in turn to love God. It feeds him and kindles his desires, so that he drinks of the dew of gladness, which becomes a "fountain of life" inside him.[17] The end result of God's seeing is the communication of immortality and, thus, "eternal happiness."[18]

For Nicholas, the *visio Dei* of the title of his book is, in the first place, a subjective genitive. It speaks of God's all-seeing, unchangeable gaze of humanity in love and mercy. To be sure, the treatise also speaks of our vision of God, but on Nicholas's understanding, our vision of God is invariably predicated on his vision of us.[19] We cannot see God without him

---

Thomas Aquinas, *Summa Theologica*, trans. Fathers of the English Dominican Province, 5 vols. [1948; reprint, Notre Dame: Christian Classics, 1981]).

15. *DVD* 4.9–10.

16. In typically Platonic fashion, Cusa maintains that God always and only looks on us in providential love and mercy, communicating to us immortality and happiness. When we miss out on the loving glance of God, it is not because he is not looking on us in love but simply because by our free will we have decided to look away from his face. Thus, Nicholas comments that God never changes his eyes or his gaze: "If you do not look upon me with the eye of grace, I am at fault because I have separated myself from you by turning away toward some other, which I prefer to you" (*DVD* 5.14). Similarly, Nicholas suggests: "And the more one strives to look on you with greater love, the more loving will one find your face. Whoever looks on you with anger will likewise find your face angry" (*DVD* 6.19).

17. *DVD* 4.12.

18. *DVD* 4.12.

19. Cf. Jean-Luc Marion's comment: "I may well say that I see God, but this can only be if God, this God who remains a hidden God, grants it to me. And he only lets himself be seen by someone else by giving himself to him, so by himself first seeing this someone who will thus eventually see him. For a face to see the face of God, God must first turn this face towards

first seeing us.[20] In fact, since Nicholas explicitly identifies God's gaze with his providential love, it would not be a stretch to suggest that Nicholas believed in a *creatio continua* of sorts, in which the created order perdures only inasmuch as it is upheld by the loving gaze of God.[21] Cusa confesses: "I exist only insomuch as you are with me. And since your seeing is your being, therefore, because you regard me, I am (*ego sum, quia tu me respicis*), and if you remove your face from me, I will cease to be."[22] For Cusa, our vision of God is always only in response to God's vision of us. Jacob Sherman rightly explains Cusa's position as follows: "In being seen we are being created, called into existence, sustained in our very being. This is the ontological key to why in seeing us the hidden God gives himself to be seen."[23] Put differently, if God's vision of the world is the loving emanation of creation from the being of God, our vision of him constitutes a deifying return to him.

We could say that God's vision of us trains us to look upon him in turn. Nicholas grounds our vision of God in the beauty of God's face, which attracts our loving gaze: "Every face has beauty, but none is beauty itself. Your face, Lord, has beauty, and this having is being. It is thus absolute beauty (*pulchritudo absoluta*) itself, which is the form (*forma*) that gives being to every form of beauty. O immeasurably lovely Face, your beauty is such that all things to which are granted to behold it are not sufficient to admire it."[24] God's face, according to Nicholas, is beauty itself. We see this "face of faces"

those who look at him" ("Voir, se voir vu: L'Apport de Nicolas de Cues dans le *De visione Dei*," *BLE* 117, no. 2 [April 2016]: 18–19 [translation mine]).

20. Cf. Andrew R. Hay's comment: "God is objectively radiant, shining forth himself, outstripping any and all conceptual notions *in toto*, and yet making himself graciously perceptible and 'speakable'" (*God's Shining Forth: A Trinitarian Theology of Divine Light*, PTMS 218 [Eugene, OR: Pickwick, 2017], 18).

21. Marion notes that for Nicholas of Cusa God's gaze is always already a loving gaze: "The intentionality [of the gaze of God] does not lead to 'objecthood,' nor does it aim at an object, but extends love and aims at a beloved, who can then in turn become a lover" ("Voir, se voir vu," 35 [translation mine]).

22. *DVD* 4.10. Cusa similarly comments a little later: "Your seeing is nothing other than your bringing to life, nothing other than your continuously imparting your sweetest love" (*DVD* 4.12). Again, he states: "You are visible by all creatures and you see all. In that you see all you are seen by all. For otherwise creatures cannot exist since they exist by your vision (*visione tua sunt*). If they did not see you who see, they would not receive being from you. The being of a creature is equally your seeing and your being seen" (*DVD* 10.40).

23. Jacob Holsinger Sherman, *Partakers of the Divine: Contemplation and the Practice of Philosophy* (Minneapolis: Fortress, 2014), 177.

24. *DVD* 6.20.

(*facies facierum*) in veiled fashion by looking into the faces of those around us.[25] But the eye desires to see the light that is beyond all visible light. As a result, the eye "knows that so long as it sees anything, what it sees is not what it is seeking." Only when we enter into the cloud—a picture derived from the Christian Platonist tradition reaching back via Dionysius to Gregory of Nyssa—do we see the invisible light of God's beauty: "The denser, therefore, one knows the cloud to be the more one truly attains to the invisible light (*invisibilem lucem*) in the cloud."[26] For Nicholas of Cusa, the notion of "invisible light" bespeaks the recognition that God can only be found after we willingly enter into the cloud, and in doing so acknowledge what Cusa terms the "coincidence of opposites" (*coincidentia oppositorum*). The deeper the obscurity of the cloud, the more clearly we see the brilliance of the light of God's face.[27] Once we are inside the cloud, the pedagogy of divine providence has reached its telos, since now we gaze upon the very love that shines from the eyes of God.

The eighteenth-century Reformed philosopher-theologian Jonathan Edwards (1703–1758) had a theological and metaphysical approach similar to that of Nicholas of Cusa. To be sure, I have no evidence that Edwards was familiar with Cusa's treatment of the beatific vision.[28] Nonetheless, had he read Cusa's *De visione Dei*, I suspect he would have sensed a certain kinship with the late medieval German theologian. Edwards's theological approach, like that of Cusa, was deeply grounded in the Christian Platonist tradition,

25. *DVD* 6.21.

26. *DVD* 6.21.

27. Cf. Nicholas's comment: "I admit that darkness is light, ignorance knowledge, and the impossible necessary. . . . We are admitting, therefore, the coincidence of contradictories (*coincidentiam contradictorum*), above which is the infinite. But this coincidence is a contradiction without contradiction, and it is an end without end" (*DVD* 13.53). For Nicholas this vision of God is presented in a profoundly Trinitarian and christological fashion—and here he clearly advances beyond Dionysius. Moving inside the cloud (or beyond the wall of the coincidence of opposites), the believer enters Paradise, where he encounters Jesus as the tree of life. Turning to him in prayer, Nicholas writes, "O Jesus, you are the Tree of Life in the paradise of delights. For none can be fed by that desirable life except from your fruit. . . . Just as everyone is bound to you, O Jesus, by a human nature common to oneself and to you, so one must also be united to you in one spirit in order that thus in one's nature, which is common with you, Jesus, one can draw near to God, the Father, who is in paradise. Therefore, to see God the Father and you, Jesus, his Son, is to be in paradise and everlasting glory. For outside paradise one cannot have such a vision since neither God, the Father, nor you, Jesus, are able to be found outside paradise. Therefore, every human being who has attained happiness is united to you, O Jesus, as a member is united to its head" (*DVD* 21.92).

28. For detailed treatment of Edwards's theology of the beatific vision, see chap. 12.

probably as a result of his reading of the Cambridge Platonists. The result is that Edwards, too, thought of the beatific vision as being caught up in God's loving gaze on us. For Edwards, as for Cusa, the beatific vision means that we enter ever more gloriously into the light of God's face.[29]

One statement of Cusa, in particular, would have held great appeal to Edwards: "In that you see all you are seen by all. For otherwise creatures cannot exist since they exist by your vision (*visione tua sunt*)."[30] For Edwards, as for Cusa, the creature exists only by God's vision. Like Cusa, Edwards was convinced that it is only in and through divine perception that created reality has being. Countering the materialism of Thomas Hobbes, therefore, Edwards writes in his "Notes on Knowledge and Existence": "All existence is perception. What we call body is nothing but a particular mode of perception; and what we call spirit is nothing but a composition and series of perceptions, or an universe of coexisting and successive perceptions connected by such wonderful methods and laws."[31] In short, for Edwards, creation exists as a result of divine perception. To be is to be perceived (*esse est percipi*).

The implication, according to Edwards, is that only one substance truly exists, namely, God himself. Edwards comments in his notebook entry "Of Atoms": "The substance of bodies at last becomes either nothing, or nothing but the Deity acting in that particular manner in those parts of space where he thinks fit. So that, speaking most strictly, there is no proper substance but God himself (we speak at present with respect to bodies only). How truly, then, is he said to be *ens entium* [being of beings]."[32] If matter exists only in the sense that God's loving gaze continually calls forth the ideas of his mind (so that there is no substratum that underlies the properties that we perceive with the senses), then we must conclude, according to Edwards, that the only substance that truly exists is God; there are no other substances.[33]

29. This is not to deny obvious (and significant) differences between Edwards and Cusa. For Edwards, the history of redemption takes on much greater prominence than for Cusa. Edwards's theology of vision does not use the "cloud" language of the apophatic tradition (and does not revel in its paradoxical language). As we saw in chap. 12, for Edwards, unlike for Cusa, the beatific vision is not just spiritual but also bodily in character. Furthermore, Edwards's occasionalism makes him resistant to free will, whereas for Cusa it is precisely free will that causes us to turn away from the vision of God and lapse into nonbeing.

30. *DVD* 10.40.

31. Edwards, "Notes on Knowledge and Existence," *WJE* 6:378.

32. Edwards, "Of Atoms," *WJE* 6:215.

33. For Edwards's immaterialism or idealism, see Oliver D. Crisp, *Jonathan Edwards on God and Creation* (New York: Oxford University Press, 2012), 33–36; Michael J. McClymond and Gerald R. McDermott, *The Theology of Jonathan Edwards* (New York: Oxford University

Edwards's understanding of matter has significant metaphysical implications. Since he maintained that creation exists from moment to moment simply by being perceived, the created order does not have independent stability for him. Created beings, he believed, are constantly in flux. Creation, explains Seng-Kong Tan, was for Edwards a "continuous *ex nihilo* operation."[34] Created entities have their being only in God's *creatio continua*, that is to say, in his continuous perception of them. Oliver Crisp terms Edwards's approach *occasionalist*, meaning that God "continually creates the world *ex nihilo* moment-by-moment" and that "God is the only causal act in the world," so that "creaturely 'acts' are merely the 'occasions' of God's activity."[35] Crisp compares God's continuous creation in Edwards to watching a movie:

> When watching a movie at the cinema we appear to see a sequence of actions across time represented in the projected images on the silver screen. But in reality, the images are a reel of photographic stills run together at speed to give the illusion of motion and action across time. Similarly with occasionalism: the world seems to persist through time, but in fact it does not. "The world" (meaning here, the created cosmos) is merely shorthand for that series of created "stills"—that is, the complete, maximal, but momentary states of affairs—God brings about in sequence, playing, as it were on the silver screen of the divine mind.[36]

By closely linking his immaterialism to his Calvinist occasionalism, Edwards devised his own unique brand of metaphysics, which he believed was the only proper antidote to the influential materialism and nominalism of Thomas Hobbes.

Edwards's Calvinism grounded the notion of *creatio continua* in the divine will. It is only the will of God, according to Edwards, that allows for the continuity of created objects and for the stability and reliability of the world around us: "When I call this an arbitrary constitution," writes Edwards, "I

Press, 2012), 112–15; Leon Chai, *Jonathan Edwards and the Limits of Enlightenment Philosophy* (New York: Oxford University Press, 1998), 56–71. Many of the essays in Joshua R. Farris, Mark Hamilton, and James S. Spiegel, eds., *Idealism and Christian Theology*, Idealism and Christianity 1 (New York: Bloomsbury Academic, 2016), also deal with idealism in Edwards.

34. Seng-Kong Tan, "Jonathan Edwards's Dynamic Idealism and Cosmic Christology," in Farris, Hamilton, and Spiegel, *Idealism and Christian Theology*, 239.

35. Oliver D. Crisp, "Jonathan Edwards's Ontology: A Critique of Sang Hyun Lee's Dispositional Account of Edwardsian Metaphysics," *RelS* 46 (2010): 10.

36. Crisp, "Jonathan Edwards's Ontology," 10.

mean, that it is a constitution which depends on nothing but the divine will; which *divine will* depends on nothing but the *divine wisdom*. In this sense, the whole course of nature, with all that belongs to it, all its laws and methods, and constancy and regularity, continuance and proceeding, is an *arbitrary constitution*."[37] Edwards's notion of an "arbitrary constitution" may well be unsettling. Clearly, his terminology at this point is the result of his Calvinist convictions. For Edwards, however, this "arbitrariness" of God does not result from a nominalist separation between nature and the supernatural. Instead, he links it to a metaphysic that is thoroughly participatory in character. "Within Edwards's metaphysical vision," comments Bruce Hindmarsh, "it was possible to discern God's presence again, not remotely, but in the world itself."[38] Divine pedagogy originates, according to Edwards, in God's loving gaze of the world, and it is this same loving gaze that leads human beings to their supernatural end of the vision of God.

Pedagogy and Salvation History

The second-century theologian Irenaeus of Lyons (ca. 130–202) was keenly aware that the eschatological vision of God in Christ is already given to us in the revelatory anticipations (or sacraments) that precede it. The bishop of Lyons repudiated the Gnostic and Marcionite devaluation of both the created order and the Old Testament narratives of ancient Israel. Through his Logos, God reveals himself in both, Irenaeus maintained, so that in some fashion one can contemplate God in both. Saint Irenaeus had a high view of the materiality of the created order.[39] He purposely used earthy vocabulary such as *plasma, plasmatio, caro, artifex Verbum, plasmare,* and *fabricare* to speak of the origin of creation.[40] Irenaeus regarded the redeemer and the

37. Edwards, *Original Sin, WJE* 3:403. Cf. Tan, "Jonathan Edwards's Dynamic Idealism," 241.

38. D. Bruce Hindmarsh, *The Spirit of Early Evangelicalism: True Religion in a Modern World* (New York: Oxford University Press, 2018), 134.

39. This stands in contrast to the Gnostics, for whom material substance originated in "ignorance and grief, and fear and bewilderment" (*Haer.* 1.2.3; quotations come from *Irenæus against Heresies,* in *ANF* 1, ed. Alexander Roberts and James Donaldson [Buffalo: Christian Literature Co., 1885]).

40. J. T. Nielsen, *Adam and Christ in the Theology of Irenaeus of Lyons: An Examination of the Function of the Adam-Christ Typology in the* Adversus Haereses *of Irenaeus, against the Background of the Gnosticism of His Time* (Assen, Neth.: Van Gorcum, 1968), 16–17. See also John Behr, *Asceticism and Anthropology in Irenaeus and Clement* (Oxford: Oxford University Press, 2000), 38.

creator as one and the same God—seeing as the "one God . . . by the Word and Wisdom created and arranged all things"[41]—so that the vision of God at the end of time meant for him the completion of a manifestation of God that began with creation itself.

Irenaeus articulated this conviction in his famous words: "For the glory of God is a living man; and the life of man consists in beholding God. For if the manifestation (*ostensio*) of God which is made by means of the creation, affords life to all living in the earth, much more does that revelation (*manifestatio*) of the Father which comes through the Word, give life to those who see God (*qui vident Deum*)."[42] For Irenaeus, we first see God in creation, and so the process leading to the beatific vision begins with his self-manifestation in creation. The created order, we could say, functions for Irenaeus as a theophany that makes God present in some way, so that to see him there—and to treat creation accordingly—is to engage in contemplation of God.[43]

In book 4 of *Against Heresies*, the bishop outlines the pedagogical process through which God slowly but surely apprentices his human creatures to enable them to see him. The entire salvation history is a narrative in which God takes his children by the hand and with pedagogic skill leads them to maturity, so that in the end they will be able to sustain the sight of God in his kingdom.[44] This divine pedagogical approach moves through three successive stages, according to Irenaeus. With *prophetic vision* the prophets saw beforehand, through the Spirit, God's coming in the flesh, when he would be seen, not according to his greatness and glory but "in regard to His love, and kindness, and as to His infinite power."[45] Next, in *adoptive vision* God manifests himself to us today through his Son. Finally, *paternal vision* is the ultimate vision of the Father, a vision of such brilliance that it will

41. *Haer.* 4.20.4.

42. *Haer.* 4.20.7.

43. Eastern theology often speaks in this connection of "noetic contemplation" (θεωρία φυσική). See Bruce V. Folz, *The Noetics of Nature: Environmental Philosophy and the Holy Beauty of the Visible* (New York: Fordham University Press, 2014).

44. Irenaeus argues that God could have created Adam and Eve perfect from the beginning but did not do so because they were mere infants. Even when in Christ God recapitulated all things, he did not come in his glory, but instead merely "as we were capable of beholding Him. He might easily have come to us in His immortal glory, but in that case we could never have endured the greatness of the glory" (*Haer.* 4.38.1). Cf. *Haer.* 3.22.4; *Dem.* 14.

45. *Haer.* 4.20.5. Statements such as this led to the Eastern distinction between the essence and energies of God. Irenaeus does not use this technical language, and we should probably read no more into it than an acknowledgment that we cannot grasp or comprehend the entirety of God's infinite life.

render human beings incorruptible in the eschaton. Irenaeus summarizes this gradual increase in vision: "For as those who see the light are within the light, and partake of its brilliancy (*claritatem*); even so, those who see God are in God, and receive of His splendour (*claritatem*). But [His] splendour (*claritas*) vivifies them; those, therefore, who see God, do receive life. And for this reason, He, [although] beyond comprehension (*incomprehensibilis*), and boundless and invisible, rendered Himself visible, and comprehensible (*comprehensibilem*), and within the capacity of those who believe, that He might vivify those who receive and behold Him through faith."[46] Salvation history, for Irenaeus, is a process of increasing perception of the light of God's brilliance (*claritas*), which gives one a share in this light and so in the divine life.[47]

The three stages are not separate, as if the saints saw a different object at each stage. Rather, according to Irenaeus, at each stage they see the same God—though both ontologically and epistemologically, the stages differ from each other in important ways, especially since only in Christ does God take on human flesh.[48] Vladimir Lossky comments that each stage "is virtually contained in the other," so that the prophetic "vision of 'the likenesses of the splendour of the Father' already contains the premises for the perfect vision which will be realized later."[49] Put differently, for Irenaeus, although the prophets did not yet see the actual face of God, the final telos was in a mysterious sense present from the beginning of God's self-manifestation. Irenaeus's understanding of the beatific vision was sacramental inasmuch as he believed that the eschatological reality was in some way already present in both of the stages leading up to it.[50]

---

46. *Haer.* 4.20.5 (brackets in original).

47. Cf. Mary Ann Donovan, "Alive to the Glory of God: A Key Insight in St. Irenaeus," *TS* 49 (1988): 288–89.

48. Although Irenaeus depicts the Logos as already present in Old Testament theophanic appearances and visions (*Haer.* 4.20.11), he regarded the Old Testament theophanies and prophetic visions as nonbodily manifestations of the Logos and as such inferior to God's physical self-manifestation in the incarnation (Jackson Jay Lashier, "The Trinitarian Theology of Irenaeus of Lyons" [PhD diss., Marquette University, 2011], 144–50).

49. Vladimir Lossky, *The Vision of God*, trans. Asheleigh Moorhouse, 2nd ed., Library of Orthodox Theology 2 (1963; reprint, Leighton Buzzard, UK: Faith Press, 1973), 34. Irenaeus takes the expression "similitudes of the splendour of the Lord" from Ezek. 1:28 (2:1) (*Haer.* 4.20.11). Ezekiel actually speaks of "the appearance of the likeness of the glory of the LORD" (cf. *Haer.* 4.20.10). For Irenaeus, the genitival construct indicates distance: the prophets did not see the Father himself; he remained invisible.

50. Irenaeus makes this particularly clear when he comments: "In this manner, therefore,

Irenaeus's understanding of salvation history, therefore, does not simply progress chronologically from creation, via the Fall, to redemption and consummation. Rather, the bishop understood this history as the progressive revelation of the Christ, who in an incipient, inchoate manner was always already present.[51] Speaking of the relationship between the (Old Testament) Scriptures and the gospel, John Behr comments as follows:

> Irenaeus does not understand this in terms of a history recorded in the "Old Testament" continuing on to a new phase in the "New Testament," as two bodies of literature between which, if we so wish, we might be able to discern correspondences, or "types," and continuities. There is, rather, *a strict identity between the Scriptures and the Gospel*, both speaking of the "once for all" work of God in Christ: at length and diachronically, on the one hand, through various figures in the Scriptures; in brief, on the other hand, recapitulated together, synchronically, in the Gospel, drawing from the Scriptures.[52]

The strict identity of which Behr speaks indicates that Christ was not just foreshadowed, but was already present within the Scriptures themselves. The difference between the various stages of God's pedagogy is the increasing clarity with which he reveals himself. Like a good teacher, God constantly adjusts himself to his students' capacity.

It is not only the overall history of salvation that is akin to a pedagogical program leading toward the *visio Dei*. When we isolate a narrow slice of this history, namely, the book of Exodus, we see that here too God makes himself increasingly visible and more intimately present, both to Moses individually and among the people of Israel corporately. Although we could turn to a variety of biblical passages, the exodus narrative is particularly instructive,

---

did they also see the Son of God as a man conversant with men, while they prophesied what was to happen, saying that He who was not come as yet *was present*; proclaiming also the impassible as subject to suffering, and declaring that He who was then in heaven *had descended* into the dust of death" (*Haer.* 4.20.8 [emphasis added]).

51. Cf. John Behr's word of caution regarding the term "salvation history": "'Salvation history' certainly unfolds in scripture as a narrative, as we read from the opening verses of Genesis onwards, but reading this narrative as 'salvation history' is nonetheless a statement of how these scriptures appear retrospectively in the light of Christ" (*The Mystery of Christ: Life in Death* [Crestwood, NY: St. Vladimir's Seminary Press, 2006], 88).

52. John Behr, *Irenaeus of Lyons* (Oxford: Oxford University Press, 2013), 139 (emphasis added).

since it forms the backdrop to the Pauline promise that in the hereafter we will see God face-to-face (1 Cor. 13:12).[53] Perhaps, therefore, we need to turn to the book of Exodus to see how it anticipates (and sacramentally instantiates) the face-to-face vision of God in the eschaton. The narrative makes clear that from the beginning God has been unveiling himself to his people, so that the beatific vision lies anchored sacramentally within the very early stages of salvation history. From the beginning, the Son of God was the treasure hidden in the field (cf. Matt. 13:44) and could be discerned by those who had eyes to see.[54]

So, how does the book of Exodus concretely depict God as the divine tutor, leading his people to the beatific vision in glory? Moses first encounters God in the burning bush (Exod. 3:1–6). It is the "angel of the LORD" who "appeared" (יֵרָא) to Moses (3:2)—though God himself then calls to Moses from the bush (3:4). Moses, awed by the appearance of the God of his fathers, "hid his face (פָּנָיו), for he was afraid to look (מֵהַבִּיט) at God" (3:6). God's appearance in created form—as the angel of the Lord in a burning bush—comes in the context of God's redemptive love for his people; the narrative is bracketed by expressions of God hearing, seeing, remembering, and knowing (2:24–25; 3:7), indicating his attentive care for his oppressed people. The theophanic experience opens up a call narrative, in which God enlists Moses to become their leader.

Once Moses has led the Israelites out of Egypt and they have arrived at Mount Sinai, God appears to him a second time. He instructs Moses to consecrate the people and to have them wash their clothes, since he will come down upon the mountain "in the sight of [לְעֵינֵי; literally, 'before the eyes of'] all the people" (19:11). To be sure, they have already experienced God's presence throughout their journey: he has traveled with them continuously in a pillar of cloud and of fire (13:21–22).[55] But the requirement of purification intimates that he is about to manifest himself in a more direct fashion.

---

53. The theology of God's progressive self-manifestation through theophanies begins in the book of Genesis. For reasons of economy I will restrict myself to some highlights from the book of Exodus.

54. For Irenaeus's use of Matt. 13:44 in support of his sacramental reading of the Scriptures, see *Haer.* 4.26.1. Cf. Hans Boersma, *Scripture as Real Presence: Sacramental Exegesis in the Early Church* (Grand Rapids: Baker Academic, 2017), 16–17.

55. Carl Friedrich Keil and Franz Delitzsch comment that "we have to imagine the cloud as the covering of the fire, so that by day it appeared as a dark cloud in contrast with the light of the sun, but by night as a fiery splendour" (*Commentary on the Old Testament*, vol. 1 [Peabody, MA: Hendrickson, 1996], 346).

Still, also this time, the divine self-revelation remains veiled and takes the form of "thunders and lightnings and a thick cloud on the mountain and a very loud trumpet blast" (19:16), with the mountain being "wrapped in smoke because the LORD had descended on it in fire" (19:18). The Lord warns Moses that the people will perish if they "break through to the Lord to look (לִרְאוֹת)" (19:21). After giving Israel the book of the covenant (20:1–23:33), God then invites Moses, Aaron, Nadab, and Abihu, as well as seventy of the elders, to "come up to the LORD" to "worship from afar" (24:1). Once they have gone up, these leaders experience an encounter with God that is much more intimate than what the rest of the people have witnessed: "They saw (וַיִּרְאוּ) the God of Israel. There was under his feet as it were a pavement of sapphire stone, like the very heaven for clearness. And he did not lay his hand on the chief men of the people of Israel; they beheld (יֶחֱזוּ) God, and ate and drank" (24:10–11). The text mentions emphatically that despite their vision of God, the leaders of the people do not perish. Instead, they celebrate a meal of fellowship in God's presence.[56] When Moses and Joshua proceed even higher up the mountain, on the seventh day Moses approaches the cloud and actually enters it (24:18). His second encounter with God thus concludes with Moses entering the very place of God's presence. The absence of a description this time around surely is an indication of the ineffably glorious character of the experience.

God then makes preparations for a more permanent presence among his traveling people. He gives detailed instructions for the building of a tabernacle (chaps. 25–31), and the book concludes with a description of its actual construction (chaps. 35–40). In between these two sections, we find the narrative of the golden calf, followed by the account of Moses's third vision of God and of his plea to God that he be allowed to accompany his people on their journey. God initially shows himself reluctant to grant this after the golden calf incident, indicating he will send an angel before them instead (33:2). This attitude toward the people contrasts sharply with God's stance vis-à-vis Moses. Moses speaks with the Lord in the tent of meeting, with the pillar of cloud standing at the entrance (33:9). The intimacy of the encounter is thus far unparalleled: "Thus the LORD used to speak to Moses face to face (פָּנִים אֶל־פָּנִים), as a man speaks to his friend" (33:11). In what

---

56. The meal is commonly interpreted as a covenant meal. For an alternative view, based on historical-critical considerations, see E. W. Nicholson, "The Interpretation of Exodus xxiv 9–11," *VT* 24 (1974): 77–97.

follows, God does end up promising that his face (פָּנַי) will accompany the Israelites, after all (33:14).

Moses, however, continues to worry whether or not God will actually be true to this promise, and he exclaims, "Please show me your glory (כְּבֹדֶךָ)" (33:18). The Lord's response makes clear that there are limits to one's ability—even that of Moses—to endure the light of God's face:

> "I will make all my goodness pass before you and will proclaim before you my name 'The LORD.' And I will be gracious to whom I will be gracious, and will show mercy on whom I will show mercy. But," he said, "you cannot see my face (פָּנַי), for man shall not see me and live." And the LORD said, "Behold, there is a place by me where you shall stand on the rock, and while my glory (כְּבֹדִי) passes by I will put you in a cleft of the rock, and I will cover you with my hand until I have passed by. Then I will take away my hand, and you shall see my back (אֲחֹרָי), but my face (פָּנַי) shall not be seen." (33:19–23)

God reveals his gracious character but stipulates that despite this unveiling of his name (and so of his identity), he will in some sense remain veiled: Moses can only see God's back.[57]

Many theologians have mulled over this passage, since God's refusal to show Moses his face (33:20, 23) seems directly to contradict the earlier statement that Moses had already seen God face-to-face (33:11). An Irenaean (and Calvinian) lens may help us make sense of this puzzle. That is to say, it seems to me that God is educating Moses, revealing himself with increasing clarity.[58] The Lord first appears to Moses in a burning bush (3:1–6). Next, he shows himself to Moses on Mount Sinai, initially in the company of the other leaders and subsequently by himself within the cloud (24:9–18). Finally, God speaks to Moses "face to face" in the tent of meeting, and Moses is allowed to see God pass by, as Moses watches within a cleft of the rock (33:7–23). Within this progression of increasingly direct and intimate contact, God's

---

57. Cf. Walter Brueggemann's comment: "The culmination of this chapter is a vision of God (vv. 22–23). It is, however, a vision that embodies exactly the tension and juxtaposition we have seen all through the chapter. Moses does get to see God—but not God's face. Moses's '*seeing*' is honored—but not fully. Moses anticipates Paul: 'For now we see in a mirror, dimly, but then we will see face to face' (1 Cor 13:12 NRSV)" ("The Book of Exodus: Introduction, Commentary, and Reflections," in *The New Interpreter's Bible*, ed. Leander E. Keck [Nashville: Abingdon, 1994], 1:942–43).

58. For Calvin's understanding of how divine pedagogy relates to face-to-face vision, see chap. 9, section entitled "Pedagogical Accommodation."

word of caution that "man shall not see me and live" (33:20) indicates that God's face-to-face encounter with Moses as his friend has not erased the creator-creature distinction. In some ways, God remains veiled, even in this remarkably personal and intimate encounter. Moses's sight of the merciful character of God (33:19; 34:6–7) does not mean that he now comprehends God. In its very nature, God's mercy is infinite and cannot be exhausted by human sight.

This inexhaustibility of God's being is precisely what Gregory of Nyssa had in mind in his reflections on Moses's ascent up the mountain: "He [i.e., Moses] shone with glory. And although lifted up through such lofty experiences, he is still unsatisfied in his desire for more. He still thirsts for that with which he constantly filled himself to capacity, and he asks to attain as if he had never partaken, beseeching God to appear to him, not according to his capacity to partake, but according to God's true being (ὡς ἐκεῖνός ἐστι)."[59] Gregory rightly postulates that regardless of the intimacy of our vision of God, we will never capture or comprehend the infinity of his being. Even in the eschaton, God continues infinitely to transcend us. Our progression into the life of God will continue forever—a teaching to which Jean Daniélou referred as *epektasis*, an eternal stretching forth into the life of God.[60] Contemplation of God progresses without end, even in the eschatological reality of the beatific vision itself.[61]

Although God allows Moses to attain astounding heights of contemplation, none of the narratives describes him as interested in the visionary experiences as such. Instead, Moses is consistently concerned for his people, as he wants the face of God to journey along with them ("Is it not in your going with us, so that we are distinct, I and your people, from every other people on the face of the earth?"; 33:16). Perhaps the most startling aspect of the book of Exodus is its ending. Once more it describes the presence of

---

59. *Vit. Moys.* 2.230.1–6. ET: *The Life of Moses*, trans. and ed. Abraham J. Malherbe and Everett Ferguson (New York: Paulist, 1978), 114.

60. Jean Daniélou, *Platonisme et théologie mystique: Doctrine spirituelle de Saint Grégoire de Nysse*, rev. ed., Théologie 2 (Paris: Aubier, 1944), 291–307. I discuss the notion of *epektasis* in greater detail in chap. 3.

61. The most weighty objection to this epektatic understanding of the beatific vision is that it does not do justice to the complete satisfaction of desire and to the restful character of eternity. I would respond in line with Edwards that the satisfaction is always complete, as it keeps pace with our increasing capacity, and that eternal progress is not a literal movement and so does not run counter to the idea of rest. Cf. chap. 12, section entitled "Beatific Vision and Progressive Happiness."

God, this time after the construction of the tabernacle is finished. At this point the glory of the Lord fills the tabernacle (40:34), and God continues to travel with his people through his presence in their midst: "The cloud of the LORD was on the tabernacle by day, and fire was in it by night, in the sight of [לְעֵינֵי; literally, 'before the eyes of'] all the house of Israel throughout all their journeys" (40:38). The book does not conclude with one of the theophanies of Moses; it ends with God's presence among his people, reminding us that contemplation is by no means an isolated activity. The beatific vision is the result of God's indwelling of his people. The various theophanies to Moses thus point beyond him, as he mediates the vision of God to the people as a whole. God will be visibly present to them on their journey to the ultimate *visio Dei* in his temple in the promised land (cf. 15:17).

Pedagogy and Christology

One of the most fascinating biblical passages dealing with the vision of God occurs in Jesus's farewell discourse to his disciples (John 13–17). As he encourages them by explaining that he is leaving them to prepare a place for them ("In my Father's house are many rooms"; 14:2), Thomas and Philip engage Jesus in discussion. Thomas expresses his incomprehension: he doesn't know where Jesus is going, let alone how to get there. In response, Jesus points to himself: "I am the way, and the truth, and the life. No one comes to the Father except through me" (14:6). In some sense, it would seem from this that the Father is the destination, while Jesus is the means through which one arrives at it. But Jesus then adds a comment that complicates this understanding. He points to the eternal mystery of the Father-Son relationship: "If you had known me, you would have known my Father also. From now on you do know him and have seen him" (14:7).[62] Jesus indicates, therefore, that when we look at him, we already see the Father as well. At

---

62. Biblical scholars commonly suggest that this passage primarily refers to the Son's mission and only in a secondary sense speaks of the ontological unity between Father and Son (e.g., Raymond E. Brown, *The Gospel according to John XIII–XXI*, Anchor Bible 29A [Garden City, NY: Doubleday, 1970], 632; Andreas J. Köstenberger, *John*, Baker Exegetical Commentary on the New Testament [Grand Rapids: Baker Academic, 2004], 431). I agree with this assessment as long as one keeps in mind that from the economy we know of the inner Trinitarian life. We need not downplay the latter in favor of the former. In and through God's self-revelation in Christ, we come to know God as he truly is.

least for those who look with eyes of faith, there is no distance separating the Father from the Son.

This gift of spiritual sight seems to be in short supply with Philip. He presses the point: "Lord, show us the Father, and it is enough for us" (14:8). Philip, like many others in John's Gospel, displays culpable ignorance: Jesus has just indicated that by knowing and seeing him, we also know the Father; yet Philip is still asking to see the Father. As Philip makes this request of Jesus, the answer is (quite literally) staring him in the face: when we contemplate Jesus, we contemplate the Father. Since the Father and the Son are one (cf. 10:30; 12:45; 13:20), it makes no sense to look for the Father behind Jesus. Though it is true that Jesus is the means to the Father, it would be erroneous to suggest that another divine person is hiding behind Jesus. To explain this to Philip, therefore, Jesus makes the matter as plain as possible: "Have I been with you so long, and you still do not know me, Philip? Whoever has seen me has seen the Father. How can you say, 'Show us the Father'? Do you not believe that I am in the Father and the Father is in me?" (14:9–10). According to Jesus's dialogue with Thomas and Philip, then, Jesus is the way to the Father, and the reason is that Father and Son are one. Seeing the Son necessarily entails seeing the Father.

One of the key lessons to draw from this dialogue is that contemplation of God is centered on the incarnate Christ. It is by seeing Christ in the flesh and by recognizing in him, through eyes of faith, the eternal "I am" that we gain life (or happiness, beatitude). We may put it even more strongly: seeing Christ with eyes of faith not only *leads* to beatitude, it *is* beatitude. In Christ, end and means converge. When we see Christ, we see God. It is with good reason that many in the tradition have taken a Christ-centered approach to the vision of God. The basis for this lies in Jesus's allusions to the doctrines of the Trinity and the incarnation. His remark to Thomas, "I am the way, and the truth, and the life" (14:6)—the sixth of seven "I am" sayings in this Gospel—is a claim of identity with the Father. When Jesus states that he is the "I am" (ἐγώ εἰμι), he identifies with the "I am" who revealed himself to Moses at the burning bush with the name "I AM WHO I AM" (Exod. 3:14).

Thus, when the prologue to John's Gospel identifies Jesus as the "true light" (John 1:9), the Evangelist is suggesting nothing less than that in Jesus the glory of God's own presence has come to dwell with his people.[63] Much like God used to come down in the theophany of fire within the pillar

---

63. Cf. Jesus's comment in John 8:12: "I am the light of the world. Whoever follows me will not walk in darkness, but will have the light of life."

of cloud in the tabernacle and in the temple (Exod. 33:9; 40:34–35; 1 Kings 8:10–11), so he has now come down in Christ in human flesh and blood: "And the Word became flesh and dwelt [or 'tabernacled'—ἐσκήνωσεν] among us, and we have seen his glory, glory as of the only Son from the Father, full of grace and truth" (John 1:14). The vision that renders us truly happy (the Latin *beatus* meaning "happy")—or, as John's Gospel would put it, the vision that genuinely gives life (1:4; 8:12)—is the vision of Jesus Christ as the eternal Son of God who has taken on flesh and blood (3:16; 6:50–54). Vision of God is always vision in and through the human Jesus who is identified as the Son of God, in and through whom alone we come to know the Father. The future beatific vision is therefore not a stage beyond the vision of Christ (though we will see God in Christ much more clearly in the beatific vision than ever before). Rather, we see God himself—the divine essence—when we indwell the incarnate tabernacle of God through union and communion with Jesus. Sacrament and reality coincide in him. The divine essence does not lie behind or beyond Christ; rather, those who have eyes of faith can see the essence of God in the unity of the person of Christ.

Jesus's conversation with Thomas and Philip in the Gospel of John is key to understanding the beatific vision, even though the passage does not mention the eschatological vision of God directly. Biblical passages that explicitly address the topic are obviously central (and there are quite a few of them), but we need to incorporate these into a broader theology of seeing God (and of contemplation of God), which we draw from the Scriptures as a whole. Since Jesus is the true and ultimate revelation of God (Heb. 1:2), Jesus manifests him in a way unmatched by any previous manifestations and unsurpassed by any future revelation: Jesus is the true and ultimate sacramental theophany of God, made present in and through the hypostatic union of the divine and human natures in the Son of God. We know about the beatific vision by turning with eyes of faith to the Christ whom we behold in the gospel and in the sacrament.[64]

---

64. Herbert McCabe comments: "The story of Jesus is nothing other than the triune life of God projected onto our history, or enacted sacramentally in our history, so that it becomes story" ("The Involvement of God," in *God Matters* [London: Continuum, 1987], 48). McCabe goes on to write, "Watching, so to say, the story of Jesus, we are watching the processions of the Trinity. . . . They are not just reflection but sacrament—they contain the reality they signify. The mission of Jesus is *nothing other* than the eternal generation of the Son" (48–49). I am indebted to Fr. John Behr for this reference. For Jesus as the "primordial sacrament" (*oersacrament*), see E. Schillebeeckx, *Christ the Sacrament of the Encounter with God*, trans. Paul Barrett (Lanham, MD: Sheed and Ward/Rowman and Littlefield, 1963).

Thus, despite the eschatological barrier, we have reliable insight into what the future beatific vision entails. The reason is that God's self-manifestation in Christ does not mislead; when in faith we look to him, we come face-to-face with God himself. In fact, the apostle Paul suggests that the new covenant in Christ is much more glorious than the old, and that when, in Moses-like fashion, we turn (ἐπιστρέψῃ) to him in faith, the veil (κάλυμμα) is removed (2 Cor. 3:16). By enjoining us to turn to "the Lord," Saint Paul plainly places Jesus in the position of God, to whom Moses also used to turn with unveiled face (Exod. 34:34). The apostle ends his reflections on our vision of God in Christ with the comment that "we all, with unveiled face, beholding the glory of the Lord, are being transformed (μεταμορφούμεθα) into the same image from one degree of glory to another" (2 Cor. 3:18). These words make an astounding claim of intimacy, especially considering that by the time Moses experienced his third theophany of God in Exodus 34, his face-to-face vision was already much more glorious than when he first saw God in the burning bush.[65] Against the backdrop of the narrative of Moses's continuous transformation in the book of Exodus, the transforming vision of Christ of which Paul speaks is simply staggering.

Interpreting the doctrine of the beatific vision christologically has implications also for the way we read the many biblical passages that explicitly mention the beatific vision. Without dealing exhaustively with the biblical witness, it may nonetheless be helpful to discuss some of the key verses. Jesus's sixth beatitude is "Blessed are the pure in heart, for they shall see God" (Matt. 5:8). Jonathan Edwards, in a 1730 sermon on this verse, makes clear that just as God once spoke to Israel on Mount Sinai, so he speaks here to his disciples on a mountain—though God reveals himself now, in the incarnate Christ, more clearly and perfectly than he once did on Mount Sinai.[66] In Christ, God is present once again, only this time in a much more glorious manner. As I observed in the previous chapter, this means, for Edwards, that the vision of God is not just *mentioned* but actually *takes place* in Jesus's preaching of the beatitudes.[67] The disciples see God in Christ in a way that used to be foreclosed to the ancient people of Israel. Or, if we wish to put it in sacramental terms: the reality of the telos of the eschatological vision of God, made present in a hidden manner already on Mount Sinai, becomes present

65. For a homily on 2 Cor. 3, see Hans Boersma, *Sacramental Preaching: Sermons on the Hidden Presence of Christ* (Grand Rapids: Baker Academic, 2016), 183–95.
66. Edwards, "The Pure in Heart Blessed," in *WJE* 17:59.
67. See chap. 12, section entitled "Beatific Vision and Christ."

much more gloriously in Jesus's preaching of the Sermon on the Mount. The eyes of the disciples (and of others interacting with Jesus on earth) may be incapable of seeing the fullness of his divine glory, but it is nonetheless present here, as it is throughout Jesus's life on earth. The incarnation—God assuming human flesh—is the continuation and climax of God's apprenticeship program of acquainting his people with the brilliance of his glory.

On my understanding, therefore, the beatitudes (and in particular, the one that holds out the vision of God to the pure in heart) have Jesus himself as their focus. Jesus does not position himself as a third party between God (the promised object) and his audience (who are told to be pure in heart); Jesus is not an outsider imposing on others an extraneous condition (purity of heart) for seeing God. Rather, in his beatitude on the *visio Dei*, Jesus puts himself forward as the subject of both the first and the second part of his saying. In terms of the first part, it seems obvious that Jesus is the very definition of what it means to be "pure in heart." We obtain purity only by participating in his purity. We participate in the life of God—in his purity—only inasmuch as we are united to Christ. The second part of Jesus's saying makes clear that this purity of heart enables us to discern who God is *in Jesus*. If Jesus is the true revelation of God, then in him we see the character or being of God. Jesus's words, then, hold out to the disciples the way to greater intimacy with himself. Both parts of this beatitude dispel any notion of Jesus standing aloof from or in between the two parties (God and man) that he reconciles. It is in the hypostatic union of the Son of God that we come to know ourselves as well as God. Jesus does not simply pronounce this beatitude; he is himself its subject. He is both the one in whom we are blessed ("blessed are the pure in heart") and the contents of the promise ("they shall see God"). Again, therefore, in Jesus means and end converge: since the three persons of the Trinity are not three individuals, but are one in substance, there is no vision of the Father outside of Jesus Christ.

The apostle Paul, in his encomium on love (1 Cor. 13:1–13), holds out this same promise of a face-to-face vision of God, saying that "now we see in a mirror dimly, but then face to face" (13:12). He explains that in this beatific vision partial (ἐκ μέρους) knowledge (13:9, 12) will give way to full knowledge (ἐπιγνώσομαι), corresponding to God's full knowledge of us (ἐπεγνώσθην) (13:12).[68] Thus, both in terms of sight and in terms of knowl-

---

68. Though Paul contrasts knowing "in part" with "knowing fully" (ἐπιγινώσκω), we should not give too much weight to the use of the prefix ἐπι in the verb. Rudolf Bultmann observes that "ἐπιγινώσκειν is often used instead of γινώσκειν with no difference in meaning"

edge, the eschaton marks a transition to a more glorious future. The Puritan theologian John Owen expounds on this transition in his posthumously published *Meditations and discourses on the glory of Christ* (1684).[69] As long as we see Christ's glory merely by faith, explains Owen, we have a view that is "obscure, dark, inevident, reflexive"[70] and thus unsteady and uneven.[71] By contrast, our vision of the glory of Christ in heaven will be "immediate, direct, intuitive," and therefore "steady, eaven, and constant."[72] Owen then goes on to say: "Christ himself, in his own person with all his glory, shall be continually with us, before us, proposed unto us. We shall no longer have an *Image*, a Representation of him, such as is the delineation of his Glory in the Gospel. We *shall see him*, saith the Apostle, *face to face*; 1 Cor. 13. 12. which he opposeth unto our seeing him *darkly as in a glass*, which is the utmost that faith can attain to."[73] Owen does not explain here the reason for his christological reading of the passage. Presumably, what drives it is his conviction that God reveals himself fully in Christ and that we can be "fully known" only when God accepts us in him. Christ, according to Owen, will forever be the means of communication between God and his saints. Owen's theological disposition seems to me exactly right: the virtue of love that abides (13:13) is the saints' eternal participation in the love that defines God in Christ, that is to say, the character or the essence of God. To know God in Christ—whether on earth today or in heaven in the hereafter—is to know (something of) the character or essence of God. There simply is no other vision of God.

Just as 1 Corinthians 13:12 contrasts today's partial knowledge (ἐκ μέρους) with the "full knowledge" (ἐπιγνώσομαι) of the hereafter, so John's first epistle too emphasizes the ineffable character of the future face-to-face vision: "Beloved, we are God's children now, and what we will be has not yet appeared; but we know that when he appears we shall be like him, because we shall see him as he is (καθώς ἐστιν)" (1 John 3:2). The meaning of this saying is not immediately transparent. What does it mean to see him "as he is"? And

---

("γινώσκω," in *TDNT* 1:703) and that "even in 1 C. 13:12 the alternation is purely rhetorical" (1:704).

69. For Owen's views on the beatific vision, see further in chap. 11.

70. John Owen, *Meditations and discourses on the glory of Christ, in his person, office, and grace with the differences between faith and sight: applied unto the use of them that believe* (London, 1684; Wing O769), 174.

71. Owen, *Meditations*, 178.

72. Owen, *Meditations*, 179 (emphasis omitted).

73. Owen, *Meditations*, 179.

who is the one John tells us we will see? Is it the Father, or is it the Son?[74] And what does "as he is" entail? The exegetical questions are numerous and complex. One thing is undisputed, however: the eschatological vision will far surpass anything we may experience by way of contemplation today.

Those who think it is the Father whom we will see "as he is" (καθώς ἐστιν) often conclude that in the eschaton (and, therefore, not today) we will see the divine essence itself. This is Thomas Aquinas's argument. After stating that face-to-face vision (1 Cor. 13:12) implies seeing God's essence, the thirteenth-century Dominican adds: "Further, it is written (1 Jo. iii. 2): *When He shall appear we shall be like to Him, because we shall see Him as He is. Therefore we shall see Him in His essence.*"[75] Now, Aquinas is appropriately cautious in *how* he affirms this vision of the divine essence. In an important sense, he acknowledges that this vision of God's essence does *not* mean that we will comprehend God.[76] This built-in reservation, meant to safeguard God's transcendence or otherness vis-à-vis the creature, seems to me important: regardless of what it means that we will see God "as he is," it cannot mean that the creator-creature distinction will disappear.

This does again raise the question of what we mean by seeing the divine essence. Eastern and Protestant theologians often—though the latter by no

74. Simon Francis Gaine argues that John has the Father in mind, since (1) John has just mentioned our adoption as "God's children" in the same verse; and (2) John also seemed to have the Father in mind as the one who "appears" in 1 John 2:28 and the one of whom we are born in 2:29 (since elsewhere in the letter John makes clear that we are born of *God*; cf. 3:9; 4:7; 5:1) (*Did the Saviour See the Father? Christ, Salvation, and the Vision of God* [London: Bloomsbury T. & T. Clark, 2015], 26–29). Others, however, maintain that John has the Son in mind: In 3:5, 8, John says the Son "appeared," and so it may seem more likely that the Son is also the subject of "he appears" in 2:28 and in 3:2 (Rudolf Bultmann, *The Johannine Epistles: A Commentary on the Johannine Epistles*, trans. R. Philip O'Hara, Lane C. McGaughy, and Robert W. Funk, Hermeneia [Philadelphia: Fortress, 1973], 48).

75. *ST* Suppl. q. 92, a. 1; cf. I, q. 12, a. 1.

76. *ST* I-II, q. 4, a. 3. Aquinas explains here that our eschatological comprehension of God is not the kind in which God (the comprehended) is included in us (the comprehensors). Instead, comprehension here means "holding something already present and possessed: thus one who runs after another is said to comprehend him when he lays hold on him." In *ST* I, q. 12, a. 1 Aquinas briefly comments that God is "not comprehended." And in *ST* I, q. 12, a. 7 he explains that no created intellect can know God infinitely, so God cannot be comprehended in the sense that he would be included within a finite being. Saint Thomas does claim, however, that in some sense it is possible to comprehend God, "for he who attains (*attingit*) to anyone is said to comprehend him when he attains to him" (*ST* I, q. 12, a. 7). Aquinas means to convey that in some way we can *reach* or *attain* the essence of God without grasping or including it within our finite being.

means universally—avoid saying that the beatific vision involves seeing God's essence. The underlying reason is the same in both traditions. Notwithstanding Saint Thomas's claim to the contrary, there is a lingering concern among Orthodox and Protestants that the prospect of an eschatological vision of God *per essentiam* entails a denial of divine transcendence. It is a concern we should not dismiss lightly. As we have noted, Thomas Aquinas speaks a great deal about seeing the divine essence, but to my knowledge he does not speak of the beatific vision as a vision of Christ. This cannot but lead to the question of whether Aquinas thought that the final object of our vision is something that lies *beyond* Christ, namely, the very essence of God.

The questions that we face here are difficult. The seventh-century theologian Saint Maximus the Confessor, in response to questions from the Libyan monk Thalassius, points out that our understanding of these matters is limited. He discusses the question of how to hold together the ignorance that John appears to confess ("Beloved, we are God's children now, and what we will be has not yet appeared"; 1 John 3:2) with Paul's claim to knowledge ("For the Spirit searches everything, even the depths of God"; 1 Cor. 2:10).[77] Maximus suggests that though the two verses both speak of the eschatological future, each deals with a different aspect of it. We already know the divine aim or σκοπός—we know that we will be deified—but we do not yet know precisely what this will entail; we do not know *how* exactly we will be deified. As Norman Russell puts it, according to Maximus "the reality of the form of future goods has not yet been revealed. For the present we walk with faith."[78] The question of how we will be deified or how we will see God is one that reason cannot adequately or fully address.[79]

Especially in the light of Maximus's word of caution, it seems to me that Saint Thomas gives an unduly speculative answer to the question of how the

77. Maximus the Confessor, *Ad Thalassium*, no. 9. Cf. Russell, *Doctrine of Deification*, 284–85.

78. Russell, *Doctrine of Deification*, 285.

79. Maximus distinguishes between essence and energies, arguing that though human beings can participate in the divine energies of God, they will never see his essence. Gregory Palamas codified this distinction in the fourteenth century. See John Meyendorff, *A Study of Gregory Palamas*, trans. George Lawrence (Crestwood, NY: St. Vladimir's Seminary Press, 1998), 202–27. If the essence-energy distinction is meant as a real rather than just a nominal distinction, it may be difficult to retain the simplicity of God—and it is unlikely that Palamas had in mind nothing more than a nominal distinction. It seems to me that we alleviate the Palamite concern about seeing the essence of God by recourse to Christology: all vision of God (and of his essence) has always been and always will be only a partial and theophanic vision of God's being in Christ.

visio Dei is possible.[80] He would not have faced this question in the same way had he not separated the light of faith (which allows for indirect vision today) and the light of glory (which enables us to see the essence of God directly in the hereafter). If we truly see the character or οὐσία of God in Christ, then it is the same God in Christ who has been seen in a variety of ways in history and whom in the hereafter we will see in glory. God's pedagogy does not mean that he reveals a different "part" or "aspect" of himself at different points during our apprenticeship, so that at death the one aspect of the program still outstanding would be the vision of the divine essence. Rather, throughout history God has trained his people to see him by means of *self*-revelation. At all times—even in the eschaton—this self-manifestation (or disclosure of the divine essence) is a manifestation of God in Christ.

The difference between Moses's vision of God and the beatific vision is not that Moses saw one thing (say, created objects) whereas the blessed see another (the divine essence). When in the Old Testament God appeared in theophanies by means of creaturely objects, it is his own being or essence that was seen (though it was seen indirectly through the veil of the bodily appearance). Similarly, when in the hereafter the blessed will see God's essence, they will see it in a theophany—that is to say, in God's ultimate self-manifestation in Christ. To be sure, in one important respect the object is different: not every theophany is an actual incarnation. As Saint Augustine reminds us in *De Trinitate*: "The Word *in* flesh is one thing, the Word *being* flesh is another; which means the Word *in* a man is one thing, the Word *being* man another."[81] While the eternal Word (his essence) is mysteriously present in the burning bush, he does not identify with it as he does with the flesh of Christ.[82] The difference between the former and the latter is not just epistemological, therefore, but also ontological: only in connection with the incarnation can we say in a univocal or straightforward manner that "the

80. Aquinas suggests that the light of glory (*lumen gloriae*) will serve as a created gift elevating the natural intellect so that it can see the divine essence (*ST* I, q. 12, a. 2). But this raises the question of how a created light can have a deifying effect. Aquinas's defense that God gives the created light of glory this deifying power seems to me inadequate: only God's own power suffices to enable us to see him. For a similar critique, see Nicholas J. Healy, *The Eschatology of Hans Urs von Balthasar: Being as Communion* (Oxford: Oxford University Press, 2005), 172. See further Michael M. Waddell, "Aquinas on the Light of Glory," *Tópicos* 40 (2011): 105–32.

81. *Trin.* 2.2.11 (WSA I/5:107).

82. On my reading of Augustine, in *De Trinitate* he too maintained that God's substance (*substantia*) was present in Old Testament theophanies, even though it could not be seen with bodily eyes. See chap. 4, section entitled "Creature Control and Sacramental Presence."

Word became flesh" (John 1:14). The reason God allows himself to be seen *as* the carpenter's son from Nazareth is that with the incarnation, the apprenticeship program has progressed to the crucial next stage.

While the same Word that appeared to Moses also appears to the blessed in heaven, only the latter see the incarnate Christ (ontological progress), and their capacity to see him will have improved drastically (epistemological progress). The face-to-face vision of the hereafter is much more intense than the face-to-face vision of Moses in part because, as a result of God's gracious pedagogy, the blessed have been habituated much more thoroughly to God's love in Christ (keeping in mind that we never fully comprehend or exhaust God's love, or his essence, in Christ). The future sight of Christ in glory will certainly change us—our physical as well as our spiritual eyes—but that will be the conclusion of a beatifying process that began much earlier. God's transfiguration or μεταμόρφωσις of us is a progressive apprenticeship, which allows for degrees of intensity. God's pedagogy gradually leads us to a fuller view of his love in Christ.

There is every reason to think that at death, the souls of the blessed are so changed that they are rendered capable of seeing God in Christ in a way that they could not during their earthly existence. Moreover, I suspect that as a result of the resurrection of the body the saints will be changed even more (cf. 1 Cor. 15:37), so that with metamorphized body and soul they will continuously arrive at a clearer apprehension of the loving character of God in Christ. In any case, whether it is Moses seeing God in the burning bush or the saints adoring God in the highest heaven, God's theophanic self-manifestation—invariably a revelation of his own self or essence—is, in varying ways, always and only revelation in Christ.

The Puritan theologian Thomas Watson may be helpful at this point. While affirming that 1 John 3:2 speaks of our vision of God as "transforming" in character, he does not conclude that this future transformation will give us a new, created habit along with a new capacity, namely, to see the divine essence. Commenting in his 1660 treatise on the Beatitudes that the saints "shall have some rayes and beams of Gods glory shining in them,"[83] Watson then makes the following comparisons: "As a man that rowles himself in the Snow, is of a Snow-like whiteness; as the Crystal by having the Sun shine on

---

83. Thomas Watson, *The beatitudes: or A discourse upon part of Christs famous Sermon on the Mount . . .* (London, 1660; Wing [2nd ed.]: W1107), 261. I discuss Watson's views on the beatific vision in more detail in chap. 11, section entitled "'Contemplative-Mystical Piety' (2): Thomas Watson and John Owen."

it, sparkles and looks like the Sun; so the Saints by beholding the brightness of Gods glory, shall have a tincture of that glory upon them; not that they shall partake of Gods very *essence*; for as the iron in the fire becomes fire, yet remains iron still; so the Saints by beholding the lustre of Gods Majesty shall be glorious creatures, but yet creatures still."[84] Watson's language is fascinating. He claims that the saints will have a "tincture" of God's own glory. And though he doesn't explicitly use the language of deification, by saying that "the iron in the fire becomes fire," the unspoken inference is that those who participate in God become divine. At the same time, to safeguard the creator-creature distinction, Watson then explains that we will not partake of the divine essence itself. As I have already made clear, I am not convinced that we need to avoid the language of seeing the divine essence: there is every reason to say that, inasmuch as God's theophanic appearances in the Old Testament Scriptures were sacramental appearances of God in Christ, God revealed himself from the beginning the way he really is. Still, Watson's underlying concern is salubrious: God's pedagogy does not allow even an already graduated student to usurp the teacher's place. God's love in Christ is infinite; our capacity properly to apprehend it is always finite.

It is hardly coincidental that the Puritans, including Watson—and, in the eighteenth century, also Jonathan Edwards—often connected the beatific vision with seeing Christ in the hereafter. It is in and by seeing Christ that we also see God himself. Through union with the humanity of Christ we will not just see *his* divinity, but inevitably we will see (in a spiritual sense) each of the divine persons, since they are one God. As we have already seen, Edwards puts this beautifully: "The spouse of Christ, by virtue of her espousals to that only begotten son of God, is as it were, a partaker of his filial relation to God, and becomes the 'King's daughter' (Ps. 45:13), and so partakes with her divine husband in his enjoyment of his Father and her Father, his God and her God."[85] Even in the eschaton, it is through union with Christ in his human nature that we attain to the eternal Word of God (because of the hypostatic union) and so also to union with the triune God.

If the argument thus far holds—namely, that we have to construct the doctrine of the beatific vision as a vision of Christ—then this means that whenever and wherever we see Christ on earth, we anticipate the beatific vision. This is the case most clearly in the incarnation—hence Jesus's com-

---

84. Watson, *Beatitudes*, 261–62.

85. Edwards, "True Saints, When Absent from the Body, Are Present with the Lord," *WJE* 25:234. Cf. above, p. 373.

ment to Philip, "Whoever has seen me has seen the Father" (John 14:9). By contemplating Christ we also contemplate the Father. We simply cannot separate seeing Christ during his sojourn on earth from seeing the Father in the eschaton. When by faith we are united to Christ, we already participate, in a proleptic way—sacramentally—in the beatific vision. Indeed, whenever and wherever we see truth, goodness, and beauty, it is as though the eschaton comes cascading into our lives and we receive a glimpse of God's beauty in Christ. While the eschatological face-to-face vision is the reality (*res*) of our deifying union with God in Christ, rays from the light of God's presence already shine into our lives today. In these rays, God himself—none other than he—appears to us; these rays are theophanies (divine appearances): sacraments (*sacramenta*) that render the future reality present to us.[86]

Pedagogy and Transformation: Bodily Vision of God

God can only apprentice us if he comes to us in a creaturely fashion. Whether we have recourse with John Chrysostom to the notion of divine condescension (συγκατάβασις)[87] or with Thomas Aquinas to the axiom that "what is received is received according to the mode of the receiver,"[88] we apprehend God in a creaturely manner. We do so in this life as well as in the next. In the remainder of this chapter I want to reflect on the question of what this means for embodiment (and vision) in the resurrection. This question has been particularly vexing in the Christian tradition. On the one hand, Christians have typically insisted that after death the soul will continue to have a personal, conscious existence, enjoying the beatific vision of God. On the other hand, Christians have also recognized the importance of the resurrection of the body and have usually regarded the soul's separated existence in the interme-

86. Cf. John Panteleimon Manoussakis's comment that "a *pre*-eschatological vision of God is precisely made possible only retrospectively by eschaton itself—that is by the kingdom—which is to come and yet always coming, flowing, as it were, into history" ("Theophany and Indication: Reconciling Augustinian and Palamite Aesthetics," *ModTh* 26 [2010]: 86).

87. David Rylaarsdam links this notion, which he translates as "adaptation," with Chrysostom's understanding of divine pedagogy (*John Chrysostom on Divine Pedagogy: The Coherence of His Theology and Preaching* [Oxford: Oxford University Press, 2014]).

88. See John F. Wippel, "Thomas Aquinas and the Axiom 'What Is Received Is Received according to the Mode of the Receiver,'" in *Metaphysical Themes in Thomas Aquinas II*, Studies in Philosophy and the History of Philosophy 47 (Washington, DC: Catholic University of America Press, 2007), 113–22.

diate state as incomplete. In other words, the fullness of the beatific vision of
God requires the reunification of body and soul. The tension between these
two aspects is tangible: Why should body and soul be reunited if the ultimate
happiness of the vision of God is already ours in the intermediate state? Or,
we may also ask, how can the separated soul already have perfect happiness
if reunification with the body will still add to it?

These questions have received sustained attention particularly in the
Thomist tradition. Briefly put, Saint Thomas argued that embodiment is
one of the reasons that here on earth we cannot yet see the essence of God.[89]
When death removes this obstacle, separated souls, according to Aquinas,
can attain "final beatitude" (*ultima beatitudo*) in the vision of God.[90] To the
obvious follow-up question, But what then of the body's function in the
hereafter?, Aquinas answered that, although the soul is completely (*totaliter*)
at rest in relation to the object of its vision, the *extent* of the soul's happiness
will increase after the resurrection.[91] Aquinas seems to have thought that
the soul's reunification with the body will expand the soul's joy, since it rejoices now in company with its erstwhile partner, the body.[92] It seems to me,

89. Aquinas comments, for example, "Now, if we are not able to understand other separate
substances in this life, because of the natural affinity of our intellect for phantasms, still less
are we able in this life to see the divine essence which transcends all separate substances. An
indication of this may also be taken from the fact that the higher our mind is elevated to the
contemplation of spiritual beings, the more is it withdrawn from sensible things. Now, the
final limit to which contemplation can reach is the divine substance. Hence, the mind which
sees the divine substance must be completely cut off from the bodily senses, either by death
or by ecstasy. Thus, it is said by one who speaks for God: 'Man shall not see me and live'
(Exod. 33:20)" (*SCG* 3.47.1–2, in *Summa contra Gentiles*, trans. Anton C. Pegis et al., 5 vols.
[1956; reprint, Notre Dame: University of Notre Dame Press, 1975]). Aquinas goes well beyond
arguing that it is the passions or the mortality of the body that prevents one from seeing God
on earth. Similarly, he comments that because the divine essence "cannot be seen by means of
phantasms," the perfect happiness of seeing the divine essence "does not depend on the body"
(*ST* I-II, q. 4, a. 5). At the very least, therefore, the absence of the body does not present an
obstacle with regard to the vision of God. Cf. Phillip Blond, "The Beatific Vision of St. Thomas
Aquinas," in *Encounter between Eastern Orthodoxy and Radical Orthodoxy: Transfiguring the
World through the Word*, ed. Adrian Pabst and Christoph Schneider (Burlington, VT: Ashgate,
2009), 194.

90. *SCG* 4.91.2.

91. *ST* I-II, q. 4, a. 5.

92. Aquinas comments that the absence of the body "is not incompatible with Happiness,
but prevents it from being perfect in every way (*omnimodae perfectioni*). And thus it is that
separation from the body is said to hold the soul back from tending with all its might to the
vision of the Divine Essence. For the soul desires to enjoy God in such a way that the enjoyment
also may overflow (*per redundantiam*) into the body, as far as possible. And therefore, as long

however, that this solution faces two difficulties: First, it seems odd that if on earth the body was an obstacle to union with God, the soul's happiness would increase precisely by being reunited with the body in the resurrection.[93] Second, the added benefit that the resurrected body will offer to the soul in its beatific vision of God seems decidedly limited if the soul's vision was already fully beatifying prior to the resurrection. In all, it seems to me that although Aquinas does anticipate that God will transform the entire human person in the eschaton, he relates the telos of the beatific vision much more directly to changes in the soul than to changes in the body. Put differently, in Aquinas's approach, the sacramental link between the pedagogical outcome (i.e., the beatific vision) and the apprenticeship leading up to it is much more obvious for the soul than it is for the body.

One solution to this problem, though perhaps a bold one, is to say that the resurrection will intensify our happiness because, in part, the vision of God will be physical—that is to say, perhaps we should take seriously the notion that we will see God with physical eyes.[94] In Western theology, this solution has often been rejected in favor of a strictly spiritual vision of the divine essence—ever since Augustine's famous letter to Bishop Fortunatian (*Ep.* 148), written in 413 or 414. In it the bishop of Hippo requests Fortunatian to intervene on his behalf with another bishop, to whom Augustine had suggested a little too bluntly that "the eyes of this body do not see and will not see God."[95] Augustine explains in his letter that he had made his sharp comments in order to exclude the viewpoint of the anthropomorphites, who claimed that God has a body, and he makes clear that he continues unflinchingly to oppose their approach.

Augustine nuances his position, however, by suggesting that he might countenance the viewpoint that by undergoing a change, the body will be

---

as it enjoys God, without the fellowship of the body, its appetite is at rest in that which it has, in such a way, that it would still wish the body to attain to its share" (*ST* I-II, q. 4, a. 5). For more in-depth discussion, see Matthew Levering, *Jesus and the Demise of Death: Resurrection, Afterlife, and the Fate of the Christian* (Waco: Baylor University Press, 2012), 109–25.

93. One could argue, of course, that the resurrected body, inasmuch as it will have changed and will no longer be subject to the passions and to mortality, will also no longer form an obstacle to the vision of God. I very much sympathize with the notion of a transfigured resurrection body, but we have already seen that for Aquinas, the body itself makes it impossible to see the essence of God in this life.

94. For the distinction between physical and spiritual sight, see Paul L. Gavrilyuk and Sarah Coakley, eds., *The Spiritual Senses: Perceiving God in Western Christianity* (Cambridge: Cambridge University Press, 2012).

95. *Ep.* 148.1.1 (WSA II/2:351).

able to see incorporeal substances in the resurrection. To be sure, Augustine is not enamored of the idea: "For they will either be the eyes of this body, and they will not see him, or they will not be the eyes of this body if they do see him, because by such a great transformation they will be the eyes of a far different body."[96] While complex questions remained for Augustine—such as whether our bodily eyes will become spiritual and whether they will help the spirit see bodily things in the eschaton[97]—his basic stance was skeptical:[98] Augustine was largely unconvinced that our bodily eyes would ever see the essence of God, though toward the end of his life he became more open to entertaining this possibility.[99] Regardless of how muted Augustine's acknowledgment of the possibility of seeing God with transformed physical eyes, I think it is a notion worthy of further exploration.[100] Perhaps it is a transfiguration of our entire being (physical eyes as well as intellect) that will enable us to see God face-to-face—keeping in mind, of course, that on my understanding the vision of God's being is one of continuous progress. (That is to say, I would not in any way suggest that the beatific vision is an actual comprehension of the divine essence.)[101]

In his *Triads in Defense of the Holy Hesychasts* (from the late 1330s), Gregory Palamas highlights the importance of both physical and intelligible sight. He mentions repeatedly that it is only possible to see God in a suprasensible

96. *Ep.* 148.2.3 (WSA II/2:352).

97. *Ep.* 148.5.16 (WSA II/2:358–59).

98. *Ep.* 148.1.2 (WSA II/2:351); 2.5 (WSA II/2:353).

99. See Augustine's discussion in *Civ. Dei* 22.29. Boyd Taylor Coolman draws not only on Augustine, but also on medieval authors such as Hugh and Richard of Saint Victor, Alexander of Ashby, and William of Auxerre, to make a case for what he calls an eschatological "sensuous beatitude," in which the physical and spiritual senses interpenetrate and are oriented toward the incarnate Christ in his two natures ("Spiritual and Sensuous").

100. Following Augustine's lead, most Western theologians have resisted the notion of seeing God with physical eyes in the hereafter. Herman Bavinck mentions that a number of Lutheran scholastic theologians (Johann Andreas Quenstedt, David Hollatz, Johann Hülsemann, Lucas Maius, and Johann Wolfgang Jäger) taught it, and that perhaps also a few Reformed theologians (Johann Heinrich Alsted and Gulielmus Bucanus) may have held to it (*Reformed Dogmatics*, vol. 2, *God and Creation*, trans. John Vriend, ed. John Bolt [Grand Rapids: Baker Academic, 2004], 187). More recently, within the neo-Calvinist tradition, G. C. Berkouwer has more radically questioned the metaphysical invisibility of God (*The Return of Christ*, trans. James Van Oosterom, ed. Marlin J. Van Elderen [Grand Rapids: Eerdmans, 1972], 359–86).

101. As I mentioned in the introduction to this chapter, in light of the traditional understanding of the beatific vision as strictly intellectual, I offer the exposition that follows more or less conjecturally, by way of hypothesis or proposal, in the hope that it will stimulate further study and discussion—though obviously I think there is a compelling logic to the argument.

and supraintelligible manner. Palamas speaks, for instance, of the "supra-sensible light" that is God,[102] of a "supra-intelligible union" with this light,[103] and of "supra-intelligible" knowledge.[104] Similarly, he refers to "a sense that exceeds the senses" and to "a mind that exceeds the mind."[105] Palamas acknowledges the importance both of sense perception and of intellectual perception, while he also recognizes that the aim of God's pedagogy is that both will be transcended in the final vision of God.[106]

Palamas goes even further in his positive embrace of the senses—and seems to have appropriated insights that percolated throughout the Eastern tradition—suggesting that physical sight is not so much replaced by spiritual sight as it is transformed into spiritual sight (without ceasing to be physical). He speaks, for instance, of a "transformation" (ἐναλλαγή) of the physical senses,[107] and he refers to eyes that are "transformed" (μετασκευασθεῖσι) by the Holy Spirit.[108] The physical, bodily character of vision is not simply set aside, therefore, in practices of contemplation or in the beatific vision. Rather, according to Palamas, God transfigures both the physical senses and the intellect, so that the entire human person is elevated to a higher level by the Spirit and at this level engages in ecstatic communion with God. As Nikolaos Loudovikos puts it: "The body and the soul in its absolute unity of mind, desire, and affectivity, become coeternal in this transforming psycho-somatic vision of the uncreated light."[109] Palamas's understanding seems to me essentially sacramental: the spiritual senses do not *replace* the physical senses but rather *transform* them and move them to a higher level.[110]

The bodily and intellectual change that the beatific vision effects is a mystery beyond our comprehension. It is impossible rationally to explain such a transformation. If he could fully and adequately explain the learning outcomes, the student would be the teacher. That said, it is possible to speak rationally about this transformation, using positive discourse: a suprasensi-

102. *Triads* 1.3.23; the quotations come Gregory Palamas, *The Triads*, trans. Nicholas Gendle, ed. John Meyendorff (New York: Paulist, 1983).

103. *Triads* 1.3.22.

104. *Triads* 2.3.68.

105. *Triads* 3.3.10.

106. See further chap. 5, section entitled "Christian Spirituality and Beatific Vision."

107. *Hom.* 34.8.

108. *Triads* 3.1.22.

109. Loudovikos, "Striving for Participation," 130.

110. Appealing to Gregory Palamas, John Behr similarly concludes: "The vision of God, and the transfiguration in that vision, is to be shared by both soul and body" (*The Mystery of Christ: Life in Death* [Crestwood, NY: St. Vladimir's Seminary Press, 2006], 158).

ble and supraintellectual apprehension of God is more compatible with some than with other metaphysical understandings. A materialist metaphysic renders a Palamite transformation of both the senses and the intellect—or, for that matter, any transformation from kernel to grain (cf. 1 Cor. 15:37)—unintelligible. By contrast, an immaterialist metaphysic would seem to allow for a transfiguration of physical eyes in the hereafter, such that perhaps they will then be equipped to see God in Christ much more clearly than today.

Let me illustrate what I have in mind by turning to the fourth-century Cappadocian Gregory of Nyssa (ca. 335–ca. 394), whose view of matter—and of the human body in particular—was quite similar to the immaterialism Edwards would later develop. Gregory, much like Edwards, regarded the human body as fluid and malleable. According to Nyssen, its characteristics can, and do, change over time. As he struggled to restrain his emotions, sitting at his sister Macrina's deathbed in 379, he recognized that his saintly sister's body had begun to take on an angelic form: "It was as if by some dispensation an angel had assumed a human form, with whom, not having any kinship or affinity with the life of the flesh, it was not at all unreasonable that the mind should remain in an unperturbed state, since the flesh did not drag it down to its own passions."[111] His sister, he insists, was rapidly losing her gendered character on her deathbed: "The subject of the tale was a woman—if indeed she was a 'woman,' for I know not whether it is fitting to designate her of that nature who so surpassed nature."[112] This destabilizing of his sister's gender did not turn her from a woman into a man; Nyssen proposed instead that neither of the two genders has ultimate, eschatological significance. He considered his sister's virtue to be of such an exalted character that he observed in her the realization of the Lord's promise that we will be like the angels (Luke 20:35–36). Gender differentiation, for Gregory, is something that only characterizes our postlapsarian situation, which is a life of food and drink, passions, sexual activity, and death.[113] The resurrection body—angelic in character as it is—leaves all this behind.

111. *Macr.* 396.1–6; quotations come from Anna M. Silvas, *Macrina the Younger, Philosopher of God*, Medieval Women: Texts and Contexts 22 [Turnhout, Belgium: Brepols, 2008]).

112. *Macr.* 371.6–9.

113. To be sure, Gregory does explain in *On the Making of Man* that God created human beings as male and female already in Paradise, but he claims that God did so only because he foreknew the Fall and wanted Adam and Eve to be prepared for their postlapsarian mode of existence. See Gregory of Nyssa, *Op. hom.* 17.4 (PG 44:189C–D; *NPNF* II/5, 407). Cf. Hans Boersma, *Embodiment and Virtue in Gregory of Nyssa: An Anagogical Approach* (Oxford: Oxford University Press, 2013), 100–109.

Gregory's insistence on the fluidity of gender is the direct result of both his Christology and—immediately linked to it—his understanding of virtue. Nyssen refuses to give autonomy to our postlapsarian natural existence. Our bodies—the "garments of skin" of Genesis 3:21 to which Gregory repeatedly alludes—do not have the kind of stability that our modern concept of *pura natura* suggests. Bodies as we know them today are deeply compromised as a result of the Fall, and it is only when they are reconfigured in Christ that they take on their proper identity as God meant them to be. That is to say, in true sacramental fashion, it is the christological telos that determines, for Gregory, the identity of the human body. The christological eschaton, not some observable, purely natural order, tells us what the body is meant to be. Saint Gregory maintains that the human body will be reconfigured in the hereafter to be conformed to Christ. It is a transformation that will involve the loss of gender, but emphatically not of the body. The body—though drastically changed—will find its ultimate destiny in the fullness (πλήρωμα) of Christ.[114]

Gregory maintains that this bodily transformation hinges on growth in virtue. It is his admiration for his sister Macrina's saintly character that makes him recognize that she has undergone a physical transformation from a female to an angelic body. Similarly, therefore, he maintains in his *Homilies on the Song of Songs* that when through a life of virtue we more and more identify with Christ, we actually "put him on," as Saint Paul words it (Eph. 4:24; Col. 3:10).[115] Along with the bride in the Song of Songs, we take off the postlapsarian garment of skin (Song 5:3) and replace it with that of Christ: "Whoever has taken off the old humanity and rent the veil of the heart has opened an entrance for the Word. And when the Word has entered her, the soul makes him her garment (ἔνδυμα) in accordance with the instruction of the apostle; for he commands the person who has taken off the rags of the old humanity 'to put on the new' tunic that 'has been created after the likeness of God in holiness and righteousness' (Eph. 4:24); and he says that this garment (ἔνδυμα) is Jesus (cf. Rom. 13:14)."[116] Jesus, explains Saint Gregory, is the new garment that replaces the garments of skin that God gave human beings

---

114. Gregory links the fullness (πλήρωμα) of Christ with the creation of "man" in the image of God (Gen. 1:27a). He distinguishes this universal, christological "man" from the creation of human beings as "male and female" (Gen. 1:27b). See *Op. hom.* 16.8–9 (PG 44:181B–C; *NPNF* II/5, 405). Cf. Boersma, *Embodiment and Virtue*, 104–5.

115. For more detail, see Boersma, *Embodiment and Virtue*, 87–92.

116. *Cant.* 328.5–11, in *Gregory of Nyssa: Homilies on the Song of Songs*, trans. and ed. Richard A. Norris, Writings from the Greco-Roman World 13 (Atlanta: Society of Biblical Literature, 2012), p. 347.

after the Fall (Gen. 3:21), and we put him on through a life of holiness and righteousness. As a result, our postlapsarian bodily constitution changes. In other words, for Gregory a change cannot only be observed in our virtuous behavior but also involves an actual physiological transformation. Putting on Christ means, for Gregory, that we replace our fallen, passible life with the eschatological impassible existence that becomes ours in and through identification with Christ. As we identify with Christ, we undergo an onto-logical—and this implies for Gregory also a physical—change in our makeup or constitution.

This bodily change—effected in Christ through a life of virtue—is pos-sible, for Gregory, inasmuch as he holds lightly to the continuity of matter. Peter Bouteneff rightly observes that for Gregory, "the difference between the body's coarseness in the present life, and the 'lighter fibres' with which our body will be spun in the resurrection . . . rests within the moral realm. For Gregory conceives of matter itself as essentially formless, not to say im-material."[117] Like Edwards would do centuries later, Gregory here appeals to the divine will as that which makes it possible for material objects to come into being out of nothing.[118] Saint Gregory maintains that nothing material underlies the properties of an object that we perceive with the senses: "If, then, colour is a thing intelligible, and resistance also is intelligible, and so with quantity and the rest of the properties, while if each of these should be withdrawn from the substratum, the whole idea of the body is dissolved; it would seem to follow that we may suppose the concurrence of those things, the absence of which we found to be the cause of the dissolution of the body, to produce the material nature."[119] For Gregory, what we call "matter" is simply the convergence of a bunch of properties, which are intelligible, not material in constitution.[120] Such an idealist view of matter allows for an

---

117. Peter C. Bouteneff, "Essential or Existential: The Problem of the Body in the Anthro-pology of St. Gregory of Nyssa," in *Gregory of Nyssa: Homilies on the Beatitudes; An English Version with Supporting Studies; Proceedings of the Eighth International Colloquium on Gregory of Nyssa (Paderborn, 14–18 September 1998)*, ed. Hubertus R. Drobner and Albert Viciano, VCSup 52 (Leiden: Brill, 2000), 418.

118. *Op. hom.* 23.5 (PG 44:212C; *NPNF* II/5, 414).

119. *Op. hom.* 24.2 (PG 44:213A; *NPNF* II/5, 414).

120. Cf. James S. Spiegel, "The Theological Orthodoxy of Berkeley's Immaterialism," *FP* 13 (1996): 216–35; Richard Sorabji, *Time, Creation, and the Continuum: Theories in Antiquity and the Early Middle Ages* (1983; reprint, Chicago: University of Chicago Press, 2006), 290–91; Stephen H. Daniel, "Berkeley's Christian Neoplatonism, Archetypes, and Divine Ideas," *JHP* 39 (2001): 239–58; Kirill Zinkovskiy, "St. Gregory of Nyssa on the Transformation of Physical Elements—in Nature and Holy Eucharistic Gifts," in *The Beauty of God's Presence in the Fathers*

eschatological view of the body as something rather ethereal, reconstituted in angelic form in the nongendered fullness of Christ.

Gregory did not, as Edwards later would, treat God's contemplation of human beings as the ground for this malleability of the body. Nor would Gregory's synergistic approach to virtue allow for the Calvinist occasionalism of Edwards's idealism. Also, although Edwards believed that the saints will have expanded possibilities of sense perception in heaven, he never connected this with his immaterialist metaphysic. With regard to this latter point, it is not clear to me why Edwards did not positively link the two.[121] As our excursus on Gregory of Nyssa illustrates, Edwards's immaterialism could have been of significant metaphysical support for his eschatological speculation. Immaterialism allows one to hold on to the Irenaean incarnational approach—and so to the confession that Christ's physical body is in heaven at the right hand of the Father and that we will be bodily raised in and through him—in combination with the spiritualizing tendencies of Gregory of Nyssa and others. Gregory's spiritualizing did not leave the body behind. Instead, his spiritualizing approach was predicated on the body's transformation and perfection in the eschatological reality of Jesus Christ.

---

of the Church: The Proceedings of the Eighth International Patristic Conference, Maynooth, 2012, ed. Janet Elaine Rutherford (Dublin: Four Courts Press, 2014), 150–60. I have also benefited from Lampros Alexopoulos, "The Theory of Non-Existence of Matter in Plotinus, Porphyry and Gregory of Nyssa" (unpublished paper); George Karamanolis, The Philosophy of Early Christianity (London: Routledge, 2014), 101–7.

121. Some have hinted that Edwards may have seen some connection between his idealism and his eschatology. Robert W. Caldwell suggests that "Edwards's reflections on the 'physics' of heaven and the nature of the saints' glorified bodies there remain some of the most fascinating (if not the most speculative) reflections in all of his writings" ("A Brief History of Heaven in the Writings of Jonathan Edwards," CTJ 46 [2011]: 66). Indeed, Edwards speculates, for instance, that in heaven the bodily senses will allow the saints to converse with people at "a thousand miles' distance" ("Miscellanies" no. 263, WJE 13:369). The bodies of the saints will be attuned, maintains Edwards, to every physical pleasure, though in such a way that this pleasure will contribute also to spiritual pleasure ("Miscellanies" no. 233, WJE 13:350–51). These eschatological musings certainly make for interesting reading. Though Edwards nowhere provides a metaphysical underpinning for these eschatological observations, it seems to me he could easily have done so.

Conclusion

Dogmatically speaking, I would articulate my hypothesis as follows: God's pedagogy arrives at its telos when, in the hereafter, his providential vision of us in Christ will transform us—body and soul—so that our physical and intellectual capacities will be healed and transfigured, as a result of which they will obtain powers of contemplation such as

> no eye has seen, nor ear heard,
>> nor the heart of man imagined. (1 Cor. 2:9)

On such an understanding, the body will no longer be conceived of in modern terms, as a self-sustained, independent entity that continues uninterruptedly through time—and perhaps into eternity—unaffected by the loving gaze of God in Christ. Instead, the body, like everything else created, is defined by its final cause as a convergence of intelligible properties conceived and perceived by God's vision, in and through Christ, and brought to its perfection and its true identity through participation in him.

The beatific vision, on this understanding, results from the eschatological brilliance of God's eternal gaze on us in Jesus Christ, a loving vision that will eternally sustain us in his presence (Cusa, Edwards). The resulting transformation is suprasensible and supraintellectual, in the (Palamite) sense that physical sight as well as intellectual sight are transfigured into a visionary capacity that far transcends the capacities of body and mind in their fallen state. All this greatly underscores the importance of the resurrection of the body. After all, the soul's reunification with the perfected, reconfigured resurrection body (Nyssen) will render the beatific vision much more glorious than it was in the intermediate state. The resurrection of the body will thus give way to an eternally progressing transfiguration of body and soul, and the clarity and enjoyment of the face-to-face vision of God will similarly progress eternally in the infinite being of God.

BIBLIOGRAPHY

Akbari, Suzanne Conklin. "Illumination and Language." In *Seeing through the Veil: Optical Theory and Medieval Allegory*, 3–20. Toronto: University of Toronto Press, 2004.

Alexopoulos, Lampros. "The Theory of Non-Existence of Matter in Plotinus, Porphyry and Gregory of Nyssa." Unpublished paper.

Allen, Michael. "The Active and Contemplative Life: The Practice of Theology." In *Aquinas among the Protestants*, edited by Manfred Svensson and David VanDrunen, 189–206. Oxford: Wiley Blackwell, 2018.

———. *Grounded in Heaven: Recentering Christian Hope and Life on God.* Grand Rapids: Eerdmans, 2018.

Ambrose, Isaac. *Looking unto Jesus a view of the everlasting Gospel, or, the souls eying of Jesus as carrying on the great work of mans salvation from first to last.* London, 1685; Wing A2956.

Ameen, Alyia Shahnoor. "The Response of John Donne to the New Philosophy." *ASA University Review* 5 (2011): 285–95.

Annas, Julio. *Platonic Ethics Old and New.* Ithaca, NY: Cornell University Press, 1999.

Anselm. *Proslogium.* In *Basic Writings*, translated by S. N. Deane. 2nd ed. Chicago: Open Court, 1962.

Aristotle, *Metaphysics.* Translated and edited by Hugh Lawson-Trancred. Rev. ed. London: Penguin, 2004.

———. *Physics.* Translated by Robin Waterfield. Edited by David Bostock. Oxford: Oxford University Press, 1996.

Armstrong, John M. "After the Ascent: Plato on Becoming Like God." *OSAP* 26 (2004): 171–83.

Arnold, Alec Andreas. "Christ and Our Perception of Beauty: The Theological Aesthetics of Dionysius the Areopagite and Hans Urs von Balthasar." ThM thesis, Regent College, 2015.

Asselt, Willem J. van. *Introduction to Reformed Scholasticism.* Translated by Albert Gootjes. Grand Rapids: Reformation Heritage, 2010.

Auerbach, Erich. *Dante: Poet of the Secular World.* Translated by Ralph Manheim. Rev. ed. New York: New York Review of Books, 2007. Original 1929.

Augustine. *Agreement among the Evangelists*. In *The New Testament I and II*, translated by Kim Paffenroth, edited by Boniface Ramsey. WSA I/15, I/16. Hyde Park, NY: New City Press, 2014.

———. *Confessions*. Translated by Henry Chadwick. Oxford: Oxford University Press, 1991.

———. *Eighty-Three Different Questions*. Translated by David L. Mosher. Edited by Hermigild Dressler. FC 70. Washington, DC: Catholic University of America Press, 1982.

———. *The Greatness of the Soul*. In *Augustine: The Greatness of the Soul, the Teacher*, translated by Joseph M. Colleran, edited by Johannes Quasten and Joseph C. Plumpe. ACW 9. New York: Newman, 1978.

———. *Letters 100–155*. Translated by Roland J. Teske. Edited by Boniface Ramsey. WSA II/2. Hyde Park, NY: New City Press, 2002.

———. *The Literal Meaning of Genesis*. Translated by John Hammond Taylor. Edited by Johannes Quasten, Walter J. Burghardt, and Thomas Comerford Lawler. 2 vols. ACW 41–42. New York: Newman, 1982.

———. *On Christian Teaching*. Translated by R. P. H. Green. Oxford: Oxford University Press, 2008.

———. *The Trinity*. Translated by Edmund Hill. Edited by John E. Rotelle. 2nd ed. WSA I/5. Hyde Park, NY: New City Press, 2012.

———. *The Works of Saint Augustine: A Translation for the 21st Century*. Translated by Edmund Hill. Edited by John E. Rotelle. Hyde Park, NY: New City Press, 1990–2005.

Ayres, Lewis. *Augustine and the Trinity*. Cambridge: Cambridge University Press, 2010.

Bacon, Francis. *The New Organon*. Edited by Lisa Jardine and Michael Silverthorne. Cambridge: Cambridge University Press, 2000.

Bacote, Vincent E. *The Spirit in Public Theology: Appropriating the Legacy of Abraham Kuyper*. Grand Rapids: Baker Academic, 2005.

Baert, Edward. "Le Thème de la vision de Dieu chez S. Justin, Clément d'Alexandrie et S. Grégoire de Nysse." *FZPhTh* 2 (1965): 439–97.

Balás, David L. *Μετουσια Θεου: Man's Participation in God's Perfections according to Saint Gregory of Nyssa*. Rome: Herder, 1966.

Balthasar, Hans Urs von. "Eschatology in Outline." In *Explorations in Theology*, vol. 4, *Spirit and Institution*, translated by Edward T. Oakes, 423–67. San Francisco: Ignatius, 1995.

———. *The Glory of the Lord: A Theological Aesthetics*. Vol. 1, *Seeing the Form*. Translated by Erasmo Leiva-Merikakis. Edited by Joseph Fessio and John Riches. San Francisco, CA: Ignatius, 1983

———. *The Glory of the Lord: A Theological Aesthetics*. Vol. 3, *Lay Styles*. Translated by Andrew Louth et al. Edited by John Riches. 1986. Reprint, San Francisco: Ignatius, 2004.

———. "Some Points of Eschatology." In *Explorations in Theology*, vol. 1, *The Word Made Flesh*, translated by A. V. Littledale with Alexander Dru, 255–77. San Francisco: Ignatius, 1989.

———. *Theo-Drama: Theological Dramatic Theory*. Vol. 5, *The Last Act*. Translated by Graham Harrison. San Francisco: Ignatius, 1998.

———. *A Theology of History*. 1963. Reprint, San Francisco: Ignatius, 1994.

Barnes, Michel René. "Exegesis and Polemic in Augustine's *De Trinitate* I." *AugStud* 30 (1999): 43–59.

———. "The Visible Christ and the Invisible Trinity: Mt. 5:8 in Augustine's Theology of 400." *ModTh* 19 (2003): 329–55.

Barney, Rachel. "*Eros* and Necessity in the Ascent from the Cave." *AncPhil* 28 (2008): 357–72.

Barth, Karl. *The Epistle to the Romans*. Translated by Edwyn C. Hoskyns. Oxford: Oxford University Press, 1968.

Bates, William. *The four last things viz. death, judgment, heaven, hell, practically considered and applied in several discourses*. London, 1691; Wing B1105.

Bavinck, Herman. *Reformed Dogmatics*. Vol. 1, *Prolegomena*. Translated by John Vriend. Edited by John Bolt. Grand Rapids: Baker Academic, 2003.

———. *Reformed Dogmatics*. Vol. 2, *God and Creation*. Translated by John Vriend. Edited by John Bolt. Grand Rapids: Baker Academic, 2004.

———. *Reformed Dogmatics*. Vol. 3, *Sin and Salvation in Christ*. Translated by John Vriend. Edited by John Bolt. Grand Rapids: Baker Academic, 2006.

———. *Reformed Dogmatics*. Vol. 4, *Holy Spirit, Church, and New Creation*. Translated by John Vriend. Edited by John Bolt. Grand Rapids: Baker Academic, 2008.

Baxter, Richard. *The Autobiography of Richard Baxter*. Edited by J. M. Lloyd Thomas and N. H. Keeble. Everyman's University Library 863. Totowa, NJ: Rowman and Littlefield, 1974.

———. *The saints everlasting rest, or, A treatise of the blessed state of the saints in their enjoyment of God in glory . . .* London, 1651; Wing B1384.

Behr, John. *Asceticism and Anthropology in Irenaeus and Clement*. Oxford: Oxford University Press, 2000.

———. *Irenaeus of Lyons*. Oxford: Oxford University Press, 2013.

———. *The Mystery of Christ: Life in Death*. Crestwood, NY: St. Vladimir's Seminary Press, 2006.

Benedict XII. "Benedictus Deus." January 29, 1336. In Xavier LeBachelet, "Benoît XII," in *Dictionnaire de Théologie Catholique*, vol. 2, pt. 1, cols. 657–58. Paris: Letouzey et Ané, 1932. ET: http://www.papalencyclicals.net/Ben12/B12bdeus.htm.

Berger, Peter L. *The Sacred Canopy: Elements of a Sociological Theory of Religion*. Garden City, NY: Doubleday, 1967.

Berkouwer, G. C. *The Return of Christ*. Translated by James Van Oosterom. Edited by Marlin J. Van Elderen. Grand Rapids: Eerdmans, 1972.

Bett, Richard. "Immortality and the Nature of the Soul in the *Phaedrus*." *Phronesis* 31 (1986): 1–26.

Billings, J. Todd. *Union with Christ: Reframing Theology and Ministry for the Church*. Grand Rapids: Baker Academic, 2011.

———. "United to God through Christ: Assessing Calvin on the Question of Deification." *HTR* 98 (2005): 315–34.

Bintsarovskyi, Dmytro. "God Hidden and Revealed: A Reformed and an Eastern Orthodox Perspective." PhD diss., Theologische Universiteit Kampen, 2018.

Blankenhorn, Bernhard. "Balthasar's Method of Divine Naming." *NV Eng* 1 (2003): 245–68.

Blond, Phillip. "The Beatific Vision of St. Thomas Aquinas." In *Encounter between Eastern*

Orthodoxy and Radical Orthodoxy: Transfiguring the World through the Word, edited by Adrian Pabst and Christoph Schneider, 185–212. Burlington, VT: Ashgate, 2009.

Bockmuehl, Klaus. *Listening to the God Who Speaks: Reflections on God's Guidance from Scripture and the Lives of God's People*. Edited by Kathryn Yanni. Colorado Springs: Helmers and Howard, 1990.

Boersma, Corine. "A Comparative Analysis of Sacramentality in Augustine and Dionysius." MA thesis, Regent College, 2016.

Boersma, Gerald P. *Augustine's Early Theology of Image: A Study in the Development of Pro-Nicene Theology*. New York: Oxford University Press, 2016.

Boersma, Hans. "Ascension of an Immaterial Body: With Contributions of Nicholas of Cusa, Jonathan Edwards, and Gregory of Nyssa." In *The Book of Acts: Theological-Ecumenical Readings*, edited by Charles Raith II. Washington, DC: Catholic University of America Press, forthcoming.

———. "Becoming Human in the Face of God: Gregory of Nyssa's Unending Search for the Beatific Vision." *IJST* 17 (2015): 131–51.

———. "Blessing and Glory: Abraham Kuyper on the Beatific Vision." *CTJ* 52 (2017): 205–41.

———. *Embodiment and Virtue in Gregory of Nyssa: An Anagogical Approach*. Oxford: Oxford University Press, 2013.

———. *Heavenly Participation: The Weaving of a Sacramental Tapestry*. Grand Rapids: Eerdmans, 2011.

———. *Nouvelle Théologie and Sacramental Ontology: A Return to Mystery*. Oxford: Oxford University Press, 2009.

———. "The Real Presence of Hope and Love: The Christocentric Legacy of Pope Benedict XVI." *Books & Culture* 19, no. 5 (September/October 2013): 11–14.

———. *Sacramental Preaching: Sermons on the Hidden Presence of Christ*. Grand Rapids: Baker Academic, 2016.

———. *Scripture as Real Presence: Sacramental Exegesis in the Early Church*. Grand Rapids: Baker Academic, 2017.

———. *Violence, Hospitality, and the Cross: Reappropriating the Atonement Tradition*. Grand Rapids: Baker Academic, 2004.

Bolt, John. *A Free Church, a Holy Nation: Abraham Kuyper's American Public Theology*. Grand Rapids: Eerdmans, 2001.

Bolton, Robert. *Mr. Boltons last and learned worke of the foure last things, death, iudgement, hell, and heauen. With an assise-sermon, and notes on Iustice Nicolls his funerall. Together with the life and death of the author*. Edited by Edward Bagshaw. London, 1632; *STC* (2nd ed.) 3242.

Bonaventure. *Itinerarium mentis in Deum*. Translated by Zachary Hayes. Edited by Philotheus Boehner. *Works of Saint Bonaventure* 2, pp. 35–39. Saint Bonaventure, NY: Franciscan Institute, 2002.

———. *On the Reduction of the Arts to Theology*. Translated and edited by Zachary Hayes. *Works of Saint Bonaventure* 1. Saint Bonaventure, NY: Franciscan Institute, 1996.

Boring, M. Eugene. *Mark: A Commentary*. NTL. Louisville: Westminster John Knox, 2006.

Bouteneff, Peter C. "Essential or Existential: The Problem of the Body in the Anthropology of St. Gregory of Nyssa." In *Gregory of Nyssa: Homilies on the Beatitudes; An*

English Version with Supporting Studies; Proceedings of the Eighth International Collo-quium on Gregory of Nyssa (Paderborn, 14–18 September 1998), edited by Hubertus R. Drobner and Albert Viciano, 409–20. VCSup 52. Leiden: Brill, 2000.

Bras, Kick. *Een met de ene: Protestantse mystiek van Abraham Kuyper tot Maria de Groot.* Vught, Neth.: Skandalon, 2013.

Bratt, James D. *Abraham Kuyper: Modern Calvinist, Christian Democrat.* Grand Rapids: Eerdmans, 2013.

Bremmer, R. H. *Herman Bavinck als dogmaticus.* Kampen: Kok, 1961.

Brinkman, M. E., and C. van der Kooi, eds. *Het calvinisme van Kuyper en Bavinck.* Sleu-telteksten in godsdienst en theologie 22. Zoetermeer, Neth.: Meinema, 1997.

Brown, Raymond E. *The Gospel according to John XIII–XXI.* Anchor Bible 29A. Garden City, NY: Doubleday, 1970.

Brueggemann, Walter. "The Book of Exodus: Introduction, Commentary, and Reflec-tions." In *The New Interpreter's Bible*, edited by Leander E. Keck, 1:942–43. Nashville: Abingdon, 1994.

Bruijne, Ad de. "Midden in de wereld verliefd op God: Kuypers aanzet tot een neocal-vinistische spiritualiteit." In *Godsvrucht in geschiedenis: Bundel ter gelegenheid van het afscheid van prof. dr. Frank van der Pol als hoogleraar aan de Theologische Universiteit Kampen*, edited by Erik A. de Boer and Harm J. Boiten, 441–53. Heerenveen, Neth.: Groen, 2015.

Bucur, Bogdan G. "Theophanies and Vision of God in Augustine's *De Trinitate*: An East-ern Orthodox Perspective." *SVTQ* 52 (2008): 67–93.

Bultmann, Rudolf. *The History of the Synoptic Tradition.* Translated by John Marsh. Ox-ford: Blackwell, 1963.

———. *The Johannine Epistles: A Commentary on the Johannine Epistles.* Translated by R. Philip O'Hara, Lane C. McGaughy, and Robert W. Funk. Hermeneia. Philadelphia: Fortress, 1973.

Bynum, Caroline Walker. *The Resurrection of the Body in Western Christianity, 200–1336.* Lectures on the History of Religions 15. New York: Columbia University Press, 1995.

Caldwell, Robert W. "A Brief History of Heaven in the Writings of Jonathan Edwards." *CTJ* 46 (2011): 48–71.

Calvin, John. *Calvin's Commentaries.* 45 vols. Edinburgh: Calvin Translation Society, 1846–1851.

———. *The Institutes of the Christian Religion.* Translated by Ford Lewis Battles. Edited by John T. McNeill. Vol. 1. Library of Christian Classics 20. Philadelphia: Westmin-ster, 1960.

———. *Psychopannychia.* In *Tracts*, translated by Henry Beveridge, vol. 3. Edinburgh: Calvin Translation Society, 1851.

Cameron, Michael. *Christ Meets Me Everywhere: Augustine's Early Figurative Exegesis.* New York: Oxford University Press, 2012.

———. "The Emergence of *Totus Christus* as Hermeneutical Center in Augustine's *Enar-rationes in Psalmos*." In *The Harp of Prophecy: Early Christian Interpretation of the Psalms*, edited by Brian Daley and Paul R. Kolbet, 205–26. Notre Dame: University of Notre Dame Press, 2015.

———. "Sign." In *Augustine through the Ages: An Encyclopedia*, edited by Allan D. Fitz-gerald, 793–98. Grand Rapids: Eerdmans, 1999.

Canlis, Julie. "Calvin, Osiander and Participation in God." *IJST* 6 (2004): 169–84.

Canty, Aaron. *Light and Glory: The Transfiguration of Christ in Early Franciscan and Dominican Theology*. Washington, DC: Catholic University of America Press, 2011.

Capitain, Francis de. "Dante's Conception of the Beatific Vision." *ACQR* 27 (1902): 417–32.

Cary, Phillip. *Outward Signs: The Powerlessness of External Things in Augustine's Thought*. Oxford: Oxford University Press, 2008.

Casarella, Peter. "*His Name Is Jesus*: Negative Theology and Christology in Two Writings of Nicholas of Cusa from 1440." In *Nicholas of Cusa on Christ and the Church: Essays in Memory of Chandler McCuskey Brooks for the American Cusanus Society*, edited by Gerald Christianson and Thomas M. Izbicki, 281–307. Leiden: Brill, 1996.

Casey, John. *After Lives: A Guide to Heaven, Hell, and Purgatory*. New York: Oxford University Press, 2009.

Cavallera, Ferdinand. "La Vision corporelle de Dieu d'après Saint Augustin." *BLE* 7 (1915–1916): 460–71.

Chai, Leon. *Jonathan Edwards and the Limits of Enlightenment Philosophy*. New York: Oxford University Press, 1998.

Cherniss, Harold Fredrik. *The Platonism of Gregory of Nyssa*. Berkeley: University of California Press, 1930.

Coakley, Sarah. "Gregory of Nyssa." In *The Spiritual Senses: Perceiving God in Western Christianity*, edited by Paul L. Gavrilyuk and Sarah Coakley, 36–55. Cambridge: Cambridge University Press, 2012.

Coe, John H. "Musings on the Dark Night of the Soul: Insights from St. John of the Cross on a Developmental Spirituality." *JPT* 28 (2000): 293–307.

Coffin, Charles Monroe. *John Donne and the New Philosophy*. Columbia University Studies in English and Comparative Literature 126. New York: Columbia University Press, 1937.

Constas, Nicholas. "'To Sleep, Perchance to Dream': The Middle State of Souls in Patristic and Byzantine Literature." *DOP* 55 (2001): 91–124.

Coolman, Boyd Taylor. "Spiritual and Sensuous: The Christian Doctrine of the Spiritual Senses of the Soul, Eschatologically Considered." In *Sensing Things Divine: Towards a Constructive Account of Spiritual Perception*, edited by Frederick D. Aquino and Paul L. Gavrilyuk. Oxford: Oxford University Press, forthcoming.

Cooper, Tim. *John Owen, Richard Baxter, and the Formation of Nonconformity*. Burlington, VT: Ashgate, 2011.

Crisp, Oliver D. *Jonathan Edwards on God and Creation*. New York: Oxford University Press, 2012.

———. "Jonathan Edwards's Ontology: A Critique of Sang Hyun Lee's Dispositional Account of Edwardsian Metaphysics." *RelS* 46 (2010): 1–20.

Cullmann, Oscar. *Christ and Time: The Primitive Christian Conception of Time*. Translated by Floyd V. Filson. Rev. ed. Philadelphia: Westminster, 1964.

Daley, Brian E., ed. *Light on the Mountain: Greek Patristic and Byzantine Homilies on the Transfiguration of the Lord*. Crestwood, NY: St. Vladimir's Seminary Press, 2013.

Dalzell, Thomas G. *The Dramatic Encounter of Divine and Human Freedom in the Theology of Hans Urs von Balthasar*. Studies in the Intercultural History of Christianity 105. Bern: Peter Lang, 2000.

Daniel, Stephen H. "Berkeley's Christian Neoplatonism, Archetypes, and Divine Ideas." *JHP* 39 (2001): 239–58.

Daniélou, Jean. "La Chronologie des œuvres de Grégoire de Nysse." *SP* 7 (1966): 159–69.

———. *The Lord of History: Reflections on the Inner Meaning of History*. Translated by Nigel Abercrombie. 1958. Reprint, Cleveland: Meridian/World, 1968.

———. *Platonisme et théologie mystique: Doctrine spirituelle de Saint Grégoire de Nysse*. Rev. ed. Théologie 2. Paris: Aubier, 1944.

Dante Alighieri. *Paradiso*. Translated by Jean Hollander and Robert Hollander. Edited by Robert Hollander. New York: Doubleday, 2007.

———. *Purgatorio*. Translated by Jean Hollander and Robert Hollander. Edited by Robert Hollander. New York: Doubleday, 2003.

Davison, Andrew. *The Love of Wisdom: An Introduction to Philosophy for Theologians*. London: SCM, 2013.

Deck, John N. *Nature, Contemplation, and the One: A Study in the Philosophy of Plotinus*. Toronto: University of Toronto Press, 1967.

de Lubac, Henri. *Augustinianism and Modern Theology*. New York: Crossroad/Herder and Herder, 2000.

Descartes, René. *The Philosophical Writings of Descartes*. Edited by John Cottingham, Robert Stoothoff, and Dugald Murdoch. Vol. 2. Cambridge: Cambridge University Press, 1984.

———. *Principles of Philosophy*. Translated and edited by Valentine Rodger Miller and Reese P. Miller. Synthese Language Library 15. Dordrecht, Neth.: Kluwer Academic, 1983.

Dillard, Peter. "Keeping the Vision: Aquinas and the Problem of Disembodied Beatitude." *NB* 93 (2012): 397–411.

DiPasquale, Theresa M. *Literature and Sacrament: The Sacred and the Secular in John Donne*. Medieval and Renaissance Literary Studies. Pittsburgh: Duquesne University Press, 1999.

Divry, Édouard. *La Transfiguration selon l'Orient et l'Occident: Grégoire Palamas– Thomas d'Aquin vers un dénouement œcuménique*. Croire et Savoir 54. Paris: Téqui, 2009.

Doerksen, Daniel W. "Polemist or Pastor? Donne and Moderate Calvinist Conformity." In *John Donne and the Protestant Reformation: New Perspectives*, edited by Mary Arshagouni Papazian, 12–24. Detroit: Wayne State University Press, 2003.

Dondaine, H.-F. "L'Object et le 'medium' de la vision béatifique chez les théologiens du XIIIe siècle." *RTAM* 19 (1952): 60–99.

Donne, John. *John Donne: The Divine Poems*. Edited by Helen Gardner. 2nd ed. Oxford: Clarendon, 1978.

———. *John Donne: Selections from Divine Poems, Sermons, Devotions, and Prayers*. Edited by John Booty. Mahwah, NJ: Paulist, 1990.

———. *The Sermons of John Donne*. Edited by George R. Potter and Evelyn M. Simpson. 10 vols. Berkeley: University of California Press, 1953–1962.

———. *The Variorum Edition of the Poetry of John Donne*. Vol. 6, *The Anniversaries and the Epicedes and Obsequies*. Edited by Paul A. Parrish. Bloomington: Indiana University Press, 1995.

Donovan, Mary Ann. "Alive to the Glory of God: A Key Insight in St. Irenaeus." *TS* 49 (1988): 283–97.

Driel, Edwin Chr. van. "'Too Lowly to Reach God without a Mediator': John Calvin's Supralapsarian Eschatological Narrative." *ModTh* 33 (2017): 275–92.

Duba, William. "The Beatific Vision in the *Sentences* Commentary of Gerald Odonis." *Vivarium* 47 (2009): 348–63.

Dupré, Louis. "The Mystical Theology of Nicholas of Cusa's *De visione Dei*." In *Nicholas of Cusa on Christ and the Church: Essays in Memory of Chandler McCuskey Brooks for the American Cusanus Society*, edited by Gerald Christianson and Thomas M. Izbicki, 205–20. Leiden: Brill, 1996.

———. *Passage to Modernity: An Essay in the Hermeneutics of Nature and Culture*. New Haven: Yale University Press, 1993.

Dykmans, Marc. *Les Sermons de Jean XXII sur la vision béatifique*. Miscellanea Historiae Pontificiae 34. Rome: Presses de l'Université Grégorienne, 1973.

Edwards, David L. *John Donne: Man of Flesh and Spirit*. London: Continuum, 2001.

Edwards, Jonathan. *The Works of Jonathan Edwards*. New Haven: Yale University Press, 1977–2009. Online: edwards.yale.edu.

Eglinton, James Perman. *Trinity and Organism: Towards a New Reading of Herman Bavinck's Organic Motif*. T. & T. Clark Studies in Systematic Theology 17. New York: T. & T. Clark, 2012.

Ettenhuber, Katrin. "'The Evidence of Things Not Seen': Donne, Augustine, and the Beatific Vision." In *Donne's Augustine: Renaissance Cultures of Interpretation*, 205–24. Oxford: Oxford University Press, 2011.

Eubank, Nathan. "Ineffably Effable: The Pinnacle of Mystical Ascent in Gregory of Nyssa's *De vita Moysis*." *IJST* 16 (2014): 25–41.

Evans, Craig A. *Mark 8:27–16:20*. Word Biblical Commentary 34B. Nashville: Nelson, 2001.

Farris, Joshua R., Mark Hamilton, and James S. Spiegel, eds. *Idealism and Christian Theology*. Idealism and Christianity 1. New York: Bloomsbury Academic, 2016.

Fasolini, Diego. "'Illuminating' and 'Illuminated' Light: A Biblical-Theological Interpretation of God-as-Light in Canto XXXIII of Dante's *Paradiso*." *L&T* 19 (2005): 297–310.

Ferguson, Everett. "God's Infinity and Man's Mutability: Perpetual Progress according to Gregory of Nyssa." *GOTR* 18 (1973): 59–78.

———. "Progress in Perfection: Gregory of Nyssa's *Vita Moysis*." *SP* 14 (1976): 307–14.

Ferguson, John. "Sun, Line, and Cave Again." *ClQ* 13 (1963): 188–93.

Festugière, A.-J. *Contemplation et vie contemplative selon Platon*. 2nd ed. Le Saulchoir: Bibliothèque de philosophie 2. Paris: Vrin, 1950.

Fiedrowicz, Michael. General introduction to Augustine, *Expositions of the Psalms 1–32*, edited by John E. Rotelle, 13–66. WSA III/15. Hyde Park, NY: New City Press, 2000.

Fitzpatrick, Antonia. "Bodily Identity in Scholastic Theology." PhD diss., University College, London, 2013.

Foley, Richard. "The Order Question: Climbing the Ladder of Love in Plato's *Symposium*." *AncPhil* 30 (2010): 57–72.

Foltz, Bruce V. *The Noetics of Nature: Environmental Philosophy and the Holy Beauty of the Visible*. New York: Fordham University Press, 2014.

Foster, Kenelm. *The Two Dantes and Other Studies*. Berkeley: University of California Press, 1977.

Foster, M. B. "The Christian Doctrine of Creation and the Rise of Modern Natural Science." *Mind* 43 (1934): 446–68.

Franks, Angela Franz. "Trinitarian *Analogia Entis* in Hans Urs von Balthasar." *Thomist* 62 (1998): 533–59.

Freccero, John. "An Introduction to the *Paradiso*." In *Dante: The Poetics of Conversion*, edited by Rachel Jacoff, 209–20. Cambridge, MA: Harvard University Press, 1986.

Frontain, Raymond-Jean. "Donne's Protestant *Paradiso*: The Johannine Vision of the *Second Anniversary*." In *John Donne and the Protestant Reformation: New Perspectives*, edited by Mary Arshagouni Papazian, 113–42. Detroit: Wayne State University Press, 2003.

Frost, Stefanie. *Nikolaus und Meister Eckhart. Rezeption im Spiegel der Marginalien zum Opus tripartitum Meister Eckharts*. Beiträge zur Geschichte der Philosophie und Theologie des Mittelalters, n.s., 69. Münster: Aschendorff, 2006.

Führer, M. "The Consolation of Contemplation in Nicholas of Cusa's *De visione Dei*." In *Nicholas of Cusa on Christ and the Church: Essays in Memory of Chandler McCuskey Brooks for the American Cusanus Society*, edited by Gerald Christianson and Thomas M. Izbicki, 221–40. Leiden: Brill, 1996.

Gaine, Simon Francis. *Did the Saviour See the Father? Christ, Salvation, and the Vision of God*. London: Bloomsbury T. & T. Clark, 2015.

————. "Thomas Aquinas and John Owen on the Beatific Vision: A Reply to Suzanne McDonald." *NB* 97 (2016): 432–46.

Garrett, Stephen M. *God's Beauty-in-Act: Participating in God's Suffering Glory*. PTMS 196. Eugene, OR: Pickwick, 2013.

Gavrilyuk, Paul L., and Sarah Coakley, eds. *The Spiritual Senses: Perceiving God in Western Christianity*. Cambridge: Cambridge University Press, 2012.

Geljon, Albert-Kees. "Divine Infinity in Gregory of Nyssa and Philo of Alexandria." *VC* 59 (2005): 152–77.

Gerson, Lloyd P. *Plotinus: The Arguments of the Philosophers*. Edited by Ted Honderich. New York: Routledge, 1994.

Gibson, Michael. "The Beauty of the Redemption of the World: The Theological Aesthetics of Maximus the Confessor and Jonathan Edwards." *HTR* 101 (2008): 45–76.

Goodblatt, Chanita. "The Penitential Psalm 32: The Sacred Philology of Sin." In *The Christian Hebraism of John Donne*, 77–107. Pittsburgh: Duquesne University Press, 2010.

Gorman, Michael J. *Inhabiting the Cruciform God: Kenosis, Justification, and Theosis in Paul's Narrative Soteriology*. Grand Rapids: Eerdmans, 2009.

Gosseye, Lise. "Salutary Reading: Calvinist Humanism in Constantijn Huygens' *Ooghentroost*." In *The Turn of the Soul: Representations of Religious Conversion in Early Modern Art and Literature*, edited by Lieke Stelling, Harald Hendrix, and Todd Richardson, 225–46. Intersections: Interdisciplinary Studies in Early Modern Culture 23. Leiden: Brill, 2012.

Grafton, Anthony, and Megan Williams. *Christianity and the Transformation of the Book: Origen, Eusebius, and the Library of Caesarea*. Cambridge, MA: Belknap Press of Harvard University Press, 2006.

Gregorios, Paulos Mar. *Cosmic Man: The Divine Presence; The Theology of St. Gregory of Nyssa (ca 330 to 395 A.D.)*. New York: Paragon, 1988.

Gregory, Brad S. *The Unintended Reformation: How a Religious Revolution Secularized Society*. Cambridge, MA: Belknap Press of Harvard University Press, 2012.

Gregory of Nyssa. *Contra Eunomium Liber II*. In *GNO*, vol. 1, edited by Wernerus Jaeger, 226–409. Leiden: Brill, 2002.

———. *De beatitudinibus*. In *GNO*, vol. 7/2, edited by Johannes F. Callahan, 75–170. Leiden: Brill, 1992.

———. *De perfectione*. In *GNO*, vol. 8/1, edited by Wernerus Jaeger, 173–214. Leiden: Brill, 1986.

———. *De vita Moysis*. In *GNO*, vol. 7/1, edited by Hubertus Musurillo. Leiden: Brill, 1991.

———. *Gregory of Nyssa: Homilies on the Beatitudes; An English Version with Supporting Studies*. Translated by Stuart George Hall. Edited by Hubertus R. Drobner and Albert Viciano. Leiden: Brill, 2000.

———. *Gregory of Nyssa: Homilies on the Song of Songs*. Translated and edited by Richard A. Norris. Writings from the Greco-Roman World 13. Atlanta: Society of Biblical Literature, 2012.

———. *Gregory, Bishop of Nyssa: Homilies on Ecclesiastes*. In *Gregory of Nyssa: Homilies on Ecclesiastes; An English Version with Supporting Studies*, translated by Stuart George Hall and Rachel Moriarty, edited by Stuart George Hall, 31–144. Berlin: de Gruyter, 1993.

———. *Gregory, Bishop of Nyssa: The Second Book against Eunomius*. Translated by Stuart George Hall. In *Gregory of Nyssa: Contra Eunomium II; An English Version with Supporting Studies; Proceedings of the 10th International Colloquium on Gregory of Nyssa (Olomouc, September 15–18, 2004)*, edited by Lenka Karfíková, Scot Douglass, and Johannes Zachhuber, 59–201. VCSup 82. Leiden: Brill, 2007.

———. *In ecclesiasten homiliae*. In *GNO*, vol. 5, edited by Paulus Alexander, 195–442. Leiden: Brill, 1996.

———. *The Life of Moses*. Translated and edited by Abraham J. Malherbe and Everett Ferguson. New York: Paulist, 1978.

———. *On Perfection*. In *Saint Gregory of Nyssa: Ascetical Works*, translated by Virginia Woods Callahan, 91–122. FC 58. 1967. Reprint, Washington, DC: Catholic University of America Press, 1999.

———. *On the Making of Man*. In *NPNF* II/5, translated and edited by H. A. Wilson, 386–427. Buffalo: Christian Literature Co., 1893.

Gregory Palamas. *Défense des saints hésychastes*. Edited by John Meyendorff. Études et Documents 30–31. 2 vols. 2nd ed. Louvain: Spicilegium Sacrum Lovaniense, 1973.

———. *The Homilies*. Translated and edited by Christopher Veniamin. Waymart, PA: Mount Thabor Publishing, 2009.

———. *The Triads*. Translated by Nicholas Gendle. Edited by John Meyendorff. New York: Paulist, 1983.

Grumett, David. "De Lubac, Grace, and the Pure Nature Debate." *ModTh* 31 (2015): 123–46.

Hadot, Pierre. *Plotinus, or, the Simplicity of Vision*. Translated by Michael Chase. Chicago: University of Chicago Press, 1993.

Hahn, Scott W., and Benjamin Wiker. *Politicizing the Bible: The Roots of Historical Criticism and the Secularization of Scripture, 1300–1700*. New York: Herder and Herder/Crossroad, 2013.

Bibliography

Hambrick-Stowe, Charles E. "Practical Divinity and Spirituality." In *The Cambridge Companion to Puritanism*, edited by John Coffey and Paul C. H. Lim, 191–205. Cambridge: Cambridge University Press, 2008.

Hanby, Michael. *Augustine and Modernity*. London: Routledge, 2003.

Harinck, George. "'Met de telephoon onzen God oproepen': Kuypers meditaties uit 1905 en 1906." In *Godsvrucht in geschiedenis: Bundel ter gelegenheid van het afscheid van prof. dr. Frank van der Pol als hoogleraar aan de Theologische Universiteit Kampen*, edited by Erik A. de Boer and Harm J. Boiten, 454–56. Heerenveen, Neth.: Groen, 2015.

Harl, Marguerite. "Recherches sur l'originisme d'Origène: La 'satiété' (κόρος) de la contemplation comme motif de la chute des âmes." *SP* 8 (1966): 373–405.

Harmless, William. "Mystic as Cartographer: Bonaventure." In *Mystics*, 79–105, 283–87. New York: Oxford University Press, 2008.

Harrison, Carol. *Rethinking Augustine's Early Theology: An Argument for Continuity*. Oxford: Oxford University Press, 2006.

Harrison, Verna E. F. *Grace and Human Freedom according to St. Gregory of Nyssa*. Lewiston, NY: Edwin Mellen, 1992.

———. "Receptacle Imagery in St. Gregory of Nyssa's Anthropology." *SP* 22 (1989): 23–27.

Hart, David Bentley. "The Bright Morning of the Soul: John of the Cross on *Theosis*." *ProEccl* 12 (2003): 324–44.

Hay, Andrew R. *God's Shining Forth: A Trinitarian Theology of Divine Light*. Eugene, OR: Pickwick, 2017.

Hayes, Cory J. "*Deus in se et Deus pro nobis*: The Transfiguration in the Theology of Gregory Palamas and Its Importance for Catholic Theology." PhD diss., Duquesne University, 2015.

Healy, Nicholas J. *The Eschatology of Hans Urs von Balthasar: Being as Communion*. Oxford: Oxford University Press, 2005.

Heath, J. M. F. *Paul's Visual Piety: The Metamorphosis of the Beholder*. Oxford: Oxford University Press, 2013.

Heine, Ronald E. *Perfection in the Virtuous Life: A Study in the Relationship between Edification and Polemical Theology in Gregory of Nyssa's De vita Moysis*. Cambridge, MA: Philadelphia Patristic Foundation, 1975.

Heslam, Peter S. *Creating a Christian Worldview: Abraham Kuyper's Lectures on Calvinism*. Grand Rapids: Eerdmans, 1998.

Hillebert, Jordan, ed. *T&T Clark Companion to Henri de Lubac*. London: Bloomsbury T. & T. Clark, 2017.

Hindmarsh, D. Bruce. *The Spirit of Early Evangelicalism: True Religion in a Modern World*. New York: Oxford University Press, 2018.

Hinson, E. Glenn. "Ignatian and Puritan Prayer: Surprising Similarities; A Comparison of Ignatius Loyola and Richard Baxter on Meditation." *TMA* 20 (2007): 79–92.

Hoekema, Anthony A. *The Bible and the Future*. Grand Rapids: Eerdmans, 1979.

Hoff, Johannes. *The Analogical Turn: Rethinking Modernity with Nicholas of Cusa*. Grand Rapids: Eerdmans, 2013.

Holmes, Jeremy. "Aquinas' *Lectura in Matthaeum*." In *Aquinas on Scripture: An Introduction to His Biblical Commentaries*, edited by Thomas G. Weinandy, Daniel A. Keating, and John P. Yokum, 73–97. London: T. & T. Clark, 2005.

Hooker, Morna D. *A Commentary on the Gospel according to St. Mark*. Black's New Testament Commentaries. London: A. & C. Black, 1991.

Howe, John. *The blessednesse of the righteous discoursed from Psal. 17, 15*. London, 1668; Wing H3015.

Hoye, William J. "Die Vereinigung mit dem gänzlich Unerkannten nach Bonaventura, Nikolaus von Kues und Thomas von Aquin." In *Die Dionysius-Rezeption im Mittelalter. Internationales Kolloquium in Sofia vom 8. bis 11. April 1999 unter der Schirmherrschaft der Société internationale pour l'étude de la philosophie médiévale*, edited by Tzorcho Boiadjiev, Georgi Kapriev, and Andreas Speer, 477–504. Rencontres de Philosophie Médiévale 9. Turnhout, Belgium: Brepols, 2000.

Huijgen, Arnold. "Divine Accommodation in Calvin: Myth and Reality." In *The Myth of the Reformation*, edited by Peter Opitz, 248–59. Refo500 Academic Studies 9. Göttingen: Vandenhoeck & Ruprecht, 2013.

———. *Divine Accommodation in Calvin's Theology: Analysis and Assessment*. Reformed Historical Theology 16. Göttingen: Vandenhoeck & Ruprecht, 2011.

Huttinga, Wolter. *Participation and Communicability: Herman Bavinck and John Milbank on the Relation between God and the World*. Amsterdam: Buijten & Shipperheijn Motief, 2014.

Irenaeus. *Irenæus against Heresies*. In *ANF* 1, edited by Alexander Roberts and James Donaldson. Buffalo: Christian Literature Co., 1885.

———. *Proof of the Apostolic Preaching*. Translated by Joseph P. Smith. ACW 16. New York: Paulist, 1952.

Irigaray, Luce. "Sorcerer Love: A Reading of Plato's *Symposium*, Diotima's Speech." Translated by Eleanor H. Kuykendall. *Hypatia* 3, no. 3 (1989): 32–44.

Jenson, Robert W. *Systematic Theology*. Vol. 2, *The Works of God*. New York: Oxford University Press, 1999.

John of the Cross. *The Collected Works of Saint John of the* Cross. Translated by Kieran Kavanaugh and Otilio Rodriguez. Rev. ed. Washington, DC: ICS, 1991.

Johnson, Adam. "The Crucified Bridegroom: Christ's Atoning Death in St. John of the Cross and Spiritual Formation Today." *ProEccl* 21 (2012): 392–408.

Johnson, Jeffrey. *The Theology of John Donne*. Cambridge: Brewer, 1999.

Johnson, Luke Timothy. *The Gospel of Luke*. Sacra Pagina 3. Collegeville, MN: Glazier/Liturgical Press, 1991.

———. *Hebrews: A Commentary*. NTL. Louisville: Westminster John Knox, 2006.

Jorgenson, Allen G. "Martin Luther on Preaching Christ Present." *IJST* 16 (2014): 42–55.

Kapic, Kelly M. *Communion with God: The Divine and the Human in the Theology of John Owen*. Grand Rapids: Baker Academic, 2007.

Karamanolis, George. *The Philosophy of Early Christianity*. London: Routledge, 2014.

Kavanaugh, Kieran. *John of the Cross: Doctor of Light and Love*. New York: Crossroad, 1999.

Keil, Carl Friedrich, and Franz Delitzsch. *Commentary on the Old Testament*. Vol. 1. Peabody, MA: Hendrickson, 1996.

Kenney, John Peter. *Contemplation and Classical Christianity: A Study in Augustine*. Oxford: Oxford University Press, 2013.

Kilby, Karen. "Hans Urs von Balthasar on the Trinity." In *The Cambridge Companion to the Trinity*, edited by Peter C. Phan, 208–22. Cambridge: Cambridge University Press, 2011.

Kirk, Kenneth E. *The Vision of God: The Christian Doctrine of the Summum Bonum; The Bampton Lectures for 1928*. London: Longmans, Green, 1932.

Kitanov, Severin Valentinov. *Beatific Enjoyment in Medieval Scholastic Debates*. Lanham, MD: Lexington, 2014.

Kittel, Gerhard, and Gerhard Friedrich, eds. *Theological Dictionary of the New Testament*. Translated by Geoffrey W. Bromiley. 10 vols. Grand Rapids: Eerdmans, 1964–1976.

Kloos, Kari. *Christ, Creation, and the Vision of God: Augustine's Transformation of Early Christian Theophany Interpretation*. Ancient Christianity 7. Leiden: Brill, 2011.

Kooi, Cornelis van der. *As in a Mirror: John Calvin and Karl Barth on Knowing God—a Diptych*. Translated by Donald Mader. Studies in the History of Christian Traditions 120. Leiden: Brill, 2005.

Köstenberger, Andreas J. *John*. Baker Exegetical Commentary on the New Testament. Grand Rapids: Baker Academic, 2004.

Krivochéine, Basil. *In the Light of Christ: Saint Symeon the New Theologian (949–1022); Life—Spirituality—Doctrine*. Translated by Anthony P. Gythiel. Crestwood, NY: St. Vladimir's Seminary Press, 1986.

Kuipers, Tjitze. *Abraham Kuyper: An Annotated Bibliography, 1857–2010*. Translated by Clifford Anderson with Dagmare Houniet. Brill's Series in Church History 55. Leiden: Brill, 2011.

Kuyper, Abraham. *Abraham Kuyper: A Centennial Reader*. Edited by James D. Bratt. Grand Rapids: Eerdmans, 1998.

———. *De gemeene gratie*. Vol. 1. Leiden: Donner, 1902.

———. *Dictaten Dogmatiek*. Vol. 1, *Locus de Deo*. 2nd ed. 1891. Reprint, Kampen: Kok, 1910.

———. *Dictaten Dogmatiek*. Vol. 2, *Locus de Creatione*. 2nd ed. 1891. Reprint, Kampen: Kok, 1911.

———. *Dictaten Dogmatiek*. Vol. 5, *Locus de Consummatione Saeculi*. 2nd ed. 1892. Reprint, Kampen: Kok, 1913.

———. *Drie kleine vossen*. Kampen: Kok, 1901.

———. *Encyclopædie der heilige godgeleerdheid*. 3 vols. Amsterdam: Wormser, 1894.

———. *E voto Dordraceno: Toelichting op den Heidelbergschen Catechismus*. Vol. 2. Amsterdam: Wormser, 1893.

———. *In de schaduwe des doods: Meditatiën voor de krankenkamer en bij het sterfbed*. Amsterdam: Wormser, 1893.

———. *In Jezus ontslapen: Meditatiën*. Amsterdam: Höveker & Wormser, 1902.

———. *Lectures on Calvinism: Six Lectures from the Stone Foundation Lectures Delivered at Princeton University*. 8th ed. Grand Rapids: Eerdmans, 1987.

———. *Nabij God te zijn*. 2 vols. Kampen: Kok, 1908.

———. "Sphere Sovereignty." In *Abraham Kuyper: A Centennial Reader*, edited by James D. Bratt, 461–90. Grand Rapids: Eerdmans, 1998.

———. *Van de voleinding*. Edited by H. H. Kuyper. 4 vols. Kampen: Kok, 1929–1931.

———. *Voor een distel een mirt: Geestelijke overdenkingen bij den Heiligen Doop, het doen van belijdenis en het toegaan tot het Heilig Avondmaal*. Amsterdam: Wormser, 1891.

Laird, Martin. "Apophasis and Logophasis in Gregory of Nyssa's *Commentarius in Canticum Canticorum.*" *SP* 37 (2001): 126–32.

———. "Darkness." In *The Brill Dictionary of Gregory of Nyssa*, edited by Lucas Francisco Mateo-Seco and Giulio Maspero, translated by Seth Cherney, 203–5. Leiden: Brill, 2010.

———. *Gregory of Nyssa and the Grasp of Faith: Union, Knowledge, and Divine Presence.* Oxford: Oxford University Press, 2004.

Lane, Belden C. "Two Schools of Desire: Nature and Marriage in Seventeenth-Century Puritanism." *CH* 69 (2000): 372–402.

Langley, Silas. "Aquinas, Resurrection, and Material Continuity." *PACPhA* 75 (2001): 135–47.

Lashier, Jackson Jay. "The Trinitarian Theology of Irenaeus of Lyons." PhD diss., Marquette University, 2011.

Lee, Dorothy. *Transfiguration.* New Century Theology. London: Continuum, 2004.

Lee, Yang-Ho. "Calvin on Deification: A Reply to Carl Mosser and Jonathan Slater." *SJT* 63 (2010): 272–84.

Levering, Matthew. "Balthasar on Christ's Consciousness on the Cross." *Thomist* 65 (2001): 567–81.

———. *Jesus and the Demise of Death: Resurrection, Afterlife, and the Fate of the Christian.* Waco: Baylor University Press, 2012.

———. *Participatory Biblical Exegesis.* Notre Dame: University of Notre Dame Press, 2008.

Lewalski, Barbara Kiefer. *Donne's* Anniversaries *and the Poetry of Praise: The Creation of a Symbolic Mode.* Princeton: Princeton University Press, 1973.

Liere, F. A. van. "Johannes XXII en het conflict over de visio beatifica." *NedTT* 44 (1990): 208–22.

Long, Steven A. *Natura Pura: On the Recovery of Nature in the Doctrine of Grace.* New York: Fordham University Press, 2010.

Lossky, Vladimir. *The Mystical Theology of the Eastern Church.* 1957. Reprint, Cambridge: Clarke, 2005.

———. *The Vision of God.* Translated by Asheleigh Moorhouse. 2nd ed. Library of Orthodox Theology 2. 1963. Reprint, Leighton Buzzard, UK: Faith Press, 1973.

Loudovikos, Nikolaos. "Striving for Participation: Palamite Analogy as Dialogical Syn-Energy and Thomist Analogy as Emanational Similitude." In *Divine Essence and Divine Energies: Ecumenical Reflections on the Presence of God in Eastern Orthodoxy*, edited by Constantinos Athanasopoulos and Christoph Schneider, 122–48. Cambridge: Clarke, 2013.

Louth, Andrew. *The Origins of the Christian Mystical Tradition: From Plato to Denys.* Oxford: Oxford University Press, 1981.

———. "Patristic Mysticism and St. John of the Cross." In *The Origins of the Christian Mystical Tradition: From Plato to Denys*, 179–90. Oxford: Oxford University Press, 1981.

Maloney, George. Introduction to *The Discourses*, by Symeon the New Theologian. Translated by C. J. de Catanzaro, 1–36. New York: Paulist, 1980.

Manoussakis, John Panteleimon. "Theophany and Indication: Reconciling Augustinian and Palamite Aesthetics." *ModTh* 26 (2010): 76–89.

Marion, Jean-Luc "Voir, se voir vu: L'Apport de Nicolas de Cues dans le *De visione Dei*." *BLE* 117, no. 2 (April 2016): 7–37.

Marsh, Harry Clarke. "Cosmic Structure and the Knowledge of God: Thomas Aquinas' 'In Librum beati Dionysii de divinis nominibus expositio.'" PhD diss., Vanderbilt University, 1994.

Marshall, Bruce D. "Action and Person: Do Palamas and Aquinas Agree about the Spirit?" *SVTQ* 39 (1995): 379–408.

Martin, Catherine Gimelli. "Unmeete Contraryes: The Reformed Subject and the Triangulation of Religious Desire in Donne's *Anniversaries* and *Holy Sonnets*." In *John Donne and the Protestant Reformation: New Perspectives*, edited by Mary Arshagouni Papazian, 193–220. Detroit: Wayne State University Press, 2003.

Maspero, Giulio. *Trinity and Man: Gregory of Nyssa's Ad Ablabium*. Leiden: Brill, 2007.

Mateo-Seco, Lucas F. "Epektasis—Ἐπέκτασις." In *The Brill Dictionary of Gregory of Nyssa*, edited by Lucas Francisco Mateo-Seco and Giulio Maspero, translated by Seth Cherney, 263–68. Leiden: Brill, 2009.

———. "1 Cor 13, 12 in Gregory of Nyssa's Theological Thinking." *SP* 32 (1997): 153–62.

Maurer, Margaret, and Dennis Flynn. "The Text of *Goodf* and John Donne's Itinerary in April 1613." *TC* 8 (2013): 50–94.

May, Gerhard. "Die Chronologie des Lebens und der Werke des Gregor von Nyssa." In *Écriture et culture philosophique dans la pensée de Grégoire de Nysse: Actes du colloque de Chevetogne (22–26 septembre 1969)*, edited by Marguerite Harl, 51–67. Leiden: Brill, 1971.

Mazzotta, Giuseppe. *Dante, Poet of the Desert: History and Allegory in the Divine Comedy*. Princeton: Princeton University Press, 1987.

McClymond, Michael J. "Salvation as Divinization: Jonathan Edwards, Gregory Palamas and the Theological Uses of Neoplatonism." In *Jonathan Edwards: Philosophical Theologian*, edited by Paul Helm and Oliver Crisp, 139–60. Burlington, VT: Ashgate, 2003.

———. "Spiritual Perception in Jonathan Edwards." *JR* 77 (1997): 195–216.

McClymond, Michael J., and Gerald R. McDermott. *The Theology of Jonathan Edwards*. New York: Oxford University Press, 2012.

McCormack, Bruce L. "Union with Christ in Calvin's Theology: Grounds for a Divinization Theory?" In *Tributes to John Calvin: A Celebration of His Quincentenary*, edited by David W. Hall, 504–29. Phillipsburg, NJ: Presbyterian and Reformed, 2010.

McDonald, Suzanne. "Beholding the Glory of God in the Face of Jesus Christ: John Owen and the 'Reforming' of the Beatific Vision." In *The Ashgate Research Companion to John Owen's Theology*, edited by Kelly M. Kapic and Mark Jones, 141–58. Burlington, VT: Ashgate, 2012.

McDuffie, Felicia Wright. *"To Our Bodies Turn We Then": Body as Word and Sacrament in the Works of John Donne*. New York: Continuum, 2005.

McGibben, D. D. "The Fall of the Soul in Plato's *Phaedrus*." *ClQ* 14 (1964): 56–63.

McGinn, Bernard. *The Flowering of Mysticism: Men and Women in the New Mysticism—1200–1350*. Vol. 3 of *The Presence of God: A History of Western Christian Mysticism*. New York: Crossroad Herder, 1998.

———. "God as Eros: Metaphysical Foundations of Christian Mysticism." In *New Perspectives on Historical Theology: Essays in Memory of John Meyendorff*, edited by Bradley Nassif, 189–209. Grand Rapids: Eerdmans, 1995.

———. *The Harvest of Mysticism in Medieval Germany*. Vol. 4 of *The Presence of God: A History of Western Christian Mysticism*. New York: Herder and Herder, 2005.

———. "Seeing and Not Seeing: Nicholas of Cusa's *De visione Dei* in the History of Western Mysticism." In *Cusanus: The Legacy of Learned Ignorance*, edited by Peter Casarella, 26–53. Washington, DC: Catholic University of America Press, 2006.

McGuckin, John Anthony. "The Luminous Vision in Eleventh-Century Byzantium: Interpreting the Biblical and Theological Paradigms of St. Symeon the New Theologian." In *Work and Worship at Theotokos Evergetis, 1050–1200: Papers of the Fourth Belfast Byzantine International Colloquium, Portaferry, Co. Down, 14–17 September 1995*, edited by Margaret Mullet and Anthony Kirby, 90–123. Belfast Byzantine Texts and Translations 6.2. Belfast: Belfast Byzantine Enterprises, 1997.

———. *The Transfiguration of Christ in Scripture and Tradition*. Lewiston, NY: Edwin Mellen, 1986.

McMahon, Robert. *Understanding the Medieval Meditative Ascent: Augustine, Anselm, Boethius, and Dante*. Washington, DC: Catholic University of America Press, 2006.

McNair, Philip. "Dante's Vision of God: An Exposition of *Paradiso* XXXIII." In *Essays in Honour of John Humphrey's Whitfield: Presented to Him on His Retirement from the Serena Chair of Italian at the University of Birmingham*, edited by H. C. Davis et al., 13–29. London: St. George's Press, 1975.

McNulty, Robert. "The Protestant Version of Robert Parsons' *The First Book of the Christian Exercise*." *HLQ* 22 (1959): 271–300.

Meconi, David Vincent. "Heaven and the *Ecclesia Perfecta* in Augustine." In *The Cambridge Companion to Augustine*, edited by David Vincent Meconi and Eleonore Stump, 251–72. Cambridge: Cambridge University Press, 2014.

Meyendorff, John. *A Study of Gregory Palamas*. Translated by George Lawrence. Crestwood, NY: St. Vladimir's Seminary Press, 1998.

Middleton, J. Richard. *A New Heaven and a New Earth: Reclaiming Biblical Eschatology*. Grand Rapids: Baker Academic, 2014.

Migne, J.-P., ed. Patrologiae Cursus Completus, Series Graeca. Paris: Migne, 1857–1866.

Milbank, John. *The Suspended Middle: Henri de Lubac and the Renewed Split in Modern Catholic Theology*. 2nd ed. Grand Rapids: Eerdmans, 2014.

———. *Theology and Social Theory: Beyond Secular Reason*. 2nd ed. Malden, MA: Wiley-Blackwell, 2006.

Miles, Margaret. "Vision: The Eye of the Body and the Eye of the Mind in Saint Augustine's *De Trinitate* and *Confessions*." *JR* 63 (1983): 125–42.

Miller, Clyde L. "The Icon and the Wall: *Visio* and *Ratio* in Nicholas of Cusa's *De visione Dei*." *PACPhA* 64 (1990): 86–98.

Moevs, Christian. *The Metaphysics of Dante's Comedy*. Oxford: Oxford University Press, 2005.

Moltmann, Jürgen. *The Coming of God: Christian Eschatology*. Translated by Margaret Kohl. Minneapolis: Fortress, 1996.

———. *Crucified God: The Cross of Christ as the Foundation and Criticism of Christian Theology*. Translated by John Bowden. Minneapolis: Fortress, 1993.

———. *God in Creation: A New Theology of Creation and the Spirit of God*. Translated by Margaret Kohl. San Francisco: Harper and Row, 1985.

Mosser, Carl. "The Greatest Possible Blessing: Calvin and Deification." *SJT* 55 (2002): 36–57.

Moutsoulas, Elie D. "'Essence' et 'énergies' de Dieu selon St. Grégoire de Nysse." *SP* 18 (1989): 517–28.

Mulcahy, Bernard. *Aquinas's Notion of Pure Nature and the Christian Integralism of Henri de Lubac: Not Everything Is Grace.* American University Studies 7: Theology and Religion 314. New York: Peter Lang, 2011.

Muller, Richard A. "Christ in the Eschaton: Calvin and Moltmann on the Duration of the *Munus Regium.*" *HTR* 74 (1981): 31–59.

———. *Post-Reformation Reformed Dogmatics: The Rise and Development of Reformed Orthodoxy, ca. 1520 to ca. 1725.* 4 vols. Grand Rapids: Baker Academic, 2003.

———. *The Unaccommodated Calvin: Studies in the Foundation of a Theological Tradition.* New York: Oxford University Press, 2000.

Murray, Russel. "Mirror of Experience: Palamas and Bonaventure on the Experience of God—a Contribution to Orthodox–Roman Catholic Dialogue." *JES* 44 (2009): 432–60.

Nicholas of Cusa. *On the Vision of God.* In *Nicholas of Cusa: Selected Spiritual Writings*, translated and edited by H. Lawrence Bond. Mahwah, NJ: Paulist, 1997.

Nicholson, E. W. "The Interpretation of Exodus xxiv 9–11." *VT* 24 (1974): 77–97.

Nielsen, J. T. *Adam and Christ in the Theology of Irenaeus of Lyons: An Examination of the Function of the Adam-Christ Typology in the* Adversus Haereses *of Irenaeus, against the Background of the Gnosticism of His Time.* Assen, Neth.: Van Gorcum, 1968.

Noble, Ivana. "Religious Experience—Reality or Illusion: Insights from Symeon the New Theologian and Ignatius of Loyola." In *Encountering Transcendence: Contributions to the Theology of Christian Religious Experience*, edited by Lieven Boeve, Hans Geybels, and Stijn van den Bossche, 375–93. Annua Nuntia Lovaniensia 53. Leuven: Peeters, 2005.

Nye, Andrea. "The Subject of Love: Diotima and Her Critics." *J Value Inq* 24 (1990): 135–53.

Nygren, Anders. *Agape and Eros: The Christian Idea of Love.* Translated by Philip S. Watson. Chicago: University of Chicago Press, 1982.

Oakes, Edward T. "Balthasar and Ressourcement: An Ambiguous Relationship." In *Ressourcement: A Movement for Renewal in Twentieth-Century Catholic Theology*, edited by Gabriel Flynn and Paul D. Murray, 278–88. Oxford: Oxford University Press, 2012.

O'Brien, Dennis. "Plotinus on Matter and Evil." In *The Cambridge Companion to Plotinus*, edited by Lloyd P. Gerson, 171–95. Cambridge: Cambridge University Press, 1996.

O'Leary, Peter. "Imparadising, Transhumanizing, Intrining: Dante's Celestial Vision." *Postmed* 6 (2015): 154–64.

Ollerton, A. J. "*Quasi Deificari*: Deification in the Theology of John Calvin." *WTJ* 73 (2011): 237–54.

O'Meara, Dominic J. *Plotinus: An Introduction to the* Enneads. Oxford: Clarendon, 1993.

O'Meara, John J. *The Young Augustine: The Growth of St. Augustine's Mind up to His Conversion.* 2nd ed. New York: Alba, 2000.

Origen. *Spirit and Fire: A Thematic Anthology of His Writings.* Edited by Hans Urs von Balthasar. Translated by Robert J. Daly. Washington, DC: Catholic University of America Press, 1984.

Ortlund, Gavin. "Ascending toward the Beatific Vision: Heaven as the Climax of Anselm's *Proslogion*." PhD diss., Fuller Theological Seminary, School of Theology, 2016.

Owen, John. *Christologia, or, A declaration of the glorious mystery of the person of Christ, God and man with the infinite wisdom, love and power of God in the contrivance and constitution thereof . . .* London, 1679; Wing O762.

———. *Meditations and discourses on the glory of Christ, in his person, office, and grace with the differences between faith and sight: applied unto the use of them that believe.* London, 1684; Wing O769.

Pabst, Adrian. *Metaphysics: The Creation of Hierarchy.* Grand Rapids: Eerdmans, 2012.

Packer, J. I. *A Quest for Godliness: The Puritan Vision of the Christian Life.* Wheaton, IL: Crossway, 1990.

Papanikolaou, Aristotle. "Personhood and Its Exponents in Twentieth-Century Orthodox Theology." In *The Cambridge Companion to Orthodox Christian Theology*, edited by Mary B. Cunningham and Elizabeth Theokritoff, 232–45. Cambridge: Cambridge University Press, 2008.

Patterson, Paul A. *Visions of Christ: The Anthropomorphite Controversy of 399 CE.* Studies and Texts in Antiquity and Christianity 68. Tübingen: Mohr Siebeck, 2012.

Patterson, R. F., ed. *Ben Jonson's Conversations with William Drummond of Hawthornden.* London: Blackie, 1923.

Pauw, Amy Plantinga. "'Heaven Is a World of Love': Edwards on Heaven and the Trinity." *CTJ* 30 (1995): 392–401.

Pelikan, Jaroslav. *Christianity and Classical Culture: The Metamorphosis of Natural Theology in the Christian Encounter with Hellenism.* New Haven: Yale University Press, 1993.

———. *The Christian Tradition: A History of the Development of Doctrine.* Vol. 1, *The Emergence of the Catholic Tradition (100–600).* Chicago: University of Chicago Press, 1971.

Penkett, Robert. "Symeon the New Theologian's Visions of the Godhead." *Phronema* 15 (2000): 97–114.

Perrin, David B. "The Unique Contribution of John of the Cross to the Western Mystical Tradition." *ScEs* 51 (1999): 199–230.

Pertile, Lino. "A Desire of Paradise and a Paradise of Desire: Dante and Mysticism." In *Dante: Contemporary Perspectives*, edited by Amilcare A. Iannucci, 148–63. Toronto: University of Toronto Press, 1997.

Pfau, Thomas. *Minding the Modern: Human Agency, Intellectual Traditions, and Responsible Knowledge.* Notre Dame: University of Notre Dame Press, 2015.

Phillips, John F. "Plotinus and the 'Eye' of the Intellect." *Dionysius* 14 (1990): 79–103.

Pitstick, Alyssa. *Light in Darkness: Hans Urs von Balthasar and the Catholic Doctrine of Christ's Descent into Hell.* Grand Rapids: Eerdmans, 2007.

Plato. *Phaedrus.* Translated and edited by Robin Waterfield. Oxford: Oxford University Press, 2000.

———. *Republic.* Translated and edited by Robin Waterfield. Oxford: Oxford University Press, 1998.

———. *Statesman.* Translated by Robin Waterfield. Edited by Julia Annas and Robin Waterfield. Cambridge: Cambridge University Press, 1995.

———. *Symposium.* Translated and edited by Robin Waterfield. Oxford: Oxford University Press, 1994.

———. *Timaeus and Critias.* Translated by Robin Waterfield. Edited by Andrew Gregory. Oxford: Oxford University Press, 2008.

Plested, Marcus. *Orthodox Readings of Aquinas.* Oxford: Oxford University Press, 2012.

Pliny. *Natural History.* Vol. 3. Translated by H. Rackham. LCL 353. 1940. Reprint, London: Heinemann, 1967.

Plotinus. *Enneads.* Translated and edited by A. H. Armstrong. 6 vols. LCL 440–45. Cambridge, MA: Harvard University Press, 1966–1988.

Polanyi, Michael. *Knowing and Being: Essays by Michael Polanyi.* Edited by Marjorie Grene. Chicago: University of Chicago Press, 1969.

———. *The Tacit Dimension.* Garden City, NY: Doubleday, 1966.

Pollack, Tamara. "Light and Mirror in Dante's *Paradiso*: Faith and Contemplation in the Lunar Heaven and the *Primo Mobile.*" PhD diss., Indiana University, 2008.

———. "Light, Love and Joy in Dante's Doctrine of Beatitude." In *Reviewing Dante's Theology,* vol. 1, edited by Claire E. Honess and Matthew Treherne, 263–319. Leeds Studies on Dante. Oxford: Lang, 2013.

Pollard, Alfred W., and G. R. Redgrave, eds. *A Short-Title Catalogue of Books Printed in England, Scotland, and Ireland and of English Books Printed Abroad, 1475–1640.* 3 vols. Rev. ed. London: Bibliographical Society, 1976–1991.

Porphyry. *On the Life of Plotinus and the Order of His Books.* In Plotinus, *Enneads,* vol. 1, translated and edited by A. H. Armstrong, 1–87. LCL 440. Cambridge, MA: Harvard University Press, 1966.

Press, Gerald A. *Plato: A Guide for the Perplexed.* London: Continuum, 2007.

Pseudo-Dionysius. *Pseudo-Dionysius: The Complete Works.* Translated by Colm Luibheid. Edited by Paul Rorem. Mahwah, NJ: Paulist, 1987.

Pusey, Edward. "Lectures on Types and Prophecies in the Old Testament." Unpublished lectures, 1836.

Quistorp, Heinrich. *Calvin's Doctrine of the Last Things.* Translated by Harold Knight. London: Lutterworth, 1955.

Ratzinger, Joseph. *The Theology of History in St. Bonaventure.* Translated by Zachary Hayes. Chicago: Franciscan Herald Press, 1989.

Ray, Robert H. *A John Donne Companion.* 1990. Reprint, New York: Routledge, 2014.

Rehnman, Sebastian. *Divine Discourse: The Theological Methodology of John Owen.* Grand Rapids: Baker Academic, 2002.

Roberts, Alexander, and James Donaldson, eds. *The Ante-Nicene Fathers: Translations of the Fathers Down to A.D. 325.* Edited by Alexander Roberts and James Donaldson. Rev. ed. A. Cleveland Coxe. 10 vols. Buffalo: Christian Literature Co., 1885–1896.

Rorem, Paul. "Dionysian Uplifting (Anagogy) in Bonaventure's *Reductio.*" *FcS* 70 (2012): 183–88.

Rudnytsky, Peter L. "'The Sight of God': Donne's Poetics of Transcendence." *TSLL* 24 (1982): 185–207.

Russell, Jeffrey Burton. "The Heavenly Paradise." In *A History of Heaven: The Singing Silence,* 165–85. Princeton: Princeton University Press, 1997.

Russell, Norman. *The Doctrine of Deification in the Greek Patristic Tradition.* Oxford: Oxford University Press, 2004.

Ryan, Christopher. *Dante and Aquinas: A Study of Nature and Grace in the Comedy.* Edited by John Took. London: Ubiquity Press, 2013.

Rylaarsdam, David. *John Chrysostom on Divine Pedagogy: The Coherence of His Theology and Preaching*. Oxford: Oxford University Press, 2014.

Schaff, Philip, and Henry Wace, eds. *A Select Library of Nicene and Post-Nicene Fathers*. Second Series. 14 vols. Buffalo: Christian Literature Co., 1886–1900.

Schilder, Klaas. *Wat is de hemel?* Edited by Koert van Bekkum and Herman Selderhuis. Introduction by Barend Kampuis. 1935. Reprint, Barneveld, Neth.: Nederlands Dagblad, 2009.

Schillebeeckx, E. *Christ the Sacrament of the Encounter with God*. Translated by Paul Barrett. Lanham, MD: Sheed and Ward/Rowman and Littlefield, 1963.

Schufreider, Gregory. *Confessions of a Rational Mystic: Anselm's Early Writings*. West Lafayette, IN: Purdue University Press, 1994.

Schumacher, Lydia. *Divine Illumination: The History and Future of Augustine's Theory of Knowledge*. Malden, MA: Wiley-Blackwell, 2011.

Schwanda, Tom. "The Saints' Desire and Delight to Be with Christ." In *Puritanism and Emotion in the Early Modern World*, edited by Alec Ryrie and Tom Schwanda, 70–93. New York: Palgrave Macmillan, 2016.

———. *Soul Recreation: The Contemplative-Mystical Piety of Puritanism*. Eugene, OR: Pickwick, 2012.

———. "'Sweetnesse in Communion with God': The Contemplative-Mystical Piety of Thomas Watson." *JHRP* 1, no. 2 (2015): 34–63.

Schwarz, Hans. *Eschatology*. Grand Rapids: Eerdmans, 2000.

Schweitzer, William M. *God Is a Communicative Being: Divine Communicativeness and Harmony in the Theology of Jonathan Edwards*. T. & T. Clark Studies in Systematic Theology 14. London: Bloomsbury, 2012.

Selderhuis, Herman J., ed. *A Companion to Reformed Orthodoxy*. Leiden: Brill, 2013.

Serrán-Pagán y Fuentes, Cristóbal. "Mystical Vision and Prophetic Voice in St. John of the Cross: Towards a Mystical Theology of Final Integration." PhD diss., Biola University, 2003.

Shami, Jeanne. "Anatomy and Progress: The Drama of Conversion in Donne's Men of a 'Middle Nature.'" *UTQ* 53 (1984): 221–35.

———. "Donne's Decision to Take Orders." In *The Oxford Handbook of John Donne*, edited by Jeanne Shami, Dennis Flynn, and M. Thomas Hester, 523–36. Oxford: Oxford University Press, 2011.

———. "The Sermon." In *The Oxford Handbook of John Donne*, edited by Jeanne Shami, Dennis Flynn, and M. Thomas Hester, 318–47. Oxford: Oxford University Press, 2011.

———. "'Speaking Openly and Speaking First': John Donne, the Synod of Dort, and the Early Stuart Church." In *John Donne and the Protestant Reformation: New Perspectives*, edited by Mary Arshagouni Papazian, 35–65. Detroit: Wayne State University Press, 2003.

Sherman, Jacob Holsinger. *Partakers of the Divine: Contemplation and the Practice of Philosophy*. Minneapolis: Fortress, 2014.

Sia, Marian F., and Santiago Sia. *From Suffering to God: Exploring Our Images of God in the Light of Suffering*. New York: St. Martin's Press, 1994.

Silvas, Anna M. *Macrina the Younger, Philosopher of God*. Medieval Women: Texts and Contexts 22. Turnhout, Belgium: Brepols, 2008.

Slater, Jonathan. "Salvation as Participation in the Humanity of the Mediator in Calvin's *Institutes of the Christian Religion*: A Reply to Carl Mosser." *SJT* 58 (2005): 39–58.

Slotemaker, John T. "'"*Fuisse in Forma Hominis*" Belongs to Christ Alone': John Calvin's Trinitarian Hermeneutics in His *Lectures on Ezekiel*." *SJT* 68 (2015): 421–36.

Smith, Christian, with Melinda Lundquist Denton. *Soul Searching: The Religious and Spiritual Lives of American Teenagers.* New York: Oxford University Press, 2005.

Smith, Christian, with Patricia Snell. *Souls in Transition: The Religious and Spiritual Lives of Emerging Adults.* New York: Oxford University Press, 2015.

Smith, J. Warren. *Passion and Paradise: Human and Divine Emotion in the Thought of Gregory of Nyssa.* New York: Herder and Herder/Crossroad, 2004.

Smith, James K. A. *How (Not) to Be Secular: Reading Charles Taylor.* Grand Rapids: Eerdmans, 2014.

Socrates. *Selected Myths.* Edited by Catalin Partenie. Oxford: Oxford University Press, 2004.

Sorabji, Richard. *Time, Creation, and the Continuum: Theories in Antiquity and the Early Middle Ages.* 1983. Reprint, Chicago: University of Chicago Press, 2006.

Spence, Alan. *Incarnation and Inspiration: John Owen and the Coherence of Christology.* New York: T. & T. Clark, 2007.

Spiegel, James S. "The Theological Orthodoxy of Berkeley's Immaterialism." *FP* 13 (1996): 216–35.

Stanwood, P. G. "'Essentiall Joye' in Donne's *Anniversaries*." *TSLL* 13 (1971): 227–38.

Starr, James. "Does 2 Peter 1:4 Speak of Deification?" In *Partakers of the Divine Nature: The History and Development of Deification in the Christian Traditions*, edited by Michael J. Christensen and Jeffery A. Wittung, 81–92. Grand Rapids: Baker Academic, 2007.

Stathopoulos, Demetri. "The Divine Light in the Poetry of St. Symeon the New Theologian (949–1025)." *GOTR* 19 (1974): 95–111.

Stethatos, Niketas. *The Life of Saint Symeon the New Theologian.* Translated by Richard P. H. Greenfield. Dumbarton Oaks Medieval Library 20. Cambridge, MA: Harvard University Press, 2013.

Stevenson, Kenneth. "From Origen to Gregory of Palamas: Greek Expositions of the Transfiguration." *BBGG*, ser. 3, vol. 4 (2007): 197–212.

Strezova, Anita. "Doctrinal Positions of Barlaam of Calabria and Gregory Palamas during the Byzantine Hesychast Controversy." *SVTQ* 58 (2014): 177–215.

Strobel, Kyle. "Jonathan Edwards' Reformed Doctrine of the Beatific Vision." In *Jonathan Edwards and Scotland*, edited by Kelly Van Andel, Adriaan C. Neele, and Kenneth P. Minkema, 163–80. Edinburgh: Dunedin, 2011.

———. *Jonathan Edwards's Theology: A Reinterpretation.* T. & T. Clark Studies in Systematic Theology 19. London: T. & T. Clark, 2013.

———. "Theology in the Gaze of the Father: Retrieving Jonathan Edwards's Trinitarian Aesthetics." In *Advancing Trinitarian Theology: Explorations in Constructive Dogmatics*, edited by Oliver D. Crisp and Fred Sanders, 147–70. Grand Rapids: Zondervan, 2014.

Studebaker, Steven M., and Robert W. Caldwell. *The Trinitarian Theology of Jonathan Edwards: Text, Context, and Application.* Burlington, VT: Ashgate, 2012.

Studer, Basil. *Zur Theophanie-Exegese Augustins: Untersuchung zu einem Ambrosius-Zitat in der Schrift* De videndo Deo *(Ep. 147).* SA 59. Rome: Herder, 1971.

Symeon the New Theologian. *Catéchèses.* Translated by Joseph Paramelle. Edited by Basile Krivochéine. 3 vols. Sources Chrétiennes 96, 104, 113. Paris: Cerf, 1963–1965.

———. *Hymns of Divine Love.* Translated and edited by George A. Maloney. Denville, NJ: Dimension, 1975.

Tan, Seng-Kong. "Jonathan Edwards's Dynamic Idealism and Cosmic Christology." In *Idealism and Christian Theology,* edited by Joshua R. Farris, S. Mark Hamilton, and James S. Spiegel. Idealism and Christianity 1. New York: Bloomsbury Academic, 2016.

Targoff, Ramie. *John Donne, Body and Soul.* Chicago: University of Chicago Press, 2008.

Tayler, Edward W. *Donne's Idea of a Woman: Structure and Meaning in* The Anniversaries. New York: Columbia University Press, 1991.

Taylor, Charles. *A Secular Age.* Cambridge, MA: Belknap Press of Harvard University Press, 2007.

Tertullian. *Against Praxeas.* In *ANF* 3, translated by Peter Holmes, edited by Alexander Roberts, James Donaldson, and A. Cleveland Coxe. Buffalo: Christian Literature Co., 1885.

Teske, Ronald J. "St. Augustine and the Vision of God." In *Augustine: Mystic and Mystagogue,* edited by Frederick Van Fleteren, Joseph C. Schnaubelt, and Joseph Reino, 287–308. New York: Peter Lang, 1994.

Thomas Aquinas. *Catena Aurea: Commentary on the Four Gospels, Collected out of the Works of the Fathers.* Translated by John Henry Newman. 4 vols. Oxford: Parker, 1841–1845.

———. *Commentary on the Gospel of Matthew.* Translated by Jeremy Holmes. Edited by the Aquinas Institute. Biblical Commentaries 34. Lander, WY: Aquinas Institute for the Study of Sacred Doctrine, 2013.

———. *On Love and Charity: Readings from the* Commentary on the Sentences of Peter Lombard. Translated by Peter A. Kwasniewski, Thomas Bolan, and Joseph Bolin. Edited by Peter A. Kwasniewski. Washington, DC: Catholic University of America Press, 2008.

———. *Scriptum super Sententiis: An Index of Authorities Cited.* Edited by Charles H. Lohr. Avebury, NY: Fordham University Press, 1980.

———. *Summa contra Gentiles.* Translated by Anton C. Pegis et al. 5 vols. 1956. Reprint, Notre Dame: University of Notre Dame Press, 1975.

———. *Summa Theologica.* Translated by Fathers of the English Dominican Province. 5 vols. 1948. Reprint, Notre Dame: Christian Classics, 1981.

———. *Super Evangelium S. Matthaei Lectura.* In *Commentary on the Gospel of Matthew,* translated by Jeremy Holmes, edited by the Aquinas Institute. Biblical Commentaries 34. Lander, WY: Aquinas Institute for the Study of Sacred Doctrine, 2013.

Tollefsen, Torstein Theodor. *Activity and Participation in Late Antique and Early Christian Thought.* Oxford: Oxford University Press, 2012.

Torrance, Alexis. "Precedents for Palamas' Essence-Energies Theology in the Cappadocian Fathers." *VC* 63 (2009): 47–70.

Trottmann, Christian. *La Vision béatifique des disputes scolastiques à sa définition par Benoît XII.* Bibliothèque des écoles françaises d'Athènes et de Rome 289. Rome: École française de Rome, 1995.

Bibliography

Trueman, Carl R. *John Owen: Reformed Catholic, Renaissance Man*. 2007. Reprint, New York: Routledge, 2016.

Turner, Denys. *The Darkness of God: Negativity in Christian Mysticism*. Cambridge: Cambridge University Press, 1995.

———. "Hierarchy Interiorised: Bonaventure's *Itinerarium Mentis in Deum*." In *The Darkness of God: Negativity in Christian Mysticism*, 102–34. Cambridge: Cambridge University Press, 1995.

Tylenda, Joseph N. "Calvin and the Avignon Sermons of John XXII." *ITQ* 41 (1974): 37–52.

Van Fleteren, Frederick. "Augustine and the Possibility of the Vision of God in This Life." In *SMC*, vol. 11, edited by John R. Sommerfeldt and Thomas H. Seiler, 9–16. Kalamazoo, MI: Medieval Institute/Western Michigan University, 1977.

———. "Mysticism in the *Confessiones*—a Controversy Revisited." In *Augustine: Mystic and Mystagogue*, edited by Frederick Van Fleteren, Joseph C. Schnaubelt, and Joseph Reino, 309–36. New York: Peter Lang, 1994.

———. "Videndo Deo, De." In *Augustine through the Ages: An Encyclopedia*, edited by Allan D. Fitzgerald, 869. Grand Rapids: Eerdmans, 1999.

Van Rossum, Joost. "Deification in Palamas and Aquinas." *SVTQ* 47 (2003): 365–82.

Vella, John A. *Aristotle: A Guide for the Perplexed*. New York: Continuum, 2008.

Veniamin, Christopher. "The Transfiguration of Christ in Greek Patristic Literature: From Irenaeus of Lyons to Gregory Palamas." PhD diss., University of Oxford, 1991.

Voegelin, Eric. *Plato*. 1957. Reprint, Columbia: University of Missouri Press, 2000.

Vree, J. "More Pierson and Mesmer, and Less Pietje Baltus: Kuyper's Ideas on Church, State, Society and Culture during the First Years of His Ministry (1863–1866)." In *Kuyper Reconsidered: Aspects of His Life and Work*, edited by Cornelis van der Kooi and Jan de Bruijn, 299–310. VU Studies on Protestant History 3. Amsterdam: VU Uitgeverij, 1999.

Waddell, Michael M. "Aquinas on the Light of Glory." *Tópicos* 40 (2011): 105–32.

Wainwright, William W. "Jonathan Edwards." In *The Spiritual Senses: Perceiving God in Western Christianity*, edited by Paul L. Gavrilyuk and Sarah Coakley, 224–40. Cambridge: Cambridge University Press, 2012.

Wallace, Ronald S. *Calvin's Doctrine of the Word and Sacrament*. 1953. Reprint, Eugene, OR: Wipf and Stock, 1997.

Watson, Thomas. *The beatitudes: or A discourse upon part of Christs famous Sermon on the Mount* . . . London, 1660; Wing [2nd ed.] W1107.

———. *A body of practical divinity consisting of above one hundred seventy six sermons on the lesser catechism composed by the reverend assembly of divines at Westminster* . . . London, 1692; Wing W1109.

Weakland, John E. "Pope John XXII and the Beatific Vision Controversy." *AnM* 9 (1968): 76–84.

Westhaver, George. "The Living Body of the Lord: E. B. Pusey's Types and Prophecies of the Old Testament." PhD diss., Durham University, 2012.

Whidden, David L. "The Theology of Light in Thomas Aquinas." PhD diss., Southern Methodist University, 2011.

Wilken, Robert L. *The Christians as the Romans Saw Them*. New Haven: Yale University Press, 1984.

————. *The Spirit of Early Christian Thought: Seeking the Face of God*. New Haven: Yale University Press, 2003.

Williams, A. N. "The Doctrine of God in San Juan de la Cruz." *ModTh* 30 (2014): 500–524.

————. *The Ground of Union: Deification in Aquinas and Palamas*. New York: Oxford University Press, 1999.

Williams, D. H. "Polemics and Politics in Ambrose of Milan's *De Fide*." *JTS* 46 (1995): 519–31.

Wilson-Kastner, Patricia. "God's Infinity and His Relationship to Creation in the Theologies of Gregory of Nyssa and Jonathan Edwards." *Foundations* 21 (1978): 305–21.

Wing, Donald Goddard, et al., eds. *A Short-Title Catalogue of Books Printed in England, Scotland, Ireland, Wales, and British America, and of English Books Printed in Other Countries, 1641–1700*. Rev. ed. 3 vols. New York: Modern Language Association of America, 1994.

Wippel, John F. "Thomas Aquinas and the Axiom 'What Is Received Is Received according to the Mode of the Receiver.'" In *Metaphysical Themes in Thomas Aquinas II*, 113–22. Studies in Philosophy and the History of Philosophy 47. Washington, DC: Catholic University of America Press, 2007.

Wirzba, Norman. "Christian *Theoria Physike*: On Learning to See Creation." *ModTh* 32 (2016): 211–30.

Wojtyla, Karol. *Faith according to St. John of the Cross*. Translated by Jordan Aumann. San Francisco: Ignatius, 1981.

Wolterstoff, Nicholas. *Until Justice and Peace Embrace: The Kuyper Lectures for 1981 Delivered at the Free University of Amsterdam*. Grand Rapids: Eerdmans, 1983.

Wright, N. T. *Simply Jesus: A New Vision of Who He Was, What He Did, Why It Matters*. London: SPCK, 2011.

————. *Surprised by Hope: Rethinking Heaven, the Resurrection, and the Mission of the Church*. New York: HarperOne, 2008.

Zachman, Randall C. *Image and Word in the Theology of John Calvin*. Notre Dame: University of Notre Dame Press, 2007.

Zaleski, Carol. *Otherworld Journeys: Accounts of Near-Death Experience in Medieval and Modern Times*. New York: Oxford University Press, 1987.

Ziebart, Meredith. "Laying Siege to the Wall of Paradise: The Fifteenth-Century Tegernsee Dispute over Mystical Theology and Nicholas of Cusa's Strong Defense of Reason." *JMRCul* 41 (2015): 41–66.

Zinkovskiy, Kirill. "St. Gregory of Nyssa on the Transformation of Physical Elements—in Nature and Holy Eucharistic Gifts." In *The Beauty of God's Presence in the Fathers of the Church: The Proceedings of the Eighth International Patristic Conference, Maynooth, 2012*, edited by Janet Elaine Rutherford, 150–60. Dublin: Four Courts Press, 2014.

INDEX OF AUTHORS

INDEX OF SUBJECTS

8–10; vision of the Father, 135–38. *See also* Christ's humanity: in transfiguration; Christ's role in beatific vision; Mediated vision; Transfiguration

Christ as the essence of God: Gregory of Nyssa on, 88–94, 95; John's Gospel on, 409–10; Nicholas of Cusa on, 398n27. *See also* Christ's role in beatific vision; Divine essence, comprehension of; Divine essence, sight of

Christian Platonism, 45–47, 50, 194, 395n14, 395n16; of Augustine, 97, 102n17, 118–24, 126; and the body, 356–59; critique of, 28n26, 33; of Dante, 249; of Edwards, 354–56, 383, 398; of Gregory of Nyssa, 77n2, 80n10; of Nicholas of Cusa, 398. *See also* Philosophy

Christ's humanity: in beatific vision (Edwards), 367–75; in beatific vision (Owen), 322–27; in transfiguration, 135–44, 149–50, 155, 158, 161

Christ's role in beatific vision, 12–14, 37, 50–51, 74–75, 198–200, 391–92, 409–20; I. Ambrose on, 316–19; Aquinas on, 51, 159–62, 367, 415–16; Augustine on, 99–101; Calvin on, 272–78; Donne on, 295–301, 310–12; Edwards on, 363–75, 384; Kuyper on, 340–52; Nicholas of Cusa on, 213–26; Owen on, 321–27. *See also* Christ as the essence of God; Christ's humanity; Divine essence, comprehension of; Divine essence, sight of

Contemplation (this-worldly), 13, 24–26, 401; I. Ambrose on, 317–19; Baxter on, 327–32; Bonaventure on, 202–3; Dante on, 223–24; Donne on, 308–13; of the incarnation (I. Ambrose), 332–34; Kuyper on, 347–51; Nicholas of Cusa on, 209. *See also* Ecstatic experience; Experience of God

Creation: continual, Edwards on, 400–401; continual, Nicholas of Cusa on, 397, 400. *See also* Contemplation (this-worldly); Sacramental ontology; Theophany

Creator-creature distinction, 35–36, 53n16, 61–62, 73, 394, 408, 415; Aquinas on, 234, 238, 375n83; Calvin on,

274, 278; Gregory of Nyssa on, 95; John of the Cross on, 182–84, 187n48; Watson on, 419. *See also* Deification; Participatory ontology; Union

Darkness: John of the Cross on, 177–93

Deification, 31–33, 51, 61n30, 64, 393; Donne on, 306–7, 313; and mystical union (Symeon the New Theologian), 173n26; and transfiguration, 130, 158; Watson on, 419. *See also* Creator-creature distinction; Union

Desire: Dante on, 228–39; Gregory of Nyssa on, 87–88, 90–93, 94; infinite nature of (Gregory of Nyssa), 90–93. *See also* Affect

Divine accommodation: Calvin on, 261–75. *See also* Divine pedagogy

Divine energies (operations), 12, 29, 38, 62, 73, 391n7, 416n79; Gregory of Nyssa on, 79–80, 84–85, 94–95; and transfiguration (Palamas), 146–55

Divine essence, comprehension of, 415–16, 418, 423; Aquinas on, 238, 312n62, 380, 415–16; Donne on, 312; Kuyper on, 344; Owen on, 323n16, 324–25. *See also* Contemplation (this-worldly); Divine energies (operations); Divine essence, sight of

Divine essence, sight of, 12–14, 32, 35–36, 51, 229, 391, 415–16; I. Ambrose on, 319–20, 323; Aquinas on, 13, 32, 51, 116, 149–50, 161–62, 380–83, 415–17; Augustine on, 112–17; Dante on, 236–38; Calvin on, 264n25, 273–75, 278; Donne on, 311–12, 314; John of the Cross on, 187–88, 190; Kuyper on, 343–47, 350–52; Palamas on, 146; Watson on, 335, 419. *See also* Christ's role in beatific vision; Contemplation (this-worldly); Divine energies (operations); Divine essence, comprehension of

Divine incomprehensibility: Gregory of Nyssa on, 79–80, 85–88, 93. *See also* Apophaticism; *Epektasis* (infinite progress); Ineffability of God

Divine infinity: Gregory of Nyssa on, 83–84, 93, 94; Palamas on, 154–55. *See also* Apophaticism; *Epektasis* (infinite progress)

INDEX OF SCRIPTURE REFERENCES